GLOBALIZATION

Written by two leading scholars of global politics, *Globalization: The Return of Borders to a Borderless World?* is a major new book for students of globalization. It describes and explains globalization and its origins, and examines its future in light of key recent political and global events.

The text:

- Identifies the key attributes of globalization.
- Examines its historical origins into the twenty-first century.
- Describes the multiple attributes and effect on the sovereignty of the nation state.
- Discusses recent trends such as the increased use of social media and events like the Arab Spring.
- Assesses the normative implications of globalization.
- Analyzes the challenges to globalization posed by contemporary events such as the global financial crisis.

This book will be essential reading for all students of globalization, and will be of great interest to students of global politics and global governance.

Yale H. Ferguson is Professorial Fellow and former Co-Director of the Division of Global Affairs, Rutgers University-Newark, and Honorary Professor, University of Salzburg, Austria. He is a Member of the European Academy of Sciences and Arts, and has been a Visiting Fellow at the University of Cambridge, the Norwegian Nobel Institute, and the University of Padua, as well as Fulbright Professor at Salzburg.

Richard W. Mansbach served as political science chair at Rutgers University-New Brunswick and Iowa State University, and is currently Professor of Political Science at ISU. Formerly a Marshall Scholar, he has received three Fulbright fellowships – to Singapore, Seoul, and Vienna.

GLOBALIZATION

The return of borders to a borderless world?

Yale H. Ferguson and Richard W. Mansbach

Taylor & Francis Group

LONDON AND NEW YORK

First published 2012
by Routledge
2 Park Square, Milton Park, Abingdon, Oxon, OX14 4RN

Simultaneously published in the USA and Canada
by Routledge
711 Third Avenue, New York, NY 10017

Routledge is an imprint of the Taylor & Francis Group, an informa business

© 2012 Yale H. Ferguson and Richard W. Mansbach

The right of Yale H. Ferguson and Richard W. Mansbach to be identified as the authors of this work has been asserted by them in accordance with the Copyright, Designs and Patents Act 1988.

All rights reserved. No part of this book may be reprinted or reproduced or utilised in any form or by any electronic, mechanical, or other means, now known or hereafter invented, including photocopying and recording, or in any information storage or retrieval system, without permission in writing from the publishers.

Trademark notice: Product or corporate names may be trademarks or registered trademarks, and are used only for identification and explanation without intent to infringe.

British Library Cataloguing in Publication Data
A catalogue record for this book is available from the British Library

Library of Congress Cataloging in Publication Data
Ferguson, Yale H.
  Globalization : the return of borders to a borderless world? / Yale H. Ferguson & Richard W. Mansbach.
    p. cm.
  Includes bibliographical references and index.
  1. Globalization—Textbooks. 2. Globalization—History—Textbooks.
  I. Mansbach, Richard W., 1943– II. Title.
  JZ1318.F465 2012
  303.48'2—dc23   2011042744

ISBN: 978–0–415–52196–3 (hbk)
ISBN: 978–0–415–52197–0 (pbk)
ISBN: 978–0–203–12138–2 (ebk)

Typeset in Garamond by
Keystroke, Station Road, Codsall, Wolverhampton

Printed and bound in Great Britain by
TJ International Ltd, Padstow, Cornwall

To James N. Rosenau – pioneer, mentor, friend

CONTENTS

List of tables   xi

Introduction   1

Background to this book   2
Can globalization be reversed?   10

1 What is globalization?   16

The meaning(s) of globalization   17
   Skeptics   18
   Hyperglobalists   21
   Transformationalists   25
The multiple and interdependent dimensions of globalization   26
Transformational theory: territory, actors, and identity   28

2 Globalization in historical perspective   40

Early respacializations   42
The ancient Mediterranean   43
Intercontinental linkages from Late Antiquity to the dawn of Europe's "Age of Discovery"   50
The Atlantic bridged, European sovereign states, empires, and global capitalism   54
From the Cold War to twenty-first-century globalization   62
Conclusion   67

3 The essentials of globalization   75

Spreading capitalism   75
Global governance   78
The triumph of democracy?   84
Global civil society   85
Cultural homogenization?   89
English as the *lingua franca*   91
Transgovernmental linkages and networks   93
Diffusion of global power?   94

Collective environmental degradation 96
From military to human security 97
The changing nature of military security 98

4 Globalization and information and communication technologies 109

ICT, geography, and territory 112
Skilled and participant publics 113
ICT and political participation 114
Economic implications of ICT 117
Security implications 120
ICT, globalization, and localization 123

5 The global versus the local 131

Deterritorialization and denationalization 136
Glocalization 138
The dialectical relationship between the global and the local 140
Globalizing versus localizing cultural currents 143
A world of shifting boundaries and evolving authority 145

6 The normative implications of globalization 152

Central normative issues 155
    A "democratic deficit"? 155
    A cut-throat world of neoliberal capitalism 157
    Reactive and structural violence 161
    The erosion of human rights? 162
    A race to the bottom? 164
    Cultural conformity or modernity? 166
    Migrants, drugs, bugs, trafficking, and terrorism 167
    States, war, and violence 170
    Sovereignty and its discontents 171
The counter-globalization movement 172
A mixed verdict 176

7 Regional dynamics: Europe and Asia 186

Globalization and Europe 188
    Western Europe 188
    Post-communist Central Europe 192
Globalization and Asia 194
    Southeast Asia 196
    East Asia 198
    Central Asia 204
    South Asia 207

8 Regional dynamics: Russia, Latin America, the Middle East, and Africa — 220

Globalization and the Russian Federation — 221
Latin America — 226
The Middle East — 231
Africa — 234

9 Two steps forward, one step back? — 247

Anti-globalization currents — 249
Nationalism and ethnicity — 249
   The return of the state — 252
   State failure — 254
   Opposition to immigration — 256
Neomercantilism — 261
Environmental nationalism — 266

10 The balance sheet — 277

The political dialectic — 281
The cultural dialectic — 282
The military dialectic — 283
The economic dialectic — 283
The environmental dialectic — 285
Enfin — 285

Index — 291

TABLES

Table 4.1 Internet usage statistics   111
Table 7.1 Non-US technology leaders and challengers   188

Introduction

Globalization is certainly a source of anxiety in the U.S. academic world.[1] And the sources of this anxiety are many: Social scientists . . . worry about whether markets and deregulation produce greater wealth at the price of increased inequality. Political scientists worry that their field might vanish along with their favorite object the nation-state, if globalization truly creates a "world without borders." Cultural theorists, especially cultural Marxists, worry that in spite of its conformity with everything they already knew about capital, there may be some embarrassing new possibilities for equity hidden in its workings. Historians, ever worried about the problem of the new, realize that globalization may not be a member of the familiar archive of large-scale historical shifts.[2]

Globalization lies at the heart of virtually all the concerns that have preoccupied us as scholars and co-authors for over three decades. It affects peoples everywhere (whether they recognize it or not) in innumerable ways, some small and some large. It continues to engage numerous scholars in diverse disciplines as well as policy-makers and citizens.

The origin of the term "globalization," like almost everything about the topic, is contested. At one point it was incorrectly credited to Theodore Levitt, a professor at the Harvard Business School,[3] but in fact it was in use earlier. Although the term gained currency in the 1960s, its current popularity dates to the 1990s after the end of the Cold War. Since then globalization has spawned an immense literature. Globalization theory owes much to a group of political scientists who did pioneering work during an era that was otherwise dominated by state-centric thought: Karl W.

Deutsch's path-breaking study of security communities, integration theory, and transaction data; Hedley Bull's development of the concept of international society; Robert O. Keohane's and Joseph S. Nye, Jr.'s theories of complex interdependence and transnational politics; Susan Strange's advancement of the subfield of international political economy; and James N. Rosenau's exploration of national/international linkages and post-international politics. We are delighted to acknowledge our debt to these and to other scholars, many of a later generation, in the pages that follow. We dedicate this book to Rosenau, whom we first knew as a fellow member of the Rutgers University faculty and who became a mentor, source of inspiration, and longstanding friend.

BACKGROUND TO THIS BOOK

The most important of our own concerns for over four decades has been the evolution of the territorial state or "Westphalian polity" (our term) and the so-called state system that has been central to conceptions of *international* politics. Since the 1970s, we have argued that the role and nature of the state were continuing to change; that borders were becoming more porous and penetrable; that state autonomy and capacity were being challenged by transnational linkages; that territory was losing much of its significance in the face of new communications, improvements in transportation, and changing military technology; and that states are increasingly required to share the global stage with a host of nonstate actors, both nongovernmental and intergovernmental.

Our first book together,[4] in 1976, examined the growing role of nonstate actors in global politics, focusing on the impact of transnational corporations in Latin America, terrorist groups in the Middle East, and Europe's emerging regional community. We were conscious even then of the diminished role of state sovereignty and of the declining autonomy and capacity of territorial states that had to cope with more encompassing communities as well as transnational and subnational groups. Transnational politics and interdependence among peoples as well as states were changing international politics into global politics, and cooperation in the face of collective dilemmas was becoming as central as the traditional concern with interstate conflict.

We soon argued that the timeless, state-centric world of realists and neorealists – what one observer calls a "real estate vision of history"[5] – that dominated international relations theory impeded theoretical growth and ignored the shift from international to global politics.[6] By contrast, we viewed the Westphalian state as contingent and time-bound, the product of a particular constellation of historical factors. Certainly, the state had *never* been the only significant type of actor in global politics.[7] Moreover, contemporary states, as well as other actors, far from showing the functional similarity often claimed for them by structural realists, undertake profoundly different and often more specialized functions. The tidy world of interstate theory, with its notion of territorial states enjoying exclusive control of a defined territory, in an anarchic global system featuring competition for power and unrelieved conflict, was a gross distortion and hopelessly anachronistic. State-centric theorizing, with its absence of historical sensitivity, carried conceptual baggage that made it difficult to "remap" political reality.[8] Our present is a different era, one Rosenau labeled "postinternational politics," characterized by a world that is increasingly complex and, at least until recently, was globalizing at an accelerating pace.[9]

The role of territory has changed, and more and more observers believe, in a globalized world, there is no longer "a direct correspondence between society, economy and polity within an exclusive and bounded national territory."[10] Naturally, not everyone agrees. Linda Weiss argues that the phrase "without regard to country/territory/national boundary" "cannot mean 'without regard to *any and every* territory'" because "every relationship and transaction (even those using electronic means, in so-called cyberspace) takes place within nationally defined borders – and is thereby subject, *in principle,* to the rules and laws of the nation-state in which it transpires (including intrafirm trade which is often misleadingly cited as evidence of 'transborder' activity)." She concludes that, at most, operating "in a transborder or global capacity . . . does not create a transcendent reality" but "is more appropriately a 'globalization with borders'."[11] Of course, we might respond, there is typically a huge gap between subjection "in principle" and actual practice; moreover, although the presence of state borders is undeniable, the question remains as to their continued relevance with respect to particular purposes. That question – along with the nature and probable future of globalization – are the central concerns of this book.

Part of what made it difficult for theorists to discern what was transpiring was a breakdown of conventional levels of analysis.[12] Many of the new entities were nonterritorial, had overlapping memberships, and were based on identities other than that of citizenship. There was a need to contend with multiple identities, many of which are not anchored in territory, and contingent identity hierarchies. As Jan Aart Scholte observed in 1996, "matters of identity have until recently received little attention in international studies" and for traditional analysts of "social relations on a world scale . . . identity boiled down to nationality and loyalty to the corresponding territorial state."[13]

The "levels-of-analysis problem,"[14] in our view, was exaggerated because it was actually a logical problem of parts and wholes rather than an empirical issue. Only by a conceptual leap to what we termed "a world of polities"[15] could we overcome the artificial limitations posed by levels-of-analysis thinking, begin to break down the barriers between the social science disciplines and their outdated subfields, and move towards a theory or at least unified approach towards understanding *politics*. The study of globalization takes us in this direction.

The concepts of "global governance"[16] and "global civil society" – central to globalization discourses – reflect the reality of the coalescing and fragmentation of effective authority or influence in different locations and point up that "world order," in any meaningful sense, necessarily involves much more than interacting sovereign states.

Effective authority or influence and legitimacy may or may not coincide, vary by issue, and are not necessarily vested in the same actors or polities. Moreover, as we shall see, the "local" and "global" continuously shape each other. Instead of a static state-centric world, we perceive "a seamless web, encompassing numerous layered, overlapping, and interacting political authorities."[17] For us, the essence of global politics is "the relationships and evolution of many polities of different types" that typically share "political space."[18]

Globalization, as Philip Cerny contends, has made the levels-of-analysis puzzle obsolete, because the political universe "should not be seen as an all encompassing, seamless process of 'level shift' but as the result of the addition and interaction of a complex set of intertwined processes on a range of diverse, intersecting and overlapping, and often quite uneven levels and playing fields."

These processes include the development of denser relations among states (usually called "internationalisation"), growing below-the-border dealings cutting across states ("transnationalisation"), denser interactions among localities and regions ("translocalisation" or "glocalisation"), and the transformation of social, economic and political relations and processes at the domestic and local levels themselves – the macrocosm within the microcosm. More important than any one of these levels, however, are the interaction effects among them. It is these *interaction effects* that destabilise the structural equilibrium underpinning the levels of analysis distinction, thereby undermining the path dependency of the international system as we have known it, and lay the foundations for ongoing and future developments.[19]

In *The Elusive Quest*, in 1988, we suggested that five conditions were crucial for theoretical progress in our field: (1) overcoming historical selectivity, (2) de-emphasizing strict empiricism, (3) liberating ourselves from state-centric realism, (4) erasing the boundary between the "international" and "domestic" arenas, and (5) moving freely among levels of analysis.[20] All have become central issues of the globalization debate. Additionally, we confronted the claim by positivists that empirical and normative theorizing are separable, arguing to the contrary that any effort to separate facts and values ignores much of what is genuinely political in our field. Normative and empirical claims infuse and shape one another, and the dichotomy is impossible to sustain. In fact, realism and liberalism – rather than providing persuasive explanations or predictions – are normative ideals. Similarly, those who favor globalization (however defined) tend to see it as irreversible,[21] whereas those who are critical of globalization are apt to believe it can be reversed.[22] "Almost invariably," as Matthew Hannah observes, "organizations which benefit from globalization in its current form will represent it as *natural* or *inevitable*," because in "encouraging people the world over to accept the inevitability of globalization, they help fulfill their own prophecy and ensure their own prosperity."[23] Of course, those who perceive themselves or others as poorly served or disadvantaged by globalization are likely to downplay any benefits and insist that it *can* and *ought to be* reversed or at least reformed.

Positivists affirm the interstate model of global politics as reality partly because it facilitates data collection and comparison and uses history only selectively or ignores it entirely. For the most part, positivists neglect values, culture, identity, and other subjective and difficult-to-quantify factors that are central to globalization discourses. Partly owing to this neglect, *The Elusive Quest* expressed our growing disenchantment with inductive empiricism, and pessimism about the prospects for theoretical innovation.

Our work over the years has consistently emphasized the necessity for historical analysis to make sense of change and its relationship to continuity. Shifting authority patterns reflect changing identities and loyalties and also can give rise to the same.[24]

In *Polities* we analyzed authority patterns in six historical systems that antedated the post-Westphalian era in order to identify alternatives to modern interstate politics and, in a broader sense, to establish the degree to which contemporary global politics is both the same as and different from the past. Analysts of globalization must concern themselves with its historical origins and trajectory, which is the subject of Chapter 2.

Although this book builds on our joint scholarship over several decades, it is specifically a sequel to our *Remapping Global Politics* (2004). At the conclusion of that work, we admitted that "we are more sympathetic to the pro- than anti-globalization narrative" and that we believed "that globalizing trends are less and less reversible."[25] We then offered three possible future scenarios, arguing that there already existed some evidence for each. The first two were premised on an acceleration of globalizing trends. The first foresaw a minimalist state, having evolved from a national to civic culture in the Western liberal tradition, principally concerned with assuring the "rules of the game" and distributing public goods in a world characterized by a dense network of subnational and transnational civic associations. The second anticipated a world governed by the norms and institutions of interstate and transnational cooperation, aided by liberal states, to assure democracy, peace, and human security. The third entailed a stagnation or retreat of globalization during a period of chaos that would raise popular anxiety and encourage statist authoritarianism.[26] "The shape of post-Westphalian global politics," we concluded, "remains obscure."[27] *Globalization: The Return of Borders to a Borderless World?* revisits our earlier conclusions in light of recent perspectives and tumultuous events that provide additional evidence of the direction of global politics in general and of globalization in particular. As we shall see, in many respects globalization persists; in others, it has strengthened; in still others, it has slowed, stagnated, or even retreated.

Whether globalization is good or bad is a valid question, but such a broad one that it invites either sweeping generalization or an exceedingly long list of pluses and minuses. The contagion of financial panic[28] or the global health hazard of avian or swine influenza[29] and the trafficking in women and drugs[30] facilitated by new technologies and porous borders are patently undesirable. By contrast, many would regard the spread of human-rights norms and transnational epistemic communities that deal with human rights and environmental issues as positive developments. Nevertheless, we repeat, it is crucial to recognize the connection between normative judgments about globalization and empirical claims regarding the directions that it is taking.

We must avoid two other common pitfalls. The first is to assume that globalization *necessarily* erodes state capacity and authority. The second is to believe that the increasing "internationalization" of states is producing a globalized world.

The territorial state has been the focus of international relations for over three centuries, and the lives of citizens and subjects have been largely guided by the laws and practices of states. However, like all polity types, the state has continually evolved, and that evolution has produced an enormous variety of actual state polities.

One of the most ambitious analyses of state evolution and resulting diversity is that of Philip Bobbitt. State evolution, he argues, is a consequence of the interaction of history, military strategy, and law. "The State exists," he writes, "by virtue of its purposes" among which "are a drive for survival and freedom of action, which is strategy; for authority and legitimacy, which is law; for identity, which is history."[31] The first of Europe's states – "princely states" Bobbitt calls them – emerged from Europe's medieval society in the city-states of Italy at the end of the fifteenth century.[32] These polities, unlike the scattered dynastic territories of medieval rulers, were geographically compact and lacked a clear distinction between the "domestic" and "foreign" realms. They featured a common culture and a monetized economy that financed the employment of mercenaries and the reconstruction of walled fortresses to reduce the impact of cannon. Princely states also saw themselves as "juridical entities separate from . . . the civil society" at a time when "human traits" were "transposed to the State itself." Princes needed professional bureaucrats to cope with military threats from one another and from outside Italy, and they were legitimated by Machiavelli's version of *ragione di stato* under which a prince does not serve his personal interests but instead watches over the interests of his state and its inhabitants. The features of these highly personalized "princely states," when imported to the larger territories of Spain, England, and France, took the form of "kingly states" with the added dimension of dynastic legitimacy.

For Saskia Sassen the transition to kingly states, especially the provision of legitimacy and the accompanying shift in norms and identities, came earlier, with France's Capetian monarchs. "The Capetian project," she argues,

> and its claim to divinity as a source of authority autonomous from the papacy was . . . an innovative epistemic shift and, thus a critical development of capabilities for the national state, not merely a fight between those who wanted centralization and those who wanted decentralization. In addition, sovereign territorial authority entailed recognizing a mutually agreed upon spatial demarcation of political authority. It demanded a principle of juridical equivalence. Thus the emergence of the sovereign territorial state and the interstate system is a critical component of that larger epistemic shift and also represents a cognitive shift.[33]

Bobbitt locates Europe's transition from "kingly" to "territorial" states between the early sixteenth to the late seventeenth centuries, an era featuring religious wars and the efforts of the Habsburgs to establish imperial dominion over the continent. During this time the kingly state – "a domain of absolute authority that made the king the personification of the State"[34] – was the dominant state polity. Small firearms organized into rotating rows of highly disciplined musketeers and fortified cities that could withstand lengthy sieges changed warfare and made standing armies necessary. Such states were "machines built for the battlefield,"[35] and they reflected a merging of economic and military capabilities. The logic of kingly states was to extend the power of sovereignty to personify the state and enhance dynastic interests. That logic motivated the efforts of Louis XIII and XIV to end religious strife within France and secularize political life, overthrow Habsburg power, place Bourbons on the thrones of France's neighbors, and impose French hegemony on Europe. France emerged from the Thirty Years' War as an archetypal kingly state, legitimated by divine right and dynastic continuity, and featuring "the transformation of the princely Valois state into the Bourbon kingly state, a centralization, secularization, and nationalization of state authority along absolutist lines famously identified with the principle of *raison d'état*."[36]

Benno Teshke agrees up to a point, adding the caveat that "1648, far from signaling a breakthrough to modern inter-state relations, was the culmination of the epoch of absolutist state formation."[37] He contends that

> the bellicose nature of absolutist states was the external expression of political strategies of accumulation rooted in a social property regime characterized by a tax/office state taking coerced rents from a peasantry in possession of its means of subsistence.[38]

Instead of focusing on Westphalia and French absolutism, Teshke emphasizes England's Glorious Revolution of 1688 as beginning state modernization and inter-state relations by the "formation of capitalism."[39]

Unlike kingly states, Bobbitt contends, "the territorial state was identified by its contiguity." "For the territorial state, its borders were everything – its legitimacy, its defense perimeter, its tax base"; it was "a state of definite limits" that "was characterized by a shift from the monarch-as-embodiment of sovereignty to the monarch as minister of sovereignty."[40] Its armies, observes James Sheehan, "were made up of the unskilled, the unwilling, and the unlucky, who were turned into soldiers by endless drill, brutal discipline, and the threat of draconian punishment."[41]

Bobbitt claims that the territorial state rested upon *Staats raison*, which he contrasts with *ragione di stato* and *raison d'état*, describing it as "an imperative that compels its [the state's] strategic designs" and "identifies the state with the country, the land."[42] Of all the state types that Bobbitt describes, the territorial state comes closest to the model international-relations polity. He maintains that the territorial state was ratified as a model, not by the Treaty of Westphalia (1648) that (in his view) legitimized kingly states, but by the Treaty of Utrecht (1713), "the first European treaty that explicitly establishes a balance of power as the objective of the treaty regime."[43] In doing so, the treaty recognized the existence of rules, practices, and norms within an interstate society. The system of territorial states promoted limited (though often bloody) warfare featuring trained professional armies seeking modest territorial adjustments that did not threaten ruling houses or the independence of great powers.

Bobbitt argues that the French revolutionary and Napoleonic wars ushered in yet another variant of the state, the "state-nation." This is "a state that mobilizes a nation – a national ethnocultural group – to act on behalf of the State" that "can thus call on the revenues of all society and on the human talent of all persons" but "does not exist to serve or take direction from the nation, as does the nation-state" which "creates a state in order to benefit the nation which it governs." In other words, the state-nation "was not responsible *to* the nation; rather it was responsible *for* the nation," a relationship that the nation-state would reverse.[44] The state-nation was energized by mass conscription, citizen soldiers, and standing armies; and, as Sheehan contends, "the more universal military service became . . . the more tightly the strands of identity and obligation, welfare and duty, were knitted in a single category of citizenship."[45] One consequence was the emergence of enormous armies driven by aggressive expansionism in the nation's name. The nineteenth-century British, Russian, and French Empires were, Bobbitt argues, state-nations. The wedding of state and nation produced a powerful polity, just as the increasing separation of state and nation under the influence of contemporary regionalization and globalization is producing increasing numbers of weak and divided polities.

Bobbitt's differentiation of "kingly" from "territorial" states and "state-nations" from "nation-states" is unusual, and theorists often conflate these. Typical is Rodney Bruce Hall's two-fold typology of "territorial-sovereign state actors whose regimes relied upon dynastic legitimating principles" and "national-sovereign actors whose regimes have relied upon the 'imagined community' of the nation as a legitimating principle."[46]

In Bobbitt's view, the transition from state-nations to nation-states accelerated throughout the nineteenth century and featured the 1848 revolutions, the Crimean War, extensions of suffrage in much of Europe, climaxing in the unification of Germany. Nation-states were legitimized by the principle of national self-determination: the "nation" was the repository of sovereignty, and embraced "democracy" to an unprecedented degree. The doctrine of self-determination, proclaimed by Europe's colonizers, would, in turn, ultimately destroy the colonial empires of Europe's state-nations.[47] Their colonial wars and the world wars they fought between one another were total, identity-based, conflicts fuelled by industrialization and advancing military technologies.[48] The transition from state-nations to nation-states that privileged citizens who, in turn, assumed exclusive allegiance to "their" states.

Decolonization has led to the proliferation of what Robert Jackson calls "quasi-states" that have "negative" sovereignty or "juridical statehood" but lacking in empirical capacity to ensure citizens' security or welfare.[49] A similar distinction between formal/juridical "sovereignty" and the empirical capacity of "autonomy" is put forward by Kjell Goldmann.[50]

Many globalization enthusiasts believe that state capacity and autonomy – even of well-established states – are currently eroding or, at a minimum, evolving. Some even predict the demise of the nation-state. These include Arjun Appadurai who bluntly predicts that "the nation-state, as a complex modern political form, is on its last legs."[51] Kenichi Ohmae, a strong advocate of this position, declares that the "nation state is increasingly a nostalgic fiction."[52] He argues:

> In the world of near instant communications, the nation-state is irrelevant. One of the outward symbols of its existence is the national border, staffed by uniformed officials checking papers and manning barricades. But what use are such border controls in the world of the Internet, for example? Does a stream of data passing along a fiber-optic cable stop at each national border it crosses so it can be inspected for contraband?[53]

Unfortunately for Ohmae's example, asserting controls over internet content is precisely what some authoritarian countries like China seem increasingly intent on doing.

As we have observed, states are subject to *both* globalizing and localizing dynamics. It is hardly surprising that "failed states" are among the least integrated into global processes and structures,[54] unless they come under the administration of international peacekeeping forces and/or humanitarian agencies. As Rosenau expresses it, "it may well be that in the emergent epoch national states and societies are no longer *the* terminal entities around which people and their institutions are organized. Conceivably, fragmegrative processes may in the long run lead to a proliferation of authority structures above and below the national level that undermines the authority that states and societies can wield."[55]

Michael Mann and Roland Axtmann take more nuanced positions. Mann argues that during the twentieth century what he terms "the modest nation-state" triumphed over dynastic empires and the fascist and communist advocates of "a much stronger, authoritarian state."[56] European states and their white colonies in time "relinquished powers over moral regulation" and "much of social life remained or became *more* private, outside the sphere of competence of the nation-state, even during its great period of expansion."[57] He suggests that those who now perceive the erosion of the state base their claims on four trends: "capitalist transformation, environmental limits, identity politics and post-militarism [or 'post-nuclearism']", but cautions that: "We must beware the more enthusiastic of the globalists and transnationalists."

> With little sense of history, they exaggerate the former strength of the nation-states; with little sense of global variety, they exaggerate their current decline; with little sense of their plurality, they downplay inter-national relations. In all four spheres of "threat" we must distinguish: (a) differential impacts on different types of state in different regions; (b) trends weakening *and* some trends strengthening nation-states; (c) trends displacing national regulation to inter-national as well as to transnational networks; (d) trends simultaneously strengthening nation-states *and* transnationalism.[58]

Axtmann, for his part, concludes that "the changes we witness in the structure of the state are unlikely to lead to its demise" for a variety of reasons. These include the state's role as mediator between the supranational and subnational arenas, its contribution to "collective learning about functional linkages and material interdependencies" among diverse polities, a continuing need to regulate global markets, and the importance of managing social conflicts.[59]

Stephen Krasner represents what is probably the most unyielding realist skepticism about the impact of globalization on the territorial state and change in global politics. He admits: "Some aspects of the contemporary environment are unique – the number of transnational nongovernmental organizations has grown dramatically, international organizations are more prominent, cyber crime could not exist without cyber space" and that such "developments do challenge state control."[60] Nevertheless, the global system remains anarchic, thereby limiting the variation in global rules, actors, and practices. In any event, "Globalization and intrusive international norms," Krasner argues, "are not new phenomena,"[61] and he contends that relatively little has changed over the centuries:

> States have always struggled to control the cross-border flow of ideas, goods, and people. The right of rulers to unilaterally and autonomously establish laws for their own polities has been challenged by external actors concerned about international security, minority rights, and fiscal responsibility. Power holders in the present system do not have an incentive to devise a new set of rules that would displace

those associated with sovereignty because existing arrangements can coexist with alternatives that can be constructed either voluntarily or through coercion when conventional norms provide less attractive outcomes.[62]

Thus, "it is too early to schedule a wake for the sovereign-state system."[63]

CAN GLOBALIZATION BE REVERSED?

A key issue in this book is whether globalization, in whole or in substantial part, is reversible or whether it will overcome obstacles and intensify in future decades. Will global "flows" (a term frequently used in this chapter) – what Appadurai terms "objects in motion"[64] – be seriously impeded or even brought to a halt?

Even before the global recession that began with the subprime mortgage crisis in the United States, some observers concluded that the 9/11 terrorist attacks on New York and Washington were assaults on globalization and its symbols – "dangerous enemies of civilized modernity"[65] – and that the responses to these attacks heightened anti-globalization sentiments. Nicholas Rengger and Caroline Kennedy-Pipe, for example, view 9/11 as having falsified the idea that globalization had helped "to tame war" and make it unthinkable.[66] Economic liberalism became associated with militant US unilateralism. "Certainly," argue David Held and Anthony McGrew, "measured solely in terms of flows within the circuits of the world economy . . . economic globalization temporarily stalled" after 9/11. However, they also note that "[d]espite the war on terror, patterns of global interconnectedness appear to have proven extremely resilient; global economic flows, in fact, soon picked up and intensified."[67]

Held and McGrew maintain that empirical evidence shows that globalization is more "socially embedded" than critics claim and rests on "a number of 'deep drivers'." These include "the changing infrastructure of global communications linked to the IT revolution; the development of global markets in goods and services, connected to the worldwide distribution of information; the new global division of labour driven by multinational corporations; the end of the Cold War and the diffusion of democratic and consumer values across many of the world's regions (alongside some marked reactions to this); and the growth of migration and the movement of peoples, linked to shifts in patterns of economic demand, demography and environmental degradation."[68] "The *social* facts of globalization," Ronaldo Munck observes, "are myriad, from transnational migration to the rise of the 'global city', from new forms of community to the flourishing of global crime."[69] In McGrew's view:

> Explanations of economic globalization tend to focus on three interrelated factors or social forces; *technics* (technological change and social organization); *economics* (markets and capitalism); and *politics* (ideas, interests, and institutions). Since they are so closely interrelated, the principal methodological problem for analysis lies in unbundling the causal mechanisms involved.[70]

Even in the economic sphere globalization remains a contested concept. The agenda behind Paul Hirst's definition of globalization becomes apparent when he stresses that not only did its first two periods not "undermine the nation-state," but also, in fact, that "many modern nation-states were forged during the *belle époque* and sustained by rapid industrial growth." And he argues that, between 1950 and 1973, supposedly the "heyday of autonomy in national economic policy and of Keynesian demand management," when governments cooperated, they could exercise a considerable amount of "supranational governance."[71]

So has nothing changed? Hirst acknowledges that direct merchandise trade has become much less significant as capital flows have increased, but he avoids asking whether the vast speculative flows of currency that characterize the present are unprecedented and does not address what impact they and other globalizing trends might have upon state autonomy and capacity. For instance, between 1998 and 2010, currency trading exploded from $1.5 trillion per day to $4 trillion per day.[72]

Are current capital flows, other than daily financial speculation, global in scope? Hirst notes that over 90 percent of foreign direct investment still takes place between and among rich countries, representing just over a quarter of the world's population. His intention is twofold, first to demonstrate that a great deal of investment is not actually global but concentrated and, second, that as long as this is the case, the potential for the relatively small group of affected countries to design joint strategies for regulation remains high. He concludes that global "governance [is] possible, given the political will and a measure of international consensus,"[73] thereby introducing a powerful qualification of his forecast.

The claim that the spatial scope of globalizing trends is limited is also implicit in observations that much of global economic activity emanates from and links a few "world cities"[74] that "are locations through which global goods and services reach their markets and are consumed and from which surplus values are extracted."[75] "A focus on cities," argues Sassen, "decomposes the national economy into a variety of subnational components. Some are profoundly articulated with the global economy and others not," and it "also signals the declining significance of the national economy as a unitary category."[76]

A similar implication is found in the claim that globalization is more intense in particular bilateral relationships and/or in certain regions. Thus, it is hotly debated whether bilateral trade agreements and regional arrangements such as the EU, ASEAN, NAFTA, Mercosur, and the like are building blocks of globalization or are impediments to it.[77] C. Fred Bergsten does not believe regionalization needs to impede global trade, but he strongly prefers globalization "because it maximizes the number of foreign markets involved and avoids the economic distortions (and political risks) of discrimination among trading partners."[78] Whatever one's view of this matter, regional arrangements probably do encourage the fragmentation of states into smaller components because the regional grouping provides local producers with larger markets than the states of which they had been a part. In addition, markets in the microstates that have emerged from the fragmentation of countries like the Soviet Union and Yugoslavia are tempted to cooperate and interact informally for economic survival.[79]

The globalizing process also knits people in distant places together, thereby producing, not simply worldwide interdependence, but "a structural shift . . . in the organization of human affairs: from a world of discrete but interdependent national states to the world as a shared social space,"[80] and featuring the rapid and large-scale movement of persons, things, and ideas across space. "It is now possible," Thomas Friedman argues, "for more people than ever to collaborate and compete in real time with other people on more different kinds of work from more different corners of the planet and on a more equal footing than at any previous time in the history of the world – using computers, e-mail, fiber-optic networks, teleconferencing, and dynamic new software."[81] Globalization challenges the unity and capacity of states and cultures, threatening unique traditions and cultures and reducing the authority of nation-building leaders.[82] "If physical borders separate states spatially and are zealously maintained in order to assert the identity of the state, then cultural boundaries are equally important in distinguishing different groups in the minds of the population for the same end."[83] Of course, cultural tensions are not solely transnational; they are frequently intrastate as well.[84] Whatever the source of cultural challenges, the result has been a combination of acceptance and resistance on the part of local elites bent on anchoring nationalism, preserving power, and reinforcing traditional normative structures linked to religion, language, and/or ethnicity.

Although we have examined some the features of globalization and described how the present authors came to write this book, we must now consider systematically how to define globalization. Our answer conditions the rest of this book.

NOTES

1. This is also true of academia elsewhere.
2. Arjun Appadurai, "Grassroots Globalization and the Research Imagination," in A. Appadurai, ed., *Globalization* (Durham, NC: Duke University Press, 2001), 1.
3. See Barnaby J. Feder, "Theodore J. Levitt, 81, Who Coined the Term 'Globalization', Is Dead," *New York Times*, July 6, 2006, http://www.nytimes.com/2006/07/06/business/06levitt.html.
4. Richard W. Mansbach, Yale H. Ferguson, and Donald E. Lampert, *The Web of World Politics* (Englewood Cliffs, NJ: Prentice Hall, 1976).
5. Jan Nederveen Pieterse, *Globalization and Culture* (Lanham, MD: Rowman & Littlefield, 2004), 116.
6. See Yale H. Ferguson and Richard W. Mansbach, *The State, Conceptual Chaos, and the Future of International Relations* (Boulder, CO: Lynne Rienner, 1989).
7. Yale H. Ferguson and Richard W. Mansbach, *Polities: Authority, Identities, and Change* (Columbia, SC: University of South Carolina Press, 1996).
8. Yale H. Ferguson and Richard W. Mansbach, *Remapping Global Politics* (Cambridge: Cambridge University Press, 2004).
9. James N. Rosenau, *Turbulence in World Politics* (Princeton, NJ: Princeton University Press, 1990), 6.
10. David Held and Anthony McGrew, "The Great Globalization Debate: An Introduction," in D. Held and A. McGrew, eds., *The Global Transformations Reader: An Introduction to the Globalization Debate*, 2nd edn (Cambridge: Polity Press, 2003), 8.
11. Linda Weiss, "Globalization and National Governance: Antinomy or Interdependence?" *Review of International Studies* 25 (December 1999), 61, 62. Emphasis in original.
12. Yale H. Ferguson and Richard W. Mansbach, *The Elusive Question Continues* (Upper Saddle River, NJ: Prentice Hall, 2003), 204.
13. Jan Aart Scholte, "The Geography of Collective Identities in a Globalizing World," *Review of International Political Economy* 3:4 (Winter 1996), 567.
14. See J. David Singer, "The Level-of-Analysis Problem in International Relations," *World Politics* 14:1 (October 1961), 77–92.

15 Yale H. Ferguson and Richard W. Mansbach, *A World of Polities* (London: Routledge, 2008).
16 For an analysis of the characteristics of global governance, see James W. Nickel, "Is Today's International Human Rights Regime System a Global Governance Regime?" *The Journal of Ethics* 6:4 (2002), 354–6.
17 Ferguson and Mansbach, *Polities*, 33–4.
18 Ibid., 43.
19 Philip Cerny, "Multi-nodal Politics: Globalisation Is What Actors Make of It," *Review of International Studies* 35:2 (April 2009), 424. Emphasis in original.
20 Yale H. Ferguson and Richard W. Mansbach, *The Elusive Quest* (Columbia, SC: University of South Carolina Press, 1988), 367–75.
21 See, for example, Moisés Naím, "Globalization," *Foreign Policy* 171 (March/April 2009), 28–34.
22 Martin Wolf, an advocate of globalization, argues that it is irreversible in the long run but reversible in the short run, by which he appears to mean a century or more. Martin Wolf, *Why Globalization Works* (New Haven, CT: Yale University Press, 2004), 96. In discussing the long run, Wolf leans heavily on Robert Wright, *Nonzero: The Logic of Human Destiny* (New York: Vintage Books, 2000) and his view of cultural evolution. Nevertheless, as we stress in subsequent chapters, almost any logic also suggests that, insofar as globalization is a multifaceted phenomenon, certain dimensions will be more (or less) reversible than others – or perhaps irreversible.
23 Matthew Hannah, "Representation/Reality," in Noel Castree, Alistair Rogers, and Douglas Sherman, eds., *Questioning Geography* (Oxford: Blackwell Publishing, 2005), 164. Emphasis in original.
24 See Ferguson and Mansbach, *Polities*, and Yale H. Ferguson and Richard W. Mansbach, "Polities, the Past, and the Present," *Millennium* 37:2 (December 2008), 365–79.
25 Ferguson and. Mansbach, *Remapping Global Politics*, 338.
26 Ibid., 314–19.
27 Ibid., 340.
28 See, for example, "The Cracks Spread and Widen," *The Economist*, May 1, 2010, 63–5, and Graham Bowley, "Wall St. Slides, Fearing a Return to Recession," *New York Times*, May 14, 2010, http://www.nytimes.com/2010/05/15/business/15markets.html.
29 Jonathan Cheng, "Changing Season in Asia Revives Avian Flu Threat to Humans and Birds," *Wall Street Journal*, December 15, 2008, A12, "Watching Nervously," *The Economist*, May 2, 2009, 69–70, Keith Bradsher, "Assessing the Danger of New Flu," *New York Times*, April 27, 2009, http://www.nytimes.com/2009/04/28/health/28hong.html, and Betsy McKay, "As Flu Retreats, Scientists Brace for Its Return," *Wall Street Journal*, May 28, 2009, A10.
30 See, for example, James C. McKinley Jr., "Mexican Cartels Lure American Teens as Killers," *New York Times*, June 22, 2009, http://www.nytimes.com/2009/06/23/us/23killers.html.
31 Philip Bobbitt, *The Shield of Achilles: War, Peace, and the Course of History* (New York: Random House, 2002), 6.
32 Ibid., 81.
33 Saskia Sassen, *Territory, Authority, Rights* (Princeton, NJ: Princeton University Press, 2006), 80–1. Sassen (43–5) explains: "The economic transformations between 1000 and 1300 brought with them political innovations. Monetization, trade, and the growing wealth and numbers of towns altered the political organization of the times in that they weakened the system of in-kind transfers crucial to earlier feudal organization. . . . It is also the period when territorial state sovereignty is invented . . . In addition, it was at this time that the notion itself of boundaries was established . . . It is then out of these self-apotheosized weak kings that the origins of the European sovereign territorial state can be traced. . . . By the time their dynasty ended they had claimed full authority over all inhabitants of the territory, within fixed boundaries and held no claims beyond these."

34 Bobbitt, *The Shield of Achilles*, 95.
35 Bill Jordan, *The State: Authority and Autonomy* (Oxford: Basil Blackwell, 1985), 152.
36 Bobbitt, *The Shield of Achilles*, 109. Bourbon France was less absolutist than commonly thought. See Perry Anderson, *Lineages of the Absolutist State* (London: New Left Books, 1974), 5, and Bertrand Badie and Pierre Birnbaum, *The Sociology of the State*, trans. A. Goldhammer (Chicago, IL: University of Chicago Press, 1983), 105 ff.
37 Benno Teshke, *The Myth of 1648* (London: Verso, 2003), 3.
38 Ibid., 10.
39 Ibid., 248.
40 Bobbitt, *The Shield of Achilles*, 120, 139, 143.
41 James J. Sheehan, *Where Have All the Soldiers Gone?* (Boston, MA: Houghton Mifflin, 2008), 15.
42 Bobbitt, *The Shield of Achilles*, 135–6. According to Bobbitt (136): "The *raison d'état* is a reason invoked on behalf of a king, justifying his acts as being those imposed on him by the State" and *ragione di stato* "are reasons that distinguish the state code of behavior from the moral code of the prince" as a private individual.
43 Ibid., 129.
44 Ibid., 146, 196, 178. Emphasis in original.
45 Sheehan, *Where Have All the Soldiers Gone?*, 14.
46 Rodney Bruce Hall, *National Collective Identity* (New York: Columbia University Press, 1999), 4. Unlike Bobbitt, Hall sees colonial expansion as characteristic of nation-states, which he interprets as the "global transmission of bourgeois-national identity and culture" (214–47). For a concise description of the modern nation-state, see Roland Axtmann, "The State of the State: The Model of the Modern State and Its Contemporary Transformation," *International Political Science Review* 25:3 (July 2004), 259–79.
47 Robert H. Jackson, "The Weight of Ideas in Decolonization: Normative Change in International Relations," in Judith Goldstein and Robert O. Keohane, eds., *Ideas and Foreign Policy* (Ithaca, NY: Cornell University Press, 1993), 119–26.
48 Michael Geyer, "German Strategy in the Age of Machine Warfare, 1914–1945," in Peter Paret, ed., *Makers of Modern Strategy* (Princeton, NJ: Princeton University Press, 1986), 527–97.
49 Robert Jackson, *Quasi-States: Sovereignty, International Relations and the Third World* (Cambridge: Cambridge University Press, 1990), 168–9.
50 Kjell Goldmann, *Transforming the European Nation-State* (London: Sage, 2001), 62–5. Axtmann believes that for democratic states, at least, Goldmann's distinction "is unintelligible" because having "sovereign rights" requires the capability to act upon those rights. See Axtmann, "The State of the State," 263.
51 Arjun Appadurai, *Modernity at Large* (Minneapolis, MN: University of Minnesota Press, 1996), 19.
52 Kenichi Ohmae, *The End of the Nation State* (New York: Free Press, 1995), 12.
53 Kenichi Ohmae, *The Next Global Stage* (Upper Saddle River, NJ: Pearson Education, 2005), 91.
54 Gearóid Ó Tuathail, Andrew Herod, and Susan M. Roberts, "Negotiating Unruly Problematics," in A. Herod, G. Ó. Tuathail, and S. M. Roberts., eds., *An Unruly World? Globalization, Governance and Geography* (London: Routledge, 1998), 11–12.
55 James N. Rosenau, *Distant Proximities* (Princeton, NJ: Princeton University, 2003), 85–6. Emphasis in original.
56 Michael Mann, "Has Globalization Ended the Rise and Rise of the Nation-State?" *Review of International Political Economy* 4:3 (Autumn 1997), 477.
57 Ibid. Emphasis in original.
58 Ibid. Emphasis in original.
59 Axtmann, "The State of the State," 271.
60 Stephen D. Krasner, "Abiding Sovereignty," *International Political Science Review* 22:3 (July 2001), 248.

61 Ibid.
62 Ibid.
63 Ibid., 231. Sassen points out that that mobility also entails "fixity." Thus, "capital fixity" is a precondition for "hypermobile dematerialized financial instruments." See Saskia Sassen, "Spatialities and Temporalities of the Global: Elements for a Theorization," in Appadurai, ed., *Globalization*, 263.
64 Appadurai, "Grassroots Globalization and the Research Imagination," 5.
65 Wolf, *Why Globalization Works*, 10.
66 Nicholas Rengger and Caroline Kennedy-Pipe, "The State of War," *International Affairs* 84:5 (September 2008), 891. See also Caroline Kennedy-Pipe and Nicholas Rengger, "Apocalypse Now? Continuities or Disjunctions in World Politics after 9/11," *International Affairs* 82:3 (May 2006), 427–30.
67 David Held and Anthony McGrew, "Introduction: Globalization at Risk?" in David Held and Anthony McGrew, eds., *Globalization Theory* (Cambridge: Polity Press, 2007), 1.
68 Ibid., 4.
69 Ronaldo Munck, *Globalization and Contestation* (London: Routledge, 2007), 8. Emphasis in original.
70 Anthony McGrew, "The Logics of Economic Globalization," in John Ravenhill, ed., *Global Political Economy*, 2nd edn (Oxford: Oxford University Press, 2008), 296. Emphasis in original.
71 Paul Hirst, "The Global Economy – Myths and Realities," *International Affairs* 73 (1997), 410–12.
72 Tom Lauricella and Dave Kansas, "Currency Trading Soars," *Wall Street Journal*, September 1, 2010, A1, A2.
73 Paul Hirst, "The Global Economy," 425.
74 Paul L. Knox and Peter J. Taylor, *World Cities in a World-System* (Cambridge, UK: Cambridge University Press, 1995), Saskia Sassen, *The Global City*, 2nd edn (Princeton, NJ: Princeton University Press, 2001), and Peter Dicken, *Global Shift: Mapping the Changing Contours of the World Economy*, 5th edn (New York: Guilford Press, 2007), 62–4.
75 David Clark, *Urban World/Global City*, 2nd edn (London: Routledge, 2003), 11.
76 Saskia Sassen, *Globalization and Its Discontents* (New York: New Press, 1998), xix.
77 For a negative view of such arrangements, see "Doing Doha Down," *The Economist*, September 5, 2009, 15, 18.
78 C. Fred Bergsten, "Globalizing Free Trade," *Foreign Affairs* 75:3 (May/June 1996), 106.
79 See, for example, "Entering the Yugosphere," *The Economist*, August 22, 2009, 45–6, which describes the restoration of economic links among the former Yugoslav republics in an informal regional successor to Yugoslavia.
80 David Held and Anthony McGrew, *Globalization/Anti-Globalization*, 2nd edn (Cambridge: Polity Press, 2007), 3.
81 Thomas L. Friedman, *The World Is Flat* (New York: Farrar, Straus & Giroux, 2005), 8.
82 See, for example, Somini Sengupta, "Attack on Women at an Indian Bar Intensifies a Clash of Cultures," *New York Times*, February 9, 2009, http://www.nytimes.com/2009/02/09/world/asia/09india.html in which one woman declared: "We are globalized in our lifestyle, but very Indian at heart."
83 Tong Chee Kiong and Lian Kwen Fee, "Cultural Knowledge, Nation-States, and the Limits of Globalization in Southeast Asia," in Shinji Yamashita and Jeremy Seymour Eades, eds., *Globalization in Southeast Asia: Local, National, and Transnational Perspectives* (Oxford: Berghahn Books, 2002), 44.
84 See, for example, Sengupta, "Attack on Women at an Indian Bar."

CHAPTER 1

What is globalization?

What Nandan is saying, I thought to myself, is that the playing field is being flattened ... Flattened? I rolled that word around in my head for a while and then, in the chemical way that these things happen, it just popped out: My God, he's telling me the world is flat![1]

What does globalization mean for labor markets and fair wages? How will it affect chances for real jobs and reliable rewards? What does it mean for the ability of nations to determine the economic futures of their populations? What is the hidden dowry of globalization? Christianity? Cyber-proletarianization? New forms of structural adjustment? Americanization disguised as human rights or as MTV?[2]

Practically everyone is touched by globalization, and the term, as Zygmunt Bauman observes, is "on everybody's lips, a fad word fast turning into a shibboleth."[3] Susan Strange's warning that globalization "can refer to anything from the Internet to a hamburger"[4] should be kept in mind. The forces driving the process are said to include "deterritorialization, digitization, internationalization, liberalization, modernization, privatization, regionalization, universalization, weaponization, Westernization, etc."[5]

It quickly becomes evident, then, that globalization is poorly understood and its impact is fiercely debated, partly because "it is such a big idea, a 'grand theory' or meta-narrative which seeks to account for many, indeed most, of the social, economic, geographical and political characteristics of the contemporary world."[6] It is, as Jan Nederveen Pieterse's puts it so well, "like a prism in which major disputes over the collective human condition are now refracted: questions of capitalism, inequality, power, development, ecology, culture, gender, identity, population, all come back in a landscape where 'globalization did it,'" and it "crosses boundaries of government and business, media and social movements, general and academic interest."[7]

Definitional issues also muddy efforts to generalize about the consequences of globalization. Are globalizing trends making for the continued advance of a "human web,"[8] a global "network society,"[9] a "flat,"[10] "bumpy,"[11] or "spiky"[12] world, selective "denationalization,"[13] or "fragmegration"?[14] Or, are state borders regaining significance as governments and international institutions respond to current global financial and economic crises caused by unregulated markets and the spread of global financial networks?[15] Has a failure of risk management by major financial institutions around the world involving the proliferation of derivatives and securitization of arcane assets undermined the essential ideational and economic bases of globalization?

Is there an emergent "end-of-history"[16] consensus around free market capitalism and political democracy? Or, is ideological support for neoliberal capitalism eroding as suggested by a 2011 poll that indicated that between 2002 and 2010 the percentage of Americans who believe that the free market system is the world's best declined from 80 to 59 percent.[17] To what extent is globalization still advancing, stalling, or in retreat? To what degree are sovereign states losing their authority, merely adapting to globalizing processes, or reasserting their authority and control over their borders and citizens?

THE MEANING(S) OF GLOBALIZATION

Unfortunately, though perhaps not surprisingly, just as there is disagreement about most aspects of globalization, there is no single, agreed-upon definition of the phenomenon itself. As Thomas Risse suggests, "explanations for its origins as well as its consequences are equally varied."[18] Again, normative preferences intervene and preclude consensus. "For some," as Risse declares, "globalization means the internationalization of financial markets and of production networks. Others understand globalization as the erosion of borders and the end of the nation-state as we know it."[19]

Defining globalization might seem to some a nominal task suitable only for introductory texts, yet research agendas are repeatedly confounded by the confusion that flows from defining the concept in different ways. Hence both the range of useful notions and our own definition of globalization must be clear for the analysis that follows to be meaningful.

An attractive definition is provided by David Held and his colleagues who declare globalization to be "the widening, deepening and speeding up of worldwide interconnectedness in all aspects of contemporary social life, from the cultural to the criminal, the financial to the spiritual."[20] It consists of the "multiplicity of linkages and interconnections that transcend the nation-state (and by implication the societies) which make up the modern world system." It "defines a process through which events, decisions, and activities in one part of the world can come to have significant consequences for individuals in quite distant parts of the globe."[21] The combining of the local and global in this way leads James Rosenau to view the phenomenon as a matter of "distant proximities."[22]

The way in which globalization is conceptualized is surely critical to any assessment of whether the current era is unique in human history, and the comprehensive history of globalization that we provide later bears witness to our own conviction that historical perspective is crucial. We subscribe, for example, to the multidimensional and deeply historical view of Barry Gills and William Thompson who write of "globalizations" in the plural, arguing that globalization processes "have long pedigrees" and "are anything but novel."[23] As they see it, the reason that we think of globalization as novel "has to do with the way we tell stories about the past" that focus on "relatively local and largely disconnected events."[24] "History," they conclude, "is a matter of perspective. Local perspectives yield local histories. Global perspectives yield global perspectives."[25]

In his popular text, Jan Aart Scholte identifies five different definitions of globalization, all of which treat it as a *process*. The first is *internationalization* meaning "cross-border relations between countries" and the "growth of international exchange and interdependence."[26] This definition emphasizes the nature of relations among sovereign states and retains a state-centric focus. As such, it implies that little is new about contemporary globalization or, as Scholte puts it: "Global relations of this kind can be examined on the same ontological and methodological grounds as international relations" and "gives the comforting message that the new can be wholly understood in terms of the familiar."[27] This definition has roots in earlier communications/transactions approaches to political integration in which it was thought that data concerning the absolute volume of interstate transactions, the relative amount of transactions among actors, the geographic concentration of transactions, the ratio of interstate to intrastate transactions, and the percentage change in volume of transactions indicated the direction and velocity of interstate integration.[28]

Scholte's other four definitions extend the range of potential understandings and hence, of course, potential confusion. His second usage is globalization as economic *liberalization* that removes artificial state restrictions on borderless markets. A third conception is *universalization*, a reassuring notion (to some) that local cultures will somehow be synthesized into a sort of "planetary humanism." A fourth definition is globalization as *Westernization or modernization*, a trajectory that may be viewed with alarm in non-Western traditional societies and by fundamentalist religious movements. Scholte's fifth approach is *respacialization*, which is rather like Rosenau's distant proximities mentioned earlier, and emphasizes "increased transplanetary connections" among persons.[29] We will have more to say about Scholte's definitions shortly. Suffice it to say here that they intersect and diverge in complicated ways with the three orientations towards globalization that Held and his colleagues label *hyperglobalist, skeptical,* and *transformationalist*.[30]

Skeptics

Skeptics insist that contemporary globalization is neither new nor revolutionary.[31] Typical is the view of Tom Nairn and Paul James who contend that "globalization is treated mythically as the latest thing, the all-encompassing process that itself explains all that happens on this planet." As they see it, "moving from the ridiculous to the sublimely stupid, some globalization ideologues have just begun proclaiming its 'true meaning' as the natural condition of the planet, pushing globalization back to the beginning of time and naturalizing as if it has always been with us."[32] As we shall explain later, the true situation is exactly the reverse: it is the sublimely stupid, or, more kindly, ideologically blinkered, who cannot read the clear historical trajectory.

However, skeptics should not be dismissed lightly. Although the present authors are generally unsympathetic to their perspective, the traumatic events that followed America's subprime mortgage crisis and the later threats of European and American sovereign default should alert us to the real possibility that the global economic system could contract, that barriers to human and economic movement could be reestablished, and that authoritarian solutions to economic and social woes might be sought. Is the economic downturn merely a blip in a long-term trend towards greater globalization, or does it signify a more fundamental turning point in economic, political, and social life? Finally, social science has repeatedly toyed with "fad words." Might globalization be another? These are the central questions that lie behind this book.

Skeptics observe that governments still retain the formal authority to regulate the global economy. Interdependence, they argue, is no higher today than it was in the late nineteenth century – another claim we address later. In their view, developments such as the simultaneous lowering in 2008 of US interest rates by the Federal Reserve, the Bank of England, and the European Central Bank, as well as a strong yen and a reduction in Japanese exports, simply reflect traditional interstate interdependence. Yet governments were also confronting a threatened collapse of a far more complex global economy (not least in terms of variety of actors) than anything that existed in the nineteenth century or even the Great Depression of the 1930s.

Skeptics focus on the economic dimension of globalization, arguing that it features high levels of interstate trade and the expansion of regional and exclusive common markets such as the European Union (EU) and the North American Free Trade Agreement (NAFTA) that, they claim, reduce global economic integration.[33] This is the view of Paul Hirst and Grahame Thompson who stress "the continued dominance of the Triad economic blocs – North America, Europe and Japan – in trade, in FDI [foreign direct investment] flows and stocks and in world income distribution."[34] As skeptics see it, states retain a dominant role in these activities, including an ability to regulate or unravel economic integration. The power of governments, in other words, has not ebbed; state sovereignty has not eroded; and transnational corporations remain under national control and retain national characteristics. States can reassert sovereign prerogatives any time they choose to do so, even though the costs of doing so may be high. States, not least the United States and China, are responsible for higher levels of transborder economic activities and the existence and survival of global institutions like the World Trade Organization (WTO) and the International Monetary Fund (IMF).

Hirst and Thompson summarize the skeptical view of globalization:

> The present highly internationalized economy . . . is not unprecedented: it is one of a number of distinct conjunctures of states of the international economy that have existed since the economy based on modern industrial technology began to

be generalized from the 1860s. In some respects the current international economy is *less* open and integrated than the regime that prevailed from 1870 to 1914.[35]

Even the magnitude of migration in the nineteenth century, they declare, was greater than at present. Elsewhere, Hirst observes that the growth in international trade and investment "has been going on, punctuated by the interruptions of severe economic crises and wars, for well over a century." "By the late nineteenth century, the whole world had become part of a developed and interconnected commercial civilization." A second phase began at the end of World War II, lasting until the OPEC oil crisis of 1973, when trade and output grew significantly; and a third took place between 1973 and 1979, when capital movements grew dramatically owing to the deregulation of financial markets and floating exchange rates.[36]

Hirst and Thompson retain a highly state-centric perspective, limiting themselves to interstate transactions. Hence, they conclude:

So long as governments continue to target their current accounts, retaining some sovereignty within their borders ... and differentially regulate their financial systems, investors cannot think about domestic and foreign assets in the same way. Different national financial systems are made up of different institutions and arrangements, with different conceptions of the future and assessments of past experience, and thus operate with different modalities of calculation. *All these features factor into a continued diversity of expectation and outlooks which cannot all be reduced to a single global marketplace or logic.*[37]

For Scholte, as for the present authors, this line of reasoning is seriously misleading. He observes that economic liberalization "has generally ranked as policy orthodoxy in respect of contemporary globalization" because of its "hold on élite circles," but he concludes that this definition is an "analytical dead-end."[38] It is deficient not least because it relies so heavily on states and intergovernmental institutions and bargaining. For instance, while the governments of states go on wrangling with diminishing returns over the familiar agendas of tariff and non-tariff barriers to trade, corporations are organizing their own supply chains and negotiating a wide range of accommodations directly with governments and their counterparts abroad.

Historian Niall Ferguson adopts a similar "it-all-happened-before" perspective. "From around 1870 until World War I," he argues, "the world economy thrived in ways that look familiar today."

The mobility of commodities, capital, and labor reached record levels; the sea-lanes and telegraphs across the Atlantic had never been busier, as capital and migrants traveled west and raw materials and manufactures traveled east. In relation to output, exports of both merchandise and capital reached volumes not seen again until the 1980s. Total emigration from Europe between 1880 and 1910 was in excess of 25 million. People spoke euphorically of 'the annihilation of distance.'[39]

According to Ferguson, World War I brought an end to this happy era of globalization. "International trade, investment, and migration all collapsed."[40] Thereafter, the

Great Depression fostered inward-looking and "beggar-thy-neighbor" policies, with America's 1930 Smoot-Hawley tariff raising tariffs to new heights on some 20,000 imports. If history is any guide, then globalization, according to Ferguson, is reversible.

Still another but quite different skeptical perspective is provided by Alexander Cooley and Hendrik Spruyt who contend that "the common proposition that the twin forces of internationalization and globalization are eroding state sovereignty is a clumsy conceptual approach to the topic."[41] Theirs is a nuanced view to the effect that "exclusive sovereignty as a right and even entitlement of modern states"[42] is a fiction; instead, contemporary global politics, they argue, features a variety of subtle arrangements featuring "intermediary," "incomplete," "mixed," or "hybrid" sovereignty in which sovereign rights are shared. They interpret sovereignty as a dynamic contractual form of governance, in which a distinction must be made between the right of ownership ("residual rights") and the right to make use of the territory and other assets of a polity. In other words, "sovereignty consists of a bundle of rights."

> Some polities maintain most, and perhaps almost all, such rights for themselves. Others, willfully or by force, relinquish considerable rights to external powers. Yet others, as polities in some regional organizations, surrender some sovereign rights to new institutional sites while they retain others for themselves. Like property rights, aspects of sovereignty can be split or shared by states and other international actors.[43]

Territoriality from this perspective is no longer exclusive. Nor is it exclusive when dealing with outer space or with the seabed where countries are increasingly making claims to exploit resources.

Another form of skepticism is expressed by Robert Keohane and Joseph Nye, who suggest their "characterization of interdependence more than 20 years ago now applies to globalization at the turn of the millennium."[44] In their view, globalization assumes "that something is increasing," so they prefer to use the term "globalism," "a condition that can increase or decrease." "Globalism" they define as "a state of the world involving networks of interdependence at multicontinental distances" that has "ancient roots."[45] They conclude that globalization can be analyzed much as they had analyzed "complex interdependence," that is, in terms of sensitivity and vulnerability.[46]

Hyperglobalists

Like skeptics, hyperglobalists focus largely on the economic dimension of globalization. They include (interestingly enough) both economic neoliberals and Marxists. Among the most committed of the hyperglobalists are the vigorous proponents of neoliberal economics who are committed to economic efficiency rather than equality or abstract justice. As Peter Dicken observes: "To the 'neo-liberals' on the right – the pro-globalizers – globalization is a political economic project, one which, it is argued, will bring the greatest benefit for the greatest number ... The 'rising tide' of globalization will 'lift all boats'; human material well-being will be enhanced ..."[47]

Dicken also captures the views of hyperglobalists who criticize globalization and who value equality and justice above efficiency. "To the hyper-globalizers of the left – the *anti*-globalizers – the problem is globalization itself. The very operation of those market forces claimed to be beneficent by the right are regarded as the crux of the problem: a malign and destructive force . . . Unregulated markets inevitably lead to a reduction in well-being for all but a small minority in the world . . ."[48]

Hyperglobalists believe that changes in the global economy are ushering in a novel historical era in which territorial states have become obsolete economic units. Fixation on territorial states, they argue, reflects an outdated (even for Europe) Eurocentric view of the world. Instead, globalization, as they see it, is producing a single, integrated global market in which transnational corporations (TNCs) from many countries vigorously compete with one another, and capital is immensely mobile.[49] Contemporary capital mobility contrasts dramatically with what Moisés Naím calls the "pre-reform era" in which "most countries either banned or tightly limited foreign currency transactions" and in which "[f]oreign investment was closely screened and regulated, and 'export of capital' was a crime."[50]

Hyperglobalists reject the skeptics' contention that the nineteenth century saw a higher level of global economic integration than the present, pointing out, among other things, that trade relative to the production of merchandise goods is much higher today. This is because "the barriers that inhibit trade and prevent exchange from taking place are lower today than they were a century ago."[51] Transportation costs remain low, tariff barriers are lower, and information about foreign markets is greatly improved.[52]

In addition, trade in services among developed countries has replaced trade in manufactured goods as "GDP [gross domestic product] in current prices has become increasingly dominated by services. In 1913 about two-thirds of GDP in advanced countries, in current prices, consisted of the production of goods; today, services make up the same proportion."[53] And, as Hamilton and Quinlan observe,

> The internet is to trade and services what the advent of container shipping was to trade in goods – a transforming capability that enables faster, cross-border delivery of a variety of activities that were once considered non-tradable . . . advertising, education, medicine, data processing, consulting, legal services, engineering and a host of other functions.[54]

This reveals that the technological capacity of TNCs is actually altering the very meaning of competition. "Traditionally," declare Hamilton and Quinlan, "competition was defined within specific sectors of the economy – clearly understood market segments with understandable sets of competitors." Manufacturers of automobiles, bicycles, and airplanes were rarely, if ever, in competition.

> Now, due to these transformative technologies, falling barriers and relative ease of movement, a company's toughest competition might come not from its traditional rivals, but from another sector entirely . . . Competition is between various economic areas that utilize new technologies in ways that cut across traditional economic sectors, producing new "value domains" and new customers.[55]

This phenomenon is evident, for example, in Apple's "tablet computer" that combines elements of a laptop and a smart phone that competes with firms that make computers, cell phones, televisions, and so forth.[56] These changes encourage enterprises "to move from geographically concentrated production networks to geographically dispersed networks."[57] Production is global, and trade and investment are fused.

For such reasons, today's global economic integration, in the view of hyperglobalizers, is without precedent, and "economic globalization is bringing about a 'denationalization' of economies through the establishment of transnational networks of production, trade, and finance,"[58] a "borderless economy" in which "national governments are relegated to little more than transmission belts for global capital."[59] Denationalization is visible in the emergence of a new economic class, often associated with transnational corporations, whose members are separated from fellow citizens by barriers of language, knowledge, wealth, and tastes and to whom they may be physically proximate but psychologically remote. Wealth only partly explains the status of the globalized elite. Access to knowledge and information is even more significant.[60] "The growing disparity in what information is becoming available to mass populations," argues Edward Comor, "relative to what is becoming available to elites, signals little hope that the information revolution will result in much more than the liberation of the most powerful."[61] The new class is profoundly pro-globalization.

Instead of a world of distinctive local cultures and traditional values, then, globalization promotes a globalized wealthy, highly educated, and upwardly mobile sector, which places a premium on possessive individualism, consumerism, secularism, and neoliberal capitalism. Its members are psychologically close to others like themselves, who may be geographically remote, but with whom they regularly communicate by email, fax, and telephone and whose tastes, norms, and values they share.

It is less important that urban managerial, knowledge, and technocratic elites dress much the same, eat some of the same foods, and listen to some of the same music than that they substitute these norms and values for socially stabilizing customs and norms on which traditional authority structures rest. Their norms are on view at annual meetings of the World Economic Forum in Davos, Switzerland, and at international academic and institutional conferences that collectively reflect transnational epistemic communities. In sum, the division of the world between a relatively small number of globalized elites and the masses of citizens has created new horizontal, class-like we–they boundaries that transcend national boundaries.

Hyperglobalizers also contend that the growth of a single global market and the declining capacity of states to determine their economic destiny are among the most important factors characterizing contemporary globalization. Transnational corporations, capital markets, and related activities no longer have a true territorial home, and many are cross-border and transnational in nature.[62] Neoliberal hyperglobalizers applaud the resulting growth in overall wealth and, as noted earlier, tend to play down the claims of inequality within and among states, whereas Marxist hyperglobalizers focus on the growth of intrastate and interstate inequality.

Hyperglobalizers gather considerable data to buttress their claims. With the collapse of the communist bloc at the Cold War's end, the capitalist economic system finally became genuinely global in scope. The last fifty years of the twentieth century witnessed a twenty-fold increase in merchandise trade, a far greater increase than in merchandise production, indicating that ever more production was being traded internationally.[63] Between 1973 and 1995, the ratio of daily foreign exchange trading ($10–$20 billion) to world trade grew from 2/1 to 70/1, with daily foreign exchange trading at $1,260 billion.[64] By 2007, *daily* foreign exchange turnover was $3.2 trillion, increasing some 69 percent since 2004.[65] Global trade reached new heights before recession began to take its global toll at the end of 2007, and the concentration of trade in North America and Europe was declining as China, India, and Brazil rapidly emerged as global economic players. Global interest rates increasingly converged, reflecting the growing interdependence of key economies.

The conception of hyperglobalism is akin to Scholte's *liberalization*, emphasizing the speed and volume of economic exchange across sovereign borders. Globalization in this perspective owes much to neoliberal economics and is to be measured by "removal of official interventions in the market, especially through measures of deregulation, privatization, and fiscal constraint."[66] Transnational corporations increasingly have spatial characteristics – sales, customers, production facilities, and currency holdings – that distinguish them from national enterprises. Corporate leaders are designing transnational and sometimes global and regional strategies, and production and management structures that integrate more and more enterprises around the world.[67] "Some smart organizations," argues William Greider, "are even reconfiguring themselves into what business futurists have dubbed 'the virtual corporation,' a quick-witted company so dispersed that it resembles the ganglia of a nervous system, a brain attached to many distant nodes but without much bodily substance at the center."[68] "More than any other institution," as Dicken explains, "the transnational corporation has come to be seen as the primary shaper of the contemporary global economy and a major threat to the economic autonomy of the nation-state"; such corporations are best understood "as networks within networks" and "the threads from which the fabric of the global economy is woven."[69] Corporations focus their activities where value added is offered, perhaps by reduced costs, high-quality infrastructure, or advanced technology. States, for their part, try to compel corporations to adhere to national rules, and corporations frequently confront different standards, for instance antitrust rules, in different countries and regions.

What differentiates contemporary economic globalization from that of the nineteenth century and therefore undermines the argument of those who contend that contemporary globalization is not novel is that, even though most contemporary TNCs still profit most from operations within their own region, economic integration before World War I was, as Dicken describes it, "*shallow* integration," involving trade in goods and services between different corporations and the straightforward movement of relatively limited investment among countries. By contrast, today's global economic system reflects "*deep integration*, organized primarily within and between geographically extensive and complex *transnational production networks*."[70] FDI inflows reached a record level of $1,979 billion in 2007, driven by transnational mergers and acquisitions, and then receded during the global recession to $1,697 billion in 2008 and declined a further 44 percent during the first quarter of 2009.[71]

According to Sassen, the global distribution of factories reflects "highly integrated corporate structures with strong tendencies towards concentration in control and profit appropriation." "In terms of sovereignty and globalization," she suggests, the fact that globalization produces markets that extend beyond any single country's ability to impose regulation "is only half the story: the other half is that these central functions are disproportionately concentrated in the national territories of the highly developed countries,"[72] especially in "global cities" like New York, Shanghai, and London that remain under the sovereign authority of the states in which they are located.

Notwithstanding the hyperglobalizers' claim that the degree of contemporary economic interdependence is unprecedented, economic integration is far from complete. "Our analysis," argue Scott Bradford and Robert Lawrence, "suggests that internal market fragmentation remains considerable, even among countries with low tariff barriers."[73] They point to significant price differences for comparable goods in the developed world that *cannot* be explained by transportation costs, and their data "underscore the relative openness and strength of competitive conditions in North America and the much weaker competitive conditions in Japan and, to a lesser degree, in Europe."[74] Japanese consumer and producer prices are significantly higher than the average, indicating that the country is not highly integrated in the global economy, and Japan might therefore be the world's largest beneficiary of greater economic integration.

Hyperglobalizers and skeptics, as we have seen, are both inclined to emphasize the economic dimension of globalization but in different ways. Held and McGrew succinctly summarize the four key issues between the two perspectives as: "the extent to which the evidence shows that economic activity is being globalized"; "whether a new form of global capitalism, driven by the 'third industrial revolution', is taking hold across the globe"; "how far economic globalization remains subject to proper and effective national and international governance"; and "whether global competition spells the end of national economic strategy and the welfare state."[75]

Transformationalists

Transformationalists stress that globalization has multiple dimensions – economic, cultural, security, environmental, and so forth.[76] Those dimensions are linked. Consider, for instance, the complex relationship of economic globalization and human rights. "The emergence of a global economy," as Rosenau argues, has had both positive and negative impacts on human rights. On the one hand, workers are vulnerable to large and rapid capital movements:

> If one is inclined to view these economic deprivations generated by the global economy as an assault on human rights (as many observers do), or if one is disposed to view the global economy as producing like-minded consumers who have little choice about the commodities and values they hold dear (as more than a few observers do), then clearly those who initiate and sustain these economic dynamics can be treated as actors who undermine human rights in significant ways.

On the other hand, "to the extent that the same dynamics raise standards of living, reduce the unfairness of the system, and lessen the rich-poor gap . . . then to that extent they brighten and accelerate the processes favoring human rights."[77]

Similar linkages are apparent among all of globalization's dimensions. Thus, economic or ecological disasters can produce massive migrations, which in turn can trigger violent social and political confrontations. By contrast, diasporas are frequently a significant source of economic benefit to their countries of origin, returning some $328 billion in remittances – compared to $120 billion in official aid flows from Organisation for Economic Co-operation and Development (OECD) members – in 2008 to their homelands. India alone received $52 billion from its citizens living overseas.[78] In these and other ways, the dimensions of globalization are complexly interdependent.

With such complexity in mind, Luke Martell argues that transformationalists – the "third wave" of globalization theory – have "tried to construct a more complex framework" that "undermines skeptics' claims that we, at best, live in an era of internationalization rather than on a new global plane above and beyond the international."[79] For their part, hyperglobalists, Martell continues, even while trying to refute the skeptics actually reach conclusions that accept many of the skeptics' arguments. Both accept that globalization must move in only one of two possible directions and that globalization compels states to act in certain ways. Martell's contention is based on the transformationalists' recognition that globalization may *either* retreat *or* advance and that globalization may as much be a *result* of state behavior as a *cause* of that behavior. Nevertheless, Martell does not take sufficient account of what makes the transformational view unique. And it is illogical to suggest that states' roles in enabling globalization necessarily means that they still can control the horse they have let out of the barn.

In addition to the indeterminacy of the direction globalization may take, what perhaps distinguishes transformational theory from the work of skeptics and hyperglobalists most clearly is the transformationalists' recognition that globalization is not only an economic phenomenon but also encompasses a variety of other dimensions and processes that are indubitably linked.

THE MULTIPLE AND INTERDEPENDENT DIMENSIONS OF GLOBALIZATION

Unlike hyperglobalizers and skeptics, transformational theorists view globalization as both multidimensional and as a dynamic "set of processes that operate unevenly across space and time to shape global geographies and in so doing constantly rework the relative positions of peoples, places, and states."[80] Held, McGrew, Goldblatt, and Perraton, for their part, describe globalization as a set of processes that involve not only the world economy and technology but also include governance, military, cultural, demographic, human rights, migration, and environmental dimensions.[81]

Just as the global economy features a dense web of public and private economic institutions, the political realm is characterized by a dense web of international and regional organizations and nongovernmental organizations (NGOs), often with overlapping memberships. In the military arena, few states any longer seek to assure their security unilaterally, and joint ventures, specialization, co-production arrangements, and transnational subcontracting increasingly characterize the production and distribution of weapons.[82] According to Rachel Epstein:

> The perceived imperatives to capture new markets and economies of scale have driven contractors toward cross-national mergers, joint ventures, and licensing arrangements [and have produced] incentives to export, enter into offset arrangements, and likewise pursue short-term gains at the expense of suffering long-term security costs of destabilizing proliferation.[83]

In addition, military security has itself been increasingly "marketized," a fact made clear after the 2003 Anglo-American intervention in Iraq. As Deborah Avant declares, "private military and security companies now sell more services, some of which are core military capabilities"; "changes in the nature of conflicts have led tasks less central to the core of modern militaries (such as technical support and policing) to become more important, and private security companies provide these services readily"; and "states are no longer the only organizations that purchase security services."[84] "War," as McGrew insists, "is not only an example of globalization. It is one of the principal mechanisms of globalization. A globalizing force."[85]

Although globalization's dimensions are *analytically* separable, they rarely change independently of one another. Greater or lesser globalization in one or another dimension may be increased or even balanced by a retreat in others. Consider Jan Nederveen Pieterse's assertion that the "essential problem of globalization is that technological capabilities and economic changes are ahead of institutional and political capacities."[86] Or Jonathan Kirshner's insistence that "monetary phenomena are always and everywhere political." "States routinely try and shape the nature and extent of their interactions with the international monetary system, either to enhance domestic autonomy, advance foreign policy goals, or accommodate demands for national security." Indeed, "every choice about money reflects the outcome of a political contest."[87] Moreover, the movement of persons frequently influences the movement of ideas and goods; the movement of ideas, the movement of persons and goods; and the movement of goods, the movement of persons and ideas.

Global war and resulting insecurity may undermine and reverse economic and cultural globalization and trigger large-scale migrations. Economic globalization may encourage transborder migration that can produce cultural hybridization. However, migration may also stimulate a local backlash against cultural "invasion" and help reverse economic globalization in the face of economic downturns, perceived security threats, and the inability or unwillingness of migrants to assimilate into new cultures. Even major countries like the United States seem incapable of controlling streams of illegal migrants and drugs from abroad and their citizens no doubt rightly worry, despite extraordinary precautions, about the likelihood of dedicated foreign terrorists penetrating their defenses.[88]

"Frequently" does not mean "inevitably" or "necessarily," and the dimensions of globalization are interdependent only up to a point. Whether they will move in the same or opposite directions is probably contextually determined. Trade, for example, surely affects culture,[89] but spreading economic globalization may *either* facilitate or impede cultural and security globalization. Lags are certain to occur in changes among even linked dimensions of globalization. Moreover, it is possible that changes may occur in one or another dimension without any apparent impact on other dimensions. For example, a high level of cultural globalization may exist and persist even in the absence of economic or security globalization. (Whether such independence is merely *perceived* owing to temporal lags rather than genuine is unclear.)

The impact of any dimension of globalization on other dimensions may also be indirect and therefore not immediately visible. For instance, economic globalization enlarges the global middle class whose perceptions of the world around them generally differ from those of either the poor or the very affluent. Citing a 2007 Pew survey, *The Economist* concludes: "Middle-income people are more likely than the poor to say they want competitive elections with at least two parties; more likely to demand fair treatment under the law; and more disposed to back freedom of speech and the press."[90] This suggests the larger the middle class, the more likely it is that democracy will take root.

The perception of such relationships often generates controversy among theorists. For example, since both political democratization *and* economic globalization are frequently thought to be Western in origin, some critics of globalization believe that globalization per se is a form of "cultural imperialism" or hegemony and an extension of "Westernization" or "Americanization."[91] In this vein, Heather Viles groups globalization with other "broad geographic projects of domination" such as imperialism, transatlantic slavery, colonization of Africa, and "white flight" in cities.[92] Not least of the visible icons of globalization are American firms such as McDonald's, Coca-Cola, and Disneyland. Disney, which already has theme parks in Paris, Tokyo, and Hong Kong, will soon add an additional Disneyland in Shanghai.[93]

Again, there is no consensus on this issue. The idea that globalization is no more than an imperial project is vigorously contested by those like John Tomlinson who argues that "it was and is a mistake to confuse the broader phenomenon of cultural globalization with cultural imperialism."[94] Anthony Giddens takes much the same position, arguing that globalization "is more than a diffusion of Western institutions across the world, in which other cultures are crushed"; instead, it "is a process of uneven development that fragments as it coordinates – introduces new forms of world interdependence, in which . . . there are no 'others'."[95] For Giddens, globalization *is* equivalent to modernity that emerges in part from revolutionary new technologies and scientific breakthroughs.[96] Globalization compresses both time and space, even while space "is increasingly dislocated from place, and networked to other social contexts across the globe."[97]

TRANSFORMATIONAL THEORY: TERRITORY, ACTORS, AND IDENTITY

In addition to what may be happening "globally" in any one of these dimensions, we must recognize that there are important hegemonic, regional, subregional, bilateral, and city-to-city patterns in the overall picture as well, thereby creating still greater complexity. Change ripples up and down as well as among dimensions of globalization. Polymorphous international regimes are proliferating in additional issue areas. In this sense, formal governance is multilayered or at best fragmented, and by any measure political and economic influence remains widely diffused. In any event, however conceived, there are no universally accepted benchmarks against which to measure globalization or localization or even which dimensions are most important to consider.

Transformational theorists emphasize the declining significance of geography and territory, focusing on interconnectedness among *individuals, groups, and various institutions* rather than only among *states*. Transformationalists are persuaded that "globalization is a central driving force behind the rapid social, political and economic changes that are reshaping modern societies and world order"[98] and entails "the stretching of political relations across space and time and across the boundaries of the modern nation-state."[99] More than ever before, events, ideas, and decisions have an impact on far-distant persons and places. In this respect, contemporary globalization has no close historical parallel. For transformational theorists, "globalization brings into question the core organizing principles of modern social science – namely the state, society, political community, the economy – and the classical inheritance of modern social theory which takes these for granted as the metrics or focus of social explanation."[100]

Our description of the transformational perspective overlaps with Scholte's *respatialization* – "a reconfiguration of social with increased transplanetary connections between people" and "a shift in the nature of social space" – that he believes "opens up new knowledge and engages key challenges of current history in a constructively critical manner."[101] This entails "the spread of 'supraterritorial' or 'transborder relations'." The "re-imagination of social space inspired by the spectre of globalization," suggests Sarah Whatmore, involves "new spatial metaphors, like networks, topologies and folds."[102]

What Scholte finds "distinctive" about contemporary globalization is that it entails "a fundamental transformation of human geography" in which the world has "acquired a (rapidly growing) global dimension alongside the territorial framework of old" that is reflected in spheres such as telecommunications, marketing, and "transworld finance." As a result, he believes that "the territorialist assumptions which underpin modern understandings of 'international relations' have become untenable." "[B]orders are not so much crossed as *transcended*."[103] In sum, the global political and economic worlds are not entirely old or new; they are worlds in transition.

Scholte contrasts the transformational perspective with *universalization* or "the process of spreading various objects and experiences to peoples at all corners of the earth,"[104] whether popular music, modes of dress, business practices, or anything else. This perspective is less state-centric, adds a cultural/ideational dimension, and can apply to any issue area. However, for Scholte, universalization is a "cul-de-sac"[105] because he finds it difficult to identify the political or spatial implications of this approach.

Among the key consequences of interconnectedness, transformationalists believe, are a merging of the foreign (external) and domestic (internal) policy arenas and the reduced importance of physical distance and territory. As early as 1969, Rosenau was struck by anomalies that defied the classic distinction between "foreign" and "domestic," declaring: "Almost every day incidents are reported that defy the principles of sovereignty. Politics everywhere, it would seem, are related to politics everywhere else."[106] In his view, globalization involves the ways in which people change local behavior and decisions in response to the flood of economic, social, and political events that cross their national borders. States lose authority and capacity as they are pulled in different directions by simultaneous processes of globalization (integration) and localization (fragmentation). As a result, Rosenau concludes that there is "a mismatch between the rapid extension of boundary-crossing activities and the authority necessary to give direction to them."[107]

Peter Taylor writes that "political, social and economic activities are becoming global in scope and dissolving the internal/external distinction crucial to the orthodox definition of sovereignty."

> If globalization has blurred the distinction between national and international, transformed the conditions of nation decision-making, altered the legal framework and administrative practices of states, obscured lines of responsibility, and changed the institutional and organizational content of national politics, then sovereignty as a doctrine is of limited relevance. In this sense, globalization refers to more than the erosion of autonomy. It highlights a change in the political landscape and requires an adaptation of political practice.[108]

"Relations across the world," as John Urry insists, "are complex, rich and non-linear, involving multiple negative and, more significantly, positive feedback loops."[109] Under these conditions, governance becomes increasingly difficult to impose or observe.

Transformational theorists contend that international, subnational, and transnational groups are all growing more important as state power ebbs, and, therefore, by inference (as we have mentioned) that traditional levels of analysis are collapsing. This also exacerbates the theoretical problem in relating parts and wholes. And with the declining capacity of sovereign states and the reduced importance of territory, the role of identity – what Manuel Castells describes as "process of construction of meaning on the basis of a cultural attribute, or a related set of cultural attributes, that is given priority over other sources of meaning"[110] – has grown. Identities and interests constitute each other. Neither remains stable; instead, they are repeatedly modified and reconstituted, and, as they mix under the simultaneous impact of globalization and localization, they become hybrid.

The increasing variety of nonstate identities undermines the assumption that citizenship is inevitably the source of one's highest loyalties. The porosity of state frontiers, the growing separation of nationality from citizenship, the degree to which new technologies conspire to make it easier for ideas and values to be communicated instantly at vast distances and for groups to be mobilized and coordinated in cyberspace creates a dramatically different global context than that of earlier centuries. "'Global' conditions," as Scholte observes, "are relatively placeless, distanceless, borderless interactions and interdependencies between persons . . . unfold in *the world as a single place*." One result is "that globalization has unsettled long dominant territorially based constructions of collective identities, including in particular the nationality principle."[111]

Perceptions of the dehumanizing and homogenizing impact of the global economy and culture tend to reinvigorate identities associated with religion, ethnicity, tribe, class, gender, race, and civilization. Groups based on some of these identities lead the backlash against globalization, and their aspirations for autonomy within or for secession from or even for enhanced participation in existing polities threatens a host of states, from the Middle East to Nigeria, Russia, Indonesia, and Pakistan. China is challenged by ethno-national resistance to Han dominance among its Uighur, Tibetan, and Vietnamese minorities. All this led Strange to observe with typical perspicacity: "Loyalty of the kind that is ready to die for a cause is more often found among ethnic or religious minorities . . . than it is among the ordinary citizens in an average state."[112]

Identities other than citizenship can provide what Doreen Massey terms a "global sense of place,"[113] although some do not require a territorial home and are not coextensive with or anchored in any particular state or group of states. Instead, they have boundaries that, as Anssi Paasi observes, "are no longer understood as physical, immovable spatial entities."[114] Religion, notably political Islam, is particularly important in this regard.

Militant Islamists seek to replace the interstate system with "the construction of the *umma*, or worldwide community of the believers, transcending the boundaries of nation-states"[115] governed by putatively literal interpretation of Islamic law and tradition. It has its own globalized vision, "an alternative form of globalization," Stephen Vertigans and Philip Sutton contend, distinguished "from the currently dominant, and made to seem inevitable Western capitalist one."[116] Groups like Al Qaeda are what Oliver Roy calls advocates of neofundamentalism, "a closed, scripturalist and conservative view of Islam that rejects the nationalist and statist dimensions in favour of the *ummah*, the universal community of all Muslims, based on *sharia* (Islamic law)." Such groups represent Muslims who are "uprooted migrants and/or living in a minority" and are experiencing "the deterritorialization of Islam."[117] "Islam is not tied to territory and has never accepted the division of the *umma* into nation-states. It is embodied in people – mobile, deterritorialized people carrying ideas and practices," and it "has been powerfully reshaped by globalization processes, particularly information and migration."[118]

Castells attributes "the explosion of Islamic movements . . . to both the disruption of traditional societies (including the undermining of the power of traditional clergy), and to the failure of the nation-state, created by nationalist movements, to accomplish modernization, develop the economy, and/or distribute the benefits of economic growth among the population at large." Militant Islamists oppose capitalism, socialism, and nationalism, all viewed as "failing ideologies of the post-colonial order."[119] "Islamic movements," as Mustapha Kamal Pasha contends, "are not simply a response to Western conquest and control, but a movement, promoted by fractions *within* Muslim society, and a movement *for* realizing an alternative to secular nationalism."[120]

Identity shifts, as reflected in the growing intensity of religion and ethnic consciousness, are significant elements in the transformationalist version of globalization. In examining the transformation of hierarchical institutions like the state by economic, political, and social networks, Joachim Blattner summarizes four changes that "contribute to the fact that the identity-providing and mobilizing dimension of political institutions (and political actions) is increasingly important." These are (1) the key role played by information and communication in societies and economies, (2) "the paradigmatic change from 'government' to 'governance'," (3) the growing importance of identity politics ("race, gender, and ethnicity"), and (4) "processes of internationalization/globalization and processes of decentralization/devolution" that "undermine the 'natural' political ties of citizens to the nation-state and lead to the creation of many supranational, transnational, and 'subnational' political communities and institutions."[121]

As we have seen, Rosenau, like the present authors, embraces what is essentially a transformationalist perspective and adopts the term "postinternationalism" to describe "an apparent trend in which more and more of the interactions that sustain world politics unfold without the direct involvement of nations and states."[122] He examines "multiple contradictions" and anomalies in global politics, especially the tension between globalization and localization, and describes "a new and wide political space" that he terms "the domestic-foreign frontier":

> The international system is less commanding, but it is still powerful. States are changing, but they are not disappearing. State sovereignty has been eroded, but it is still vigorously asserted. Governments are weaker, but they can still throw their weight around. At certain times publics are more demanding, but at other times they are more pliable. Borders still keep out intruders, but they are also more porous.[123]

"What distinguishes globalizing processes," Rosenau perceives, "is that they are not hindered or prevented by territorial or jurisdictional barriers. They can spread readily across national boundaries and are capable of reaching into any community everywhere in the world." And, "they consist of all those forces that impel individuals, groups, societies, governments, institutions, and transnational organizations toward engaging in similar forms of behavior or participating in *more encompassing* and coherent processes, organizations, or systems."[124] In this respect, epistemic communities, for example, contribute to globalizing dynamics. Likewise, Rosenau believes that "the dynamics at work in the realm of economics are powerful sources of centralizing tendencies" and that "financiers, entrepreneurs, workers, and consumers" are "now being deeply enmeshed in transnational networks that have superseded the traditional political jurisdictions of national scope."[125]

States and sovereignty matters ever less in a world in which "the transformations wrought by economic globalization have lessened national controls" and in which "the world's producers, consumers, traders, investors, makers, and all the other actors who sustain economies tend to conduct themselves in terms of global rather than national markets." National borders only hinder economic life in a world in which corporations and their subsidiaries exist in many states, vast amounts of money move instantaneously around the world, and corporate leaders are constantly in contact or on the move. Rosenau concludes:

> In a like manner, producers move or build their plants where labor costs are cheapest, develop products to cater to regional and local tastes far removed from

corporate headquarters, and disperse their research, advertising, accounting, and legal staffs to service corporate needs in far-flung markets.[126]

Services, too, are being globalized. For example, "medical tourism" has become increasingly fashionable for individuals seeking timely high-quality medical care at lower cost, and an increasing number of countries are competing in this field.[127] Various countries such as Antigua, Liechtenstein, and the British-owned Cayman Islands provide tax havens where the wealthy can leave funds and evade taxes in their own countries.[128] In addition, the enrollment of students in foreign universities has increased to such an extent that higher education has become a globalized service industry.[129] As Ben Wildavsky explains: "In the worlds of business and culture, the globalization trend is so well known as to be a cliché. But a lesser known phenomenon, the globalization of universities, is equally important and has perhaps even more far-reaching consequences."[130] Globalized universities play a key role in spreading ideas, and "students and faculty everywhere are conscious that they are in an academic competition that extends well beyond the campus gates."[131] The United States remains the most popular destination of international students but is being challenged by universities in other countries such as the United Kingdom, Australia, China, and Japan. Some countries, for example, Qatar in the Middle East, are attracting "branch campuses" and investing heavily in their own universities to keep students at home.

Some of its enthusiasts go so far (perhaps too far) as to argue that as globalization thickens, it will be accompanied by the spread of cosmopolitan identities that encourage individuals to view themselves as members of a single global community, imbued with "the idea that citizenship can be based not on exclusive membership of a territorial community, but on general rules and principles which can be entrenched and drawn upon in diverse settings."[132]

Whether or not some aspects of contemporary globalization are unique, there is no question that much of what we see today has deep historical roots. The next chapter explores these roots.

NOTES

1 Friedman, *The World Is Flat*, 7.
2 Arjun Appadurai, "Grassroots Globalization and the Research Imagination," in A. Appadurai, ed., *Globalization: Public Culture* 12:1 (Winter 2000), 2.
3 Zygmunt Bauman, *Globalization: The Human Consequences* (Cambridge: Polity, 1998), 1.
4 Susan Strange, *The Retreat of the State* (Cambridge: Cambridge University Press, 1996), xiii.
5 Peter Kien-hong Yu, *International Governance Regimes, and Globalization* (Boca Raton: BrownWalker Press, 2008), 76.
6 Clark, *Urban World/Global City*, 13.
7 Nederveen Pieterse, *Globalization and Culture*, 7.
8 J. R. McNeill and William H. McNeill, *The Human Web* (New York: Norton, 2003).
9 Manuel Castells, *The Rise of Network Society*, I, 2nd edn (Oxford: Blackwell, 2000).
10 Friedman, *The World Is Flat*.
11 David S. Hamilton and Joseph P. Quinlan, *Globalization and Europe* (Washington, DC: Center for Transatlantic Relations, 2008), 182.

12 Richard Florida, "The World Is Spiky," *Atlantic Monthly* (October 2005), 48–51.
13 Sassen, *Territory, Authority, Rights*, 13–14. By "denationalization," Sassen means "the reorienting of national agendas towards global ones, and the circulation of private agendas inside the state apparatus where they get dressed up as public policy." See S. Sassen, "The Places and Spaces of the Global: An Expanded Analytic Terrain," in Held and McGrew, eds., *Globalization Theory*, 78.
14 James N. Rosenau, *Along the Domestic–Foreign Frontier: Exploring Governance in a Turbulent World* (Cambridge: Cambridge University Press, 1997), 30.
15 During the second half of 2008, global trade experienced a significant decline led by the US whose combined imports and exports dropped by 18 percent between July and November of that year. See Kelly Evans, John W. Miller, and Mei Fong, "Global Trade Posts Sharp Decline," *Wall Street Journal*, January 14, 2009, A1, A10.
16 Francis Fukuyama, *The End of History and the Last Man* (New York: Free Press, 1992).
17 "Market of Ideas," *The Economist*, April 9, 2011, 70.
18 Thomas Risse, "Social Constructivism Meets Globalization," in Held and McGrew, *Globalization Theory*, 126.
19 Ibid. Risse adds: "Last but not least, some focus on the global diffusion of norms and other cultural scripts."
20 David Held, Anthony McGrew, David Goldblatt, and Jonathan Perraton, "The Globalization Debate," in Stuart Hall, David Held, and Tony McGrew, eds., *Classic Readings and Contemporary Debates in International Relations*, 3rd edn (Belmont, CA: Wadsworth, 2006), 5.
21 Anthony McGrew, "A Global Society," in Stuart Hall, David Held, and Tony McGrew, eds., *Modernity, and Its Futures* (Cambridge: Polity Press, 1992), 65–6.
22 Rosenau, *Distant Proximities*.
23 Barry K. Gills and William R. Thompson, "Globalizations, Global Histories and Historical Globalities," in Gills and Thompson, eds., *Globalization and Global History* (Oxford: Routledge, 2006), 19.
24 Ibid.
25 Ibid., 20.
26 Jan Aart Scholte, *Globalization: A Critical Introduction*, 2nd edn (London: Palgrave Macmillan, 2005), 16. See also Scholte, "Global Capitalism and the State," *International Affairs* 73:3 (1997), 427–52.
27 Scholte, *Globalization*, 55.
28 See Karl W. Deutsch, "Towards Western European Integration: An Interim Assessment," *Journal of International Affairs* 16:1 (1962), 89–101, and Donald J. Puchala, "International Transactions and Regional Integration," *International Organization* 24:4 (Autumn 1970), 732–63. This approach is reflected in globalization indexes constructed by the following: A. T. Kearney and the journal *Foreign Policy* since 2001, "Measuring Globalization," *Foreign Policy* 122 (January/February 2001), 56–65, the Center for the Study of Globalization and Regionalism at Warwick University since 2005, Ben Lockwood and Michela Redoano, The CSGR Globalisation Index (2005), http://www2.warwick.ac.uk/fac/soc/csgr/index, and the KOF Swiss Economic Institute Index of Globalization, http://globalization.kof.ethz.ch/. See Scholte, *Globalization*, 55.
29 Scholte, *Globalization*, 16–17.
30 See David Held, Anthony McGrew, David Goldblatt, and Jonathan Perraton, *Global Transformations: Politics, Economics and Culture* (Stanford, CA: Stanford University Press, 1999), 2–10. Others utilize a similar Tripartite Set of Definitions. Duncan S. A. Bell discusses these orientations in "History and Globalization: Reflections on Temporality," *International Affairs* 79:4 (July 2003), 803–6. Robert J. Holton in *Making Globalization* (London: Palgrave Macmillan, 2005), 5, differentiates among "three broad waves of analysis," hyper-globalism, skepticism, and post-skepticism. Held and McGrew, "Introduction," (6) add a fourth wave that "reflects the influence of post-structuralist and constructivist thinking across the social sciences, from Open Marxism

to postmodernism" involving analysis of the "making, unmaking and remaking of globalization understood as both a historical process and as a hegemonic discourse." See also Anthony McGrew, "Globalization and Global Politics," in John Baylis, Steve Smith, and Patricia Owens, *The Globalization of World Politics*, 4th edn (Oxford: Oxford University Press, 2008), 14–33. Manfred B. Steger differentiates among "rejectionists," "skeptics," and "modifiers." The first group "dismiss the utility of globalization as a concept"; the second "emphasizes the limited nature of current globalizing processes"; and the third "disputes the novelty of the process, implying that the label 'globalization' has often been applied in a historically imprecise manner." See Steger, *Globalisms*, 3rd edn (Lanham, MD: Rowan & Littlefield, 2009), 24, 25, 26.

31 Held and McGrew contrast "skeptics" – those who see globalization "as a primarily ideological or social construction which has marginal explanatory value" – with "globalists" – "those who consider that contemporary globalization is a real and significant historical development." See Held and McGrew, "The Great Globalization Debate," 2.
32 Tom Nairn and Paul James, *Global Matrix* (London: Pluto Press, 2005), 4.
33 For an argument that firms should pursue regional rather than global strategies, see Alan M. Rugman, *The End of Globalization* (London: Random House, 2000).
34 Paul Hirst and Grahame Thompson, *Globalization in Question*, 2nd edn (Cambridge: Polity Press, 1999), 16. The authors doubt "whether a regime of free trade and capital mobility would lead to a market-based take-off by most of the developing world – large countries like China, India, Indonesia and Brazil included" (ibid., 17). The past decade should dispel this doubt.
35 Hirst and Thompson, *Globalization in Question*, 2. Emphasis in original. See also Dani Rodrik, *Has Globalization Gone Too Far?* (Washington, DC: Institute for International Economics, 1997), 7.
36 Hirst, "The Global Economy – Myths and Realities," 410–12.
37 Hirst and Thompson, *Globalization in Question*, 39. Emphasis added.
38 Scholte, *Globalization*, 39, 56.
39 Niall Ferguson, "Sinking Globalization," *Foreign Affairs* 84:2 (March/April 2005), 64.
40 Ibid.
41 Alexander Cooley and Hendrik Spruyt, *Contracting States: Sovereign Transfers in International Relations* (Princeton, NJ: Princeton University Press, 2009), 205–6.
42 Ibid., 206.
43 Ibid., xi.
44 Robert O. Keohane and Joseph S. Nye, "Globalization: What's New? What's Not? (And So What?)," *Foreign Policy* 118 (Spring 2000), 104.
45 Ibid., 105, 106.
46 Robert O. Keohane and Joseph S. Nye, *Power and Interdependence*, 3rd edn (New York: Longman, 2001), 10–14.
47 Dicken, *Global Shift*, 6.
48 Ibid. Emphasis in original.
49 See, for example, Winfried Ruigrok and Rob van Tulder, *The Logic of International Restructuring* (London: Routledge, 1995), 119. Wolf, *Why Globalization Works*, 14–15, terms this "liberal globalization."
50 Moisés Naím, *Illicit: How Smugglers, Traffickers, and Copycats Are Hijacking the Global Economy* (New York: Random House, 2005), 22.
51 Michael D. Bordo, Barry Eichengreen, Douglas A. Irwin, Jeffrey Frankel, and Alan M. Taylor, "Is Globalization Today Really Different from Globalization a Hundred Years Ago?" *Brookings Trade Forum* (1999), 15.
52 Ibid., 15–20.
53 Wolf, *Why Globalization Works*, 111.
54 Hamilton and Quinlan, *Globalization and Europe*, 27.

55 Ibid., 22.
56 Brad Stone, "With Its Tablet, Apple Blurs Line between Devices," *New York Times*, January 27, 2010, http://www.nytimes.com/2010/01/28/technology/companies/28apple.html?ref=business.
57 Hamilton and Quinlan, *Globalization and Europe*, 22.
58 See Sassen, "The Places and Spaces of the Global," 94–8, and Clark, *Urban World/Global City*, Table 4.1, 90.
59 Held, McGrew, Goldblatt, and Perraton, "The Globalization Debate," 550.
60 Robert Reich argues that "knowledge workers" or "symbolic analysts" are conscious of a kinship to others with similar skills that are geographically remote. See R. Reich, *The Work of Nations* (New York: Alfred A. Knopf, 1991), 177–80.
61 Edward S. Comor, "Governance and the Nation-State in a Knowledge-Based Political Economy," in Martin Hewson and Timothy J. Sinclair, eds., *Approaches to Global Governance Theory* (Albany, NY: State University of New York Press, 1999), 129.
62 Rob van Tulder and Alex van der Zwart reach a more nuanced view of TNCs, arguing that "it is not easy to identify a dominant/particular trend in the international repertoires of leading (core) firms"; "A very limited number of firms can be classified as truly 'global'." See *International Business–Society Management* (Oxford: Routledge, 2006), 67.
63 Dicken, *Global Shift*, 36.
64 John Eatwell and Lance Taylor, *Global Finance at Risk* (New York: New Press, 2000), 3–4.
65 Bank for International Settlements, "Triennial Bank Survey," December 2007, http://www.bis.org/publ/rpfxf07t.pdf.
66 Scholte, *Globalization*, 38. See also Philip G. Cerny, "Globalization and the Changing Logic of Collective Action," *International Organization* 49:4 (Autumn 1995), 595–625, Cerny, "What Next for the State?" in Eleonore Kofman and Gillian Youngs, eds., *Globalization: Theory and Practice*, (London: Pinter, 1996), 123–37, and Cerny, "Globalization and Other Stories: Paradigmatic Selection in International Politics," in Axel Hülsemeyer., ed., *Globalization in the Twenty-First Century* (New York: Palgrave Macmillan, 2003), 51–66.
67 By contrast, Hirst maintains that most corporations "are still multinational, not transnational; that is, they have a home base in one of the Triad [Europe, Japan, and North America] countries" and "are not footloose capital but are rooted in a major market." See Hirst, "The Global Economy – Myths and Realities," 418.
68 William Greider, *One World Ready or Not* (New York: Simon & Schuster, 1997), 25.
69 Dicken, *Global Shift*, 106, 154.
70 Ibid., 7. Emphasis in original.
71 United Nations Conference on Trade and Development, *World Investment Report 2009: Transnational Corporations, Agricultural Production and Development*, http://www.globalbioenergy.org/uploads/media/0909_UNCTAD_-_WIR2009.pdf, 20.
72 Sassen, "The Places and Spaces of the Global," 85, 86. By "central functions," Sassen means "all the top-level financial, legal, accounting, managerial, executive, planning functions necessary to run a corporate organization in more than one country" (86).
73 Scott C. Bradford and Robert Z. Lawrence, *Has Globalization Gone Far Enough?* (Washington, DC: Institute for International Economics. 2004), 6.
74 Ibid., 7.
75 Held and McGrew, "The Great Globalization Debate," 19.
76 Constructivists like Thomas Risse emphasize the cultural and normative dimensions of globalization and the ability of "agents" to intensify or slow globalization processes. See Risse, "Social Constructivism Meets Globalization," 133–6. By contrast, materialist perspectives such as realism and Marxism stress the economic and political dimensions of globalization and focus on structural conditions at the expense of agency. The present authors see structure and agency as interacting and, therefore, are in sympathy with Anthony Giddens's theory of structuration that neither privileges "the experience of the

individual actors, nor the existence of any form of social totality." See Anthony Giddens, *The Constitution of Society* (Cambridge: Polity Press, 1984), 2.
77 Rosenau, *Distant Proximities*, 330–1.
78 "The Aid Workers Who Really Help," *The Economist*, October 10, 2009, 61–2. The World Bank's estimate for 2008 was $444 billion, of which $338 billion went to developing countries. See World Bank's Migration and Development Brief 11 (November 3, 2009): Migration and Remittance Trends 2009, http://go.worldbank.org/5YMRR0VW80.
79 Luke Martell, "The Third Wave in Globalization Theory," *International Studies Review* 9:2 (Summer 2007), 193.
80 Michael Bradshaw, "Globalization, Regional Change, and the Territorial Cohesion of the Russian Federation," in Douglas W. Blum, ed., *Russia and Globalization: Identity, Security, and Society in an Era of Change* (Baltimore, MD: Johns Hopkins University Press, 2008), 79. See also John Tomlinson, "Globalization and Cultural Analysis," in Held and McGrew, eds., *Globalization Theory*, 150, and Barrie Axford, *The Global System: Politics, Economics, and Culture* (New York: St. Martin's Press, 1995), 33.
81 Held, McGrew, Goldblatt, and Perraton, *Global Transformations*. The A. T. Kearney/*Foreign Policy* Globalization Index measures countries' level of globalization along four dimensions: technology, political engagement, personal contact and economic integration. See "Globalization's Last Hurrah?" *Foreign Policy* 128 (January/February 2002), 38–51. Other indexes also utilize multiple though not identical dimensions in measuring levels of state globalization.
82 Russia is a prominent exception to this. See Alla Kassianova, "The Russian Defense Industry in the Age of Globalization," in Blum, ed., *Russia and Globalization*, 153–80.
83 Rachel Epstein, "Divided Continent: Globalization and Europe's Fragmented Security Response," in Jonathan Kirshner, ed., *Globalization and National Security* (New York: Routledge, 2006), 251.
84 Deborah Avant, "The Marketization of Security: Adventurous Defense, Institutional Malformation, and Conflict," in Kirshner, ed., *Globalization and National Security*, 107, 108.
85 Anthony McGrew, "Organized Violence in the Making (and Remaking) of Globalization," in Held and McGrew, eds., *Globalization Theory*, 32.
86 Jan Nederveen Pieterse, "Globalization, Kitsch and Conflict: Technologies of Work, War and Politics," *Review of International Political Economy* 9:1 (March 2002), 27–8.
87 Jonathan Kirshner, "Money Is Politics," *Review of International Political Economy* 10:4 (November 2003), 645, 646.
88 The use of inexpensive fiberglass submarines by Latin American drug smugglers illustrates the point. They not only pose difficulties in reducing the influx of narcotics into the United States but there is the additional threat of their being used by terrorists. See William Booth and Juan Forero, "Undersea Smuggling," *Washington National Post Weekly*, June 15–21, 2009, 20.
89 See Tyler Cowen, *Creative Destruction: How Globalization Is Changing the World's Cultures* (Princeton, NJ: Princeton University Press, 2002), 2.
90 John Parker, "Burgeoning Bourgeoisie: A Special Report on the New Middle Classes in Emerging Markets," *The Economist*, February 14, 2009, 12. The article points up the myriad difficulties in defining "middle class" and notes that findings differ by country and region. See also "Two Billion More Bourgeois," *The Economist*, February 14, 2009, 18.
91 See, for example, Roger Burbach, Orlando Núñez, and Boris Kagarlitsky, *Globalization and Its Discontents* (London: Pluto Press, 1997), and Samir Amin, *The Liberal Virus: Permanent War and the Americanization of the World* (New York: Monthly Review Press, 2004). For a critique of this argument, see Nederveen Pieterse, *Globalization and Culture*, 49–52.
92 Heather Viles, "A Divided Discipline?" in Castree, Rogers, and Sherman, eds., *Questioning Geography*, 45.

93 Brooks Barnes, "China Approves Disney Theme Park in Shanghai," *New York Times*, November 3, 2009, http://www.nytimes.com/2009/11/04/business/global/04disney.html.
94 Tomlinson, "Globalization and Cultural Analysis," 148.
95 Anthony Giddens, *The Consequences of Modernity* (Stanford, CA: Stanford University Press, 1990), 175.
96 Ibid., 64.
97 See James H. Mittelman, *The Globalization Syndrome* (Princeton, NJ: Princeton University Press, 2000), 6.
98 Held, McGrew, Goldblatt, and Perraton, "The Globalization Debate," 554.
99 Held, McGrew, Goldblatt, and Perraton, *Global Transformations*, 49. See also Eric Sheppard, "The Spaces and Times of Globalization: Place, Scale, Networks and Positionality," *Economic Geography* 78:3 (2002), 307–30.
100 Held and McGrew, "Introduction," 5.
101 Scholte, *Globalization*, 16, 59, 84.
102 Sarah Whatmore, *Hybrid Geographies* (London: Sage Publications, 2002), 35.
103 Scholte, "Global Capitalism and the State," 429–30, 432. Emphasis in original.
104 Scholte, *Globalization*, 6.
105 Ibid., 57.
106 James N. Rosenau, "Introduction: Political Science in a Shrinking World," in J. Rosenau, ed., *Linkage Politics: Essays on the Convergence of International and National Systems* (New York: Free Press, 1969), 2.
107 Rosenau, *Along the Domestic–Foreign Frontier*, 99; see 99–117 concerning "fragmegration."
108 Peter J. Taylor, "The Modern Multiplicity of States," in Eleonore Kofman and Gillian Youngs, eds., *Globalization: Theory and Practice* (London: Pinter, 1996), 117–18.
109 John Urry, *Global Complexity* (Cambridge: Polity Press, 2003), 130.
110 Manuel Castells, *The Power of Identity: The Information Age: Economy, Society and Culture*, II, 2nd edn (Oxford: Blackwell Publishing, 2004), 6.
111 Scholte, "The Geography of Collective Identities in a Globalizing World," 571, 573. Emphasis in original. Scholte also notes that some preexisting collective identities have vanished under the pressure of globalization (576).
112 Strange, *The Retreat of the State*, 72.
113 Doreen Massey, *Space, Place, and Gender* (Cambridge: Polity Press, 1994), 146–56.
114 Anssi Paasi, "Boundaries as Social Processes: Territoriality in the World of Flows," in David Newman, ed., *Boundaries, Territory and Postmodernity* (Abingdon, UK: Frank Cass, 1999), 86.
115 Ibid., 111.
116 Stephen Vertigans and Philip Sutton, "Globalisation Theory and Islamic Praxis," *Global Society* 16:1 (2002), 32. See also Brian Beeley, "Global Options: Islamic Alternatives," in James Anderson, Chris Brook, and Allan Cochrane, eds., *A Global World?* (Oxford: Oxford University Press, 1995), 167–208.
117 Oliver Roy, *Global Islam: The Search for a New Ummah* (New York: Columbia University Press, 2004), 1, 2.
118 Marc Lynch, "Globalization and Arab Security," in Kirshner, ed., *Globalization and National Security*, 190.
119 Castells, *The Power of Identity*, 17.
120 Mustapha Kamal Pasha, "Globalization, Islam and Resistance," in Barry K. Gills, ed., *Globalization and the Politics of Resistance* (London: Macmillan Press, 2000), 245. Emphasis in original.
121 Joachim Blattner, "Beyond Hierarchies and Networks: Institutional Logics and Change in Transboundary Spaces," *Governance: An International Journal of Policy, Administration and Institutions* 16:4 (October 2003), 519–20.
122 Rosenau, *Turbulence in World Politics*, 6.
123 Rosenau, *Along the Domestic–Foreign Frontier*, 4.
124 Ibid., 80, 83. Emphasis in original.

125 Rosenau, *Distant Proximities*, 75.
126 Ibid., 76.
127 Choe Sang-Hun, "South Korea Joins Lucrative Practice of Inviting Medical Tourists to Its Hospitals," *New York Times*, November 16, 2008, http://www.nytimes.com/2008/11/16/world/asia/16medical.html, and "Importing Competition," *The Economist*, August 10, 2008, 12.
128 The issue was raised at the 2009 G-20 summit meeting. See Jonathan Weisman, David Crawford, and Stephen Fidler, "Member Nations Haggle Over Tax-Haven Roster," *Wall Street Journal*, April 1, 2009, A6.
129 See Susan Kinzie, "The Cachet of a Degree from the U.S.," *Washington Post National Weekly Edition*, May 11–17, 2009, 34.
130 Ben Wildavsky, *The Great Brain Race* (Princeton, NJ: Princeton University Press, 2010), 2.
131 Ibid., 3.
132 David Held, "Reframing Global Governance: Apocalypse Soon or Reform!" in Held and McGrew, eds., *Globalization Theory*, 255.

CHAPTER 2

Globalization in historical perspective

In the *longue durée* historical perspective globalization has been growing ever since homo sapiens settled into sedentary cultures in river valleys. Connections that began as short forays for trading, exploration, evangelism, and imperial expansion have accelerated over the millennia.[1]

[I]t certainly is plausible to suggest that, whatever the historical precedents or antecedents, at least the pace of change is accelerating, with important qualitative differences.[2]

Debate about the precise definition or even most useful understanding of the term "globalization" makes the task of tracing the history of globalization all the more difficult. As Scholte remarks, "Different definitions generate different chronologies and periodizations."[3]

Consider again his list of alternative definitions.[4] If globalization is *internationalization*, then its history began with the emergence of sovereign nation-states in Europe; or, if "nation" is the key term embedded in "international," much earlier, with what Armstrong described as "nations before nationalism."[5] If globalization is *liberalization* of state-imposed restrictions, then its history may go no further back than the abolition of British Corn Laws affecting trade in the mid-nineteenth century; and in any event pre-sovereign state history is excluded unless one expands the notion of "state" (as archaeologists tend to do) to include early kingly or tribal polities. If globalization is *universalization* in the sense of a "planetary synthesis of cultures," we may perhaps ignore regional patterns and conclude that any truly global synthesis is to date very modest at best. If globalization is *Westernization* or "modernization, especially in an 'Americanized' form," we have additional muddles. What exactly is "the West," and when did it arise? Do we start with the ancient Mesopotamians and Egyptians, or Greece, the Romans, or Renaissance Europe? Or are Westernization or modernization much later developments? If the United States is the primary influence, when did US influence begin to have a global effect?

We ourselves have written extensively about thinking in terms of "political space" and the need for "remapping global politics"[6] in order to capture far more than sovereign state boundaries. Thus we are somewhat more comfortable with Scholte's fifth definition, *respatialization*, "a reconfiguration of social geography with increased transplanetary connections among people," although his adjective "social" is perhaps too limited. He also introduces what seems to us to be an even more helpful notion of respatialization as "globality," essentially the emergence and evolution of transworld ideas and activities.[7] Indeed, without a qualifier like globality, respatialization is little more than a process, with no indication of the location or dimensions of the space affected, activities involved, or the direction of change.

Similarly, although in Chapter 1 we associated ourselves with Held's and his colleagues' "transformationalist" version of globalization, there remains a need to be clearer about who or what is being transformed and how. Much the same might be said of the definition offered by the Princeton/Washington project on "Mapping Globalization," as follows:

> We have adopted a comprehensive definition of globalization that is simply based on geographically expanding networks of transactions, where transactions may be of any type, and may have occurred at any time. This naturally supports a strongly historical perspective that includes trade, migration, transportation, communication, empires, and so on.[8]

In our view, globalization is an evolutionary non-unilinear process that has multiple interrelated dimensions: ecology, disease, demography, economics, technology, culture, politics, military, and society. These categories are by no means the only possible ones, nor are they mutually exclusive. They overlap and can easily be subdivided. For example, "culture" may be interpreted to encompass most of human affairs. "Military" and "economics" are often highly "political," as indeed is immigration in the realms of "demography" and "society." "Technology" applies equally well to military as to communications and transportation or to the production of goods. "Economics" may be subdivided into production, trade, and finance. And on and on.

The following, then, are *essential* parts of our larger conception of globalization: It is a non-unilinear evolutionary process: that is, it ebbs and flows and typically does so unevenly in its different dimensions. Therefore, speaking of globalization as a single phenomenon is highly misleading. It is multidimensional, however those dimensions may be grouped, divided, and subdivided. Different dimensions routinely overlap to some degree and also influence one another. Since globalization is an evolutionary process, in any dimension it may be considered to have begun long before "globality" is fully achieved.

At any given time with respect to any dimension, the globalization process has geographical scope, volume and density of transactions, and a pace and direction of change. As Richard L. Smith comments, "there can be simultaneous regional 'world' systems, each in a sense comprising its own 'world.'"[9] Nonetheless, the "known world" at any time may be broader than one or more regional systems. Paradoxically, even as globalization bridges wider geographical space, it makes for a "smaller" more connected world, a phenomenon Rosenau describes as "distant proximities."[10] Of course, it can also increase the psychological distance and potential for conflict between and among groups and individuals.

Globalization from the outset has involved different actors and types of polities, with some similar and also different motivations. Different polity types have taken the lead at different times in pushing the process forward – or in curbing or even reversing it. The "local" and the "global" (of the day) have continuously interacted. Those polities engaging with the external universe have inevitably altered it and also have themselves been affected by the experience, often profoundly so. Hence transformation may sometimes be an entirely appropriate characterization of the process. Yet perhaps even more frequently, the changes involved have been incremental, simple addition to previous patterns, consolidation, or even subtraction.

The foregoing considerations inform our historical narrative in this chapter.

EARLY RESPACIALIZATIONS

The globalization story begins with the biological emergence of a very small number of our human ancestors who walked out of Africa and possibly Eurasia as well,[11] and whose descendants by about 10,000 years ago had reached every continent except Antarctica. By modern standards, the pace of migrations was glacially slow, 700 generations from Africa to Australia. But considering the transportation available at the time, the migration was amazingly fast and it is no exaggeration to speak, for example, of an "express train" to Australia.[12]

Around 10,000 BC, the Ice Age receded, and hunting-and-gathering gradually gave way to agriculture. Small settlements and then cities appeared, and agricultural surplus made possible the emergence of chiefs, priests, kings, and craft labor. Nayan Chanda writes:

> Essentially, the basic motivations that propelled humans to connect with others – the urge to profit by trading, the drive to spread religious belief, the desire to explore new lands, and the ambition to dominate others by armed might – all had been assembled by 6000 BCE to start the process we now call globalization.[13]

However, one might also insist that the "start" of the globalization process had already been the earliest migration stage, albeit lacking some motivations and dimensions that manifested themselves more clearly later.

Nor should we underestimate the complexity of motivations involved at the very outset. The search for more food when population increased, the desire for certain items not found locally, and the appeal of exploring beyond the immediate horizon no doubt inspired Neolithic migrants and traders. Agriculture, to be sure, wrought huge changes, but, as Robert Wright observes, those should not be exaggerated: "Toward the end of the hunter-gatherer era there were more storage huts and other capital projects requiring political leadership, more long-distance alliances, and more trade – not to mention more kinds of food and tools than ever before."[14] Note here, already at this prehistoric stage, the need for an unfolding respacialization narrative of economics, politics, alliances, ecology, and technology.

That said, it is equally important to acknowledge the central role of agriculture. As Jared Diamond explains, "only a few areas of the world developed food production independently, and they did so at widely different times." Peoples of other environmentally suitable areas learned to domesticate plants and animals either from neighbors that already had that knowledge or from invaders. However they acquired the capacity, those who had a "head start on food production thereby gained a head start on the path leading towards guns, germs, and steel." That, according to Diamond's seminal argument, goes a long way towards accounting for the modern-day distribution of haves and have-nots.[15]

THE ANCIENT MEDITERRANEAN

Smith observes:

> Larger, more stable communities attracted people with something to swap. Between 6250 and 5400 BCE, the largest of these communities was Catal Huyuk in south central Anatolia . . . Its inhabitants grew wheat and barley and traded cattle, which had the great advantage of transporting itself. They also traded obsidian from a nearby source, for which there was a great demand elsewhere.

Around the Mediterranean, even before cities and regional polities, much long-distance trade went by boat. "This varied in scale from fishermen who did part-time trading to peddlers who stopped at villages along the coast to see what the locals had to offer."[16]

It is currently accepted that the first "civilization," substantial city-polities, and empire emerged in Sumer in southern Mesopotamia.[17] The Tigris and Euphrates provided water for irrigation that produced a large food surplus, but the area lacked minerals to forge into metal, as well as stone and wood suitable for building. Trade thus was important not only to supply temple-priests and rulers with luxury items, but also to raise the temples and cities in which elites dwelled; indeed, notes Smith, trade "became an engine in driving socio-political complexity."[18] Karl Moore and David Lewis observe that as early as 3500–3200 BC the trading posts of the city of Uruk's "temple-oriented economy" reached to the Levant and modern-day Iran, and suggest that this "represented the first halting steps toward the multinational enterprise." "Here were operations internalized, managed from abroad, and set up as permanent establishments on foreign territory to seek out both resources and eventually markets."[19]

Two closely related trading systems developed, one involving expeditions sent out directly by temple-priests and kings, and the other a relay trade through merchant middlemen who did not constitute a middle class but were military or high government officials. Over time, especially by the third and second millennia, the role of private entrepreneurship became increasing prominent.[20] From about 2600 to 2400 BC, another Early Bronze Age city, Ebla, in today's northwest Syria, presided over "a magnificent trading empire." It controlled some seventeen other polities – all of Syria and Palestine – and had trading links into the Mediterranean as far as Cyprus. "Eblaite treaties ... show an understanding of business law, international taxation, and territorial jurisdictions."[21]

By the Akkadian period of Sargon's empire and his successors (2350–2160 BC), Mesopotamia had become "the hub of a system that stretched from India and Central Asia on the one side to northeast Africa and the borderlands of Europe on the other."[22] "Sargon's trade, still dominated by temple and palace, was nevertheless more and more in the hands of a rising class of private merchants. These were known as *damgara* in Sumer and Akkad, and *tamkarum* (plural *tamkaru*) in Babylonia and Assyria."[23] Trade continued to prosper under the Third Dynasty of Ur, the collapse of which allowed the emergence of an Old Assyrian–Cappadocian trading system based even more on private enterprise. "[M]erchants ... now increasingly operated on their own as international trade began to pass into the hands of the self-employed, rather than crown merchants."[24] An association (karum) represented the interests of merchants engaged in Anatolian trade vis-à-vis political authorities, which continued to tax and partially regulate that trade. A network of karums established general standards, sometimes operated warehouses for what was essentially a large-scale wholesale operation, and even occasionally lent money. Silver and gold were the units of exchange,[25] and Akkadian became "the new common language of the ancient Near East."[26]

By Hammurabi's time (1792–1750 BC) in Babylon, as Niall Ferguson mentions, lending had become still more "sophisticated." "Debts were transferable," and interest was charged. Most of the loans "were simple advances from royal or religious storehouses." However, by the sixth century BC, "families like the Babylonian Egibi had emerged as powerful landowners and lenders, with commercial interests as far afield as Uruk over a hundred miles to the south and Persia to the east."[27]

The Euphrates and Tigris were both navigable for long stretches, and there were many canals in the south. Remarkable reed and skin boats compensated for the lack of timber. Sumerians ventured out into the Persian Gulf as early as the third millennium and later empires followed suit, encouraging a reorientation of trading activities from north and west to south and east. Dilmun (probably Kuwait to Bahrain) acted as a meeting point for merchants far and wide. Magan (Oman) was an important source of copper. Trade into the Indian Ocean was mainly with the Harappans in the Indus River Valley and lasted until their civilization began to decline around 1800 BC[28] "As well as vital grain exports, the merchants of the Indus traded in finished industrial products, notably cotton cloth (the earliest found anywhere) that was spun and woven in the numerous cities."[29]

Although Egyptian civilization emerged only slightly later than that in Mesopotamia, its political and economic focus was the Nile. There were contacts with the outside world in two directions, one north through the Nile delta into the Mediterranean and eastward to Asia, and the other south into Nubia and beyond.

Indeed, suggests Smith, "the struggles between warrior groups up and down the Nile Valley for control over internal trade and access to external routes were a major factor leading to the unification of Egypt."[30] By at least the 1st Dynasty a newly unified Egyptian polity had established a busy trade route into southern Palestine and was also gaining access to the gold and tropical products of Lower Nubia.[31] "Old Kingdom Egypt was both an intense theocracy *and* the closest parallel to a developed socialist state. There was little *visible* private sector." Trade was an almost complete monopoly of the pharaohs, by contrast with the pattern in Mesopotamia.[32]

Overland trade via Palestine gave way to sea contact with Lebanon/Syria, which provided not only the legendary cedars of Lebanon but also "plugged Egypt into the main trunk line of the long-distance commercial network that ran from Anatolia to Afghanistan."[33] From the 5th Dynasty well into the New Kingdom, another key destination was the Kingdom of Punt, perhaps modern Somalia or (it is now thought) either southern Sudan or Eritrea.[34] Middle and New Kingdom imperial incursions into Palestine/Syria also resulted in a substantial trading relationship with the major Canaanite/Phoenician center of Byblos on the coast north of modern Beirut.[35] By 2300 BC, Egyptian fleets of forty cargo vessels over 100 feet in length, known as Byblos ships, were carrying Egyptian exports of glass, jewelry, perfumes, and papyrus, and returning with timber. Egyptian trade remained tightly controlled by the pharaohs, while the Canaanite pattern was one of merchant families often in partnerships, prefiguring later developments.[36]

The famous Amarna letters that cover a brief period of thirty years from about 1365 to 1335 BC offer a unique glimpse into Egypt's diplomatic relations with its neighbors during the reign of Amenhotep III and his son Akhenatan. There were close ties among the kings of the leading polities at the time: Babylonia, Assyria, Mittani, Hatti, Alashiya, and Arzawa. Van de Mieroop writes:

> All participants in this system knew what their place was in the political hierarchy and how to interact with others. They behaved as if they lived in a large village where communications were close and people were related to each other. In order to maintain the system, they were in constant contact with one another, sending envoys back and forth with oral and written messages. All courts had a chancellery where scribes worked, writing in Babylonian, the international language of diplomacy.[37]

Most of the correspondence between the kings themselves was not about political issues but "the diplomatic exchange of messengers, goods, and women."[38] Royal weddings linking polities were a common practice.

Egypt's dual access routes to the outside world experienced reverse flows after the Third Intermediate Period (1069–715 BC) and Late Period (747–732 BC). In 945 BC, Libyan prince Shoshenq I established control over Lower Egypt and founded the Babasite Dynasty that ruled for more than 200 years. Kushite kings from Nubia conquered the whole of Egypt and established the 25th Dynasty (747–656 BC) of Black Pharaohs. The next arrivals were the Assyrians, ruling as 26th Saite Dynasty, and then the Persians, who constituted both the 27th and 31st Dynasties, the last ending with Alexander the Great's arrival in 332 BC.

From about 1500 BC there was a "shift of attention" in the Near East from east to west. Cyprus and Aegean polities became "regular trading partners" and trade with Egypt intensified.[39] Mediterranean trade seems to have flowed counterclockwise from Egypt to the Levantine cities and then to Cyprus, along the Anatolian coast to Crete, the Greek Islands and mainland, south to the African coast, and finally back to Egypt. Some ships may have ventured to collect metals from Sardinia and as far as Spain. However, it is uncertain when large-scale direct trade from the Aegean to Egypt and the Levant began. The Minoan civilization on Crete (c. 1600 BC) was "100% maritime in orientation," although using smaller ships than the Byblos vessels. They traded timber, olive, wine, woolen textiles, and pottery containers for a variety of products.[40] Trade was almost entirely in the hands of a "palace-temple hierarchy."[41]

Trade may have played a role in the decline of the Minoans and rise of mainland Mycenaean city-polities. The Mycenaeans might have been pirates who eventually got the upper hand, or Minoan trade might have declined because of natural disasters or other reasons. In any event, the Mycenaeans proved to be "aggressive traders" who maintained commercial outposts in Ugarit and elsewhere in the Levant and traded west to Sicily, Italy, and Sardinia, and north to the amber-rich Nordic–Baltic region. Palace-centered bureaucracies continued to exercise tight control over economic activities, but, as in Mesopotamia, private traders seem to have become more involved over time.[42]

Smith observes that, thus, by the late Bronze Age there existed "a series of overlapping commercial exchange systems" that "extended from the western Mediterranean to Afghanistan and India." However, the transition to the Iron Age towards the end of the second millennium was tumultuous in the extreme. The Hittite Empire and Mycenaean civilization disintegrated, Ramses III in New Kingdom Egypt narrowly fended off attacks by the "Sea Peoples," and new groups like the Philistines and Dorians appeared. Smith's general description of the period is grim:

Farmers, craftsmen, and miners stopped producing for a market economy, sea lanes swarmed with pirates, roads fell into disuse, trading centers were abandoned, and whole trade systems became dislocated. . . . The cause of this cataclysm has not been completely sorted out, but the usual suspects – warfare, demographic shifts, large-scale migrations, social upheaval, famine from poor harvests, epidemics, and natural catastrophes – have all come in for a share of the blame, One factor is certain: the magnitude of this phenomenon can be explained only by the interconnectedness of the Bronze Age world . . . [T]he domino theory was played out with a vengeance. The result was a near total systems collapse.[43]

Into the relative vacuum left by the Bronze Age systems collapse first sailed the Levant Canaanites who hailed from independent city-polities under their new Greek name, the Phoenicians. Their various merchant houses traded with and paid tribute to the mighty Assyrian Empire that by 640 BC extended from today's western Iran to Egypt[44] and forcefully resettled an estimated 4.5 million people from one part of the empire to another.[45] But the Phoenicians set their sights westward in search of a monopoly of trade.[46] Enroute they established a number of cities in North Africa, Sicily, Sardinia, and along the coast of Spain.[47], the most important of which was Carthage, which eventually inherited Phoenician trade routes.[48] The Levantine cities were adversely affected by the decline of the Assyrians and rise of the short-lived Neo-

Babylonian Empire. Neo-Babylonians unsuccessfully besieged the key Phoenician center of Tyre, although it recovered enough from that ordeal to provide the emergent Persian Empire with a major portion of its fleet.[49] The Persian Empire came to control the Phoenician harbor cities and immense territories from Egypt to the Indus Valley. Darius dug a canal from the Nile to the Red Sea, and trade throughout the vast empire flourished.[50]

From the eight century BC until Alexander's arrival, the Greeks were the main competitors of the Phoenicians and the Persians.[51] An "entrepreneurial spirit"[52] arose after the Dark Age. The Iron Age Revolution in tools and weaponry encouraged individualism in agriculture, artisan production, warfare, and politics. Moore and Lewis explain:

> Independent farming and enterprise was free to flourish in what could be called a more "Jeffersonian" society . . . Any peasant could afford an iron axe . . . and iron ploughshares . . . Every hoplite farmer could afford a bronze helmet and breastplate and an iron sword.[53]

In what was to be one of the most important milestones in global political history, free Greeks became *citizens* of their own *polis* communities, rather than *subjects* of tribal kingdoms.[54] A phase of rule by tyrants in several *poleis* helped to undermine aristocratic control, and gradually there was more popular participation in politics, whether the resulting form of government was oligarchy, limited democracy, or authoritarian (e.g. Sparta).

Greek population and surplus goods soared, metal coinage was introduced,[55] and merchants were soon setting forth in double-banked fifty-oared pentekontor ships up to 80 feet long.[56] Because the well-born typically regarded commerce as below their station, most trade was conducted by "metics", or foreigners. Greek cities early-on established colonies throughout the Mediterranean as far as Italy and Sicily and north to the Black Sea, partly to relieve land pressures but also to create trading links with distant peoples like the Etruscans.[57] Moore and Lewis describe the economic effects:

> Wheat flowed into the Aegean from the new overseas colonies, inevitably spurring urbanization and encouraging metropolitan Greeks to become ever more organized and specialized. Even the farmers of the Peloponnesus, Attica, and Ionia emerged as rural entrepreneurs raising increasing quantities of wine, oranges, and the ubiquitous olives. The market revolution was on!

A strong majority of Greek cities briefly united to repulse two major Persian invasions (499–449 BC), but subsequent rivalry between Athens and Sparta and their respective allies degenerated into the devastating Peloponesian War. Victorious Athens achieved a measure of regional integration via its own Empire (the Delian League), one significant commercial feature of which was the creation of a respected international coinage, the tetradachm,[58] and a uniform system of weights and measures. Chanda comments: "The silver Athenian coin . . . [was] to traders then what Visa and Mastercard are today."[59] As it had much earlier in Babylon, a system of banking also developed; money-lenders exchanged currencies and, along with temples, accepted deposits and made loans.[60]

The next major cataclysm to sweep the Mediterranean region and well beyond was Alexander the Great's campaigns of conquest of 334–323 BC. Alexander cut the Gordian Knot of established regimes, most notably the powerful Persian Empire in Asia Minor, and gave birth to a substantially new Hellenistic world. The long-range results were at once unifying, fragmenting, and preservative. Alexander's campaigns ranged across three continents, and his short-lived empire encompassed 2 million square miles. It stretched from the Greek lands of the west, north to the Danube, south into Egypt, and east to the Indian Punjab. Alexander thus established the footprint for a vast imperial polity that would not be fully realized and consolidated until the Romans. He also established no fewer than seventy new cities and made it clear that his intention – building upon the Persian precedent established by Cyrus and Darius – was to create a kind of cosmopolitan conglomerate, respecting traditional customs and patterns of rule. When he moved on to the next conquest, he often left local satraps in control, and he encouraged his soldiers to marry foreign women, setting the example himself by taking as a wife the late Great King's daughter Roxanne.

Following his death, Alexander's generals struggled among themselves for control of his legacy and four main dynastic polities emerged: the Antigonid in Macedon and Greece, the Ptolemaic in Egypt based at Alexandria, the Seleucid in Syria and Mesopotamia ruling from Antioch, and the Attalid in Anatolia at Pergamum. Two more major kingdoms later appeared, the Greco-Bactrian and the Indo-Greek. Although the original conquered territories were thus divided, the post-Alexander arrangements were stable enough to usher in an unprecedented Hellenistic era of flourishing trade and commerce, demographic mobility, spread of a common Greek culture along with local cultural adaptation, new intellectual currents, and rapidly shifting loyalties and identities. Not unlike our own time, albeit on a much smaller scale and at a far slower pace, the period was one of great fluidity and ferment, promise as well as uncertainty.

Trade and commerce advanced in part because of improved ships and ports, and also because money-lending became the business of large institutions that could transfer money from place to place using letters of credit. Kings owned all land and controlled economic activity, especially in Egypt, but "side-by side" a "more free-wheeling system" persisted. Alexandria with its famous lighthouse was the leading commercial center. There were other important transit cities too, and Rhodes had the largest commercial fleet. Nabatean Petra prospered because it was a crossroads for regional caravan routes. Camels were introduced as a beast of burden for trade and – since they needed less water, moved faster, and carried twice as much as a horse or mule – improved the competitiveness of land routes through arid territory.

A century or so after Alexander, Rome began to march. After the Romans secured their Italian homeland and finally defeated the Carthaginians[62] in the Punic Wars (264–146 BC), they rapidly extended their imperial conquests in every direction to become the largest empire the world had ever known. It was to persist, in one form or another, until the Arab conquests overcame the last remnants of the Eastern Empire in AD 641. Chester Starr describes the sheer magnitude of Roman accomplishments as "an impossibility." At its fullest extent under the Emperor Trajan in AD 117, the Empire stretched 3,000 miles from southern Scotland to southern Egypt, west to the Atlantic, and east to the upper plains of the Euphrates River. Observes Starr: "This huge block was larger than the whole earth today, if measured in terms of ancient communications and transportation."[63]

Roman rule and culture spread across Hellenic Greek and other cultures throughout the Empire. Rome provided an overarching administrative structure, sufficient Roman law and military might to maintain order, a tax structure, and an imperial monetary regime.[64] What was demanded in return, in addition to payment of taxes, was obedience to and at least outward respect for the Roman Emperor and officialdom, Roman decrees, and Roman gods. Roman citizenship was relatively restricted in the beginning but was ultimately extended as political circumstances seemed to dictate to almost all free subjects of the Empire. As a general policy – in the tradition of relative tolerance prefigured by the Persians and Alexander – "client kings"[65] and other native authorities and peoples were allowed to manage their own affairs.

There was "an extraordinary level of uniformity," including the degree of urbanization. Hosts of new and older cities served as centers of cultural life, economic activity, and Roman and local administration. They "thrived as part of a system," relying on their rural hinterlands, other cities in their network, and the larger Empire as well. There was a "prodigious increase in inter-regional mobility" of peoples and an "explosion of mercantile activity in the Mediterranean." Road-building and the harnessing of water power were Roman preoccupations. Roads were mainly for military and local use, for, despite advances in the design and mass production of carts and wagons, overland transport was still difficult and expensive.[66]

Sea transport was less expensive, but weather was only favorable from April to October.[67] Romans built ships of 245–450 tons as early as the 1st century BC, which were mainly useful for transporting grain from Egypt and North Africa to Rome,[68] and also developed better rigging and navigational aids, harbors, warehouses, and lifting devices. Rhodes produced the first code of maritime law.[69] Roman officials engaged large naval contractors,[70] and by the late Imperial period the government kept grain shipments under tight control. Rich senatorial families owned huge latifundia worked by slave labor and often had family ships. "Merchants could own their own ships, rent space on someone else's ship, or serve as agents for goods owned by someone else." In due course "a class of middlemen emerged" that would deal in any goods that turned a profit.[71]

Even as Roman politics in the late Republic became increasingly polarized and dangerous – with "peasantry, proletariat, slaves, freedmen, and other polities divided along class, ethnic and occupational lines" – enterprising wealthy families or *publicani* "reached their zenith."[72] "Next to agriculture, military contracts were the major business in Rome" and ensured a steady stream of additional income to the *publicani*.[73] Moore and Lewis write:

> Beginning as large partnerships working in the free-market milieu of Roman Italy, they evolved into modern-style conglomerates or non-specialized mega-firms ... Associations of partners came together to carry out a contract and then disbanded – the virtual corporation management form model ... [T]he Roman *publicani* of the second and first centuries BCE were transacting business on a much larger scale than had any private firm in the Near East or Mediterranean before them.[74]

Rome also engaged *publicani* as tax collectors in much of the Empire and promised triple money to those who were venturesome enough to invest in such far-flung domains as Syria and Judea.[75]

INTERCONTINENTAL LINKAGES FROM LATE ANTIQUITY TO THE DAWN OF EUROPE'S "AGE OF DISCOVERY"

During the first millennium AD, the Mediterranean became increasingly linked with other regions of the world that themselves had previously been experiencing substantial economic and other forms of integration. Intercontinental trade routes carried a much greater diversity and volume of goods. Major new religions arose and gained converts far and wide. And in Central Asia, especially, tribal peoples were on the move.

As Smith observes: "Three great corridors, the Red Sea, the Persian Gulf, and the Malacca Straits leading into the China Sea connected East, South, and West Asia and Africa and Europe." The Indian Ocean was the first to become a "commercial zone" or, rather, divided as it is by the South Asian continent, "two arcs" that constituted "a set of interrelated commercial systems, each with overlapping circuits."[76] Traders discovered how to work the monsoon wind and currents between India and Egypt to cut sailing time to three months from the previous thirty months.[77] Arab traders operating from east Africa were the pioneers of trade with India. However, the Roman Empire stretched to the Red Sea by the first century AD,[78] and Mediterranean traders were soon able to bypass the Arabs in improved ships and trade directly with India,[79] a principal factor, incidentally, in the decline of Petra as a caravan crossroads. Roman authorities encouraged private merchants and investment in trade, and imports boomed in spices, perfumes, medicines, and many other goods.[80] Meanwhile, "a merchant ship left Egypt for India almost every day of the season carrying tin, wine, coral, glass, and gold and silver coins."[81] But since Roman demand for luxuries was so great and about the only major Roman export in continual demand in India was wine, a serious balance of trade problem developed,[82] which was to prove to be a perennial issue in West-to-East trade.

Apart from the Americas and the South Pacific, China was the farthest frontier for the West, not least because the Chinese were relatively self-sufficient and uninterested in connections with the West. For several millennia BC there was frontier trade with China's immediate north and west. China imported jade (the Jade Road) and fur and gold (the Fur Road) from Tibet and Siberia, respectively, and other gemstones and metals, animals, wool, hides, and wood from various sources. Silk was a major Chinese export at least as early as the second century BC. The Chinese attitude towards large-scale commerce became somewhat more positive during the Period of Warring States (403–221 BC), when iron technology and the introduction of coinage contributed to economic expansion, but relations with Central Asian steppe nomads were always fraught with danger as well as potential reward. The Emperor Qin Shihuangdi, who first unified China, built the Great Wall in a largely unsuccessful effort to keep out the Xiongnu.[83]

The Han Dynasty (202 BC–AD 220) initially concluded a treaty under which the Chinese agreed to supply silk, grain, and alcoholic beverages to the Xiongnu, and border markets were created to encourage local trade.[84] The official Han ideology of Confucianism (rather like the attitude of classical Greek aristocrats) was disdainful of merchants and craftsmen, but the government found their activities useful, taxed them heavily, and occasionally assumed direct control of trade.[85] Emperor Han Wudi (141–87 BC) engaged in almost continual skirmishes with the Xiongnu and reportedly besieged the distant Ferghana until they supplied him with the Heavenly Horses he most desired. He also sent his emissary Zhang Qian west on an arduous quest to conclude an alliance with the Xiongnu's former enemies the Yuezhi, whom he finally found in Bactria. Zhang Qian failed to enlist them as allies, but brought back reports of a host of exotic lands. The Chinese became increasingly interested in opportunities for trade as far west as Persia, Mesopotamia, and the Roman Empire.[86]

Smith suggests that the Chinese were actually entering in a more intensive way a system that had been operational for millennia, since the start of the Jade Road.[87] By the first century AD, the Silk Road was "carrying silk and lacquerware to the Roman Empire and woolen and linen textiles, glass, coral, amber, and pearl to China."[88] As Smith concludes, the "larger picture was that the sustained, systematic, large-scale movement of goods across a fully integrated land system and a parallel [Indian Ocean] sea system had become a reality."[89] The Silk Road reached its height much later, during the thirteenth century, when the Mongol Empire controlled its full length and the Road's terminus in the Tang Dynasty capital, present-day Xian, was the largest and most cosmopolitan city in the world.[90]

Intellectual currents and religions with potential transnational appeal also traveled the new connecting routes. Chanda observes: "The rise of monotheistic religion, centered on the belief in one god for all, could unshackle humans from their animistic local gods. Freed from local settings, religion could travel and become global, and yet a god could be personal."[91] According to the Bible and subsequent tradition, the world's three great monotheistic religions all had their origin in Bronze Age Mesopotamia (Genesis 11 says Ur of the Chaldees) in the person of Abraham (Ibrahim), whose first son Isaac fathered the nation of Israel and thus Judaism, and whose second son Ishmael (Isma'il), fathered the Arab people and Islam (via the medieval Prophet Muhammad, regarded as his direct descendant). Christianity also traces it history to Abraham, incorporating the Hebrew Scriptures as the "Old Testament," and worshipping the Jewish-born Jesus of Nazareth as the Son of God (Christ).

Both Judaism and Christianity are also associated with Roman rule in the Near East. Rome inadvertently facilitated the dispersal of both Judaism and Christianity in the first century AD by crucifying Jesus and warring on Jewish rebels at Masada (recounted by Josephus) and elsewhere. Of the two religions, Judaism was to prove much more inward-looking and closely associated with preserving Jewish ethnicity and culture in what was to become a widespread Jewish diaspora, rather than proselytizing for new converts. In contrast, Christianity – although often persecuted by Rome – rapidly made converts throughout the Empire and eventually the Emperor Constantine (312–37) himself. He convened the Council of Nicea in 325, partly to address disputes with Arianism, and the Nicene Creed over time came to be accepted by both Catholics and Orthodox. Under later emperors, most notably, the Emperors Theodosius I (379–95) and Justinian (518–65), Christianity became firmly established as the official religion and paganist practices were outlawed.[92]

A strikingly different version of a new universalistic religion that did not have a single god, but taught the need for individuals to pursue a path of enlightenment and salvation available to all, was Buddhism. Buddhism was unusually tolerant of other faiths and "perfectly suited for the life of itinerant traders."[93] In 623 BC, Siddharta Gautam, a prince in a small northern India kingdom, received *bodhi* (enlightenment), and his message spread to today's eastern Iran and Central Asia and even to Japan and Vietnam. The Mauyran Emperor Asoka who conquered India in the third century BC actively promoted Buddhism, as did the Han Emperor Mingdi in the first century AD, and the famous monk/scholar preacher Xuanzang who in 629 began a twelve-year journey to India and back to China.[94]

Even as the new religions were establishing their own spheres of influence, the Roman Empire started a long decline. The Empire was formally divided between West (Rome) and East (Constantinople) following the death of Constantine, and Rome soon found itself facing successive incursions by Germanic tribes (Visigoths, Huns, Ostrogoths, and Vandals) from Central Asia. The deposition of the child emperor Romulus Augustulus in 476 and elevation of the Visigoth Odoacer as effective king of Italy marks what historians accept as the final death knell of the Western Empire. However, the Eastern Empire continued for nearly a millennium in the form of the Greek Byzantine Empire, and the Eastern Emperor Justinian did briefly reconquer the west and restore some of its former glory.[95]

During Europe's Middle Ages and Early Modern periods, Christianity under the authority of the Pope in Rome (or two or three at different places during times of schism) – and the Greek Orthodox Patriarch in the east – remained the dominant religion. Venice, founded ca. 568 by refugees from the Lombards, in late medieval times became in William H. McNeill's words, the "hinge of Europe,"[96] linking Frankish kingdoms and the Holy Roman Empire (the Pope's principal temporal competitor) with Byzantium and a newly militant Islam.

Fundamental changes occurred in the former Roman Eastern Empire in the late sixth and early seventh centuries. Indo-European Slavs invaded the Balkans from the north, and the Eastern Empire engaged in a protracted struggle with the Sassanian Persians that exhausted both sides. Inspired by the preaching and leadership of the Prophet Muhammad and his successors, the Arabs rapidly conquered Syria and Palestine (630s), the Persian Empire (637), Egypt (641), and Roman Africa (by the end of the century).[97] Mitchell argues that two main factors account for Arab successes: they "developed a high level of military organization and a capacity for aggressive warfare" and a "complete fusion of political and religious loyalty, in a form that was completely independent of the monotheism of the Christian empire or the Mazdaean traditions of the Sassanians." "The Islamic state was based on the notion of *umma*, the community of believers, which transformed Arab tribal society." For these reasons, the "holy war of the Christian empire was outmatched by a *jihad*."[98]

In the centuries that followed the initial Arab victories there was both "bloody and lucrative interchange between European Christendom and Middle Eastern Islam."[99] Part of the conflict was about religion, converting heathens for Christ and reclaiming the Holy Land, but it was also a matter, as Niall Ferguson reminds us, of plundering the Muslim world's precious metals to overcome a chronic shortage especially of silver in Western Europe.[100] A Pisan customs official, Fibonacci, based in today's Algeria introduced Hindu–Arabic numbers and the decimal system to Europe and "showed how it could be applied to commercial bookkeeping, to currency conversions, and, crucially, to the calculation of interest." "Venice . . . became Europe's great lending laboratory,"[101] its money-lenders providing ample finance for Venetian merchants' ambitious trading ventures. However, it was the Florentines who pioneered modern banking. Fourteenth-century finance in Italy featured the three Florentine houses of Bardi, Peruzzi, and Acciaiuoli, who all went bankrupt lending to high-risk clients like Britain's King Edward II and King Robert of Naples. The Medici banking enterprise was on a different plane, starting as simple foreign-exchange dealing, then issuing bills of exchange, becoming a full-fledged bank with "multiple related partnerships, each based on a special, regularly renegotiated contract," and finally underpinning a powerful Florentine city-polity hereditary monarchy.[102]

Venice, in particular, and other Italian city-polities profited from their relationships with all sides to almost any conflict. Venice gradually established a major trading empire in the Mediterranean as it built ships for Crusaders and sold them supplies. Later Venice financed an Ottoman fleet to make war on the Portuguese in the Red Sea. The "Genovese sold Christian and pagan slaves to the Mamlukes in Egypt who then trained them as soldiers to be used against the Crusaders."[103] Venice built its Arsenal shipyard and, along with Genoa, radically improved ship technology by adding the Arab lanteen sail to square and staysails – for three-masted vessels – and the Chinese sternpost rudder. The compass also came into regular use, perhaps another import from China.[104] Even as money-lenders provided basic financing for risky trading voyages, Venetian merchants found ways of sharing the risk through contracts that echoed some ancient world practices and also foreshadowed later corporations and insurance.

Islamic warriors eventually defeated the waves of Crusaders, the Byzantine Empire expired after the fall of Constantinople in 1453, and, following struggles among Turkish tribes, Mongols, Persians, and Mamlukes, the Mamlukes gained the upper hand. The Mamluke "structures and prosperous relationship" with Venice involved the latter's military might keeping Europeans from seizing Egypt and accessing Red Sea links with India and China, while "Venetians docked in Alexandria to wait for access to spices, dyes, pepper, silk, cotton and porcelains from Malaysia, India, and China." Meanwhile, Arab traders along Africa's eastern coast and Zanzibar conducted a lively exchange with India and elsewhere in Southeast Asia, leading in part to the enormous Muslim populations of modern-day Malaysia and Indonesia.[105]

The Ottomans eventually succeeded the Mamlukes and, although the Ottoman Empire was to persist until 1922, its height was under Suleiman the Magnificent (1566–74) when it expanded to include the Balkans and Hungary and first unsuccessfully besieged Vienna. Severe setbacks were the Ottoman defeat in the naval Battle of Lepanto in 1571 by the Holy League (a coalition of Spain, Venice, the Papacy, the Duchy of Savoy, the Knights Hospitaller, and others), and the failure of the Ottomans' second siege of Vienna in 1683.

Marco Polo made his legendary journeys (by sea and land) to and within China in the second half of the thirteenth century, to the court of the Mongol ruler of China, Kublai Khan. The later Ming Dynasty (1368–1644) forced the Mongol rulers out, and for nearly a century Ming emperors seemed determined to continue exploring opportunities in the outside world. Chinese ships were the wonder of the age, with multiple decks, an unprecedented number of cannons, and a cargo capacity of 1520–1860 tons. Chinese admiral Zheng He's trading voyages (1405–33) commanded "treasure ships" with nine masts, 400 feet long, and a maximum crew of 1,000.[106] They reputedly reached numerous ports in East Africa, South Asia, and Southeast Asia into the South Pacific, and indeed such ships could have carried the Chinese as far as the Americas or Italy.[107] Then, for reasons not yet entirely clear, the Ming Dynasty precipitously halted most expeditions and retired its sea-going fleet. Explanations include fear of cultural pollution, court politics (concern about the influence of eunuchs like Zheng He), preoccupation with internal development, reduced likelihood of attack by sea when the capital moved to Beijing, or simply a lack of sufficient evidence that goods obtained from abroad would ever justify the trouble and expense of procuring them.[108]

Chinese retreat from the outside world may have made good sense to the Mings, but it left the field wide-open for the Europeans, who were just reaching a point in their own development to be able to take full advantage of it. A case in point was Spain, which in 1492 had finally completed a *reconquista* of its South from the Moors that had been in progress since 711 and witnessed the union in marriage of King Ferdinand and Queen Isabella of Aragon and Castile. Once again, the Italian city-polities were quick to make an additional profit. Chanda states:

> The Ottoman Empire was a barrier [to trade], and the Atlantic Ocean was increasingly seen as a way to get around it. Merchants and financiers from Venice, Genoa, Florence, and Livorno were ready to back adventurers who would find another way to Asia for silk, spice, and diamonds.[109]

THE ATLANTIC BRIDGED, EUROPEAN SOVEREIGN STATES, EMPIRES, AND GLOBAL CAPITALISM

O'Brien and Williams's adaptation of Abu-Lughod's map of fifteenth-century regional economic systems[110] shows twelve overlapping systems, including ten that linked various areas of Europe, Asia, and Africa. The other two systems had emerged in the Americas, unbeknownst to traders elsewhere in the world. One was in Mesoamerica,[111] in Teotihuacán in the Basin of Mexico, then one of the largest cities in the world and an important center for crafts and trade as well as the hub of an empire that reached as far south as the Maya Lowland Petén subregion in today's Guatemala. Another smaller polity, Monte Albán, controlled the Valley of Oaxaca and adjoining areas. When both centers collapsed around 700, control passed successively to the Toltecs and the Aztec Empire, which rested on fearsome domination and tribute rather than trade. The second regional system was the Inca Empire, centered in modern-day Peru, whose impressive roads and administrative structure stretched as far south as Chile.

After the early migrations across the Siberian peninsula, the first documented Eurasian visitors and brief settlers on the North American continent were the Norse, who colonized Iceland and Greenland and established temporary camps as far south as Newfoundland. We have mentioned possible Chinese visits before the Ming retreat, but Columbus still retains the rightful title of the first European "discoverer" of the Americas on his several voyages beginning in 1492. To be sure, Columbus was initially looking for a new route to the Indies and his major achievement was part of a much wider European "Age of Discovery." Vasco da Gama soon pioneered a sea route to India by way of the Cape of Good Hope, and Ferdinand Magellan in 1519–22 circumnavigated the globe. Where Spain and Portugal ventured, other Europeans were quick to follow.

It is hard to underestimate the significance of the European bridging of the Atlantic. It transformed world history – with a broad range of positive and negative consequences – by closing the last intercontinental transactions gap after millennia of separate development and regional integration. Diamond describes the period as one of "Hemispheres Colliding"[112] and Alfred Crosby somewhat more positively as "the Columbian Exchange."[113]

European settlement began in the West Indies with Columbus's arrival in 1492. Another colony was established in Panama in 1508, and the Aztecs and Inca empires fell to Cortés and Pizarro, respectively, in 1519–20 and 1532–3. Successful conquests owed partly to military superiority and cooperation of some tribes hostile to their overlords, but also the devastating impact of European diseases like smallpox and measles. In later years up to 95 percent of the total Native American population failed to survive forceful elimination or relentless microbes.[114] Diamond estimates that the total human population of the Americas today is about ten times what it was in 1492, almost entirely because of the arrivals of Old World peoples (Europeans, Africans, and Asians). He characterizes the "demographic shift of the last 500 years" as "the most massive shift on any continent except Australia."[115]

Added to the other major consequences of the Spanish Conquest were the combined effects of the introduction of European technology and what Crosby calls "the greatest biological revolution in the Americas since the end of the Pleistecene era."[116] The Spanish introduced the horse, donkey, mule, and ox, as well as a range of cattle, pigs, sheep, goats, new breeds of dogs and cats, and various domesticated fowls, into the Western Hemisphere. The Conquest also doubled or tripled the number of cultivatable food plants in the New World, bringing wheat, sugar cane, bananas, grapes, chickpeas, cauliflowers, cabbages, various orchard fruits, salad greens, radishes, onions, and European melons.[117] Many new grasses and wildflowers arrived, too, to the extent that today "an American botanist can easily find whole meadows in which he is hard put to find a single species of plant that grew in America in pre-Columbian times."[118] On the severely negative side, the Spanish ruthlessly exploited native labor and New World reserves of gold and silver, and the European plow caused widespread erosion in former grassland areas.

The other side of the story is the reverse impact of New World trade on Spain and the Old World generally. Plants new to Europe included maize, manioc, potato, pumpkin, a variety of table beans, cacao, tobacco, paprika, and American cotton – and probably played a role in the subsequent population increase in the Old World. Indeed, the Industrial Revolution might not have happened without the potato, a source of cheap calories for the laboring poor. Although the new supply of precious metals seemed to provide a bonanza for Spain, its eventual effect was devastating. Prices in Spain rose about 400 percent in the sixteenth century, pushed wages up, discouraged new technological advances, made Spanish goods uncompetitive, and ultimately had much to do with Spain's decline as a world power.[119]

Spain's consolidation as a sovereign state and imperial expansion was the leading edge of a political and economic revolution in Europe that began in the late Middle Ages into the Early Modern era. Medieval fairs in such places as Champagne and Frankfurt were early hubs of commerce. As we have seen, Venice, Genoa, Florence, and other Italian city-polities prospered during the Crusades, engaged in a lively trade with the Near and Far East, and made remarkable institutional innovations in banking, credit, and risk-sharing companies. A "second Venice" was the northern Belgian city of Bruges, which anchored a new generation of Flemish fairs, had an extremely successful textile industry, and established the first stock market, the Bourse. Meanwhile, the Hansa group of merchants created a highly successful trading operation that connected Baltic city-polities with others as far as the North Sea, English Channel, and Irish Sea.

The Italian banking system inspired forerunners of modern central banks in Amsterdam, London, and Stockholm.[120] The Amsterdam Exchange Bank (1609) accepted deposits in multiple currencies and allowed depositors to write checks or make direct debits or transfers denominated in a single currency. The Swedish Riksbank (1656) engaged in lending that exceeded its actual monetary reserves. The Bank of England (1694) issued its own stock and enjoyed a partial monopoly on the issue of banknotes. One might say a divergence between "real" and "virtual" money had thus begun.

All was not entirely well, for, as O'Brien and Williams observe, there was a continued imbalance in trade: "Money drained from the north of Europe to the south and eventually to the east of the Mediterranean and beyond. High priced and desirable goods came into Europe from China, India, the Middle East and Africa." The West had some large bulk goods to exchange and a few luxuries, but this was not sufficient. "Luxury goods that could not be offset with trade had to be purchased with silver or gold," which left the Europeans with three fundamental choices: They "could find new sources of silver and gold; they could try to seize the goods they wanted by force; or they could develop more desirable goods for trade purposes."[121] In the end, they pursued all three courses of action, often to their benefit but also sometimes ultimately (as with Spain) for the worse.

The political institution-building side of the European revolution from the Medieval to Early Modern periods was, of course, the emergence and consolidation of sovereign territorial states.[122] Although we have termed such polities "Westphalian States," the process took hundreds of years rather than a literal "Westphalian moment." The triumph of the European state over its feudal-era rivals was gradual, tentative, and uneven. Tilly argues, "as seen from 1600 or so, the development of the state was very contingent; many aspiring states crumpled and fell along the way."[123] Princes wrested exclusive control of what became dynastic domains and gained the loyalty of a new urban commercial class that was attracted by the significant advantages the larger centralized units offered them, including uniform laws of property, a common currency, standard weights and measures, better infrastructure, and protection both from predatory nobles and highway brigands.[124] All of this had important implications for encouraging both internal and external trade and markets.

There was another crucial external dimension to state-building. Physical security for rulers and subjects was an age-old problem that, if anything, increased with the rivalries engendered by the new system of sovereign states. Although an overstatement, there is much truth in Tilly's famous aphorism that "War made the state and vice versa."[125] Michael Mann observes that "both military technique and economic expansion favoured the consolidation of larger territorial states and the alliance of kings and merchants."[126] As Niall Ferguson emphasizes, war was also "the father of the bond market" for government debt – yet another "invention of the Italian Renaissance" – and helped provide the requisite finance to supplement taxes, confiscation (e.g. Henry VIII's seizure of English monasteries), and plunder of foreigners. The bond market itself evolved from its Florentine and Venetian origins as forced loans that then could be traded, through the issuance of annuities in the Low Countries, to a positively "thriving" bond market that gave England a critical edge in defeating Napoleon and later made the Rothschild family's fortunes.[127]

Although the process of consolidation was somewhat different in each country and remained incomplete nearly everywhere – especially in Germany and Italy – the Westphalian State prospered because it was better able at the time than any other institution to reduce violence within its boundaries, manage and channel violence externally, and mobilize the abilities and resources of subjects. People did not immediately sublimate their local or transnational identities as villagers, Christians, or subjects of the Holy Roman Empire, but those identities became relatively less central to their lives as the state increased its extractive and regulatory capacities. Henry VIII's establishment of an English church was at once a means to his divorce, a power statement, an appropriation of wealth, and a nation-building symbol. Loyalties to states further intensified with the explosion of nationalism that accompanied and followed the French Revolution, a trend towards constitutional monarchies and increased popular participation, and finally the creation of the modern welfare state.

It is surely one of the greatest ironies in history that the rise of the nation-state is so closely intertwined with what also might correctly be described as an Age of Empires. No sooner were the foundations of European states laid than many of those same states embarked on campaigns of exploration, trade, and conquest to the farthest reaches of the world. Thus, paradoxically, the hardening of boundaries of new states spurred transnational expansion, and the gains from that expansion helped them to consolidate within those selfsame boundaries. In almost all cases, state boundaries were anything but permanent. Consider the fact that the only European state to retain today exactly the same boundaries as at Westphalia is Portugal, which subsequently gained and in due course lost most of its empire! Ironically, the state model and its associated concept of national self-determination were carried on the banners of European empires, thus planting in every imperial bosom the seeds of its own destruction – the eventual creation of yet more states. No clearer general example could be found of what we have called the dynamics of fusion/fission – or "fragmegration" in Rosenau's terminology – that are inherent in the multiple processes of globalization.

Spain's empire encompassed the immense riches of Mexico and Peru and stretched as far as Manila. Portugal's empire was "no less profitable" and "even more extensive," spreading "outwards from the Atlantic islands of Madeira and São Tomé to include the vast territory of Brazil and numerous trading outposts in West Africa, Indonesia, India and even China."[128] By the Pope's Bull, the Spanish got the trade and mineral wealth of the Americas, and the Portuguese had the sugar, spices, and slaves.[129] The French, Dutch, and British entered the race for empire mainly from the seventeenth century. The French acquired extensive territories in North America and colonies in the Caribbean and India. After losing Canada and other New World colonies to the British and US purchase of the Louisiana Territories, the French switched their colonial focus to Africa and Southeast Asia. The Netherlands was the leading global commercial power during the Dutch Golden Age of the second half of the seventeenth century. Theirs was primarily a trading empire that included some former Spanish and Portuguese possessions, and it was they who pioneered colonialism by state-sponsored corporations, the Dutch East and West India Companies.

As Niall Ferguson remarks, the British were "late beginners" in the imperial game; rather than acquiring their empire "in a fit of absence of mind," as is sometimes suggested, in fact "it was a conscious act of imitation."[130] What the British initially wanted mainly was the gold and silver the Spanish found in the Americas, but finding none of significance in their own transatlantic explorations, they became adept at commissioning privateers to steal it from Spanish galleons. However, Ferguson observes, what subsequently drove the later British Empire was "less . . . the Protestant work ethic or English individualism than . . . the British sweet tooth," the development of "the world's first consumer society" and its "insatiable appetite" for sugar and a host of other imported commodities like raw cotton, tobacco, tea, and coffee.[131] The British unsuccessfully fought three wars against the Dutch in the mid-seventeenth century and lost their West African outposts in the process. Yet the "Glorious Revolution" of 1688 – in addition to its political affirmation of British parliamentary monarchy – also involved what Ferguson terms an "Anglo-Dutch business merger." The British founded what was to become the fabulously wealthy and powerful East India Company and learned other Dutch lessons about "modern finance," which inspired the creation of the Bank of England, a "national public debt . . . funded through a Stock Exchange," and a national currency. However belatedly acquired or imitative, the resulting British Empire at its peak was considerably more than a later Rome – except that Rome at the same stage had fewer rivals. In fact, Britain had "the biggest Empire ever" "that governed roughly a quarter of the world's population, covered about the same proportion of the earth's land surface, and dominated nearly all its oceans."[132]

Again in the historical record we encounter the fusion/fission dynamic in globalization and its complexity, both tendencies happening simultaneously rather than "simply" in reaction to one another. The Seven Years' War of 1756–63 (the French and Indian War in North America) has sometimes been regarded, with good reason, as the first global war. In Ferguson's words:

> Like the global wars of the twentieth century, it was at root a European war. Britain, France, Prussia, Austria, Portugal, Spain, Hanover, Russia and Sweden

were all combatants. But the fighting ranged from Coromandel to Canada, from Guinea to Guadeloupe, from Madras to Manila. Indians, native Americans, African slaves and American colonists all became involved. At stake was the future of empire itself. The question was simply this: Would the world be French or British?[133]

Our own assessment here is yes, but in significant ways, no – and also, much more. To be sure, the British acquired Canada, the French ceded the Louisiana territory, and Napoleon was eventually defeated. But victorious Britain still had imperial rivals and, with fateful consequences (symbolized by the "shot heard round the world" at the 1775 battle of Lexington and Concord, Massachusetts), drew precisely the wrong lessons from its military experience in the North American colonies that it had heretofore treated with benign neglect. The British got a good look at the prosperity of the colonies they had protected with blood and treasure, and sought to recoup some of the costs through increased taxation. The result a few years later was revolution and independence, which happened – it should be stressed – long before the British Empire reached its fullest extent.

The US Declaration of Independence (1776), Haitian independence from the French (1804), Spain's loss of much of Spanish America after 1810, and Brazil's separation from Portugal (1822) began the lengthy forced retreat of European empires. Yet some empires like the British and the French in Africa and Southeast Asia continued to expand, and new ones were created. Perhaps predictably, Germany and Italy – late arrivals to state consolidation – were late aspirants to empire, and the United States and Japan as well, in the late nineteenth and first half of the twentieth century. The United States wrested Texas, most of New Mexico and Arizona, and California from Mexico. Moreover, after a brief period of European "gunboat diplomacy," the Caribbean effectively became a US lake, and US marines repeatedly intervened throughout much of the subregion. The United States reached its probable height of influence as a hegemon ("informal" empire) after World War II, and its height of nonsensical hubris with the neoconservative G. W. Bush administration's vision of "American empire." Russia meanwhile expanded from a large national state, to a Tsarist empire that included its "near abroad," to an "informal" Soviet empire that after 1945 also dominated Eastern Europe. Neither US nor Russian empires endured indefinitely in substantial form, and it is an open question today whether "empire" is any longer even a viable political option.

But we are now well ahead of our loose chronology and should return to pick up more of the economic side of the globalization story. Let us resume with textile production in Britain around 1750 and the ensuing Industrial Revolution.[134] A series of technological innovations – notably the spinning jenny, the waterframe, and the introduction of steam power ca. 1790 – transformed production. The factory system emerged, and workers gravitated to large industrial cities like Manchester. There was also a global shift in patterns of supply and demand for cotton. More than half now came not from the Caribbean but from the United States, where cotton harvested using mainly slave labor accounted for over 50 per cent of US exports. Trade in slaves had, of course, existed since ancient times, and in the period of the European empires was "pioneered" by the Portuguese and their African partners. However, the "triangular trade" – slaves from Africa to North America and the Caribbean, commodities from North America and the Caribbean to Britain and Europe, and British and European manufactures to Africa and beyond – was a particularly ugly dimension of the European economic boom that followed the Industrial Revolution. In the mid-nineteenth century, developing iron and coal industries made possible major growth in railroad building and steel-hulled ships powered by steam that soon were routinely plying transatlantic and Asian waters. By 1900, railroads had cut land transportation costs by over four-fifths, and the steamship reduced the cost of shipping by more than two-thirds.[135] The completion of the Suez Canal (1869) and the Panama Canal (1915) greatly facilitated inter-oceanic trade. Late industrial bloomers Germany and the United States made remarkable strides in chemicals and electricity, and Japan also rapidly entered the ranks of industrial powers.

Revolutionary changes in production and transport had the additional effect of altering the prevailing formal and informal rules and practices of global commerce and international finance. The emergence of far-flung European empires to some extent had an integrative effect, insofar as vast regions of the world were grouped under individual imperial banners. But the mercantile ideology initially pursued by the empires involved containing trade within their own imperial realms and limiting transactions with others. Yet, as Jeffrey Frieden explains, increasingly there were reasons not to adopt such an exclusive policy: "By the 1820s British factories could undercut competitors in virtually every market. The economic interests created by Britain's Industrial Revolution saw mercantilism as irrelevant or harmful."[136] British manufacturing elites and financiers in the City of London, now the world's leading financial center, mounted a concerted attack on mercantilism. Adam Smith's argument for free markets in his *The Wealth of Nations* (1776) and later David Ricardo's theory of comparative advantage provided powerful intellectual support for the reformers. Their key success was the repeal in 1846 – over the spirited opposition of British farmers – of the Corn Laws, taxes imposed on grain imports during the Napoleonic Wars. Free trade ideas gradually made headway both on the European continent and across the Atlantic. The British and French signed a major commercial treaty in 1860 that freed their bilateral trade, and when "the German states moved toward unification in 1871, they created a free trade area among themselves, then opened trade with the rest of the world."[137]

A common argument of some analysts who are skeptical about the novelty of present-day globalization is that the world was at least as globalized, and possibly even more so, in the late nineteenth and early twentieth centuries. Although we believe the argument is fundamentally flawed, there is nonetheless some evidence to support it. European empires continued to rule much of the world at a time of so-called Pax Britannica, but old-fashioned mercantilism was essentially dead. The trade of advanced countries increased two to three times as fast as their national economies, and by about 1900 trade accounted for seven or eight times its share of the world economy than a century earlier.[138] Some private corporations grew to resemble today's giant firms and a number of global brands appeared, although few corporations were yet multinational to the degree of having production facilities abroad. Most countries followed the British example and supported a gold monetary standard, which was the dominant "organizing principle of global capitalism"[139] between 1875 and 1914.

International finance boomed, and some banks opened foreign branches. The revolution in transportation dramatically reduced the expense of moving people as well as goods, which fostered a dramatic surge in migration, the creation of new diasporas, and the beginnings of mass tourism. Another revolution occurred in communications, with the arrival of the telegraph, submarine cables, the telephone, and wireless transmission.

There were also new international governmental organizations (IGOs), the expansion of international law, and many more multilateral treaties. One trend was multilateral conference diplomacy, beginning after 1815 with the Concert of Europe, which attempted to address such problems as arms races and potential clashes over imperial expansion. The Hague Conferences of 1899 and 1907 banned aerial bombing, chemical warfare, and the use of hollow point bullets; tried to curb the proliferation of submarines and armed merchant vessels; and created the Permanent Court of Arbitration. Meanwhile, starting with the 1826 Panama Congress, there was a series of inter-American and pan-Latin American conferences, culminating in the establishment of the Pan American Union in 1910. Another parallel trend was the emergence of new functional and regulatory agencies dealing with matters of growing global or regional concern, including the International Telecommunications Union (1865), the Universal Postal Union (1874), and the Pan American Sanitary Bureau (1902).

Not everything, of course, went smoothly. As Frieden explains, New World grain flooded world markets, and traditional small-scale agriculture began a long retreat. From 1873 to 1896, most prices and earnings declined while debt obligations stayed constant. France and Italy had a lengthy trade dispute. Germany became more protectionist, and the United States remained consistently so. Italy, Spain, and Portugal dropped the gold standard, and Russia and Austria–Hungary never adopted it. The 1893 collapse of Baring Brothers of London caused a global financial panic.[140] As for military security, the imperial contests and arms races that concerned the Concert and Hague Conferences were real enough, new technology produced ever more destructive weaponry, and the need for possible quick mobilization around complicated railroad timetables became a hair-trigger obsession for national decision-makers.

Such were the prevailing patterns in the world prior to World War I. All things considered, despite familiar tensions and inevitable reversals, there were then strong reasons to be optimistic about the future. Norman Angell, sadly, is best remembered for his entirely logical but ill-fated prediction in 1909 that the economies of the great powers were so closely interdependent that war had become almost unthinkable.

Globalization did continue – a crucially important point! – but mostly in negative and even horrific ways that threatened and indeed savaged many of the positive accomplishments of the previous century of significant transnational engagement and integration. Nothing could have been more atavistic or pitifully futile than the desperate trench warfare in World War I that wiped out a generation of Europe's young men. The only "victors" were the United States and, oddly, Soviet Russia after the Tsarist regime's demise. The League of Nations, established after the Versailles Peace Conference, was gravely undermined from the outset by the US failure to join. Although it was to provide a model of sorts for the later United Nations, the League proved incapable of curbing the expansionist ambitions of what were to be the Axis powers and general military tensions and arms races. A killer flu epidemic of 1918–19 provided a foretaste of pandemics to come. The US Smoot–Hawley Tariff of 1930 raised US tariff levels to historic highs, but was actually a response – albeit one that only made matters worse – to the onset of the Great Depression following the US stock market collapse of 1929. In 1939, World War II officially began – a global war, to be sure, that caused almost unimaginable material destruction, loss of life and genocide, and finally ushered in the nuclear age at Hiroshima and Nagasaki. Could anything be more fully "global" than a vision of "mutually assured destruction" (MAD) – possibly of the planet – that was soon to arise?

FROM THE COLD WAR TO TWENTY-FIRST-CENTURY GLOBALIZATION

From World War II to the present, and especially since the Cold War's end in 1989, globalization has vastly accelerated. Much of this story is well known and is analyzed elsewhere in this book, so we confine ourselves here to an overview. There have been ebbs as well as flows in particular dimensions of globalization, but mostly the pattern has been flows. "Thin" globalization has become far "thicker"; the density of transborder transactions has increased dramatically and, at least until recently, at an ever-faster pace. What the McNeills[141] term "the human web" has become so interwoven and complex that it almost defies description. Although sovereign nation-states and their associated identities remain an integral part of the global system, state boundaries have been both transcended and penetrated to such an extent that, as Sassen argues, the "global" has become substantially "embedded" in the "local,"[142] even as many local actors – cities, businesses, NGOs, organized crime, terrorists, and others – have become more "global."

The predominant feature of the post-World War II world was, of course, the existence of two competing superpowers, the United States and the Soviet Union, with opposite political and economic ideologies. Both soon possessed giant arsenals of transcontinental missiles armed with nuclear warheads. Soviet domination over Eastern Europe and the Warsaw Pact alliance was an "informal" empire only insofar as it was "undeclared." Whether United States influence over the so-called Free World after World War II reached the level of "informal" empire, the US until the 1970s was clearly a "hegemon" and in that role profoundly shaped prevailing institutions, rather like the British Empire did during its heyday. The postwar Western alliance network included both NATO and the Organization of American States, which alone among alliances included a process for resolving disputes among its own members.

At the end of World War II, the victorious Big Five allies founded the United Nations, with its declared primary mission of preserving international peace and security. Although the UN was severely hampered by Cold War rivalry and other divisions among the five permanent members of the Security Council, it nonetheless played a significant role in legitimizing the Korean War and First Gulf War and, still today, is engaged in some fifteen peacekeeping missions deployed on four continents. Its list of member states has swelled from 51 to 193. The rise in membership is itself a testament to the rapid emergence of new states as the old European empires disintegrated. Some states in what was then dubbed the "Third World" chose to play at least a nominally nonaligned role in the Cold War.

Addressing a widespread assumption that World War II had derived in part from the deprivations of the Great Depression, the 1944 Bretton Woods Conference created an International Bank for Reconstruction and Development (the World Bank ir IBRD) and the International Monetary Fund (IMF). The core membership of the World Bank and IMF has grown from thirty to 187. The IBRD was to assist, along with the Marshall Plan, in rejuvenating war-torn economies especially in Europe. It has shifted its aid emphasis over the years to developing countries. Under the IMF, exchange rates would be fixed, but the international reserve currency was initially the dollar, theoretically convertible into gold. Both the World Bank and the IMF have widely been viewed, with considerable justice, as purveyors of liberal capitalist models of economic development and international markets. A planned International Trade Organization (ITO) never fully materialized, although a less ambitious General Agreement on Tariffs and Trade (GATT) was concluded in 1947. Member countries negotiated tariff reductions, which – following a "most favored nation" requirement – were extended to all GATT members. GATT was also charged with defining and curbing "unfair" trading practices and other non-tariff barriers to trade. GATT's successor, the World Trade Organization, launched in 1986, enjoyed most of the powers originally envisaged for the ITO, particularly a capacity to adjudicate disputes and legitimize sanctions against violators of the liberal trade regime.

One major characteristic of the global system since World War II has been a veritable explosion of institutions and organizations of different types and with different memberships, geographical scopes, and purposes. *The Yearbook of International Organizations, 2004/2005* listed 245 "conventional" IGOs and 1,743 under the heading of "other international bodies."[143] The International Court of Justice succeeded the PCIJ, and more recently an International Criminal Court has been created to address genocide, crimes against humanity, and war crimes. Functional IGOs to date include a total of nineteen UN specialized agencies – among them, such organizations as the World Health Organization (WHO), the United Nations Children's Fund (UNICEF), the Food and Agriculture Organization (FAO), the International Civil Aviation Organization (ICAO), and the International Maritime Organization (IMO) – as well as numerous others within the UN system, for example, the International Atomic Energy Association (IAEA). Many IGOs have been regional, such as the European Common Market and subsequent European Union, the OAS, the North American Free Trade Agreement (NAFTA), Mercosur, League of Arab States, Organization of African Unity (ONU), APEC, and ASEAN. The London School of Economics and Politics Library's "IGOs: Regional Organizations" website[144] lists sixteen in Africa, twenty-two in the Americas and Caribbean, seven in Arabia, fourteen in Asia, one in the Baltic Region, two in the Black Sea Region, two in Eurasia, fourteen in Europe, eleven in the Pacific, two in Scandinavia, and four Other.

There has also been a proliferation of nongovernmental organizations (NGOs). The same reference work we cited earlier[145] for IGO numbers lists 7,261 "conventional" NGOs and an additional 13,590 under the heading of "other international bodies." This is a very conservative estimate. Even the most "local" of millions of

NGOs are often concerned with issues that also resonate at regional and global levels, and many NGOs are networked with others that advance their joint positions transnationally. Many NGOs also have institutionalized relationships or are at least selectively engaged with IGOs regarding issues and projects of mutual concern. The literature on globalization has tended to describe the increasing number and transnational activism of NGOs as the rise of "global civil society" and, further, to suggest that many NGOs – like IGOs – have a "democratic deficit" that can have the effect of undermining their legitimacy.[146]

Perhaps an even greater transformation has occurred in the global economy and markets. Martin Wolf notes that some describe the growth of the past two centuries as "Promethean," to distinguish it "from the earlier 'Smithian,' described in Adam Smith's *The Wealth of Nations* (1776)." Wolf writes: "To describe what happened in the early nineteenth century as an 'industrial' or even 'energy' revolution is misleading. It would be more accurate to describe it as a culmination and acceleration of a market revolution that became far more powerful with the mass application of physical energy."[147] He offers impressive statistics supporting the notion of Promethean growth: world gross domestic product (at purchasing power parity) increasing thirteen times as fast as population, a thousand-fold increase in the average standard of living, and an almost doubling of life expectancy in most of the world. "Almost every economy is richer than it was two centuries ago, but some have done much better than others."[148] The latter clause is a remarkable understatement (see below), and there is obviously more to the global economy story, much of which, to be fair, Wolf does tell elsewhere. However, at this juncture, a crucial point is that most of the Promethean changes happened after World War II, suggesting that the Industrial Revolution was perhaps no more significant than the globalization accelerators of the 1970s and 1990s.

As O'Brien and Williams point out, after 1945 world trade grew at a rate twice that of global production. Total trade in 1997 was fourteen times the level in 1950. Early in the second half of the twentieth century, most trade was still in manufactures, but services became the fastest-growing sector.[149] Trade growth was initially concentrated among main developed market economies – the US, Europe, and Japan – but over time began significantly to reflect some of the principal emerging economies: Mexico, South Korea, and the so-called BRICs, that is, Brazil, Russia, India, and China. Overall trade growth amounted to about 10 percent annually, with occasional downturns, including the sharpest drop in seventy years (12.2 percent) during the global recession of 2009; yet the WTO expected the rate to rebound to 9.5 percent in 2010.[150] The EU came to rival the United States for the rank of the largest economy – if indeed the EU is a single economy – while Japan by most measures was number two until China managed to overtake it in 2011.

The expansion in the global economy is owed to at least five major and interrelated factors. The first was the success of GATT in lowering overall barriers to trade to something like a quarter of what they had been in 1945. Trade liberalization continued under the WTO, but at a much slower pace, not least because what remained were the most entrenched forms of protectionism. Developed countries' complaints about remaining barriers to trade and investment and lack of protection for intellectual property have been met by developing countries' complaints about remaining restrictions on their exports and agricultural subsidies especially in the EU and the US.

A second change was a revolution in communications and information, with the advent of television, computers, the internet (the World Wide Web became widely available in 1991), mobile phones, satellites, fiber-optic cables, and various social networks. The increase in human mobility was almost equally impressive, with the average number of persons crossing state borders each day rising from 69,000 in 1950 to over 2 million in 2000.[151]

A third monumental shift was China's re-engagement with the West and acceptance of substantial market capitalism and then, after the Cold War's end in 1989, the incorporation into the global capitalist economy of the former Soviet Union and Eastern Europe. Western-style democracy made significant headway in most of Eastern Europe, although China remained staunchly authoritarian and initial hopes for full-fledged democracy in Russia have gradually dimmed. The recent "Arab Spring" has raised hopes for at least modest democratic progress in the Middle East.

A fourth major trend, facilitated by the IT/communications revolution and expanded opportunities in the world economy, has been a vast increase in the number, size, and innovative strategies of transnational corporations (TNCs). The number of TNCs has risen from a few thousand in the late 1960s to an estimated 82,000 in 2008.[152] There has also been an upsurge in mergers and acquisitions, strategic alliances and networks, joint ventures, and corporate supply chains.[153] Today some fifty-one of the 100 largest economies are not states but corporations, and TNCs account for nearly 70 percent of world trade.[154] Foreign direct investment (FDI) is expected to be about $1.3–1.5 trillion in 2011. O'Brien and Williams highlight the fact that here has been a transition from Fordist to post-Fordist organization of manufacturing activities, involving a change in priorities "from labour costs and mass production to product innovation." "Factors that now affect location choice include proximity to suppliers and markets, and the availability of skilled labour and specialized technology," as well as better "infrastructure requirements which many countries specializing in cheap labour are unable to meet." "[M]any TNCs need to have entire production chains occurring in one region," a consideration that to date has helped give East Asia a significant competitive advantage over Africa.[155]

A fifth development in the 1990s was the liberalization of national and world financial markets. Frieden explains:

> As trade was liberalized, governments of developed countries also removed the last barriers to the free flow of money and capital, and many developing countries reduced controls on cross-border investment. By the late 1990s international financial activities were so intertwined with domestic financial markets that for all intents and purposes there was one global financial system that included all the developed countries and many developing and formerly Communist countries. Pensioners and small investors routinely included foreign stock and bond funds in their portfolios, even when the foreign securities were Chilean, Czech, or Korean. Most countries also liberalized domestic banking, leading to a wave of mergers of the world's leading financial institutions.[156]

There was a healthy expansion in the amount and mobility of capital in the world economy. Soon the amounts traded around-the-clock at digital speed greatly exceeded those required to finance actual trade in goods and non-financial services. New entities like hedge funds emerged to do much of the trading, and the instruments traded evolved to include a wide range of so-called derivatives. Quantitative models dictated rapid purchases or sell-offs. The "real economy" became increasingly divorced from the "virtual economy."

However, the unhealthy dimension of global financial liberalization was a risk of volatility and even collapse. Strains became apparent in the developing country debt crisis of the early 1980s. In 1992, speculation by currency traders caused a run on the pound and the lira, destroying the fledgling European Economic and Monetary Union (EMU). The Mexican peso and banking system collapsed in 1994. In 1997, a financial panic spread from Thailand and the Philippines to Indonesia and Malaysia and Taiwan and Korea. Frieden summarizes: "International financial organizations and creditor nations mobilized over $50 billion for Mexico in 1995, almost $120 billion for the three principal Asian crisis nations (Indonesia, Korea and Thailand), and another $70 billion for Russia and Brazil in 1998 and 1999." Prefiguring debates a decade later: "Critics charged that taxpayers were being forced to bail out foolish investors and bad governments, but financial leaders insisted on the need for quick response to avoid financial contagion."[157] For a time it appeared that a measure of stability had been achieved, and it was further encouraging that the EU was able to launch a single euro currency in 2001.

However, in 2008 in the United States, inflated housing prices suddenly began to drop, concessionary mortgages proved to be uncollectible, bank failures loomed, and the global economy was soon plunged into the worst recession since the 1930s. Public complaints about "bail-outs" of banks, other financial and insurance firms, and the auto industry (in the US) contributed to what had already been a rising mistrust of governments and politicians throughout much of the developed world. Although at the time of writing, a variety of financial reforms is being adopted at the national and international levels, most analysts are skeptical that adequate controls are now in place to avoid yet another collapse. In 2011, a sovereign debt crisis in several EU countries and political paralysis over the US debt ceiling that threatened an unprecedented default provided painful evidence of grave structural problems.

Finally, it should be stressed that global economic growth has not only been uneven chronologically but also in terms of beneficiaries. Upper- and middle-class elites – and now including BRIC countries – have experienced better living standards. Health and longevity are also improving, as well as a global capacity to respond to pandemics like AIDs, SARS, and avian flu. But, generally speaking, inequality may be rising across the state system and within some countries; the rich have been getting much richer, while the lot of the poorest has either remained the same, improved at a much slower pace, or actually declined. Consider the United States: In 1915, the richest 1 percent of the population possessed 15 percent of total national income; currently, the top 1 percent hold 24 percent. From 1980 to 2005, more than 80 percent of the increase in US national income went to the top 1 percent, even though there was a 20 percent increase in productivity.[158] Regarding China, although there has been notable success in reducing the most extreme poverty (now 1 percent of the population), a 2009 World Bank report concludes:

> Not everyone has participated in the economic success equally. Income inequality in China has increased significantly since the start of economic reforms, and China is no longer the low-inequality country it was a quarter century ago. [The level of inequality is now similar to that in] many other middle-income economies, including some in the East Asia region such as Thailand and Malaysia, though lower than that in many Latin American countries. Where China stands out is in the magnitude of the increase in inequality and the pace at which it has occurred. The rise in inequality is the result of both a widening income gap between the cities and the countryside, as well as growing inequality within rural and urban areas.[159]

Statistics from the WTO website give some sense of the situation worldwide. In 1999, the world's poorest countries' share of world trade had declined by more than 40 percent since 1980 to 0.4 percent. In 2001, the poorest 49 countries with 10 percent of the world's population had the same 0.4 percent share of world trade. Between 1980 and 2000, the number of people living on less than $2 day rose by almost 50 percent to 2.8 billion or about half of the world's population. In 1999, the richest fifth had 80 percent of the world's income and the poorest fifth had 1 percent. Trade liberalization in many cases seems to have increased income inequality, although such data tell us nothing about the trade-generated portion of increases in total national income or in living standards other than income inequality.

One last (possibly in every sense) trend is clear, and it is demonstrated elsewhere in this volume: economic development associated with globalization, along with population growth, has dangerously increased the threat to our planet's environment. Energy consumption is rising at an alarming pace; greenhouse gases are exacerbating climate turbulence and global warming; air pollution especially in developing-country cities is reaching deadly levels; there has been a radical decline in biodiversity and loss of rainforests; overfishing is reducing stocks and threatening some key species with extinction; and so on and on. Not all of this, of course, is directly attributable to globalization and even the indirect links are attenuated. But it does raise a serious question. Regardless of how desirable and inexorable many aspects of globalization are, how sustainable are its human subjects and the world in which they live?

CONCLUSION

What "lessons" might we draw from our review of thousands of years of globalization history? That question presupposes (1) that we have adequate information and understanding of the past, and (2) that the past is not so different from the present as to make comparison and generalizations meaningless. We have wrestled with these issues at length elsewhere,[160] so we make only a few comments on the central debates here.

Concern (1) raises all the epistemological/philosophical issues about how we "know" what we know, the problems inherent in language and concepts, the impact of values on the choice and interpretation of information, and so on. We are particularly limited as to sources with regard to ancient history. Nonetheless, we do know a great deal about the ancient world, and addressing contemporary events may actually in some respects be harder than dealing with much earlier eras because of the lack of temporal "distance" and sheer information overload.

Concern (2) highlights assertions both from some ancient historians and modern globalization theorists about the "primitive" nature and therefore incomparability of the past with the present.[161] For example, eminent classicist M. I. Finley created a controversy during the 1970s and 1980s[162] by insisting that ancient economies bore little or no resemblance to the national and international economies that evolved after the Industrial Revolution. For Rosenau, anything before the vast expansion of globalization in the 1990s represents a "difference in kind."[163]

Although some distinguished scholars tell us either to study the past (as best we can) only for its own sake or to ignore it altogether, we insist that their arguments miss the *main* point about globalization: Globalization has multiple dimensions and has always been – and today remains – an evolutionary process. To be sure, globalization was not anywhere near as advanced in any dimension in the ancient world as it is in the twenty-first century, nor has its course in any dimension over time been unilinear. But the *process* has been operating from the dawn of human history and, viewed across the millennia, looks to have been an almost inexorable one. That is lesson one.

The history of that process does offer additional important perspectives on the present and possible future of globalization. A second lesson is that most of the changes have been incremental – a new trade route here, better technology introduced there, another conquest, and so on. Third, there have been major reversals and even near-complete breakdowns, for example, the end of the Bronze Age in the Mediterranean, the demise of the Roman Empire in the West, the Chinese Ming decision to turn inward, and the Great Depression of the 1930s. Fourth, despite breakdowns, the globalization process has always resumed, because some actor(s) somewhere have taken up the slack. The Phoenicians sailed into the power vacuum left by the Bronze Age collapse. The Islamic conquests and Chinese progress kept things moving when even the Byzantine legatees of the Eastern Roman Empire were gone. Just when the Mings gave up on foreign adventures, the Europeans launched their own voyages of discovery. Fifth, sometimes it is difficult to distinguish between a breakdown and advance. For instance, World War I was a disaster for economic integration and prosperity but was, after all, a *world* war. World War II, another *world* war, similarly disrupted normal economic activities; but military spending played an important role in stimulating national economies out of 1930s stagnation, and wartime horrors (added to the 1930s experience) proved to be a powerful spur to the most innovative era to date in international institution-building.

Sixth, the drivers of globalization have been different types of actors – pursuing their own ends and most of the time not all advancing simultaneously – as well as more anonymous forces like technology, weather, and disease. Chanda spotlights traders, preachers, adventurers, and warriors.[164] Noticeably absent from this list are political entities like kings (of course, until recently, many were warriors too), states, and empires. As kings illustrate, sometimes it is difficult to distinguish between drivers. Conquistadors were adventurers who were warrior agents of monarchy, looking for precious metals and trade and marching with clerics intent on saving heathen souls at any cost. Sometimes early kings reserved trade for palace agents, and sometimes they allowed private traders more freedom. Even during the relative absence of any political center, some forms of trade usually continued. Moore and Lewis rightly comment on "how variegated has been ... the world's experience with capitalist models – from temple capitalism in Egypt to maritime capitalism in Phoenicia to Roman family capitalism."[165]

Seventh, as we stressed in our narrative, the "local" and the "global" (of the day) have continuously interacted. Actors and polities engaging with the external world have inevitably altered their environment and often, as a consequence, have themselves been transformed. States and the state system in Europe evolved as they did in part because imperial expansion went hand-in-hand with state-building. Also, tribal or extended-family polities grouped into imperial units eventually became states partly because their metropoles inadvertently brought them the concepts of state sovereignty and nation-state identity. Traders invented contracts to share risk, larger companies, and better ships because commercial opportunities abroad could not be effectively exploited without them. Military technology would obviously have developed far more slowly without foreign enemies, and banking vastly expanded to finance governments and wars as well as commerce.

Eighth and finally, both in terms of the drivers and process, globalization has involved increasing geographical scope, volume and density of transactions, and pace of change. Globalization has now come to engage (or at least affect) virtually all of humanity and to have generated much (if not most) of the complexity that characterizes the contemporary world. As our own work on *Polities* has demonstrated, paradoxically, some of that complexity is the persistence of political forms and ideas from much earlier historical eras. *The past is embedded in the present fully as much as the global, which observation helps to account for why present-day global governance lags so far behind the issues it urgently needs to address.* Some of that embedded past is well worth preserving and possibly essential to human identity and well-being. Some should have died and been buried long ago. The difficulty is agreeing on which bits of the past are which! Meanwhile, complexity seems continually to increase, despite or even because of downturns like the recent financial crisis, and raises the risk of another general system collapse. There is no reason, especially because of its potentially true global reach, why such a collapse should be any less catastrophic than much earlier ones – quite the contrary. Where thereafter will the drivers be?

NOTES

1 Nayan Chanda, "Runaway Globalization Without Governance," *Global Governance* 14 (2008), 119.
2 Jack Donnelly, "Human Rights, Globalizing Flows, and State Power," in Alison Brysk, ed., *Globalization and Human Rights* (Berkeley, CA: University of California Press, 2002), 226.
3 Scholte, *Globalization*, 85.

4 Ibid., 16–17.
5 John A. Armstrong, *Nations before Nationalism* (Chapel Hill, NC: University of North Carolina Press, 1982).
6 See Yale H. Ferguson and Richard W. Mansbach, "Remapping Political Space: Issues and Non-Issues in Analyzing Global Politics in the Twenty-First Century," in Y. Ferguson and R. J. Barry Jones, eds., *Political Space: The New Frontier of Global Politics* (Albany, NY: State University of New York Press, 2002), 87–111, and Ferguson and Mansbach, *Remapping Global Politics*.
7 Scholte, *Globalization*, 67 ff.
8 *Mapping Globalization* is a collaborative project of Princeton University's Niehuas Center for Globalization and Governance (NCGG) and the University of Washington. The definition is from the project's website, https://qed.princeton.edu/index.php/MG.
9 Richard L. Smith, *Premodern Trade in World History* (London: Routledge, 2009), 6. Smith's book is the most useful study of its kind in the literature, and our own survey of premodern trade relies heavily upon it. See also Philip D. Curtin, *Cross-Cultural Trade in World History* (Cambridge: Cambridge University Press, 1984), which traces the title subject from earliest times through the nineteenth century and is particularly helpful for patterns on the African continent.
10 Rosenau, *Distant Proximities*.
11 In the 1980s, "Out of Africa" contenders argued with those who adopted a "multiregional" explanation for the emergence and spread of early homo sapiens. Modern evidence seems to suggest that a complex mix of the two may be the best explanation. Cf. Michael Haederle, "The Ancestor Hunter," *Miller McCune Online*, August 31, 2009, http://www.miller-mccune.com/science-environment/the-ancestor-hunter-3496/.
12 Nayan Chanda, *Bound Together: How Traders, Preachers, Adventurers, and Warriors Shaped Globalization* (New Haven, CT: Yale University Press, 2007), 9.
13 Ibid., 23.
14 Robert Wright, *NonZero: The Logic of Human Destiny* (London: Little Brown, 2000), 76.
15 Jared Diamond, *Guns, Germs, and Steel* (New York: Norton, 1999), 103.
16 Smith, *Premodern Trade*, 15.
17 On ancient Mesopotamia, see Ferguson and Mansbach, *Polities*, chs. 3–4.
18 Smith, *Premodern Trade*, 24.
19 Karl Moore and David Lewis, *The Origins of Globalization* (London: Routledge, 2009), 24–5. We have made extensive use of this pioneering analysis in this chapter. Moore and Lewis focus on the variety of ancient world economic systems and the early evolution of the multinational corporation.
20 Smith, *Premodern Trade*, 25–6.
21 Moore and Lewis, *The Origins of Globalization*, 34.
22 Smith, *Premodern Trade*, 28.
23 Moore and Lewis, *The Origins of Globalization*, 43.
24 Ibid., 48.
25 Smith, *Premodern Trade*, 31.
26 Moore and Lewis, *The Origins of Globalization*, 85.
27 Niall Ferguson, *The Ascent of Money: A Financial History of the World* (New York: Penguin, 2008), 30–1.
28 Smith, *Premodern Trade*, 33–6.
29 Moore and Lewis, *The Origins of Globalization*, 58.
30 Smith, *Premodern Trade*, 40–1.
31 Ian Shaw, "Egypt and the Outside World," in I. Shaw, ed., *The Oxford History of Ancient Egypt* (Oxford: Oxford University Press, 2000), 314.
32 Moore and Lewis, *The Origins of Globalization*, 38. Emphasis in original.
33 Smith, *Premodern Trade*, 41.

34 Shaw, "Egypt and the Outside World," 316–17.
35 Ibid., 320–1.
36 Smith, *Premodern Trade*, 46–8.
37 Marc Van de Mieroop, *A History of the Ancient Near East: ca. 3000–323 BC*, 2nd edn (Oxford: Blackwell, 2007), 134.
38 Ibid., 136.
39 Ibid., 124.
40 Smith, *Premodern Trade*, 55. A major addition to our knowledge about second millennium trade was the 1982 discovery of a shipwreck with a large, diverse cargo from that era off Uluburun in Turkey.
41 Moore and Lewis, *The Origins of Globalization*, 76.
42 Smith, *Premodern Trade*, 56–8.
43 Ibid., 58–9. See also Van de Mieroop, *A History of the Ancient Near East*, ch. 10.
44 Smith, *Premodern Trade*, 64.
45 Van de Mieroop, *A History of the Ancient Near East*, 233.
46 Smith, *Premodern Trade*, 64.
47 Chanda, *Bound Together*, 44. See map of Phoenician settlements in Van de Mieroop, *A History of the Ancient Near East*, 221.
48 Smith, *Premodern Trade*, 66.
49 Ibid., 66–7.
50 Van de Mieroop, *A History of the Ancient Near East*, 299.
51 On classical Greece, see Ferguson and Mansbach, *Polities*, chs. 5–6.
52 Smith, *Premodern Trade*, 67.
53 Moore and Lewis, *The Origins of Globalization*, 123.
54 Ibid., 125.
55 See ibid., 123–4. The Kingdom of Lydia in northwestern Asia Minor usually gets credit for "perfecting the use of metal coins as currency."
56 Smith, *Premodern Trade*, 67.
57 Ibid., 68.
58 Moore and Lewis, *The Origins of Globalization*, 122.
59 Niall Ferguson notes that the earliest known coins date back to 600 BC electrum ovular Lydian coins found in the Temple of Artemis at Ephesus. See Ferguson, *Ascent of Money*, 24.
60 Chanda, *Bound Together*, 58.
61 Smith, *Premodern Trade*, 72–3.
62 On the Carthage inheritance and extension of Phoenician trade and mining enterprises in the western Mediterranean, see Moore and Lewis, *The Origins of Globalization*, 145–63.
63 Chester G. Starr, *The Roman Empire 27B.C.–A.D.476* (New York: Oxford, 1982), 3.
64 N. Ferguson notes: "The Roman system of coinage outlived the Roman Empire itself. Prices were still being quoted in terms of silver denarii in the time of Charlemagne." See Ferguson, *Ascent of Money*, 24.
65 David C. Braund, "Client Kings," in *The Administration of the Roman Empire: 241 B.C.–A.D. 193* (Exeter: University of Exeter, 1988), 69–96.
66 Stephen Mitchell, *A History of the Later Roman Empire: A.D. 284–641* (Oxford: Blackwell, 2007), 301–5.
67 Peter Garnsey and Richard Saller, *The Roman Empire: Economy, Society and Culture* (London: Duckworth, 1987), 52.
68 Ibid., 49.
69 Smith, *Premodern Trade*, 78.
70 Mitchell, *History of the Later Roman Empire*, 304.
71 Smith, *Premodern Trade*, 76–7. Smith (76) reports: "Traders identified as 'Roman' could come from anywhere in the empire except the region they were operating in, so, for example, Roman traders in Greece were often Italians, including Greek Italians, but

Roman traders in the Indian Ocean trade were more likely to be Syrians or Egyptian Greeks."
72 Moore and Lewis, *The Origins of Globalization*, 168.
73 Ibid., 166–7.
74 Ibid., 168–9.
75 Ibid., 170.
76 Smith, *Premodern Trade*, 84–5.
77 Chanda, *Bound Together*, 45.
78 Ibid., 44.
79 Smith, *Premodern Trade*, 86–7.
80 Ibid., 89–94.
81 Chanda, *Bound Together*, 45.
82 Smith, *Premodern Trade*, 95–8.
83 Ibid., The foregoing paragraph summarizes information from pp. 121–8.
84 Ibid., 128.
85 Ibid., 124.
86 Ibid., 130–3.
87 Ibid., 134.
88 Chanda, *Bound Together*, 41–2.
89 Smith, *Premodern Trade*, 136.
90 Chanda, *Bound Together*, 42–3.
91 Ibid., 110.
92 Cf. Christopher MacKay, *Ancient Rome: A Military and Political History* (Cambridge: Cambridge University Press, 2004), ch. 22.
93 Chanda, *Bound Together*, 110.
94 Ibid., 114–16.
95 Cf. MacKay, *Ancient Rome*, ch. 24.
96 William H. McNeill, *Venice: The Hinge of Europe, 1081–1797* (Chicago, IL: University of Chicago Press, reprinted 2009).
97 McKay, *Ancient Rome*, 355.
98 Mitchell, *History of the Later Roman Empire*, 421. On Medieval Islam, see also Ferguson and Mansbach, *Polities*, chs. 11 and 12.
99 Robert O'Brien and Marc Williams, *Global Political Economy*, 2nd edn (London: Palgrave, 2007), 46.
100 Ferguson, *Ascent of Money*, 24–5.
101 Ibid., 32–4.
102 Ibid., 41–5.
103 O'Brien and Williams, *Global Political Economy*, 47.
104 Chanda, *Bound Together*, 49.
105 This paragraph tracks O'Brien and Williams, *Global Political Economy*, 47.
106 Chanda, *Bound Together*, 49.
107 See Gavin Menzies, *1421: The Year China Discovered America*, 2nd edn (New York, Harper Collins, 2008), and Gavin Menzies, *1434: The Year a Magnificent Chinese Fleet Sailed to Italy and Ignited the Renaissance* (New York: Morrow, 2008).
108 O'Brien and Williams, *Global Political Economy*, 48.
109 Chanda, *Bound Together*, 159.
110 O'Brien and Williams, *Global Political Economy*, 45.
111 For discussion of pre- and post-Conquest Mesoamerica, see Ferguson and Mansbach, *Polities*, chs. 9 and 10.
112 Diamond, *Guns, Germs, and Steel*, ch. 18.
113 Alfred W. Crosby, *The Columbian Exchange: Biological and Cultural Consequences of 1492* (Westport, CN: Greenwood, 1972).
114 Diamond, *Guns, Germs, and Steel*, 373–5.
115 Ibid., 375.

116 Crosby, *The Columbian Exchange*, 66. This paragraph and the two that follow reproduce material from Ferguson and Mansbach, *Polities*, 270–1.
117 Crosby, *The Columbian Exchange*, 107.
118 Ibid., 72–3.
119 J. H. Parry, *The Spanish Seaborne Empire* (Berkeley, CA: University of California Press, 1966), 244.
120 Discussed in Ferguson, *The Ascent of Money*, 48–9.
121 O'Brien and Williams, *Global Political Economy*, 52–3.
122 We draw here upon our earlier discussion of the rise of the state in Ferguson and Mansbach, *Remapping Global Politics*, 120–2.
123 Charles Tilly, "Reflections on the History of European State-Making," in C. Tilly, *The Formation of Nation-States in Western Europe* (Princeton, NJ: Princeton University Press, 1975), 7.
124 See Hendrik Spruyt, *The Sovereign State and Its Competitors* (Princeton, NJ: Princeton University Press, 1994).
125 Charles Tilly, *Coercion, Capital, and European States, AD 990–1990* (Oxford: Blackwell, 1990), especially ch. 3.
126 Michael Mann, *States, War and Capitalism* (Oxford: Blackwell, 1988), 112.
127 Ferguson, *Ascent of Money*, 176–8.
128 Niall Ferguson, *Empire: The Rise and Demise of the British World Order and the Lessons for Global Power* (New York: Basic Books, 2002), 5.
129 Ibid., 6.
130 Ibid., 4–5.
131 Ibid., 14–15.
132 Ibid., xii.
133 Ibid., 34–5.
134 Our summary discussion in this paragraph is mostly drawn from O'Brien and Williams, *Global Political Economy*, 78–81, 65–7 (triangular trade), 85 (later industrializers).
135 Jeffrey A. Frieden, *Global Capitalism* (New York: Norton, 2006), 5.
136 Ibid., 3.
137 Ibid., 4.
138 Ibid.
139 Ibid., 6.
140 Ibid., 7–9.
141 J. R. McNeill and William H. McNeill, *The Human Web* (New York: Norton, 2003).
142 Cf. Sassen, *Territory, Authority, Rights*.
143 Union of International Organizations, ed., *Yearbook of International Organizations, 2004/2005* (Munich: K. G., 2004), appendix 3, table 1.
144 www2.lse.ac.uk/library/collections/govtpub/igos/IGO_web_regional.aspx.
145 Union of International Organizations, ed. *Yearbook of International Organizations, 2004/2005*, appendix 3, table 1.
146 See, for example, Eva Erman and Anders Uhlin, eds., *Legitimacy Beyond the State? Re-examining the Democratic Credentials of Transnational Actors* (London: Palgrave, 2010).
147 Wolf, *Why Globalization Works*, 41–3.
148 Ibid., 43–4.
149 O'Brien and Williams, *Global Political Economy*, 148–9.
150 World Trade Organization, "International Trade Statistics," Press Release 598 (March 26, 2010), http://www.wto.org/english/news_e/pres10_e/pr598_e.htm.
151 Scholte (citing French), *Globalization*, 104.
152 UNCTAD, *World Investment Report* (New York and Geneva, 2010).
153 See, for example, O'Brien and Williams, *Global Political Economy*, 193–4 (especially table 6.4).
154 www.gatt.org/trastat_e.html (citing CorpWatch).
155 O'Brien and Williams, *Global Political Economy*, 192–3.

156 Frieden, *Global Capitalism*, 383.
157 Ibid., 390–1.
158 Timothy Noah, "The United States of Inequality," *Slate*, September 3, 2010, www.slate.com/id/2266025/entry/2266026.
159 World Bank, "From Poor Areas to Poor People: China's Evolving Poverty Reduction Agenda: An Assessment of Poverty and Inequality in China" (March 2009), site resources.worldbank.org/CHINAEXTN/Resources/318949-1239096143906/China_PA_Report_March_2009_eng.pdf.
160 See especially Ferguson and Mansbach, *The Elusive Quest Continues: Theory and Global Politics* (Upper Saddle River, NJ: Prentice-Hall), 2003, and Ferguson and Mansbach, *A World of Polities*, chs. 1–4, 8, and 12.
161 See Moore and Lewis, *The Origins of Globalization*, preface and ch. 1.
162 See, for example: M. I. Finley, *The Ancient Economy*, 2nd edn (London: Hogarth Press, 1985), J. G. Manning and Ian Morris, eds., *The Ancient Economy* (Stanford, CA: Stanford University Press, 2005), and Walter Scheidel and Sitta von Reden, eds., *The Ancient Economy* (Edinburgh: Edinburgh University Press, 2002).
163 Rosenau, *Along the Domestic–Foreign Frontier*, 22.
164 Chanda, *Bound Together*.
165 Moore and Lewis, *The Origins of Globalization*, 3.

CHAPTER 3

The essentials of globalization

> Globalization is a package of transnational flows of people, production, investment information, ideas, and authority (not new, but stronger and faster).[1]

> The Bible tells us that God created the world in six days and on the seventh day he rested. Flattening the world took a little longer. The world has been flattened by the convergence of ten major political events, innovations, and companies.[2]

Has increased "globality" in contemporary life significantly reshaped the primary structures of social relations as transformational theorists believe? Or has globalization merely generated relatively superficial shifts at the level of objects, institutions, and perceptions, while leaving the underlying framework intact?

Globalization has a number of interrelated features that both enthusiasts and many critics regard as novel and even to be accelerating, but that skeptics see as either having existed in the past and/or as being less extensive and important than others claim. In any event, these features are producing shared fates among individuals and groups geographically remote from one another who may not even be aware of one another's existence.

SPREADING CAPITALISM

> *The global spread of market capitalism and neoliberal economic orthodoxy that transcend state boundaries and limits states' control of their economies are also driving and sustaining*

economic globalization. "Neoliberalism has, in short," declares David Harvey, "become hegemonic as a mode of discourse" and "has become incorporated into the common-sense way many of us interpret, live in, and understand the world."[3] "It's hard," as one commentator observes, "to imagine alternatives to neo-liberal perspectives and post-developmental governance in an age of accelerating globalization."[4] With the end of the Cold War, free-market capitalism spread to the former Soviet bloc and China as well as many emerging economies of the developing world that had previously sought to develop mainly through export-substitution policies. Marxist theorist Alex Callinicos, for example, accepts the dominance of neoliberalism as a fact, admitting that "the lens through which to view globalization is that of the historical development of capitalism as a world system."[5] To increasing numbers of people, neoliberal economic policies seemed the path to modernization.

However, with the global financial crisis and prolonged economic slump that began in 2007, there has been renewed interest in state capitalism, a possible Asian variant, and growing caution about continuing privatization and unbridled neo-liberalism. Many commentators and policy-makers have urged rethinking the role of states in Keynesian-style pumping-priming and re-regulation, to stimulate healthy growth and decrease volatility in national and global markets. Critics like Harvey contend that "neoliberalization" has "entailed much 'creative destruction', not only of prior institutional frameworks and powers . . . but also divisions of labour, social relations, welfare provisions, technological mixes, ways of life and thought, reproductive activities, attachments to the land and habits of the heart."[6] Ronaldo Munck similarly denounces it as "an economic process leading to the commodification of life itself" in which everything is for sale, "from health to education, from knowledge to our genes."[7]

There remain a variety of "capitalisms" – European social democracy, US neo-liberalism, Chinese and East Asian state capitalism – but the need to compete in an increasingly global marketplace does tend to trump national preferences regarding such crucial matters as interest rates, prices, welfare, and wages. Despite some disagreement as to its accuracy,[8] a widespread impression exists that competition for foreign investment and market share forces governments to pursue policies favored by transnational corporations and financial markets, which generally seek out countries with less regulation, lower taxes, and limited welfare costs. Austerity policies, reflecting harsh neoliberal financial discipline, have generated domestic resentment and instability in Iceland, Ireland, Greece, Portugal, Spain, and Italy. Previously prosperous France and Germany, as well, have been buffeted by financial markets concerned about their exposure to sovereign debt in the Eurozone. Markets in mid-2011 even had the temerity to challenge the United States, threatening grave consequences in the event of a "technical" default, caused by political deadlock over budget deficit-reducing priorities and a related increase in the legal debt ceiling. The symbolism of a private bond-rating agency, Standard & Poor's, downgrading the US credit rating – *despite* eventual legislative action to avoid default – speaks volumes.

Hence it is relatively easy to establish that neoliberal globalization saps the authority of states and to some extent "denationalizes" their economies.[9] Critical theorist Robert Cox believes that in a neoliberal world the autonomous capacity of *all* states has been reduced and that they "are, by and large, reduced to the role of adjusting national economies to the dynamics of an unregulated global economy."[10] From a Marxist perspective, Michael Hardt and Antonio Negri reach a similar conclusion: "In a previous period nation-states were the primary actors in the modern imperialist organization of global production and exchange, but to the world market they appear increasingly as mere obstacles."[11] Strange – neither a critical theorist nor a Marxist – likewise argued "that the impersonal forces of world markets, integrated over the postwar period more by private enterprise in finance, industry and trade than by the cooperative decisions of governments, are now more powerful than the states to which ultimate political authority over society and economy is supposed to belong. Where states were once the masters of markets, now it is the markets which, on many crucial issues, are the masters over the governments of states."[12]

Others, like Layna Mosley, offer a more nuanced view of state impotence. She maintains that "while capital market openness does influence some aspects of government policymaking, this influence is by no means omnipotent or omnipresent."[13] Mosley insists that there are "myriad reasons to be skeptical of the claim," notably the differential impact of domestic institutions and citizens' demands.[14] As she sees it, domestic structures vary in capacity and can often modify the impact of global pressures. Linda Weiss adopts a related position. Empirical studies, she declares, do not support the belief that state welfare policies are inversely related to globalization and she suggests, instead, that reduced welfare is mainly the product of slow economic growth.[15] Weiss denies that globalization necessarily reduces "autonomy, capacity, or effectiveness for national decision-making vis-à-vis the domestic economy."[16] In her view, the growing influence of international institutions actually *extends* state capacity. If state autonomy has declined in some respects, it is not due so much to globalization as to reduced interstate cooperation, for example, the end of the Bretton Woods system of fixed exchange rates. "State capacity," she concludes, "far from becoming irrelevant, has acquired new significance in a changing world economy," and "the contest between competing capitalisms . . . will be increasingly a contest between strong and weak state capacities in the domestic arena."[17]

Other globalization scholars support the arguments of Mosley and Weiss that states are hardly cat's-paws in the face of neoliberal globalization. John Hobson suggests that, contrary to the notion of a "race to the bottom," "states have room for fiscal manoeuvre under globalization" and that "reports of the death of taxation and the welfare state remain greatly exaggerated."[18] Duane Swank provides additional evidence for the claim that, unlike uncoordinated market economies, "globalization has not led to significant welfare retrenchment in coordinated market economies; coordinated market institutions shape the interests, strategic choices, and capacities of labour, capital, and the state in ways favourable to the maintenance of social protection."[19] Thomas Risse likewise writes: "Many approaches to globalization are committed to an overly structuralist ontology. Structuralists tend to argue that some anonymous forces – be they financial markets, be they global production networks – command the global economy as a result of which states and political decision-making have lost almost all autonomy and freedom of choice." "All states," declares Risse, "can do is to adapt and to conform to the forces of the neoliberal world economy," resulting in "a 'race to the bottom' with regard to social policies and to the end of the welfare state as we knew it."[20] Risse, a social constructivist, takes a very different view, arguing that "globalization is reinforced and reproduced by and through social and political practices" that "can change as a result of which globalization will change."[21] Risse would almost certainly accept Manfred Steger's contention that "globalization is also a linguistic and ideological practice" rather than "merely a set of material processes anchored in economics and technology."[22]

Which countries have been most successful competitively in the course of economic globalization? According to the *Global Competitiveness Report 2009–2010*, developed by the World Economic Forum, competitiveness is defined as *"the set of institutions, policies, and factors that determine the level of productivity of the country."*[23] In 2009–2010, Switzerland was the world's most competitive country. The United States was ranked second, having been first the previous year. Other countries ranked among the top ten were Singapore, Sweden, Denmark, Finland, Germany, Japan, Canada, and the Netherlands. Interestingly, for all its progress, China ranked twenty-ninth. Seven of the least competitive economies were African.[24]

GLOBAL GOVERNANCE

Multilateral institutions and transnational corporate networks, as well as other public and private institutions that have encouraged and/or been fostered by globalization, are actual or potential sources of global governance. Governance, according to Rosenau, "encompasses the activities of governments, but it also includes any actors who resort to command mechanisms to make demands, frame goals, issue directives, and pursue policies,"[25] especially in regard to issues that have a global impact. In his view, governance is related to the erosion of state authority in the course of globalization,[26] and it involves the provision of collective goods that states are ever less able to provide for their citizens.

The provision of order and coordination is also central to governance. Thus, Scholte describes it "as processes whereby peoples formulate, implement, enforce and review rules to guide their common affairs,"[27] and Ian Douglas argues that globalization and governance are virtually equivalent and that both reflect Michel Foucault's idea that "*spatialization* and *deterritorialization*" are characteristics of modernity that may produce greater injustice along with new regulatory mechanisms.[28] An example of the provision of order through governance is the Kimberley Process, "a joint governments, industry and civil society initiative to stem the flow of conflict diamonds – rough diamonds used by rebel movements to finance wars against legitimate governments"[29] that was established in 2003. The purpose was to prevent the sale of "blood diamonds" that in recent decades have been used to finance violence in countries such as Angola, Ivory Coast, the Democratic Republic of Congo, Sierra Leone, and Zimbabwe. Member states must certify the diamonds that they sell are "conflict-free."[30]

Governance, unlike government, does not necessitate hierarchical relationships. Instead, it frequently involves interactions among and decisions by institutions from the local to global levels that are organized as networks rather than hierarchies. Global life, then, as Rosenau suggests, is "dense with organized activities," and contemporary global complexity "is partly because the world is host to ever greater numbers of organizations in all walks of life and in every corner of every continent,"[31] producing a significantly less coherent authority structure than that of the interstate world. This is a result of the shift from a state-centric universe to what Scholte terms "polycentrism," in which "states themselves have become more decentred and fragmented" and regulation "has been increasingly diffused from states to other sites 'above' and 'below' the country government." "Whereas statism concentrates the construction and application of social rules in centralized national territorial governments, polycentrism disperses regulation across multiple, substate and private sites, as well as dense networks that interlink these many points of governance."[32]

Globalization institutions, however, confront new challenges posed by the growing importance of emerging economies and their discontent with OECD domination of global governance and the consequent need to revise and reinvigorate the roles of those institutions in the global economy.[33] As we saw in Chapter 2, postwar US policy aimed at providing a foundation for international economic cooperation and stability by establishing the International Monetary Fund (IMF), the World Bank (IBRD), and the GATT (General Agreement on Tariffs and Trade). One aim was to avoid future economic disorder like the Great Depression. Today, especially since China joined the World Trade Organization (WTO), these institutions have become staunch advocates of globalization. They also serve as forums for poor countries and nongovernmental organizations (NGOs) to express their views and try to limit what they regard as the negative consequences of globalization. Some NGOs even assist in mediating international disputes, as did a group called the Center for International Dialogue during the political violence that wracked Kenya after that country's 2007 disputed election.[34] In the words of O'Brien, Goetz, Scholte, and Williams, the combination of NGOs and international institutions constitutes "complex multilateralism."[35]

Multilateral economic institutions are among the most public sources of economic governance. They continue to play key roles in sustaining globalization, and their future is tied up with their ability to persuade developing countries that they are dedicated to ending poverty and encouraging growth. "As interdependence among countries intensifies," declare Stephen Brooks and William Wohlforth, "and the list of global problems that the United States cannot resolve on its own grows, the benefits of international institutions will increase."[36] One of these, as Susan Roberts observes, is governance of world trade:

> From a system characterized by a mixture of consolidating free trade areas (most notably the European Union) in a sea of trade agreements negotiated between countries on a bilateral basis (with the exception of previous GATTs), the world is moving towards a system based on multilateral agreements policed and enforced by one transnational regulatory institution – the WTO.[37]

For its part, the WTO also encourages the informal rule-making and arbitration described above.

Roberts also praises international institutions for providing governance in respect to economic development and capital flows. "The crises in exchange rate management and in sovereign indebtness ... have been met by the rising regulatory power of two

Bretton Woods institutions: the World Bank and the International Monetary Fund" which "have become major influences through their policies of structural adjustment which for many countries in the global South are tied to development priorities and access to international capital flows."[38] The World Bank initiated its program of Structural Adjustment Loans in February 1980 following the second oil crisis. Their purpose was to "finance over a period of several years in return for reform in trade protection and price incentives for efficient resource use,"[39] encouraging free markets and reducing state intervention.

The recent global economic and financial crises also reversed what had appeared to be the growing irrelevance of the IMF. Prior to these crises, few states were seeking IMF loans. This has changed significantly, even as the institution assumes a greater advisory role to beleaguered governments,[40] including those in Europe such as Greece,[41] Ireland, Spain, and Portugal that face the prospect of sovereign default that would shut them out of global capital markets and undermine major banks that had made loans to these countries.[42]

Emerging market economies in general, especially those in Asia, have been dissatisfied with what they view as the Western dominance of international institutions and, therefore, of global governance.[43] Reflecting recognition of the growing economic role of both Asia and Latin America, as well as demands of major emerging economies for greater political influence,[44] it was agreed in September 2009 that the G-7 (G-8 when Russia is represented) would be replaced by the Group of 20 (G-20), which includes the so-called "BRIC" countries – Brazil, Russia, India, and China – as members.[45] The BRICs have formalized their relations and have added South Africa to their number. Although the BRICs reflect the growing economic clout and self-confidence of emerging economies, they are sufficiently diverse so as not to constitute a bloc.[46] Thus, Brazil and Russia depend on commodity exports, and China is a major commodities importer. Nevertheless, their combined share of global output grew from 16 to 22 percent between 2000 and 2008, or roughly 60 percent of the global increase during that period.[47]

In future, G-20 members will peer-review one another's economic policies and try to persuade one another to follow through on commitments. In addition, the IMF is assuming the additional role of providing the newly energized G-20 with staff support[48] and, on behalf of that group, has evaluated how a global tax on financial institutions might be levied.[49] It has also increased its funding, begun to overcome its reputation for ideological neoliberalism, and has, for the first time, successfully issued bonds. Finally, the G-20 must deal with the questions of whether the US dollar should remain the world's major reserve currency, how to slow the influx of foreign exchange into emerging economies, and how to manage the volatility of capital flows.[50]

The major institutions we have described are only a few of the diverse formal and informal international and transnational institutions and networks that have emerged with the authority to perform tasks that states once performed for themselves or to steer people and groups in performing these tasks. For example, the World Trade Forum, the Bilderberg group, the Trilateral Commission, and the Indus Enterprise are "clubs" at which elites gather to discuss global economic and other relevant issues. Think-tanks and institutes like Brookings, the Hoover Institution, the Carnegie

Foundation, and the Heritage Foundation mobilize expertise and coordinate epistemic communities to influence global policies.

In another issue area, Interpol and the United Nations are pooling resources for a "global policing doctrine" that would enable them to train police peacekeepers and centralize criminal information.[51] The International Criminal Court (ICC) is becoming an important instrument, along with NGOs like Amnesty International, in a global human rights regime. Similarly, the US Center for Disease Control and Prevention in Atlanta is at the center of an international regime aimed at controlling the spread of diseases. The CDC maintains six centers outside the United States in Kenya, Egypt, Thailand, Kazakhstan, China, and Guatemala where US experts work with local officials to prevent or cope with the spread of diseases.[52]

We will shortly have more to say about global civil society. Suffice it to observe here that global civil society and its networks of private groups are diverse, some in favor of existing globalization and others seeking to reform or even reverse the process. According to Salamon, Wojciech Sokolowski, and List:

> A global "associational revolution" is underway around the world, a massive upsurge of organized private, voluntary activity in virtually every corner of the globe [which is] . . . the product of new communications technologies, significant popular demands for greater opportunity, and dissatisfaction with the operations of both the market and the state in coping with the inter-related social and economic challenges of our day.[53]

The democratic legitimacy and accountability of some of these groups are themselves limited. However, some observers regard these networks as correctives to the "democratic deficit" that globalization critics decry, promising "new governing arrangements that enable something like effective and democratically accountable government, the rule of law and more equitable and freer social relations."[54] Jonathan Fox, for instance, describes how transnational civil society tried to influence the World Bank to take account of human rights. "A combination of symbolic and leverage politics pressured the World Bank to create an innovative pro-accountability institution, the Inspection Panel" that "is mandated to investigate claims from directly affected people that the Bank's reform policies have been violated."[55] Unfortunately, the panel has enjoyed only limited success, and the Bank has rejected most of its recommendations.[56]

NGOs, along with government bureaucracies and international institutions, coalesce into international regimes that are meta-institutions at the heart of global governance and that coordinate decisions and policies in particular issue areas. The idea behind global governance owes much to the concept of international regimes. Such regimes are defined by Stephen Krasner as "principles, norms, rules, and decision-making procedures."[57] The role of regimes appears when Weiss and Thakur declare:

> "Global governance" – which can be good, bad, or indifferent – refers to existing collective arrangements to solve problems [and] . . . is the sum of laws, norms, policies, and institutions that define, constitute, and mediate relations among

citizens, society, markets, and the state in the international arena – the wielders and objects of international public power.[58]

Along with international economic institutions, transnational corporations (TNCs) are key elements in international economic regimes and major players in providing governance for the global economy. William Tabb points out that:

> National sovereignty in an anarchic world has had a powerful hold on the thinking of international relations theorists. Such a framing is restrictive if not misleading in the era of corporate globalization in which transnational capital and international financial institutions shape and constrain the possibilities of nation states and global state economic governance institutions take on crucial elements of stateness.[59]

Informal modes of governing economic practices of the sort prevalent in medieval Europe are becoming critical intermediaries between national and transnational law. "In the era of globalization," Tabb declares, "the law merchant is being reconfigured, reconstituted in a contemporary form as a handmaiden of transnational capital."[60] Thus, Tabb sees a revival of merchant law or *lex mercatoria*, encouraged by deregulation, by which private actors established rules of economic conduct during the era of European state-building. In a globalizing world: "The interplay between the *lex mercatoria* and not only state power but also global state economic governance institutions suggests the importance of pre-public negotiation and private consensus formation as well as a continuing interpenetration of private, governmental, and intergovernmental consensus," that contain, among other things, industry agreement "on definitions, standards, and rules." In sum, economic governance is achieved through "soft law," and "the medieval law merchant, which operated outside of both the local political economy and the local state" has reappeared and is "freeing merchant laws and institutions from national controls."[61] Practices such as informal arbitration, accounting standards, or investment agreements, fostered by groups such as the International Chamber of Commerce and the International Accounting Standards Committee, facilitate dispute-resolution, especially in the absence of mature international law or compatible legal systems. They also help harmonize rules and procedures among transnational firms.

Today's transnational corporations (TNCs) are pillars and drivers of economic globalization. From only a few thousand in 1990, following the collapse of the Soviet bloc and the USSR, the numbers of TNCs soared to over 82,000 with some 810,000 foreign affiliates. By 2008, TNCs employed 77 million people, the 100 largest alone accounted for 4 percent of the gross world product, and the 1,000 largest corporations provided 80 percent of the world's industrial output. By 2007, the 100 largest TNCs had assets of $10.7 trillion (declining slightly in 2008), sales in 2008 worth over $8.5 trillion, and over 15 million employees.[62]

In fact, relatively few TNCs are genuinely global, defined by Rugman and Verbeke as having "at least 20% of their sales in all three regions of the triad [NAFTA, the EU, and Asia], but less than 50% in any one region." Of the 365 corporations for which data were available, only nine "are unambiguously 'global'"[63] – IBM, Sony,

Royal Philips Electronics, Nokia, Intel, Canon, Coca-Cola, Flextronics International, and LVMH.[64] Instead, an overwhelming majority of TNCs are focused on their home region (320 firms) and a minority (twenty-five) of them have at least 20 percent of their sales in two core regions. "Regionalization," Rugman and Verbeke argue, "should be viewed as an expression of semi-globalization" which "implies that we observe neither extreme geographical fragmentation of the world in national markets nor complete integration."[65]

Although the largest number of the wealthiest transnational corporations have their headquarters in the United States, many transnational corporations are relatively small, and, surprisingly, Denmark, Germany, and Sweden were the sites of the largest number of TNC headquarters, and South Korea and Japan hosted more TNCs than did the United States.[66] Overall, North America, Europe, and Japan hosted some 445 of the 500 largest TNCs.[67] Among the growing number of TNCs were defense industries unable to survive by relying solely on national contracts. European corporations were the most internationally organized, with British firms scoring highest in this respect.[68]

Notwithstanding the dominance of Western and Japanese corporations, an increasing number of major TNCs such as Suzlon and Tata Motors of India, which has built the world's least expensive automobile, are from emerging markets. Instead of focusing on specialized economic sectors, many of these are conglomerates. By 2008, sixty-two of the world's 500 largest corporations were from BRIC countries, double the number in 2003 and reflecting the increasing interdependence of the West and major emerging economies. Some of the largest of these – such as China's Sinopec, State Grid, and China National Petroleum, Russia's Gazprom and Lukoil, Brazil's Petrobras, and India's Indian Oil – are involved in resource extraction.[69]

For transnational corporations, global economic integration is critical to achieve efficiency. Technological changes both compel and permit firms to develop global products, and these reflect a growing homogenization of consumer tastes.[70] The cost of R&D is an additional spur to global integration, and TNCs are major sources of R&D investment.[71] The global integration of production and distribution is also encouraged by what Bartlett, Ghoshal, and Birkinshaw term "a competitive strategy called 'global chess'."

> The game could only be played by companies managing their worldwide operations as interdependent units guided by a coordinated global strategy. Whereas the traditional multinational approach assumed that each national market was unique and independent of others, this strategy emphasized the effect of financial interdependence. Regardless of consumer tastes or manufacturing scale economies, the corporation with worldwide operations was advantaged because it could use funds generated in one market to subsidize its position in another. These same factors encouraged global alliances among firms.[72]

When all is said and done, however, global governance remains fragile. As Weiss and Thakur remind us: "The starting point about international public policy is that governance for the planet is weak ... No matter how strong the contributions of informal and formal networks are, no matter how plentiful the resources from private organizations and corporations are, no matter how much goodwill from governments exists, the striking reality is that there is no central authority."[73]

THE TRIUMPH OF DEMOCRACY?

The spread of democratic norms from the core areas of North America, Western Europe, and Japan to Latin America, Asia, the countries of the former Soviet bloc, and even to Africa[74] *and now perhaps the Middle East has accompanied globalization.* This process, it has been suggested, is partly a result of neoliberal economic policies that create wealth and enlarge the middle class who demand democratic rights. According to one analysis, the middle class in Asia and the Pacific increased from 315 million in 1990 to over 1.1 billion by 2005; in China alone it increased from 173 to 806 million people.[75]

Not all agree that globalization spreads democracy. Barry Gills takes issue with the claim, at least at the system level, arguing that "it is still the most powerful governments of the world that determine the primary course of action and define the parameters of mainstream discussion whenever there is a crisis." Gills calls for "a common set of core values that will lead to new democratic and popular forms of global governance, which go beyond the confines of the existing power structure."[76]

For liberals at least, globalization is believed to promote democracy and wealth, and democracy and wealth promote the "democratic peace." In other words, globalization is viewed as increasing the prospects for a peaceful world, both domestically and internationally. Paul Collier disputes this claim, or at least modifies it by arguing that elections in poor countries have "increased political violence instead of reducing it"; in these societies elections are confused with true democracy, which "has rules for the conduct of those elections" and "checks and balances that limit the power of a government once elected."[77] Recent elections in Iran, Iraq, and Afghanistan are examples of exercises in democratic form rather than substance.

Although globalization has been accompanied by growing acceptance of individual rights for several decades, including that of choosing one's own leaders, it is decidedly premature to declare the triumph of *liberal* democracy and "the end of history."[78] Democracy remains fragile at best in some countries and regions, is non-existent in others, and generally is violently contested by those whose authority would vanish in the face of free elections. Indeed, in some respects democracy may appear to be in retreat. According to a 2010 Freedom House report, "2009 marked the fourth consecutive year in which global freedom suffered a decline – the longest consecutive period of setbacks for freedom in the nearly 40-year history of the report."[79] The areas criticized were Sub-Saharan Africa, notably Kenya, Nigeria, Ethiopia, Guinea, Madagascar, Niger, Eritrea, and the Democratic Republic of Congo, much of the Middle East and Central America, as well as Russia, Kazakhstan, and Kyrgyzstan. By contrast, on the whole, democracy continued to advance in Asia.[80]

Although history did not end following the Cold War and authoritarian rule persisted in many countries, the link between globalization and democracy became clear in early 2011. Then, in a rapid series of events that shook North Africa and the Middle East, authoritarian leaders were swept from power in Tunisia and Egypt, their successors as well as the King of Jordan were forced to make concessions to the popular aspirations of their countries' citizens. Violence erupted in Bahrain, and civil war convulsed Libya and Yemen. Underlying the dramatic events was the role of the new information and communication technologies described in the next chapter. The internet and its social networks, email, and mobile phones, especially those capable of transmitting videos and photographs, helped undermine the hierarchical structures of authority and the capacity of governments to manage and limit what citizens could know about events. The rapid spread of news among individuals and the role of new technologies in facilitating their mobilization were profoundly democratizing (and destabilizing).[81] Whether the wave of democratic aspirations that swept these regions will bring real democratic change remains, at present, unanswered.

Democratic values and informed citizens with access to information and able to communicate their views across vast distances are prerequisites for the spread of civil society. Civil society, in turn, reinforces democratic self-consciousness and is a potentially critical element in establishing global governance.

GLOBAL CIVIL SOCIETY

Global civil society, notably the proliferation of international (INGOs)[82] and non-governmental organizations (NGOs) and NGO networks, including giant transnational firms, is beginning to coalesce and, as we have seen, constitutes a potentially key foundation for revitalizing global governance.[83] Today, "a veritable 'global associational revolution' appears to be underway, a massive upsurge of organized private, voluntary activity in literally every corner of the world," that is produced in part "by growing doubts about the capability of the state to cope on its own with the social welfare, developmental and environmental problems that face nations today."[84]

According to Peter Willetts, "many NGOs ... have their membership measured in millions, whereas 42 of the 192 countries in the UN have populations of less than one million, of which 12 are less than 100,000."[85] These institutions and networks are both drivers and consequences of globalization. "By imagining the growth of the idea of a transnational citizenship as a well-spring for transnational forms of social mobilization," declare Randall Germain and Michael Kenny, "some commentators are able to invest in the achievement of a global civil society the hope of a new kind of progressive alternative to neo-liberal globalization."[86] Normatively, some even see civil society as a site for "moralities of all kinds."[87] We should not forget, however, that religious militants, groups of political extremists of all stripes, anarchists, and others who oppose globalization also form part of global civil society.

Well over a century ago, Hegel had given "civil society," including private corporations and associations, "a pivotal sociological and normative role in linking the individual to the wider community realized in the state," viewing it as "a historically concrete space of social interaction among individuals."[88] Some advocates of civil society like Mary Kaldor see it in the tradition of Kantian cosmopolitanism.[89] The mention of Hegel and Kant as progenitors of civil society suggests that Alejandro Colás is correct in describing it as "a specifically modern site of socio-political struggle which contains very diverse, often incompatible ideological projects."[90]

At least as envisaged by liberals,[91] civil society "champions the political vision of a world founded on non-violent, legally sanctioned power-sharing arrangements among many different and interconnected forms of socio-economic life that are distinct from governmental institutions."[92] This definition reflects what Gideon Baker calls "the 'globalisation from below' model," the theorists of which "look to the agency of 'bottom up', 'solidarist' transnational social movements" for the "growth of an increasingly norm-governed world system."[93] John Naisbitt agrees: "Globalization," he writes, "is a bottom-up phenomenon with all actions initiated by millions of individuals, the sum total of which is 'globalization'," a process in which "no one can anticipate what the sum of all the individual initiatives will be before the result is manifest."[94]

Another liberal claim about civil society is that the increasing globalization of the media serves to liberalize the perspectives of the non-governmental sector by spreading concern for human welfare transnationally and creating pressure on states and international institutions to act. This is Martin Shaw's view. "The internationalized political order has been increasingly liberal in content, facilitating transnational and globalized communications and culture ... Although many have located the emergence of a global civil society in globalist social movements – environmental, feminist, human rights, and so on – the common framework of this emerging form has been the transformed public sphere of the mass media."[95] Global media, in effect, bridge "emotional and psychological distance."[96]

A growing number of NGOs are indeed committed to finding cooperative solutions to collective dilemmas. They are also sources of activism and expertise and are welcomed by many countries seeking to manage change in non-violent ways. Although organizations and movements have different aims, many collaborate for a perceived collective good. According to Gideon Baker and David Chandler:

> For an increasing number of commentators, global civil society represents nothing less than the outline of a future world political order within which states will no longer constitute the seat of sovereignty [that] . . . is revolutionising our approach as new non-state-based and border-free expressions of political community challenge territorial sovereignty as the exclusive basis for political community and identity.

In effect, it is "a challenge 'from below' to the nation-state system."[97] Writing of the economic sphere, Sassen partially agrees: "While the state participates in enabling the expansion of the global economy, it does so in a context increasingly dominated by deregulation, privatization, *and the growing authority of nonstate actors*, some of which assume new normative roles."[98]

In all events, global networks of individuals and NGOs now exist[99] – made possible by new technologies – that are concerned with issues as varied as capital flows, human rights, women's rights, economic development, and the degradation of the environment. Private charitable organizations provide enormous amounts of aid to the developing world, often focusing their assistance on particular problems. The Bill & Melinda Gates Foundation, for instance, has committed almost $23 billion since it was founded, including $3 billion in 2009, mainly towards coping with improving health and agriculture in Africa.[100] The Clinton Foundation provided over $200 million in 2009 to improve health care, initiate climate control programs, and support sustainable growth.[101]

Leaders of some countries like Russia, China, and Iran recoil at the democratizing potential of these networks and have taken steps to suppress them.[102] By contrast, NGOs are finding greater acceptance in other countries like Japan where, according to Hugo Dobson, "a more audible civil society is beginning to make itself heard." It could, of course, be argued, as does Dobson, "that many NGOs and citizens' movements have been subject to approval from and supervised by government, and as a result are beholden to and suffer from the same symptoms of fatigue and rigidity as traditional structures of government in responding to the demands of globalization."[103] Still, even in China, "it is in the void left by declining Communist Party power that we began to see autonomous organizations and the makings of a civil society."[104]

NGO networking, aided by agencies like the World Bank and the globalization of the media, fosters the global spread of values, forcing governments at least to acknowledge them. Munck uses human rights to make the point. "Human rights activism – mainly organized through NGOs – has successfully put together transnational coalitions of considerable effectiveness."[105] As a result, "human rights are no longer tied exclusively to national sovereignty," and one consequence is "growing levels of transnational accountability."[106]

The issue of women's rights has also been significantly globalized by civil society, climaxing in the Fourth World Conference on Women meeting in Beijing, China, in 1995, at which then first-lady Hillary Clinton famously declared that the time had come for the world to hear

> that it is no longer acceptable to discuss women's rights as separate from human rights ... It is a violation of human rights when babies are denied food, or drowned, or suffocated, or their spines broken, simply because they are born girls ... It is a violation of human rights when women are doused with gasoline, set on fire and burned to death because their marriage dowries are deemed too small.[107]

"What the feminist international lobby has achieved," Munck suggests, "is the legitimacy of an international women's regime,"[108] leading Castells to a premature celebration of "the end of patriarchalism."[109]

Nevertheless, many women's groups, as well as other globalized issue networks vigorously criticize aspects of globalization such as human trafficking, outsourcing of jobs, environmental damage, and income disparities. Wolf asserts:

> The new actors are idealistic, not narrowly self-interested. Their goals are also generous, not narrow. They include conservationists and environmentalists, fearful that the liberal world economy will sweep away hard-won domestic regulations or exacerbate perceived global environmental damage; lobbies for development, concerned about debt burdens or the devastation allegedly caused by the structural adjustment and liberalization imposed by the International Monetary Fund and

World Bank under the so-called "Washington consensus"; consumer groups worried about product safety and consumer health; human rights groups, troubled by exploitation and political oppression in mainland China, Myanmar and other parts of the developing world; Church groups of all denominations; women's groups; and campaigners for indigenous groups and traditional ways of life.[110]

Jagdish Bhagwati is much less complimentary, arguing that many critics of globalization, including labor unions, "are also proceeding instead from *self-interest* actuated by *fear*," and "mask their concerns by claiming to be altruistic as well."[111]

How important and laudatory are such civil society groups? Pessimists like Shaw contend that "civil society is not only too weak to take the full weight of global transformation, it is also still too national in form."[112] Although globalization enthusiasts believe that NGO networks are potentially critical sources of global governance, not all observers hold that view. Thus, Rudra Sil argues that "new global networks . . . have had an impact on the environment within which states seek to exercise influence, but such networks are too segmented, each focusing on issue-specific transnational ties to supplant the nation-state as the ultimate guarantor of contracts or laws over a given domain."[113]

Partly owing to the criticism of globalization by some NGOs, international institutions like the United Nations, the IMF and the WTO, as well as many governments, have consulted with selected NGOs involved in global civil society, for example, during UN-sponsored issue-specific conferences, and have profited from their expertise and experience. In this role, these groups, as Colás rightly points out, "are fundamentally pressure groups which do not contest the overall legitimacy of a specific regime but merely seek to alter a particular policy – on human rights, environmental law, women's rights and so forth," "eschew campaigning for structural socio-political change," and are not concerned with producing "grand-scale transformations at an inter-state level."[114] As a result, he concludes that "the form, content and eventual outcomes of such gatherings are so heavily circumscribed by the interests of states that it is difficult to see how the agents of global civil society can be said to be genuinely representative of an autonomous and undifferentiated 'global citizenry'." With a nod to Alexander Wendt's familiar characterization of anarchy, Colás declares that "global civil society is what states make of it."[115]

As the limitation on global civil society described by Colás suggests, not all observers are persuaded that it will transform global politics. Indeed, some are genuinely scathing about the prospects for global civil society. Kenneth Anderson and David Rieff, for example, deride "the claim that transnational or international NGOs constitute 'global civil society' at least if this term is intended to draw upon the conceptual machinery of 'civil society' as understood to apply in a settled domestic democratic society," and they "find the term 'global civil society' conceptually incoherent."[116]

The global diffusion of common individual skills and values (including democracy), the spread of civil society, and the emergence of institutions of transnational and global governance suggest that globalization may also produce cultural homogenization and reduce the space for cultural uniqueness.

CULTURAL HOMOGENIZATION?

Western culture, with its norms of secularism, democracy, and mass consumerism, has been spreading globally by means of mass media, migration, tourism, and music. Westernization has raised concerns, especially but not exclusively in traditional societies, about a threatened homogenization of mass culture. For example, Blum writes of "an inundating wave of uniformity that threatens to wash away all cultural difference, undermining the foundation of distinct social and political institutions,"[117] and Sarah Armstrong argues that "Canadians' access to the diversity of their nation's cultures" is "threatened by forces of economic globalization,"[118] including information technology that facilitates evasion of national trade regulations and the liberalization of trade in goods and services.

Frequently, the spread of a homogenizing global culture is equated with the spread of US culture. Thus, "global popular culture dominated by American products and ideas destroys this diversity of cultural production. So there is a fear and backlash against what is viewed as a leveling force, a sweeping homogeneity or Disneyfication of culture."[119] Culture in this sense is "soft power," that is, "the ability to obtain preferred outcomes through attraction."[120]

Homogenization, it is argued, can be seen in everything from dress, diet, and education to advertising and the spreading belief in democracy and human rights; it ranges from Big Macs and designer jeans to abhorrence of torture. "McDonalds," writes Benjamin Barber, "serves 20 million customers around the world every day, drawing more customers daily than there are people in Greece, Ireland, and Switzerland together."[121]

Scholte describes the spread of mass culture as "*westernization* or *modernization* ... a dynamic whereby the social structures of modernity (capitalism, rationalism, industrialism, bureaucratism, individualism, and so on) are spread the world over, frequently destroying pre-existing cultures and local self-determination in the process."[122] This line of argument is essentially pejorative and sometimes state-centric, viewing globalization as part of a "hegemonic discourse"[123] around American hegemony or imperialism.[124] Thus, Callinicos conceives of globalization "not as a secular tendency, but as a highly specific political and economic project represented notably by the neo-liberal policies of the Washington Consensus ... and informed by the drive to maintain and even extend the position of the United States as the dominant global power."[125]

"That American hegemony and economic globalization are connected," observes G. John Ikenberry, "is not surprising" because "[a]t various historical junctures – such as after great wars and other upheavals in international relations – leading states are presented with unusual opportunities to shape the basic organization and rules of regional and global markets."[126] As World War II came to a close, the United States, having achieved economic hegemony, took the lead at Bretton Woods in establishing a new multilateral economic architecture. As Ikenberry explains: "The post-1945 era is marked by two great developments: the emergence of an open world economy and the American construction of a hegemonic order. These global transformations in markets and geopolitics are deeply intertwined."[127] The United States successfully sought to reintegrate Japan and Germany into the world economy and, as the Cold War emerged, to encourage cooperation within Western Europe. Thus, "the American-centered security system served as the political foundation that supported the expansion of world markets," and "[t]his hegemonic structure – liberal, institutionalized, open, and expansive – provided the political and strategic infrastructure for an explosion in trade and investment."[128]

The perspectives of Callinicos and Ikenberry, though ideologically antithetical, imply that little is genuinely novel in contemporary globalization. We have seen it all before, earlier imperialisms and hegemonic epochs from Rome and Imperial China to Europe's imperial expansion. In all cases, the hegemon imposes its norms and practices upon those whom it conquers or influences. Rosenau views this as "oversimplified." "McDonald's may be thriving in Asia and thousands of other locations around the world, but so are Chinese, Japanese, Vietnamese, and Korean restaurants frequented widely in the United States and Europe, and much the same can be said about the direction of intercultural flows in the fields of medicine, education, and religion."[129] Westernization is only one source of cultural globalization.

Still, the spread of a global culture *may* threaten some local cultures and religious beliefs, undermine traditional norms and elites, erode national autonomy, and dilute individual and collective identities. The latter, Ronald Suny explains, are "embedded in the stories we tell about ourselves individually and collectively, implied in the way individuals and groups talk and give meaning to their being, their selves, their roles" and "are part of a search for a usable past and an acceptable modernity to stave off anxiety about the present and future."[130]

Social subjectivities are fundamental to globalization, but in our view cultural homogenization is less likely than cultural complexity and hybridization. There is no fully effective way to stop the exchange of ideas and styles in cyberspace or through travel and migration. As Tyler Cowen observes: "A typical American yuppie drinks French wine, listens to Beethoven on a Japanese audio system, uses the Internet to buy Persian textiles from a dealer in London, watches Hollywood movies funded by foreign capital and filmed by a European director, and vacations in Bali; an upper-middle-class Japanese may do much the same."[131] Elites and an affluent middle class are similarly engaged the world over, and the masses cannot but be affected by the likes of media influences too. As the security of place vanishes, fear of the unknown may intensify, even as new possibilities present themselves. Rosenau writes of "workers threatened by a loss of their jobs to competitors; citizens convinced that local cultures are being overwhelmed by Westernization and its corollary, Americanization, and thus fearful that globalizing dynamics are generating an undesirable degree of homogeneity." As he sees it, "these are among the more conspicuous individuals who seek to preserve the meaning of local space by resisting the encroachment of global forces."[132]

But must globalization *necessarily* trample upon and stamp out local cultures? Tomlinson vigorously takes issue with this proposition. "There are," he insists, "good reasons to doubt the most pessimistic predictions of depletion in the variety of global cultural experience. Not the least of these is that they tend to radically underestimate both the adaptive and, indeed, the resistive resources of local culture." He continues: "Far from being the fragile flower that globalization tramples, identity is seen here as the upsurging dynamic of local culture that offers *resistance* to the centripetal force of capitalist globalization."[133] Constructivists like Risse also reject the idea that globalization is eradicating local cultures and imposing a single, homogenous culture on the world as a whole. "People," he argues, "will continue to enact their local scripts and follow local norms of appropriate behavior," and "hybrid cultures are likely to emerge which incorporate some global scripts into the local habits, while rejecting others."[134]

Paradoxically, by threatening sovereignty, tradition, and national identity, focusing attention on "outsiders," and triggering internal efforts to emphasize shared values and reinforce collective identity, globalization may actually reinforce state autonomy. As a result, cultural homogenization is not a *necessary* consequence of globalization. "Rather," as Featherstone suggests:

> the globalization process should be regarded as opening up the sense that now the world is a single place with increased contact becoming unavoidable, we necessarily have greater dialogue between various nation-states, blocs, and civilizations: a dialogical space in which we can expect a good deal of disagreement, clashing of perspectives and conflict, not just working together and consensus.[135]

To the extent that global culture is becoming homogenized, one of the trends that contribute to this process is the growing dominance of a single language, English. Alternatively, it can be argued that there is no *single* language called "English," but instead that the spread of many variations of English reflect the continued cultural idiosyncrasies of those who speak and read it.

ENGLISH AS THE *LINGUA FRANCA*

The spread of English as a global language links cultural and business elites across the globe much as Latin and French did in earlier epochs. As Robert McCrum, an associate editor of the British newspaper *The Observer*, declares, "rarely has a language and its hegemony been more pervasive than Anglo-American culture," and "the globalization of English, and English literature, law, money and values, is the cultural revolution" of his generation.[136] In a much simplified form of the language that McCrum calls "Globish," English serves to permit communication among people who do not speak each other's native tongue.[137] In its numerous local variations and patois, "English was becoming a global phenomenon with a fierce, inner multinational dynamic, an emerging *lingua franca* described by the anthropologist Benedict Anderson as 'a kind of global-hegemonic post-clerical Latin'."[138]

Lieber and Weisberg see the spread of English as central to America's cultural hegemony and a key source of soft power. "A century ago," they write, "French was the language of diplomacy and German was the leading scientific language as well as extensively used in Central and Eastern Europe. By the mid-twentieth century, Russian was the predominant second language throughout the Soviet sphere in Central Asia and Eastern Europe. Now, however, it is English that prevails."[139]

Today, seven of the twenty most culturally globalized countries (United States, United Kingdom, Canada, Australia, Ireland, Singapore, and Israel) are among the ten leading English-speaking countries in the world.[140] Indeed, English enjoys a special status in seventy-five countries. "One dimension of the 'flattening' of the world in the age of globalization," declares Harm De Blij, "is the cultural convergence of which linguistic homogenization is a key component."[141] English is spoken as a native language by between 300 and 400 hundred million people and as a second language by about 375 million others, although in many cases it is a local version of English mixed with local languages. Everywhere, the demand to learn English is intense, because it has become the language of commerce, science, and technology. Although more people are actually native speakers of Mandarin Chinese[142] and Hindi, what makes English dominant is that it is spoken so widely compared to other languages – in 104 countries. English is used by some 478 million internet users and Chinese by 378 million, with other languages far behind.[143] De Blij concludes: "Chinese still is in the numerical lead, but Chinese is hardly on track to become a world language to compete with English: it remains geographically confined and would require an unlikely conversion of communication technologies."[144]

"Based on English as its *lingua franca* and on the rise of the internationally mobile knowledge worker," writes Michael Talalay, "a type of international citizenry is appearing. In the office of one of my consultancy clients in Switzerland, the native languages of the staff include Italian, Croatian, Russian, Serbian, Portuguese, Hindi, French, Greek and German. The working language, however, is English. This is the official policy of the company, not merely a *de facto* development."[145] "It's no longer just top execs who need to speak English," declare two observers. "Everyone in the corporate food chain is feeling the pressure to learn a common tongue as companies globalize and democratize. These days in formerly national companies such as Renault and BMW, managers, engineers, even leading blue-collar workers are constantly calling and e-mailing colleagues and customers in Europe, the United States, and Japan."[146]

Even in remote Azerbaijan and Kazakhstan the "ability to speak English is also considered essential, providing not only a gateway to knowledge but also a tool for national development."[147] Countries like India, Pakistan, and Ghana that were formerly British colonies can be grateful to the imperial power for spreading English, at least among local elites. However, countries and individuals that lack English are markedly disadvantaged in a globalized world. "For those outside the West who wish to have their ideas taken seriously in the global field," as Featherstone contends, "the English language-dominated academic investment curve is steep," making it "difficult to shift the existing power balances and patronage networks in the production and dissemination of global knowledge."[148] In sum, as Jacques Maurais and Michael Morris observe: "A globalising world poses a challenge of rising interdependence for all languages, since no linguistic sphere is protected or assured and a more tightly integrated world generally favours the spread of English."[149]

Sadly, many languages are disappearing, and "the protection of endangered species is closely linked to the preservation of tongues."[150] Nevertheless, it is worth recalling that other languages have been dominant for a period of time and then lost that status, and that notwithstanding "regionalization and globalization, local identities remain the most ingrained," thereby creating resistance to linguistic homogenization.[151] Welsh and Celtic languages have been revived, and still others like Hebrew have been reinvented. These are not supplanting but supplementing English and are a distinct source of pride among ethnic minorities at home and abroad.

Communication and information technologies, skilled individuals, and common cultural touchstones enable the formation of transgovernmental networks, even while the effort to spread civil society and create governance institutions encourages the formation of such networks.

TRANSGOVERNMENTAL LINKAGES AND NETWORKS

The growth of complex transgovernmental linkages stands in contrast to the expansion in authority and autonomy that state bureaucracies enjoyed in earlier decades. "Though the details varied," argues Martin van Creveld, "in all countries the century and a half after 1648 was characterized by the growth in the power of state bureaucracy, both that part whose function was internal administration and the division responsible for external affairs."[152] The twentieth century witnessed the birth of new national bureaucracies to administer the host of tasks associated with providing collective social and economic goods. The welfare state was a bargain struck between citizens and the state in which the latter provided social and economic protection to the former. The normative context came to be what John Ruggie famously called "embedded liberalism" – "a framework which would safeguard and even aid the quest for domestic stability without, at the same time, triggering the mutually destructive external consequences that had plagued the interwar period."[153] "Under embedded liberalism," as Sean Ó Riain argues, "states could maintain a janus-faced posture, dealing relatively separately with negotiating international markets, with other states, and with balancing domestic social and political pressures. Now that the buffering institutions of embedded liberalism have been weakened, states are increasingly faced with the integration of domestic and international policy."[154]

The proliferation of economic, environmental, security, and other issues that transcend national boundaries and that often provoke bureaucratic contests within governments have also produced transgovernmental alliances and networks. For example, wealthy countries and corporations that find it difficult to reduce their own emissions have joined in a novel program to pay local people *not* to cut down trees in order to prevent deforestation. Both state and society are increasingly fragmented and penetrated by external economic, political, and social forces.

Cerny, for instance, describes "systematic linkages between state actors and agencies within particular jurisdictions and sectors, cutting across different countries and including a heterogeneous collection of private actors and groups in interlocking policy communities."[155] Transnational bureaucratic alliances owe much to "the ability of firms, market actors and competing parts of the national state apparatus itself to defend and expand their economic *and* political turf through activities such as transnational policy networking ... [which] has both undermined the control span of the state from without and fragmented it from within."[156]

Like transnational corporations, national bureaucracies increasingly organize transnational networks and coalitions to promote their objectives in a globalized world. Sassen writes of "transnational networks of government officials" and "novel types of networks" that "connect corporate globalization and the globalizing of governmental responsibilities and aims," examples of which include "judges having to negotiate a growing array of international rules and prohibitions that require some measure of cross-border standardization," "immigration officials needing to co-ordinate border controls," and "police officials in charge of discovering financial flows that support terrorism."[157]

Such networks point up how political space is being transformed in a globalizing world, and they suggest the degree to which globalized issues and international and transnational governance – linking governments and societies – are facts of global life.[158] Indeed, political space is constantly in flux owing to processes that entail the formation of extensive networks of interaction and interdependence, along with the division, even disintegration, of polities into smaller more localized political entities.

To the extent that governance is shared and that values are authoritatively allocated by transnational networks of varied polities and actors, global power, too, is diffused. In addition, the emergence of new centers of innovation and economic growth and the spread of competitive capitalism – along with the declining capacity or necessity of actors to occupy territory – greatly complicates the capacity of any single polity to act as a hegemon.

DIFFUSION OF GLOBAL POWER?

The diffusion of global power is eroding the brief post-Cold War era of what many observers thought of as United States unipolarity.[159] This change has been accelerated by the global economic recession and makes it unlikely that any hegemon or group of leading states exists to reform the world financial system or provide the leadership to do so. The United States remains "a beacon of entrepreneurialism," but that beacon has been shining rather less brightly in recent years.[160] The relative decline of the United States is connected to the country's enormous current-accounts deficit and its emergence as the world's leading debtor country and resulting dependence on foreign purchases of American securities to finance its overseas military and political commitments.[161]

"How long," asked President Barack Obama's economic adviser, Lawrence Summers, "can the world's biggest borrower remain the world's biggest power?"[162] China, which holds much of America's debt, is reconsidering its purchase of US securities,[163] and the United States is encouraging a rebalancing of Sino-American economic relations.[164] Ultimately, this problem reflects overconsumption and inadequate saving by Americans and underconsumption and unnecessarily high saving rates in China. US–Chinese trade tensions may moderate if China encourages greater domestic consumer spending, a step it has begun to take, albeit tentatively.[165] A seriously undervalued Chinese currency is also a factor, and Beijing has agreed to take only minimal steps to remedy this.[166] Only a reversal in these habits can restore a reasonable semblance of economic balance between China and the United States. China's economy, writes Gideon Rachman, "has been growing by 9 to 10 percent a year, on average, for roughly three decades. It is now the world's leading exporter and its biggest manufacturer, and it is sitting on more than $2.5 trillion of foreign reserves. Chinese goods compete all over the world. This is no Soviet-style economic basket case."[167]

Although the United States is bogged down in several regional conflicts, it remains the world's leading military power. However, countries like China and India are rapidly developing a capacity to project force at greater distances.[168] "A China with global economic interests," declares one observer, "is already a China with global political interests, and increasingly, a China with expanding security interests."[169] China has significantly expanded its naval capabilities,[170] and neighbors are increasingly wary of that country's growing assertiveness, for example in the South China Sea and its territorial claims to several regional island groups like the Senkaku (known in China as the Diaoyi).[171] Beijing has shown it is prepared to use economic leverage to achieve political objectives.[172] Growing Chinese military and economic power has led to discussion of balancing or containing China in Asia,[173] and US relations with India, Japan, Vietnam, and other Asian countries have warmed[174] even as regional tensions have increased. The question remains whether the United States and China are becoming serious adversaries or can somehow manage to fashion a strategic partnership.[175]

How much a change in the military balance matters is debatable. Military superiority is no guarantee, for example, that the United States can realize its objectives. Andrew Krepinevich argues:

> Several events in recent years have demonstrated that traditional means and methods of projecting power are growing increasingly obsolete ... The diffusion of advanced military technologies, combined with the continued rise of new powers, such as China, and hostile states, such as Iran, will make it progressively more expensive in blood and treasure – perhaps prohibitively expensive – for US forces to carry out their missions in areas of vital interest, including East Asia and the Persian Gulf.[176]

American efforts to spread democracy have had some successes but have also triggered considerable resistance. The American goal to win the War on Terror remains elusive as do US efforts to prevent proliferation of weapons of mass destruction. China has been especially difficult in a number of ways, including its reluctance to participate in imposing sanctions on Iran, allow its currency to float freely, or agree to verifiable limits on carbon emissions.[177]

Although the United States remains the world's leading economic power, its superiority in this realm, too, is eroding quickly. Other centers of economic power, especially the European Union, Japan, India, Brazil, and China, are able competitors. American dependence on foreign energy and investment remains high. The global economic crisis has had a particularly negative impact on the United States and Europe. "The United States," argues Roger Altman, "will now be focused inward and constrained by unemployment and fiscal pressures," and, because much of the world blames US policies for the widespread economic distress, "the US model of free-market capitalism" is "out of favor."[178] European disunity has also been evident during the crisis, which has recently undermined the euro. "The one clear winner," Altman concludes, "is China, whose unique political economic-model has come through unscathed,"[179] and which is recovering more rapidly from the crisis than any other major state. For its part, China extended loans to countries in financial distress and blamed the West and its neoliberal philosophy for global financial disarray.

Does declining American hegemony matter? Paul Krugman thinks so and suggests how the erosion of US power also endangers globalization:

> By itself ... the war in Georgia isn't that big a deal economically. But it does mark the end of the Pax Americana – the era in which the United States more or less maintained a monopoly on the use of military force. And that raises some real questions about the future of globalization. Most obviously, Europe's dependence on Russian energy, especially natural gas, now looks very dangerous – more dangerous, arguably, than its dependence on Middle Eastern oil. After all, Russia has already used gas as a weapon: in 2006, it cut off supplies to Ukraine amid a dispute over prices. And if Russia is willing and able to use force to assert control over its self-declared sphere of influence, won't others do the same? Just think about the global economic disruption that would follow if China – which is about to surpass the United States as the world's largest manufacturing nation – were to forcibly assert its claim to Taiwan.[180]

This, of course, *only* speaks to greater diffusion of authority within the state system. However, as we have seen earlier in discussing global governance, an even greater source of diffusion of power and authority has been *from states* themselves to a vast array of subnational, transnational, international, and even supranational institutions. Some of these are formal organizations, and others are informal congeries of individuals and groups; some are public, but many are private.

Diffusion of global authority and the decline in hegemonic power make it difficult to coordinate responses to collective challenges or to provide global collective goods. Civil society and new governance institutions may compensate in time for such diffusion, but at present they remain relatively nascent.

COLLECTIVE ENVIRONMENTAL DEGRADATION

Environmental degradation including depletion of fossil fuels, fish, fresh water, and arable land continues. Human wealth and welfare are threatened by global warming, deforestation, desertification, and the loss of biodiversity. Concern is reflected in debates over the global spread of genetically modified (GM) grains and the loss of rain forests in Latin America and Asia. The global nature of environmental issues and the relatively weak governance associated with them are also illustrated by the problem of waste disposal. Wealthy states seek to ship toxic wastes to poor countries that can earn income by accepting it.[181] Observes *The Economist*: "The stretch of the Pacific between Hawaii and California is virtually empty. There are no islands, no shipping lanes, no human presence for thousands of miles – just sea, sky and rubbish."[182]

Environmental problems are palpably linked. Waste in oceans, lakes, and rivers, for instance, produces water pollution, algae blooms, and massive fish kills. Efforts to bury waste in dumps allows rotting organic material to give off methane – a powerful greenhouse gas – and produces acids that dissolve toxic heavy metals that may leach into aquifers. Garbage such as electronic appliances, batteries, paint, and the like produces toxic chemicals, and efforts to incinerate such garbage release toxic gases into the atmosphere. Thus, the incineration of trash and coal-fired enterprises in China not only produce methane, but are also responsible for a significant amount of the toxic mercury falling into North American lakes.[183]

To date, collective global responses to environmental challenges have been (not to mince words) pathetic, and vested economic interests have vigorously resisted concerted global policies. The 1992 Kyoto Protocol on global warming never attracted anywhere near universal support, and the 2009 Climate Conference in Copenhagen, intended to update the Kyoto Protocol, ended in disagreement with key powers like the United States, China, and India unwilling to adhere to mandatory and verifiable limits on carbon emissions.

It is difficult to achieve a focus on these trends because many of them pose long-term rather than imminent hazards. However, since such threats pose growing economic burdens, markets may begin to facilitate investments in technological solutions such as wind and solar energy. In addition, science may provide partial answers to some of these problems, for example, the use of non-polluting hydrogen as a fuel in automobiles. Finally, concerned individuals and groups have mobilized their skills and influence transnationally to find answers and have created global networks to lobby for cooperative responses to environmental challenges.[184]

Collective environmental afflictions, it can be argued, have already surpassed interstate warfare as a threat to human welfare and survival. In consequence, the essential meaning of security is changing. No longer are threats to the state regarded as identical to threats to individual citizens.

FROM MILITARY TO HUMAN SECURITY

The essential meaning of security is changing. Victor Cha argues that "the basic transaction processes engendered by globalization – instantaneous transportation and communication, exchanges of information and technology, flow of capital – catalyze certain dangerous phenomena or empower certain groups in ways unimagined previously."[185] Human mobility and interaction, as Cha observes, are associated with disease and environmental deterioration, and the "skills revolution" – coupled with the movement of illegal arms and dangerous technologies – abet transnational crime, terrorism, and ethnic insurgency. Cultural globalization is associated with local resistance and identity conflicts. Other global problems, including poverty, drugs, famine, and human-rights abuses, also imperil human well-being and survival. Climate change is now viewed by some as a threat to American security owing to its association with possible political unrest and violence resulting from pandemics, mass migration, and natural disasters.[186]

Globalization, then, with its culture of modernity has helped to produce what Ulrich Beck calls a risk society on a global scale in which "the national perspective on the dynamics of risk conflicts in world risk society is outdated."[187] Beck distinguishes between "side effect catastrophes, such as those associated with the new cutting-edge technologies, but also with climate change" or financial meltdown, and intentional catastrophes like "transnational suicide terrorism."[188] "The disregard for the globalizing risks," he concludes succinctly, "aggravates the globalization of risk."[189]

Among the most publicized of human-security issues are human-rights abuses including genocide and ethnic cleansing. Despite setbacks in countries like Myanmar and Uzbekistan and the continued reluctance of countries like China and Belarus to accept human-rights norms, these norms are deepening and will continue to elicit widespread support, especially as more people become prosperous and as states and international organizations adopt new human-rights conventions and set legal precedents that can gradually earn broader acceptance.

There is, of course, another side to this coin, exemplified by America's invasion of Iraq in 2003 and Russia's invasion of Georgia in 2008. "Appeals for justice and human rights," argues Beck, "are being used to legitimize invasions of other countries."

> How can one advocate a cosmopolitan form of legitimation when it leads to crises and wars and hence to the bloody refutation of the idea itself? Who will rein in the side effects of a cosmopolitan moral principle that speaks of peace while promoting war? What does 'peace' mean when it universalizes the possibility of war?[190]

As awareness of these problems grows, so does recognition that security encompasses more than guarding against military threats. Recognition of these additional threats is widening as more information becomes available to more people, networks of international and nongovernmental organizations form, and potential solutions emerge to problems that for most of history have been regarded as insoluble. Beck refers to this as *cosmopolitan realpolitik.* "In an age of global crises and risks, we need a politics of 'golden handcuffs' – the creation of a dense network of transnational interdependencies."[191]

Although interstate warfare is no longer the only or even the principal threat to human welfare, violence ranging from terrorism and civil disorder to abuses of human rights and brutality against women remains an existential source of insecurity. Indeed, the horizontal proliferation of weapons of mass destruction (WMD) to additional states and potentially to terrorist groups has raised the likelihood of apocalyptic conflict perhaps higher than it was during the Cold War.

THE CHANGING NATURE OF MILITARY SECURITY

A shift from conventional to irregular warfare is increasing violence that is subnational or transnational rather than between sovereign states even as nuclear proliferation continues. Although interstate warfare will inevitably erupt from time to time, a combination of factors will minimize its occurrence and relative significance. These include the declining importance of territory and the growing difficulty in occupying countries, the role of economic interdependence, the proliferation of weapons of mass destruction, the spread of civil strife, and the proliferation of nonstate sources of violence. "The consequences of globalization," concludes Jonathan Kirshner, "have reshaped incentives in ways that make traditional interstate war between relatively advanced, relatively large states less likely."

> Liberalization in trade and investment and the fragmentation of production, the greater share and significance of knowledge intensive sectors, and globalization of finance have raised the opportunity costs of going to war, reduced the expected gains from territorial conquest, and diluted pristine formulations of the 'national interest' that can be effectively advanced by interstate war.[192]

Even as the probability of interstate conflict declines, intrastate violence continues to spread, especially into less-developed and globally integrated regions and countries, and "into the void of diminished state capacity will flow participants in the illicit economy, entrepreneurs of violence, criminal gangs, separatist and insurgent groups, and terrorist organizations."[193] As Cha concludes, "with globalization terms such as global violence and human security become common parlance, where the fight is between irregular substate units such as ethnic militias, paramilitary guerrillas, cults and religious organizations, organized crime and terrorists."[194]

The distinction between legitimate war and crime will continue to blur, and violence among groups competing for power over the carcasses of failed or failing states or over sources of wealth like diamonds, coltan, lithium, oil, and cocaine will increase. Terrorism will surely persist, as fanatical individuals and groups of political extremists seek vengeance for real or imagined wrongs or try to spread messianic ideologies.

Globalization facilitates the spread of terrorism[195] much as it does the spread of disease[196] and famine.[197] Porous boundaries, the ability to mobilize, coordinate and communicate in cyberspace, the ease of transportation, the legal and illegal transnational arms trade[198] and transnational criminal networks, failed and failing states like Somalia and Yemen and the sanctuaries they provide, and access on the internet to information about how to make and use weapons are among the factors that contribute to the spread of terrorism and revolutionary violence. In sum, as Nederveen Pieterse concludes:

> With regard to violence, as with production, the state no longer holds the pre-eminent position it used to. Economies no longer necessarily hinge on the national market and states no longer hold a monopoly on the means of coercion. Criminal organizations and paramilitaries also organize flexibly, embrace the free market and source internationally for contraband, weapons, allies and profit. They too represent the 'magic of the market place'. Urban gangs, rural militias and warlords replay the game of states.[199]

As a result, in a globalized world the distinction between public and private violence and security is blurring, and "the 'Criminal–Industrial Complex' is anticipated to be a major growth industry."[200] Thus, the "essential problem of contemporary globalization is that technological capabilities and economic changes are ahead of institutional and political capacities; in a word growing capacities, also for conflict, and inadequate institutions."[201]

The United States and perhaps other countries may launch preventive or pre-emptive wars, but they will have only very limited success as long as poverty, religious and political extremism, and political oppression persist. These are the fundamental conditions that give rise to dissatisfaction, hatred, and violence, while globalization reduces the relative capacity of territorial states to respond effectively either domestically or beyond their borders to spreading forms of irregular violence.

The proliferation of weapons of mass destruction (WMD) will continue to be a major challenge in coming years, especially in an environment in which knowledge and information are ever more accessible. "Building an inefficient fission weapon capable of killing 100,000 in an urban center or cultivating cultures for biological use is child's play relative to the past."[202] US anti-proliferation policy is in tatters, and the use of force against potential proliferators may actually provoke such countries to acquire WMD for protection. North Korea has acquired nuclear weapons, and Iran is nearing that goal. When such countries acquire WMD, those who fear them may be convinced to develop their own WMD. Moreover, especially cash-poor nuclear states like North Korea will be tempted to provide other states or even terrorist groups with WMD. Although deterrence threats may prevent countries from using WMD, elusive terrorist groups are far more difficult to control, and are presumably more inclined to apocalyptic violence. Although renewed efforts are underway to reduce existing nuclear stockpiles, the real concern has shifted to potential new and decidedly irregular members of the WMD club.

Information and communication technologies constitute what are probably the most novel aspect and foundation of contemporary globalization. The next chapter examines these additional "essentials" of globalization.

NOTES

1 Alison Brysk, "Introduction: Transnational Threats and Opportunities," in A. Brysk, ed., *Globalization and Human Rights* (Berkeley, CA: University of California Press, 2002), 1.
2 Friedman, *The World Is Flat*, 1.
3 David Harvey, *A Brief History of Neoliberalism* (Oxford: Oxford University Press, 2005), 3.
4 Mark Baildon, "'Being Rooted and Living Globally': Singapore's Educational Reform as Post-Developmental Governance," in Rahil Ismail, Brian Shaw, and Ook Giok Ling, *Southeast Asian Culture and Heritage in a Globalising World: Diverging Identities in a Dynamic Region* (Farnham, UK: Ashgate Publishing, 2009), 73.
5 Alex Callinicos, "Globalization, Imperialism and the Capitalist World System," in Held and McGrew, eds., *Globalization Theory*, 65. See Giovanni Arrighi, *The Long Twentieth Century: Money, Power and the Origins of Our Time*, rev. edn (London: Verso, 2009). Castells, *The Rise of the Network Society*, 124, argues that the high concentration of R&D and of modern technologies in a few OECD countries "would run against the idea of a knowledge-based global economy, except under the form of a hierarchical division of labor between knowledge-based producers, located in a few 'global cities and regions,' and the rest of the world, made up of technologically dependent economies," except for intense communication among scientists around the world in a global epistemic community.
6 Harvey, *A Brief History of Neoliberalism*, 3.
7 Munck, *Globalization and Contestation*, 2.

8 One of those who take issue with this claim is Nathan M. Jensen who argues that "the fiscal competition among governments to attract FDI [foreign direct investment] has been grossly exaggerated" and ignores "the major political determinants of FDI flows." See N. Jensen, *Nation-States and the Multinational Corporation* (Princeton, NJ: Princeton University Press, 2006), 1.
9 See A. Claire Cutler, "Locating 'Authority' in the Global Political Economy," *International Studies Quarterly* 43:1 (March 1999), 59–81.
10 Robert W. Cox with Timothy J. Sinclair, *Approaches to World Order* (Cambridge: Cambridge University Press, 1996), 528. See also Rodrik, *Has Globalization Gone Too Far?* 6.
11 Michael Hardt and Antonio Negri, *Empire* (Cambridge, MA: Harvard University Press, 2000), 150.
12 Strange, *The Retreat of the State*, 4.
13 Layna Mosley, "The Political Economy of Globalization," in Held and McGrew, *Globalization Theory*, 107. See also James Anderson, "The Exaggerated Death of the Nation-State," in Anderson, Brook, and Cochrane, eds., *A Global World?*, 65–112.
14 Mosley, "The Political Economy of Globalization," 111. Concerning welfare, see Elmar Rieger and Stephan Leibfried, *Limits to Globalization* (Cambridge: Polity Press, 2003). See also Mauro F. Guillén, *The Limits of Convergence: Globalization and Organizational Change in Argentina, South Korea, and Spain* (Princeton, NJ: Princeton University Press, 2001).
15 Weiss, "Globalization and National Governance," 73–7.
16 Ibid., 64.
17 Linda Weiss, *The Myth of the Powerless State* (Ithaca, NY: Cornell University Press, 1998), 13.
18 John M. Hobson, "Disappearing Taxes or the 'Race to the Middle'? Fiscal Policy in the OECD," in Weiss, ed., *States in the Global Economy*, 37.
19 Duane Swank, "Withering Welfare? Globalisation, Political Economic Institutions, and Contemporary Welfare States," in Weiss, ed., *States in the Global Economy*, 58.
20 Risse, "Social Constructivism Meets Globalization," 128.
21 Ibid., 129.
22 Steger, *Globalisms*, 18, ix.
23 Jennifer Blanke, Clara Browne, Margareta Drzeniek Hanouz, Thierry Geiger, Irene Mia, and Xavier Sala-i-Martin, *The Global Competitiveness Report 2009–2010* (Davos: World Economic Forum, 2009), http://www3.weforum.org/docs/WEF_GlobalCompetitiveness Report_2010–11.pdf. Emphasis in original. The index uses data consisting of indicators such as strength of public and private institutions, population and per capita GDP, infrastructure such as airline passenger-carrying capacity and telephone lines per 100 population, macroeconomic stability such as government budget balance, national savings rate and inflation, health and primary education, and higher education and training.
24 Ibid., table 4, "The Global Competitiveness Index 2009–2010 rankings and 2008–2009 comparisons," http://www.weforum.org/pdf/GCR09/GCR20092010fullrankings.pdf.
25 Rosenau, *Along the Domestic–Foreign Frontier*, 145.
26 See James N. Rosenau, "Governance in a New Global Order," in David Held and Anthony McGrew, eds., *Governing Globalization: Power, Authority, and Global Governance* (Cambridge: Polity Press, 2002), 70–86.
27 Scholte, *Globalization*, 140.
28 Ian R. Douglas, "Globalization *as* Governance: Toward an Archaeology of Contemporary Political Reason," in Aseem Prakash and Jeffrey A. Hart, eds., *Globalization and Governance* (London: Routledge, 1999), 147. Emphasis in original.
29 Kimberley Process, "What Is the Kimberley Process?" http://www.kimberleyprocess.com/.
30 Sarah Childress and Sara Toth Stub, "World Diamond Monitors Hit Deadlock," *Wall Street Journal*, June 25, 2010, A8.
31 Rosenau, *Along the Domestic–Foreign Frontier*, 150, 151.
32 Scholte, *Globalization*, 202, 140.

33 For an overview of different approaches on the issue of governance, see especially Martin Hewson and Timothy J. Sinclair, *Approaches to Global Governance Theory* (Albany, NY: State University of New York Press, 1999), and Craig N. Murphy, "Global Governance: Poorly Done and Poorly Understood," *International Affairs* 76:4 (October 2000), 789–803.
34 "The Discreet Charms of the International Go-Between," *The Economist*, July 5, 2008, 71–2.
35 Robert O'Brien, Anne Marie Goetz, Jan Aart Scholte, and Marc Williams, *Contesting Global Governance* (Cambridge: Cambridge University Press, 2000), 3.
36 Stephen G. Brooks and William C. Wohlforth, "Reshaping the World Order: How Washington Should Reform International Institutions," *Foreign Affairs* 88:2 (March/April 2009), 51.
37 Susan M. Roberts, "Geo-Governance in Trade and Finance and Political Geographies of Dissent," in Herod, Ó Tuathail and Roberts, eds., *An Unruly World?*, 119. For a trenchant criticism of international economic institutions and their neoliberal bent, see Walden Bello, *Deglobalization: Ideas for a New World Economy*, rev. edn (London: Zed Books, 2005).
38 Roberts, "Geo-Governance in Trade and Finance and Political Geographies of Dissent," 119–20.
39 William Easterly, "What Did Structural Adjustment Adjust? The Association of Policies and Growth with Repeated IMF and World Bank Adjustment Loans," *Journal of Development Economics* 76:1 (February 2005), 2.
40 Anthony Faiola, "A Bigger, Bolder Role," *Washington National Weekly Edition*, April 27–May 3, 2009, 22.
41 Bob Davis, "IMF's Reach Spreads to Western Europe," *Wall Street Journal*, May 11, 2010, A15, and "High Stakes," *The Economist*, May 15, 2010, 85.
42 See "The Sad End of the Party," *The Economist*, May 8, 2010, 51–2, and Stephen Fidler, "EU Bailout Sparks New Challenge in Free-Spending Countries," *Wall Street Journal*, May 11, 2010, A15.
43 The term "emerging markets" was coined by Antoine W. van Agtmael in 1981. Agtmael, Chairman and Chief Investment Officer of Emerging Markets Management LLC, recalls that he rejected the term "Third World" because it "suggested stagnation; 'emerging markets' suggested progress, uplift and dynamism." See "A Bigger World: A Special Report on Globalization," *The Economist*, September 20, 2008, 10.
44 See "Wrestling for Influence," *The Economist*, July 5, 2008, 33–6.
45 Edmund L. Andrews, "Global Economic Forum to Expand Permanently," *New York Times*, September 25, 2009, http://www.nytimes.com/2009/09/25/world/25summit.html.
46 BRIC was coined by Jim O'Neill of Goldman Sachs. See "The Trillion-Dollar Club," *The Economist*, April 17, 2010, 64–6.
47 "Not Just Straw Men," *The Economist*, June 20, 2009, 63–4.
48 Bob Davis, "IMF Gets New Role of Serving the G-20," *Wall Street Journal*, October 5, 2009, A10.
49 Bob Davis, "IMF Mulls a Global Bank Tax," *Wall Street Journal*, October 3, 2009, A8.
50 "Beyond Bretton Woods 2," *The Economist*, November 6, 2010, 85–7.
51 Doreen Carvajal, "Interpol and U.N. Back 'Global Policing Doctrine'," *New York Times*, October 11, 2009, http://www.nytimes.com/2009/10/12/world/europe/12iht-interpol.html.
52 Kevin Sullivan and Mary Jordan, "Diseases Travel Fast, but So Do Tools to Fight Them," *Washington Post National Weekly Edition*, May 4–10, 2009, 13.
53 Lester Salamon, S. Wojciech Sokolowski, and Regina List, "Global Civil Society: An Overview," in L. Salamon, S. Wojciech Sokolowski, and R. List, and Associates, *Global Civil Society: Dimensions of the Nonprofit Sector*, vol. 2 (Bloomfield, CT: Kumarian Press, 2004), 3.
54 John Keane, "Cosmocracy and Global Civil Society," in Gideon Baker and David Chandler, eds., *Global Civil Society: Contested Futures* (New York: Routledge, 2005), 35.

55 Jonathan Fox, "Transnational Civil Society Campaigns and the World Bank Inspection Panel," in Brysk, ed., *Globalization and Human Rights*, 172.
56 Ibid., 179, 180, 182.
57 Stephen D. Krasner, "Structural Causes and Regime Consequences: Regimes as Intervening Variables," in S. D. Krasner, ed., *International Regimes* (Ithaca, NY: Cornell University Press, 1983), 2. See also Andreas Hasenclever, Peter Mayer, and Volker Rittberger, *Theories of International Regimes* (Cambridge: Cambridge University Press, 1997).
58 Thomas G. Weiss and Ramesh Thakur, *Global Governance and the UN* (Bloomington, IN: Indiana University Press, 2010), 6
59 William K. Tabb, *Economic Governance in the Age of Globalization* (New York: Columbia University Press, 2004), 151.
60 Ibid., 156.
61 Ibid., 157, 158. See also Axtmann, "The State of the State," 271. For corporate self-regulation, see Virginia Haufler, "Globalization and Industry Self-Regulation," in Miles Kahler and David A. Lake, eds., *Governance in a Global Economy* (Princeton, NJ: Princeton University Press, 2003), 226–54.
62 *World Investment Report 2009*, 17 and table 1.7, 19.
63 Alan M. Rugman and Alain Verbeke, "A Perspective on Regional and Global Strategies of Multinational Enterprises," *Journal of International Business Studies* 35:1 (January 2004), 6–7.
64 Ibid., table 2, 8. Several other firms may be global, but there were insufficient data to determine this.
65 Ibid., 6.
66 Medard Gabel and Henry Bruner, *Globalinc: An Atlas of Multinational Corporations* (New York: New Press, 2003), 4.
67 Ibid., 5.
68 *World Investment Report 2009*, table 1.9, 52.
69 "A Bigger World," 3–4.
70 Christopher A. Bartlett and Sumantra Ghoshal, *Managing Across Borders* (Cambridge, MA: Harvard Business School Press, 1998), 6–7.
71 Ibid., 7.
72 Christopher A. Bartlett, Sumantra Ghoshal, and Julian Birkinshaw, *Transnational Management*, 4th edn (New York: McGraw-Hill/Irwin, 2003), 556–644.
73 Weiss and Thakur, *Global Governance and the UN*, 29.
74 Held, McGrew, Goldblatt, and Perraton, *Global Transformations*, 69–70.
75 "Burgeoning Bourgeoisie: A Special Report on the New Middle Classes in Emerging Markets," *The Economist*, February 14, 2009, 4.
76 Barry K. Gills, "Democratizing Globalization and Globalizing Democracy," *Annals of the American Academy of Political and Social Science*, 581 (May 2002), 159, 167.
77 Paul Collier, *Wars, Guns, and Votes* (New York: HarperCollins, 2009), 11, 15.
78 Harold James reminds us "ideas move in great pendulum swings, and that triumphalism invariably provokes a sharp reaction." See H. James, *The End of Globalization: Lessons from the Great Depression* (Cambridge, MA: Harvard University Press, 2001), 210.
79 "Freedom in the World 2010: Global Erosion of Freedom," *Freedom House*, January 12, 2010, http://www.freedomhouse.org/template.cfm?page=505.
80 "Press Release: Freedom in the World 2010: Global Erosion of Freedom," January 12, 2010, http://www.freedomhouse.org/template.cfm?page=70&release=1120.
81 See Christine Hauser, "New Service Lets Voices from Egypt Be Heard," *New York Times*, February 1, 2011, http://www.nytimes.com/2011/02/02/world/middleeast/02twitter.html.
82 For an analysis of how INGOs tend to be federations of national NGOs and how they expand in order to secure additional resources, see Johanna Siméant, "What Is Going Global? The Internationalization of French NGOs 'Without Borders'," *Review of International Political Economy* 12:5 (December 2005), 851–83.

83 There are innumerable definitions of "global civil society." See Rupert Taylor, "Interpreting Civil Society," *Voluntas* 13 (December 2002), 339–47, and Ashwani Kumar, Jan Aart Scholte, Mary Kaldor, Maries Glasius, Hakan Seckinelgin, and Helmut K. Anheier, eds., *Global Society Yearbook 2009: Poverty and Activism* (London: Sage Publications, 2009).

84 Lester M. Salamon, Helmut K. Anheier, and Associates, "Civil Society in Comparative Perspective," in Lester M. Salamon, Regina List, Stefan Toepler, S. Wojciech Sokolowski and Associates, *Global Civil Society: Dimensions of the Nonprofit Sector* (West Hartford, CT: Kumarian Press, 1999), 4.

85 Peter Willetts, "Transnational Actors and International Organizations in Global Politics," in Baylis, Smith, and Owens, eds., *The Globalization of World Politics*, 332.

86 Randall Germain and Michael Kenny, "Understanding Global Civil Society: Contestation, Citizenship, Governance," in Germain and Kenny, eds., *The Idea of Global Civil Society*, 197. See also Darren J. O'Byrne, *The Dimensions of Global Citizenship* (London: Frank Cass, 2003).

87 John Keane, *Global Civil Society?* (Cambridge: Cambridge University Press, 2003), 197.

88 Alejandro Colás, *International Civil Society* (Cambridge: Polity Press, 2002), 40.

89 Mary Kaldor, "The Idea of Global Civil Society," in Gideon Baker and David Chandler, eds., *Global Civil Society* (New York: Routledge, 2005), 103–13.

90 Alejandro Colás, "Global Civil Society: Analytical Category or Normative Concept?" in Baker and Chandler, eds., *Global Civil Society*, 17.

91 Adam A. Seligman, "Civil Society as Idea and Ideal," in Simon Chambers and Will Kymlicka, eds., *Alternative Conceptions of Civil Society* (Princeton, NJ: Princeton University Press, 2001), 1–12.

92 Keane, *Global Civil Society?*, 62.

93 Gideon Baker, "Saying Global Civil Society with Rights," in Baker and Chandler, eds., *Global Civil Society*, 115.

94 John Naisbitt, *Mind Set! Eleven Ways to Change the Way You See – and Create – the Future* (New York: HarperCollins, 2009), 164.

95 Martin Shaw, "Media and Public Sphere Without Borders? News Coverage and Power from Kurdistan to Kosovo," in Brigitte L. Nacos and Robert Y. Shapiro, eds., *Decisionmaking in a Glass House* (Oxford: Rowman & Littlefield, 2000), 32.

96 Martin Shaw, *Civil Society and Media in Global Crises* (London: Pinter, 1996), 8. Transnational media do not necessarily entail homogenized interpretations of meaning.

97 Gideon Baker and David Chandler, "Introduction: Global Civil Society and the Future of World Politics," in Baker and Chandler, eds., *Global Civil Society*, 1.

98 Sassen, *Territory, Authority, Rights*, 269. Emphasis added.

99 See Margaret E. Keck and Kathryn Sikkink, *Activists Beyond Borders* (Ithaca: Cornell University Press, 1998), and Thomas Risse, Stephen C. Ropp, and Kathryn Sikkink, *The Power of Human Rights* (Cambridge: Cambridge University Press, 1999).

100 Bill & Melinda Gates Foundation, "Foundation Fact Sheet," http://www.gatesfoundation.org/about/Pages/foundation-fact-sheet.aspx. See also Robert A. Guth and Roger Thurow, "Weaving Africa's Breadbasket," *Wall Street Journal*, September 25, 2008, A18. For an analysis of the impact of the Gates Foundation, see "The Side-Effects of Doing Good," *The Economist*, February 23, 2008, 77–8.

101 Clinton Foundation, *Annual Report 2009*, http://www.clintonfoundation.org/files/reports_cf/annualReport_cf_2009.pdf, 50.

102 See Andrew Jacobs, "Hepatitis Group Is Harassed in China," *New York Times*, July 31, 2009, http://www.nytimes.com/2009/07/31/world/asia/31hepatitis.html, "Open Constitution Closed," *The Economist*, July 25, 2009, 38–9, and "Bertelsmann Stiftung, BTI 2008 – Russia Country Report" (Gütersloh: Bertelsmann Stiftung, 2007), http://www.bertelsmann-transformation-index.de/159.0.html.

103 Hugo Dobson, "Social Movements and Society in Japan," in Catarina Kinnvall and Kristina Jönsson, eds., *Globalization and Democratization in Asia* (New York: Routledge, 2002), 146, 147.

104 Doug Guthrie, *China and Globalization* (New York: Routledge, 2006), 271.
105 Munck, *Globalization and Contestation*, 77.
106 Ibid., 78.
107 Cited in Patrick E. Tyler, "Hillary Clinton in China, Details Abuse of Women," *New York Times*, September 6, 1995, A1. As US Secretary of State, Mrs. Clinton has also highlighted gender issues. See Mary Beth Sheridan, "Women's Rights as Foreign Policy," *Washington Post Weekly Edition*, August 24–30, 2009, 18, and US Department of State, "Hillary Rodham Clinton, Remarks at the UN Commission on the Status of Women," March 12, 2010, http://www.state.gov/secretary/rm/2010/03/138320.htm.
108 Munck, *Globalization and Contestation*, 81.
109 Castells, *The Power of Identity*, 192–302.
110 Wolf, *Why Globalization Works*, 6.
111 Jagdish Bhagwati, *In Defense of Globalization* (Oxford: Oxford University Press, 2004), 268. Emphasis in original.
112 Martin Shaw, *Theory of the Global State: Globality as an Unfinished Revolution* (Cambridge: Cambridge University Press, 2000), 264.
113 Rudra Sil, "Globalization, the State, and Industrial Relations: Common Challenge, Divergent Transitions," in T. V. Paul, G. John Ikenberry, and John A. Hall, eds., *The Nation-State in Question* (Princeton, NJ: Princeton University Press, 2003), 286.
114 Colás, *International Civil Society*, 62.
115 Ibid., 153.
116 Kenneth Anderson and David Rieff, "'Global Civil Society': A Sceptical View," in Anheier, Glasius, and Kaldor, eds., *Global Civil Society 2004/5*, 26.
117 Douglas W. Blum, *National Identity and Globalization* (Cambridge, Cambridge University Press, 2007), 12.
118 Sarah Armstrong, "Magazines, Cultural Policy and Globalization: The Forced Retreat of the States," *Canadian Public Policy* 26:3 (September 2000), 370.
119 Robert J. Lieber and Ruth E. Weisberg, "Globalization, Culture, and Identities in Crisis," *International Journal of Politics, Culture, and Society* 16:2 (Winter 2002), 281.
120 Joseph S. Nye, Jr., *Foreign Affairs* 88:4 (July/August 2009), 160.
121 Benjamin Barber, *Jihad vs. McWorld* (New York: Times Books, 1995), 23.
122 Scholte, *Globalization*, 16. Emphasis in original.
123 Ibid., 58.
124 Niall Ferguson, "Sinking Globalization," 73, argues that the United States is "an empire in all but name." See also Held and McGrew, "Introduction," 7. See Ferguson and Mansbach, "Superpower, Hegemony, Empire," Ferguson and Mansbach, *A World of Polities*, 200–15.
125 Callinicos, "Globalization, Imperialism and the Capitalist World System," 62. For a discussion of dissatisfaction with the Washington Consensus, see Robin Broad, "The Washington Consensus Meets the Global Backlash: Shifting Debates and Policies," *Globalizations* 1:2 (December 2004), 129–54.
126 G. John Ikenberry, "Globalization as American Hegemony," in Held and McGrew, eds., *Globalization Theory*, 41.
127 Ibid.
128 Ibid., 57.
129 Rosenau, *Distant Proximities*, 188, 189.
130 Ronald Grigor Suny, "Provisional Stabilities: The Politics of Identities in Post-Soviet Eurasia," *International Security* 24:3 (Winter 1999/2000), 144.
131 Cowen, *Creative Destruction*, 4.
132 Rosenau, *Distant Proximities*, 97–8.
133 Tomlinson, "Globalization and Cultural Analysis," 161. Emphasis in original. Castells argues that "resistance" identities can be differentiated from "legitimizing" and "project" identities. See Castells, *The Power of Identity*, 8.
134 Risse, "Social Constructivism Meets Globalization," 135.

135 Mike Featherstone, *Undoing Culture: Globalization, Postmodernism and Identity* (London: Sage, 1995), 102.
136 Robert McCrum, *Globish: How the English Language Became the World's Language* (New York: W. W. Norton, 2010), 277, 5.
137 Ibid., 11.
138 Ibid., 7.
139 Lieber and Weisberg, "Globalization, Culture, and Identities in Crisis," 277.
140 Randolph Kluver and Wayne Fu, "The Cultural Globalization Index," *Foreign Affairs* (February 2004), Web Exclusive, http://www.foreignpolicy.com/story/cms.php?story_id=2494#.
141 Harm De Blij, *The Power of Place: Geography, Destiny, and Globalization's Rough Landscape* (Oxford: Oxford University Press, 2009), 31. Of major developed countries, Japan has probably been the most immune to English linguistic dominance. Ibid., 49.
142 Kien-hong Yu points out that "there are many Chinese characters that cannot find their equivalent in English." See *International Governance, Regimes and Globalization*, 80.
143 "Internet World Users by Language," *Internet World Stats* (2009), http://www.internetworldstats.com/stats7.htm.
144 De Blij, *The Power of Place*, 38.
145 Michael Talalay, "Technology and Globalization: Assessing Patterns of Interaction" in Randall D. Germain ed., *Globalization and its Critics* (New York: St. Martin's Press, 2000), 220.
146 Stephen Baker and Inka Resch, with Kate Carlisle and Katharine A. Schmidt, "The Great English Divide," *Business Week Online*, August 13, 2001, http://www.businessweek.com/magazine/content/01_33/b3745009.htm.
147 Blum, *National Identity and Globalization*, 163.
148 Mike Featherstone, *Consumer Culture and Postmodernism* (London: Sage, 2002), 151.
149 Jacques Maurais and Michael A. Morris, "Introduction," in J. Maurais and M. A Morris, eds., *Languages in a Globalising World* (Cambridge: Cambridge University Press, 2003), 9.
150 "When Nobody Understands," *The Economist*, October 25, 2008, 73. See also Sam Roberts, "Listening to (and Saving) the World's Languages," *New York Times*, April 28, 2010, http://www.nytimes.com/2010/04/29/nyregion/29lost.html.
151 Joshua A. Fishman, "The New Linguistic Order," *Foreign Policy* 113 (Winter 1998–9), 32.
152 Martin van Creveld, *The Rise and Decline of the State* (Cambridge: Cambridge University Press, 1999), 141–2.
153 John Gerard Ruggie, "International Regimes, Transactions, and Change: Embedded Liberalism in the Postwar Economic Order," *International Organization* 36:2 (Spring 1982), 393.
154 Sean Ó Riain, "States and Markets in an Era of Globalization," *Annual Review of Sociology* 26 (2000), 190.
155 Philip G. Cerny, "Globalization and Other Stories," 65. Pioneering research about transgovernmental politics includes Robert W. Russell, "Transnational Interaction in the International Monetary System, 1960–1972," *International Organization* 27:4 (Autumn 1973), 431–64, C. Robert Dickerman, "Transnational Governmental Challenge and Response in Scandinavia and North America," *International Organization* 30:2 (Spring 1976), 213–40, Raymond F. Hopkins, "The International Role of 'Domestic' Bureaucracy," *International Organization* 30:3 (Summer 1976), 405–32, and Robert O. Keohane, "The International Energy Agency: State Influence and Transgovernmental Politics," *International Organization* 32:4 (Autumn 1978), 929–51.
156 Cerny, "What Next for the State?" 123–4. Emphasis in original.
157 Sassen, *Territory, Authority, Rights*, 298. Another area of transgovernmental bureaucratic cooperation is in civil liberties. See also Sassen, "Places and Spaces of the Global," 88–90, and Abraham L. Newman, "Building Transnational Civil Liberties: Transgovernmental

Entrepreneurs and the European Data Privacy Directive," *International Organization* 62:1 (Winter 2008), 103–30.
158 See Kjell Goldmann, *Transforming the European Nation-State* (London: Sage Publications, 1991).
159 Charles Krauthammer, "The Unipolar Moment," *Foreign Affairs* 70:1 (Winter 1990/1), 23–33.
160 "The United States of Entrepreneurs: Special Report on Entrepreneurship," *The Economist*, March 14, 2009, 9.
161 See Gideon Rachman, "This Time It's for Real," *Foreign Policy* 184 (January/February 2011), 59–61.
162 Cited in David E. Sanger, "Deficits May Alter U.S. Politics and Global Power," *New York Times*, February 1, 2009, http://www.nytimes.com/2010/02/02/us/politics/02deficit.html.
163 See Keith Bradsher, "China Losing Taste for Debt from U.S.," *New York Times*, January 7, 2009, http://www.nytimes.com/2009/01/08/business/worldbusiness/08yuan.html.
164 See "A Wary Respect: A Special Report on China and America," *The Economist*, October 24, 2009, 5–6.
165 Edward Wong, "China's Export Economy Begins Turning Inward," *New York Times*, June 24, 2010, http://www.nytimes.com/2010/06/25/world/asia/25china.html.
166 Rebecca Blumenstein, Andrew Browne, and Dinny McMahon, "China Deflects Pressure for Yuan Rise," *Wall Street Journal*, September 1, 2010, A9.
167 Rachman, "This Time It's for Real," 59.
168 See Anand Giridharadas, "Land of Gandhi Asserts Itself as Global Military Power," *New York Times*, September 22, 2008, http://www.nytimes.com/2008/09/22/world/asia/22iht-22india.16352927.html, and Jeremy Page and Julian E. Barnes, "China Shows Its Growing Might," *Wall Street Journal*, January 12, 2011, A1, A10.
169 Cited in Jeremy Page, "China's Army Extends Sway," *Wall Street Journal*, October 4, 2010, A10.
170 "Distant Horizons," *The Economist*, April 25, 2009, 47–8.
171 See "Getting Their Goat," *The Economist*, September 18, 2010, 56, and "Deng's Heirs Ignore His Advice," *The Economist*, September 25, 2010, 54.
172 This was evident in China's temporary ban on the export of rare earths to Japan and the US. See Keith Bradsher, "China Is Said to Widen Its Embargo of Minerals," *New York Times*, October 19, 2010, http://www.nytimes.com/2010/10/20/business/global/20rare.html.
173 See Mark Landler and Sewell Chan, "Taking Harder Stance Toward China, Obama Lines Up Allies," *New York Times*, October 25, 2010, http://www.nytimes.com/2010/10/26/world/asia/26china.html.
174 Mark Landler, Jim Yardley, and Michael Wines, "China's Fast Rise Leads Neighbors to Join Forces," *New York Times*, October 30, 2010, http://www.nytimes.com/2010/10/31/world/asia/31china.html.
175 See Mark Landler, "Leaving for Asia, Clinton Says China is Not an Adversary," *New York Times*, October 28, 2010, http://www.nytimes.com/2010/10/29/world/29diplo.html.
176 Andrew F. Krepinevich, Jr., "The Pentagon's Wasting Assets," *Foreign Affairs* 88:4 (July/August 2009), 18.
177 John Pomfret, "China's Strident Tone Raises Concerns among Western Governments' Analysts," *Washington Post*, January 31, 2010, http://www.washingtonpost.com/wp-dyn/content/article/2010/01/30/AR2010013002443.html.
178 Roger C. Altman, "Globalization in Retreat: Further Geopolitical Consequences of the Financial Crisis," *Foreign Affairs* 88:4 (July/August 2009), 2. See also Altman, "The Great Crash, 2008," *Foreign Affairs* 88:1 (January/February 2009), 2–14.
179 Altman, "Globalization in Retreat," 3.
180 Paul Krugman, "The Great Illusion," *New York Times*, August 15, 2008, http://www.nytimes.com/2008/08/15/opinion/15krugman.html. See also Keith Bradsher, "U.S.

Deal with Taiwan Has China Retaliating," *New York Times*, January 30, 2010, http://www.nytimes.com/2010/01/31/world/asia/31china.html.
181 See "'Toxic' US Ship Banned in India," *BBC News*, November 10, 2009, http://news.bbc.co.uk/2/hi/8351957.stm.
182 "Talking Rubbish," Special Report on Waste, *The Economist*, February 26, 2009, 3. See also Juliet Eilperin, "Finding Space for All in Our Crowded Seas," *Washington Post*, May 4, 2009, http://www.washingtonpost.com/wp-dyn/content/article/2009/05/03/AR2009050301930.html. For debris in space, see "Flying Blind," *The Economist*, February 21, 2009, 10.
183 Keith Bradsher, "China's Incinerators Loom as a Global Hazard," *New York Times*, August 11, 2009, http://www.nytimes.com/2009/08/12/business/energy-environment/12incinerate.html.
184 See Steven Yearly, "The Transnational Politics of the Environment," in Anderson, Brook and Cochrane, eds., *A Global World?* 209–48.
185 Victor D. Cha, "Globalization and the Study of International Security," *Journal of Peace Research* 37:3 (May 2000), 394.
186 John M. Broder, "Climate Change Seen as Threat to U.S. Security," *New York Times*, August 9, 2009, http://www.nytimes.com/2009/08/09/science/earth/09climate.html.
187 Ulrich Beck, *World at Risk* (Cambridge: Polity Press, 2009), 76. See also Beck, *Risk Society* (London: Sage Publications, 1992).
188 Beck, *World at Risk*, 77, 78.
189 Ibid., 47.
190 Ibid., 66.
191 Ibid. Emphasis in original.
192 Jonathan Kirshner, "Globalization, Power, and Prospect," in Kirshner, ed. *Globalization and National Security*, 335.
193 Ibid.
194 Cha, "Globalization and the Study of International Security," 393–4.
195 See Audrey Kurth Cronin, "Behind the Curve: Globalization and International Terrorism," *International Security* 27:3 (Winter 2002/3), 30–58.
196 See Katherine F. Smith, Dov F. Sax, Steven D. Gaines, Vanina Guernier, and Jean-François Guégan, "Globalization of Human Infectious Disease," *Ecology* 88:8 (August 2007), 1903–10.
197 Andrew Martin, "So Much Food, So Much Hunger," *New York Times*, September 19, 2009, http://www.nytimes.com/2009/09/20/weekinreview/20martin.html.
198 Thom Shanker, "Despite Slump, U.S. Role as Top Arms Supplier Grows," *New York Times*, September 7, 2009, http://www.nytimes.com/2009/09/07/world/07weapons.html. As for illegal arms, according to Naím, *Illicit*, 56, the "illicit weapons trade looks very much like an adaptation to the political conditions and commercial possibilities of globalization."
199 Jan Nederveen Pieterse, "Globalization, Kitsch and Conflict: Technologies of Work, War and Politics," *Review of International Political Economy* 9:1 (March 2002), 2.
200 Ibid., 3.
201 Ibid., 35–6.
202 Cha, "Globalization and the Study of International Security," 396.

CHAPTER 4

Globalization and information and communication technologies

> Technological change has played a leading role in devaluing territory with regard to the world economy, warfare, political mobilization, and identity formation – and thus is one of the major reasons why the task of remapping postinternational global politics is so urgently required.[1]

> It is technology that has profoundly altered the scale on which human affairs take place, allowing more people to do more things in less time and with wider repercussions than could have been imagined in earlier eras. It is technology, in short, that has fostered an interdependence of local, national, and international communities that is far greater than any previously experienced.[2]

Technological change has been a driver as well as a consequence of globalization (as we have defined the process) since ancient times. The inventions of improved tools, better ships, more effective weapons, and sophisticated machines have been instrumental in shrinking space, making connections, and generally moving history along. Arguably, technological change has always been a necessary but not sufficient "cause" of globalization. Wolf rightly cautions us to beware the trap of "technological determinism" that he attributes to Thomas Friedman.[3] Technology has provided the *means*, although the main *motives* for forward momentum, as Chanda suggests, have been such factors as trade, religion, adventure, and war.[4] Technological change has tended to be cumulative and often has reverberated across a wide range of human activity. The printing press, for example, revolutionized the diffusion of information and helped to undermine elite control of politics and religion. Of course, some subjectivity and, therefore, differences of opinion are inevitable whenever one highlights particular inventions and their effects. Rather than emphasizing the role of information technologies, for instance, Vaclav Smil argues that the "prime movers of [economic] globalization" were "high-compression non-sparking internal combustion engines invented by Rudolf Diesel" and gas turbines, owing to their role in making possible ever larger sea-going vessels and jet aircraft respectively.[5]

Most of those who focus on the uniqueness of contemporary globalization see the microelectronic revolution as the principal technological feature of globalization. To some extent, they are surely correct, although we would stress that such technologies are themselves the fruit of long-term historical processes.

The communications network of the internet originally developed for use by the Pentagon burst upon the global scene only in 1995 and soon became worldwide, enabling and enhancing the globalization of business and professional services.[6] Recognition of the globalization of production and demand came with the Information and Technology Agreement in 1997, when forty-four countries accounting for more than 90 percent of trade agreed to eliminate all tariffs on six categories of key products related to ICT (Information and Communication Technologies) by 2000. Certainly the story of the globalization of the US economy, as well as dynamic economies elsewhere such as China and India, has been intimately bound up with ICT.[7] The technology sector has seen extraordinarily rapid innovation and dramatic declines in quality-adjusted prices of computer hardware and software. Such innovation, according to the Organisation for Economic Co-operation and Development (OECD), is intimately associated with progress in education, research, and infrastructure that supports and diffuses knowledge.[8] Michael Connors views those countries that are developing these new technologies as involved in a competitive "race to the intelligent state," in which "info-tigers" like Israel and India move to the fore.[9] Access to advanced technology facilitates acquisition of technological skills, and income inequality both between and within countries appears to be related to the level of workers' technological skills.[10]

The role of powerful computers and microelectronic technologies in shrinking geographic distance and transcending sovereign boundaries is reflected in new terminology ranging from "cyberspace," "electronic highway," "electronic mail," "infobahn," "infosphere," and "information superhighway," to "online community," "virtual community," and "virtual reality." ICT enables individuals and groups to communicate almost instantaneously by email, fax, and cellular and satellite telephones, and also to move vast amounts of money and information with equal ease. Technological diffusion also encompasses satellites for television and radio, as well as global marketing of films and television programs. The internet and especially its social networks like Facebook (which is the second most-visited internet site after Google)[11] and Twitter permit diasporas to communicate and keep alive their identities and languages, thereby reducing the pressure to assimilate within dominant cultures and regimes.[12] ICT obviously plays a critically important role in linking the emerging global corporate and political elite as well as the elites within diaspora communities such as Indian and Chinese scientists, educators, and business people.[13] Indeed, with over 660 million users by 2011, Facebook has been described as an "imagined community," "a liberal polity," and a virtual cyber-state.[14] Perhaps the most extraordinary aspect of these communities is that, unlike traditional media that report news, Twitter, YouTube, and the like, not only report events, but also participate in them and "make news."

By any measurement the rate of internet expansion has accelerated over time. As of 1996, there were fewer than 10 million internet hosts. By the beginning of the year 2000, there were over 72 million, and only six months later over 93 million. By mid-2009, this figure had soared to over 681 million.[15]

As of the end of June 2010, there were almost 2 billion internet users, unequally distributed globally in the manner shown in Table 4.1. Asia hosts the largest number, with over 828 million internet users. This includes 384 million internet users and 346 million broadband subscribers in China alone.[16] By contrast, Africa and the Middle East host relatively few users, some 111 and 63 million respectively. The "digital divide" is even more evident in internet penetration, which ranges from a high of over 77 percent in North America, 61 percent in Oceania, and 58 percent in Europe to a low of under 11 percent in Africa.

The divide is, however, likely to diminish rapidly as cell phones with internet capacity become increasingly available in the developing world.[17] Thus, even though relatively few Africans at present have access to the internet or to mobile phones, the numbers who do are increasing dramatically. Some 22 percent of Kenyans, for example, already bank by mobile phone, and Safaricom's M-PESA service transfers the equivalent of 11 percent of Kenya's gross domestic product (GDP) annually.[18] "Since 2000," writes Ethan Kapstein, "growth in cell-phone usage has been greater in Africa than in any other region of the world: it has increased tenfold, to about 80 million subscribers. Internet growth has been even more impressive: the number of people with Internet access has quadrupled since 2000."[19] Moreover, until recently, the internet was limited to Latin script. Now, however, in the spirit of globalization, Arabic and Cyrillic scripts have been added, and it is likely that in the near future Chinese logograms will follow.[20]

Table 4.1 Internet usage statistics

Region	Population	Internet users	Penetration (% Population)
Asia	3,834,792,852	828,930,856	21.6%
Europe	813,319,511	475,121,735	58.4 %
North America	344,124,450	266,224,500	77.4 %
Latin America	550,924,250	195,042,230	30.4 %
Africa	1,013,779,050	110,948,420	10.9%
Middle East	212,336,924	63,240,946	29.8 %
Oceania, Australia	34,700,201	21,272,470	61.3 %
Total world	6,845,609,960	1,970,837,003	28.8 %

Source: Internet World Stats, estimates for August 31, 2010. Copyright © 2010, www.internetworldstats.com.

Could Alexander Graham Bell have imagined that someday people would acquire Infosat's MSAT Mobile System that "extends modern fixed and mobile, wireless voice, fax, and data services throughout North and Central America including the northern tip of South America, Hawaii, the Caribbean and Alaska,"[21] or make and receive calls and email from vehicles, planes, or ships, or an Inmarsat mobile satellite service that provides telephone and fax access to over 98 percent of the world, including areas beyond the reach of any other communications?[22] Or that the development of credit card scanners that plug into cell phones would enable individuals to settle debts without cash or checks wherever they might find themselves.[23]

In sum, for better or worse, the internet, cell and mobile phones, and other new technologies are revolutionizing the way we produce, sell, consume, communicate, learn, educate, socialize, and coordinate our lives.

ICT, GEOGRAPHY, AND TERRITORY

ICT technologies have reduced geography and physical distance in politics, economics, and war and have rendered territory less important than in any previous historical epoch. The decreased utility of physically occupying territory may help reduce the incentives to conquer and directly control other countries. To be sure, territory will remain important if it contains strategic raw materials like lithium, coltan (Columbite-tantalite), or oil or, like national homelands and religious shrines, is symbolically central to particular identities and cultures. The key point, however, is that, with contemporary ICT, distance poses diminishing obstacles to innumerable global activities ranging from transacting business and mobilizing political activity to projecting military force and exchanging ideas and information. Moreover, the boundaries of states are ever less able to keep out subversive ideas, ideologies, and practices. Ultimately, with "the relative decline of distance and territory," we may "have moved from a world of spatially delimited 'enemies' to a world of spatially diffuse and omnipresent 'dangers' – global environmental destruction, drugs, terrorism."[24] Merely adjusting to new conceptions of geography is, by itself, difficult enough.

Naeem Inayatullah and David Blaney declare that "alternative constructions of space – as overlapping, heterogeneous, and relative – may compete with modern visions that subscribe to the magic of straight lines." Consequently, "the separate and overlapping character of group relations and ambitions might be recognized and negotiated where relative notions of space . . . are also put into play."[25] But, why, as they ask, should we accept "the assumption that property/sovereignty should be governed by the logic of straight lines"? Instead, we should be keenly aware that "territorial spaces are historically constructed, entailing a set of social relationships and processes, and not a universal and fixed category within a Euclidean geometry or Newtonian cosmology."[26]

Global politics no longer reflects (if it ever really did, in practice) the neat, exclusive territorial boxes and the solid lines between countries on state-centric maps. We need to rethink this and design a wide variety of maps that take account of many forms of political activity. Considering globalization and the processes and links that it engenders, it is important," as Held suggests, "to explore the way in which the sovereign state is now criss-crossed by a vast array of networks and organizations that have been established to regulate and manage diverse areas of international and transnational activity – trade, communications, crime, and so on."[27] "Political communities," he continues, "can no longer be considered (if they ever could with any validity) as simply 'discrete worlds'; they are enmeshed in complex structures of overlapping forces, relations and networks," and "even where sovereignty still appears intact, states do not retain sole command of what transpires within their own territorial boundaries."[28]

SKILLED AND PARTICIPANT PUBLICS

Knowledge and skills are spreading as a result of the explosion in political communication, mobilization, and participation. Whether or not there is a "democratic deficit" in a globalized world, as some contend, it is also the case that individuals have been increasingly empowered. The communications and transportation revolutions enable many more people, even in remote corners of the globe, to be informed about the world, form opinions about events, and get involved in politics in ways that were previously unimaginable. "Globalization processes," as Mike Featherstone observes, "not only mean the intensification of flows of goods, people, information, data, money but also academic knowledge too," frequently from the West "to the peripheries, with raw data moving the other way."[29]

Rosenau views information, communication, and transportation technologies and more education at all levels as producing a revolution in human skills that, among its consequences, is raising questions about the legitimacy of the sovereign state or at least those who presume to govern it.[30] He argues that the impact is mainly at what he calls the "micro level," that is, at the level of individuals. The skills being acquired "range from advanced learning to street smarts, from reflective to judgmental capacities, from technical training to native intelligence, and from experiential wisdom to intellectual curiosity."[31] Such skills, Rosenau believes, do not necessarily spread democratic or capitalist values. Instead, the "presumption is, rather, that individuals and officials are differently, if not more, skilled in terms of their culture."[32]

Cable and satellite television provide exposure to an almost infinite variety of opinion and information. And, with the increasing availability of inexpensive computers – some powered by hand cranking or even bicycle in the developing world – the internet is becoming the most important tool of all in facilitating the exchange of views, the dissemination of information and propaganda, and the mobilization and coordination of activities.[33] Internet blogs and bloggers are hugely influential in spreading a vast diversity of opinion. Before leaving this issue, we should also recognize that many people may choose not to be exposed to a diversity of views and can more that in the past limit themselves to blogs, sites, and television stations that reflect only the views of others like themselves.

Skilled and self-confident individuals do not necessarily translate into conventional democratic institutions and practices such as political parties and formal elections, but, along with the growth of a global middle class, make more possible the spread of democratic values. Although globalization may weaken conventional forms of state-based democracy, access to greater information and opinion is likely to intensify the desire of people to control their destinies. Thus, political participation will continue to grow and manifest itself in unconventional ways ranging from street demonstrations and formation of new political parties to terrorism. The internet, as we shall see, is particularly useful as a means of mobilizing and coordinating such activities.

One consequence of greater popular awareness, we have emphasized, is that it will become ever more difficult for states to conquer and occupy one another as they have for centuries. Colonialism was only possible when populations were politically inert and foreign rulers needed merely to conquer or co-opt relatively small local elites to establish imperial rule. Today, the mobilization of significant portions of the population against foreign occupation, as illustrated by events in Iraq and Afghanistan, increasingly makes the costs of such efforts prohibitively high.

Individuals, in Rosenau's view, are acquiring a growing sense of self-efficacy as microelectronic advances give them the information needed to discover whether their interests are being served by their governments. The "printing press, telephone, radio, television, and personal computer have created conditions for skill development among citizenries that governments could not totally control and that have helped make citizenries more effective in relation to the centers of authority."[34]

As the next section reveals, when individuals' competence increases, their sense of empowerment and self-efficacy grows along with their willingness to act outside the traditional avenues of political expression. In some countries, irreverent investigative media give them exactly the "facts" they need to find out whether their interests are being sacrificed to those of national governments that are often incompetent, frequently corrupt, definitely expensive, and sometimes venal. "People may be experiencing uncertainty over where their lives are headed, and they may have a greater sense of remoteness from the centers of decision, but they nonetheless seem ready to act on their convictions."[35]

ICT AND POLITICAL PARTICIPATION

ICT has been central to the emergence of global civil society that we described in the last chapter. For example, internet, cell phones, and other digital technologies have enabled anti-globalization activists to mobilize and publicize their activities globally. Jeffrey Juris writes:

> First, they send e-mails to each other and to their friends and families, facilitating action coordination, while rapidly circulating information about events on the ground. Second, activists generate formal updates, which are instantly posted and distributed through global distribution lists. Third, protesters can also immediately upload and disseminate video and image files. Fourth, IMCs [Independent Media Centers] also provide workshops for carrying out more complex operations, including live video and audio streaming as well as documentary film editing . . . Finally, such temporary media labs have also facilitated the exchange of infor-

mation, ideas, and resources, as well as experimentation with new digital technologies through which media activists inscribe their emerging political ideas within new forms of networked space, a practice I call "information utopics."[36]

ICT has also gradually emerged as a powerful weapon of opponents of authoritarian regimes, including the recent popular revolutions in North Africa and the Middle East. After the initial uprising in Tunisia, *Al Jazeera*, the Qatar-based satellite channel, played a critical role in spreading the news of rebellion and stimulating additional unrest, not only in Egypt, but also throughout the Middle East and beyond.[37] One report on the downfall of Egypt's President Hosni Mubarak commented: "Fear is the dictator's traditional tool for keeping the people in check. But by cutting off Egypt's internet and wireless service . . . in the face of huge street protests, President Hosni Mubarak betrayed his own fear – that Facebook, Twitter, laptops and smartphones could empower his opponents, expose his weakness to the world and topple his regime."[38] Despite the regime's interference with the web, Twitter, with the help of Google, continued to function via its "speak-to-tweet" system.[39]

It is hardly surprising that authoritarian regimes in Myanmar, Moldova, Pakistan, and China have felt threatened by contemporary ICT. Myanmar military authorities closed off internet access to curtail news of the uprising against their tyrannical rule that was coordinated by Buddhist monks in 2007.[40] Young Moldovans used Twitter to protest their country's elections in 2009, and, in reaction, the government shut down the internet service.[41] In 2010, the Pakistan authorities blocked access to YouTube for "growing sacrilegious content,"[42] and also Facebook, for a page that solicited images of the Prophet Muhammad.[43] Makeshift antennas have, however, enabled internet users to circumvent such shutdowns.[44]

In 1989, China's democracy movement used the fax to provide information to the world during the Tiananmen crackdown, and more recently – along with the Falun Gong – has employed ICT in all its forms to mobilize and coordinate activities. Chinese authorities blocked YouTube in March 2009 because it had shown videos of Chinese soldiers beating Tibetan monks,[45] and even tightened control over printing and photocopying shops in Lhasa lest these be used to spread anti-Chinese views.[46] Beijing also blocked internet service for ten months to Xinjiang after ethnic Uighurs rioted in Urumqi, the region's capital, in 2009.[47] Disputes between China's government and Google almost led to a complete cessation of Google's services in that country in 2010, and Chinese hackers stole the Google passwords of Chinese activists, journalists, and American officials the following year.[48] Then, in the wake of the turmoil in the Middle East and North Africa in 2011, all Chinese internet services were heavily censored. Since then, Chinese authorities have established a new agency, the State Internet Information Office, that combines a variety of other agencies with authority to oversee internet content.[49]

Iranian authorities, too, have felt endangered by the new technologies. In 2009, Iranians protesting the country's rigged presidential elections made use of Twitter,[50] Facebook, and YouTube to keep the world informed of events as they unfolded. In Iran, Twitter proved "to be a crucial tool in the cat-and-mouse game between the opposition and the government over enlisting world opinion."[51] In December 2009, a pro-government group in Iran calling itself "the cyber army" hacked and interrupted Twitter and disrupted an Iranian opposition website.[52] In addition, the government blocked internet sites used to download "resistance music," songs of protest that have helped mobilize opponents of the regime.[53] As foreign journalists reported, "this revolution is being tweeted, blogged and Facebooked."[54] In recognition of the potential political clout of ICT, the Obama administration granted a general license for the export of free internet services including Facebook and Twitter not only to Iran but also to Cuba and Sudan in the hope that they will help to open up these societies.[55]

For its part, the US government was roundly embarrassed by the release of confidential material on the internet by the WikiLeaks website. WikiLeaks, a small nonprofit group dedicated to publishing classified information from around the world, was established in December 2006 by Australian Julian Assange. The group describes itself as "a multi-jurisdictional public service designed to protect whistleblowers, journalists and activists who have sensitive materials to communicate to the public."

> Since July 2007, we have worked across the globe to obtain, publish and defend such materials, and, also, to fight in the legal and political spheres for the broader principles on which our work is based: the integrity of our common historical record and the rights of all peoples to create new history. We believe that transparency in government activities leads to reduced corruption, better government and stronger democracies ... We believe this scrutiny requires information. Historically that information has been costly – in terms of human life and human rights. But with technological advances – the internet, and cryptography – the risks of conveying important information can be lowered.[56]

In 2008, a classified report from the Army Counterintelligence Center declared that WikiLeaks "represents a potential force protection, counterintelligence, operational security (OPSEC) and information security (INFOSEC) threat to the U.S. Army."[57] In April 2010, WikiLeaks put a video online that showed an American helicopter in Baghdad killing a dozen Iraqis including two journalists. In October 2010, the WikiLeaks website released detailed logs of events in the Iraqi and Afghan wars, and the following month began to publish 250,000 classified US diplomatic cables that had been passed to it by an American soldier. A global sensation ensued when disturbing confidential information about the candid views of American diplomats regarding foreign leaders and policies were publicized worldwide.

In reaction, there were efforts to hack the WikiLeaks website and retaliatory hacking by WikiLeaks supporters – many of whom belonged to the Anonymous internet subculture – of government agencies and firms like Google, PayPal, and Visa that had taken steps to stem the release of the confidential cables.[58]

As the WikiLeaks case emphasizes, there are pluses and minuses to the new technologies. "Purloining secret documents is an old business," but "technology has hugely increased the ease and potential quantity of theft and the ubiquity of publication."[59] Twitter and similar technologies can also be used by governments or others to misinform. Some commentators like Evgeny Morozov regard as "cyber-utopian" what he calls "the Google doctrine," the belief that the internet, Twitter, YouTube, and similar communities and sites constitute a liberating force that will bring an end to power politics. "The fervent conviction that given enough gadgets, connectivity, and foreign funding, dictatorships are doomed . . . reveals the pervasive influence of the Google doctrine."[60] Morozov argues that the reaction of authoritarian leaders has simply been to take control of these technologies, make use of them, get a lot of demonstrators killed or imprisoned, and thereby reinforce their hold on power.

According to Marcus Alexander, Vladimir Putin's Russia has chosen a subtle alternative: "to promote Internet access and ICP proliferation, and then use the Internet for direct and indirect propaganda." Alexander warns that "what may seem more freedom could mean less freedom in the short run and a danger of yet-to-be-conceived opportunities in the long run."[61] Countries, as Jonathan Kirshner suggests,

> can employ both reactive and proactive strategies for addressing the challenges raised by the Internet . . . Reactive strategies involve restrictions on Internet use, filters to block proscribed sites, and, perhaps most significantly, monitoring . . . Proactive strategies include using the Internet as a conduit for government authority, information, and propaganda, as well as the construction of closed, government-run national intranets.[62]

China, as we have seen, has been proactive concerning what it views as a threat to its internal security that is posed by the internet, Twitter, and other high-tech communications facilities,[63] and it has sought to limit access to these media.[64] Beginning in 1998, Beijing initiated the Golden Shield Project, known as the "Great Firewall of China," which blocks selected internet addresses, thereby effectively censoring the internet.[65] Online blogs are also seen by Chinese officials as sites for mobilizing undesirable public protests.[66]

ECONOMIC IMPLICATIONS OF ICT

Knowledge and information have become key commodities in the global economy.[67] ICT are critical for the continuing operation of global markets and transnational corporations seeking to pursue their activities worldwide. "What characterizes the current technological revolution," declares Castells, "is not the centrality of knowledge and information, but the application of such knowledge generation and information processing/communication devices, in a cumulative feedback loop between innovation and the uses of innovation."[68] Financial markets have begun to function twenty-four hours every day, a wide range of derivatives and other non-traditional forms of investments have evolved, and e-commerce, with its own electronic money, has come into its own. "Private e-currencies," according to Stephen Kobrin, "will make it difficult for central bankers to control – or even measure or define – monetary aggregates. Several forms of money, issued by banks and nonbanks, will circulate. At the extreme . . . currencies issued by central banks may no longer matter."[69]

Global finance has changed almost beyond recognition in recent decades. Castells captures the fundamentals involved in this transformation. He observes that "throughout the world major mergers between financial firms led to the consolidation of the industry in a few mega-groups, capable of a global reach, covering a wide range of financial activities, in an increasingly integrated manner." In Castell's view, technology was the principal driver behind changes in the conduct of financial markets and transactions, including the integration of financial markets and the direct access of investors to those markets: "Powerful computers, and advanced mathematical models, allowed for sophisticated designing, tracking, and forecasting of increasingly complex financial products, operating both in real time and in future time."[70] What results is "an economy with the capacity to work as a unit in real time on a planetary scale."[71]

The potentially volatile combination of the ICT revolution, the substantial deregulation of financial markets that started in the 1990s, and the development of new financial instruments proved to be disastrous in 2007–8. A subprime mortgage meltdown in the United States quickly developed into a global financial crisis and deep recession that was worse than anything the world had seen since the Great Depression. Such a crisis had been brewing for years, not only because of a host of dubious practices pursued by banks and investment companies but also because of an ICT multiplier that quickly spreads and amplifies any "contagion."

As Moisés Naím pointed out in the wake of the Mexican debt crises of 1992 and 1994, "increasingly financial markets tend to cluster those countries perceived to be in the same 'neighborhood' and to treat them roughly along the same lines." The "defining criterion is the potential volatility of the countries; the contagion spread inside risk-clusters, or volatility neighborhoods" that are "no longer defined solely in terms of geography." [72] Naím's "neighborhood effect" was also very much in evidence during the 1997–8 Asian financial crisis, as well as the fear of sovereign default that gripped Europe beginning in 2008. The collapse of Icelandic and Irish banks soon raised concern about possible debt defaults in Eurozone countries Greece, Ireland, Portugal, Spain, and Italy.

Another downside to ICT is its contribution to a different sort of economic activity, that of transnational criminal groups. As Naím observes:

> [T]he entire legal and technological apparatus of globalization has made the illicit drug trade faster, more efficient, and easier to hide . . . Not only can drug wholesalers use express delivery services, but by tracking a shipment online they can know whether it has arrived or whether it has been held up, alerting them to a possible interception and narrowing the window in which authorities can intervene before the traffickers take evasive action. Drug sales are routinely arranged on cell phones that are discarded after no more than a week's use; traffickers coordinate by means of Instant Messaging, Webmail accounts, and chat rooms.[73]

Criminal syndicates are even developing the capacity to hack into the records of law enforcement agencies and to encrypt their own records and transactions. In addition to other criminal activities, the internet facilitates the spread of cybercrime, including identity theft, with as many as 10 million victims in 2009 alone.[74]

A different but no less significant concern is the uneven economic impact of new technologies. In Friedman's view, as we have noted, new technologies are making the world "flat." Many regard his claim as exaggerated at best. William Thompson and Rafael Reuveny insist that Friedman "knows the world is not really flat and that there are a very large number of people living in what he calls the 'unflat world'." Using a world-systems perspective, Thompson and Reuveny conclude that the economic gap between the developed and developing worlds will actually widen as globalization continues, owing in large measure to the digital divide involved in a high concentration of technology in the developed world. Almost two-thirds of "technologies producing hubs" are in North America and Europe.[75]

The World Economic Forum that meets annually in Davos, Switzerland, along with the European Institute of Business Administration (INSEAD), in 2002 developed a Global Information Technology Report based on a Networked Readiness Index (NRI) to measure how prepared countries are to take advantage of information and communications technologies that are vital "to leapfrog stages of development or, more generally, to enhance their competitiveness."[76] The survey of 234 polities that account for 98 percent of the world's GDP uses survey data and hard data including internet users per 100 population, internet bandwidth measured in megabytes per second per 10,000 population, and mobile telephone subscribers per 100 population.

Of the ten most networked-ready countries in 2008–9, seven were European, especially Nordic (Denmark ranking 1st, Sweden 2nd, Switzerland 5th, Finland 6th, Iceland 7th, Norway 8th, and the Netherlands 9th), two were North American (the United States ranking 3rd and Canada 10th), and one was Asian (Singapore 4th). China ranked 46th and India 51st, indicating that these two emerging economic superpowers, although having advanced significantly in ICT in recent years, still have much ground to cover before reaching the top technologically. Nevertheless, *Fortune 500* corporations have opened ninety research and development (R&D) facilities in China and sixty-three in India, and both consumers and firms in emerging markets are "moving upmarket."[77] Four of the ten least networked-ready are sub-Saharan African countries, four are Asian, and two are Latin American.[78]

An additional aggregate measure has been developed by Daniele Archibugi, Mario Denni, and Andrea Filippetti based on 1995–2005 data of three "pillars" – "firm activities and outputs," "human resources," and "infrastructures and absorptive capacity"[79] – to assess "the main trends, results and determinants of the innovative performance of countries across the world." Their conclusion is:

> The results show that over the last decade there is a stable group of countries which are firmly within the top performers, which includes Sweden, Switzerland, Finland, Israel and Japan . . . These countries base their innovative performance mainly on the innovative activities of their business sector. However, behind the leaders, there is a large group of countries which has been remarkably narrowing the gap with respect to the *leaders*, and it includes emerging countries like the Republic of Korea and Singapore. At the bottom of the ranking there are emerging countries, such as three of the four BRIC countries, Brazil, China and India, which have undertaken a catching-up process by considerably increasing their innovative performances.[80]

SECURITY IMPLICATIONS

Given the growing importance of cyberspace, it is hardly surprising that it is becoming an arena of intense conflict,[81] with significant security implications. Cyberspace has become warfare's "fifth domain" after land, sea, air, and space.[82] However, theory about information warfare has lagged.[83] "Information dominance – for intelligence, surveillance, reconnaissance, and real time military operations," argues Kirshner, "enhances the relative power of great powers," but "both civilian and military dependence on computers and other forms of information technology may raise new vulnerabilities."[84]

Although some observers believe the threat of cyberwar has been exaggerated,[85] many analysts have argued that cyberwar – featuring computer viruses, worms, logic bombs, and trojan horses instead of bullets and bombs – can involve espionage or, worse, massive destruction. "Cyberspace is ideal for spies. Digitally disguised and undeterred by borders or passports, they can pick locks anywhere in the world, pilfer secrets without trace and even leave toxic traps for the unwary."[86] Espionage was the aim of a "vast electronic spying operation" that "infiltrated computers and has stolen documents from hundreds of government and private offices around the world."[87] Known as "Ghost-Net," the operation, which was discovered in 2009, was centered in China. "Ghost-Net is capable of taking full control of infected computers, including searching and downloading specific files, and covertly operating attached devices, including microphones and web cameras," and "it demonstrates the ease by which computer-based malware can be used to build a robust, low-cost intelligence capability and infect a network of potentially high-value targets."[88] Cyber espionage was also involved in the theft, probably by China, of information about the Pentagon's Joint Strike Fighter project,[89] and "a foreign intelligence service" hacked into one of the Pentagon's corporate contractors, stealing over 24,000 Department of Defense (DOD) files in a single attack.[90]

Controversy over Google in China and elsewhere threatens to fracture the internet. Chinese officials hacked into Google's search engines and violated the privacy of Google Mail, leading to a temporary decision by Google to resist censorship by transferring its operations from China to Hong Kong.[91] American diplomats reported that the hacking attack on Google was personally directed by Li Changchun, a member of the Chinese Communist Party's Politburo Standing Committee.[92] Chinese and European hackers also apparently broke into some 2,400 corporate and government computers over an eighteen-month period,[93] as well as the email accounts of academics and journalists.[94] Such espionage led Britain's MI5 Centre for the Protection of National Infrastructure to give a formal warning to British businesses "that Chinese intelligence agencies were engaged in a wide-ranging effort to hack into British companies' computers and to blackmail British businesspeople over sexual relationships and other improprieties."[95] According to Richard Clarke and Robert Knake, "the extent of Chinese government hacking against U.S., European, and Japanese industries and research facilities is without precedent in the history of espionage. Exabytes of data have been copied from universities, industrial labs, and government facilities."[96]

The potential destructiveness of cyberwar was brought home by cyberattacks on Estonia (2007) and Georgia (2008) by Russian hackers,[97] both involving "distributed denial of service" (DDOS) attacks that utilize networks of computers under remote control to flood and overwhelm an adversary's computer systems with incoming messages. In July 2009, US and South Korean computer networks were "besieged for days" by a cyberattack, from North Korea,[98] and in September 2010 Iranian nuclear facilities were attacked with apparently devastating effect by a worm called Stuxnet.[99] The worm was designed to attack a particular Iranian nuclear facility utilizing software provided by the German firm Siemens. Its attack reflected knowledge of the company's production processes and control system and the nuclear facility's blueprints[100] and "was perfectly calibrated in a way that could send nuclear centrifuges wildly out of control."[101] Such events raise the question of whether cyberattacks should be regarded as armed attacks subject to military retaliation.

Estonia was especially vulnerable because the country is a leader in internet connectivity both at the individual and government levels, and most Estonians use online banking.[102] Between 2000 and 2007, the percentage of Estonians who were internet users increased from 28 to 57 percent.[103] Beginning in the evening of April 26, 2007, and "fueled with step-by-step instructions so simple that any Internet user could follow,"[104] the cyberattack began, in apparent retaliation for the removal of a Soviet war memorial from central Tallinn, the so-called "Bronze Soldier of Tallinn."

Estonia thus became the first country in the world to come under a broad and sustained attack from the internet. Continuing for several weeks, anonymous foreign networks comprising hundreds of thousands of computers repeatedly disabled Estonia's internet servers used by the government, banks, media, and other organizations by bombarding them with information requests. During two episodes, "the attacks, simultaneously harnessing as many as 1 million remotely controlled computers across the world, infected with malicious software without their owners' knowledge, brought down the internet servers of Estonia's biggest bank, Hansapank, among others. People paying for their gasoline, milk, and bread – not to mention other purchases – suddenly found that their bank cards didn't work. It was a rude awakening for a country where connectivity is a way of life."[105]

In general, offensive cyber capabilities have outpaced defensive capabilities. Geography is no impediment to a cyberattack that may only take seconds to carry out. The United States, which has a robust cyberattack capability organized by NSA and DOD, is nonetheless poorly prepared to defend itself against attack, especially in the private sector, and overall existing American cybersecurity has been described as "embarrassing."[106] American efforts to deter cyberattacks have thus far been largely unsuccessful.[107] For instance, in 2008, it was discovered that cyber spies had penetrated America's electrical grid and planted software that could be used to degrade the system.[108] According to Tom Burling of Tulip Systems, "the U.S. is probably more Internet-dependent than any place in the world. So to that extent we're more vulnerable than any place in the world to this kind of attack."[109] Owing to this dependence, the United States has embarked on a new effort called "Perfect Citizen" using sensors in computer networks to detect cyberattacks on government agencies and private companies managing such services as the electric grid and nuclear power.[110]

Andrew Krepinevich argues that cyber warfare could "inflict crippling damage on the U.S. economy" and could make US military capability "the modern equivalent of the Maginot Line."[111] Clarke and Knake draw a genuinely apocalyptic picture of the possible results of a large-scale cyberattack on the United States:

> It's now 8:15 p.m. Within a quarter of an hour, 157 major metropolitan areas have been thrown into knots by a nationwide power blackout hitting during rush hour. Poison gas clouds are wafting toward Wilmington and Houston. Refineries are burning up oil supplies in several cities. Subways have crashed in New York, Oakland, Washington, and Los Angeles. Freight trains have derailed outside major junctions and marshaling yards on four major railroads. Aircraft are literally falling out of the sky as a result of midair collisions across the country. Pipelines carrying natural gas to the Northeast have exploded, leaving millions in the cold. The financial system has also frozen because of the terabytes of information at data centers being wiped out. Weather, navigation, and communications satellites are spinning out of their orbits into space. And the U.S. military is a series of isolated units, struggling to communicate with each other.[112]

Such scenarios led to the introduction of a "kill switch" bill in the US Senate giving the president authority to close down part of the internet in the event of a cyber-attack.[113]

Even individuals can penetrate highly valued secure sites,[114] and in one case a single hacker "with a junior high school education slapped cartoon pandas onto millions of computers to hide a destructive spy program. The Panda Burns Incense computer worm, created by 27-year-old Li Jun, wreaked havoc for months in China in 2006 and 2007."[115] In some cases, individual hackers attack computer sites as a means of political protest.[116] The technology needed for hacking is inexpensive and readily available. Insurgents in Iraq and Afghanistan, using off-the-shelf SkyGrabber, a downloadable program costing $26, have even hacked into unmanned American drones.[117]

President Obama declared that "in today's world, acts of terror could come not only from a few extremists in suicide vests but from a few key strokes on the computer – a weapon of mass disruption . . . From now on, our digital infrastructure – the networks and computers we depend on every day – will be treated as they should be: as a strategic national asset."[118] The growing threat of cyberattacks has led to cyberwar games at the US Military Academy,[119] and the Obama administration has created a cybersecurity office in the White House run by Howard Schmidt, former head of security at Microsoft.[120] Moreover, the Department of Defense has created a new Cyber Command led by a four-star general.[121] Its establishment reflects the growing Pentagon belief that future wars will involve cyberattacks.[122] The DOD's Cyber Command is located near the National Security Administration (NSA) because the latter, as a civilian agency, may conduct espionage but not launch military operations.

The United States and Russia have held talks aimed at improving internet security and limiting the likelihood of cyberwar, and, in July 2010, the two countries agreed, along with thirteen other countries, to a series of steps towards this end.[123] In early

2011, the United States and Russia declared that "Rules of Engagement" were necessary in order to render "the Geneva and Hague conventions in cyberspace."[124] The US–Russian proposal, based on a report of the EastWest Institute, grew out of recognition that the distinction between civilian and military targets is difficult to maintain in cyberspace, as is establishing the source of cyberattacks. For its part, the Pentagon, which refers to internet attacks as "hybrid warfare,"[125] has been generally reluctant to launch cyberattacks against adversaries, for example, Iraq in 2003, because of the potential for extensive collateral damage.[126]

ICT has been shaping the conduct of asymmetrical warfare in physical as well as cyberspace battlefields. Consider the insights of former US commander in Afghanistan General Stanley A. McChrystal: "ICT has been shaping the conduct of asymmetrical warfare in physical as well as cyberspace battlefields." Describing the enemy he confronted in Afghanistan, McChrystal terms the Taliban

> a uniquely 21st-century threat. Enjoying the traditional insurgent advantage of living amid a population closely tied to them by history and culture, they also leverage sophisticated technology that connects remote valleys and severe mountains instantaneously – and allows them to project their message worldwide, unhindered by time or filters ... And just like their allies in al Qaeda, this new Taliban is more network than army ... In bitter, bloody fights in both Afghanistan and Iraq, it became clear to me and to many that to defeat a networked enemy we had to become a network ourselves.[127]

Cyberwar is by no means the only security concern arising out of evolving ICT. For the West, the reverse image of authoritarian regimes in places like Iran and China clamping down on internet freedom to curb political protest is the potential challenge political democracies face from homegrown radical extremism that might encourage terrorist acts. The same free ICT sources that help preserve, for example, a healthy multiculturalism or diversity of political opinions across the ideological spectrum also frequently carry messages of hate and incitements to violence. Mobile phones have also provided effective aid to Islamic extremists.[128] These may even extend to what some have termed "video terrorism," including video broadcasts by suicide bombers, explaining their actions, or even of beheadings of those taken captive by terrorist groups. In addition, individual privacy is endangered by the information collected by firms such as Google, Amazon, Facebook, and Netflix.[129]

ICT, GLOBALIZATION, AND LOCALIZATION

It is crucial to understand that the new ICT technologies are central *both to globalization and to the efforts of those who would defend against its effects*. Taking account of the widespread use of English and the diffusion of ICT, Michael Talalay suggests that "the entire world is heading for a common culture."[130] However, there is a widespread tendency, as Friedman famously put it, for individuals to prize both an "olive tree" – "everything that roots us, anchors us, identifies us and locates us in this world"[131] – and a "Lexus," a symbol for the advanced technology of a globalizing world. ICT culture and the new social and economic elites that have adopted it are associated with individualism, consumerism, and secularism. More traditional individuals and societies are much more selective in their embrace of these values, or reject them entirely.

Political and commercial interests threaten the early naive belief that the internet would unify humanity and afford everyone equal access to information and an ability to communicate directly with anyone else. On the one hand, there are China's firewall and other state-sponsored efforts to manage internet links with the outside world. Then there are controls by companies like Facebook and Google designed to limit selected web-based services to customers, as well as corporate efforts to provide proprietary web services and the exclusivity of "clouds" to those who pay for them. The collective effect is to reduce the universality of the internet and threaten to divide it into pieces.[132]

There is also growing interest outside of the West in finding alternatives to an internet so closely identified with its original sponsoring country, the United States.[133] Even more fundamental is the issue Kobrin raises of "whether, or to what extent, national territorial jurisdiction applies to cyberspace."[134] He concludes that cyberspace "is inherently international; every website can be accessed by every computer connected to the Internet,"[135] and, in consequence, cyberspace can and should be regulated only internationally. But a universal internet regime still seems a distant goal. Meanwhile, more limited arrangements like the US–Russian "Rules of Engagement" are probably the best that can be achieved in the foreseeable future.

Overall, globalization is perceived as the antithesis of localization, and in some respects this is true. In other ways, however, the global and the local are two sides of the same coin. In the next chapter, we shall examine the relationship between globalizing and localizing processes.

NOTES

1 Ferguson and Mansbach, *Remapping Global Politics*, 273.
2 Rosenau, *Turbulence in World Politics*, 17.
3 Wolf, *Why Globalization Works*, 16–17.
4 Chanda, *Bound Together*.
5 Vaclav Smil, "The Two Prime Movers of Globalization: History and Impact of Diesel Engines and Gas Turbines," *Journal of Global History* 2 (2007), 374.
6 For the evolution of the internet, see Janet Abbate, *Inventing the Internet* (Cambridge, MA: MIT Press, 2000), and John Naughton, *A Brief History of the Future: From Radio Days to Internet Years in a Lifetime* (Woodstock, NY: Overlook Press, 2001).
7 Catherine L. Mann with Jacob Funk Kirkegaard, *Accelerating the Globalization of America* (Washington, DC: Institute for International Economics, 2006), 2.
8 "Growing on the Cheap," *The Economist*, May 29, 2010, 64.
9 Michael Connors, *The Race to the Intelligent State*, 2nd edn (Oxford: Capstone Publishing, 1997), xi–xii.
10 Sebastian Moffett, "Technology Widens Gap between Rich and Poor," *Wall Street Journal*, May 4, 2011, A12.
11 David Pogue, "Humanity's Database," *New York Times*, June 24, 2010, http://www.nytimes.com/2010/07/04/books/review/Pogue-t.html.
12 "A New Sort of Togetherness," *The Economist*, May 22, 2010, 64–5.

13 See "The Few: A Special Report on Global Leaders," *The Economist*, January 22, 2011, 17–18.
14 As of March 31, 2011, Facebook had over 664 million users and was spreading rapidly. See "Facebook World Statistics," *Internet World Stats News*, 062, April 12, 2011, and "The Future is Another Country," *The Economist*, July 24, 2010, 59–60.
15 Internet Systems Consortium, https://www.isc.org/solutions/survey/history, table 2.1. An internet host is a computer or an application connected to the internet that has an Internet Protocol address. That address identifies every internet host. The origin of the terms "host" and "server" is that a computer "hosts" or "serves" its user(s). See InetDaemon, http://www.inetdaemon.com/tutorials/internet/ip/whatis_ip_host.shtml.
16 "Internet Stats Today," *Internet World Stats News*, January 2010, http://internetstatstoday.com/?p=1295.
17 "Technology Quarterly," *The Economist*, September 6, 2009, 3–4.
18 "Out of Thin Air," *The Economist*, June 12, 2010, 85.
19 Ethan B. Kapstein, "Africa's Capitalist Revolution," *Foreign Affairs* 88:4 (July/August 2009), 122.
20 "'Historic' Day as First Non-Latin Web Addresses Go Live," *BBC News*, May 6, 2010, http://news.bbc.co.uk/2/hi/10100108.stm.
21 MSAT Mobile System, http://www.infosat.com/prod_serv/voice/mobile/msat/.
22 See the Inmarsat website at http://www.inmarsat.com/.
23 Claire Cain Miller and Nick Bilton, "Cellphone Payments Offer Alternative to Cash," *New York Times*, April 28, 2010, http://www.nytimes.com/2010/04/29/technology/29cashless.html.
24 Ó Tuathail, Herod, and Roberts, "Negotiating Unruly Problematics," 12.
25 Naeem Inayatullah and David L. Blaney, *International Relations and the Problem of Difference* (New York: Routledge, 2004), 191, 210.
26 Ibid., 189, 191.
27 David Held, *Global Covenant* (Cambridge: Polity Press, 2004), 74–5.
28 Ibid., 87.
29 Featherstone, *Consumer Culture and Postmodernism*, 151.
30 Rosenau, *Distant Proximities*, chs. 10–11. For a historical analysis of the role of education in the rise of nationalism, see Ernest Gellner, "Nationalism and Modernization," in John Hutchinson and Anthony D. Smith, eds., *Nationalism* (New York: Oxford University Press, 1994), 55–63.
31 Rosenau, *Distant Proximities*, 235.
32 Ibid., 245.
33 For the impact of information technologies in China, see Guthrie, *China and Globalization*, 282–6.
34 Rosenau, *Turbulence in World Politics*, 239.
35 Ibid., 249.
36 Jeffrey S. Juris, "The New Digital Media and Activist Networking within Anti-Corporate Globalization Movements," *Annals of the American Academy of Political and Social Science* 597 (January 2005), 201.
37 Robert F. Worth and David D. Kirkpatrick, "Seizing a Moment, Al Jazeera Galvanizes Arab Frustration," *New York Times*, January 27, 2011, http://www.nytimes.com/2011/01/28/world/middleeast/28jazeera.html.
38 Scott Shane, "Spotlight Again Falls on Web Tools and Change," *New York Times*, January 29, 2011, http://www.nytimes.com/2011/01/30/weekinreview/30shane.html?ref=scottshane.
39 "Egypt Protesters Use Voice Tweets," *BBC News*, February 1, 2011, http://www.bbc.co.uk/news/technology-12332850.
40 Seth Mydans, "Monks Are Silenced, and for Now, Internet Is, Too," *New York Times*, October 4, 2007, http://www.nytimes.com/2007/10/04/world/asia/04info.html.

41 Ellen Barry, "Protests in Moldova Explode, with Help of Twitter," *New York Times*, April 7, 2009, http://www.nytimes.com/2009/04/08/world/europe/08moldova.html.
42 Sabrina Tavernise, "Pakistan Widens Ban to Include YouTube," *New York Times*, May 20, 2010, http://www.nytimes.com/2010/05/21/world/asia/21pstan.html.
43 Adam B. Ellick and Waqar Gillani, "Pakistani Court Orders Access to Facebook Restored," *New York Times*, May 31, 2010, http://www.nytimes.com/2010/06/01/world/asia/01pstan.html.
44 "Signalling Dissent," *The Economist*, March 19, 2011, 89–90.
45 Quentin Sommerville, "China 'Blocks YouTube Video Site'," *BBC News*, March 24, 2009, http://news.bbc.co.uk/2/hi/7961069.stm.
46 Sharon LaFraniere, "China Aims to Stifle Tibet's Photocopiers," *New York Times*, May 20, 2010, http://www.nytimes.com/2010/05/21/world/asia/21tibet.html.
47 Edward Wong, "After Long Ban, Western China Is Back Online," *New York Times*, May 14, 2010, http://www.nytimes.com/2010/05/15/world/asia/15china.html.
48 John Markoff and David Barboza, "Google Says Hackers Stole Gmail Passwords," *New York Times*, June 1, 2011, http://www.nytimes.com/2011/06/02/technology/02google.html?pagewanted=all.
49 Michael Wines, "China Creates New Agency for Patrolling the Internet," *New York Times*, May 4, 2011, http://www.nytimes.com/2011/05/05/world/asia/05china.html.
50 For analysis of the claim that Twitter increases access to politicians, see "Sweet to Tweet," *The Economist*, May 8, 2010, 61.
51 Noam Cohen, "Twitter on the Barricades: Six Lessons Learned," *New York Times*, June 21, 2009, http://www.nytimes.com/2009/06/21/weekinreview/21cohenweb.html?pagewanted=print.
52 "Pro-Iranian Hackers Hit Twitter and Opposition Websites," *BBC News*, December 18, 2009, http://news.bbc.co.uk/2/hi/8420369.stm.
53 Nazila Fathi, "Music Stirs the Embers of Protest in Iran," *New York Times*, June 5, 2010, http://www.nytimes.com/2010/06/06/world/middleeast/06iranmusic.html.
54 John Palfrey, Bruce Etling, and Robert Faris, "Reading Twitter in Tehran?" *Washington Post National Weekly Edition*, June 29–July 12, 2009, 26–7.
55 Mark Landler, "U.S. Hopes Exports Will Help Open Closed Societies," *New York Times*, March 7, 2010, http://www.nytimes.com/2010/03/08/world/08export.html?emc=eta1. The countries with the world's largest number of registered Facebook users are the US, UK, Indonesia, Turkey, France, Italy, Canada, Philippines, Mexico, and Spain. See also Norimitsu Onishi, "Debate on Internet's Limits Grows in Indonesia," *New York Times*, April 19, 2010, http://www.nytimes.com/2010/04/20/world/asia/20indonet.html?ref=world.
56 "WikiLeaks: About," http://www.wikileaks.org/wiki/WikiLeaks:About.
57 Cited in Peter Grier, "Video of Iraqi Journalists' Killings: Is WikiLeaks a Security Threat?" *Christian Science Monitor*, April 6, 2010, http://www.csmonitor.com/USA/Military/2010/0406/Video-of-Iraqi-journalists-killings-Is-WikiLeaks-a-security-threat.
58 "Unpluggable," *The Economist*, December 4, 2010, 33.
59 Cohen, "Twitter on the Barricades."
60 Evgeny Morozov, *The Net Delusion* (New York: PublicAffairs, 2011), 1–2. See also "Caught in the Net," *The Economist*, January 8, 2011, 82–3.
61 Marcus Alexander, "The Internet in Putin's Russia: Reinventing a Technology of Authoritarianism," paper presented at the Annual Conference of the Political Studies Association (2003), 23, 24, http://www.psa.ac.uk/journals/pdf/5/2003/Marcus%20Alexander.pdf.
62 Jonathan Kirshner, "Globalization and National Security," in Kirshner, ed., *Globalization and National Security*, 19.
63 Sharon LaFraniere and Jonathan Ansfield, "China Alarmed by Security Threat from Internet," *New York Times*, February 11, 2010, http://www.nytimes.com/2010/02/12/world/asia/12cyberchina.html.

64 "Internet Restrictions Curtail Human Rights, Says US," *BBC News*, March 11, 2010, http://news.bbc.co.uk/2/hi/americas/8563084.stm.

65 Jonathan Watts, "War of the Words," *The Guardian*, February 20, 2006, http://www.guardian.co.uk/technology/2006/feb/20/news.mondaymediasection/print.

66 Keith B. Richburg, "A Place for Public Protest," *Washington Post National Weekly Edition*, November 16–22, 2009, 18. Individual Chinese bloggers try to evade the censorship.

67 See Carl Shapiro and Hal K. Varian, *Information Rules* (Cambridge, MA: Harvard Business School Press, 1999).

68 Castells, *The Rise of the Network Society*, 31.

69 Stephen Kobrin, "Electronic Cash and the End of National Markets," *Foreign Policy* 107 (Summer 1997), 71. See also Benjamin M. Friedman, "The Future of Monetary Policy: The Central Bank as an Army with Only a Signal Corps?" *International Finance* 2:3 (November 1999), 321–38. Kobrin's position is refuted by Charles Helleiner, who argues that "new forms of electronic money are unlikely to pose a significant threat to the power of the sovereign state." See C. Helleiner, "Electronic Money: A Challenge to the Sovereign State?" *Journal of International Affairs* 51:2 (Spring 1998), 399–400.

70 Castells, *The Rise of the Network Society*, 153.

71 Ibid., 92.

72 Moisés Naím, "Mexico's Larger Story," *Foreign Policy* 99 (Summer 1995), 125.

73 Naím, *Illicit*, 77, 78.

74 "Good for Some," *The Economist*, February 13, 2010, 34.

75 William R. Thompson and Rafael Reuveny, *The Limits of Economic Globalization: The North–South Gap* (New York: Routledge, 2010), 7.

76 Soumitra Dutta and Irene Mia, "Executive Summary," in S. Dutta and I. Mia, eds., *Global Information Technology Report 2008–2009: Mobility in a Networked World* (INSEAD and World Economic Forum: 2009), http://www.insead.edu/v1/gitr/wef/main/fullreport/index.html.

77 "The New Masters of Management," *The Economist*, April 17, 2010, 11.

78 Dutta and Mia, eds., *Global Information Technology Report 2008–2009*.

79 Daniele Archibugi, Mario Denni, and Andrea Filippetti, "The Global Innovation Scoreboard 2008: The Dynamics of the Innovative Performances of Countries," report prepared for Pro Inno Europe: Inno Metrics, March 2009, http://www.danielearchibugi.org/downloads/papers/scoreboard.pdf, 33. Each of these three metrics is a composite of specific measures. The authors also summarize alternative efforts to measure innovation and compare the consistency of their results (12–22).

80 Ibid., 3. Emphasis in original. The United States "drops out of the leaders in 2005" (34), falling from 3rd in 1995 to 6th globally.

81 See "Age of Cyber 'Warfare' Is Dawning," *BBC News*, November 17, 2009, http://news.bbc.co.uk/2/hi/8363175.stm.

82 "War in the Fifth Domain," *The Economist*, July 3, 2010, 25–6, 28.

83 See John Erikkson and Giampiero Giacomello, "The Information Revolution, Security, and International Relations: (IR) Relevant Theory?" *International Political Science Review* 27:3 (July 2006), 221–44.

84 Kirshner, "Globalization and National Security," 17.

85 Maggie Shiels, "Cyber War Threat Exaggerated Claims Security Expert," *BBC News*, February 16, 2011, http://www.bbc.co.uk/news/technology-12473809.

86 "A Chinese Ghost in the Machine," *The Economist*, April 4, 2009, 62. See also David Barboza and Kevin Drew, "Security Firm Sees Global Cyberspying," *New York Times*, April 3, 2011, http://www.nytimes.com/2011/08/04/technology/security-firm-identifies-global-cyber-spying.html.

87 John Markoff, "Vast Spy System Loots Computers in 103 Countries," *New York Times*, March 29, 2009, http://www.nytimes.com/2009/03/29/technology/29spy.html.

88 "Tracking *GhostNet*: Investigating a *Cyber Espionage* Network," *Information Warfare Monitor* (Munk Centre for International Studies, University of Toronto), March 29,

2009, http://www.scribd.com/doc/13731776/Tracking-GhostNet-Investigating-a-Cyber-Espionage-Network. See also "Shadow Cyber Spy Network Revealed," *BBC News*, April 6, 2010, http://news.bbc.co.uk/2/hi/technology/8605548.stm.

89 Siobhan Gorman, August Cole, and Yochi Dreazen, "Computer Spies Breach Fighter-Jet Project," *Wall Street Journal*, April 21, 2009, A1, A2.

90 Thom Shanker and Elisabeth Bumiller, "Hackers Gained Access to Sensitive Military Files," *New York Times*, June 14, 2011, http://www.nytimes.com/2011/07/15/world/15cyber.html?pagewanted=all.

91 "Flowers for a Funeral," *The Economist*, January 16, 2010, 41–2. China disrupted Google services again at the end of March 2010. See Jessica E. Vascellero and Loretta Chao, "Google Runs into China's 'Great Firewall'," *Wall Street Journal*, March 31, 2010, B1.

92 James Glanz and John Markoff, "Vast Hacking by a China Fearful of the Web," *New York Times*, December 4, 2010, http://www.nytimes.com/2010/12/05/world/asia/05wikileaks-china.html.

93 Siobhan Gorman, "Hackers Mount New Strike," *Wall Street Journal*, February 18, 2010, A3.

94 Andrew Jacobs, "Journalists' E-Mails Hacked in China," *New York Times*, March 30, 2010, http://www.nytimes.com/2010/03/31/world/asia/31china.html.

95 John F. Burns, "Britain Warned Businesses of Threat of Chinese Spying," *New York Times*, January 31, 2010, http://www.nytimes.com/2010/02/01/world/europe/01spy.html.

96 Richard A. Clarke and Robert K. Knake, *Cyber War* (New York: HarperCollins, 2010), 59.

97 "Marching Off to Cyberwar," *The Economist*, December 6, 2008, http://www.economist.com/sciencetechnology/tq/displayStory.cfm?story_id=12673385, and Siobhan Gorman, "Cyber Attacks on Georgia Used Facebook, Twitter, Stolen IDs," *Wall Street Journal*, August 17, 2009, A5.

98 Siobhan Gorman and Evan Ramstad, "Cyber Blitz Hits U.S., Korea," *Wall Street Journal*, July 9, 2009, A1, A4.

99 David E. Sanger, "Iran Fights Malware Attacking Computers," *New York Times*, September 25, 2010, http://www.nytimes.com/2010/09/26/world/middleeast/26iran.html.

100 "A Worm in the Centrifuge," *The Economist*, October 2, 2010, 63–4.

101 William J. Broad and David E. Sanger, "Worm Was Perfect for Sabotaging Centrifuges," *New York Times*, November 18, 2010, http://www.nytimes.com/2010/11/19/world/middleeast/19stuxnet.html.

102 Gadi Evron, "Battling Botnets and Online Mobs: Estonia's Defense Efforts during the Internet War," *Georgetown Journal of International Affairs* 9:1 (Winter/Spring 2008), 121–6.

103 "Estonia: Internet Usage Stats and Market Report," *Internet World Stats* (2009), http://www.internetworldstats.com/eu/ee.htm.

104 Evron, "Battling Botnets and Online Mobs," 123.

105 Ahto Lobjakas, "How Vulnerable Are Countries to Cyberattacks? Ask Estonia!" *Radio Free Europe/Radio Liberty*, April 29, 2008, http://www.rferl.org/content/article/1109653.html.

106 Maggie Shiels, "US Cyber-security 'Embarrassing'," *BBC News*, April 29, 2009, http://news.bbc.co.uk/2/hi/technology/8023793.stm.

107 John Markoff, David E. Sanger, and Thom Shanker, "In Digital Combat, U.S. Finds No Easy Deterrent," *New York Times*, January 25, 2010, http://www.nytimes.com/2010/01/26/world/26cyber.html.

108 Siobhan Gorman, "Electricity Grid in U.S. Penetrated by Spies," *Wall Street Journal*, April 8, 2009, A1, A2.

109 Cited in Brandon Griggs, "U.S. at Risk of Cyberattacks, Experts Say," *CNN.com*, August 18, 2008, http://edition.cnn.com/2008/TECH/08/18/cyber.warfare/index.html.

110 Siobhan Gorman, "U.S. Plans Cyber Shield for Utilities, Companies," *Wall Street Journal*, July 8, 2010, A3.
111 Krepinevich, "The Pentagon's Wasting Assets," 25.
112 Clarke and Knake, *Cyber War*, 67.
113 "Reaching for the Kill Switch," *The Economist*, February 12, 2011, 67–8. The shutdown of internet and mobile phone services in Egypt and elsewhere during turmoil in the Middle East in 2011 dampened enthusiasm for the bill.
114 See John F. Burns, "Hacker's Extradition to U.S. More Likely," *New York Times*, July 31, 2009, http://www.nytimes.com/2009/08/01/world/europe/01britain.html.
115 James T. Areddy, "People's Republic of Hacking," *Wall Street Journal*, February 20–1, 2010, A1.
116 "Political Hacktivists Turn to Web Attacks," *BBC News*, February 10, 2010, http://news.bbc.co.uk/2/hi/8506698.stm.
117 Siobhan Gorman, Yochi J. Dreazen, and August Cole, "Insurgents Hack U.S. Drones," *Wall Street Journal*, December 17, 2009, A1, A21.
118 "Remarks by the President on Securing Our Nation's Cyber Infrastructure," *The White House*, May 29, 2009, http://www.whitehouse.gov/the_press_office/Remarks-by-the-President-on-Securing-Our-Nations-Cyber-Infrastructure/. "In 2007 alone the Pentagon reported nearly 44,000 incidents of what is called malicious cyber activity carried out by foreign ministries, intelligence agencies and individual hackers." "US Launches Cyber Security Plan," *BBC News*, May 29, 2009, http://news.bbc.co.uk/2/hi/americas/8073654.stm.
119 Corey Kilgannon and Noam Cohen, "Cadets Trade the Trenches for Firewalls," *New York Times*, May 11, 2009, http://www.nytimes.com/2009/05/11/technology/11cybergames.html.
120 Ellen Nakashima and Brian Krebs, "Obama Says He Will Name New Cybersecurity Adviser," *Washington Post*, May 30, 2009, http://www.washingtonpost.com/wp-dyn/content/article/2009/05/29/AR2009052900350.html, and "War in the Fifth Domain."
121 Thom Shanker, "Cyberwar Nominee Sees Gaps in Law," *New York Times*, April 14, 2010, http://www.nytimes.com/2010/04/15/world/15military.html?ref=world.
122 Patrick Jackson, "Meet USCybercom: Why the US is Fielding a Cyber Army," *BBC News*, March 15, 2010, http://news.bbc.co.uk/2/hi/8511711.stm.
123 John Markoff, "Step Taken to End Impasse over Cybersecurity Talks," *New York Times*, July 16, 2010, http://www.nytimes.com/2010/07/17/world/17cyber.html. The US views computer hacking in terms of law enforcement, whereas Russia views it in views terms. See Andrew E. Kramer, "Hacker's Arrest Offers Peek into Crime in Russia," *New York Times*, August 23, 2010, http://www.nytimes.com/2010/08/24/business/global/24cyber.html. Russia originally sought an international treaty to prevent cyberwar attacks, while the United States prefers cooperation among international law enforcement groups.
124 Cited in Susan Watts, "Proposal for Cyber War Rules of Engagement," *BBC News*, February 3, 2011, http://news.bbc.co.uk/2/hi/programmes/newsnight/9386445.stm.
125 David E. Sanger, John Markoff, and Thom Shanker, "U.S. Steps Up Effort on Digital Defenses," *New York Times*, April 28, 2009, http://www.nytimes.com/2009/04/28/us/28cyber.html.
126 John Markoff and Thom Shanker, "Halted '03 Iraq Plan Illustrates U.S. Fear of Cyberwar Risk," *New York Times*, August 2, 2009, http://www.nytimes.com/2009/08/02/us/politics/02cyber.html.
127 Stanley A. McChrystal, "Becoming the Enemy," *Foreign Policy* 185 (March/April 2001), 67.
128 "Jihadists Use Mobiles as Propaganda Tools," *BBC News*, April 21, 2011, http://www.bbc.co.uk/news/technology-13149571.
129 Eli Pariser, *The Filter Bubble: What the Internet Is Hiding from You* (New York: Penguin Press, 2011).

130 Talalay, "Technology and Globalization: Assessing Patterns of Interaction," 211.
131 Thomas L. Friedman, *The Lexus and the Olive Tree* (New York: Farrar, Strauss & Giroux, 1999), 27.
132 "The Web's New Walls," *The Economist*, September 4, 2010, 11–12, and "A Virtual Counter-Revolution," *The Economist*, September 4, 2010, 75–7.
133 The central role of the internet in globalization has produced controversy over whether regulation of internet addresses should continue to be controlled by a private, non-profit US-based agency called ICann (Internet Corporation for Assigned Names and Numbers). See Eric Pfanner, "New Chief Defends U.S. Base for Agency that Manages Web," *New York Times*, July 12, 2009, http://www.nytimes.com/2009/07/13/technology/internet/13iht-icann13.html, and "ICAAN Be Independent," *The Economist*, September 26, 2009, 78.
134 Stephen J. Kobrin, "Territoriality and the Governance of Cyberspace," *Journal of International Business Studies* 32:4 (2001), 692.
135 Ibid.

CHAPTER 5

The global versus the local

It is clear to me that to be successful, to continue growth and to be sustainable, *globalization is wholly dependent on the degree to which the world continues to decentralize.*[1]

On a recent global brand manager development programme, the participants were asked to bring examples of their global products. In one case a cleaning product that was a leading "global" brand for the organization had 14 variations to accommodate various markets . . .[2]

Global politics features both globalizing and localizing dynamics as well as "the production of new spatialities and temporalities" that "belong to both the global and the national, if only to each in part."[3] Frank Lechner illustrates the way the two coexist in his description of how the Tokyo fish market is at once "a very Japanese place," while also serving a global clientele:

The Tsukiji fish market in Tokyo is the largest in the world. Six days a week, traders buy thousands of pounds of fish at dockside auctions in order to resell it to chefs and retailers – 50,000 people working to satisfy the needs of the region's more than 20 million residents. Tsukiji is a very Japanese place, with its own Japanese trading customs, linked to distinctively Japanese businesses, and catering to Japanese tastes in seafood. At the same time, it serves as the central hub of the global fishing industry. Thanks to modern shipping technology – the more valuable flies via Narita International Airport – it enjoys a global supply, ranging from Canadian salmon and Maine sea urchin roe to Okhotsk crab and Thai shrimp.[4]

Fans of globalization applaud the global, whereas critics tend to celebrate the local. Globalization enthusiasts regard the local as parochial and divisive, whereas globalization opponents praise the local because they prefer diversity and autonomy. Globalization, argues David J. Keeling, "has emerged as the ultimate expression both of an increasingly interconnected global society and of a socio-economic Trojan Horse that will wreak deprivation and degradation on local communities."[5] Thus, there is a "dynamic tension between the global and the local"[6] in which the local is frequently both a refuge from and a reaction to the global.

Education, for example, consists of both globalizing and localizing dynamics. Governments utilize education and media to socialize youth in national norms and values. On the one hand, educational institutions have a globalizing function, a "central role in the development of the knowledge economy," including the spread of English and modern technology. On the other hand, education can reinforce the local in teaching national history, language, and literature that "fuels conflict at all levels through racism, religious conflict, prejudice against refugees and ultimately warfare."[7] In the case of Estonia, for instance, language was the "pointed response to what Stalin wrought."[8]

Education instills values, whether global and/or local, and such socialization matters greatly. "The key political tension in the coming era," argues globalization critic Gills, "will be between the forces of neoliberal economic globalization, seeking to expand the freedom on capital, and the forces of social resistance, seeking to preserve and to redefine community and solidarity."[9] Interestingly, a preference for the local is vigorously criticized by Hardt and Negri, who are Marxist critics of globalization, as "both false and damaging."[10]

Globalization and localization are occurring at the same time, and it is frequently difficult to see which is dominant. Castells comments: "While capital flows freely in the electronic circuits of global financial networks, labor is still highly constrained, and will be for the foreseeable future, by institutions, culture, borders, police, and xenophobia."[11] Castells notwithstanding, labor unions are also becoming transnational, as is illustrated by the successful negotiations in 2008 between Great Britain's Unite union that represented British airline flight attendants and the United Steelworkers Union in the United States. The merger produced a new transnational labor group called Workers Uniting that represents over "three million active and retired workers from the United States, Canada, Great Britain and the Republic of Ireland who work in virtually every sector of the global economy, including manufacturing, service, mining and transportation."[12] Labor problems in any single unit of a giant transnational corporation (TNC) can bring a production standstill elsewhere in the corporation, including units in other countries. Of course, TNCs can fight back by threatening to outsource production from countries with labor unrest.[13]

The local and global, in fact, are inextricably linked. As Nederveen Pieterse argues: "What globalization means in structural terms . . . is the *increase in the available modes of organization*: transnational, international, macroregional, national, microregional, municipal, and local."[14] Globalization can simultaneously reinforce "both supranational and subnational regionalism," for example, when "constituencies in Northern Ireland can appeal to the European Court of Human Rights in Strasbourg on decisions of the British courts" or when "Catalonia can outflank Madrid and Brittany and outmaneuver Paris by appealing to Brussels or by establishing links with other regions (e.g. between Catalonia and the Ruhr area)."[15] In reality, one of the reasons it is sometimes difficult to tell globalization and localization apart is because regionalism contains elements of both. On the one hand, it involves enlarging the scope of political and economic activities beyond the territorial state; on the other, it may act as a barrier to further enlargement or, at least, an alternative to globalization. For instance, Allen Morrison, David Ricks, and Kendall Roth argue that "international corporations should view with skepticism much of the current discussion on" globalization, and "should reassess their strategies with the objective of strengthening regional competitiveness"[16] in light of problems posed by diverse industry standards and customer tastes, and the advantages of being an "insider."

The links between the global and the local reflect what Appadurai describes felicitously as "relations of disjuncture," by which he means that the paths taken by various flows "of objects, persons, images, and discourses – are not coeval, convergent, isomorphic or spatially consistent."[17] Appadurai cites as an example of such disjunctions media "flows across national boundaries that cannot be satisfied by national standards of living and consumer capabilities" and "flows of discourses of human rights that generate demands from workforces that are repressed by state violence which is itself backed by global arms flows."[18] Globalization has focused global attention on the collective rights of local groups of indigenous peoples, women as a class, and environmental and health protection.[19] Disjunctions like these, according to Appadurai, produce *"problems that manifest themselves in intensely local forms but have contexts that are anything but local."*[20] Sassen emphasizes that the local and the global do not exclude each other. "To the contrary, they significantly overlap and interact in ways that distinguish our contemporary moment."[21] Globalization "entails not only a focus on that which is explicitly global in scale but also a focus on the multiplication of horizontal cross-border connections among various localities," as well as recognition "that many of the globally scaled dynamics, such as the global capital market, actually are partly embedded in subnational sites and move between these differently scaled practices and organizational forms."[22]

The "contemporary moment" is indeed unique in important ways, but overlapping and interacting as characteristics of political and socio-economic systems are nothing new. For example, scholars have been intrigued for some time by similarities between the overlap and layering of local, regional, national, and transnational authorities in a globalizing world and the overlapping of authority and governance in medieval Europe. Over three decades ago, Hedley Bull described five trends that he regarded as harbingers of what he called a potential "new medievalism." These were regional integration of sovereign states, fragmentation of such states, a renewal of private violence internationally, a proliferation of transnational institutions, and the emergence of technologies that unified peoples around the world.[23] In fact, all five of these trends have become increasingly evident in subsequent years. Kobrin adopted the medieval metaphor to capture changes in the global political economy regarding "space, geography and borders," "the ambiguity of authority," "multiple loyalties," "transnational elites," "distinctions between public and private property," and "unifying belief systems and supranational centralization."[24]

Overall, as Shaw explains:

> The dominant trend is the complex globalization of authority. This involves the extension of globally legitimate international institutions. It also involves the transformation of national forms of state – including concepts of sovereignty . . . However, at the same time there is a dissolution of legitimate national authority which produces atavistic, exclusive, ethnic–nationalist caricatures of state power.[25]

As this suggests, the overlap of authority and governance among subnational, national, transnational, and international polities is fraught with difficulties.

Difficulties manifest themselves in phenomena like the growing extraterritorial claims of powerful states. Whether pursuing terrorists or lobbying foreign legislators, states such as the United States, China, and Russia seek to extend their practices extraterritorially well beyond their borders in order to protect and assist their citizens and firms. Among the most highly publicized manifestations of extraterritorial activity were the US practice of "extraordinary rendition" as part of its War on Terror and the indictment of foreign leaders by European magistrates for alleged human-rights abuses. It is ironic that, although globalization has limited state autonomy in a variety of ways, it has also encouraged such behavior. "In increasingly globalized state relations," writes Shaw, "extraterritorial action by juridical state entities is becoming normal. Within the Western state, especially, it is a routine component of the internationalization of the state."[26] "Extra-territorial disputes arise due to competing jurisdictional claims, in which multiple regulatory authorities seek to set the rules of the game for a particular space and/or issue area,"[27] the solutions to which require (but do not always generate) new institutional forms.

Hence it makes little sense to treat global and local as dichotomous. Instead, the two processes constitute a continuum along which different spaces and places are complexly linked. "In a tightly networked political and social world where speed is a paramount feature," argues Brunn, "scale questions become fuzzy."

> The question arises: what is local? What is regional and what is global? In short, they become mixed and somewhat confused, which poses a problem for the local state, the national state and also interstate relations. The reason is that local issues, events or problems have or can have far-reaching impacts that may extend not only into local areas in an adjacent state, but into states and territories in another part of the world. The result is that "the local becomes global", and "the global becomes local".[28]

Turkey is

> a key example of the contending dynamics in the Middle East of regionalism, localism, and globalization . . . It has felt the attractions of European (and Western) trade, exported labour to Europe, been exposed to Western media and cultural exports, contended with the difficult dynamics of democratization, and aspired to membership in the European Union."[29]

In consequence, Turkey retains links to both Europe and the Middle East and is increasingly characterized by a moderate hybridized form of Islam, and the country is viewed by observers as a possible "bridge" between the two regions.

Caroline Humphrey, a professor at Cambridge University, has been studying the "border country" of Inner Asia for forty years. She says she is still interested "in the meeting of Russia and China and in the way that the countries of this region are so different from ours. So many things that seem natural to us, like having a home in one place, or owning property, or having an address, just don't exist in the same way there." Interestingly, however, when asked which is the more "exotic," Humphrey answers:

> It has to be Cambridge – it has so many peculiar and traditional ways of doing things that it must seem quite strange for people from outside. You can live in Cambridge for years and still not quite get it because each college does things differently . . . Whereas Mongolia is nowadays a very restless, changeable new capitalist country – skyscrapers go up, new businesses are started. And I think that's probably more characteristic of the world in general.[30]

So, Cambridge is "exotic" because each of its thirty-two colleges is, in a way, its own little world – a local within a local within a local – while what makes traditional back-of-beyond Mongolia more familiar is the fact that it is being transformed economically rather like the rest of the newly capitalist globalizing world.

Everywhere, migration is an issue that is shaped by the interaction of local and global conditions. Local demographic and economic conditions trigger or impede global flows of migrants, and "through the interaction of the global and the national, the refugee is policed into deterritorialized frontierlands."[31] "For men and women alike," as Arlie Russell Hochschild suggests, "migration has become a private solution to a public problem."[32] And, this migration "is historically and structurally linked to the uneven development of the global economy, the legacy of colonialism, and the indebtedness of Third World countries."[33]

Regarding migration, Nikos Papastergiadis describes how "concepts like deterritorialization and hybridity do not reside exclusively in any particular discipline."[34] "The globalization of migration," he suggests, "can be defined through the following features: multiplication of migratory movements; differentiation in the economic, social and cultural backgrounds of immigrants; acceleration of migration patterns; expansion in the volume of migrants; feminization of migration; deterritorialization of cultural communities; and multiple loyalties of diasporas."[35] Papastergiadis likewise maintains that "the cultural dynamic of deterritorialization has decoupled previous links between space, stability and reproduction; it has situated the notion of community in multiple locations; it has split loyalties and fractured the practices that secure understanding and knowledge within the family and social unit," and the result has been "more ambivalent images of homeland" and "greater stress on the need for re-imagining the possibilities of belonging."[36] In this we see an attenuation of the connection between place and culture.

DETERRITORIALIZATION AND DENATIONALIZATION

Globalization, Steger declares (and we have previously noted), is not "merely a set of material processes anchored in economics and technology"; it is also "a linguistic and ideological practice."[37] In other words, culture is a key dimension of globalization, and the overlap of the local and global is especially visible in the cultural realm. In this respect, Nederveen Pieterse persuasively describes cultural mixing or hybridization through migration and through cyberspace as subverting "nationalism because it privileges border crossing" and diminishes "identity politics such as ethnic or other claims to purity and authenticity because it starts out from the fuzziness of boundaries."[38] Culture is "a translocal learning process" rather than a "learning process that is, in the main, localized."[39] Migration, for example, mixes language, religions, and tastes. Hybridity has an additional temporal dimension in its "coexistence and interspersion of premodernity, modernity, and postmodernity."[40] As we shall see in Chapters 7 and 8, various regions and countries have mixed globalized values with indigenous norms and practices. In some cases, as in Europe, the mix highlights the globalized side of the equation, and in others, as in Central Asia, it stresses local norms. Nevertheless, even in North America and Europe, the main sources of globalized values, migration has resulted in the importation of the norms and practices by Asian, African, and Latin American diasporas.

We are back to the important point that culture is increasingly deterritorialized in the course of globalization. "Globalized culture," as Tomlinson emphasizes, "is less determined by location because location is increasingly penetrated by 'distance' – by the integration of structures of global connectivity."[41] Thus, "globalization reveals the possibility of – indeed makes possible – the relative independence of culture from place, and ... this, rather than any idea of the dominance of one geographically defined culture is its most significant effect."[42] The reduction in cultural territoriality is partly a function of what Tomlinson calls "telemediazation" by which he means "the increasing implication of electronic communications and media systems in both the reach of global connectivity into everyday experience, and the 'accessing of the world' by locally situated individuals" resulting in "time-space bridging."[43] Global media have to some degree made the idea of "world public opinion" a reality. They have also sensitized people to and made them aware of natural disasters and large-scale violence in remote corners of the globe, creating unprecedented pressures for "humanitarian relief" and "humanitarian intervention."

Ideas travel from place to place almost seamlessly and instantaneously. However, greater velocity may not always be a virtue in global politics. "Speed," cautions Nick Stevenson, "destroys thought and the possibility of democratic deliberation. Ideas concerning the possibility of using technology to enhance democracy are mistaken in that what is more likely is a culture of conditioning where communications are used to condition the responses of the public."[44] Spatial reality can be virtual reality. And "time" loses meaning as it is ever more compressed and equivalent to instantaneous. To Harvey, "time-space compression" refers to "processes that so revolutionize the objective qualities of space and time that we are forced to alter, sometimes in quite radical ways, how we represent the world to ourselves."[45]

What is true of culture, of course, is perhaps even more evident in the realms of economics and politics, where the logic of territory no longer determines organization or distribution. Held describes "the growing deterritorialization of economic activity as production and finance increasingly acquire a global and transnational dimension,"[46] and Held and McGrew write of "a process of relative deterritorialization: as social, political and economic activities are significantly 'stretched' across the globe."[47] Papastergiadis prefers to speak of both the "dematerialization and deterritorialization of the global economy" because "the bulk of world trade is now focused on speculative options, future shares, insurance, finance and real estate, rather than in the commodity market."[48]

Associated with the deterritorialization of economics and politics "is the growing articulation of globalization with national economies and the associated withdrawal of the state from various spheres of citizenship entitlements, with the possibility of a corresponding dilution of loyalty to the state."[49] Globalization blurs the distinction between domestic and foreign politics, between the public and private arenas, and between public and private goods. What is distinctive about the institutional order of the current epoch of globalization, as far as Sassen is concerned, "is its capacity to privatize what was heretofore public and to denationalize what were once national authorities and policy agendas,"[50] and she focuses on "processes that take place deep inside territories and institutional domains that have largely been constructed in national terms,"[51] which, although nationally or locally organized, are elements in transnational networks. Bob Jessop adds the idea of "destatization" to "denationalization," defining the first as "redrawing the public–private divide, reallocating tasks, and rearticulating the relationship between organizations and tasks across this divide on whatever territorial scale(s) the state in question acts."[52]

Denationalized activities include environmental and human rights activist networks. Sassen also includes "non-cosmopolitan forms of global politics and imaginaries that remain deeply attached or focused on localized issues or struggles, yet are – knowingly or not – part of global lateral networks containing multiple other such localized efforts."[53] Globalization has even denationalized campaign finance in the sense that "the emergence of vast new wealth around the globe, tethered to no single nation, has become a weapon for buying influence and a force for local and global corruption. Campaign finance, know-how, and even skullduggery have gone global, while national mechanisms for regulating them have failed to keep pace."[54]

One must be careful here. Deterritorialization and denationalization are not necessarily the same, and there are perceptive critics of the claim that globalization induces deterritorialization. Stuart Elden, for example, "takes issue with understandings of globalization as deterritorialization, which claim that territory no longer occupies the foundational geographical place, claiming that they misconceive the very basis of this crucial term."[55] He argues that "space and place should not be distinguished on the basis of scale, but that space emerges in Western thought through a particular way of grasping place ... as something extensible and calculable, extended in three dimensions and grounded on the geometric point."[56] The idea of deterritorialization needs to be reconsidered when "territory" is taken to mean "place" or "point." By contrast, global simultaneity or instantaneity are temporal factors and are not equivalent to deterritorialization. "If there is a shift today beyond [the traditional conception]," Elden believes, "it is that the space is no longer that of a single country (or later, nation), but that of the world as a whole. The abstract space is extended to the globe, which is understood as a geometrical object. Conceived in this way it can be divided, or ordered as a whole."[57]

GLOCALIZATION

Although the term "glocalization" has several usages, it was coined to refer in particular to the simultaneous presence of globalizing and localizing dynamics[58] and to "the more or less deliberate filtering or adaptation of global models and practices within particular local contexts that in turn reshapes these models and practices."[59] It is a helpful concept because "we can no longer draw clear and firm boundaries between local and global spheres or between national and international spheres of social life," and "cannot separate the 'in here' of the city, community or locality in which we live from the 'out there' of global flows of money, capital, people, power and dominance."[60]

"Globalization," as Nederveen Pieterse reminds us, "can mean the reinforcement of or go together with localism, as in 'Think globally, act locally,'" and such a "tandem operation of local/global dynamics, or glocalization, is at work in the case of minorities who appeal to transnational human rights standards beyond state authority, or indigenous peoples who find support for local demands from transnational networks."[61] What it does *not* mean is that the local has been erased or absorbed by the global. In other words, the global and local are complexly related and may simultaneously compete with or reinforce each other. Thus, "glocalization" signifies the existence of complex "parallel, irreversible and mutually interdependent processes by which globalization-deepens-localization-deepens-globalization and so on." "The global and the local are inextricably and irreversibly bound together through a dynamic relationship, with huge flows of 'resources' moving backwards and forwards between the two. Neither the global nor the local exists without the other."[62]

Glocalization, as Erik Swyngedouw contends, modifies the general assumption that globalization *only* erodes state capacity. He sees this dual process manifested in the state intervention in the economy that can occur either downward to the local level or upward to regional groups such as the European Union (EU) and the North American Free Trade Agreement (NAFTA) or global institutions like the World Trade Organization (WTO) and the International Bank of Reconstruction and Development (IBRD – the World Bank).[63]

Munck further illustrates the impact of local and regional events on global affairs that he calls "local transnationalism" by pointing to the impact that local labor unions, peasant movements like Brazil's MST, and environmental nongovernment organizations (NGOs) such as Friends of the Earth and Greenpeace can have on corporate networks and government decision-making.[64] Such NGOs as the Nature Conservancy and Conservation International have received funds from TNCs, including the oil giant BP, and have assisted corporations to improve their environmental practices as did the Environmental Defense Fund for McDonald's. The Environmental Defense Fund has also sought to use a corporate–NGO alliance, US Climate Action Partnership, to lobby for a law to cap America's carbon emissions. Not surprisingly, however, the disastrous oil spill in the Gulf of Mexico in 2010, caused by an explosion that destroyed a BP offshore oil platform, revealed serious strains in corporate–NGO relations.[65]

Many of these NGOs are what Neil Washbourne describes as "translocal," by which he means they are able to connect directly "to other places without having to go via centres."[66] Environmental groups, in particular, "have the ability to bridge the gap between the local and the global, the space of places and the space of flows" that "will combine the new communication-based mechanisms of power with the creation of a new politics attuned to the Information Age."[67] Activities like these suggest that we are confronting growing "interdependence and intermingling of global, distant and local logics."[68] For instance, anti-globalization demonstrations routinely mix opponents of local and national policies with those opposed to international actions and policies.

Successful transnational corporations, almost by definition, combine the local and the global. On the one hand, Bartlett and Ghoshal write, "Many companies have exploited – and accelerated – the convergence of tastes and preferences by developing products that can be sold worldwide." On the other hand,

> even this trend toward standardized products has a flip side. In many industries, a large and growing group of consumers rejects homogenized product design and performance and wants to reassert its traditional preferences, thereby creating openings – often very profitable ones – for competitors willing to meet this need for locally differentiated products and services.[69]

Transnational corporations thus require "local sensitivity and market understanding" and a need to be keenly aware of "national differences and local interests in the host countries where they operate."[70] Japanese firms came to appreciate the need for localization earlier than did their Western competitors, a fact that was at least partly responsible for Japan's growing economic competiveness in the 1970s and 1980s.[71] "At the same time," as Scholte observes, "local particularities are sometimes reproduced in supraterritorial space, as witnessed in the contrasts between Japan-based and US-based global automobile manufacture, for example."[72]

Information technologies are crucial in linking the "global" and the "local." "Telemediazation" matters greatly. Major "local" events, such as the Beijing Olympics, an anti-globalization protest, or an Asian tsunami, have an immediate "global" reach owing to technologies that enable "extensive corporeal, imaginative and virtual travel."[73] The sources of information are no longer only local; rather they have become "placeless," with no or at least few boundaries to their movement. "Information flows," Urry argues, "have been dematerialized from place. With digitization, information adopts patterns and modes of mobility substantially separate from material form or presence. Information gets everywhere (or nowhere) travelling more or less instantaneously along the fluid networks of global communications."[74] What is available locally is virtually the same as what is available globally. Indeed, among the reasons why the territorial boundaries of state are ever less congruent with political, economic, and cultural life is "the significance of various transnational media, both economic and cultural, in constituting the ways in which people live."[75] Sources of information may be "placeless", but "the globalization process contributes to strengthening the role of the cultural intermediaries who administrate the new global media distribution chains (via satellite etc.)," and "draws in the intellectuals to interpret traditions and styles in a new global circumstance which is one of polyculturalism."[76]

Global cities are archetypal "glocalized" worlds. Sassen, who has pioneered our theoretical understanding of the role of such cities, explains that they are sites for managerial skills needed by the global economy, for private governance functions performed by corporations, and for state-of-the-art infrastructure. They are also sites where cultures meet, sometimes clash, and frequently evolve hybrid forms. She writes:

> The space constituted by the worldwide grid of global cities ... is perhaps one of the most strategic spaces for the formation of transnational identities and communities ... a space that is both place-centered, in that it is embedded in particular and strategic cities, and transterritorial because it connects sites that are not geographically proximate yet are intensely connected to each other.[77]

Economic "core" and "periphery" exist in close proximity, and one can "see most clearly an incipient, highly specialized and partial denationalization of specific components of national states."[78] "If we consider further that large cities concentrate a growing share of disadvantaged populations ... then we can see that cities have become a strategic terrain for a whole series of conflicts and contradictions."[79]

THE DIALECTICAL RELATIONSHIP BETWEEN THE GLOBAL AND THE LOCAL

The proliferation of subnational, transnational, international, and supranational actors, sharing adherents with states, as we observed earlier, seems to have returned global politics in some respects to the overlapping and crosscutting political life of far earlier eras and away from the neat, exclusive territorial boxes characteristic of state-centric maps. One natural result is the proliferation of links between the global and the local. As Marc Williams puts it, "the primacy given to territoriality and the importance of the internal/external distinction are undermined by the process of globalization."[80] We are seeing the "dialectic of fractionalisation and reorganization."[81] This dialectic has much in common with what Karl Polanyi meant by his concept of "double movement" – a movement met by a countermovement "checking the expansion in definite directions,"[82] which Polanyi applied mainly to the relationship between self-regulating market and society.

History is not unilinear, as we emphasized earlier. Globalization and localization processes wax and wane. Although there are genuinely novel aspects to contemporary globalization, earlier epochs have witnessed a retreat from or movement towards highly globalized worlds. Some periods feature integration of independent polities into larger entities characterized by economies of scale, cultural homogenization, and centralized governance – and sometimes the reverse. As James observes:

> Often we believe that this process [globalization] is irreversible, that it provides a one-way road to the future. But historical reflections lead to a more sober and more pessimistic assessment. There have already been highly developed and highly inte-

grated international communities that dissolved under the pressure of unexpected events. But in every case the momentum was lost; the pendulum swung back. In Europe, for instance, the universal Erasmian world of the Renaissance was destroyed by the Reformation and its Catholic counterpart, and separatism, provincialism, and parochialism followed.[83]

As we have seen, there were periods in ancient history – for example, the Mediterranean at the height of the Roman Empire – when at least a part of the world was highly integrated. In China, even during the warring states era, a sense of cultural unity produced a common identity among the Han Chinese, notwithstanding localized security arrangements. In medieval Europe, before local identities had hardened into full-fledged national identities, Christianity provided cultural cohesion; political boundaries were indeterminate; and merchants, artisans, and clerics moved across the continent with little attention to legal frontiers. A form of globalization (or at least regionalization) also characterized the world of Europe's colonial empires from the seventeenth to the early twentieth century. Economic interdependence deepened when mercantilism gave way to economic liberalism and free trade. As Krugman recalls, "our great-great grandfathers lived, as we do, in a world of large-scale international trade and investment, a world destroyed by nationalism." Krugman quotes John Maynard Keynes's description of prewar Europe: "The inhabitant of London could order by telephone, sipping his morning tea in bed, the various products of the whole earth . . . he could at the same moment and by the same means adventure his wealth in the natural resources and new enterprises of any quarter of the world." "But then," continues Krugman,

> came three decades of war, revolution, political instability, depression and more war. By the end of World War II, the world was fragmented economically as well as politically. And it took a couple of generations to put it back together. So, can things fall apart again? Yes, they can.[84]

"Globalization," as Rosenau declares, "is but one component of the transformative dynamics that underlie the emergence of a new epoch"; "localization is also a powerful force at work throughout the world"; the two processes appear to be "pervasive contradictions."[85] The world is driven by dynamic and interdependent processes of centralization, which produces "intermestic" politics, and decentralization of political authority. Rosenau describes these processes collectively as "fragmegration" precisely because the term "serves to underscore the contradictions, ambiguities, complexities, and uncertainties that have replaced the regularities of prior epochs."[86]

Contradictions were evident in the decades after World War II, which simultaneously witnessed centralizing processes associated with the institutionalization of the Bretton Woods system and the decentralizing dynamics of decolonization. As Elisa Reis observes: "Under the impact of global processes that make the world a single unit, on the one hand, and of a global trend toward decentralization and fragmentation, on the other, great transformations are taking place."[87] Simultaneously, "centripetal forces . . . are making groups and nations more and more interdependent even as centrifugal forces are increasingly fragmenting them into subgroups and subnations."[88] Global stability urgently requires a balance between these forces, but of course this is easier to recognize than to achieve. Friedman captures this when he declares: "The challenge in this era of globalization – for countries and individuals – is to find a healthy balance between preserving a sense of identity, home and community and doing what it takes to survive within the globalization system."[89]

We are in "a period in which the competition between alternative intersubjective agreements relative to borders intensifies as those fearful of immigration vie with those who are open to the values and practices of globalization."[90] Consider the US–Canadian and US–Mexican borders. In both cases, "the closer the transition gets to stripping the border of meaning, the greater will be the tensions as localizing reactions to the globalizing dynamics become increasingly defensive, articulate, and resistant."[91] This is Friedman's "olive tree backlashing against the Lexus,"[92] and, for Nederveen Pieterse, it is how cultural interaction produces "intense and dramatic nostalgia politics, of which ethnic upsurges, ethnicization of nations, and religious revivalism form part."[93]

Focusing on security, Ian Clark also foresaw simultaneous processes of globalization and fragmentation beginning after the Cold War:

> Although the state remained central to discussions of security, its monopoly was challenged by its submergence into wider patterns of transnational activity, nowhere more apparent than in the case of international financial flows or in what some saw as the emergence of a global civil society: at the other end, fragmentation has challenged the state's capacity to manage its own domestic economic, political, security agenda as well, whether it be in the form of separatism, regionalism, or organized crime.

And, in words reminiscent of Rosenau's "fragmegration," Clark concluded: "What is happening to security is but one manifestation of what is happening to the state in general and reflects the twin pressures exercised by both globalization and fragmentation,"[94] which he regards as cyclical historical phases.

Expressed metaphorically, Barber contrasts "Babel" and "Disneyland." At one extreme is

> the grim prospect of a retribalization of humankind by war and bloodshed: a threatened balkanization of nation-states in which culture is pitted against culture, people against people, tribe against tribe, a Jihad in the name of a hundred narrowly conceived faiths against every kind of interdependence, every kind of artificial social cooperation and mutuality: against technology, against pop culture, and against integrated markets; against modernity itself.[95]

On the one hand, critics of economic globalization insist that globalization has increased unemployment, created greater economic inequality, and produced social and gender gaps. "In short, there are winners and losers everywhere."[96] Barber describes the other extreme as a "future in shimmering pastels, a busy portrait of onrushing economic, technological, and ecological forces that demand integration and uniformity that mesmerizes people everywhere with fast music, fast computers, and fast food . . . one McWorld tied together by communications,[97] information, entertainment, and commerce."[98]

The processes of centralization and decentralization of authority are linked *dialectically*, a point we shall return to later. Clark writes of a "dialectic between globalization and fragmentation," though he also gainsays the claim by describing them as "two facets of the same process."[99] Hoffmann contemplates how

> the spread of chaos in the state system might lead to a two-tier international milieu, produced by the dialectic of globalization and fragmentation: at one level, all the effective states engaged in the ups and downs, the gains and losses, of world capitalism, and at the other, a set of poor and either disintegrating or isolated societies left to fend – and feud – for themselves.[100]

Even with the addition of new information and communication technologies, centralization of authority produces difficulties in managing disparate peoples with disparate interests, while intensifying their desire for local autonomy and governance and nourishment of local culture, norms, and identity. Decentralization simplifies problems of control but reduces functional efficiency and economies of scale, even while sustaining and deepening intimacy and tradition. The virtues of localization appear in numerous and unexpected settings, including urban street gangs that jealously guard their "turf."[101]

Thus, as Alison Brysk argues in her work on indigenous peoples, globalization entails a paradox:

> The consequences of globalization are substantial but by no means uniform or homogenizing. Rather, globalization can strengthen local differences through access to information, audiences, markets, foreign policy processes, and transnational pressure points. Increasing interpenetration across borders is not a single process but encompasses linking subsidiary logics of interactions based on power, profit, and principle. When these coincide, globalization tends to erase the tribal village. *But when the international relations of states, markets, and civil societies are disparate, local forces have increased opportunities to construct a response.*[102]

GLOBALIZING VERSUS LOCALIZING CULTURAL CURRENTS

The interdependence of globalization and localization is evident in how cultural homogenization may encourage localization. "Modernization, economic development, urbanization, and globalization," as Samuel Huntington suggested, "have led people to rethink their identities and to redefine them in narrower, more intimate, communal terms."[103] Globalization has not eliminated local diversity, but, instead, has frequently deepened local identities and territorial attachments, for example, among ethnic groups. In some cases, loyalties to states have also become more deeply anchored.[104] These are some of the ways globalization and localization are entwined.

"In the former Soviet Union," writes Douglas Blum, "one finds a veritable preoccupation with cultural globalization," experienced by many "as Westernization (or, often, as 'Americanization'),[105] which is widely understood as conveying a massive pressure for homogeneity. This in turn generates a powerful mix of emotions: excitement, pride, anxiety, and disgust."[106] The spread of Islamic zealotry also reflects this backlash, engendering fears of social pollution and moral collapse, and a search for cultural refuge.

The idea of a cultural refuge is evident in Huntington's provocative analysis of a shift in global politics away from a European era of clashing states towards an era of clashing civilizations – the antithesis of globalization.[107] Huntington feared that relentless globalization would undermine national cultures that he regarded as territorially anchored and perhaps even national independence. He believed that "cultural characteristics and differences are less mutable and hence less easily compromised and resolved than political and economic ones."[108] Analogous to Huntington's position is Sarah Armstrong's "local cultural model, which defines culture as a way of life and deserving of state support" which she contrasts with "the global market model, which defines culture as a commodity to be treated like other commodities."[109]

Nederveen Pieterse regards Huntington's thesis as one of three cultural paradigms, the others of which he terms "McDonaldization" and "Hybridization."[110] He interprets Huntington's "Clash of Civilizations" as a romantic vision that assumes cultures to be pure and closed and reflect permanent differences, and its "fallacy is the reification of the local, sidelining the interplay between the local and the global."[111] It represents the "paradigm of differentialism following the principle of *purity*,"[112] as reflected in the burning of churches by militant Muslims in Egypt and Malaysia. By contrast, "McDonaldization" assumes cultural homogenization owing to diffusion from a hegemonic cultural core via transnational corporations that produces convergence, a trend that Armstrong fears "could produce the marginalization of local cultures within their own borders," thereby threatening a local community's survival.[113] Finally, hybridization, as we have noted, assumes a mixing of cultural traits "that resolves the tension . . . between the local and the global." "Each paradigm involves a different take on *globalization*:"

> According to cultural differentialism, globalization is a surface phenomenon only: the real dynamic is regionalization, or the forming of regional blocs, which tend to correspond with civilizational clusters. Therefore the future of globalization is interregional rivalry. According to the convergence principle, globalization is westernization or Americanization writ large . . . According to the mixing approach, the outcome of globalization processes is open-ended and current globalization is as much a process of easternization as westernization.[114]

Hybridization is plainly interdependent in a variety of ways. "We are," declare Lieber and Weisberg, "constantly borrowing, imitating and incorporating just as we are distinguishing and differentiating ourselves by innovative, exclusive or singular expressions."[115] "Globalization itself," Cerny, Menz, and Soederberg write,

> is . . . reshaped by and through local conditions and domestic political objectives; it is not just imposed from outside. It starts from the competing goals of people in everyday politics and economics . . . and seeps into the deepest nooks and crannies of everyday life. International and domestic politics are therefore *not* two separate arenas, but parts of an interpenetrated set of webs of politics and governance that increasingly cut across and entangle the nations of the world, summoning forth and molding the actions of ordinary people.[116]

Terrorists, traffickers, and drug dealers, and corporations, among others, also function both locally and globally. Problems posed by water rights, water pollution, and water conservation are only a few illustrations of how crucial policy issues have both local and global dimensions.

Still, in most respects, global in contrast to local governance remains an aspiration of cosmopolitan scholars rather than a reality. In the area of human rights, according to Chris Brown, such scholars contend that "the ultimate referent object of international society ought to be individual human beings rather than states as such" and "that it is already possible to discern the outlines of a global civil society in our current situation."[117] They believe, Brown continues, "that such developments are backed by, indeed immanent in, the processes of global social and economic change summarized by the term globalization."[118] However, such governance is vigorously resisted by many countries, especially in the developing world, that see it as part of an effort to increase the influence of "those already rich and powerful."[119] Brown is what we earlier described as a "skeptic," and he concludes:

> Certainly some of the rhetoric of globalization – a "borderless world", for example – looks even more silly today than it did originally; the world has never been borderless for those flying economy class, and the security checks and controls that are being introduced today for all travelers simply extend to the privileged the surveillance and harassment that were previously reserved for the proles.[120]

Moreover, the great powers have no interest in a borderless world and, unlike many Europeans, still value "the importance of brute military force."[121]

A WORLD OF SHIFTING BOUNDARIES AND EVOLVING AUTHORITY

Brown's view notwithstanding, the porosity of borders *does* play an important role in the transformative perspective regarding globalization. "Globalization," argues Rosenau,

> is rendering boundaries and identity with the land less salient, while localization, being driven by pressures to narrow and withdraw, is highlighting borders and intensifying the deep attachments to land that can dominate emotions and reasoning ... In short, *globalization is boundary-eroding and localization is boundary-strengthening.*[122]

Although Rosenau captures an essential feature of globalizing, the spatial issue is even more complex because, as Sassen stresses, "the global – whether an institution, a process, a discursive practice, or an imaginary – simultaneously transcends the exclusive framing of national states yet partly inhabits national territories."[123] Roger Keil follows Sassen, arguing that global cities (which he equates with "local states") are spaces within which "the dominant culture and the multiplicity of cultures and identities are inscribed."[124] Criticizing Mann for underestimating "subnational networks in the globalization process," Keil contends that globalization is driven by "agency" and that: "The argument of an ascending replacement of local by supra-local networks is ultimately a surprisingly linear and undialectical historico-geographical view, which almost posits a teleologically guided historical process and equates spatial relationships with physical distance."[125]

In contrast to globalization, Rosenau observes, "localization derives from all those pressures that lead people, groups, societies, governments, institutions, and transnational organizations to *narrow* their horizons and withdraw to *less encompassing* processes, organizations, or systems."[126] Beggar-thy-neighbor economic policies, anti-immigration sentiments, or cultural exclusion activities, xenophobic nationalism, or ethno-national secessionism all constitute the faces of localization. A resurgence of power politics and arms racing, great power unilateralism, and ethnic or religious communalism and separatism also involve localizing dynamics.

Normatively, there is no reason to assume that the centralizing of authority implicit in globalization is preferable to the decentralizing consequences of localization.

> Clearly, neither globalizing nor localizing dynamics are innately desirable or noxious. Considered normatively, there is a good deal to be said for and against both of them, depending on the nature of the arrangements they foster and the perspective from which they are assessed.[127]

Rosenau's definitions of globalization and localization provide reasonably clear criteria to determine the direction or impact of any particular event or trend. An event such as the splitting off of South Ossetia and Abkhazia from Georgia by Russian military force is a "localizing event" because it produces smaller polities, emphasizes the role of territory, and creates additional impediments to the free movement of things, peoples, and ideas. Such diverse events as an airline strike, a cyberattack, or the requirement for visas to cross borders are all localizing. By contrast, allowing free competition among airlines, enlarging the number of people with access to the internet, and reducing restrictions on immigration are "globalizing events."[128]

Given accelerating change, Rosenau asks:

> How do we assess a world in which the Frontier is continuously shifting, widening and narrowing, simultaneously undergoing erosion with respect to many issues and reinforcement with respect to others? How do we reconceptualize political space so that it connotes identities and affiliations (say, religious, ethnic, and professional) as well as territorialities?[129]

His own view is that globalizing processes are overwhelming localizing processes. For his part, Scholte insists that the "local coexists with, is not wholly subordinate to, and indeed shapes the global at the same time that it is shaped by the supraterritorial realm."[130] Whether Rosenau or Scholte is closer to the mark, a reshuffling of authorities and identities has and continues to take place, a reshuffling that led the present authors to call for a "remapping of global politics."

Rosenau's conceptual criteria for evaluating globalization and localization are enriched by the work of Held and his colleagues who elaborate several dimensions along which to conceptualize the direction and magnitude of change in globalization. They offer several "spatio-temporal" dimensions: "(1) the extensiveness of networks of relations and connections; (2) the intensity of flows and levels of activity within these networks; (3) the velocity or speed of interchanges;[131] and (4) the impact of these phenomena on particular communities."[132] The admission of new members to the WTO reflects growing extensiveness; the proliferation of mobile phones and internet availability produce greater intensity and velocity in the flow of ideas; the introduction of mobile money using such phones is having a profound impact on the economies of poor states;[133] and the consequences of higher commodity and energy prices illustrate the growing impact of shortages of raw materials. Held and his colleagues also identify several descriptive organization variables: infrastructures, institutionalization, stratification, and modes of interactions that should be kept in mind in considering the nature of globalization over time.[134]

Globalization owes much to United States hegemony after World War II and the desire of Western leaders to encourage and sustain an open trading system, global economic growth, and the spread of values such as individualism, democracy, and free enterprise. Some argue that globalization could not survive if major countries no longer supported it. They believe that, if today's major powers were to become disillusioned with globalization's consequences, their withdrawal could bring about the collapse of key public and private institutions that sustain it. Others argue that the process is so far along that it can no longer be reversed, that it is no longer controlled by any country or countries, and that the costs for a country to cut the web of interdependence in which it is enmeshed is simply too high to consider.

Views about whether globalization is reversible are linked to judgments about whether the globalization process is, on balance, beneficial or harmful. After all, globalization has "losers" as well as "winners," and individuals everywhere are increasingly discovering that their welfare is determined by remote forces beyond their control or even the control of their governments. Yet the choices (if there are choices) are not made any simpler by the fact that one may be simultaneously gaining from some aspect(s) of globalization and losing from others. The next chapter examines the vigorous normative debate over globalization and the central arguments that inform the debate.

NOTES

1 Naisbitt, *Mind Set!*, 166. Emphasis in original.
2 Paul Kirkbride, Paul Pinnington, and Karen Ward, "Globalization: Where Is Your Organization Today?" in Paul Kirkbride and Karen Ward, eds., *Globalization: The Internal Dynamic* (Chichester, UK: John Wiley, 2001), 8.
3 Sassen, "Spatialities and Temporalities of the Global: Elements for a Theorization," in Appadurai, ed., *Globalization*, 260.
4 Frank J. Lechner, *Globalization: The Making of World Society* (Oxford: Wiley-Blackwell, 2009), 13.
5 David J. Keeling, "Latin American Development and the Globalization Imperative: New Directions, Familiar Crises," *Journal of Latin American Geography* 3:1 (2004), 2.
6 Annabelle Sreberny-Mohammadi, "The Global and the Local in International Communications," in Kelly Michelle Askew and Richard R. Wilk, eds., *The Anthropology of Media: A Reader* (Oxford: Blackwell Publishing, 2002), 341.
7 David Coulby and Evie Zambeta, "Introduction: Trends in Globalization," in David Coulby and Evie Zambeta, eds., *World Yearbook of Education 2005: Globalization and*

Nationalism in Education (Abingdon, UK: RoutledgeFalmer, 2005), 1. For the globalizing impact of education, notably in the global "knowledge economy," see David Coulby, "The Knowledge Economy: Technology and Characteristics" and Coulby, "The Knowledge Economy: Institutions," both in ibid., 19–29 and 30–46. For the nationalist impact of education, see Evie Zambeta, "The Survival of Nationalism in a Global System" and Masako Shimbata, "Education, National identity and Religion in Japan in an Age of Globalization," both in ibid., 48–72 and 73–94.

8 Clifford J. Levy, "Soviet Legacy Lingers as Estonia Defines Its People," *New York Times*, August 15, 2010, http://www.nytimes.com/2010/08/16/world/europe/16estonia.html.
9 Barry K. Gills, "Introduction: Globalization and the Politics of Resistance," in Gills, ed., *Globalization and the Politics of Resistance*, 3.
10 Hardt and Negri, *Empire*, 44.
11 Castells, *The Rise of the Network Society*, 247. For an analysis of the effects of growing labor mobility on national sovereignty, see Jonathan W. Moses, "Exit, Vote and Sovereignty: Migration, States and Globalization," *Review of International Political Economy* 12:1 (February 2005), 53–77.
12 Workers Uniting: About Us, http://www.workersuniting.org/default.aspx?page=1.
13 "You Ain't Seen Nothing Yet," *The Economist*, April 24, 2010, 59–60.
14 Nederveen Pieterse, *Globalization and Culture*, 65–6. Emphasis in original.
15 Ibid., 65.
16 Allen J. Morrison, David A. Ricks, and Kendall Roth, "Globalization versus Regionalization: Which Way for the Multinational," in Franklin R. Root and Kanoknart Visudtibhan, eds., *International Strategic Management* (New York: Taylor & Francis, 1992), 88.
17 Appadurai, "Grassroots Globalization and the Research Imagination," 5.
18 Ibid., 6.
19 See Sumner B. Twiss, "History, Human Rights, and Globalization," *Journal of Religious Ethics* 32:1 (Spring 2004), 39–70.
20 Appadurai, "Grassroots Globalization and the Research Imagination." Emphasis added.
21 Sassen, "Spatialities and Temporalities of the Global: Elements for a Theorization," in Appadurai, ed., *Globalization*, 260.
22 Sassen, "The Places and Spaces of the Global," 90.
23 Hedley Bull, *The Anarchical Society* (New York: Columbia University Press, 1977), 264–76. See also James Anderson, "The Shifting Stage of Politics: New Medieval and Postmodern Territorialities?" *Environment and Planning: Society and Space* 14:2 (1996), 133–53.
24 Stephen Kobrin, "Back to the Future: Neomedievalism and the Postmodern Digital World Economy," *Journal of International Affairs* 51:2 (Spring 1998), 362, 369, 366.
25 Shaw, *Theory of the Global State*, 193–4.
26 Ibid., 225.
27 Alan Hudson, "Beyond the Borders: Globalisation, Sovereignty and Extra-Territoriality," in David Newman, ed., *Boundaries, Territory and Postmodernity* (Abingdon, UK: Frank Cass, 1999), 102.
28 Stanley D. Brunn, "A Treaty of Silicon for the Treaty of Westphalia? New Territorial Dimensions of Modern Statehood," in Newman, ed., *Boundaries, Territory and Postmodernity*, 117.
29 Ersel Aydinli, "Globalization of a Torn State: Turkey from the Middle East to European Integration," in Bassel F. Salloukh and Rex Brynen, eds., *Persistent Permeability? Regionalism, Localism, and Globalization in the Middle East* (Aldershot, UK: Ashgate Publishing, 2004), 149.
30 Humphrey profiled in Leigh Brauman, "Border Country," *CAM*, Issue 62 (Lent 2011), 31.
31 Richard Devetak and Christopher W. Hughes, *The Globalization of Political Violence* (New York: Routledge, 2008), 108.

32 Arlie Russell Hochschild, "Love and Gold," in Barbara Ehrenreich and Arlie Russell Hochschild, eds., *Global Women: Maids and Sex Workers in the New Economy* (New York: Henry Holt, 2002), 18.
33 Pei-Chia Lan, "Among Women: Migrant Domestics and Their Taiwanese Employers Across Generations," in Ehrenreich and Hochschild, eds., *Global Women*, 172.
34 Nikos Papastergiadis, *The Turbulence of Migration: Globalizations, Deterritorialization and Hybridity* (Oxford: Blackwell, 2000), 5.
35 Ibid., 86. See also M. Kearney, "The Local and the Global: The Anthropology of Globalization and Transnationalism," *Annual Review of Anthropology* 24 (October 1995), 559–60.
36 Papastergiadis, *The Turbulence of Migration*, 117.
37 Steger, *Globalisms*, ix, 18.
38 Nederveen Pieterse, *Globalization and Culture*, 53.
39 Ibid., 78.
40 Ibid., 67.
41 Tomlinson, "Globalization and Cultural Analysis," 153.
42 Ibid., 164.
43 Ibid., 156.
44 Nick Stevenson, "Media, Cultural Citizenship and the Global Public Sphere," in Randall D. Germain and Michael Kenny, eds., *The Idea of Global Civil Society: Politics and Ethics in a Globalizing Era* (Oxford: Routledge, 2005), 80.
45 David Harvey, *The Condition of Postmodernity* (Oxford: Blackwell, 1990), 240.
46 Held, McGrew, Goldblatt and Perraton, "The Globalization Debate," 555.
47 Held and McGrew, *Globalization/Anti-Globalization*, 4.
48 Papastergiadis, *The Turbulence of Migration*, 78.
49 Sassen, *Territory, Authority, Rights*, 283.
50 Ibid., 20.
51 Saskia Sassen, "Globalization or Denationalization?" *Review of International Political Economy* 10:1 (February 2003), 1.
52 Bob Jessop, *The Future of the Capitalist State* (Cambridge: Polity Press, 2002), 202.
53 Sassen, "Globalization or Denationalization?," 2.
54 Jane Bussey, "Campaign Finance Goes Global," *Foreign Policy* 118 (Spring 2000), 75.
55 Stuart Elden, "Missing the Point: Globalization, Deterritorialization and the Space of the World," *Transactions of the Institute of British Geographers* 30:1 (March 2005), 9.
56 Ibid., 8.
57 Ibid., 16.
58 See, for example, Roland Robertson, "Glocalization: Time–Space and Homogeneity–Heterogeneity," in Michael Featherstone, Scott M. Lash, Roland Robertson, eds, *Global Modernities* (London: Sage, 1995), 25–44.
59 Lechner, *Globalization*, 28.
60 Munck, *Globalization and Contestation*, 5. Transnational corporations are becoming ever more skilled in planning globally while appealing to local tastes. See, for example, Miguel Bustillo, "After Early Errors, Wal Mart Thinks Locally to Act Globally," *Wall Street Journal*, August 14, 2009, A1, A10.
61 Nederveen Pieterse, *Globalization and Culture*, 64.
62 Urry, *Global Complexity*, 84.
63 Erik Swyngedouw, "Neither Global nor Local: 'Glocalization' and the Politics of Scale," in Kevin R. Cox, ed., *Spaces of Globalization: Reasserting the Power of the Local* (New York: Guilford Press, 1997), 137–66.
64 Munck, *Globalization and Contestation*, 94–106.
65 "Reaching for a Longer Spoon," *The Economist*, June 25, 2010, 69–70.
66 Neil Washbourne, "Information Technology and New Forms of Organizing? Translocalism and Networks in Friends of the Earth," in Frank Webster, ed., *Culture and Politics in the Information Age: A New Politics?* (London: Routledge, 2001), 132.

67 Alan Dordoy and Mary Mellor, "Grassroots Environmental Movements: Mobilization in an Information Age," in Webster, ed., *Culture and Politics in the Information Age*, 168.
68 Ash Amin, "Placing Globalization," *Theory, Culture & Society* 14:2 (1997), 133.
69 Bartlett and Ghoshal, *Managing Across Borders*, 10.
70 Ibid., 9, 10. See also Bartlett, Ghoshal, and Birkinshaw, *Transnational Management*, 4th edn, 91–153.
71 Bartlett and Ghoshal, *Managing Across Borders*, 8–12.
72 Scholte, "The Geography of Collective Identities in a Globalizing World," 577.
73 Urry, *Global Complexity*, 87.
74 Ibid., 84–5.
75 Axford, *The Global System*, 28.
76 Featherstone, *Consumer Culture and Postmodernism*, 91.
77 Saskia Sassen, *Cities in a World Economy*, 3rd edn (London: Sage Publications, 2006), 73.
78 Sassen, "Globalization or Denationalization?" 4.
79 Sassen, *Cities in a World Economy*, 198.
80 Marc Williams, "Rethinking Sovereignty," in Kofman and Youngs, eds., *Globalization*, 120.
81 Cerny, "Multi-Nodal Politic," 444.
82 Karl Polanyi, *The Great Transformation: The Political and Economic Origins of Our Time* (Boston, MA: Beacon Press, 1944), 138. For a succinct analysis of Polanyi's relevance to globalization, see Munck, *Globalization and Contestation*, especially 14–19.
83 James, *The End of Globalization*, 1.
84 Krugman, "The Great Illusion."
85 Rosenau, *Distant Proximities*, 8. Rosenau provides instances of globalizing and localizing forces in ibid., table 1.1, 15.
86 Ibid., 12.
87 Elisa Reis, "The Lasting Marriage between Nation and State despite Globalization," *International Political Science Review* 25:3 (2004), 252.
88 James N. Rosenau, "A Pre-Theory Revisited: World Politics in an Era of Cascading Interdependence," *International Studies Quarterly* 28:3 (September 1984), 257.
89 Friedman, *The Lexus and the Olive Tree*, 41.
90 Rosenau, *Distant Proximities*, 36.
91 Ibid., 37.
92 Friedman, *The Lexus and the Olive Tree*, 35.
93 Nederveen Pieterse, *Globalization and Culture*, 81.
94 Ian Clark, *Globalization and Fragmentation* (Oxford: Oxford University Press, 1997), 180.
95 Barber, *Jihad vs. McWorld*, 11.
96 Rosenau, *Distant Proximities*, 386–7.
97 See ibid., 256–72.
98 Barber, *Jihad vs. McWorld*, 4. Lechner uses the spread of McDonald's in East Asia to illustrate what he calls "the Third Wave of globalization." See Lechner, *Globalization*, 26–9.
99 Clark, *Globalization and Fragmentation*, 189, 36.
100 Stanley Hoffmann, "The Politics and Ethics of Military Intervention," *Survival* 37:4 (1995/6), 32.
101 Michel Maffesoli describes such groups as "tribus." See M. Maffesoli, *The Time of the Tribes* (London: Sage, 1996), 140.
102 Alison Brysk, *From Tribal Village to Global Village* (Stanford, CA: Stanford University Press, 2000), 284. Emphasis added.
103 Samuel Huntington, *Who Are We? The Challenges to America's National Identity* (New York: Simon & Schuster, 2004), 13.
104 Paul Kennedy, "Globalization and the Crisis of Identities," in P. Kennedy and Catherine J. Danks, eds., *Globalization and National Identities: Crisis or Opportunity?* (New York: Palgrave, 2001), 1–28.

105 For a rebuttal of globalization-as-Americanization, see Naím, "Globalization," 30.
106 Blum, *National Identity and Globalization*, 74.
107 Samuel Huntington, *The Clash of Civilizations: Remaking of World Order* (New York: Simon & Schuster, 1996). Huntington feared a "Confucian–Islamic connection" (188) reflected in Chinese and North Korean nuclear and conventional arms transfers to Iran and Pakistan.
108 Samuel Huntington, "The Clash of Civilizations?" *Foreign Affairs* 72:3 (Summer 1993), 27.
109 Armstrong, "Magazines, Cultural Policy and Globalization: The Forced Retreat of the State?" 370.
110 Nederveen Pieterse, *Globalization and Culture*, 42–8. The author criticizes (56) Barber's *Jihad vs. McWorld* for considering only the first two paradigms, while neglecting the third.
111 Ibid., 47.
112 Ibid., 56. Emphasis in original.
113 Armstrong, "Magazines, Cultural Policy and Globalization: The Forced Retreat of the State?" 372.
114 Nederveen Pieterse, *Globalization and Culture*, 57. Emphasis in original.
115 Lieber and Weisberg, "Globalization, Culture, and Identities," 281.
116 Philip D. Cerny, Georg Menz, and Susanne Soederberg, "Different Roads to Globalization," in Soederberg, Menz, and Cerny, eds., *Internalizing Globalization* (New York: Palgrave Macmillan, 2005), 1.
117 Chris Brown, "Reimagining International Society and Global Community," in Held and McGrew, eds., *Globalization Theory*, 179, 180.
118 Ibid., 180. For a cogent analysis of different levels of global governance, see Michael Walzer: "Governing the Globe," in M. Walzer: *Arguing about War* (New Haven, CT Yale University Press, 2004), 171–91.
119 Ibid., 182. Human-rights governance is variable, with some international courts that depend on states' willingness to cooperate with them, and some national authorities claiming authority to prosecute citizens from other countries for human-rights abuses. See Craig Whitlock, "To the Ends of the Earth: Spain's Judges Cross Borders to Pursue Human Rights Cases," *Washington Post National Weekly Review*, June 1–7, 2009, 20–1.
120 Brown, "Reimagining International Society and Global Community," 184.
121 Ibid.
122 Rosenau, *Along the Domestic–Foreign Frontier*, 81. Emphasis added.
123 Sassen, "The Places and Spaces of the Global," 79.
124 Roger Keil, "Globalization Makes States: Perspectives of Local Governance in the Age of the World City," *Review of International Political Economy* 5:4 (Winter 1998), 630.
125 Ibid., 623.
126 Rosenau, *Distant Proximities*, 81. Emphasis added.
127 Rosenau, *Along the Domestic–Foreign Frontier*, 85.
128 The internet can be used for purposes of localization rather than globalization. Video terrorism, internet hacking, and cyberwar are intended to foster ethnic conflict, and blogs and websites may be used for parochial messaging.
129 Rosenau, *Along the Domestic–Foreign Frontier*, 5.
130 Scholte, "The Geography of Collective Identities in a Globalizing World," 577.
131 Tomlinson argues that globalization is producing an "era of immediacy" in which "the gap between departure and arrival, here and elsewhere, now and later, indeed, a certain order of desire and its fulfillment, has been closed by a sort of technological *legerdemain*." See Tomlinson, "Globalization and Cultural Analysis," 158.
132 Held et. al., *Global Transformations*, 17.
133 "The Power of Mobile Money," *The Economist*, September 26, 2009, 13.
134 Held et. al., *Global Transformation*, 16–20.

CHAPTER 6

The normative implications of globalization

The interesting contribution of globalization is that it produces new threat scenarios by overriding or eroding some of the old interstate dichotomies – the *familiar* structure of uncertainty and threat. It produces "risks" . . . largely because it promises to eliminate old hazards, enemies, boundaries, and battle lines and to replace them with the "asymmetrical" unknown of ethnic and cultural mixing, transborder economic flows, global communication, civilizational encounters, supranational hegemonies, Islamic extremism, natural disasters, and much more – all of which people more or less indiscriminately associate with globalization.[1]

Globalization is now on trial because on the other side of all these virtual fences are real people, shut out of schools, hospitals, workplaces, their own farms, homes and communities. Mass privation and deregulation have bred armies of locked-out people, whose services are no longer needed, whose lifestyles are written off as "backward," whose basic needs go unmet.[2]

Globalization incites passionate advocacy and criticism. Has globalization been "oversold" and become "misshapen," as Joseph Stiglitz insists? Has the governance of globalization, as he claims, "been determined by the advanced industrial countries, for their interests, or more precisely for the interests of special interests, often to the marked disadvantage of the developing world"?[3] Globalization advocate Bhagwati argues, to the contrary, that the opposition includes a multitude of hard-core protesters who "buy into a linked trilogy of discontents that take the form successively of an ethos composed of an anti-capitalist, anti-globalization, and acute anti-corporation mind-set."[4] In his view, many young protesters are influenced by "old Marxist thought" that sees "capitalism as a system that cannot meaningfully address questions of social justice." They and others are the products of an education that also applauds postmodernist deconstruction which "often has nihilistic overtones, with the paradoxical result that many of its followers now turn to anarchy."[5]

In fact, critiques of contemporary globalization can be interest-based or norm-based – or both. Critics encompass inefficient industries seeking protection, labor unions fearful of job losses, environmentalists concerned that globalization is producing ecological disaster, anarchists who detest institutional authority, Islamists who oppose globalization norms and customs, nationalists who fear the erosion of states and cultural hybridization, and those who contend that economic globalization accelerates economic inequality.

Norm-based critiques frequently regard economic, cultural, and social equality and/or diversity more highly than economic efficiency and economies of scale and see the state as the guardian of liberty and welfare. Some academic critics seek inspiration from Marxism (rather less fashionable today), critical theory, world system theory, or postmodernism, while others less theoretically inclined rely on "simple" conceptions of justice, environmental sustainability, and equal opportunity.

Many critics declare that they seek to reform rather than reverse contemporary globalization. The self-styled "alter-globalization" or "global justice" movement, as Charles Lindholm and José Zúquete suggest, attempts to distinguish itself from strictly "*anti*globalist groups."[6] The movement calls for "*the renewal of political citizenship and activism* . . . [and] practices through which citizens, social movements and civil society attempt to have an impact on the course of things."[7] Typical is the work of Nancy Fraser, who detects "a new sense of vulnerability to transnational forces" and states: "Faced with global warming, the spread of AIDS, international terrorism and superpower unilateralism, many believe that their chances for living good lives depend at least as much on processes that trespass the borders of territorial states as on those contained within them."[8] Similarly, Jackie Smith focuses on new forms of transnational activism and democratic participation.[9]

The divisions between advocates and critics of globalization are at the heart of Manfred Steger's distinction between "*globalization*" – "a set of social processes of increasing interdependence" – and "*globalisms*" – "political ideologies . . . that endow globalization with their preferred norms, values, and meanings."[10] Steger identifies three conflicting ideologies or "globalisms" that contest the meaning of globalization and the ability of agents to shape its social processes. These are market globalism, justice globalism, and jihadist globalism. "By the end of the 1990s," he writes, "market globalism had managed to spread to all parts of the world by employing its dominant codes and hegemonic meanings through its powerful arsenal of ideological representation, co-optation of loyal elites, and economic power." "Despite their formidable efforts, however, the dominant vision of neoliberal globalization became increasingly tarred by the reality of growing social inequalities and rising cultural tensions. 'Global justice' networks sprang up, and justice–globalist demonstrations erupted. . . ." Then came 9/11 carried out by a "jihadist–globalist network led by Osama bin Laden and Ayman al-Zawahiri" whose followers "incorporate into militant Islam a populist style of rhetoric that decontests 'the people' as the umma of *tawhid* – the *global* Islamic community of believers in the oneness of the one and only God."[11]

Neoliberal capitalism, free trade, and market manipulation have been particular targets of globalization critics.[12] In *The Great Transformation*, originally published in 1944, Polanyi decried "the idea of a self-adjusting market" as "a stark utopia" that "could not exist for any length of time without annihilating the human and natural substance of society" and that "would have physically destroyed man and transformed his surroundings into a wilderness."[13] Nevertheless, Polanyi believed, paradoxically, that only "a self-regulating market on a world scale could ensure the functioning"[14] of the global economy. He argued that the state must initially establish the free market and then must intervene to provide welfare and social control and stabilize society – in doing so, however, the state would create a dilemma by constraining self-regulation, thereby producing market distortions. In addition, he denounced the idea that labor should be regarded as a commodity. "Labor is only another name for a human activity which goes with life itself, which in its turn is not produced for sale but for entirely different reasons, nor can that activity be detached from the rest of life, be stored or mobilized."[15] Beverly Silver elaborates this when she declares: "By Polanyi-type labor unrest, we mean the backlash resistances to the spread of a global self-regulating market, particularly by working classes that are being unmade by global economic transformations as well as by those workers who had benefited from established social compacts that are being abandoned from above."[16]

From the other end of the political spectrum, Edward Luttwak argues that we have entered a world of "private enterprise liberated from government regulation, unchecked by effective trade unions, unfettered by sentimental concerns over the fate of employees or communities, unrestrained by customs barriers or investment restrictions, and unmolested as little as possible by taxation," a world of privatization featuring "turbo-charged capitalism," or, for short, "turbo-capitalism."[17]

The rapid spread of financial and economic distress globally that began in 2007–8 suggests that major economic outcomes remain the result of market forces that governments can soften but cannot resist. Asia's 1997 financial crisis was a harbinger of the more recent global crisis.[18] The institutions of globalization, notably the IMF, did not serve Asia well at that time, but the Asian economies recovered quickly and Asians did not turn their backs on globalization. Whether the current crisis will have a similar outcome remains to be seen, but Asia's experience with globalization and its stake in maintaining a liberal economic system suggest that, while the world may seek a different institutional architecture in which countries other than the G-8 have a greater voice, it will not be able to reject globalization in a wholesale way.

Some win, and some lose in the process of globalization. Globalization is, as Dani Rodrik argues, "exposing a deep fault line between groups who have the skills and mobility to flourish in global markets and those who either don't have these advantages or perceive the expansion of unregulated markets as inimical to social stability or deeply held norms."[19]

CENTRAL NORMATIVE ISSUES

Globalization's critics and advocates seem to be looking at entirely different worlds. They attach starkly different meanings to many of the same issues and concepts and reach dramatically different conclusions. Critics seek to reinforce state capacity, limit the role of transnational corporations (TNCs) and at least some international institutions, and foster an alternative to neoliberal globalization that stresses equality and justice. Globalization enthusiasts favor a world with minimal interference by sovereign states and see transnational corporations, international institutions, and global civil society as pathways to efficiency, prosperity, peace, and cosmopolitanism.

A "democratic deficit"?

Many critics of globalization reserve their highest loyalties for the sovereign state which they alone believe is accountable to citizens and exists to protect their interests. Strange held no such illusions, decrying the state's "retreat" and the palpable incapacity and incompetence of national leaders of even the well-established states. She wrote: "Politicians everywhere talk as though they have the answers to economic and social problems, as if they are really in charge of their country's destiny. People no longer believe them." Her firm belief was that "the perceptions of ordinary citizens are more to be trusted than the pretensions of national leaders and the bureaucracies who serve them."[20] Unfortunately, Strange contended, it is equally true that "none of the non-state authorities to whom authority has shifted, is democratically governed." For example, comparing corporate CEOs to renaissance princes, she observed: "No single elected institution holds them accountable. The cartels and oligopolists that practise private protectionism and manage markets for their own comfort and convenience are even less accountable."[21]

Although Strange was hardly sanguine about how states would fare in practice, she did believe they offer the last best hope for reining in the worst practices of markets, corporations, banks, and mafias. Critics of globalization tend to be rather more optimistic about the prospects for reforming states. For many of them, globalization "challenges clearly defined national boundaries which have traditionally demarcated the basis on which individuals are included and excluded from participation in decisions affecting their lives," and states "are vehicles to achieve self-determination, which means that nationalism or the search for a lost identity becomes a solution to the privatizing effects of the market."[22] "When broad-based, mass groups have claimed new rights, equality, prosperity and greater security," writes Cerny, "they have done so by demanding democratic accountability and redistributive public policies from and through national states. And when political philosophers have defined normative social and political values such as justice, civic virtue and the public good, they have expected these to be embodied in better, fairer, or more just states."[23] The changes wrought by globalization limit states' control of their economic destiny while altering citizens' perceptions of the role of politics.

Globalization's critics assert that in democratic states, such as those in Europe and North America, citizens enjoy a voice in determining their own fates but, in contrast, have little or no voice in determining the policies of giant corporations,[24] remote international bureaucracies like the European Union (EU) or the World Trade Organization (WTO),[25] economic markets, or many nongovernmental organizations (NGOs), however well intentioned. In consequence, argues Noreena Hertz, "the corporation is king, the state its subject, its citizens consumers."[26] Technocracy outweighs democracy. In addition, growing reliance on private security companies by democratic societies like the United States and the UK "reduces both the institutional checks on foreign policy and the amount of transparency in the process."[27] As for institutions like the EU and the International Monetary Fund (IMF) or, for that matter, Standard & Poor's, they have the ability to makes countries like Greece, Ireland, Portugal, and even the United States accept their demands and impose economic, political, and social policies on electorates in those countries. In general, then, the emerging institutions of global governance tend to be seen as obstacles to democracy. "The relationships between the sites of governance and accountability is subtle," and even when "formally democratic . . . decentralized governance may also be liable to capture."[28]

In sum, globalization, its critics argue, has created a "democratic deficit" by empowering institutions in which people have no voice and by unleashing economic and cultural forces over which people have no control.[29] Growing interdependence reduces national autonomy and, as Michael Doyle argues, "no strong version of global democracy is viable at the present time."[30] The result is alienation and anxiety, as people's lives are buffeted by remote forces beyond their control or understanding. Although some believe that global civil society is creating new democratic spaces, this too is highly debatable.[31]

If states lose authority, who will assume responsibility for welfare, uphold citizens' rights, or safeguard their economic interests and deliver justice? "No one," answer critics – certainly not corporate executives who are globalization's main beneficiaries.[32] One result has been – as Andrews, Henning, and Pauly observe – the emergence of an epistemic community:

> focusing attention on whether the webs of monetary and financial interdependence now being so tightly woven together will someday constitute the sinews of new forms of governance beyond the territorial state. Simply put, is the raw power inherent in border-spanning capital markets . . . reconstructing fundamental political relations across the international system and creating a new kind of governing authority? . . . The legitimacy of such an order is at issue.[33]

Advocates of globalization argue in response to democratic-deficit critics that new technologies, such as the internet, mobile phones, the fax, the personal computer, and cable television, and other mass media provide new opportunities for democracy, individual self-determination, and diverse sources of information, as well as new public spaces based on access to information and an ability to educate, communicate with, and mobilize groups at vast distances.[34] In addition, these technologies provide new access for those seeking public office and even raise the eventual prospect of "e-democracy."

A cut-throat world of neoliberal capitalism

Jeffrey Ayres observes that criticism of globalization has "been shaped by an underlying and quite ferocious contest over people's interpretations and understandings of the supposed benefits of neoliberal economic policies," with the result that critics "by the late 1990s successfully developed a contentious, increasingly transnationally accepted master collective action frame to challenge the prevailing neoliberal orthodoxy."[35] Globalization's critics denounce an era in which the rigors of the global marketplace force countries and industries to eliminate jobs, gut welfare programs, relocate peasants, lower real wages, impose austerity, and become more efficient to survive in a cut-throat capitalist world.[36]

As Cerny argues, "The state itself – although still the most important single organization level and institutional structure in the world – has been transformed by and through the globalization process ... This transformation involves a fundamental shift of organizational goals and institutional processes within state structures themselves, as the 'industrial welfare state' has been replaced by the 'competition state'."[37] "[S]tate structures today are being transformed into more and more market-oriented and even market-based organizations themselves, fundamentally altering the way that public and private goods are provided."[38] "The functions of the state," Cerny maintains, "although central in structural terms, are becoming increasingly fragmented, privatized and devolved."[39] The "ongoing division of labor ('globalization')" places states "under ever-increasing pressure, and with it sovereignty-based IR [international relations] theory."[40] Moreover, under the pressure of globalization, there is increasing convergence among states' regulatory policies and practices.[41]

Critics are quick to argue that recent market turmoil points up the global economy's unpredictability, the rapid spread of economic distress, and the concentration of power in a relatively few global corporations and banks. In a prescient observation, William Greider declared over a decade ago:

> In the history of capitalism's long expansionary cycles, it is finance capital that usually rules in the final stage, displacing the inventors and industrialists who launched the era, eclipsing the power of governments to manage the course of economic events. As capital owners and financial markets accumulate greater girth and a dominating influence, their search for higher returns becomes increasingly purified in purpose – detached from social concerns and abstracted from the practical realities of commerce. In this atmosphere, investors develop rising expectations of what their invested savings ought to earn and the rising prices in financial markets gradually diverge from the underlying economic reality. Since returns on capital are rising faster than the productive output that must pay them, the process imposes greater and greater burdens on commerce and societies – debt obligations that cannot possibly be fulfilled by the future and, sooner or later, must be liquidated, written off or forgiven.[42]

The claim that growing economic inequality accompanies globalization is among the most contested of the normative arguments offered by globalization's opponents.

Critics like Robert Wade charge that neoliberals "claim that income inequality is not something to worry about" because economic efficiency is of greater importance and, in any event, that "inequality is, first, an inevitable consequence of private property rights, and second, a necessary condition for effort, risk taking and entrepreneurship, and thereby for efficiency, innovation, competitiveness and panache."[43] In contrast, he argues that belief in the "Washington Consensus" with its emphasis on free trade and the unfettered movement of capital and the refusal to consider alternative policies or recognize the inadequacy of World Bank data "is faith-based social science."[44] Instead of the economic growth applauded by neoliberals, Wade sees "a dramatic growth slowdown in both developed and developing countries" during the past twenty-five years, an increase in those living on $2 a day, and a rise in inequality if one excludes China. He also maintains that growing income inequality within countries

> goes with: (1) higher poverty . . . ; (2) higher unemployment; (3) higher crime; (4) lower average health; (5) weaker property rights; (6) more skewed access to public services and state rule-setting fora, and lower standards of public services; and (7) slower transition to democratic regimes, and more fragile democracies.[45]

In sum, "the liberal theory of capitalist politics and economics suffers from glaring inadequacies for grasping the central dynamics of industrial capitalism and late development," and "the people whose authority and opinions have propelled the drive to liberalism worldwide live high up the income pyramid of the high-income states."[46] Another critic, Nederveen Pieterse, agrees with Wade that neoliberal policies "widen the global inequality that poverty reduction strategies seek to mitigate."[47]

History might suggest a different conclusion, at least in comparing countries' living standards. Jeffrey Williamson's analysis of globalization between 1850 and 1914 suggests that it was accompanied by "convergence" in living standards in rich and poor countries involved in the process, and he concludes that this was "due to the open economy forces of trade and migration." He notes that "convergence stopped between 1914 and 1950 because of," he believes, "deglobalization and implosion into autarchy."[48]

In reality, the picture is *not* clear and is muddied by different definitions of concepts such as "inequality" and "poverty" and by significant differences over how to measure these concepts empirically.[49] As Bob Sutcliffe observes, the concept "inequality" remains murky because "[w]e could be interested in inequality of income, welfare, health, education, power, and so on" and "in inequality between nations, regions, genders, ethnic groups, social classes, individuals and so on."[50] What many globalization critics also willfully neglect is the plain and crucial facts (see below) that, especially in places like China and India, globalization-led development has brought many out of poverty, raised general living standards for much of the population, and created an increasingly prosperous middle class. Nevertheless, however measured, inequality obviously matters in a globalizing world not only in itself but also because the mutual awareness that results from information and communication technologies produces a sense of relative deprivation among the poor who remain at the bottom of the ladder and perhaps, even more so, among middle classes who feel their lot is not improving rapidly enough.

Branko Milanovic examines how different conclusions emerge from three different ways of measuring inequality,[51] and he concludes that "*inequality among people in the world today is extremely high, though its direction of change is unclear,*" and that "withinnation inequalities . . . increased almost everywhere,"[52] especially between rural and urban regions. James Galbraith insists: "Everywhere – and continually for 20 years . . . – global inequalities rose"[53] owing to a change in global governance and to neoliberal policies that produced mountains of debt in the developing world, high interest rates, and a strong dollar. For their part, Kanbur and Venables emphasize regional disparities, especially rural–urban inequality. They describe what they call "spatial inequality" within countries that potentially exacerbates "political and ethnic tensions to undermine social and political stability." In their view, this form of inequality "is high and, in many countries, rising" as a result of uneven economic development that, in turn, derives from export-driven policies that facilitate "the development of new coastal or border located clusters."[54] More generally, according to Esping-Andersen, a comparison of household incomes reveals "a remarkable increase in income inequality and poverty," and, although this varies by country, "that the top incomes are pulling ahead of the rest."[55] It is highly significant that the rise in the Gini coefficient (measuring inequality) over recent years in some countries including the United States and China is largely a consequence of the accumulation of wealth by the relatively few "super rich" at the very top and masks the *reduction* in poverty at the bottom.[56]

Milanovic, like most other observers,[57] also recognizes that conclusions about trends in inequality depend heavily on whether one includes or excludes China which, along with India, account for much of the global reduction in poverty. Weighting calculations to account for their enormous populations reduces apparent inequality in contrast with counting all countries the same. Referring to the decline in extreme poverty since 1981, Wade tersely declares that "the fall depends entirely on China."[58] As for the future, Milanovic views technological change as the critical determinant of inequality, anticipating that the technology gap between rich and poor will grow.[59] Demography also matters as the "one group that clearly has suffered deterioration in a major way" are "young adults, who face an erosion of relative wages at all skill levels and who, especially in Europe, are hugely overrepresented among the unemployed and those with precarious, short-term employment contracts."[60]

Recent decades have produced shifts in the location of poverty. Until the 1990s, most of the world's poor lived in the world's poorest countries. Currently, however, as many as three-quarters of the world's poor– earning less than $1.25 a day – live in middle-income countries. This trend exists even if one does *not* include China and India, both of which are now regarded as middle-income countries.[61]

According to some observers and perhaps not surprisingly, empirical analyses suggest that neoliberal policies lead to greater economic inequality and unemployment within *some* states but not necessarily in others, especially during periods of instability. In other words, there are regional and national differences in economic trends. "Regionally," declares Milanovic, "the last 20 to 25 years have been characterized by the following basic trends: China and India pulled ahead, Latin America and Eastern Europe – the middle-income countries – declined, and Africa's position grew even worse."[62] Latin America suffered greater inequality and unemployment in the 1990s, while East Asia benefited from growing exports of labor-intensive products. As for Africa, "remoteness" helps explain poverty by "being a function not just of distance but lack of transport connections to the capital city and the coast."[63]

"While trade liberalization likely improved the income distribution in the exporters of labour-intensive manufacturers with strong domestic institutions," declares Giovanni Cornia, "it had the opposite effect in low-income, commodity-dependent countries. At the global level, it is thus difficult to identify a systemic effect of trade liberalization on inequality due to the heterogeneity of the situations analysed."[64] Nevertheless, Cornia, Addison, and Kiiski find that recent decades "have been characterized by a surge of within-country inequality in about two-thirds of the developing, developed, and transitional countries analysed,"[65] which slowed reduction in poverty in countries where inequality was already high.

The impact of neoliberal economic policies is mixed in other ways as well, notably in their relative impact on the developed and developing worlds. Income gaps have grown in the United States and the UK, owing especially to growth at the top end of the income scale and the demand for skilled rather than unskilled workers. Global trade, which has risen overall since World War II, has tended to benefit wealthy countries more than poorer ones, with trade balances between the two favoring the former. Again, China is a major exception! Surging imports into developed countries from low-wage countries did not consistently produce greater unemployment.[66] Not surprisingly, disparities in education are at once a source and a consequence of income inequality and are most evident in Africa and Latin America, and low levels of education obviously hamper the infusion of technology.[67] In addition, rural poverty has increased in recent decades in the developing world, intensified by impediments to their exports of agricultural products to the developed world and by low agricultural prices during much of that time.[68] For the most part, these inequalities stem from market forces which states have not or, as some argue, cannot effectively resist owing to the need to remain competitive.

In stark contrast to Milanovic and others, David Dollar argues that globalization has alleviated poverty and has, in a modest way, reduced global inequality. He declares that growth rates in poor countries "have accelerated and are higher than growth rates in rich countries for the first time in modern history"; that those living on less than $1 a day have "declined significantly;"[69] that the decline in global inequality since 1980 has reversed "a 200-year trend towards higher inequality"; that intra-state inequality is not growing; but that wage inequality is rising worldwide because of the greater increase in wages in "more globalized developing economies" – especially among women and skilled workers – than in "less globalized developing economies."[70] Moreover, the reason some countries have fallen further behind may not lie in globalization per se but in their *exclusion* from the globalized economy by such factors as protectionism in developed countries, especially in the form of agricultural subsidies that prevent agricultural products in the developing world from gaining entry into the markets of rich countries. "The developing world," Dollar and Kraay argue, "can be divided into a 'globalizing' group of countries that have seen rapid increases in trade and foreign investment over the last two decades . . . and a 'nonglobalizing' group that trades even less of its income today than it did 20 years ago."[71] The clear road to progress, for the latter, is thus much more globalization rather than less.

Regardless of whether or not economic inequality (again, however defined) is growing, globalization proponents argue that the economic pie *as a whole* is getting larger and that global poverty is declining, notably in formerly impoverished regions such as Southeast Asia, China, and India.[72] The poverty rate in East Asia declined from about 80 to under 20 percent between 1981 and 2005, while remaining at around 50 percent in sub-Saharan Africa during this period. "Living standards," according to the World Bank,

> have risen dramatically over the last decades. The proportion of the developing world's population living in extreme economic poverty – defined as living on less than $1.25 per day (at 2005 prices, adjusted to account for the most recent differences in purchasing power across countries) – has fallen from 52 percent in 1981 to 26 percent in 2005.[73]

In the developing world, this means a decline of 1.9 billion (one in two) below the poverty line in 1981 to 1.4 billion (one in four) in 2005.[74]

Prosperity, argue globalization's advocates, is fostered by the free movement of capital and labor and by competition among states and corporations. Although critics of globalization insist that competition is driving firms from the market and is producing market oligopolies and monopolies, the evidence does not support this. In fact, according to Pankaj Ghemawat,

> the data do not show much of a tendency at all toward increasing concentration among market leaders. Although the number of industries in the sample that experienced concentration increases is slightly greater than the number that experienced decreases, the average share of the market held by the five largest firms in each industry actually declined.[75]

Globalization enthusiasts believe that a global market with ever fewer barriers to trade provides consumers with an unprecedented choice of increasingly inexpensive goods. Overall, globalization, they conclude, has been accompanied by sustained growth and low inflation and has brought countless workers around the world new jobs and higher living standards. Losers are associated with obsolete or uncompetitive enterprises, but without losers, there could be no winners.

Reactive and structural violence

Globalization critics insist that disquiet about the political, economic, and cultural consequences of globalization are producing reactive violence by groups animated by nationalism, religion, and ethnic xenophobia that fear their loss of status, cultural uniqueness, autonomy, and authority. In addition, they observe that interstate and corporate competition for increasingly scarce resources such as oil and rare metals has intensified. In some cases, the erosion of state authority has produced failed states wracked by civil violence that provide sanctuaries for terrorists. In other cases, the result has been increased authoritarianism, leading to violations of democratic principles and widespread human-rights abuses.

Critics also claim that the operations of giant and greedy transnational conglomerates and financial institutions undermine national economic and social policies, intensify economic insecurity, and, consequently, constitute a form of structural violence against the poor. They argue that international institutions such as the IMF and the WTO serve corporate interests, force countries to adopt policies that are not in citizens' interests, and place harsh conditions on loans against which populations can only feebly protest. As events from the 1997–8 "Asian contagion"[76] to the 2008 collapse of subprime mortgage instruments suggest, huge and rapid movements of capital, often speculative in nature, can overwhelm central banks and create financial volatility that threatens national and even global economic stability. As Sergio L. Schmukler warned in 2004, "international market imperfections, such as herding, panics, and boom–bust cycles, and the fluctuating nature of capital flows can lead to crises and contagion, even in countries with good economic fundamentals."[77]

In sum, critics assert that growing inequality within and among countries may fracture global order and produce ever greater conflict.[78] Whatever the truth of broad claims like these, it is indisputably the case that *some* countries in Africa, Latin America, and parts of Asia are deprived of many of the fruits of globalization, as are the most impoverished and other disadvantaged citizens wherever they may reside.

The erosion of human rights?

It remains hotly debated whether "[i]nternational human rights are globalized," "operate beyond all borders and state mechanisms," and "have become part of the discourse in almost all societies, speaking to both the elites and the oppressed, to institutions and communities."[79] "Globalization," writes Clifford Bob, "is often seen as a double-edged sword for human rights. On one hand new technologies and new international norms may be a boon for victims and activists, binding the world together and making it harder for repressive regimes to act with impunity against their own citizens. On the other hand, the ideology of free trade and the spread of multinational corporations may infringe on labor rights, threaten environments, and destroy local control."[80] In any event, new technologies have helped spread demands for economic and political rights across national frontiers, for example, in North Africa and the Middle East in 2011.

Rosenau captures Bob's notion of globalization as a double-edged sword for human rights, notably in the growing skills of individuals owing (in part) to the spread of information and the communications technologies. He writes:

> [T]he "skill revolution" . . . has inhibited the rights violators by enabling people everywhere to more clearly assess the violations and how they affect their victims. [However] the efforts of those who perpetrate human rights violations can be enhanced as well as inhibited by the skill revolution. For just as those who abhor rights violations are more easily mobilized, so are those who subscribe to value systems that justify the violations . . . Put differently, a major consequence of the skill revolution is that people everywhere are increasingly able to know when,

where, and how to engage in collective actions, a capacity that can be just as put to the service of supporting as of opposing what are regarded as human rights violations.[81]

Nevertheless, and despite the proliferation of human-rights international law and human-rights NGOs, "unaccountable flows of migration and open markets present new threats" to human rights "which are not amenable to state-based human-rights regimes."[82] Sweatshops, child labor, the physical danger in migrating,[83] and exploitation associated with human trafficking all constitute human-rights abuses. Moreover, noncitizens typically enjoy fewer rights than citizens. Some observers allege that the United States repeatedly violates migrants' rights, for example, in the case of anti-terrorist legislation.[84] Indeed, as Donnelly reminds us, "Until we develop institutional mechanisms to implement and protect internationally recognized human rights, an active positive role for states will remain essential."[85]

Global capitalism encourages economic outsourcing as well as migration. Corporate outsourcing to the developing world is seen by some as violating human rights by underpaying workers and providing poor working conditions. However, according to Richard Falk, "more empirically grounded work has argued" that "the more receptive to foreign investment and the operation of MNCs a country is, the better its human rights record is likely to be."[86] "This capacity to publicize repressive practices," argues Falk, "is especially effective, given the shifts in the character of much multinational enterprise in the direction of consumers, and the overall rise of consumer-oriented 'franchise-capitalism'."[87] In a similar vein, Wesley Milner finds empirically that trade openness is positively associated with "security rights" such as protection from torture and unlawful imprisonment but is negatively associated with "subsistence rights" such as sufficient food, clean air, and basic health care.[88]

Women are often particular victims of human-rights abuses associated with globalization. Sassen emphasizes how globalization has "increased the demand in global cities for low-wage workers to [occupy jobs with] few advancement possibilities"[89] that can be filled only by hiring women and immigrants, frequently hidden in the "informal" underground economy. "Thanks to the process we loosely call 'globalization'," write Barbara Ehrenreich and Arlie Russell Hochschild, "women are on the move as never before in history," and many have succeeded professionally "only by turning over the care of their children, elderly parents, and homes to women from the Third World. This is the female underside of globalization, whereby millions of Josephines from poor countries in the south migrate to do the 'women's work' of the north."[90] "Due to globalization," argues Helma Lutz, "house- and carework is a cheap product that can be 'bought in': the impoverished and completely de-regularized labour markets of the world offer a large reservoir for these services."[91] Female migrants who work as domestic servants are usually poorly paid, and their own children at home are deprived of their mothers. Women are

> known to suffer under conditions that look very much like slavery after they legally enter the United States as domestic workers ... In the case of slavery and human trafficking ... an unpaid or poorly paid person becomes a commodity that can be used again and again for accumulating profit.[92]

Globalization has also increased "sex tourism"[93] and the importation of "pliant" brides, for example, from Asia to the West.[94] In the case of the Dominican Republic, "[t]he new social and cultural shifts created by the globalization of the tourism and sex industries have generated for women new forms of race, gender and class inequality."[95] Sex tourism produces abuse by public officials and sometimes the captivity of women and children of both sexes by foreigners. Such abuse has encouraged some victims to organize themselves and demand humane treatment. Although corporations can hire cheap labor, their very presence may encourage labor activism. Media exposure may help improve working conditions, even perhaps for prostitutes. Such publicity Debora Spar calls "the spotlight phenomenon."[96] In fact, some analysts insist that "trade globalization has a generally positive influence on women's status,"[97] as does foreign direct investment (FDI).[98]

The consequences of structural adjustment programs imposed on developing countries by international institutions like the IMF are also characterized by some scholars as human-rights abuses. According to Abouharb and Cingranelli, "while some regimes may positively impact human rights, two important protagonists involved in the international financial regime, the World Bank and International Monetary Fund, have negatively impacted the levels of respect governments provide for the economic, social, and physical integrity rights of their citizens."[99] Of course, these institutions have provided large amounts of aid as well.

As implied by Spar's "spotlight phenomenon," the revolution in information and communication technologies has been a boon to NGOs, including those that foster human rights. Computers enable the assembling and analysis of information about human rights, and the internet facilitates the coordination of NGO activities, although the computers are vulnerable to sabotage and irrelevant information ("noise") and may allow the airing of disagreements among groups and individuals.[100]

The dissemination of information raises the awareness of citizens and recruits activists to the cause of human rights, but not all groups or causes receive equal attention. For example, Bob describes how one group, the Movement for the Survival of the Ogoni People (MOSOP), among the many that were protesting Nigerian oil policies, was able to attract the attention of human-rights activists from around the world to their demand for political autonomy and a share of the country's oil wealth.[101]

A race to the bottom?

Globalization's critics contend that corporate policies and the movement of investment capital to countries with poor environmental and labor standards threaten reductions in living, working, and environmental conditions. In a globalized world, oligarchic corporations and banks search the world for cheap labor, move jobs from country to country, force workers into sweatshop conditions, use child labor,[102] and, despite growing global awareness, destroy the environment in a competitive "race to the bottom."[103] The central argument, as Silver describes it, is that "the hypermobility of productive capital . . . has created a single labor market in which all the world's workers are forced to compete" and that "as states become incapable of effectively controlling flows of capital, their capacity to protect their citizens' livelihoods and other workers' rights and substantive democracy, also declines."[104] In sum, globalization threatens a reduction in the rights and responsibilities of citizenship, in the state's capacity to ensure public welfare, and in the possibilities for serious democratic participation.

Many industrial workers have lost their jobs owing to outsourcing to countries that can produce goods less expensively, and this has been accompanied by growing numbers of part-time workers who lack many of the benefits associated with unionized industries. These phenomena are no longer limited to the developed world. For instance, developing countries like Mexico, as well as sub-Saharan African countries, find themselves having to compete with China and India. Indeed, Chinese growth has been so rapid that it, too, is running out of surplus labor. This is forcing up wages and will, in time, lead to outsourcing from coastal to inland China and from China to countries like Bangladesh and Vietnam.[105] Reducing costs in order to improve competitiveness is only one of the reasons for outsourcing, which is why companies sometimes choose countries that are not at the bottom of the scale. Other motivations include investing close to and penetrating key regional markets, obtaining access to intellectual property or skilled workers, improving product quality, and integrating corporate production and sales on a global basis. However, most critics conclude that competition for foreign investment and jobs leads to a deterioration of the status and welfare of the poorest and most vulnerable citizens, especially in less economically developed countries, whose dilemma is exacerbated by the neoliberal policies of the IMF and World Bank.

Nita Rudra advances an alternative thesis, arguing that it is *not* the poorer citizens of developing countries who lose the most when governments reduce welfare assistance because they had been largely ignored by their governments in the first place. Instead, Rudra's data suggest it is the middle classes that, having received the most benefits from their governments, are the most vulnerable to cuts in budgets and benefits. As she puts it "the nature of ongoing welfare retrenchment in LDCs [less developed countries] does not represent the race to the actual *bottom*; rather, *the retrenchment reflects the general downward pressure from globalization on middle-class benefits.*"[106]

In reality, as Cohen contends, the argument as to whether TNCs are "good" or "bad" is not the most intellectually productive avenue of inquiry into this subject of a supposed race to the bottom, because of the heterogeneity of FDI and corporations. Instead, "FDI in the form of foreign-owned or controlled subsidiaries is sometimes a positive thing on balance, sometimes a bad thing on balance, sometimes neutral or irrelevant on balance, and sometimes has an indeterminate effect."[107] Whether or not FDI benefits or harms host countries may vary by industry as well as country. After a balanced analysis of "positive and negative spillovers" of TNCs in developed countries, Klaus Meyer concludes that in most cases they "play a positive role in the development of host economies."[108] Perhaps it is best simply to agree with Cohen that: "Massive numbers of foreign subsidiaries operating in hundreds of different national and regional environments generate a sliding scale of economic effects that ranges from highly deleterious to highly beneficial."[109]

These are all extremely controversial issues. On the one hand, labor and human-rights advocates, as noted above, argue that there is a need for enforceable global standards. "Poor countries, on the other hand," suggests Raul Pangalangan, "see this as disguised protectionism" and "argue that wages and standards of living will improve only as their economies develop and that sanctions will only stunt that development."[110] Hamilton and Quinlan observe of Europe: "Seen from 15,000 meters, globalization is a clear and beneficial force. Seen from the street, the view is muddled and the winds of change appear more threatening. Europe as a whole has gained from globalization. But tell that to the assembly worker without a job or the IT technician forced to take a pay cut."[111] And, as for the environment, Wirth suggests that it would be good to have "an approach that seeks to demonstrate a cause-and-effect relationship between globalization and environmental effects, either beneficial or negative, to serve as a helpful analytic tool."[112] Yes, of course, but the fact remains that we are far from having anything of the sort!

Cultural conformity or modernity?

Globalization's critics also decry the way in which the global economy and culture have homogenized distinctive local tastes, traditions, and even languages. "At present," writes Harm De Blij, "about 7,000 languages remain, half of them classified by linguists as endangered."[113] The ability to speak English, the language of globalization, and other core languages is highly advantageous. "On the inhabitants of the global core as well as the periphery," he continues, "language confers advantages and imposes liability."

> Being born into a family whose mother tongue is regionally dominant and globally dispersed (English, Spanish, French) endows a child with a lifetime of opportunity that begins in preschool and continues beyond retirement, a cultural legacy of imperial times. Being born into a family whose home language is that of a minority, or a society whose linguistic mosaic is variegated, confronts a youngster with far greater challenges. The former is the good fortune of hundreds of millions of globals. The latter is the fate of billions of locals.[114]

Ancient cultures and ways of living, critics contend, are giving way before the onslaught of a relatively few, universally and instantly recognizable consumer brands, which generates a superficial "Coca-Cola/McDonald's/Levi's Jeans" culture. This consumerist culture promotes individualism, narcissism, and greed; spreads sexually suggestive and violent images; and undermines ethical and religious values and beliefs.

For instance, Kinnvall complains that globalized culture "is only another term for Western colonization and a buzzword to denote the latest phase of capitalism" with "no place" for "non-Western values."[115] Other critics insist that global media are mostly controlled by the West,[116] and even the "increasing globalization of training, the development of international MBAs and distance learning programmes, are all part and parcel of this dynamic, the export of Western bureaucratic ideology, sometimes its process, to the South."[117]

Not surprisingly, ethnic, national, and religious groups bridle at the threat they perceive to their uniqueness, dignity, and values. Unlike earlier eras when territorial states provided a measure of physical and psychological security for citizens, a clear identity, and a sense of belonging, globalized culture leaves a psychological void. "Citizens," Kinnvall concludes, "may respond to this crisis by turning to leaders who they hope will solve their problems of material deprivation, psychological uncertainty, and ideological absence."[118]

Globalization's proponents regard the threat of cultural homogenization as highly exaggerated and believe some homogenization is beneficial. Local cultures can thrive alongside the global culture of modernity. Latin American novelist Mario Vargas Llosa maintains that "contrary to the warnings of those who fear globalization, it is not easy to completely erase cultures . . . if behind them is a rich tradition and people who practice them, even in secret. And, today, thanks to the weakening of the nation-state, we are seeing marginalized, and silenced local cultures reemerging and displaying dynamic signs of life in the great concert of this globalized planet."[119] Tyler Cowen also believes that local cultures are resilient. "Cross-cultural exchange brings a clash of values and priorities that are not susceptible to easy scientific resolution," *but* "cultural clash arises in the first place only because many people wish to shift cultural markers, create new ones, or share cultural markers with new and broader communities." In any event: "The more populous and economically large the culture, the less risk it runs of being swamped by cross-cultural contact," and "wealth, technology, and cross-cultural exchange drive many cultural blossomings."[120] Furthermore, globalization defenders point out, the defense of local cultures can mean the defense of reprehensible practices and conditions that *should* disappear, such as genital mutilation of women in Africa, the Muslim practice of polygamy, the Indian caste system, and honor killings of women in Hindu and Muslim societies. Although such practices are illegal in the West, the cultural background of immigrants is gradually earning acceptance as a legal defense even when local laws are violated.[121]

Globalization advocates also reject critics' concerns about modern technology, arguing that globalization's adversaries are Luddites who reject modernity and ignore the beneficial impact that such technologies play in expanding the global economy and widening political participation. More information creates an informed citizenry, makes it harder for politicians to mislead citizens, enhances democracy, and increases individuals' ability to mobilize in cyberspace, thereby contributing to a diversity of views and the networking of civil society NGOs. And, although a digital divide exists, new technologies are reaching more and more people and accelerating economic development in poor countries. By one estimate, the addition of ten mobile phones per 100 people in poor countries translates into an increase of 0.8 percent in GDP.[122]

Expanding global governance, including numerous UN-sponsored conferences, provides better information and creates norms in areas such as the status of women and the deterioration of the environment. The result, argue globalization advocates, is growing recognition of collective problems and of potential solutions that may involve the formation of new international regimes or the strengthening of old ones. Corporations, too, are becoming more aware of environmental dangers to their own well-being as well as to the world more generally. They increasingly realize that customers want them to be environmentally conscious and recognize that climate change could causes raw materials shortages and supply-chain disruptions owing to severe weather.[123] Growing environmental concerns in the United States and other countries is resulting in real changes in attitudes and behavior.[124]

Migrants, drugs, bugs, trafficking, and terrorism

Other negative consequences of globalization, according to critics, are massive migrations of people, who leave in search of employment or are fleeing violence. Such migrations may disrupt communities, create cultural ghettos, foster transnational criminal industries in drug smuggling and human trafficking, and lead many women to become trapped in domestic or sexual servitude.[125] As of 2008, there were roughly 214 million migrants globally, accounting for about 3.1 percent of the world's population.[126] Fiona Adamson attributes increasing migration rates to

> declining transportation costs and the ease of travel; continuing levels of economic inequality among states; the fall of the Iron Curtain and the opening up of borders in the former Soviet bloc; the loosening of emigration restrictions in other states, such as China; refugee-generating conflict and violence, such as in the Balkans and sub-Saharan Africa; state policies of forced migration; and the growth of human smuggling as a form of organized crime.[127]

She also points out that migration may affect national security by threatening border security and diluting national identity, strengthening or eroding economic and military power, and fostering internal conflict, crime, and even terrorism.[128]

Human trafficking is the "underbelly of globalism."[129] The global sex trade is related to "the combination of local conditions and the forces of economic globalization,"[130] including the reduction in social welfare programs for women. "Human trafficking," as Naím observes, "is not yet the most profitable illicit trade – that honor goes to drugs – but it is very likely the fastest growing."[131] "Traffickers," writes Gargi Bhattacharyya, "abduct their victims and transport them against their will, usually for profit – they are a contemporary version of slave traders."[132]

Nevertheless, globalization defenders insist that labor mobility is a key ingredient in producing economic efficiency. If surplus labor in the developing world does not migrate to where jobs are available in the developed world, the alternative is sending jobs from the developed to the developing world where there is surplus labor and hence lower production costs. In addition, aging populations in wealthy countries means an increase in welfare costs for the growing number of elderly, and a reduction in young workers, especially those willing to take low-paying jobs, who can pay the taxes needed to pay for burgeoning health and retirement entitlements for the elderly. And migration from developing to developed countries benefits the former in three additional ways. "First, it reduces the South's labor force and thus raises wages for those who remain behind. Second, migrants send remittances of hard currency back home. Finally, migration bolsters transnational trade and investment networks."[133]

Transnational crime has had to adapt to globalization in many of the same ways as other business enterprises, utilizing partnerships, diversification, and financial expertise.[134] Guns, for instance, flow across the US border with Mexico, arming the Mexican drug cartels, even as drugs flow northward,[135] and cooperation between drug cartels and terrorists is widespread.[136] Some criminal links are amazingly complex. Referring to an Indian-born banker who was extradited from Canada to Thailand to face criminal charges regarding a bank failure, former British foreign secretary

Robin Cook spoke of "an Indian businessman, travelling on the passport of a dead Serb, awaiting extradition from Canada for alleged embezzlement from a bank in Thailand."[137]

Transnational crime's "horizontal networks," according to Frank Madsen, survive in part because of their "non-transparency, flexibility, and self-repair capabilities."[138] They are "glocalized," simultaneously extending their global reach, while becoming stronger locally.[139] Glocalization is readily apparent in the drug trade. "The enormous profits generated by drugs," declares Stephen Flynn, "provide terrorists and insurgents with hard currency to purchase weapons" and "makes it possible for transsovereign criminal organizations to corrupt officials at every level of government, thereby undermining the legitimacy of political and judicial institutions" and accentuating "social cleavages already fueled by the pain and dislocations connected with modernization and post-communist and postindustrial societal transitions."[140]

All this leads Naím to conclude: "Global criminal activities are *transforming the international system*, upending the rules, creating new players, and reconfiguring power in international politics and economics."[141] Criminal networks enjoy significant political influence and have been empowered by globalization because they "thrive on international mobility and their ability to take advantage of the opportunities that flow from the separation of marketplaces into sovereign states with borders"[142] – borders that limit the mobility and effectiveness of law enforcement agencies.

Critics also contend that globalization facilitates transnational terrorism by making it possible for terrorists and terrorist groups to coordinate in cyberspace, increasing the porosity of borders, and fostering the illegal transnational trade in arms.[143] Arms are also sold to repressive regimes such as those in Sudan and Myanmar. The UN estimates there are about 500 million small arms circulating in the world of which roughly 70 million are Soviet-designed Kalashnikovs.[144] A Russian arms dealer, Viktor Bout, arrested in Thailand and deported to the United States, is said to have "smashed arms embargoes and struck deals with a remarkable axis of ne'er-do-wells: supplying weapons and air-transport to the Taliban, abetting despots and revolutionaries in Africa and South America, aiding Hizbullah in Lebanon and Islamists in Somalia. He also found time to supply US forces in Iraq, perhaps al-Qaeda too, and maybe even Chechen rebels."[145]

"The increased exploitation of criminality by terrorists," suggests Madsen, "was facilitated by a number of relatively new phenomena, linked to the globalization of our societies, namely the remarkable expansion of international trade, travel, and communications," because "the sheer volume made illicit international trade, travel, etc., much more difficult to identify among the licit activities."[146] The globalization of mass media also figures here. Although a terrorist attack in any specific location is extremely improbable, "the globalization of the terrorist threat first manifests as the globalization of the expectation of possible terrorist attacks almost anywhere in the world at any moment."[147]

Disease, of course, travels with people. Historically, from the medieval Black Death to Europe's export of smallpox, influenza, and diphtheria to the New World, diseases have been disseminated globally. The spread of diseases globally has been facilitated by easier and cheaper air and sea travel, tourism, migration, and "the integration of world food markets."[148] In the United States, for example, parasitic diseases and infections normally found in the developing world, including toxocariasis, cysticercosis, chagas, and cytomegalovirus, are appearing, especially in poor communities located near the border with Mexico and in Appalachia.[149] In recent decades, the H1N1 influenza and the HIV/AIDS virus have also been globalized.

On the positive side, globalization of communications has made it much more possible and far quicker to coordinate teams of specialists in medical communities and governments to mount an effective transborder campaign against nascent pandemics. Partly because of early, informed, and coordinated action, for example, SARS and H1N1 proved much less devastating than might otherwise have been the case.

States, war, and violence

Globalization opponents tend to view states as created to wage wars that benefit rulers but not citizens. In Charles Tilly's words: "War made the state, and the state made war."[150] Despite the spread of popular sovereignty, the allegation is that decisions about war and peace, as well as the distribution of wealth, remain mainly in the hands of ruling elites who cultivate and manipulate nationalism to rally followers and paper over domestic woes.

Historically, as noted in Chapter 2, wars have both contributed importantly to producing globalization and resulted in destruction that at least temporarily hindered its advance. "From the Chinese armadas of the thirteenth century," writes McGrew, "through the medieval Crusades, to the New Imperialism of the late nineteenth century, military conquest and force have been vital instruments in drawing the world's distant regions and discrete civilizations into tightening webs of recursive interaction."[151] The twentieth century witnessed three wars of global scope and "strategic globality" – and "the transworld projection, organization and social relations of organized violence"[152] persists.

However, proponents argue that globalization has actually *reduced* the probability of war by creating greater interdependence among states and peoples, spreading democratic values globally, reducing national exclusiveness, and enmeshing people in a collective global venture. Thus, James Putzel identifies neoliberals and advocates of global governance as sharing "a deep skepticism of the 'state.' The advocates of liberalization condemn the state's meddling in what is best left to market actors, and the advocates of 'global governance' point to the state's tendency to make war and trample the rights of individuals."[153] "Only by elaborating a single, complex global structure of political authority, meshing national democracy with international integration," argues Shaw, "is there any realistic possibility of constraining large-scale violence and sustaining peaceful social development."[154] Katherine Barbieri sees globalization as reducing the dependence of any one country on any other and allows countries to identify new trade opportunities, suggesting that "the expansion of trade globally may be beneficial for peace, since it leads to less dependence at the dyadic level."[155] However, she does acknowledge an absence of consensus on this issue.

Globalization's advocates further claim that nation-states, with their emphasis on cultural uniqueness and association with a territorial homeland, have erected barriers between peoples, stymied efforts to deal with global problems, and produced ever bloodier wars between and within states. Nations that have a homeland seek to keep "aliens" out, while those that lack a homeland demand one for themselves. Even today nationalism plays a central role in conflicts involving Palestinians, Bosnians, Kashmiris, Kosovars, Basques, Catalans, Uighurs, Kurds, Cypriots, and others. Globalization supporters applaud processes that produce transnational economic and identity links, spread human-rights norms, facilitate the coordination of humanitarian relief and intervention, create transnational institutions, erode state exclusivity, reduce the centrality of territory and geography, encourage migration, integrate languages and cultures, and make people more prosperous and interdependent. As a result of such processes, they contend, the barriers of nationalism are dissolving, the number of interstate wars is declining, and the human-rights abuses committed by governments are losing the protection of state sovereignty. Shaw again: "It is the political conflict of global democracy versus anti-globalist nationalism that has already stimulated the development of those global state institutions which most reflect global principles – international policing, law and humanitarian action."[156]

Those favoring globalization also claim that it is replacing ideologies that divided the world in the twentieth century with a single ideology based on liberal democracy that will assure the "democratic peace." In this spirit, international law has most recently expanded to protect *people* rather than states. As publics come to recognize that states cannot deal with collective dilemmas like environmental pollution, they are placing their faith in NGOs and international institutions that can coordinate people's activities to cope with global challenges.

Sovereignty and its discontents

As the previous section implies, globalization advocates view the decline of state sovereignty as a major achievement. Sovereignty, they believe, legitimated a world in which states dominated war-making, economic policy-making, and even cultural and social policy. By contrast, today's trade is largely *among* corporations and corporate subsidiaries, and the boundaries of national economic units are no longer congruent with the transnational reach of markets. A large proportion of transnational trade is between TNCs and independent firms to which the corporations have outsourced production or services offshore. Nike, for example, outsources virtually all of its production far offshore even though a majority of its sales are in the Americas.[157]

Outsourcing is beneficial for recipient countries by integrating them into corporate production networks and sending intermediate products "home" where they are finished and are competitively exported. According to Hamilton and Quinlan: "Globally dispersed production networks have generated a huge increase in both intra-industry and intra-firm trade" with as much as "30–40 percent of overall trade among companies transferring materials, component parts and finished goods to other units within the same firm."[158] At present, the resources controlled by large corporations and banks, and by certain super-rich individuals, dwarf the resources of most governments, and the wealth of large corporations exceeds the gross domestic product of most countries.

Agriculture, too, is highly globalized. In recent years, some food-importing countries like Saudi Arabia, Kuwait, South Korea, and China that have insufficient arable land have outsourced agricultural production by purchasing farmland in countries such as Mali, Senegal, Sudan, Cambodia, and Ethiopia that already suffer malnutrition and occasional famine. Many indigenous farmers have been displaced as a consequence."[159] Some believe that such investments are a new form of imperialism – "agro-imperialism."[160]

State sovereignty and autonomy, according to globalization advocates, perpetuate economic inefficiency. Why, asks Wolf, "would humanity be better off for having its economy broken up into more than 200 entirely self-sufficient pieces?"

> Furthermore, why should one stop at 200 pieces? Why not break the world economy up into 10,000 countries, 600,000 tribes, or 6 billion self-sufficient human beings? . . . The view that the present political division of humanity is natural and inevitable is nonsensical. The parallel idea that each unit should be economically self-sufficient is equally absurd. Today's states are arbitrary products of recent history. The logical destination of a movement to self-sufficiency must be the atomization of humanity, perhaps into family bands.[161]

On the other hand, globalization critics like Putzel are likely to argue that the neoliberal variety of globalization is actually inimical to peace and development at least in the developing world. He is especially critical of the impact of neoliberal policies of privatization and small government on the capacity of developing states. He contends that such policies decrease the state's capacity to provide social cohesion and have weakened legislatures and political parties, while increasing the likelihood of corruption and political and economic inequality among social groups. These conditions promote state collapse and civil violence. His conclusion is that "it is difficult to imagine that the policies of liberalization have not had an impact on the patterns of state breakdown and violence, especially in Africa."[162]

Sovereignty no longer (if it ever did) provides significant protection for state autonomy or freedom from external intervention. Today, sovereignty tells us little about real states. The world's 200 states include a single hegemon, a number of potential challengers, and a multitude of scarcely viable "mini-states." Quite apart from issues of economic size and viability, eighty-seven countries have fewer than 5 million inhabitants, fifty-eight have fewer than 2.5 million, and thirty-five fewer than 500,000.

The contrast between the prosperous city-state of Singapore and the remains of Somalia is dramatic indeed. In failed states like Somalia, the idea of sovereignty is turned on its head; instead of providing citizens with security from foreign aggression by guarding the state's borders, armed militias *are a source of insecurity* for citizens who desperately flee them by crossing those borders into Kenya and Ethiopia. In recent decades, sovereignty in much of the world has been little more than what Robert Jackson calls "negative sovereignty," that is, protection for corrupt regimes in "quasi-states."[163] All in all, there has been a growing gap between the promise of sovereignty and the reality of global politics. With few exceptions, states are less autonomous and less able to protect or inspire citizens than at any time in recent centuries.

THE COUNTER-GLOBALIZATION MOVEMENT

The critics of contemporary globalization have not limited their concerns to the printed word but have increasingly taken to the streets to protest what they regard as its unjust outcomes. In the process, a loosely organized movement has come into being that appears wherever meetings of institutions which foster globalization, such as the WTO or G-20, take place. This movement involves an array of individuals and groups, using different methods, including nonviolent and violent direct action.[164]

Much of the violence at counter-globalization demonstrations is the work of anarchist groups in the larger mix. "Many among today's young radical activists," Barbara Epstein writes, "especially those at the center of the anti-globalization and anti-corporate movements, call themselves anarchists," meaning that they support, in this context, "egalitarianism; opposition to all hierarchies; suspicion of authority, especially that of the state; and commitment to living according to one's values."[165] The links to militant libertarianism are obvious.

Groups critical of neoliberal capitalism of an alter-globalization persuasion protest "those global and regional institutions whose main task is to promote, develop, or implement corporate globalization through neoliberal free-market policies."[166] Some observers identify more than a single anti-neoliberal element. Greg Buckman, for example, distinguishes between a reformist fair-trade school and a more extreme element anchored in churches.[167]

Although the broad opposition to globalization has come to represent diverse and sometimes conflicting interests and visions, including labor unions, environmental and gay rights advocates, indigenous peoples, anarchists, libertarians, Islamic militants, and even racist militias,[168] its roots are in the central normative concerns we have just described. Wolf, a globalization enthusiast, divides what he terms "anti-globalization.com" into "old-fashioned economic interests, on the one hand, and, more important today, single-issue non-governmental organizations, often with mass memberships, on the other."[169] Bhagwati similarly characterizes the movement as a "fortuitous alliance struck between young agitators, conventional lobbies such as the labor movement, new pressure groups such as the environmentalists, and human rights crusaders."[170] "Taking on the characteristics of a multitude," as Luis Alberto Fernandez contends, "the movement appears throughout the world in surprising locations."

> Social movement scholars see it in the water wars of Cochabamba, Peru, in the Zapatista struggle in Mexico, in indigenous resistance to genetically modified agriculture, in the peasant occupation of lands in Brazil, and even in the protest against gentrification in downtown Tempe, Arizona. The anti-globalization movement is also located in labor disputes over free-trade agreements, in the fight against sweatshop labor, and in the symbolic manipulation of corporate symbols.[171]

In consequence, "Holy ghosts of all sorts are haunting global politics: 'global civil society', 'international public opinion', 'the peoples' (or 'the women' or 'the workers' or 'the poor') of the world," "[p]erhaps, we are living at the beginning of a global social revolution that will challenge governance's attempt at a political revolution."[172]

According to Fernandez, there is disagreement about the movement's origins, ranging from those who believe it began in the Seattle protest against the WTO in 1999, the anti-IMF agitation of the 1970s, or even "when the indigenous peoples of the Americas fought European colonizers"[173] hundreds of years ago. At a minimum, it can be traced back to the 1970s protests, especially in the developing world, against IMF neoliberal policies, and was revived in the 1990s era of democratization, with the IMF and World Bank as principal targets.[174]

Protests against symbols and institutions of globalization such as the WTO, the IMF, the G-20, and the proposed Free Trade Area of the Americas (FTAA) – that have taken place in Seattle, Washington, DC, Genoa,[175] Prague, Québec City, Seoul, Pittsburgh, Toronto, and elsewhere – are not spontaneous. Some 200 groups with quite different concerns, in an uneasy coalition, were trained for the Seattle protest, the most important of which were People for Fair Trade/Network Opposed to WTO, the Direct Action Network of anarchists, the AFL–CIO and its local affiliate, as well as environmental groups like the Sierra Club.[176] One target of many of the demonstrators was the WTO's 1998 decision "which declared that U.S. attempts to protect endangered sea turtles to be a violation of world trade rules."[177] Gillian Murphy sees the Seattle protest as reflecting a cosmopolitan global civil society. "By linking the fates of distant individuals and ecosystems to global action, the global justice movement that expressed its opposition to the WTO has helped create a 'global citizen' identity much like other movements have created identities for women, minority groups, and gays and lesbians as part of the process of effecting change."[178] "The shutting down of the meeting of the World Trade Organization in Seattle on November 30, 1999, as a result of the actions of tens of thousands of demonstrators," writes Castells, "signaled the coming of age of a major social movement that opposes, on a global scale, the values and interests shaping the globalization process." Seattle "struck the public mind around the world, via their impact on the global media, bringing to everybody's attention the fact that globalization was not a natural process, but a political decision."[179]

A variety of groups combat globalization and the values they believe it spreads, despite their huge ideological differences in other respects. These include Mexico's Zapatistas (EZLN), the US's right-wing militias, and Al Qaeda, all of which are themselves transnationally networked and skillfully utilize the internet to further their objectives. The Zapatistas, for example, were formed in Chiapas in 1994, and their "media-oriented strategy was particularly explicit, and skillfully executed," as they "tried carefully to minimize violence and to work via the media and the Internet to reach out to the world."[180] "If the *Zapatistas* were the first informational guerrillas," declares Castells, "the anti-globalization movement generalized this strategy to a whole array of convergent struggles against the capitalist global order," with "the minds of people around the world" as their real target.[181]

The diverse movement further crystallized in the World Social Forum (WSF). The Forum first gathered in Porto Alegre, Brazil, in 2001 and was intended to be a mirror image of the annual World Economic Forum[182] of public and private economic movers and shakers that was founded in 1971 and meets in Davos, Switzerland. The World Social Forum's Charter of Principles issued in June 2001 emphasized its intent to serve as a source of alternative ideas to mainstream globalization as articulated at

Davos. Those ideas "stand in opposition to a process of globalization commanded by the large multinational corporations and by the governments and international institutions at the service of those corporations' interests, with the complicity of national governments" and emphasized reflexivity, democratic decision-making, universal human rights, non-violent resistance, and cultural and ethnic pluralism.

The Charter emphasized the local nature of many of the groups opposing particular local manifestations of globalization and described the WSF as "a plural, diversified, non-confessional, non-governmental and non-party context that, in a decentralized fashion, interrelated organizations and movements engaged in concrete action at levels from the local to the international to build another world."[183] The localism of many of globalization's opponents, however, leads Harvey to warn against the blinkered vision of those groups whom he terms "militant particularist movements" that ignore the tension between economic and environmental injustice and that do not "transcend the narrow solidarities and particular affinities shaped in particular places." "They can," he writes, "either ignore the contradictions, remain within the confines of their own particular militancies – fighting an incinerator here, a toxic waste dump there, a World Bank dam project somewhere else, and commercial logging in yet another place – or they can treat the contradictions as a fecund nexus to create a more transcendent and universal politics."[184] Only by doing the latter will they recognize the tradeoff between social and economic justice.

Subsequent meetings of the WSF have been held annually in cities in the developing world, including Durban, Mumbai, Bamako, and Belém where they have attracted radical leaders like Hugo Chávez of Venezuela and have become increasingly strident in opposing policies of the developed world. Thus, the Final Declaration of the February 2009 WSF meeting in Brazil, which took place in the midst of the global financial crisis, was loudly and radically anti-mainstream Western capitalism:

> We won't pay for the crisis. The rich have to pay for it! Anti-imperialist, anti-capitalist, feminist, environmentalist and socialist alternatives are necessary. . . . Over the last few years, in Latin America highly radical social struggles have resulted in the overthrow of neoliberal governments and the empowerment of governments that have carried out many positive reforms such as the nationalization of core sectors of the economy and democratic constitutional reforms . . . The international capitalist crisis manifests itself as detrimental to humankind in various ways: it affects food, finance, the economy, climate, energy, population migration, and civilization itself . . . We are facing a global crisis which is a direct consequence of the capitalist system and therefore cannot find a solution within the system . . . The present system is based on exploitation, competition, promotion of individual private interests to the detriment of the collective interest, and the frenzied accumulation of wealth by a handful of rich people.[185]

As this suggests, many of the WSF's positions reflect a revival of Marxist rhetoric, mixed with and influenced by feminist, anarchist, labor activist, and pro-Palestinian groups under a "progressive" umbrella. Nevertheless, many of the national delegates remain preoccupied by issues within their own countries, rather than by global challenges. The WSF, and, indeed, the movement as a whole, find support from those like Douglas Kellner who states that "in opposition to the globalization from above of corporate capitalism, I would advocate a globalization from below, one which supports individuals and groups using the new technologies to create a more multicultural, egalitarian, democratic, and ecological world."[186]

A MIXED VERDICT

As Held and McGrew suggest, "Deliberations about globalization, whether in the academy or beyond, are inescapably inflected – whether explicitly or implicitly – with normative reasoning."[187] Notwithstanding the arguments of proponents, reformers, or outright adversaries, any reasoned normative judgment of such a complex, multidimensional phenomenon as globalization will necessarily be mixed. Indeed, as Urry declares, "global ordering is so immensely complicated that it cannot be 'known' through a single concept or set of processes."[188] Stanley Hoffmann points up a variety of contradictions.[189] Globalization thickens interstate interdependence but does not eliminate interstate rivalries. Interstate war has become less common, but intrastate and transnational warfare has spread. Global forces and networks limit state autonomy, while domestic publics place governments under intense pressures to protect them from these forces. Globalization enriches many but spreads economic instability quickly and excludes some poor states from its benefits, and it "poses a central dilemma between efficiency and fairness."[190] Cultural globalization pits the virtues of "uniformization" against the virtues of "diversity"; political globalization entails a proliferation of international and nongovernmental organizations along with "the preponderance of the United States"; civil society exists but "remains embryonic"; and "individual emancipation" does not democratize regimes.

At the end of the day, Hoffmann gloomily concludes that "the attractive idea of improving the human condition through the abolition of barriers is dubious."

> Globalization is in fact only a sum of techniques (audio and videocassettes, the Internet, instantaneous communications) that are at the disposal of states or private actors. Self-interest and ideology, not humanitarian reasons, are what drive these actors. Their behavior is quite different from the vision of globalization as an Enlightenment-based utopia that is simultaneously scientific, rational, and universal. For many reasons – misery, injustice, humiliation, attachment to traditions, aspiration to more than just a better standard of living – this "Enlightenment" stereotype of globalization thus provokes revolt and dissatisfaction.[191]

Globalization allows losers to compare their fate with winners when winners are not driven by altruistic motives, and Hoffmann's dark vision about the "Enlightenment-based utopia" resonates among postmodernists and critical theorists. The "belief in 'progress' through reason and 'instrumental' rationality has been shattered and it has become evident that 'progress' based on the application of science, has resulted in an increase in uncertainty and the creation of new risks threatening the survival of humankind."[192]

Mounting resistance to the neoliberal project embedded in the Washington Consensus, now joined by the recent near-collapse of global finance, might suggest that at least some aspects of economic globalization are beginning to slow. Will any such showdown redound to the benefit of the state? This is a question that is implicit in the title of this book and one to which we return, among others, in Chapter 10. Suffice to say here that it is not only belief in exorable liberal progress that has been shattered but also confidence in the state, as Strange recognized as early as the mid-1990s. Popular distrust of national governments and politicians that she identified as pervasive even then has, if anything, grown apace. The Tea Party movement in the United States is but one of its latest manifestations. Indeed, beyond the matter of distrust, do the governments and states and their leaders actually have adequate knowledge and capacity to address a range of crucial global issues that, by definition, are inherently transnational? For their part, are international institutions much more than the sum of the individual incapacities of their member states? Do they have either the authority or capacity to provide a genuinely alternative or even supplemental source of governance? To what extent are those governments and international institutions themselves captured by the very globalization actors and forces they might be expected to rein in and regulate?

Globalization, of course, has not had an equal impact on all regions. Indeed, its processes are routinely described as "uneven," and, as we have seen, many observers equate globalization – whether rightly or wrongly – with "Americanization" or "Westernization." Some regions and countries benefit more than others, a central claim among globalization's critics. The next two chapters examine the impact of globalization on the world's major regions.

NOTES

1 Ulf Hedetoft and Douglas W. Blum, "Introduction: Russia and Globalization – A Historical and Conceptual Framework," in Blum, ed., *Russia and Globalization*, 8. Emphasis in original.
2 Naomi Klein, *Fences and Windows* (New York: Picador, 2002), xxi.
3 Joseph E. Stiglitz, "The Overselling of Globalization," in Michael M. Weinstein, ed., *Globalization: What's New?* (New York: Columbia University Press, 2005), 228, 229. See also Joseph E. Stiglitz, *Globalization and Its Discontents* (New York: W. W. Norton, 2003). Unlike Stiglitz, some of globalization's critics are polemicists. See, for example, Viviane Forrester, *The Economic Horror* (Cambridge: Polity Press, 1999). The African Union has demanded that rich countries compensate Africa with $67 billion annually for damage done by their carbon emissions. "A Green Ransom," *The Economist*, September 5, 2009, 52.
4 Bhagwati, *In Defense of Globalization*, 4.
5 Jagdish Bhagwati, "Coping with Antiglobalization," *Foreign Affairs* 81:1 (January/February 2002), 2, 3.
6 Charles Lindholm and José Pedro Zúquete, *The Struggle for the World: Liberation Movements for the 21st Century* (Stanford, CA: Stanford University Press, 2010), 2–3.
7 Geoffrey Pleyers and Alain Tourraine, *Alter-Globalization* (Cambridge: Polity Press, 2010), 23. Emphasis in original.
8 Nancy Fraser, "Reframing Justice in a Globalizing World," in David Held and Ayse Kaya, eds., *Global Inequality* (Cambridge: Polity Press, 2007), 253.
9 Jackie Smith, *Social Movements for Global Democracy* (Berkeley, CA: Berkeley University Press, 2007).
10 Steger, *Globalisms*, 17. Emphasis in original.

11 Ibid., 15, 16, 144–5. Emphasis in original. Steger sees bin Laden's rhetoric as having similarities to the rhetoric of anti-globalization populists like Patrick Buchanan and Lou Dobbs. For a cogent argument that Islam and democracy are not incompatible, see Mustapha Kamal Pasha, "Predatory Globalization and Democracy in the Islamic World," *Annals of the American Academy of Political and Social Science* 581 (May 2002), 121–32.
12 See Michael Kitson and Jonathan Michie, "Conflict, Cooperation and Change: The Political Economy of Trade and Trade Policy," *Review of International Political Economy* 2:4 (Autumn 1995), 632–57.
13 Polanyi, *The Great Transformation*, 3. See Munck's discussion of Polanyi in *Globalization and Contestation*, 14–20, 34–9, 135–7.
14 Polanyi, *The Great Transformation*, 145.
15 Ibid., 5. See Ronaldo Munck, "Globalization and Democracy: A New 'Great Transformation'?" *Annals of the American Academy of Political and Social Science* 581 (May 2002), 17–19.
16 Beverly J. Silver, *Forces of Labor: Workers' Movements and Globalization since 1870* (Cambridge: Cambridge University Press, 2003), 20.
17 Edward N. Luttwak, *Turbo Capitalism: Winners and Losers in the Global Economy* (New York: HarperCollins, 1999), 27.
18 See Claude Smadja, "The End of Complacency," *Foreign Policy* 113 (Winter 1998–9), 67–71.
19 Rodrik, *Has Globalization Gone Too Far?* 2.
20 Strange, *The Retreat of the State*, 3
21 Ibid., 197, 198.
22 Catarina Kinnvall, "Analyzing the Global–Local Nexus," in Kinnvall and Jönsson, eds., *Globalization and Democratization in Asia*, 14.
23 Cerny, "Multi-Nodal Politics," 422. See also Goldmann, *Transforming the European Nation-State*, 8–17.
24 See, for example, David Held, "Globalization, Corporate Practice and Cosmopolitan Social Standards," *Contemporary Political Theory* 1:1 (2002), 59–78. Many TNCs do recognize the importance of global and local public opinion and wish to be viewed as "good citizens." See, for example, Guy Chazan, "Firm to Pay $48.7 Million in Ivory Coast Pollution Case," *Wall Street Journal*, September 21, 2009, A13.
25 See, for example, Smith, *Social Movements for Global Change*.
26 Noreena Hertz, *The Silent Takeover* (New York: HarperCollins, 2003), 6.
27 Avant, "The Marketization of Security," 122.
28 Miles Kahler and David A. Lake, "Globalization and Changing Patterns of Political Authority," in Kahler and Lake, eds., *Governance in a Global Economy*, 434.
29 See Michael Zürn, "The Challenge of Globalization and Individualization: A View from Europe," in Hans-Henrik Holm and Georg Sorensen, eds., *Whose World Order?* (Boulder, CO: Westview Press, 1995), 137–64, Andrew Kuper, *Democracy Beyond Borders* (Oxford: Oxford University Press, 2004), and Andrew Kuper, ed., *Global Responsibilities: Who Must Deliver on Human Rights?* (London: Routledge, 2005). For a suggestion of how to democratize globalization, see Anthony Giddens, *The Third Way: The Renewal of Social Democracy* (Cambridge: Polity Press, 1998), 75–6.
30 Michael W. Doyle, "The Liberal Peace, Democratic Accountability, and the Challenge of Globalization," in Held and McGrew, eds., *Globalization Theory*, 201.
31 The pessimistic view can be found in Anderson and Rieff, "'Global Civil Society': A Sceptical View," 29–33, while a more optimistic perspective is provided by Mario Pianta, "Democracy vs Globalization: The Growth of Parallel Summits and Global Movements," in Daniele Archibugi, ed., *Debating Cosmopolitics* (London: Verso, 2003), 232–56.
32 See Greider, *One World Ready or Not*, 335–8.
33 David M. Andrews, C. Randall Henning, and Louis W. Pauly, "Monetary Institutions, Financial Integration, and Political Authority," in D. M. Andrews, C. R. Henning, and

L. W. Pauly, eds., *Governing the World's Money* (Ithaca, NY: Cornell University Press, 2002), 10.
34 Frank Webster, *Theories of the Information Society*, 3rd edn (Abingdon, UK: Routledge, 2006), 188.
35 Jeffrey M. Ayres, "Framing Collective Action against Neoliberalism," *Journal of World-Systems Research* 10:1 (2004), 11, 14.
36 See Ethan B. Kapstein, "Workers and the World Economy," *Foreign Affairs* 75:3 (May/June 1996), 16–36.
37 Cerny, "Globalization and Other Stories," 63–4.
38 Cerny, "What Next for the State?" 124. Cerny's competition state is echoed by Bobbitt's "market-state" "which depends on the international capital markets and, to a lesser degree, on the modern multinational business network to create stability in the world economy, in preference to management by national or transnational political bodies." See Bobbitt, *The Shield of Achilles*, 229. See also John Gray, *False Dawn: The Delusions of Global Capitalism*, rev. edn (London: Granta Books, 2002), and Greider, *One World Ready or Not*, 286, 307.
39 Cerny, "Globalization and Other Stories," 65.
40 Andreas Osiander, "Sovereignty, International Relations, and the Westphalian Myth," *International Organization* 55:2 (Spring 2001), 283.
41 Sassen, "Place and Spaces of the Global," 89.
42 Greider, *One World Ready or Not*, 227. See also H. Peter Gray and John R. Dilyard, eds., *Globalization and Economic and Financial Instability* (Northampton, MA: Edward Elgar Publishing, 2006).
43 Robert H. Wade, "Should We Worry about Income Inequality?" in Held and Kaya, eds., *Global Inequality*, 104.
44 Ibid., 107.
45 Ibid., 109, 115.
46 Ibid., 124. For a similar argument and conclusions, see Thomas W. Pogge, "Why Inequality Matters," in Held and Kaya, eds., *Global Inequality*, 132–47.
47 Jan Nederveen Pieterse, "Global Inequality: Bringing Politics Back In," *Third World Quarterly* 23:6 (December 2002), 1042.
48 Jeffrey G. Williamson, "Globalization, Convergence, and History," *Journal of Economic History* 56:2 (June 1996), 278.
49 See David Held and Ayse Kaya, "Introduction," in Held and Kaya, eds., *Global Inequality*, 1–25. For such reasons, it is difficult to ascertain whether there is a trend towards greater inequality. See Vincent A. Mahler, "Economic Globalization, Domestic Politics, and Income Inequality in the Developed Countries," *Comparative Politics Studies* 37:9 (2004), 1025–53, Sudkir Anand and Paul Segal, "What Do We Know about Global Economic Inequality?" *Journal of Economic Literature* 46:1 (2008), 57–94, A. B. Atkinson and A. Brandolini, "On Data: A Case Study of the Evolution of Income Inequality Across Time and Across Countries," *Cambridge Journal of Economics* 33:3 (2009), 381–404, and Salvatore J. Balbones and Dorian C. Vonada, "Trade Globalization and National Income Inequality Are They Related?" *Journal of Sociology* 45:1 (2009), 5–30. The problem of comparing countries is reduced by translating variations in income into purchasing power parity (PPP).
50 Bob Sutcliffe, "The Unequalled and Unequal Twentieth Century," in Held and Kaya, eds., *Global Inequality*, 51.
51 Branko Milanovic, "Globalization and Inequality," in Held and Kaya, eds., *Global Inequality*, 26–8.
52 Ibid., 32, 33. Emphasis in original.
53 James K. Galbraith, "Global Inequality and Global Macro Economics," in Held and Kaya, eds., *Global Inequality*, 173. See also Grahame F. Thompson, "Global Inequality, the 'Great Divergence' and Supranational Regionalization," in Held and Kaya, eds., *Global Inequality*, 175–8.

54 Ravi Kanbur and Anthony J. Venables, "Spatial Disparities and Economic Development," in Held and Kaya, eds., *Global Inequality*, 204, 205, 209.
55 Gøsta Esping-Andersen, "More Inequality and Fewer Opportunities? Structural Determinants and Human Agency in the Dynamics of Income Distribution," in Held and Kaya, eds., *Global Inequality*, 220, 221.
56 "Unbottled Gini," *The Economist*, January 22, 2011, 71–2.
57 For example, Sutcliffe, "The Unequalled and Unequal Twentieth Century," 60.
58 Wade, "Should We Worry about Income Inequality?" 109.
59 Milanovic, "Globalization and Inequality," 42–3.
60 Esping-Andersen, "More Inequality and Fewer Opportunities? Structural Determinants and Human Agency in the Dynamics of Income Distribution," 221. A similar trend is evident in the US.
61 "Whose Problem Now?" *The Economist*, October 2, 2010, 65.
62 Milanovic, "Globalization and Inequality," 33.
63 Kanbur and Venables, "Spatial Disparities and Economic Development," 209.
64 See Giovanni Andrea Cornia, "Inequality, Growth, and Poverty: An Overview of Changes over the Last Two Decades," in Giovanni Andrea Cornia, ed., *Inequality, Growth, and Poverty in an Era of Liberalization and Globalization* (Oxford: Oxford University Press, 2004), 17.
65 Giovanni Andrea Cornia, Tony Addison, and Sampsa Kiiski, "Income Distribution Changes and Their Impact in the Post-Second World War Period," in Cornia, ed., *Inequality, Growth, and Poverty in an Era of Liberalization and Globalization*, 26.
66 Ajit Singh and Rahul Dhumale, "Globalization, Technology, and Income Inequality: A Critical Analysis," in Cornia, ed., *Inequality, Growth, and Poverty in an Era of Liberalization and Globalization*, 149–52.
67 Daniele Checchi, "Does Educational Achievement Help Explain Income Inequality?" in Cornia, ed., *Inequality, Growth, and Poverty in an Era of Liberalization and Globalization*, 81–111.
68 Robert Eastwood and Michael Lipton, "Rural and Urban Income Inequality and Poverty: Does Convergence between Sectors Offset Divergence within Them?" in Cornia, ed., *Inequality, Growth, and Poverty in an Era of Liberalization and Globalization*, 112–43.
69 However, the number of those living on $2 a day has grown.
70 David Dollar, "Globalization, Poverty and Inequality since 1980," in Held and Kaya, eds., *Global Inequality*, 73, 74, 88. For analysis of the impact of globalization on women in the developing world, see Alison M. Jaggar, "Is Globalization Good for Women?" *Comparative Literature*, 53:4 (2001), 298–314.
71 David Dollar and Aart Kraay, "Spreading the Wealth," *Foreign Affairs* 81:1 (January/February 2002), 121.
72 See Yuri Dikhanov, "Trends in Global Income Distribution, 1970–2000, and Scenarios for 2015," World Bank: Human Development Report, 2005, http://siteresources.worldbank.org/ICPINT/Resources/hdR2005_Dikhanov_Yuri_8.pdf.
73 World Bank, "Poverty Trends," *PovertyNet*, http://web.worldbank.org/WBSITE/EXTERNAL/TOPICS/EXTPOVERTY/EXTPA/0,,contentMDK:20153855~menuPK:435040~pagePK:148956~piPK:216618~theSitePK:430367,00.html. See also Surjit S. Bhalla, *Imagine There's No Country: Poverty, Inequality, and Growth in the Era of Globalization* (Washington, DC: Institute for International Economics, 2002), who argues that global inequality has been dramatically reduced in recent decades.
74 Shaohua Chen and Martin Ravallion, "The Developing World Is Poorer than We Thought, But No Less Successful in the Fight Against Poverty," *World Bank Policy Research Working Paper* 4703, August 1, 2008, http://papers.ssrn.com/sol3/papers.cfm?abstract_id=1259575.
75 Pankaj Ghemawat, "The World's Biggest Myth," *Foreign Policy* 163 (November/December 2007), 54.
76 See T. J. Pempel, ed., *The Politics of the Asian Economic Crisis* (Ithaca, NY: Cornell University Press, 1999).

77 Sergio L. Schmukler, "Benefits and Risks of Financial Globalization: Challenges for Developing Countries," paper for the World Bank Research Report (June 2004), 3, http://siteresources.worldbank.org/DEC/Resources/BenefitsandRisksofFinancialGlobalizationSchmukler.pdf.
78 See Thomas Pogge, "Reframing Economic Security and Justice," in Held and McGrew, eds., *Globalization Theory*, 207–24. See also Ankie Hoogvelt, *Globalization and the Postcolonial World*, 2nd edn (Baltimore, MD: Johns Hopkins Press, 2001), xv, and Burbach, Núñez, and Kagarlitsky, *Globalization and Its Discontents*.
79 Robert McCorquodale and Richard Fairbrother, "Globalization and Human Rights," *Human Rights Quarterly* 21:3 (August 1999), 740.
80 Clifford Bob, "Globalization and the Social Construction of Human Rights Campaigns," in Brysk, ed., *Globalization and Human Rights*, 144.
81 James N. Rosenau, "The Drama of Human Rights in a Turbulent, Globalized World," in Brysk, ed., *Globalization and Human Rights*, 150, 151.
82 Alison Brysk, "Introduction: Transnational Threats and Opportunities," in Brysk, ed., *Globalization and Human Rights*, 2. See also Munck, *Globalization and Contestation*, 75–93.
83 See, for example, Yasmine Ryan, "Exodus from North Africa Full of Perils," *New York Times*, September 9, 2009, http://www.nytimes.com/2009/09/09/world/africa/09iht-algeria.html.
84 See Kristen Hill Maher, "Who Has a Right to Rights? Citizenship's Exclusions in an Age of Migration," in Brysk, ed., *Globalization and Human Rights*, 19–43.
85 Donnelly, "Human Rights, Globalizing Flows, and State Power," 238.
86 Richard Falk, "Interpreting the Interaction of Global Markets and Human Rights," in Brysk, ed., *Globalization and Human Rights*, 65.
87 Ibid., 67. Falk cites the use of sweatshops by Nike and Gap.
88 Wesley T. Milner, "Economic Globalization and Rights: An Empirical Analysis," in Brysk, ed., *Globalization and Human Rights*, 90.
89 Saskia Sassen, "Global Cities and Survival Circuits," in Ehrenreich and Hochschild, eds., *Global Women: Nannies, Maids, and Sex Workers in the New Economy*, 257.
90 Barbara Ehrenreich and Arlie Russell Hochschild, "Introduction," in Ehrenreich and Hochschild, eds., *Global Women*, 2, 3.
91 Helma Lutz, "At Your Service Madam! The Globalization of Domestic Service," *Feminist Review* 70 (2002), 100–1.
92 Joy M. Zarembka, "America's Dirty Work: Migrant Maids and Modern-Day Slavery," in Ehrenreich and Hochschild, eds., *Global Women*, 144. Human trafficking should be distinguished from people smuggling inasmuch as the latter is with the consent of migrants and the former is without such consent. The US State Department distinguishes among three classes of countries on the basis of their effort to end human trafficking.
93 See Denise Brennan, "Selling Sex for Visas: Sex Tourism as a Stepping-Stone to International Migration," in Ehrenreich and Hochschild, eds., *Global Women*, 154–68.
94 See Hung Cam Thai, "Clashing Dreams: Highly Educated Overseas Brides and Low-Wage U.S. Husbands," in Ehrenreich and Hochschild, eds., *Global Women*, 230–53.
95 Amalia Lucia Cabezas, "Tourism, Sex Work, and Women's Rights in the Dominican Republic," in Brysk, ed., *Globalization and Human Rights*, 55. See also Kevin Bales, "Because She Looks like a Child," in Ehrenreich and Hochschild, eds., *Global Women*, 207–29.
96 Debora L. Spar, "The Spotlight on the Bottom Line: How Multinationals Export Human Rights (Child Labor and Sweatshop Abuses by Foreign Contractors of American Corporations)," *Foreign Affairs* 77:2 (March–April 1998), 7–12.
97 David L. Richard and Ronald Gelleny, "Women's Status and Economic Globalization," *International Studies Quarterly* 51:4 (December 2007), 871.
98 Ibid., 872.
99 M. Rodwan Abouharb and David Cingranelli, *Human Rights and Structural Adjustment* (Cambridge: Cambridge University Press, 2007), 239.

100 Shayne Weyker, "The Ironies of Information Technology," in Brysk, ed., *Globalization and Human Rights*, 115–32.
101 Bob, "Globalization and the Social Construction of Human Rights Campaigns," 139–44.
102 According to Wolf, *Why Globalization Works*, 166, child labor declined everywhere as globalization spread. Wolf also argues (248) that "there are worse places to work than those we call 'sweatshops'."
103 According to Pinelopi Koujianou Goldberg and Nina Pavcnik, empirical studies find little support for "race to the bottom" arguments, and there is some evidence that more openness increases the level of and compliance with minimum wages and reduces child labor. See "Trade, Inequality, and Poverty: What Do We Know? Evidence from Recent Trade Liberalization Episodes in Developing Countries Existing," *Brookings Trade Forum* (Washington, DC: Brookings Institution, 2004), 264.
104 Silver, *Forces of Labor*, 3, 4.
105 See, for example, "The Next China," *The Economist*, July 31, 2010, 48–50.
106 Nita Rudra, *Globalization and the Race to the Bottom in Developing Countries* (Cambridge: Cambridge University Press, 2008), 4. Emphasis in original.
107 Stephen D. Cohen, *Multinational Corporations and Foreign Direct Investment* (Oxford: Oxford University Press), 13.
108 Klaus E. Meyer, "Perspectives on Multinational Enterprises in Emerging Economies," *Journal of International Business Studies*, 35:4 (July 2004), 273.
109 Cohen, *Multinational Corporations and Foreign Direct Investment*, 13.
110 Raul C. Pangalangan, "Sweatshops and International Labor Standards: Globalizing Markets, Localizing Norms," in Brysk, ed., *Globalization and Human Rights*, 98.
111 Hamilton and Quinlan, *Globalization and Europe*, 87.
112 David A. Wirth, "Globalizing the Environment," in Maryann K. Cusimano, ed., *Beyond Sovereignty* (Boston, MA: Bedford/St. Martin's, 2000), 205.
113 De Blij, *The Power of Place*, 31.
114 Ibid., 33.
115 Kinnvall, "Analyzing the Global–Local Nexus," 6.
116 See, for example, Mohammed Musa, "From Optimism to Reality: An Overview of Third World News Agencies," in Peter Golding and Phil Harris, eds., *Beyond Cultural Imperialism: Communication and the New International Order* (London: Sage Publications, 1997), 117–46.
117 Anabelle Sreberny-Mohammadi, "The Many Cultural Faces of Imperialism," in Golding and Harris, eds., *Beyond Cultural Imperialism*, 61.
118 Kinnvall, "Analyzing the Global–Local Nexus," 13.
119 Mario Vargas Llosa, "The Culture of Liberty," *Foreign Policy* 112 (January/February 2001), 66–71.
120 Cowen, *Creative Destruction*, 144, 147, 63, 13.
121 Amir Efrati, "Cultural Background Gains Traction as a Legal Defense," *Wall Street Journal*, July 2, 2009, A9.
122 "The Power of Mobile Money," 13.
123 Juliet Eilperin, "A Threat to Their Bottom Lines," *Washington Post National Weekly Edition*, September 28–October 4, 2009, 37.
124 Lester R. Brown, "Optimism on Climate Change," *Washington Post National Weekly Edition*, September 28–October 4, 2009, 25.
125 For an analysis of female migration in and from Asia and of the efforts of regional governments to cooperate around the issue, see Nana Oishi, *Women in Motion: Globalization, State Policies, and Labor Migration in Asia* (Stanford, CA: Stanford University Press, 2005).
126 United Nations' Trends in Total Migrant Stock: The 2008 Revision, http://esa.un.org/migration.
127 Fiona B. Adamson, "International Migration in a Globalizing World," in Kirshner, ed., *Globalization and National Security*, 39.
128 Ibid., 46–64.

129 Gargi Bhattacharyya, *Traffick: The Illicit Movement of People and Things* (London: Pluto Press, 2005), 4.
130 Kamala Kempadoo and Jo Doezema, *Global Sex Workers: Rights, Resistance, and Redefinition* (London: Routledge, 1998), 52.
131 Naím, *Illicit*, 88.
132 Bhattacharyya, *Traffick*, 154.
133 Dollar and Kraay, "Spreading the Wealth," 132.
134 Naím, *Illicit*, 76.
135 James C. McKinley Jr., "U.S. Stymied as Guns Flow to Mexican Cartels," *New York Times*, April 14, 2009, http://www.nytimes.com/2009/04/15/us/15guns.html?pagewanted=all.
136 See Juan Forero, "Ecuadoran Town a Hub for Drug-Running Rebels, Colombia Says," *Washington Post*, May 20, 2009, http://www.washingtonpost.com/wp-dyn/content/article/2009/05/19/AR2009051903565.html.
137 Cited in "Getting Their Man," *The Economist*, November 7, 2009, 42.
138 Frank G. Madsen, *Transnational Organized Crime* (New York: Routledge, 2009), 122.
139 Ibid., 81.
140 Stephen E. Flynn, "The Global Drug Trade versus the Nation-State: Why the Thugs Are Winning," in Cusimano, ed., *Beyond Sovereignty*, 46. Also Bhattacharyya, *Traffick*, 90–121.
141 Naím, *Illicit*, 5. Emphasis in original.
142 Ibid., 13.
143 See Scott Shane, "An Arms Sales Suspect, Bargaining with Secrets," *New York Times*, August 29, 2010, http://www.nytimes.com/2010/08/30/world/30bout.html.
144 "Out of Control," *The Economist*, September 12, 2009, 54.
145 "Flying Anything to Anybody," *The Economist*, December 20, 2008, 89.
146 Madsen, *Transnational Organized Crime*, 65. See also Tamara Makarenko, "The Crime–Terror Continuum: Tracing the Interplay between Transnational Organised Crime and Terrorism," in Mark Galeotti, ed., *Global Crime Today* (New York: Routledge, 2005), 129–45.
147 Beck, *World at Risk*, 39.
148 Dennis Pirages and Paul Runci, "Ecological Interdependence and the Spread of Infectious Disease," in Cusimano, ed., *Beyond Sovereignty*, 185.
149 Stephanie Simon and Betsy McKay, "Developing World's Parasites, Disease Hit U.S.," *Wall Street Journal*, August 22–3, 2009, A3.
150 Tilly, "Reflections on the History of European State-Making," 42.
151 McGrew, "Organized Violence in the Making (and Remaking) of Globalization," 15.
152 Ibid., 23. McGrew (23–4) observes that major warfare was also "associated with the profound disruption, if not destruction, of global networks: a process of radical (if temporary) de-globalization."
153 James Putzel, "Globalization, Liberalization, and Prospects for the State," *International Political Science Review* 26:1 (January 2005), 7.
154 Shaw, *Theory of the Global State*, 268–9.
155 Katherine Barbieri, *The Liberal Illusion: Does Trade Promote Peace?* (Ann Arbor, MI: University of Michigan Press, 2002), 118. Barbieri finds that this does *not* apply to China or Russia.
156 Shaw, *Theory of the Global State*, 269.
157 Rugman and Verbeke, "A Perspective on Regional and Global Strategies of Multinational Enterprises," 10.
158 Hamilton and Quinlan, *Globalization and Europe*, 26.
159 Neil MacFarquhar, "African Farmers Displaced as Investors Move In," *New York Times*, December 21, 2010, http://www.nytimes.com/2010/12/22/world/africa/22mali.html.
160 See "Petrodollars v Smallholders," *The Economist*, April 25, 2009, 48, "Outsourcing's Third Wave," *The Economist*, May 23, 2009, 61–3, and "When Others are Grabbing Their Land," *The Economist*, May 5, 2011, 65–6.

161 Wolf, *Why Globalization Works*, 3–4.
162 Putzel, "Globalization, Liberalization, the Prospects for the State," 9.
163 Jackson, *Quasi-States*. Jackson argues that, even if there is a gap between reality and aspiration, sovereignty *does* provide states with a degree of legitimacy denied other actors.
164 See Amory Starr, *Global Revolt* (London: Zed Books, 2005), and Chanda, *Bound Together*, 271–304.
165 Barbara Epstein, "Anarchism and the Anti-Globalization Movement," *Monthly Review* 53:4 (September 2001), http://www.monthlyreview.org/0901epstein.htm.
166 Luis Alberto Fernandez, *Policing Dissent: Social Control and the Anti-Globalization Movement* (Piscataway, NJ: Rutgers University Press, 2008), 36.
167 Greg Buckman, *Globalization: Tame It or Scrap It?* (London: Zed Books, 2004).
168 See Mark Rupert, "Globalization and American Common Sense: Struggling to Make Sense of a Post-Hegemonic World," in Gills, ed., *Globalization and the Politics of Resistance*, 171–88.
169 Wolf, *Why Globalization Works*, 5.
170 Bhagwati, "Coping with Antiglobalization," 4.
171 Luis Alberto Fernandez, *Policing Dissent*, 35. Also Rong Tang, "Describe the Anti-Globalisation Movement and Identify Its Motivation and Goals," *International Journal of Business and Management* 2:6 (December 2007), 137–44.
172 André Drainville, *Contesting Globalization: Space and Place in the World Economy* (London: Routledge, 2004), 1, 162.
173 Fernandez, *Policing Dissent*, 36. Also Jackie Smith, "Globalizing Resistance: The Battle of Seattle and the Future of Social Movements," in Jackie Smith and Hank Johnston, eds., *Globalization and Resistance* (Lanham, MD: Rowman & Littlefield, 2002), 207–27.
174 Munck, *Globalization and Contestation*, 58.
175 See Massimiliano Andretta and Lorenzo Mosca, "Understanding the Genoa Protest," in Rupert Taylor, ed., *Creating a Better World: Interpreting Global Civil Society* (West Hartford, CT: Kumarian Press, 2004), 43–63.
176 For analysis of the difficulties in building a coalition from the heterogeneous protest groups in Seattle, see Margaret Levi and Gillian Hughes Murphy, "Coalitions of Contention: The Case of the WTO Protests in Seattle," *Political Studies* 54:4 (2006), 651–70.
177 Tabb, *Economic Governance in the Age of Globalization*, 343.
178 Gillian Hughes Murphy, "The Seattle WTO Protests: Building a Global Movement," in Rupert Taylor, ed., *Creating a Better World: Interpreting Global Civil Society* (West Hartford, CT: Kumarian Press, 2004), 28.
179 Castells, *The Power of Identity*, 145.
180 Ibid., 164. See also Adam David Morton, "Mexico, Neoliberal Restructuring and the EZLN: A Neo-Gramscian Analysis," in Gills, ed., *Globalization and the Politics of Resistance*, 255–79.
181 Castells, *The Power of Identity*, 156–7. See also M. Castells, *Communication Power* (Oxford: Oxford University Press, 2009).
182 See *World Economic Forum*, http://www3.weforum.org/en/index.htm. Munck, *Globalization and Contestation*, 83, refers to the World Social Forum as a "'parallel summit' to the hidden, elitist and technocratic managers of globalization symbolized by Davos." A "summer Davos" has been established and held its first meeting in Dalian, China, in September 2009. See also Jai Sen and Peter Waterman, eds., *World Social Forum: Challenging Empires*, 2nd edn (Minneapolis, MI: Black Rose Books, 2007), and Jackie Smith, Marina Karides, et al., *Global Democracy and the World Social Forums* (Boulder, CO: Paradigm Publishers, 2007).
183 "Charter of Principles of the World Social Forum, June 2001," http://faithandcohesion.org/index.php?option=com_docman&task=doc_view&gid=74&Itemid=34Diversity.
184 David Harvey, *Justice, Nature and the Geography of Difference* (Oxford: Blackwell Publishers, 1996), 400.
185 "Final Declaration of 2009 World Social Forum meeting in Brazil," http://www.

haitianalysis.com/international-relations/final-declaration-of-2009-world-social-forum-meeting-in-brazil.
186 Douglas Kellner, "Theorizing Globalization," *Sociological Theory* 23:3 (November 2002), 302.
187 Held and McGrew, "Introduction," 6.
188 Urry, *Global Complexity*, 15.
189 Hoffmann, "Clash of Globalizations," 106–12.
190 Ibid., 107.
191 Ibid., 109.
192 Axtmann, "The State of the State," 267.

CHAPTER 7

Regional dynamics
Europe and Asia

Like predecessor notions such as internationalization and interdependence, globalization does not refer to a global level playing field or to symmetric or equal international relations. Contemporary globalization is largely concentrated in the Triad of North America, Europe, and East Asia.[1]

We can all agree that America is a more globalized place today than it was in the past. The trend is true whether we look at the narrower measure of international trade – the movement of goods and services across our borders – or the broader measure of globalization, which includes not only trade but also the movement of capital and the growing integration of production across borders. In 2007, 18.7 million standard shipping containers arrived at U.S. ports carrying many of the shirts, shoes, toys, and consumer electronics that fill our closets and family rooms. That figure is an average of 2,133 containers arriving every hour of the year, 24/7.[2]

Although globalization has had an impact on virtually everyone alive today, that impact and the reaction to it have varied, in part, by region. Although most observers agree that North America, especially the United States, has to date been the world's leading beneficiary from globalization,[3] different regions have been affected to a greater or lesser extent by globalization's key processes, and states have adapted to or resisted globalization in different ways and degrees.[4] Moreover, as the global economic system has struggled to recover from the global financial crisis, regional differences are evident, with GDP growth of emerging market economies in 2010 and 2011, especially China (10 percent, 9.7 percent),[5] India (7.7 percent, 7.8 percent), and

ASEAN (4.7 percent, 5.3 percent), projected to be considerably higher than advanced economies such as the United States (2.7 percent, 2.4 percent), Japan (1.7 percent, 1.2 percent), or the Euro area (1.0 percent, 1.6 percent).[6]

Emerging market economies account for an ever greater share of global production; they compete with one another as well as with the West; and they are home to a growing number of the world's leading transnational corporations. Emerging economies are also increasingly innovative, surpassing the West "in areas such as mobile money (using mobile phones to make payments) and online games."[7] Their companies and sovereign wealth funds are purchasing Western assets, and their publics are optimistic about their economic future. Indeed, emerging economies are increasingly exporters of manufactured goods and importers of raw materials, a far cry from earlier decades and centuries in which they were dependent on exports of raw materials and were, therefore, part of the global "periphery." Much of the world's excess savings are located in these regions, and have been available as loans to the advanced economies of North America and Europe.

This chapter deals with two regions that have greatly benefited from globalization – Europe and Asia – and have opened themselves to globalization's economic, political, and cultural flows. Both regions are diverse and contain what might be termed "core" and "peripheral" countries.[8] India and China, though still home to large numbers of impoverished citizens, are included because of the immense economic progress they have made in recent decades and, as a result, their rapidly increasing influence in global markets. They currently resemble what Immanuel Wallerstein called the "semi-periphery" – "a midway point on a continuum running from the core to the periphery."[9] At the same time the two Asian giants have become potential geopolitical rivals,[10] especially along their Himalayan frontier.[11]

Similar regional differences are reflected in expenditures on regional development. Research and development are the foundations of the contemporary "knowledge economy." The long-time leaders in R&D expenditures – the United States, Europe, and Japan – have experienced a decline in R&D spending compared to the emerging economics of China, India, and Brazil. R&D expenditures in the former are largely made by private corporations, whereas in the latter governments remain key sources.

Notwithstanding the growing R&D investment in emerging economies, the United States remained the world's leader in gross domestic expenditures on R&D at almost $402 billion (almost 35 percent of world R&D expenditures) in 2010, more than all of Asia combined.[12] The European Union (EU), in particular, saw a relative decline in global R&D investment between 2008 and 2010, its share falling from 24.9 to 23.2 percent as it fell further behind the US and Japan.[13] Europe, nevertheless, remains the leading recipient of R&D investments by American transnational corporations, while the United States remains a leading recipient of European R&D (behind intra-European investment) and China and India are growing recipients of EU R&D. Table 7.1 illustrates the different research areas in which countries other than the United States excel. Moreover, survey data reflect the attraction of emerging markets by suggesting that between 2008 and 2010 the most attractive locations for foreign direct investment (FDI) were China, India, the United States, Russia, Brazil, and Vietnam,[14] and, as the global recession demonstrated, emerging markets such as these are deeply embedded in the global economy.

Table 7.1 Non-US technology leaders and challengers. Rank (1 = best)

Technology area	1	2	3	4	5
Energy and environment	Germany	China	Japan	France	UK
Health and bioscience	UK	Germany	Japan	China	France
Defense and security	China	Israel	UK	Russia	Germany
ICT	Japan	China	India	UK	Germany
Composite, nanotech, and advanced materials	Japan	China	Germany	UK	India

Source: Grueber and Studt, "Global Perspective."

We will take a further look at some of these regional differences as we go along. Among regions, Europe, North America, and East Asia are the most globalized, and Africa, Central Asia, the Middle East, and Russia are the least globalized. There is, of course, significant variation in rankings of the different dimensions of globalization.

Some dimensions, such as economic and political globalization, are relatively easy to measure, whereas others, for example, cultural globalization, require considerable creativity. Thus, using what they call "'cultural proxies' – the conduits by which ideas, beliefs, and values are transmitted," Kluver and Fu measured "each nation's exports and imports of books, periodicals, and newspapers."[15] Their results reveal that "the globalization of culture may have a significant linguistic component" and that the most culturally globalized countries (Singapore, Switzerland, and Canada) have "official bilingual policies" and "English-language permeation."[16] They are also relatively wealthy countries.

What follows is not a comprehensive analysis of all of the world's regions. Instead, it highlights similarities and differences both among and within selected regions. Thus, as we shall see, the impact of globalization varies considerably.

GLOBALIZATION AND EUROPE

Western Europe

"From the perspective of the postcolonial world," argue Ulrich Beck and Edgar Grande, "globalization is synonymous with the decline of Europe. For globalization is the materialization of the American world spirit."[17] Indeed, some observers fear what they see as a growing convergence of American and European economic and social models and values.[18] Be that as it may, Europe, especially Western Europe, is, along with North America, the most globalized region in the world, although some observers see state-based identities in Europe as still exceptionally vibrant.[19]

Europe and Europeans have benefited significantly from globalization, and Germany has been "Europe's engine."[20] A variety of forces – rapid technological diffusion, greater trade opportunities, lower barriers to investment, and policy and structural reforms at home – have generated greater flows of goods and services, people, capital, and ideas within Europe and between Europe and the rest of the world. On the whole, these forces, until quite recently, fostered large gains for Europe:

robust growth in exports and imports; strong outflows and inflows of investment; greater technological diffusion; net portfolio inflows; net inflows of labor; downward pressure on inflation and interest rates; more jobs, higher incomes, modest increases in wages; and higher GDP growth. Despite debt burdens in southern Europe and in Ireland, on balance, Europeans are living better today than they were when the Iron Curtain fell and the Cold War ended, in part because of globalization. The euro accounts for about 37 percent of daily foreign exchange turnover, "second only to the U.S. dollar,"[21] and has become a major reserve currency globally. Negatively, however, it has prevented less efficient members of the Eurozone from depreciating their currency in order to make their exports more competitive globally.

There are significant differences among countries. In describing the region, Hamilton and Quinlan conclude:

> In general, northern European countries are well positioned to cope with globalization, thanks particularly to their education levels, their focus on high-tech products, their strong innovation frameworks, and their commitment to help workers adjust as jobs come and go. Moreover, the export sectors of northern European countries (except Denmark) are geared toward fast-growing products, and have large trade surpluses in services ... In general, EU members from southern and eastern European are having a harder time coping with globalization because they score below average on all indicators, with their relatively poor human capital levels a major weakness. Not only do these countries tend to be competing head-on with rapidly developing nations, they also have less inherent strength to deal with the challenge.[22]

These differences became increasingly salient during the global recession as concern grew over the possibility of sovereign default by Greece and the prospect that it might then spread to other heavily indebted countries in the Eurozone, notably Ireland, Portugal, Spain, and Italy. Indeed, questions arose as to whether the euro could survive the divergent financial circumstances of Eurozone members.[23] One consequence was the creation of a borrowing facility by the European Union and the International Monetary Fund (IMF) and the imposition of rigorous austerity policies – including significant budget cuts – in the most financially endangered countries.[24] The fissiparous effects of financial turmoil in the Eurozone have, however, produced Franco-German efforts to thicken economic and financial integration within the region. That, in turn, has raised the question of how far the more prosperous members are willing to go, either to support failing national economies or to create a unified European financial architecture.

Fourteen of the fifteen most globalized countries in the world ranked in the 2011 KOF Index of Globalization were European (Belgium, Austria, the Netherlands, Sweden, Switzerland, Denmark, France, Hungary, Portugal, Ireland, Finland, the Czech Republic, Luxembourg, and the Slovak Republic), as were eighteen of the twenty most globalized.[25] Similarly, thirteen of the twenty most globalized countries as measured by the 2007 *Foreign Policy* Globalization Index were European.[26] This measure, developed jointly by A. T. Kearney, Inc. and the Carnegie Endowment for International Peace, scores countries in four categories, each of which consists of several factors that reflect the degree to which countries and their societies are embedded in the global system and interact with one another. These categories are Economic Integration, Personal Contact, Technology, and Political Engagement.[27] In addition, countries in Western Europe dominate both the World Economic Forum's indices of economic competitiveness and networked readiness. In terms of competitiveness Switzerland was ranked 1st, Sweden 2nd, Germany 5th, Finland 7th, the Netherlands 8th, Denmark 9th, Great Britain 12th, Norway 14th, and France 15th.[28] The United States ranked 3rd in networked readiness and 4th in competitiveness.

According to David Rae and Marte Sollie, in Europe and the United States, the share of revenues "from the rest of the world rose from 28 and 29% respectively" in 1995 to 35 percent in 2005, although for European firms "europeanisation is stronger than globalisation."[29] British, German, Italian, and French corporations have been Europe's leaders in decreasing their relative dependence on domestic markets. Based on a variety of factors including product market restrictiveness, labor market flexibility, school results, level of education, firm creation, and so forth, Rae and Sollie conclude that the countries best able to cope with the changes associated with economic globalization are the original fifteen EU members, as well as the Nordic countries (Sweden, Finland, and Denmark), while those least prepared are more recent EU members such as Poland and Hungary and poorer members from southern Europe such as Greece, Italy, and Portugal.[30] Their conclusion has been substantially borne out in recent years.

Not surprisingly, European countries dominate the economic, social, and political dimensions of globalization, with nine of the top ten ranking in political globalization and all of the top ten in social globalization. As of 2008, Singapore was number one in economic globalization, but the remaining nine were European. London and Paris ranked 2nd and 3rd behind only New York in the *Foreign Policy* Global Cities Index.[31] By 2010, however, this had changed significantly when five of the ten most globalized cities were in Asia (Tokyo, Hong Kong, Singapore, Sydney, and Seoul), three in North America (New York, Chicago, and Los Angeles), and only one in Europe (Paris ranked 4th).[32] Connectivity is very high, since almost 64 percent of individuals in the European Union are internet users.[33] There are, however, significant variations among individual countries. Generally speaking, northern European countries are more highly integrated globally than southern and eastern European countries. Their capacity for innovation remains undiminished, and their level of interdependence remains high at a time when innovation and interdependence, in the words of John de la Mothe, "are two central elements not only of advanced economies but, indeed, of human culture and societies."[34] Thus, Western Europe accounted for five of the ten leaders in innovation.[35]

"English is the lingua franca during EU discussions in Brussels," and "is spreading through the school systems of Eastern Europe in the wake of the momentous expansion of the European Union."[36] It is also spoken by large majorities in the Netherlands, Denmark, and Sweden, and by over half the population in a number of other continental European countries.[37]

Long-time members of the European Union are among the most globalized states in the world economically. For several decades, Europe has been "a principal recipient and provider of foreign direct investment," with the United States, and "the principal source of foreign direct investment in Europe," especially in Great Britain. American assets in Great Britain of $2.3 trillion in 2005 constituted "one quarter of the global total, and an amount greater than total combined U.S. assets in Asia, South America, Africa and the Middle East."[38] Not surprisingly, outward flows of FDI from EU members are largely to one another and increasingly to new community members in Central Europe such as Poland. The United States is the leading non-European destination for European FDI and a major source of Europe's foreign earnings and corporate profits. In addition, portfolio flows to and from Europe have grown and further integrated Europe's core states in the globalized economy. Overall, there is no evidence that the United States–Europe economic links have eroded as their economies have become more interdependent with China and India.

Overall, despite national differences, globalization has meant higher living standards, greater productivity, and economic growth as well as additional employment opportunities and higher incomes for Europeans, at least until the recent global financial crisis. In sum:

> Europe accounts for 7 of the top 10 and 11 of the top 20 most competitive nations in the world . . . With only 7 percent of the world's population, EU GDP . . . accounts for nearly 30 percent of the world's economic output. The U.S. accounts for 27 percent, Japan for 9 percent and China for less than 6 percent . . . European consumers have been the biggest winners from globalization because of lower cost imports, greater availability and variety of products, downward pressure on inflation and lower interest rates.[39]

These benefits flow not only from Europe's integration in the globalized economy but also from integration within Europe itself that features common national rules and standards, mobility of persons, absence of national trade barriers, cooperative ventures, common currency, assistance to poorer regions, and ability to negotiate (to some extent) jointly with non-Europeans.

The global financial crisis has, however, sorely tested European unity. The Eurozone protected its members from currency speculation, but the impact of the economic downturn has been very uneven. Several countries amassed deficits that were so large as to threaten sovereign default. The German, Dutch, and Finnish governments in particular have been reluctant to see the EU provide large-scale funding to prevent such defaults, while the European Central Bank has resisted allowing any default to occur.

Globalization is also affecting the politics and culture of Western Europe, dividing "winners" and "losers" in other ways. For example,

> new culturally defined conflicts about the integration of West European societies, unleashed by increasing numbers of immigrants and asylum-seekers, have replaced old religious conflicts; on the other hand, attitudes towards political globalization (most significantly European integration) have been of increasing importance for the formation of political identities (compared to older, liberal values).[40]

The sources of immigration in Western Europe are from newer EU member states such as Poland and Romania and from outside the European Union, especially from former colonial areas in the developing world. Although immigration is actually higher to Europe than to the United States, immigrants to Western Europe tend to be less skilled and consist of fewer professionals than those to North America.

Although immigrants, many of whom are Muslim and are from former European colonies like Pakistan and Algeria, help compensate for Western Europe's demographic decline and aging, there have been severe problems of assimilation, alienation, and fear of terrorism. One result has been a backlash among voters and the growth of political parties built on anti-immigrant sentiment. Europeans have found it difficult to accommodate Islam and its customs.[41] According to one Eurobarometer poll,

> many respondents express insecurity when it comes to the presence of people from other ethnic groups, particularly with regard to unemployment ... Less than a third of the European Union citizens believe that the arrival of immigrants can efficiently solve the problem of the Europe's ageing population.[42]

Forty-two percent of respondents also believe that: "The presence of other ethnic groups is a cause of insecurity."[43] This view is reflected in Walter Laqueur's description of Europe's immigrants: "If you ask them they will frequently tell you that they are Muslims (or Turks or Nigerians) living in Britain, France, or Germany. They get their politics, religion, and culture from Arab and Turkish television channels."[44] Germany achieved a political milestone when its Green Party selected Cem Özdemir, the son of Turkish "guest workers," to be its leader.[45] However, in February 2011, German Chancellor Angela Merkel joined British Prime Minister David Cameron, French President Nicolas Sarkozy, and the Council of Europe in denouncing "multiculturalism" as a failure and likely to lead to the radicalization of youthful immigrants.[46]

In addition, the formation of new parties resulting from globalization has destabilized Western Europe's party system and generated "a new structural cleavage in West European politics" based on a combination of economic and cultural divisions. "In all cases, with the partial exception of the UK, party systems have been destabilized and are becoming more fragmented and polarized."[47]

Post-communist Central Europe

Among the most representative of the post-communist states of Central Europe[48] in terms of globalization are Estonia, Poland, and Ukraine. The first and third were previously Soviet republics, while the second had been an independent country within the Soviet orbit. Currently, Estonia and Poland are members of the European Union and NATO, while Ukraine is unlikely to join either of these Western organizations in the near future. The three countries reflect the variation in level of globalization within the region. The 2011 KOF Index of Globalization ranked Poland 28th in overall globalization (ranging from 9th in political globalization to 49th in economic globalization), Estonia 24th of 208 political entities in terms of overall globalization (ranging from 8th in economic globalization to 78th in political globalization), and Ukraine 53rd in overall globalization (ranging from 40th in political globalization to 77th in social globalization).[49] Like Poland, several other former Soviet bloc countries have embraced globalization. Among other Central European, Balkan, and Baltic states, Hungary ranked 8th overall, the Czech Republic 12th, the Slovak Republic 15th, Slovenia 26th, Croatia 31st, Bulgaria 32nd, Lithuania 36th, Romania 39th, Latvia 41st, Montenegro 46th, Serbia 49th, Bosnia and Herzegovina 62nd, Moldova 63rd, Macedonia 65th, and Albania 87th.

Warwick University's CSGR Globalisation Index reveals that Estonia became significantly more globalized between 1995 and 2001; Poland, while growing modestly more globalized in that period, was ranked about the same; and Ukraine's ranking had risen moderately during those years.[50] In terms of networked readiness and economic competitiveness, Estonia ranked 18th and 33rd respectively, Ukraine 62nd and 89th, and Poland 69th and 39th.[51] Technology and competitiveness do not necessarily go hand in hand.

The most dramatic feature of the changes in the region is Estonia's rapid economic reforms, and the country is the most globalized in the region. "Estonia," wrote *Foreign Policy* in 2007, "having shaken itself free from its communist-era shackles, may now qualify as the first Baltic Tiger . . ."

> In keeping with [Milton] Friedman's free-market philosophy, the country's government has moved aggressively to open itself up to the outside world. For all practical purposes, Estonia has no corporate income tax, and shareholder dividends are subject to a simple flat tax . . . The World Bank ranks Estonia 17th among 175 economies in ease of doing business, and sixth in ease of trading across borders . . . The country, dubbed by some as "E-Stonia," has launched a large online government initiative and even declared Internet access a fundamental human right.[52]

The direction of Estonia's trade has altered dramatically since the end of the Cold War. In 1990, only 5 percent of the country's trade was with the developed West, while 87 percent was with the Soviet Union. Currently, Russia accounts for only 10 percent of Estonia's trade.[53]

Poland, too, is doing well and was the only member of the European Union to grow economically in 2009, registering a significant increase in GDP per capita. Although corruption remains a problem, the country has made significant improvements in infrastructure and is beginning to streamline its notoriously complex bureaucracy.[54]

At the other extreme, economically, is Ukraine, which remains outside the European Union and is heavily dependent on Russia for oil (80 percent) and natural gas (77 percent).[55] Owing partly to internal political divisions and geography, Ukraine remains relatively under-globalized. Ranked 75th in economic globalization as measured by KOF in 2011, it is among the least economically globalized states in Europe. Poland, ranking 49th (a decline from the previous year), has become significantly more globalized economically since the end of the Cold War and its admission to the European Union.

After the Cold War, all three countries have consistently become politically more integrated in global politics as measured by number of embassies, UN missions, and membership in international organizations. It is not surprising that Poland, having been an independent state prior to 1990, is far in advance of the other two in political globalization, ranking 9th in political globalization on the KOF scale, while Ukraine ranked 40th and Estonia 78th.[56]

Regarding social globalization defined as openness to ideas and measured using data on personal contact (e.g. tourists), information flows (e.g. internet users), and cultural proximity (e.g. trade in books),[57] the three countries have all become more globalized since 1991. For all three, "the dynamic linkage between national identity formation and state–society relations is influenced by two sets of cultural factors: 1) endogenous cultural legacies arising from the Soviet experience, and 2) exogenous cultural flows introduced by globalization, including prevailing ideological interpretations of globalization."[58] Imported films reflect the latter, about which Blum suggests: "This influence affects attitudes and behavior... and produces what we can call a 'cult of individualism' instead of any feeling of being part of the collective, of society."[59] The combination of endogenous and exogenous factors produces cultural hybridization in these countries as it does elsewhere.

GLOBALIZATION AND ASIA

Asia, especially China, India, and the members of ASEAN, have profited dramatically from economic globalization in recent decades. China, the ninth largest exporter in 1999, passed Germany in 2009 to become the world's leading exporter.[60] The following year, China passed the United States in terms of energy use[61] and Japan as the world's second largest economy.[62] China has also significantly increased its share of research and development in high-tech areas. "Among Asian countries, Japan has the highest density of researchers per million inhabitants, with 5,548. India has the lowest, with only 136 researchers per million inhabitants. China has 1,071, while the U.S. has 4,707."[63] Asia is a vast continent, and globalization has had different impacts on its sub-regions – Southeast Asia, East Asia, Central Asia, and South Asia. As a whole, Asia has been slower to create functioning regional groups than other regions.[64] However, Asians are increasingly linked by new roads, railways, and pipelines,[65] many of which have been financed with Chinese capital.

China and India have become export engines of global economic growth with account surpluses that provide funds to advanced economies that run deficits, favored sites for inexpensive offshore manufacturing that restrains global inflation, burgeoning markets for European and American exports, and fierce competitors for raw materials. Indian corporations like the Tata group have been diversifying by purchasing additional firms around the world. Tata now earns three-fifths of its revenue abroad and has a workforce of 395,000.[66] Nevertheless, Asia was hit hard by the global financial crisis. It suffered a dramatic reduction in exports to the West and weakening of domestic demand but, in general, fared better than other regions.[67]

Some Asians have suggested that Western values, however useful in Europe and America, are unsuited to Asian conditions and violate Asian traditions. In this view, Western social practices such as relatively weak government regulation and a minimalist welfare state are fundamentally incompatible with their own practices and traditional social values.[68] As Guthrie suggests, "economic systems are themselves cultural systems, where learned practices and behaviors become embedded in the norms and rules by which individuals operate *over time*."[69] McGrew takes this further, emphasizing that globalization owed much to regions other than the West: "By qualifying the rise of the West narrative, revisionist historians have demonstrated that the emergence of a singular global order was a much more polycentric, complex, and contingent historical process than many orthodox accounts suggest."[70]

Until the 1997–8 Asian economic crisis, Asians had pursued a path to economic growth that featured a high degree of state involvement in economic planning. As first Japan and then Asia's newly industrializing countries, notably South Korea and Taiwan, and finally the "little tigers" of Southeast Asia clawed their way from poverty to relative prosperity, a number of Asian politicians went so far as to proclaim the *superiority* of "Asian values." Articulated by regional leaders like Singapore's Lee Kwan Yew, the Asian path to economic growth combined political authoritarianism, adherence to the collective rather than the individual, and a strong state with "managed" state capitalism.[71] Japan pioneered Asia's brand of state capitalism. This suited Japan because globalization, as Paul Midford argues, challenges Japanese "goals of preserving and enhancing autonomy," including "financial autonomy," "technological autonomy," and military autonomy.[72] That said, Japan's economic progress after World War II depended heavily upon its engagement in world trade and financial markets.

China has become the most visible example of state capitalism, though it has also benefited from the proliferation of private entrepreneurs.[73] Martin Walker maintains that the Washington Consensus of free markets is being replaced by the

> Beijing model of state ownership, state-led industrial strategy, currency controls, and authoritarian policies . . . The Beijing model's attraction lies in its crude message that countries can prosper and grow without any bothersome democratic baggage such as a free press or free elections, and it includes breathtaking levels of corruption and a docile judicial system.[74]

Some of Asia's leaders view Western emphasis on individual liberty – a cornerstone of liberal democracy – and its presumed links to economic growth as mistaken. "I do not believe," declared Lee Kwan Yew, "that democracy necessarily leads to development. I believe that what a country needs to develop is discipline more than democracy."[75] While Westerners emphasized individual freedom and prosperity, many Asians remained loyal to social values like equality of outcome that are vaguely associated with the teaching of Confucius. "Asian values," in the words of one commentator

> are different in kind, not in degree. They are self-reliant, yet somehow communitarian rather than individualistic; built on personal relationships and mutual obligation . . . respectful of authority and hierarchy; and state interventionist, even into the private space of individuals. The word that summed up this – in part self-contradictory – spirit was Confucianism.[76]

Asian leaders emphasized "Confucian precepts of work, frugality, and hierarchy" that they believed,

> underlie the dramatic economic growth achieved in Asia by Japan in the 1970s and 1980s, the four 'tigers' (Korea, Taiwan, Hong Kong, and Singapore) in the 1980s

and mid-1990s, and the three aspiring tigers (Thailand, Indonesia, and Malaysia) until the middle of 1997.[77]

The degree to which Asian and Western values differ is widely debated. François Godement argues that "the secret of Asian values is to be found first and foremost in their syncretism, rather than in a distinct identity" and "lies in the connection between culture and demography, family or social behaviour."[78] Surveys conducted by Japan's Dentsu Institute for Human Studies in Japan, China, South Korea, Thailand, Singapore, and India (1998) and in Britain, France, Germany, Sweden, and the United States (1997) suggest that Asian and Western values are less dissimilar than some observers had thought and that Asians themselves differed significantly when asked about the relative importance of "financial wealth," "acquiring high-quality goods," "family relationships," "success in work," "mental relaxation," "leisure activity," "living for the present," "striving to achieve personal goals," and "having good relationships with others." On only two of the nine dimensions of value measured were Asians and Westerners significantly different.[79]

Let us now look at the several sub-regions of which Asia consists.

Southeast Asia

The ASEAN countries in Southeast Asia have been among the major beneficiaries of globalization. They are a diverse group, including the immense island country of Indonesia with vast natural resources, the fourth largest population in the world, and the largest number of Muslims; Singapore, a multinational and prosperous city-state; and Myanmar, an impoverished and closed society ruled by a military junta. Other key actors include Malaysia, Thailand, Vietnam, and the Philippines.[80] ASEAN itself was a reaction to regional developments in Europe, North America, and China. Regional leaders "had become aware that foreign investors were becoming increasingly drawn to these regional schemes, which thus posed a threat to the ASEAN countries for which FDI had become a crucial source of economic growth."[81]

According to the 2011 KOF Index of Globalization, Singapore ranked 1st globally in economic integration and 18th overall.[82] Singapore also ranked 4th globally in global networked readiness and 3rd in economic competitiveness.[83] By contrast, the Philippines ranked 84th in overall globalization, as well as 85th in both networked readiness and economic competitiveness, and Indonesia was ranked 83rd in overall globalization by KOF, as well as 83rd and 44th in networked readiness and economic competitiveness. Malaysia and Thailand, at 37th and 60th in overall globalization respectively, were in between.[84] Not surprisingly, isolated Laos (181st) and Myanmar (186th) were near the bottom of overall globalization.

Foreign direct investment proved crucial to economic development in Southeast Asia. "By 1990, total FDI stock in ASEAN accounted for 18.2 per cent of their gross domestic product (GDP) compared to 10.3–10.5 per cent for Asian and all developing countries and 8.4 per cent for the industrial countries," and FDI enabled the core ASEAN countries to emerge "from the recession of the mid-1980s to engage in outward-oriented industrialization and become significant exporters of manufactured goods."[85] FDI afforded the means for transforming the region into a major source of manufactured exports, and Southeast Asia became a focus for offshore production by transnational corporations. Singapore is especially attractive in this regard owing in part to its excellent infrastructure, the quality of its education system, and its transportation links to the rest of the region. Following the East Asian example: "The export-oriented strategy of the key Southeast Asian countries," according to Peter Coclanis and Tilak Doshi, "typically began with the manufacture of low-skill, labor-intensive goods but gained momentum with the emergence of the semiconductor industry, which increasingly set up offshore assembly plants."[86]

The region's serious financial crisis in the late 1990s arose partly because of the "close and often corrupt relationships between governments, financial institutions, and corporate borrowers,"[87] and the region's subsequent experience with the IMF, especially the neoliberal conditions set by that organization for extending loans, still rankles. Malaysia, in particular, resisted efforts to limit state intervention in its economy. "The development experience in Malaysia (as in other newly industrialized economies in East and Southeast Asia)," declares Ishak Shari, "demonstrates the possibility of different trajectories, despite being increasingly integrated in the globalised world economy, due to variations in the role of markets and the state as co-ordinating mechanism." Globalization has increased the transparency of transactions and reduced some of the cronyism characteristic of the late 1990s. Yet it has been a difficult transition. Shari concludes:

> [T]he experience of the financial crisis of the late 1990s in Malaysia as well as in other affected countries (particularly Indonesia) demonstrates that the implementation of the neo-liberal version of globalization, particularly financial liberalization, has brought about widespread hardship among the disadvantaged groups in these countries and has caused political as well as social turmoil. Policy prescriptions from the IMF, which involved tight monetary and fiscal policies, worsened the suffering of those adversely affected by the crisis.[88]

As for the post-2007 financial crisis, Singapore may actually benefit if Europe and the United States impose additional regulations on financial institutions that then flee to a less restrictive environment.

Culturally, Southeast Asia exemplifies hybridization. "Located ... at the crossroads of global maritime trading routes," writes Johannes Widodo, "Southeast Asia has been very open towards the various cultural influxes," and "[t]hese cultures were then transplanted, adopted, absorbed and nurtured locally."[89] Currently, Singapore, Malaysia, and Brunei, in particular, require bilingual education, with English as the second language. As Shinji Yamashita contends,

> the history of Southeast Asia itself can be seen to be a good example of glocalization. Early Indian and Chinese influences, followed by the introduction of Islam and European colonialism, blended with indigenous elements to create the contemporary culture of the region. Malaysia itself is a particularly interesting case in point.[90]

Education is playing a key role, for example in Singapore, "in creating new sets of skills and capacities for globalization and the information age, commitments to lifelong learning and greater flexibility and adaptability."[91] Nevertheless, efforts are underway to preserve local cultures in the face of homogenizing forces, for example, in Malay architecture.[92] Traditional identity is under siege owing to "the cultivated glamorous image for the young and trendy and the tourists" have "amplified for some members of the community how globalization has relentlessly commodified their culture faith and space."[93]

Civil society coexists uneasily with governments in Southeast Asia, especially in those countries with an authoritarian tradition. Douglass, Ho, and Ooi observe: "The interaction between state, civil society and capital" in the region "has grown increasingly complex." On the one hand, "Alarmed by a growing civil society, the state has responded in many cases to increasing regulation of public spaces to prevent popular unrest." On the other, "there have also been instances where the state has sided with civil society in preserving built heritage and green space when this has helped solidify its role as the protector of national culture and/or increased its legitimacy and popular support."[94] The authors conclude that "the propensity to form associations in civil society is viewed as being the fountain of social capital that is a crucial source of economic sustainability."[95]

East Asia

"East Asia," as Lowell Dittmer observes, "has been a conspicuous beneficiary of economic globalization."[96] In the region, opposition to economic globalization is relatively low, but as Dittmer suggests:

> Asian adoption of globalization has always been highly selective. The realm of ultimate values has typically been sheltered, in part to preserve indigenous cultural traditions, partly in deference to the interests of political and social elites. The result has been a distinctively Asian hybrid of pell-mell economic globalization and political–cultural exceptionalism.[97]

East Asia, like other regions, was seriously affected by the global economic crisis that began in late 2007. China's current account surplus alone contracted from over $191 billion in January–June 2008 to $130 billion in the same period in 2009.[98] According to *The Economist*,

> The scale and speed of that downturn is breathtaking, and broader in scope than in the financial crisis of 1997–98. China's GDP, which expanded by 13% in 2007, scarcely grew at all in the last quarter of 2008 on a seasonally adjusted basis. In the same quarter Japan's GDP is estimated to have fallen at an annualized rate of 10%, Singapore's at 17%, and South Korea's at 21%.[99]

Nevertheless, led by China, especially that country's growing domestic demand, East Asia appears to be recovering more quickly from the crisis than other regions in Asia or elsewhere.[100]

China also reflects the coexistence of globalization and localization. Indeed, as John Naisbitt observes:

> Many people worry that China may break up. Well, China is breaking up, walking the twin path of globalization and decentralizing more than any other country in the world, a process essential to China's sustainability, giving more efficiency and power to its parts – cites, provinces, and regions. The periphery is the center.[101]

China, as Adam Segal suggests, views globalization as a "double-edged sword." For example, its leaders "see the Internet as a key engine of growth in the new economy; and China continues to devote massive material and political resources to what it calls 'informatization' – the application of modern information technology (IT) tools to other economic sectors."[102] At the same time, China's leaders see this development as a threat to the government's control of information and have developed a variety of sophisticated and not-so-sophisticated ways of censoring information flows.[103] Attempts to impose government censorship escalated in 2010–11 with a confrontation with Google's email and search engine and a blanket suppression of all internet chat in response to political upheaval in the Middle East.

On a positive note, globalization is integrating the Chinese and Taiwanese economies even as Taiwan's political autonomy persists. Overall, Segal concludes that "nationalism and economic growth" are *both* necessary for the political legitimacy of China's leadership and that globalization has contributed enormously to China's economic and political clout. However, external pressures may eventually "exacerbate weaknesses in the domestic economy," threaten some state-owned enterprises, and aggravate unemployment and social instability.[104]

In East Asia, as in Southeast Asia, there is debate about the relationship between democracy and Asian values. "The notion that democracy is a peculiar Protestant Europe cultural project," declares Edward Friedman, "is belied by the strength of democracy all over Asia."[105] Obviously, the definition of democracy is key. Friedman observes that, although many Chinese contend that "[a]uthoritarian China is morally superior," "this does not stop Chinese villagers from organizing and demonstrating for fair treatment, understood as institutionalizing a politics where they have a political voice and leaders can be rendered accountable."[106] In addition, China's leadership is sometimes said to be engaged in debate over "universal values," the most important of which is democracy.[107] That may be so, but democracy in any meaningful form at the *national* level is plainly absent. Following unrest in North Africa and the Middle East, not only did the Chinese government censor information flows in a heavy-handed fashion but it also rounded up prominent dissidents, intellectuals, and artists who had had the temerity to argue for greater transparency and popular participation in Chinese government at all levels.

Guthrie maintains that a gradual sequence of changes involving the growing autonomy of markets, declining communist party control of workplaces, emergence of alternative careers in the private sector, and increasing access to information, along with the evolving role of people's congresses, local self-governance, reform-minded elites, and the impact of foreign economic penetration make democratization of China over time a virtual certainty.[108] Recent experience might suggest that "over time" may be a rather long time indeed, unless, of course, the latest crackdowns reveal that China's leadership has more to worry about than has previously been suspected.[109]

Are Asian values and the Confucian tradition from which they grow necessarily incompatible with democracy? To this question, Friedman replies that "South Korea, the most Confucian society in the world *is* democratic."[110] So are Confucian-infused democratic Japan[111] and Taiwan. "Taiwan's democracy is both as democratic and Taiwanese as Germany's is German and democratic."[112] Again, much hinges on one's conception of the central concept. Confucianism is an extraordinarily broad and vague tradition, justifying practically anything, but is perhaps associated least with democracy in either the Western tradition or popular participation in modern Asia.

For their part, even while enmeshing themselves ever more in the global economy, China and the two Koreas have repeatedly played the "national card," especially when they perceived their independence or security to be threatened. The Asian financial crisis of 1997–8 gave the region's "hybrid globalizers their first sharp setback,"[113] forcing them to reconsider many of the practices they had used to achieve rapid economic development. The event was "a test for the new global order" and "brought home a morass of self-doubt, criticism and denigration of Asia's past achievement."[114] Observes Dittmer:

> The Asian values that had facilitated the Asian miracle were now seen to be a double-edged sword. The tight family structure that fostered achievement-oriented socialization and a voluntary welfare safety net was also conducive to nepotism and cronyism. The bonds of community that underpinned social stability and civility also gave rise to corporatism, lack of transparency, and moral hazard. The respect for authority so conducive to industrial discipline also permitted blind obedience to elite corruption. Paradoxically, the same cultural values that made Asia the late twentieth century's miracle of non-Western modernization suddenly seemed to be a grave liability, giving rise to a highly effective but clearly flawed form of capitalism.[115]

In East Asia, it is revealing that in terms of globalization relatively democratic Japan ranks 28th and authoritarian China 66th among the 72 countries in *Foreign Policy*'s 2007 Globalization Index.[116] Yet, even in China: "Pro-democracy unrest in the late 1980s played a bigger role in turning China capitalist than either officials or admirers of China's supposed gradualist approach suggest," because they "triggered fierce debate among Chinese leaders about the direction of reform."[117] For its part, South Korea became even more embedded in globalization after the 1997–8 "Asian Contagion" presented the country with an unprecedented economic crisis, even as it was in the midst of a transition from an authoritarian to a democratic polity. The reduced capacity of the South Korean state may have contributed to its difficulties by encouraging its large corporations, known as *chaebols*, to get into debt and make poor investment choices.[118] By contrast, authoritarian North Korea remains a "hermit kingdom," largely untouched by globalization.

Globalization poses challenges for East Asia as a whole even as it affords special opportunities. As elsewhere, globalization "must be conceptualized as a *relationship* between the global and the local."[119] Economic globalization has helped produce dramatic reductions in overall poverty and nowhere more so than in East Asia. Between 1990 and 2002, the world's poor, defined as those earning $1 or less per day, declined from 28 to 19 percent of the population of the developing world. Much of that reduction took place in one country – China – where 400 million people emerged from poverty. China's globalization began with the reforms of Deng Xiaoping who abandoned the policies of Mao Zedong and encouraged China's citizens to pursue the "Four Modernizations" – agriculture, industry, technology, and defense. The policies of Deng and his successors, including emphasizing exports, deregulation, and the freer movement of foreign investment, allowed China to join the World Trade Organization (WTO) and achieve dramatic increases in productivity[120] even while continuing to rely heavily on state-owned enterprises.[121] In recent years, China's construction of power plants alone has accounted for 80 percent of the world's added capacity to generate energy, while at the same time vastly increasing its emissions of greenhouse gases.[122] In the course of economic growth, China has become the largest export market for countries as diverse as Brazil, South Africa, Japan, and Australia, although many of these exports are components that are then exported elsewhere.[123] Indeed, in a single decade, the five leading exporters in 1999 – the United States, Germany, Japan, France and Britain – lost a share of global exports roughly equivalent to the increase in the share of China, India, and South Korea.[124]

Growing economic interdependence is evidenced by China's enormous dollar reserves, the degree to which America's trade and budgetary deficits have been financed by Chinese purchases of American securities,[125] and the increase in China's imports from 3 to 21 percent as a percentage of GDP between 1970 and 2009.[126] Persistent US deficits have led Chinese leaders, including Zhou Xiao-chuan, the governor of the People's Bank of China, to call for the creation of a new currency to replace the dollar as the world's principal reserve currency.[127] Of course, inclusion of China in any such scheme would be contingent on the renminbi/yuan becoming a true market currency. The Chinese have deliberately kept it undervalued since 2008. Another sign of interdependence is the fact that Chinese purchases of US securities probably contributed to the housing bubble in the United States that triggered the global recession.[128] China's stake in globalization, as well as its selective embrace of liberal rules, are illustrated by the fact that half of the trade disputes filed at the WTO in 2009 involved Beijing.[129]

Huge amounts of foreign direct investment have flowed into Asia, and China in particular has become the destination of ever more direct investment by major transnational corporations. Overall, East Asia is the leading regional recipient of FDI increasing by 19 percent in 2007 to $157 billion, and China, the recipient of some $84 billion in FDI, "is the most preferred investment location."[130] Increasingly, investments in China, Hong Kong, and Taiwan have gradually shifted from low-cost and labor-intensive manufacturing to services and technologically sophisticated products.[131] FDI has also been flowing to India (though it dropped by about one-third in 2009) and Southeast Asia, although China and Hong Kong remain the two largest Asian recipients.[132] FDI to South Korea in 2007 "dropped for the third consecutive year" to "the lowest level since 1997" owing to "slower economic growth, high oil prices, appreciation of the won, and a decline in cross-border M&A sales."[133]

Given the high level of foreign investment East Asian countries have received, it is perhaps surprising that they do rank relatively low in terms of overall globalization. Of the seventy-two countries ranked by *Foreign Policy* in 2007, only Hong Kong was near the top (2nd globally), while Japan ranked 28th, Taiwan 37th, and China 66th.[134] These countries fared even worse in the 2011 KOF Index. Japan was ranked 44th, South Korea 54th, China 92nd, and North Korea 204th of the 208 entities in the survey.[135] In terms of networked readiness and economic competitiveness, Japan ranked 17th and 8th respectively, South Korea 11th and 19th, Hong Kong 12th and 11th, Taiwan 13th and 12th, and China 46th and 29th.[136] Nevertheless, East Asia is home to some of the most globalized cities in the world. Of sixty major urban areas surveyed by *Foreign Policy*, Tokyo ranked 4th, Hong Kong 5th, Seoul 9th, and Beijing 12th in terms of globalization.[137] Japan continues to spend the highest percentage of its GDP globally on R&D, but China, though still spending a much lower percentage of GDP, has equaled Japan in total R&D expenditures.[138] Although China still lags behind the leaders in networked readiness and innovative performance, it is making significant strides in both, having established some 700 independent R&D facilities since 2000.[139] As coastal China becomes wealthier and production costs rise, China will be able to outsource to its own interior to keep down costs rather than outsourcing to other countries. In addition, a declining fertility rate and the aging of China's population have begun to increase wages and produce outsourcing to still less expensive countries such as Vietnam.

In East Asia, as a whole, continuing globalization was reflected by a growing number of cross-border mergers and acquisitions (M&A). Among emerging economies, Taiwan and Hong Kong account for the largest numbers of transnational corporations, with China ranked third.[140] China is the site for over 1,200 foreign-invested R&D centers, and Beijing and Shanghai alone host some 220 regional corporate headquarters.[141] Sovereign wealth funds – for example, the China Investment Corporation with $200 billion in assets,[142] – have been established throughout Asia and reflect the region's preference for state capitalism over the neoliberal version. East Asia, notably Hong Kong, has thus become a major source as well as recipient of FDI.

Nowhere is globalizing China more visible than in Africa. China's interest in Africa is fueled by its appetite for fuel and raw materials like iron and oil for its rapidly growing economy.[143] In Ghana, for instance, China has invested heavily in developing potentially rich oil fields and in making loans to improve local infrastructure.[144] Its investments in raw materials extraction in Africa and Asia, especially in countries politically shunned by the West such as Sudan and Myanmar, as well as in Central Asia,[145] have attracted considerable public attention, as has China's occasional "strong-arming" of companies like Singapore Petroleum and Rio Tinto.[146] China's drive for resources also lies behind its disputes with its neighbors over the Senkaku Diaoyu Islands and the Spratly archipelago.[147]

In November 2006, China invited African leaders to Beijing, where President Hu Jintao announced a broad aid package including $5 billion in loans, debt relief, and technical assistance. China has become Africa's third largest trading partner after the United States and France, quadrupling its total volume with all of Africa from $10 billion in 2000 to $40 billion by 2006, with estimates that it would reach $100 billion by 2010.[148] China has invested heavily in raw materials extraction and infrastructure, including railroads in Nigeria and Angola, roadways in Rwanda, and Africa's largest hydroelectric dam in Ethiopia. Angola and Sudan alone provide China with 25 percent of its oil imports, and the dramatic rise in global commodity prices prior to the 2007–8 global financial crisis was widely attributed to Chinese imports of raw materials to feed that country's economic expansion.

In return for raw materials, China exports finished manufactured goods to Africa. In Kano, Nigeria, for example, numerous Chinese restaurants have appeared, a Chinese shoe factory employs over 2,000 workers, and Chinese products fill store shelves. Declared the owner of a Kano textile factory who had to cut his workforce dramatically: "Without a little protection, if the Chinese bring their finished cotton to Nigeria, you cannot compete with them . . . The gap is so wide that if you just allow them to come in, you are killing Nigerian companies."[149]

Overall, China's integration into the world economy has produced rapid development but exposed that country, as well as others in Asia, to the chill winds of the global financial and economic crisis.[150] The two sides of globalization in the case of China are captured by *The Economist*: "[E]ven as officials trot out a litany of achievements they attribute to the country's 'reform and opening' policy – 200m fewer citizens living in poverty, a 6% share of global GDP compared with 1.8% in 1978, a nearly 70% increase in grain production – the world financial crisis weighs heavily on their minds, and their leaders are struggling with unfinished business."[151] According to Vivienne Shue, in China,

> the state has struggled to adjust its course so as to steer between the paradigmatic extremes of modernism, on the one hand – which it finds ineradicably contaminated by Western ideals and values – and of nativism, on the other hand – which it finds ineradicably contaminated by popular mysticism and magic.[152]

Some regard China as an obstacle to globalization. "On trade," C. Fred Bergsten writes,

> China has been playing at best a passive and at worst a disruptive role. It makes no effort to hide its current preference for low-quality, politically motivated bilateral and regional trade arrangements rather than economically meaningful (and demanding) multilateral trade liberalization through the WTO. Since China is the world's largest surplus country and second-largest exporter, this poses two important challenges to the existing global regime.

These, Bergsten continues, are, first, its "refusal to contribute positively to the Doha Round of international trade negotiations" by claiming that "it should have no liberalization obligations whatsoever" and inventing "a new category of WTO membership ('recently acceded members') to justify its recalcitrance" and, second, the fact that its "pursuit of bilateral and regional trade agreements with neighboring countries is more about politics than economics." Were a Chinese-led Asian trading bloc to emerge, it "would almost certainly trigger a sharp backlash from the United States and the EU, as well as from numerous developing countries, because of its new discrimination against them."[153] "China," Bergsten concludes "continues to act like a small country with little impact on the global system at large and therefore little responsibility for it."[154] China's threat to the open trading system is exacerbated by American and European agricultural protectionism and the demand by major developing states such as Brazil and India that agricultural subsidies be abandoned by the developed states. Countries such as France and Spain have found it politically dangerous to agree to such demands, even though many of the recipients of farm subsidies, including (interestingly enough) Britain's Queen Elizabeth, are not farmers.[155]

As with other regions, then, globalization entails trade-offs for all of Asia. Economic inequality is apparently growing in much of the region.[156] Divisions between prosperous coastal and impoverished rural China threaten serious political and social unrest. Although economic globalization offers the prospect of rapid economic development, selected personality traits, notably individualism,[157] may be needed to prosper in a neoliberal world. Entrepreneurial zeal coupled with corruption may, in turn, produce greater economic and social inequality. Asian states generally have to contend with the exigencies of global markets, a growing population of ambitious, skilled, and self-confident individuals, as well as powerful transnational corporations and a host of nongovernmental organizations (NGOs).

Central Asia

Soviet successor states in Central Asia are among the least globalized countries in the world. The region is Asia's "periphery," yet, since its separation from the Soviet Union, globalization is beginning to affect it. This owes primarily to its strategic position in relation to Afghanistan and Pakistan, growing competition for its raw materials, and an increase in drug trafficking in the region. As of 2011, the KOF Index of Globalization ranked Kazakhstan 76th in overall globalization, the Kyrgyz Republic 86th, Tajikistan 152nd, Uzbekistan 153rd, and Turkmenistan 159th.[158] In terms of networked readiness, Tajikistan ranked 104th; and in economic competitiveness, Kazakhstan ranked 72nd and Tajikistan 116th. No data were available for Turkmenistan or Uzbekistan.[159]

In contrast to the relatively developed and institutionalized polities of East Asia, globalization confronts post-Soviet Central Asia with special difficulties. On the one hand, the region is in the midst of state- and nation-building where, arguably, neither had previously existed, even while economic and cultural globalization dilutes national distinctiveness and reduces national autonomy.[160] Globalization is especially challenging to relatively young societies like those in Central Asia, threatening unique traditions and cultures, reducing the authority of nation-building leaders, and "denationalizing" their economies. The result has been a combination of acceptance and resistance on the part of local elites bent on anchoring nationalism, preserving power, and reinforcing traditional normative structures linked to religion, language, and/or ethnicity.

Like East Asian societies, those of Central Asia have adapted globalization to local conditions. In trying to construct nations and states, the post-Soviet countries of Central Asia have had to overcome an absence of historical tradition, clan and tribal ties, and the Soviet inheritance,[161] while contending with growing competition between Russia and the United States[162] and the threat posed by Islamic identities[163]

– all this, even as powerful globalizing forces threaten to undermine cultural distinctiveness and collective identity. The ingenious formula that their governments have followed has been to combine those modernizing aspects of globalization deemed beneficial, while invoking cultural and normative traditions that are "often intended to make liberalization possible, either by compensating for, or denying, the reality of cultural change."[164] National identity is asserted to strengthen state legitimacy, while modern elements are accepted for both instrumental reasons and to provide governments with the added legitimacy of modernity. This results in what Blum calls "hybrid identity construction"[165] that attempts to avoid the twin dangers of political backlash and cultural homogenization. Thus, while seeking to preserve national culture, the countries of Central Asia are adapting to globalization by encouraging decentralization and governance on the part of private economic actors and by instilling the neoliberal virtues of independence and initiative, as well as modern business, technical, and language skills. As Blum observes, "instead of Homo Sovieticus ... it has been necessary to fashion a thoroughly post-Soviet person: rational, risk-acceptant, profit-oriented, and empowered to act independently in pursuit of personal and national goals."[166] These efforts promise economic benefits, technological modernity, and political legitimacy.

Acceptance of non-conformity allows Central Asia to enjoy some of the fruits of globalization, while its rejection of Soviet-era centralization and hierarchy provide additional legitimacy for its governments. However, democratization has been uneven – greater in the Kyrgyz Republic and Kazakhstan, for instance, than in Uzbekistan, and in these three countries less than in the former Soviet bloc countries of Central Europe.[167] Civil society is also making some strides. In post-Soviet Central Asia, for example, despite the absence of democratic forms in Uzbekistan, "women's NGOs appear to be growing in a number of ways that represent a substantial departure from the past: they have international links; they draw on international gender critiques; and they are developing programs that are distinctly more feminist than those of the Soviet period."[168] Overall, according to Blum, in Kazakhstan and Azerbaijan, "substate actors play a crucial role in mediating globalization" in a manner "potentially consistent with the development of civil society, understood as the expansion of social groups and organizations outside the formal jurisdiction of the state, especially on the basis of social networks which cut across heterogeneous groups."[169]

Cultural globalization with its Western roots poses problems for Asians. Hence in post-Soviet Central Asia, as elsewhere in Asia, globalized culture has been mixed with and modified by efforts to update and assert traditional values and norms.[170] Global culture is, in effect, filtered through local languages and meaning systems that help preserve local cultures.[171] From data gathered in Astrakhan, Almaty, and Baku, Blum finds simultaneous imitation of globalized mores in ways suitable to domestic norms, "a typical pattern of hybridization: selective absorption, rejection, and assertion of national identity constructs."[172] He summarizes his empirical findings of Central Asian responses to globalization as follows:

> [T]he emerging strategic narrative champions native–traditional values and patriotic attachments. At the same time it embraces modernization, while seeking to harness the latter to nation- as well as state-building goals. Along the way many

of the fundamental assumptions of neoliberalism are reproduced, including the importance of individual volition and rational action.[173]

In Central Asia, as in East Asia, as Amitav Acharya points out, "local actors" are not simply "passive targets and learners as transnational agents acting out a universal moral script to produce and direct norm diffusion in local politics." As he sees it: "Local agents also produce norm diffusion by actively borrowing and modifying transnational norms in accordance with their preconstructed normative beliefs and practices." Moreover, "norm-takers perform acts of selection, borrowing, and modification in accordance with a preexisting normative framework to build congruence between that and emerging global norms."[174]

Much of Asia, including post-Soviet societies, reveals "the reflexive embrace of neoliberal ideas underpinning the market" even though "state–society relations – like the boundaries between public and private – vary across issue-area depending on intersubjective understandings of order."[175] In Central Asia, economic decentralization is not only a consequence of the pressures of globalization but also reflects the efforts of local politicians to retain autonomy from the center,[176] and, like East Asia, economic decentralization is not only a consequence of the pressures of globalization but also reflects the efforts of local politicians to husband their autonomy. In addition, although most countries have come to applaud free trade and investment, this enthusiasm is unlikely to persist if global prosperity diminishes for a lengthy time. Another significant and prolonged economic slump may, as in the past, renew support for protectionism and other forms of economic nationalism.

Nationalism plays an even more essential role in Central than in East Asia. Following the collapse of the Soviet Union, that country's central and southwestern Asian republics achieved independence – Turkmenistan, Tajikistan, Uzbekistan, Kyrgyzstan, Armenia, Georgia, and Azerbaijan. Since newly acquired identities in post-Soviet republics in Central and Southwestern Asia are at best very shallow, the manipulation of myths and symbols played a prominent legitimating and mobilizing role, but success remains uncertain. States such as Tajikistan and Uzbekistan had *not* existed before their inhabitants were absorbed by the Soviet Union. Stalin quite literally invented "national" roots for the Soviet Union's nomadic Muslim communities in order to dilute the more threatening Turkic and Islamic identities.[177] Stalin manipulated powerful clan identities in Central Asia to preclude Islamic unity and used the system of collective and state farms to create and anchor local loyalties and identities.[178] "Informal clan networks still pervade society and play a central political and economic role, but their role and form have changed over time, and not always with positive effects on political development."[179]

"The Soviets," argues James Rupert, created five Central Asian republics and forced "on each a distinct 'national' language and culture" and "firmly established the 'nationalities' into which Central Asia is now divided." "In pre-Soviet Turkistan,[180] people had defined themselves primarily as Turkic or Tajik Muslims, identities that could have permitted the evolution of a unified polity across the region."[181]

The major effect of the Soviet period," according to Olivier Roy, "was the territorialisation and systematic ethnicisation of populations, which led to an exacerbation of regional and ethnic conflicts that had been unknown up until that point . . . [C]itizenship in relation to a Soviet state . . . foundered amid the vapours of petrol and alcohol at the end of August 1991 . . . Nationalism was [then] created by the administrative, cultural and political *habitus* installed by the colonial power, within an entity which had no antecedents of nationhood.[182]

Since national roots are not deep in the steppe lands of Central Asia, the post-Soviet states of the region had to search their mythic pasts to find nation-building (really, state-building) symbols. In the case of the Kyrgyz Republic, this led to a revival of an epic poem about a hero named Manas who is said to have resisted Chinese incursions. In Kazakhstan, the government revived interest in the nineteenth-century poet and novelist Abai Kunanbaev,[183] and in neighboring Uzbekistan, the fourteenth-century conqueror Tamerlane was lionized as a symbol of Uzbek nationalism.[184] Despite these efforts, Islamists propagating a historic religious identity threaten to undermine the regimes in the region, though their influence varies by country.[185] Balancing Islamic identities are Turkic identities, fostered by Ankara, that have put down roots in several Central Asian societies, especially Azerbaijan and Kazakhstan.[186]

South Asia

Overall, South Asia ranks low in globalization. India, the core country of South Asia, was ranked 116th of the political entities in the 2011 KOF Index of Globalization. It ranked low in all categories except political globalization,[187] and its economic growth has been largely due to domestic demand.[188] Nevertheless, in only a decade, per capita wealth has grown by 150 percent. India has also benefited significantly from outsourcing owing to a growing working-age population.[189] Other countries in South Asia – Sri Lanka, Pakistan, and Bangladesh – ranked 107th, 109th, and 157th respectively. In terms of networked readiness and economic competitiveness, India ranked 54th and 51st respectively, Sri Lanka 72nd and 62nd, Pakistan 98th and 123rd, and Bangladesh 130th and 107th.[190]

Like China, India is experiencing dramatic economic growth, following the decades after independence known as the "License Raj," a term that connotes the country's economic inefficiency, burdensome bureaucracy and red tape, and rampant public sector corruption.[191] The result was that India fell ever further behind its Asian competitors. "Between 1960 and 1990," writes S. L. Kapur, "India's G.D.P. grew by an average of a little under 4% a year – the 'Hindu rate of growth', as it came to be known."

In round numbers, Pakistan's GDP over the same period grew by 5% a year, Indonesia's by 6%, Thailand's by 7%, Taiwan's by 8% and South Korea's by 9%. India's planners had laid great emphasis on rapid industrialisation, the ostensible reason for interfering with a more market-driven course of development. Yet in India, between 1960 and 1990, industrial output grew on an average by only 6% a year. In Pakistan it grew by 8% a year, in Indonesia by 9%, in Thailand by 9%, in South Korea by 10% and in Taiwan by 12%.[192]

Thus, although in 1947, South Korea's per capita income was less than twice that of India, by 1990 it had grown to twenty times that of India.[193]

India began cautiously to introduce economic liberalization after a 1991 balance-of-payments crisis that was triggered by the loss of what had been its major trading partner, the Soviet Union, and that compelled the country to seek IMF funding. The IMF agreed but only after India had introduced reforms such as cutting license restrictions, privatizing state-owned industries, and opening the country to additional foreign investment. Currently, it is reforming its complex system of indirect taxes.[194] In part because of these reforms, India's GDP has exceeded an annual growth rate of 7 percent since 1997, reaching 9.6 percent in 2006, 9 percent in 2007, and 6.6 percent in 2008, following the onset of the global recession.[195] India's economy was expected to grow by 9.7 percent during 2010,[196] a remarkable rate during a global economic malaise. Indeed, Indian entrepreneurs have seen opportunities for innovation in the global economic crisis.[197]

According to the World Bank: "A look at the 25-year period between 1981 and 2005 shows that India has moved from having 60 percent of its people living on less than $1.25 a day to 42 percent. The number of people living below a dollar a day (2005 prices) has also come down from 42 percent to 24 percent over the same period. Both measures show that India has maintained even progress against poverty since the 1980s, with the poverty rate declining at a little under one percentage point per year," although "the number of poor below $1.25 a day has increased from 421 million in 1981 to 456 million in 2005,"[198] and almost 80 percent of all Indians subsist on less than half a dollar a day.[199] One prediction has India's economy surpassing that of Great Britain in a few years and becoming second globally behind China by mid-century.[200] In sum, only twenty years ago, according to Thomas Friedman, India "was known as a country of snake charmers, poor people, and Mother Teresa," yet today "it is also seen as a country of brainy people and computer wizards."[201]

India's growing prosperity after 1991 was accompanied, as in China, by growing economic inequality. A survey by the UN Department of Economic and Social Affairs concluded that during the 1990s "inequality increased in both rural and urban India," that "there has been a stagnation of incomes for the majority," that "income disparities between the rural and urban sectors increased," and that "urban inequality increased for all the 15 major states in India."[202] There are also significant economic disparities among India's states.

> The headcount poverty rate in rural Orissa (43 percent) and rural Bihar (41 percent) is higher than similarly measured poverty rates of African countries like Malawi or Ghana. By the same standard poverty in rural Haryana is only 5.7 percent – less than upper middle income countries like Colombia and Brazil and rural Punjab is only 2.4 percent – approaching the rates of Costa Rica.[203]

Deregulation, privatization, and inequality in India are also viewed by some as exacerbating "the already inequitable distribution of health and educational services"[204] and eroding the country's democratic tradition.[205]

India's high-tech sector, the principal beneficiary of economic liberalization, is largely urban, employs relatively few workers, and specializes in "frugal innovation,"[206] while agrarian India was left behind with perhaps no more than one-tenth of the population controlling one-third of the country's income.[207] Additionally, some groups, for instance, the Dalits, once known as "untouchables" in India's caste system, "continue to live in grinding poverty and suffer discrimination in education, jobs and health care."[208] Owing to inequality, hunger still remains a serious problem in India,[209] and the rate of malnutrition among Indian children exceeds that of children in sub-Saharan Africa.[210] Concludes the OECD:

> Over the past two decades, India has moved away from its former dirigiste model and become a market-based economy ... Direct tax rates were significantly reduced, pervasive government licensing of industrial activity was almost eliminated, and restrictions on investment by large companies were eased. Furthermore, financial markets were reformed, with banks restored to health, entry barriers lowered, equity markets transformed and new supervisory bodies introduced. The process of reform has continued in this decade with a further opening of the economy to competition. The number of industries reserved for very small firms has been significantly reduced, and foreign suppliers have been encouraged to enter the market by a progressive lowering of tariffs to an average of 10% in 2007. The rules governing foreign direct investment have been markedly eased, notably in the manufacturing sector. Last but not least, fiscal discipline has been improved by the passage of fiscal responsibility laws for the central government and all but three of the 28 state governments.

However, "the differences in economic performance across states are associated with the extent to which states have introduced market-oriented reforms."[211]

English is a major factor dividing the minority of Indians who have taken advantage of globalization and the large majority who have not done so (or not been able to do so). English is often seen as India's advantage over China, although China is currently producing more English-speakers than is India.[212] The language is recognized in India as an "official" language, as the country's "lingua franca," and as "the key to India's success in information technology industries"[213] – even though only about 5 percent of its citizens are bilingual. According to Steve Derné, the "English-language press relies on a readership of educated high-income people who are most able to take advantage of the opportunities associated with globalization."[214] Those who spoke little English "lacked skills that they could market in the international economy."[215]

It is the English-speaking minority that constitutes the country's consumerist middle class, and, because this minority maintains its lifestyle by using low-wage labor, it is not interested in the "general middle classing of society."[216] Indeed, two observers argue that "one of the great myths of the opening up of the Indian economy since 1991" is "that economic liberalisation has resulted in a massively expanded homogeneous mass of wealthy, Indian middle classes who have been the principal beneficiaries of liberalisation, profiting immensely from the new opportunities for education, jobs and consumerism."[217] Instead, the authors argue that "the past decade and a half has brought few real benefits in the lives of many of the middle classes" and that "for many families, their lives have been made more difficult due to rising prices, inflation, increasing debt, increasing competition for jobs, and a marked decline in overall living standards."²¹⁸ New opportunities have been accompanied by personal and financial stress, as well as the proliferation of the blogosphere "as a popular social space alongside the social networking sites like YouTube, FaceBook or MySpace."²¹⁹

The mixing of global and local cultural traditions is producing hybridization in India as it is doing elsewhere, but there remains tension between global and local cultural icons.²²⁰ Nevertheless, according to Nalin Mehta: "Indian television thrives on programming genres that marry older argumentative traditions with new technology and notions of liberal democracy to create new hybrid forms that strengthen democratic culture."²²¹ "The Bollywood dance craze, as may be surmisable from its *Fame* and *break-dance* air and its enthusiasm for keep fit, weight loss, personal happiness and the pursuit of a sexy, toned body, is very much an East–West hybrid cultural phenomenon."²²² Overall, globalization "is having both positive and negative effects on India's popular cultural traditions."²²³ India's economic liberalization, the reduction in its social safety net, and the spread of global culture has produced Hindu nationalism with the "deprived section forming the major chunk of the foot soldiers of the pogroms released by religious nationalism."²²⁴

This chapter has dealt with Europe and Asia, those regions that have profited most from globalization. In the following chapter, we turn to regions that, on the whole, have remained less globalized, either by intent or circumstance.

NOTES

1 Nederveen Pieterse, *Globalization and Culture*, 13.
2 Daniel T. Griswold, *Mad about Trade: Why Main Street America Should Embrace Globalization* (Washington, DC: Cato Institute, 2009), 3.
3 See, for example, Robert Hunter Wade, *Counter Punch*, January 3, 2002, http://www.counterpunch.org/wade1.html.
4 Although individual countries in several of our "core" regions are actually economically peripheral, they have been included here if one or more of the region's leaders are part of the globalized "core."
5 China's economy grew by 10.3 percent in 2010. Ian Johnson and Bettina Wassener, "China's Economy Grew 10.3 percent in 2010," *New York Times*, January 19, 2011, http://www.nytimes.com/2011/01/20/business/global/20yuan.html.
6 International Monetary Fund, *World Economic Outlook Update: A Policy-Driven Multi-Speed Recovery*, January 26, 2010, table 1.1, http://www.imf.org/external/pubs/ft/weo/2010/update/01/index.htm#fig1.
7 "The World Turned Upside Down: A Special Report on Innovation in Emerging Economies," *The Economist*, April 17, 2010, 6. See also "The New Masters of Management," *The Economist*, April 17, 2010, 11. Developing countries like China still need access to Western markets to maintain growth. See Banyan, "Afloat on a Chinese Tide," *The Economist*, September 4, 2010, 48.
8 We use the terms "core" and "periphery" not in the neo-Marxist sense employed by world system theory like Immanuel Wallerstein or in world system history like Andre Gundar Frank and Robert Denemark but merely metaphorically to denote highly globalized states ("core") and relatively unglobalized states ("periphery").
9 Immanuel Wallerstein, *The Modern World System I: Capitalist Agriculture and the Origins of the European World-Economy in the Sixteenth Century* (with a new prologue) (Berkeley, CA: University of California Press, 2011), 102–3.
10 See "Rivals on the Roof of the World," *The Economist*, September 18, 2010, 57.

11 "A Himalayan Rivalry," *The Economist,* August 21, 2010, 17–20.
12 "2010 Global R&D Funding Forecast," *R&D Magazine,* December 2009, 3, http://www.rdmag.com/uploadedFiles/RD/Featured_Articles/2009/12/GFF2010_ads_small.pdf. China accounted for 12.2 percent of global R&D spending in 2010, up from 0.1 percent in 2008.
13 Martin Grueber and Tim Studt, "Global Perspective: Emerging Nations Gain R&D Ground," *R&D Magazine,* December 22, 2009, http://www.rdmag.com/Featured-Articles/2009/12/Policy-and-Industry-Global-Perspective-Emerging-Nations-Gain-R-D-Ground/.
14 UNCTAD, *World Investment Report 2008* (New York and Geneva 2008), table 1.20, 34.
15 Kluver and Fu, "The Cultural Globalization Index."
16 Ibid.
17 Ulrich Beck and Edgar Grande, *Cosmopolitan Europe* (Cambridge: Polity Press, 2007), 3.
18 See George Ross, "European Integration and Globalization," in Ronald Axtmann, ed., *Globalization and Europe* (London: Pinter, 1998), 164–83.
19 Jean-Marie Guéhenno, *The End of the Nation-State,* trans. Victoria Elliot (Minneapolis, MI: University of Minnesota Press, 2000), 4.
20 "Europe's Engine," *The Economist,* March 13, 2010, 13.
21 Hamilton and Quinlan, *Globalization and Europe,* 29.
22 Ibid., 149.
23 Germany, with a strong economy and relatively low unemployment, favored a strong euro and higher interest rates, whereas deficit-ridden countries with higher unemployment favored a weaker euro and low interest rates. See, for example, Charlemagne, "The Euro's Existential Worries," *The Economist,* May 8, 2010, 57, and Steven Erlanger, "Two Competing Visions of a European Economy," *New York Times,* July 1, 2010, http://www.nytimes.com/2010/07/02/world/europe/02brussels.html. Similar differences, especially with Germany, had arisen earlier when Eastern European members of the EU were confronted with financial crisis. See Charles Forelle, "EU Rejects a Rescue of Faltering East Europe," *Wall Street Journal,* March 2, 2009, A1.
24 "EU Austerity Drive Country-by-Country," *BBC News,* June 16, 2010, http://www.bbc.co.uk/news/10162176.
25 "2011 KOF Index of Globalization," http://globalization.kof.ethz.ch/static/pdf/rankings_2011.pdf. In addition to the fifteen leaders, others among the top twenty were Canada, Germany, Spain, Singapore, Norway, and Cyprus.
26 "The Globalization Index," *Foreign Policy* 163 (November/December 2007), 70–1.
27 "Measuring Globalization," *Foreign Policy* 122 (January/February 2001), 56–65. *Foreign Policy* uses a somewhat different set of dimensions than KOF. Where KOF uses three dimensions – economic, social, and political – *Foreign Affairs* uses four as described in the text. For a critique of the *Foreign Policy* index, see Ben Lockwood, "How Robust is the Foreign Policy/Kearney Index of Globalisation?" University of Warwick: Centre for the Study of Globalisation and Regionalisation, Working Paper 79/01 (August 2001).
28 World Economic Forum, "The Global Competitiveness Report 2010–2011," http://www.weforum.org/en/initiatives/gcp/Global%20Competitiveness%20Report/index.htm.
29 David Rae and Marte Sollie, "Globalisation and the European Union: Which Countries Are Best Placed to Cope," OECD Economics Department Working Paper 586 (December 2007), 9, http://www.olis.oecd.org/olis/2007doc.nsf/LinkTo/NT00005 8AE/$FILE/JT03242091.PDF.
30 Ibid., figure 20, 33. The United States ranks just behind Sweden.
31 "The 2008 Global Cities Index," *Foreign Policy* 169 (November/December 2008), 70. The Global Cities Index is an aggregation of five dimensions: Business Activity, Human Capital, Information Exchange, Cultural Experience, and Political Engagement.
32 "The Global Cities Index 2010," *Foreign Policy,* http://www.foreignpolicy.com/node/373401.
33 "European Union," *Internet World Stats* (2009), http://www.internetworldstats.com/europa.htm.

34 John de la Mothe, *Innovation Strategies in Interdependent States: Essays on Smaller Nations, Regions and Cities in a Globalized World* (Northampton, MA: Edward Elgar, 2006), 1.
35 Archibugi, Denni, and Filippetti, "The Global Innovation Scoreboard 2008."
36 De Blij, *The Power of Place*, 47.
37 Ibid., 48.
38 Hamilton and Quinlan, *Globalization and Europe*, 71.
39 Ibid., 171.
40 Edgar Grande, "Globalizing West European Politics: The Change of Cleavage Structures, Parties and Party Systems in Comparative Perspective," in Hanspeter Kriesi, Edgar Grande, Romain Lachat, Martin Dolezal, Simon Bornschier, and Timotheos Frey, *West European Politics in the Age of Globalization* (Cambridge: Cambridge University Press, 2008), 324.
41 See, for example, "When Town Halls Turn to Mecca," *The Economist*, December 6, 2008, 76–7, 79.
42 Eurobarometer, "Europe's Social Reality – Special Eurobarometer 273" (2007), 68, http://ec.europa.eu/public_opinion/archives/ebs/ebs_273_en.pdf.
43 Ibid.
44 Walter Laqueur, *The Last Days of Europe: Epitaph for an Old Continent* (New York: St. Martin's, 2007), 8.
45 "In Praise of . . . Cem Ozdemir," *The Guardian*, November 18, 2008, http://www.guardian.co.uk/commentisfree/2008/nov/18/leaders-and-reply-obama-germany-green-party. See also James Angelos, "Germany Tries to Forge European Brand of Islam," *Wall Street Journal*, August 3, 2011, A9.
46 Peggy Hollinger, "Council of Europe Warns on Multiculturalism," *Financial Times*, February 16, 2011, www.ft.com/cms/s/0/72c02d9a-39c6-11e0-8dba-00144feabdc0.html#axzz1KBzh1Xbc.
47 Grande, "Globalizing West European Politics," 343, 344.
48 What is called "Eastern Europe" is a diverse group of states that fared quite differently during the post-2007 recession. See "Wrongly Labeled," *The Economist*, January 9, 2010, 50–1.
49 "2011 KOF Index of Globalization." In *Foreign Policy*'s 2007 index ("The Globalization Index," *Foreign Policy*, 70–1), Estonia ranked 10th of 72 countries overall and 3rd in economic globalization; Poland ranked 41st of 72 overall (having declined significantly since 2006); and Ukraine ranked 42nd overall.
50 Ben Lockwood and Michela Redoano, "The CSGR Globalisation Index: An Introductory Guide," Centre for the Study of Globalisation and Regionalisation working paper 155/04 (2005), http://www2.warwick.ac.uk/fac/soc/csgr/index/download.
51 Blanke, Browne, Hanouz, Geiger, Mia, and Sala-i-Martin, *The Global Competitiveness Report 2009–2010*, and Dutta and Mia, eds., *Global Information Technology Report 2008–2009*.
52 "The Globalization Index 2007," 75.
53 US Department of State, "Background Note: Estonia," August 2009, http://www.state.gov/r/pa/ei/bgn/5377.htm.
54 "Horse Power to Horsepower," *The Economist*, January 30, 2009, 60–1.
55 US Department of State, "Background Note: Ukraine," May 2009, http://www.state.gov/r/pa/ei/bgn/3211.htm.
56 "2011 KOF Index of Globalization."
57 "2011 KOF Index of Globalization: Indices and Variables," http://globalization.kof.ethz.ch/static/pdf/variables_2009.pdf.
58 Blum, *National Identity and Globalization*, 9.
59 Ibid., 1.
60 Phillip Inman, "China Becomes World's Biggest Exporter," *guardian.co.uk*, January 10, 2010, http://www.guardian.co.uk/business/2010/jan/10/china-tops-germany-exports.
61 Spencer Swartz and Shai Oster, "China Tops U.S. in Energy," *Wall Street Journal*, July 20, 2010, A1, A12.

62 David Barboza, "China Passes Japan as Second-Largest Economy," *New York Times*, August 15, 2010, http://www.nytimes.com/2010/08/16/business/global/16yuan.html.
63 Grueber and Studt, "Global Perspective."
64 Regionalization has *not* taken root in East Asia because, as one observer explains, of "modernization with insufficient globalization." See Gilbert Rozman, *Northeast Asia's Stunted Regionalism* (Cambridge: Cambridge University Press, 2004), 7.
65 Banyan, "New Silk Roads," *The Economist*, April 10, 2010, 48.
66 "Out of India," *The Economist*, March 5, 2011, 76.
67 See Bettina Wassener, "Economies in Asia Continue to Show Strong Rebound," *New York Times*, February 1, 2010, http://www.nytimes.com/2010/02/02/business/global/02asiaecon.html.
68 For a balanced analysis of this issue, see Takashi Inoguchi and Edward Newman, "Introduction: 'Asian Values' and Democracy in Asia," *Proceedings of 1997 First Shizuoka Asia–Pacific Forum: The Future of the Asia–Pacific Region*, http://www.unu.edu/unupress/asian-values.html.
69 Guthrie, *China and Globalization*, 16. Emphasis in original.
70 McGrew, "Organized Violence and Globalization," 21.
71 See Weiss, *The Myth of the Powerless State*, 41–82, and Greider, *One World Ready or Not*, 278–80.
72 Paul Midford, "Globalization and National Security: Is Japan *Still* an Island?" in Kirshner, ed., *Globalization and National Security*, 259.
73 See "Bamboo Capitalism," *The Economist*, March 12, 2011, 13.
74 Martin Walker, "Globalization 3.0," *The Wilson Quarterly* 31:4 (Autumn 2007), 22–3.
75 Cited in "Asia's Different Drum," *Time Magazine*, June 14, 1993, 18.
76 C. O. Khong, "Asian Values: The Debate Revisited," *Proceedings of 1997 First Shizuoka Asia–Pacific Forum: The Future of the Asia–Pacific Region*, http://www.unu.edu/unupress/asian-values.html.
77 Charles Wolf, Jr., "Are 'Asian Values' Really Unique?" Hoover Institution, *Hoover Digest* 2 (2000), http://www.hooverdigest.org/002/wolf.html.
78 François Godement, *The Downsizing of Asia* (London: Routledge, 1999), 112, 115.
79 Khong, "Asian Values: The Debate Revisited."
80 Laos and Cambodia are also ASEAN members.
81 Helen E. S. Nesadurai, *Globalisation, Domestic Politics and Regionalism* (London: Routledge, 2003), 72.
82 "2011 KOF Index of Globalization." *Foreign Affairs* ranked Singapore 1st overall and 2nd in terms of economic globalization in 2007.
83 Dutta and Mia, eds., *Global Information Technology Report 2008–2009*, and World Economic Forum, "The Global Competitiveness Report 2010–2011."
84 "2011 KOF Index of Globalization," Dutta and Mia, eds., *Global Information Technology Report 2008–2009*, and World Economic Forum, *The Global Competitiveness Report 2010–2011*.
85 Nesadurai, *Globalisation, Domestic Politics and Regionalism*, 74.
86 Peter A. Coclanis and Tilak Doshi, "Globalization in Southeast Asia," *Annals of the American Academy of Political and Social Science* 570 (July 2000), 58.
87 Ibid., 60–1.
88 Ishak Shari, "Economic Growth and Social Development in Malaysia, 1971–98: Does the State Still Matter in an Era of Economic Globalisation?" in Martin Andersson and Christer Gunnarsson, eds., *Development and Structural Change in Asia–Pacific: Globalising Miracles or the end of a Model?* (London: RoutledgeCurzon, 2003), 122. See also Chris Edwards, "Neo-Liberalism on the Defensive but Not Defeated? A Comparative Review of the Asian Crisis and Lessons for the Future," in ibid., 75–92, and Medhi Krongkeaw, "The IMF in the Thai Economic Crisis: Villain or Saviour?" in ibid., 93–107.
89 Johannes Widodo, "Morphogenesis and Hybridity of Southeast Asian Coastal Cities," in Ismail, Shaw, and Ooi, *Southeast Asian Culture and Heritage in a Globalising World*, 79.

90 Shinji Yamashita, "Introduction: 'Glocalizing' Southeast Asia," in Yamashita and Eades, eds., *Globalization in Southeast Asia*, 7.
91 Baildon, "Being Rooted and Living Globally," 61.
92 Rahil Ismail, "'Di waktu petang di Geylang Serai' Geyland Serai: Maintaining Identity in a Globalised World," in Ismail, Shaw, and Ooi, *Southeast Asian Culture and Heritage in a Globalising World*, 30.
93 Ibid., 35.
94 Mike Douglass, K. C. Ho, and Giok Ling Ooi, "Globalization, the City and Civil Society in Pacific Asia," in M. Douglass, K. C. Ho, and G. L. Ooi, eds., *Globalization, the City and Civil Society in Pacific Asia: The Social Production of Civic Spaces* (London: Routledge, 2007), 3.
95 Ibid., 5.
96 Lowell Dittmer, "Globalization and the Twilight of Asian Exceptionalism," in Kinnvall and Jönsson, eds., *Globalization and Democratization in Asia*, 22. East Asia includes China, Japan, Hong Kong, South Korea, and Taiwan.
97 Ibid.
98 Nevertheless, China's surplus remains as large as that of Japan's and Germany's combined.
99 "Asia's Suffering," *The Economist*, January 31, 2009, 13.
100 See, for example, "An Astonishing Rebound," *The Economist*, August 15, 2009, 9, Nelson D. Schwartz, "Asia's Recovery Highlights China's Ascendance," *New York Times*, August 23, 2004, http://www.nytimes.com/2009/08/24/business/global/24 global.html, and Keith Bradsher, "Recovery Picks Up in China as U.S. Still Ails," *New York Times*, September 18, 2009, http://www.nytimes.com/2009/09/18/business/global/18yuan.html.
101 Naisbitt, *Mind Set!*, 183.
102 Adam Segal, "Globalization Is a Double-Edged Sword: Globalization and Chinese National Security," in Kirshner, ed., *Globalization and National Security*, 294.
103 Michael Wines, Sharon Lafraniere, and Jonathan Ansfield, "China's Censors Tackle and Trip Over the Internet," *New York Times*, April 7, 2010, http://www.nytimes.com/2010/04/08/world/asia/08censor.html.
104 Segal, "Globalization Is a Double-Edged Sword," 314.
105 Edward Friedman, "On Alien Western Democracy," in Kinnvall and Jönsson, eds., *Globalization and Democratization in Asia*, 54.
106 Ibid., 55, 56.
107 "The Debate over Universal Values," *The Economist*, October 2, 2010, 43–4, and "China: A Special Report," *The Economist*, June 25, 2011, 17–18.
108 Guthrie, *China and Globalization*, 276–303. "A totally democratic system," Guthrie concludes, "may be decades down the road, but the party is now at a point where there is no turning back" (303), and "a rule-of-law society is emerging in China" (22, also 217–55). However, recent events afford little optimism as regards democracy in China. See "Big Surprise," *The Economist*, December 19, 2009, 73–4.
109 Banyan, "The Wind That Will not Subside," February 19, 2011, 46.
110 Friedman, "On Alien Western Democracy," 58. Emphasis in original. For a more critical version of South Korean "democracy," see Geir Helgesen, "Imported Democracy: The South Korean Experience," in Kinnvall and Jönsson, eds., *Globalization and Democratization in Asia*, 73–91. Helgesen describes South Korean democracy as "strongly supported, yet weak in practice" (74), and he concludes that "the present, commonly shared social morality in Korea does not support a liberalist version of democracy which hails individual freedom, freedom of choice, and political pluralism as the supreme good" (88).
111 By contrast, Hugo Dobson approvingly quotes Chalmers Johnson's description of Japan's political process as one of "soft authoritarianism" in which bureaucracy is the chief political actor. See Dobson, "Social Movements and Society in Japan," 132.
112 Friedman, "On Alien Western Democracy," 59.

113 Dittmer, "Globalization and the Twilight of Asian Exceptionalism," 22.
114 Godement, *The Downsizing of Asia*, 17, 125.
115 Dittmer, "Globalization and the Twilight of Asian Exceptionalism," 35.
116 "The Globalization Index," 70–1. However, by almost any measure such as receipt or export of FDI, corporate mergers and acquisitions, or entry into the WTO, China is rapidly globalizing. See Guthrie, *China and Globalization*, 316–29. He concludes (330) that "all indications are that China's growth will continue to integrate the country into the global economy."
117 "The Second Long March," *The Economist*, December 13, 2008, 30.
118 See Linda Weiss, "State Power and the Asian Crisis," *New Political Economy* 4:3 (1999), 317–42.
119 Catarina Kinnvall, "Analyzing the Global–Local Nexus," in Kinnvall and Jönsson, eds., *Globalization and Democratization in Asia*, 4. Emphasis in original.
120 See, for example, "Secret Sauce," *The Economist*, November 14, 2009, 90.
121 Michael Wines, "China Fortifies State Businesses to Fuel Growth," *New York Times*, August 29, 2010, http://www.nytimes.com/2010/08/30/world/asia/30china.html.
122 "Lights and Action," *The Economist*, April 29, 2010, 72.
123 "The Indispensable Economy?" *The Economist*, April 29, 2010, 77–8.
124 Floyd Norris, "A Shift in the Export Powerhouses," *New York Times*, February 19, 2010, http://www.nytimes.com/2010/02/20/business/economy/20charts.html.
125 Guthrie, *China and Globalization*, 7. China and Russia have both suggested reducing the dollar's role as the world's major reserve currency. See "Yuan Small Step," *The Economist*, July 11, 2009, 71–3.
126 Douglas A. Irwin, "Goodbye, Free Trade?" *Wall Street Journal*, October 9–10, 2010, C1.
127 Andrew Batson, "China Takes Aim at Dollar," *Wall Street Journal*, March 24, 2009, A1, A10.
128 Mark Landler, "Chinese Savings Helped Inflate American Bubble," *New York Times*, December 25, 2008, http://www.nytimes.com/2008/12/26/world/asia/26addiction.html.
129 "When Partners Attack," *The Economist*, February 13, 2010, 77.
130 United Nations Conference on Trade and Development, *World Investment Report 2008: Transnational Corporations and the Infrastructure Challenge*, Part I, http://www.unctad.org/en/docs/wir2008p1_en.pdf, 47, 33.
131 Ibid., 51.
132 Ibid., 8.
133 Ibid., 47.
134 "The Globalization Index," 70–1.
135 "2011 KOF Index of Globalization." The East Asian countries ranked highest in political globalization and, with the exception of South Korea, lowest in economic globalization. Hong Kong and Taiwan are not among the countries ranked in the KOF Index.
136 Blanke, Browne, Hanouz, Geiger, Mia, and Sala-i-Martin, *The Global Competitiveness Report 2009–2010*, and Dutta and Mia, eds., *Global Information Technology Report 2008–2009*. No information was available for North Korea.
137 "The 2008 Global Cities Index," 70.
138 "2010 Global R&D Funding Forecast," 3.
139 Hamilton and Quinlan, *Globalization and Europe*, 123.
140 *World Investment Report 2008*, 29.
141 Ibid., 47.
142 Ibid., 50.
143 "China Oil Demand Increase 'Astonishing', Says IEA," *BBC News*, March 12, 2010, http://news.bbc.co.uk/2/hi/business/8563985.stm.
144 Will Connors, "China Extends Africa Push With Loans, Deal in Ghana," *Wall Street Journal*, September 24, 2010, A15.
145 "Riches in the Near Abroad," *The Economist*, January 30, 2010, 48, 51–2.

146 See "Sino-Trojan Horse," *The Economist*, May 30, 2009, 66, and David Barboza, "China Calls Concerns on Rio Tinto 'Noise'," *New York Times*, July 17, 2009, http://www.nytimes.com/2009/07/17/world/asia/17riotinto.html.

147 See, for example, "China Accuses Vietnam in South China Sea Row," *BBC News*, June 10, 2011, http://www.bbc.co.uk/news/world-asia-pacific-13723443.

148 Jill McGivering, "China's Growing Focus on Africa," *BBC News*, January 17, 2006, http://news.bbc.co.uk/2/hi/africa/4619956.stm, and Peter Ford, "China Woos African Trade," *Christian Science Monitor*, November 3, 2006, 1, 4.

149 Craig Timberg, "From Competitors to Trading Partners: Africans Adjust as Business Ties with China Grow," *Washington Post*, December 3, 2006, A23.

150 For analysis of the economic downturn in Asia as a result of both reduced exports and insufficient domestic demand, see "Troubled Tigers," *The Economist*, January 31, 2009, 75–7.

151 "The Second Long March," 30. For a description of China's immense role in the global economy, see James McGregor, *One Billion Customers* (New York: Free Press, 2005).

152 Vivienne Shue, "China: From Heshang to Falun Gong," in Kinnvall and Jönsson, eds., *Globalization and Democratization in Asia*, 225.

153 C. Fred Bergsten, "A Partnership of Equals: How Washington Should Respond to China's Economic Challenge," *Foreign Affairs* 87:4 (July/August 2008), 59, 60.

154 Ibid., 63–4.

155 Doreen Carvajal and Stephen Castle, "European Subsidies Stray from the Farm," *New York Times*, July 16, 2009, http://www.nytimes.com/2009/07/17/business/global/17farms.html.

156 For a contrary view in the context of Asia, see Machiko Nissanke and Erik Thorbecke, eds., *Globalization and the Poor in Asia: Can Shared Growth Be Sustained?* (Basingstoke, UK: Palgrave Macmillan, 2007).

157 There is concern, however, that excessive individualism may produce "social atomization." See Blum, *National Identity and Globalization*, 88.

158 "2010 KOF Index of Globalization." None was included among the seventy-two countries ranked by *Foreign Affairs* in 2007.

159 World Economic Forum, "The Global Competitiveness Report 2010–2011," and Dutta and Mia, eds., *Global Information Technology Report 2008–2009*.

160 See Graham Smith, Edward Allworth, and Vivien Law, eds., *Nation-Building in the Post-Soviet Borderlands* (Cambridge: Cambridge University Press, 1998).

161 A number of these Central Asian societies have witnessed the continuation or revival of Soviet-era hierarchy and authoritarianism, especially Azerbaijan, Turkmenistan, and Uzbekistan.

162 See Lena Jonson, *Tajikistan in the New Central Asia* (New York: I. B. Tauris, 2006), Lena Jonson, *Vladimir Putin and Central Asia: The Shaping of Russian Foreign Policy* (New York: I. B. Tauris, 2004), and Olga Oliker and David A. Schlapak, *US Interests in Central Asia* (Santa Monica, CA: Rand Corporation, 2005).

163 See Pinar Akcali, "Nation-State Building in Central Asia: A Lost Case?" *Perspectives on Global Development and Technology* 2:3–4 (2003), 409–29, and Sébastien Peyrouse, "Toward a Connection between Religion and Nationality in Central Asia," *Central Eurasian Studies Review* 3:1 (Winter 2004), 13–16.

164 Blum, *National Identity and Globalization*, 180.

165 Ibid.

166 Ibid., 186.

167 Pauline Jones Luong, *Institutional Changes and Political Continuity in Post-Soviet Central Asia* (Cambridge: Cambridge University Press, 2002), 17–18. For data that suggest that Islamic societies value democracy as highly as non-Islamic societies, see Pippa Norris and Ronald Inglehart, "The True Clash of Civilizations," *Foreign Policy* 135 (March/April 2003), 62–70.

168 Marianne Kamp, "Between Women and the State: Mahalla Committees and Social Welfare in Uzbekistan," in Pauline Jones Luong, ed., *The Transformation of Central Asia:*

States and Societies from Soviet Rule to Independence (Ithaca, NY: Cornell University Press, 2004), 55.
169 Blum, *National Identity and Globalization*, 190, 191. See Suny, "Provisional Stabilities," 159–62.
170 According to Laura Adams, Uzbekistan utilizes Soviet-era spectacle to foster local culture "because spectacle has properties that enable elites to close inputs from below without making the masses feel left out." See L. Adams, "Cultural Elites in Uzbekistan: Ideological Production and the States," in Luong, ed., *The Transformation of Central Asia*, 116.
171 See John R. Thompson, *Ideology and Modern Culture* (Stanford, CA: Stanford University Press, 1990), 313–19.
172 Blum, *National Identity and Globalization*, 74. Blum (91) defines "assertion" as "a bid to reconstruct social identity in ways calculated to stabilize social order and legitimate the role of the state."
173 Ibid., 179. In fact, some elements of "tradition" are synthetic, invented to deflect the impact of globalization, contain ethnic friction, replace Soviet symbols, and foster national identity.
174 Amitav Acharya, "How Ideas Spread: Whose Norms Matter? Norm Localization and Institutional Change in Asian Regionalism," *International Organization* 58:2 (Spring 2004), 269. Checkel makes a similar argument, concluding that "both domestic structures and domestic norms are variables that intervene between systemic norms and nation-level outcomes." See Jeffrey T. Checkel, "Norms, Institutions, and National Identity in Contemporary Europe," *International Studies Quarterly* 43:1 (March 1999), 91. See also Ulf Hannerz, "Scenarios for Peripheral Cultures," in Bruce Mazlish and Akira Iriye, eds., *The Global History Reader* (New York: Routledge, 2004), 232–40.
175 Blum, *National Identity and Globalization*, 76, 192.
176 Alisher Ilkhamov, "The Limits of Centralization: Regional Challenges in Uzbekistan," in Luong, ed., *The Transformation of Central Asia*, 159–82.
177 However, as Suny ("Provisional Stabilities," 164–5) argues, religiosity among "Soviet Central Asians" was "exaggerated" and "in the post-Soviet period Islamic unity has proven illusory."
178 Kathleen Collins, *Clan Politics and Regime Transition in Central Asia* (Cambridge: Cambridge University Press, 2006), 88.
179 Ibid., 16.
180 Russian Turkistan (Persian for "land of the Turks") extended from west to east from the Caspian Sea to the Chinese border and from north to south from the Aral-Irtysh watershed to the borders of Iran and Afghanistan. Geographical and historical factors made the region a link between Europe and Asia, and it was ruled or conquered at various times by the Persians, Alexander the Great, the Seleucids, the Parthians, and the Kushans.
181 James Rupert, "Dateline Tashkent: Post-Soviet Central Asia," *Foreign Policy* 87 (Summer 1992), 178. See also Suny, "Provisional Stabilities," 168, who concludes that the "peoples of Central Asia were among the last of the Soviet peoples to adopt clearly differentiated 'national' identities."
182 Olivier Roy, *The New Central Asia* (New York: I. B. Tauris, 2000), 8.
183 According to Edward Schatz, the "reconstituted knowledge of local heroes" has had the undesired and undesirable effect of reviving local and tribal differences among Kazakhs. See E. Schatz, "The Politics of Multiple Identities: Lineage and Ethnicity in Kazakhstan," *Europe–Asia Studies* 52:3 (May, 2000), 502.
184 "A Time of Heroes," *The Economist*, September 23–9, 1995, 28.
185 See, for example, "The Militants Take Aim," *The Economist*, August 26–September 1, 2000, 32–3, "Islamic Nerves," *The Economist*, October 14–20, 2000, 51.
186 Blum, *National Identity and Globalization*, 102. Turkey has consistently supported Azerbaijan in its quarrel with Armenia over Nagorno-Karabakh.
187 "2011 KOF Index of Globalization." India was the second least globalized country in "The Globalization Index," *Foreign Policy* 163.

188 James Lamont, "India: Potholes in the Road," *Financial Times*, February 4, 2010, http://www.ft.com/cms/s/0/096fb72a-11c7-11df-b6e3-00144feab49a.html.

189 India's working-age population will increase by 136 million by 2020, whereas China's will grow by 23 million. See "A Bumpier but Freer Road," *The Economist*, September 30, 2010, 75.

190 World Economic Forum, "The Global Competitiveness Report 2010–2011," and Dutta and Mia, eds., *Global Information Technology Report 2008–2009*.

191 See "An Elephant, Not a Tiger: A Special Report on India," *The Economist*, December 13, 2008, 3–18. Indian development, however, still faces significant challenges. Agriculture which still accounts for most Indians' livelihoods continues to lag behind industrial and technological growth. See "Crop Circles," *The Economist*, March 13, 2010, 15–16. Caste divisions complicate matters, especially in rural India. See "Caste in Doubt," *The Economist*, June 12, 2010, 46. Infrastructure remains poor, and higher education is insufficient to meet the demands for advanced technology.

192 S. L. Kapur, "Industry Passing Through Phase of Transition," *The Tribune (India)*, n.d., http://www.tribuneindia.com/50yrs/kapur.htm.

193 "India: The Economy," *BBC News*, December 3, 1998, http://news.bbc.co.uk/2/hi/south_asia/55427.stm.

194 "Trickle Through," *The Economist*, December 19, 2009, 115–16.

195 CIA, "India," *The World Factbook*, November 18, 2009, https://www.cia.gov/library/publications/the-world-factbook/geos/in.html.

196 Unni Krishnan, "IMF Raises India's Growth Forecast to 9.7% for 2010," *Bloomberg Businessweek*, October 7, 2010, http://www.businessweek.com/news/2010-10-07/imf-raises-india-s-growth-forecast-to-9-7-for-2010.html.

197 Rama Lakshmi, "India's Young Entrepreneurs See Opportunity in Slump," *Washington Post*, May 15, 2009, http://www.washingtonpost.com/wp-dyn/content/article/2009/05/14/AR2009051404150.html.

198 World Bank, "Revised Poverty Estimates: What Does This Mean for India?" http://www.worldbank.org.in/WBSITE/EXTERNAL/COUNTRIES/SOUTHASIAEXT/INDIAEXTN/0,,contentMDK:21880804~pagePK:141137~piPK:141127~theSitePK:295584,00.html.

199 "Nearly 80 pct of India Lives on Half Dollar a Day," *Reuters*, August 10, 2007, http://www.reuters.com/article/idUSDEL218894.

200 Damian Grammaticas, "Indian Economy 'To Overtake UK'," *BBC News*, January 24, 2007, http://news.bbc.co.uk/2/hi/6294409.stm. See also Pradumma B. Rana and J. Malcolm Dowling, *South Asia: Rising to the Challenge of Globalization* (Singapore: World Scientific Publishing, 2009), 1.

201 Friedman, *The World Is Flat*, 625.

202 Parthapratim Pal and Jayati Ghosh, "Inequality in India: A Survey of Recent Trends," DESA Working Paper 45 (July 2007), http://www.un.org/esa/desa/papers/2007/wp45_2007.pdf, 25.

203 World Bank, "India Development Policy Review: Inclusive Growth and Service Delivery: Building on India's Success" (2006), http://siteresources.worldbank.org/SOUTHASIAEXT/Resources/DPR_overview.pdf, 2.

204 Parthapratim Pal and Jayati Ghosh, "Inequality in India," 25.

205 See Kaushik Basu, *The Retreat of Democracy and Other Itinerant Essays on Globalization, Economics, and India* (Delhi: Permanent Black, 2007).

206 "The World Turned Upside Down," 7.

207 India Business Directory, "Globalization, Income Inequalities and Regional Disparities in India," n.d., http://business.mapsofindia.com/globalization/income-inequalities-regional-disparities-india.html. See also Madhu Purnima Kishwar, *Deepening Democracy: Challenges of Governance and Globalization in India* (New York: Oxford University Press, 2006).

208 Emily Wax, "A 'Broken People' in Booming India," *The Washington Post*, July 21, 2007, http://www.washingtonpost.com/wp-dyn/content/article/2007/06/20/AR2007062002535.html.

209 "Mixed Messages in Hunger Report," *BBC News*, October 16, 2009, http://news.bbc.co.uk/2/hi/8309979.stm.
210 "Malnutrition among Indian Children Worse than in Sub-Saharan Africa," *Medindia*, December 22, 2007, http://www.medindia.net/news/Malnutrition-Among-Indian-Children-Worse-Than-in-Sub-Saharan-Africa-30955-1.htm.
211 Organisation for Economic Co-operation and Development, "Economic Survey of India 2007: India's Key Challenges to Sustaining High Growth" (2007), http://www.oecd.org/document/56/0,3343,en_2649_34571_39431864_1_1_1_1,00.html.
212 "India English Growth 'Too Slow'," *BBC News*, November 18, 2009, http://news.bbc.co.uk/2/hi/south_asia/8365631.stm.
213 De Blij, *The Power of Place*, 160.
214 Steve D. Derné, *Globalization on the Ground: New Media and the Transformation of Culture, Class, and Gender in India* (London: Sage Publications, 2008), 10.
215 Ibid., 16.
216 Dipankar Gupta, *Mistaken Modernity: India between Worlds* (New Delhi: HarperCollins, India, 2000), 9.
217 Ruchira Ganguly-Scrase and Timothy J. Scrase, *Globalization and the Middle Classes in India: The Social and Cultural Impact of Neoliberal Reforms* (Oxford: Routledge, 2009), 2.
218 Ibid., 3.
219 Pramad K. Nayar, "India Goes to the Blogs: Cyberspace, Identity, Community," in K. Moti Gokulsing and Wimal Dissanayake, eds., *Popular Culture in a Globalised India* (Oxford: Routledge, 2009), 207–22.
220 See, for example, M. K. Raghavendra, "Local Resistance to Global Bangalore: Reading Minority Indian Cinema," in ibid., 15–27.
221 Nalin Mehta, "'Breaking News, Indian Style': Politics, Democracy, and Indian News Television," in ibid., 35.
222 Anna Morcom, "Indian Popular Culture and Its 'Others': Bollywood Dance and Anti-*nautch* in Twenty-First-Century Global India," in ibid., 126. Advertising in India also reflects hybridization. See Lynne Ciochetto, "Advertising in a Globalised India," in ibid., 192–204.
223 K. Moti Gokulsing and Wimal Dissanayake, "Introduction," in ibid., 8.
224 Ram Puniyani, "India: Religious Nationalism and Changing Profile of Popular Culture," in ibid., 95.

CHAPTER 8

Regional dynamics
Russia, Latin America, the Middle East, and Africa

> Behind the containment perimeter [in Asia] ... the US was able to construct and defend a liberal regional order which generated the fastest economic growth of any region in the world. By the late 1980s this was inducing all the states of the region – except North Korea – to join the globalization project.[1]

> Paranoia does not necessarily invalidate existential fears. But the geopolitical situation would seem to preclude any external threats to the regime except the more subtle one brought about not by aggression or economics but by insidious globalization that could transform Burman culture over time.[2]

Unlike Europe, North America, and Asia, a number of regions have lagged in terms of globalization. Although each of them contains states that are rapidly globalizing, on the whole, lagging regions tend to be areas that are relatively isolated, economically less developed, subject to more violent conflicts and ecological degradation, and to have countries that are governed by authoritarian regimes. In some cases, relative isolation is the product of conditions beyond countries' control. In other instances, governments successfully resist globalization by isolating themselves. Globalization, as Jonathan Kirshner argues, "is not an irresistible force, nor an arbiter of unbending laws. Rather, processes of globalization reshape the costs, benefits, and consequences of pursuing different policy choices."[3]

In any event, what used to be called the "third world" – Asia, Africa, and Latin America – have endured the global recession more successfully than richer countries in Europe and North America, and are the site of some of the world's most rapidly growing economies, notably Brazil and Turkey. A number of poor countries actually enjoy higher incomes than before the global financial crisis struck.[4]

GLOBALIZATION AND THE RUSSIAN FEDERATION

Although part of the Russian Federation is European, its vast territory stretches to Asia and the Pacific so that the country merits separate treatment. "By all accounts," declares Alexander Cooley,

> globalization played a critical role in the collapse of the Soviet Union. The Soviet Union was unable to bear the opportunity costs of maintaining a completely self-sufficient system of economic organization and, by the late 1980s, no longer could compete with a Western economic community that reaped the efficiency advantages of global production chains, international financial markets, and a liberal international trading system.[5]

To this must be added a growing recognition among Soviet elites that "a moral resurrection was essential."[6]

The end of the Cold War and the collapse of the Soviet empire brought the demise of the so-called Second World, thereby creating a single global economy. No longer did Russia enjoy exclusive trading relations with the countries of the Soviet bloc. Just as the demise of the British Empire had brought an end to imperial preference, so the end of the Soviet empire exposed the bloc countries to the chill winds of a competitive global system. In addition, Russia was confronted with bureaucratic conflicts, the spread of "official" corruption, and links between officials and proliferating mafias.

The Soviet Union had been the leader of a bloc of socialist countries and a global superpower. What, then, was to be Russia's new post-Cold War identity? Was it principally European owing to culture and geography?[7] Russia is unlikely to gain admission to the European Union (EU) and has witnessed most of its former "satellites" in Central Europe joining the EU and NATO (North Atlantic Treaty Organization). It was infuriated by the willingness of the Czech Republic and Poland to accept the US-proposed ABM system, the imposition by the European Union of a visa requirement for movement between Russia and the Russian region of Kaliningrad, Russia's separation from Russian minorities in the "near abroad," the political "revolutions" in Ukraine, Georgia, and the Kyrgyz Republic, and the (increasingly unlikely) prospect that Ukraine and Georgia might be admitted to NATO.[8] Indeed, Russian leaders have expressed concern over European influence in former Soviet republics – Armenia, Azerbaijan, Belarus, Georgia, Moldova, and Ukraine.[9] Thus, a second possible identity for Russia is that of "Soviet people,"[10] that is, a sphere of influence embracing other Soviet peoples who are no longer united in a single state, with an eye towards regaining its superpower status. Such thinking is connected with an identity that Blum terms "Eurasianism."[11]

The loss of Russia's political influence led its leaders to seek alternative ties to the defunct Soviet bloc. One is the Commonwealth of Independent States, formed as the USSR was breaking up, which is a loose symbolic grouping of former Soviet republics. A second is the Shanghai Cooperation Organization established in 2001 by Russia, China, Tajikistan, Kazakhstan, Uzbekistan, and the Kyrgyz Republic. It, too, is a loose organization with the aim of building trust among members and cooperation in political, security, diplomatic, and economic matters. Some see such groups as a Russian effort to "balance" the United States, but to date China and the other members have avoided any such project. A third, and in many ways the most important grouping, is informally known as the BRIC (Brazil, Russia, India, and China).[12] As we have mentioned, the four are significant emerging economies that have found common interests in trade negotiations with the United States and the European Union and are rapidly becoming major economic actors. Russia is the economic laggard in the group, and Russia's leaders appear to be mainly interested in transforming the group into a political bloc.[13]

"As elsewhere around the world," according to Blum, "the overall tendency in Russian identity formation is what we may call hybridization, consisting of a combined effort to absorb certain hegemonic practices, while also rejecting their 'excessive' or offensive cultural concomitants, and simultaneously asserting a distinct, supposedly indigenous identity narrative." This reflects "a perceived need to engage globalization with innovative thinking, designed to embrace rationalist models – including market institutions and individualism – while at the same time retaining something quintessentially Russian in philosophical and ideological terms."[14]

Although Russia has moved up significantly since 2009, it remains only a moderately globalized country, ranking 52nd of the political entities ranked in the 2011 KOF Index of Globalization, with many of those below it from the less developed world. It remained low (110th) in economic globalization, suggesting a degree of economic isolation, while ranking relatively higher in social (39th) and political globalization (47th).[15] Russia ranked only 74th in networked readiness and 63rd in economic competitiveness,[16] a problem to which Russian President Dmitry Medvedev has repeatedly alluded in public. Russia also ranked 51st of 133 countries in innovation and tied with Guinea-Bissau, Kenya, Laos, Papua New Guinea, and Tajikistan near the global bottom of countries in regards to perceived corruption.[17] Soviet successor states in Central Asia for the most part are seen as among the most corrupt in the world and, excepting the Kyrgyz Republic, are as authoritarian as the old Soviet Union was.[18]

"Russia," concedes Solovyev, "is clearly not among the leading nations in the globalization process. But it has also ceased to be a closed society."[19] Relatively few Russian economic enterprises have concluded transnational alliances. Moscow ranked only 19th among the sixty cities measured in the *Foreign Policy* 2008 Global Cities Index.[20] What is happening is a "complex dialectic between a Russian Federation both deeply embroiled in as well as affected by globalization, and often at the same time just as actively trying to erect barriers between itself and the world of global dynamics."[21] Since the end of the Cold War and the "opening" of Russia to the world, the country has experienced economic hardship, financial volatility, demographic decline, ethnic violence, cultural dilution, and sovereign incursions. While remaining a major military power, Russia is only now trying to regain some of the status and political influence it enjoyed as the Soviet Union.

The Russian government has skillfully sought to adapt to globalization's encroachments to promote modernization, while utilizing them to rally domestic political support against the "unjust" aspects of globalization,[22] impose authoritarian policies, and reestablish control from the center. For instance, Russian educational reform has begun to promote the value of competitiveness that is necessary in a globalized world. It has become involved in Europe's Bologna Process and increasingly emphasizes "a knowledge society."[23] "These tensions," argues Blum, "are encapsulated in the notion of 'managed democracy,' understood as an attempt to achieve control and modernization by muzzling the press, curtailing independent civic organizations, eliminating open electoral politics in favor of appointment or constrained competition, and replacing formal political institutions with informal institutions answerable to the president."[24]

"It is here," Hedetoft and Blum write, "that the 'war on terrorism' enters the fray as a master signifier, allowing Vladimir Putin and his version of Russian statism simultaneously to play the globally cooperative card (pro-EU and partly pro-American, too), step up internal security measures, agitate and take action against Chechen separatists/terrorists, curtail democratic reform, nationalize energy production and other vital economic sectors, and increase his domestic approval rating – all in the name of protecting the interests of the Russian people."[25] Putin describes a country under siege by terrorists and cheated by a newly enriched class of private oligarchs such as Vladimir Gusinsky and Boris Berezhovsky.

Under Putin, Russian nationalism has acted to limit the impact of globalization and reinforce state capacity. This "strident nationalist discourse" is the result of what Blum describes as "mounting social strains, leading to widespread anxiety and defensiveness," which are "especially evident in response to migration, the still-unsettled conflict in Chechnya, and the associated threat from radical Islam."[26] Globalization combined with the end of the Soviet superpower and the search for a new national identity have produced "profound tensions emerging in the state's attempt to control borders and prevent disintegration, while at the same time seeking to advance economic integration and profitable forms of cross-border exchange."[27] A different view is expressed by Solovyev who sees Russia's "ethnic and cultural nationalism" as "a break with the prior tradition of the supranational, imperial identity," reflecting "the transformation of Russia from a supranational, missionary, and imperial state to a national state, and the need for a positive national philosophy that accompanies this change."[28]

Xenophobic Russian nationalism is fostered by the continued threat posed by secessionist currents, especially in the North Caucasus, as well as pressures for the revival of regional autonomy, and spreading Islamic fundamentalism. The tension between the regions and the center is also reflected in rivalries that, for example, led to the fall of Moscow's long-time powerful mayor, Yuri Luzhkov.[29] Whether the coterie around Putin that governs the country can remain united is an open question.[30]

As elsewhere, Russia's boundaries are increasingly porous, especially in comparison with those of the Soviet period, and Russia in a variety of ways is less isolated from the external world than in the past. Andrey Korotayev and Darya Khaltourina attribute part of the dramatic post-Cold War rise in Russia's mortality rate "to the diffusion of teen subcultures and countercultures, including the tolerance and even propagation of drug use," arguing that "Russia's inclusion in global drug trafficking networks has further exposed the Trojan Horse of globalization."[31] However, old-fashioned alcohol is still a major heath problem.

Russia remains a multinational state – a factor that complicates and in some respects encourages Russian nationalism[32] – and the center is particularly sensitive to horizontal identity links between regions in Russia and outsiders. Putin has sought to balance regional autonomy and national interests, limiting the former by institutional changes and assertive nationalist rhetoric. Although improbable, Russia itself might eventually disintegrate, especially if regional inequality and demographic disparities continue to grow. In this sense, political globalization poses perceived security perils to Russian unity. Under Boris Yeltsin, "there was a great deal of reluctance to allow high levels of cross-national, institutionalized cooperation, on the grounds that this might encourage separatism in the Far East and in regions bordering Europe,"[33] and this concern has persisted under the joint rulership of Putin and Medvedev. As Blum observes, "Chechnya doubtless looms as a cautionary tale for many would-be separatists"; and "authorities in most ethnic regions of the country have tried to manage the identity formation process, so as to limit the potentially centrifugal effects of ethnic cultural revivalism."[34] Nevertheless, insurrection in Chechnya has spread across the northern Caucasus and introduced terrorism into Russia itself.[35]

Globalization has expanded Russia's perception of security, much as it has done elsewhere. As Fenenko observes, although military issues still loom large, "the language of security has been transformed to include new ideas, such as 'global antiterrorist coalition,' 'nation building in failed states,' and 'horizontal networks' of Islamist organizations as well as criminal groups – from drug dealers and illegal suppliers of fissile materials to shadow financial associations."[36] Democracy, migration, and declining population are also viewed as security threats by many Russians, as is ethnic revivalism.

Former President Yeltsin, who sought to link Russia more closely to the West, was prepared to encourage the growth of civil society in post-Soviet Russia, especially service rather than advocacy groups. Many of Russia's new nongovernmental organizations (NGOs) were created with Western advice and funding and failed to engage and work with existing groups left over from the Soviet period. New NGOs therefore came to be regarded as potentially subversive, especially in light of the role of foreign NGOs in fostering political change in Ukraine and Georgia.[37] The transnational links of many of these groups simultaneously made them attractive to Russia's intelligentsia and objects of suspicion to Russia's leaders. Although there is regional variation in the country, post-Soviet NGOs, especially those receiving foreign funding, remain largely isolated from society partly because of their foreign origins and partly because of the continued presence of Soviet-era institutions.[38]

The status of civil society in Russia deteriorated after Putin succeeded Yeltsin as president. "Since Putin became president ... the Russian government has sought to redefine the relation between state and society to reassert the sovereign status of the state over society."[39] While Putin was prepared to encourage NGOs that would help modernize the country, much as Communist Party-controlled groups functioned in the Soviet Union, "organizations that transgress approved boundaries ... and particularly environmental and human rights organizations, have been targeted by Putin and his allies not simply as hostile to administration policies but also as alien forces outside the body politic, serving foreign interests."[40] Thus, in 2006 a Federal Registration Center was established, with authority to register and, if necessary, to close NGOs.

In sum, the prognosis for civil society in Russia remains bleak. Marc Morjé Howard concludes that for Russia, along with other post-Soviet countries, "it is unlikely that citizen participation in voluntary organizations will increase significantly" and that "barring any miraculous turnarounds, the structural impediments of the state will serve to keep organizational membership very low."[41] Richter sees in this situation a larger dilemma for Russia. "Putin," he writes, "hopes to restore the sovereignty of the Russian state, both domestically as the embodiment of collective will and internationally as a great power."

> He cannot do both. To achieve his international goals, he must be able to integrate Russia into the world economy and develop individual initiative with links to the outside world. His domestic goals, meanwhile, require a vision of Russian society as an organic body with clear boundaries with the outside world. To the extent that the state needs to patrol these boundaries to meet domestic needs, it will fail in securing international goals, and vice versa.[42]

The desire to limit trans-border identities for political reasons contrasts with recognition of the importance of trans-border economic links and the need for foreign investment and technology. Politically and economically, Russia's post-Cold War links were forged largely with the European Union, especially Germany, though, owing to disparate values and sociocultural factors, were not fully institutionalized. "For more than a decade and a half," write Vodichev and Lamin, "Russia has searched for a way to cooperate with the European Union and to find the best ways to pursue this strategy."

> However, despite expectations, this process has been far from easy. There have been many obvious reasons for these difficulties. It is widely believed that they were due to Russia's natural and geographic circumstances (i.e., its size and location on two continents), economic factors (an economy that is unstable and structurally inconsistent with European standards), and politics (the limited nature of liberal reforms and an inclination toward the political ambitions characteristic of a former "superpower").[43]

It is in the economic sphere that Russo-European relations are most significant. Each needs the other. Europe depends on Russian energy resources, and Russia depends on European purchases of its oil and gas and exports of high-tech products to Russia. The EU is the source of over 50 percent of Russian imports and in return receives almost 45 percent of Russia's exports. (The United States and China receive 6 and 5.8 percent respectively.)[44] The nationalization of Russia's energy sector and the episodic interruption by state-controlled Gazprom of Russian natural gas to Ukraine and, therefore, to other European countries that depend on pipelines running through Ukraine, have been perceived by Europeans and Americans as politically motivated and as threatening actions that raise questions about Russian reliability.

In some respects, as Bradshaw observes, "it would seem that Russia wishes to erect barriers to protect its economy and polity against globalization, which it sees as a Western neoliberal project; but Russia cannot remain immune from globalization and seemingly has no choice but to play the global game – even if the rules are not of its making – to sustain its economy, to gain recognition, and to curry influence."[45] The Russian government seeks to profit from exports, notably energy exports, but wants to limit foreign leverage in its economy. Although the last major country outside the World Trade Organization, Russia has joined the WTO but seems, at best, lukewarm about the development because of the potential impact on domestic enterprises. Russia has also pursued bilateral trade relations as well as a customs union with Belarus and Kazakhstan.[46] Liberalizing Russia's economy is a challenge, because its firms, outside of the energy sector, remain largely uncompetitive and because of uncertainty about legal property rights. Nevertheless, foreign investment remains critical owing to the need to modernize and expand the country's energy industry.

Russian exports and, therefore, the country's economic globalization, as noted above, focus on commodities. Russia is the world's largest producer of oil and largest exporter of natural gas. As of September 2011, energy exports alone accounted for 50 percent of Russia's budget revenue and commodities (metals and energy) accounted for 80 percent,[47] leading Bradshaw to declare that "Russia's international comparative advantage is as a supplier of natural resources and little else."[48] Russia's economy is heavily dependent on global commodity prices and commodity speculation. Foreign direct investment (FDI) in Russia grew significantly from 2004 ($9.4 billion) to 2007 ($27.8 billion), most of which involved commodity extraction.[49] However, that is still less than half the amount flowing into China. Potential investors became cautious about investing in Russia after the government effectively forced its biggest oil company, Yukos, into bankruptcy, sold most of its assets to Rosneft, the state oil company, arrested and imprisoned its founder Mikhail Khodorkovsky in 2005,[50] and imprisoned his attorney.[51]

Bradshaw concludes that "the sectoral and regional consequences of Russia's trade relations and pattern of foreign investment are clearly serving to aggravate regional inequality," and the country's "engagement with the global economy is serving to promote imbalance and inequality."[52] Both trends threaten political and social stability in Russia. In addition, economic liberalization has produced significant economic and status disparities at home among individuals and among regions. As Blum observes, "by accentuating the distinctions between 'winners and losers,' globalization is likely to place additional strains on Russia's still inchoate national identity"; and if "the disparity between developed and underdeveloped regions continues to grow, the combination of ethnic identities, globalization flows, and relative poverty may produce widely destabilizing results."[53]

LATIN AMERICA

In the 1960s and 1970s, much of Latin America was significantly influenced by neo-Marxist *dependencia* or dependency theory. Ramón Grosfoguel argues there were three events in the early 1960s that gave rise to the dependency school. The first was a crisis in the region's import substitution industrialization (ISI) strategy:

All the problems that the ISI strategy was supposed to solve had been aggravated instead. Rather than importing consumer goods, Latin America started importing capital goods in the early 1950s. The latter were more expensive than the former. Moreover, most of the new industries were created by multinational corporations in search of Latin America's local markets. As a result, by the early 1960s, after a decade of import substitution industrialization, balance of payments deficits, trade deficits, increased marginalized populations, and inflation continued to affect the region.[54]

The second event was the Cuban Revolution, which was seen as "living proof of the possibility for an alternative path of development 'outside the world capitalist system'."[55] The third was the emergence of a group of young intellectuals – some influenced by the Cuban Revolution and others democratic socialists – that became known as the dependency school.

After decades of economic stagnation that resulted from Latin America's flirtation with a combination of import substitution, state intervention, and autarky that produced heavy debt burdens and the "lost decade" of the 1980s,[56] Latin America began to adopt market- and trade-friendly neoliberal policies of deregulation, free movement of investment capital, regional economic integration, and trade liberalization. José Bell Lara and Delia Luisa López argue that such policies became the means of "imposing neoliberalism all across the Americas"[57] because foreign exchange was necessary to repay foreign debts, and countries had to restructure their economies towards the production of exports, as William Robinson contends, "in accordance with the changing structure of demand on the world market."[58] The debt crisis had eroded earlier gains in reducing poverty through social welfare. Among other factors influencing the shift were the Bush administration's Enterprise of the Americas initiative and President Clinton's Free Trade Area of the Americas proposal, as well as the growing emphasis on neoliberal capitalism in the United States and Great Britain.[59] Between 1989 and 1999, the trade in goods as a percentage of gross domestic product (GDP) for Latin America and the Caribbean in general grew from 10.2 to 18.2 percent,[60] although there remained considerable variation in the level of globalization across Latin America.

Overall, economic growth in Latin America jumped following the "lost decade." Between 2003 and 2008, economic growth averaged 5.5 percent annually with little inflation, and the region's economy came through the global recession relatively unscathed.[61] Nevertheless, growth in productivity remains low; income distribution, very unequal; dependence on commodity exports, high; infrastructure, inadequate; and high levels of violence are still a problem in several countries.[62]

One concern, expressed by David Keeling, is that economic development in Latin America has failed to take sufficient notice of national peculiarities and differences. "As a result, regions, peoples, and places frequently are reduced to insignificant actors or omitted from the analysis altogether," while "an increasing percentage of national income or wealth is concentrated in the hands of fewer people" producing "social polarization or the 'development gap'."[63] Carol Graham emphasizes how educational differences account for social and economic inequality: "Such inequalities are often exacerbated by integration into global markets, particularly when skilled labour benefits disproportionately from the process and increases wage gaps across sectors, as has been the case in Latin America."[64] In Latin America, "those with higher levels of education are gaining high marginal returns compared to the rest of society, while those with secondary education are seeing decreasing marginal returns compared to those with only primary education."[65]

With few exceptions, then, Latin America's abandonment of dependency theory has intensified its integration into the globalized economy. As Keeling expresses it: "The shift from an ideology of *dirigismo* (state-directed development) to one of *neoliberalismo* (state disengagement) has opened up the region to the global capitalist regime of finance, production, marketing, and consumption, which has altered irrevocably the way in which goods and services are provided, spatial relationships are structured and cultural identities are defined and understood."[66] As a result, the major countries of Latin America – Chile, Argentina, Mexico, and Brazil – are rapidly globalizing and have become middle ranking states in this respect. They were ranked 33rd, 72nd, 75th, and 78th respectively by the 2011 KOF Index, with Argentina and Brazil scoring high on political globalization and Chile the regional leader in economic globalization.[67]

In terms of global competitiveness, Chile ranked 30th of 139 countries and 39th in networked readiness. Brazil ranked 58th in competitiveness and 59th in networked readiness, having made considerable progress from 2007–8 when it ranked 72nd and 59th in these indexes. Mexico ranked 66th in competitiveness and 67th in networked readiness; and Argentina ranked 97th in competitiveness and 87th in networked readiness.[68] The percentage of internet users in Latin America and the Caribbean is, moreover, higher than the global average, at about 3.2 percent, growing from 18 million internet users at the end of 2000 to 179 million in 2009. Overall, Latin America is host to about 10 percent of the world's internet users.[69] Brazil, where Google is extremely popular,[70] accounts for 67.5 million internet users, with Mexico next with 23.9 million users and Argentina with 20 million.[71]

Some observers, nevertheless, doubt how effective Latin America's neoliberal reforms have been in fostering the region's development. Thus, Rodrik argues:

> [D]uring the 1990s Latin America grew more slowly not only compared to other parts of the world, in particular Asia, but also compared to its own performance in the 1960s and 1970s. That is a *striking* empirical fact, the importance of which is hard to downplay. After all, the Latin America of the 1960s and 1970s is a region of import substitution, macroeconomic populism, and protectionism, while the Latin America of the 1990s is a region of openness, privatization and liberalization. The cold fact is that per capita economic growth performance has been abysmal during the 1990s by any standards.[72]

Between 1980 and 2000, per capita income growth in Latin America averaged only 1.5 per cent per annum.[73]

Not surprisingly, there are still vigorous critics of globalization in Latin America and a variety of anti-neoliberal social movements.[74] Will Braun, for example, explores the tensions between Bolivians who oppose the sale of their country's oil and those corporations that seek access to it. After President Gonzalo Sánchez de Lozada agreed to sell Bolivian oil to the United States in 1996, popular opposition forced his resignation. Braun describes how Oscar Olivera, a figure in the Bolivian anti-globalization movement, views the oil issue as part of a struggle for public control of decisions that affect everyday life, notably for a greater share of oil profits, and who argues that Bolivians feel the "violence of neoliberalism" in their daily lives.[75] Walden Bello concludes that Latin America is in retreat from neoliberal globalization, a tendency that he sees most visible in Bolivia, Argentina, and Venezuela whose president Hugo Chávez is promoting a regional economic grouping called ALBA based on non-neoliberal principles.[76] And, in February 2010, Latin American leaders, led by Brazil, proposed a new regional bloc called the South American Union that would exclude the United States and Canada and diminish the prospects of the proposed Free Trade Area of the Americas.[77]

On the one hand, "The political trend in the region represents a broad turn away from the pro-globalization economic reforms that were dominant in political agendas during the 1990s" because "policies designed to open markets and increase trade liberalization did not deliver on reducing income inequality." As a result, there have emerged "populist movements that blame global capitalism for the financial setbacks and the greater volatility in economic life" and that call for "alter-globalization."[78] On the other, Peru and Colombia have signed free trade agreements (FTAs) with the US, and Chile remains committed to neoliberal globalization.

It is evident that attitudes towards globalization in Latin America vary significantly. According to a 2006 opinion poll conducted by *Barómetro Iberoamericano*, the percentage of respondents who said globalization was having a positive impact on their country ranged from a high of 80 percent in Chile to a low of 30 percent in Argentina. Among those countries in which globalization was popular were Brazil (72 percent approval), Guatemala (64 percent), Peru (61 percent), and Colombia (56 percent). By contrast, globalization had less support in Bolivia (38 percent approval), Ecuador (40 percent), and Mexico (43 percent).[79] Mexican responses may have been skewed somewhat by that country's special economic relationship through the North American Free Trade Agreement (NAFTA) with the United States.

Latin America's debt crises increased its involvement with the International Monetary Fund (IMF), and the experience was hardly an unalloyed success. "For a short period," according to John Ralston Saul, "it looked as if the IMF's punishing approach might actually work. For a dozen years most Latin American governments tried to follow the instructions laid down by the IMF, Western governments, and the private banks," but "in each case the recovery was followed, a few years later, by an even greater collapse." That seemed to reveal "that such prolonged austerity had weakened, not strengthened, the social-economic fabric."[80]

Among the myriad effects of economic globalization in at least parts of Latin America are growing public support for democracy and the market economy. This generalization obscures some real differences, however. Chile, for example, embraced neoliberal market reforms in the late 1980s and joined the Organisation for Economic Co-operation and Development (OECD) of developed countries as its 31st member in 2010. Chile's neoliberalism is exemplified by its highly competitive retail sector.[81] By contrast, Brazil only haltingly adopted neoliberal policies. It fell behind other Latin American countries that adopted pro-market reforms in the early

1990s and is in the midst of transitional reforms that began in 1986 and continue to this day, softened by vigorous anti-poverty policies. Many Brazilians blame globalization for their economic difficulties in the 1990s, but Simon Schwartzman vigorously denies their claim: "A simplified view of the 1990s period was that, as the economy opened up, the waves of globalization destroyed the country's industry, while the shrinking of the public sector led to a fall in the provision of public services, increasing poverty, social inequity, and misery."

According to this view, globalization was the main culprit. This, however, is incorrect. It ignores the long years of inflation and institutional disorganization of the previous decade, to which the policies of economic stabilization, the control of public spending, and the opening of the economy tried to respond. It ignores also the substantial gains in several indicators of social wellbeing that took place in the 1990s.[82]

An important step for Brazil before adopting reforms was the country's transition to democracy in the 1980s.[83] The government's share of GDP has continued to rise and the state is still regarded as integral to economic development, partly the result of the roots of its recent leaders, Presidents Luiz Inácio Lula da Silva and Fernando Henrique Cardoso, in the country's political left.[84] Nevertheless, as Mark London and Brian Kelly observe in relation to Brazil's eager adoption of the internet, "Brazil has joined what Tom Friedman calls the 'flat world.'"[85]

Brazil is one of the BRICs and a leading member of the G-20, and it emerged from the global recession better than most countries. It is a major source of agricultural exports and seeks to pass the United States as the world's leading source of food exports by 2025.[86] It is also becoming a key source of oil and other raw materials, even as it has enjoyed some success in reducing domestic inequality and poverty. The country accounts for roughly 40 percent of the region's GDP, and it is likely to become one alternative to China as a site for industrial outsourcing.[87] "Brazil is already the biggest economy in Latin America and the 10th-biggest in the world. By 2050, it will likely move into fourth place, leapfrogging countries including Germany, Japan and the U.K., according to a study by Goldman Sachs. Clearly, Brazil has turned a corner – and is now a nation with the heft, ambition and economic fundamentals to become a world power."[88]

The socialist turn in Venezuela, Ecuador, and Bolivia (as well as Cuba) has isolated them from globalization's neoliberal currents and made it difficult for them to attract FDI. Ecuador, for example, defaulted on a third of its foreign debt in December 2008, an action that has greatly complicated its efforts to get additional loans,[89] and the country has become an alleged "capital of financial crime."[90] Much of Central America, excepting Costa Rica and Panama, remain impoverished and are on the verge of becoming narco-states, with Guatemala, Honduras, and El Salvador among the world's most violent societies.[91]

Latin Americans seek to diversify trading partners, and the opening of Latin American economies has attracted China's attention. China seeks access to the region's raw materials, including agricultural products and oil reserves. Mandarin is beginning to compete with English as a language of trade in the region, because, as Miguel Angela Poveda, president of the Colombo-China Chamber of Commerce in Bogotá, observes, the cultural difference makes it necessary to do business "in their language."[92] Although that claim grossly underestimates China's trade personnel's command of both Spanish and English, it is an indication of shifting times.

Cultural globalization in Latin America reflects all three of Nederveen Pieterse's cultural paradigms. The initial colonization of Latin America by Spain and Portugal exemplified Huntington's clash of civilizations. In time, however, the mixing of indigenous peoples with their conquerors and/or with African slaves produced hybridization, a result especially evident in Brazil. There is also, however, widespread evidence of Westernization or Americanization. George Ritzer and Elizabeth Malone, for instance, describe Rio de Janeiro's Rock in Rio Café: although it "has its local touches," developers were "very cognizant of American theme restaurants (eatertainment) and have made it clear that they have taken the lead from them in creating a spectacular chain of restaurants that include entry via monorail, changing projected imagery on the walls, and indoor fireworks." The authors somewhat sourly add that the eating experience puts "little emphasis on the nature and quality of the food and much on the spectacular nature of the setting" and argue that the establishment poses a "threat" to "indigenous culture."[93]

THE MIDDLE EAST

"Globalization," as Masoud Kavoossi declares, "presents both opportunities and threats for the Middle East: opportunities in the sense of economic abundance, freedom of choice, and greater cultural interactions; threats in the form of economic instability, political insecurity, and cultural hegemony."[94] Transnational corporations are "the embodiments and principal agents of globalization of the region."[95] In addition, the spread of global communications and information technologies, combined with increasingly skilled young elites, have begun to undermine the region's ossified and hierarchical political structures and limit authoritarian leaders' resort to traditional instruments of control and coercion.

Although the Middle East is unusually vulnerable to external intervention, the major countries in the region are poorly integrated into global trade and financial networks[96] and rank relatively low in indexes of globalization. The Arab Middle East is, as Marc Lynch observes, characterized by "state-dominated economies, relatively closed borders, controlled flows of information, low levels of domestic liberalization, and a highly ambivalent relationship with Western cultural products." It is also "almost completely excluded from the flows of private capital that have driven globalized finance."[97] The region attracts "less than 2 percent of FDI in the developing world – and all told the entire region receives less foreign direct investment (FDI) than Sweden."[98] Regional exceptions are Jordan and Israel, although these neighbors have quite different globalization profiles. Jordan is politically more integrated globally than Israel, and Israel is economically the more integrated of the two. In addition, the region as a whole has been affected by large-scale labor migration, accompanied by the informal *hawala* system of moving funds, and transnational media such as the satellite television stations *Al Jazeera* and *al-Arabiya*.

Overall, Jordan ranked 38th (38th politically, 52nd economically, and 51st socially), and Israel ranked 34th (27th economically, 59th socially, and 57th politically) in the 2011 KOF Globalization Index. By contrast, Turkey was ranked overall 59th, Saudi Arabia 71st, Egypt 76th, Syria 141st, Iran 160th, and Iraq 196th.[99] As regards networked readiness and economic competitiveness, Israel ranked 25th and 24th, Saudi Arabia 40th and 21st, Jordan 40th and 65th, and Turkey 61st on both measures. Israel's rankings testify to its relative technological and economic prowess. Other regional states ranked much lower on these two measures, with Egypt 76th and 91st, Syria 94th and 97th, and no data for Iraq.[100] Satellite and cable usage did rise swiftly, increasing 61 percent in 1997 alone in Algeria, Egypt, Israel, Jordan, Lebanon, Morocco, Saudi Arabia, Syria, Tunisia, and Turkey and an additional 35 and 38 percent in the next two years following the arrival of *Al-Jazeera* (which played a key role in the tumultuous events that swept the region in 2011), Future TV, and LBC.[101]

Globalization, however, is widely viewed in the Middle East as a threat to indigenous Islamic culture. Anoushiravan Ehteshami argues that "the Middle East has been exposed to outside forces for a longer time than there have been modern states; on the surface globalization, following the colonial and imperial storms of recent centuries, should have posed no real new threat to the region, or at least should not be seen as threatening by these societies. Yet globalization has been seen across the MENA [Middle East and North Africa] region as posing both a challenge and a new kind of existential threat to the 'Muslim way of life'."[102]

Political Islam has been one response to the perceived threat of globalization to traditional institutions, although this is subject to different interpretations. Thus, Kurt Campbell insists that globalization per se was not the target of the 9/11 terrorist attacks. "On display is not globalization under siege, but rather the clash between modernization and tradition. Debates within Saudi Arabia, Egypt, Algeria, Pakistan, and Iran center only in the most trivial way on Western 'contamination,' such as by pop music and video games, of their cultures."[103] By contrast, Lynch argues that many in the region "worry about whether a place will remain for Islam in a globalizing world in the face of Americanization and a global culture of modernity." "Fear of this cultural onslaught has driven the efforts of Islamist conservatives, who have focused their energies on policing the public sphere for signs of blasphemy" and who see "the realm of culture as the primary battleground for the defense of Islamic authenticity and identity."[104]

In fact, the appeal of Islamic militants is rooted, as Michael Howard suggests, "in a peculiarly Islamic predicament that only intensified over the last half of the twentieth century: the challenge to Islamic culture and values posed by the secular and materialistic culture of the West, and the inability to come to terms with it." "This," he continues,

> is not a problem of poverty as against wealth, and it is symptomatic of Western materialism to suppose that it is. It is the far more profound and intractable confrontation between a theistic, land-based, and traditional culture, in a place little different from the Europe of the Middle Ages, and the secular material values of the Enlightenment.[105]

Lieber and Weisberg add that, rather than a clash of civilizations, what is taking place is a "clash *within* civilizations" involving the "transference of deep-seated rage about turmoil and humiliation within their own societies into bitter attacks upon the United States." Above all, this represents "a sublimation of anger and its redirection toward a source that has little to do with the problem in the first place."[106] Whatever the perspective, there is less in the way of cultural hybridity in the Middle East than in other regions.

Turkey is a major exception in this regard. That country still aspires to join the European Union, and its current government, while Islamic rather than secular, is moderate and generally tolerant. And, as unrest has spread across North Africa and the Middle East, Turkey as a Muslim democracy has increasingly become a model for the region and has sought to encourage the liberalization of the region's ruling authoritarian regimes, including that of neighboring Syria.[107]

Turkey, as Ersel Aydinli argues, "will benefit by coming to accept the geographic reality of its position as a bridge between East and West." Cultural hybridity is clearly the author's objective when he writes:

> As Turkey continues on its globalization journey towards the West, it will no doubt have to do so with the inclusion of its Middle Eastern identity as well. Turkey needs, therefore, to convince both itself and the West that its Middle Eastern connections can be an asset (in ideational and geopolitical terms), not just a source of insecurity and backwardness. If Turkey succeeds at doing this, the historical pendulum between globalization and security, which has always appeared as a dichotomous phenomenon, may be transformed into a complementary one.[108]

Turkey, along with Israel, is a rare example of functioning democracy in the region. In *The Economist*'s 2010 ranking of overall democracy for 167 countries, virtually all Arabic societies were ranked below 110, with Sudan (151), Djibouti (154), Libya (158), and Saudi Arabia (160) near the bottom of the rankings.[109]

Economic globalization, with the exception of oil, has only begun to permeate the region. The Middle East "has hesitated more than any other region of the world to adopt the forms needed to benefit from the new international division of labor."[110] Kavoossi argues that the region is, however, at last acquiring a larger role in global business, as countries diversify their economies and economic growth accelerates. Greater economic integration of the region would facilitate this process, but political conflicts, rapid population growth, high unemployment, authoritarian rulers, and cultural traditions pose obstacles to regional integration.[111] Political divisions in the region and within many of its countries, as well as weak state institutions, are constraints on economic development and globalization. Traditional clan and tribal affiliations persist. Aggestam et al. write that a "feature of the Arab states today . . . is their almost exclusive reliance on a neo-patrimonial or clientelist system of governance." "This mode of government can also be reinforced, depending on the country, by confessional politics and/or communitarian affiliation/cooptation whether tribal, ethnic, or religious."[112]

In 2011, the Arabic Middle East and North Africa became the scene of what may become a sea change that will involve the region more deeply in economic, political, and social globalization. After long-time authoritarian leaders in Tunisia and Egypt were overthrown by a generation of educated and technologically adept young middle-class professionals, aided by members of diasporas in the developed world,[113] a democratic "contagion" spread rapidly – Yemen, Bahrain, Jordan, and, most violently, Libya[114] and Syria.[115] Although a relative latecomer to the participation and skills revolutions brought by globalization, the region will almost certainly never be the same again. It will likely be an arena of conflict between Islamists and secular modernizers as well as between traditional elites and educated young professionals. In almost every country, the military remains an unpredictable factor in political life. One way or the other, events will profoundly alter the role of Muslim women, relations between Sunnis and Shias, and the age-old conflict between Israelis and Palestinians.

AFRICA

Africa is the world's least globalized region and constitutes much of the global "periphery." Countries such as Somalia (206th) and Equatorial Guinea (183rd) ranked near the bottom of the 2011 KOF Index of Globalization, while the Democratic Republic of Congo was dead last (208th) in economic globalization.[116] The most globalized sub-Saharan African countries according to KOF are the island nation of Mauritius (47th) and South Africa (50th), and they are also the highest-ranked sub-Saharan African countries in terms of networked readiness and economic competitiveness (Mauritius 51st and 55th; South Africa 52nd and 54th). In contrast, some of the largest African countries such as Nigeria, Angola, and the Democratic Republic of Congo rank far down at 91st, 134th, and 173rd in terms of overall globalization, with Nigeria 90th in networked readiness and 127th in economic competitiveness.[117] Warwick's CSGR Globalisation Index (2004) scores Africa's overall globalization at 0.270, vividly contrasting with North America (0.872), Western Europe (0.754), and the Pacific (0.524).[118] For decades, the major African regional group, the Organization of African States (OAS), paid little attention to globalizing dynamics; but the establishment of its successor, the African Union (AU), owed much to growing "recognition of the significance of globalization."[119]

The benefits of globalization have not been as readily apparent elsewhere in a region with twenty-two of the world's twenty-five poorest countries, where average life expectancy is only fifty-two years,[120] and where (albeit far less importantly) less than 7 percent of the population enjoys internet access.[121] However, this picture is beginning to change. Between 2000 and 2010, six of the world's ten fastest-growing economies were in sub-Saharan Africa: Angola, Nigeria, Ethiopia, Chad, Mozambique, and Rwanda.[122] African civil society has expanded rapidly,[123] and new social movements are taking advantage of cyber technology. Still, despite the hopes associated with positive developments like the recent arrival of international fiber-optic cables in Kenya,[124] Africa as a whole remains a backwater of most forms of globalization.

According to Seyni N'Diaye,

> while opening up new prospects for economic growth, the new world economy presents daunting challenges for sub-Saharan African countries. Indeed, with less than a 2 percent share of world trade, modest investment flows, widespread

poverty, and conflicts breaking out in many parts of the continent, sub-Saharan Africa is confined to the peripheries of globalization.[125]

Notwithstanding efforts to encourage regional cooperation,[126] Africa's regionalization remains modest. Moreover, failing states and ethnic rivalries repeatedly fuel violence.[127] As Deborah Avant observes,

> the increased number of civil wars in Africa has led to increased financing for security by the private sector – extractive industries that want to retain access to natural resources, conservation organizations that want to preserve species, and humanitarian organizations that want to ease suffering – further deepening the diffusion of control over violence on that continent.[128]

Some view the impact of globalization on Africa as equivalent to neo-imperialism and/or assess it in terms of Africa's relationship with the World Bank and IMF and their structural adjustment programs. Tade Akin Aina describes "globalization and structural adjustment programs as identical twins, if not one in the same";[129] Dharam Ghai sees structural adjustment as a "phenomenon with an interdependent and mutually reinforcing relationship with the globalization process";[130] and John Briggs and Ian Yeboah hold that it is "invariably the mainstay of any representation of globalization."[131]

However, N'Diaye explains some of the many reasons why African states need fundamental reform. "A restrictive regulatory framework limited private initiatives to marginal activities, stifling the emergence of a true entrepreneurial class," while "the rare foreign capital that has flowed into the region has been contingent on investors being granted monopoly rights and protection from competition."[132] Structural adjustment, he believes, is imperative.

> High inflation rates, unproductive spending, fiscal imbalances, and large balance of payments deficits need to be contained. Only then will the state be able to devote more resources to the construction of adequate infrastructure (such as roads, ports and airports, electricity, and water), consolidation of the long-term bases of development (such as education, health care, and the environment), and the struggle against poverty and exclusion.[133]

Reform requires the state – regarded as less efficient than the private sector – to reduce its intervention in national economies. This will mean privatizing public enterprises and promoting competition and a free market in order to provide collective goods and attract foreign investment.

Equally important, N'Diaye argues, is the need for good governance, which he defines as transparency, deregulation, accountability, ending corruption, democratic freedoms, and an independent legal system.[134] According to Transparency International's 2010 Corruption Perceptions Index, nine of the twenty most corrupt countries were in Africa.[135] The M. Ibrahim Foundation, aided by Harvard's Kennedy School, formulated and published an index using measures of safety and rule of law, participation and human rights, sustainable economic opportunity and human development that ranked the quality of governance in forty-eight sub-Saharan countries.[136]

Those ranked highly in 2005 included Mauritius, Seychelles, Botswana, Cape Verde, and South Africa, while those at the bottom were Somalia, the Democratic Republic of Congo, Chad, and Sudan.[137] The M. Ibrahim Foundation also established a prize for Achievement in African Leadership to encourage good governance, and its first two winners were Joaquim Chissano (2007), president of Mozambique 1986–2005, and Festus Mogae (2008), president of Botswana 1998– 2008.[138]

Good governance in Africa has been a victim of the "resource curse." There is evidence that high exports of natural resources are negatively related to GDP growth.[139] It is also suggested that rentier states have no need to collect taxes and, therefore, are less responsive to social groups and tend towards corruption.[140] Oil-rich Nigeria epitomizes such states.[141] Paul Collier, who pioneered the "resource curse" thesis, observes that "most of the societies of the bottom billion have had weak governance."

> The consequence might be summarized in another simple formula: *nature + technology – regulation = plunder.* Plunder has dominated the history of natural assets in the poorest societies. What should have been the lifeline by which these societies haul themselves out of poverty, has instead produced wasted opportunity. Although basic economics suggests that the value of natural assets is dissipated by an equally costly struggle over possession, more sophisticated analysis shows that the outcome of that struggle can be even worse. Basic economics just predicts its cost to the participants, but not to bystanders. Because of this potential for harm the discovery of natural assets can turn into a curse.[142]

Although authoritarian regimes still hold sway in many African countries like Zimbabwe,[143] parts of Africa have become more democratic since 1991, when Benin's ruler was the first in Africa to be voted out peacefully. That feat has been emulated since then in nine other African countries, and other leaders are retiring because of term limits.[144] Elections have become increasingly common in the region, although they are still frequently rigged and losing incumbents too often refuse to step aside, as happened in 2011 in the Ivory Coast.[145]

According to the World Bank and IMF, reforms grounded in neoliberal economic theory, such as abolishing fixed exchange rates and deregulating currency markets, would allow Africa to emulate the success of the "Asian Tigers."[146] The goal of structural and institutional reforms is ostensibly "to allow the region to take full advantage of the benefits of globalization while minimizing the risks" and to foster "the growth and expansion of efficient enterprises."[147] Structural adjustment, the argument goes, is particularly important in overcoming the gap between society's urban and rural sectors. According to the "urban coalition thesis," African governments can gain sufficient votes to retain power by appeasing urban centers so they have no incentive to provide resources to their rural areas.[148] In much of Africa poverty has traditionally been rural (although it is becoming increasingly urbanized), and the agrarian sector of the economy receives little assistance. Hence, "the theoretical premise upon which SAP [structural adjustment programs] was constructed was to stand in defence of the rural poor against the 'rent seeking' and 'politically powerful' urban population." The aim was to "deconstruct most of the barriers that stifled rural agricultural production, increase the income level of the farmers, and adjust a government expenditure profile that was excessively in favour of the 'parasitic' urban population."[149]

The debate about the utility of structural adjustment programs is at the heart of discussions of globalization in the African context. Critics contend that globalization has exacerbated poverty in Africa. "Unlike most regions of the world," wrote Adejumobi, "as noted by the United Nations Economic Commission for Africa (UNECA), poverty in Africa is on the rise, despite an upward trend in real growth rate over the last five years."[150] Moreover, according to Logan and Mengisteab, "strong reform countries" have fared only moderately better than "weak reform countries." Their agricultural production and export volume is higher, but their GDP growth and export earnings remain roughly the same.[151] The overall impact of structural adjustment on poverty, while positive, thus is unclear.

Opponents make four distinct arguments against structural reform programs in Africa. The first is that such programs reflect Western values and that globalization has reduced the political influence of poor countries in global politics.

> Conditions in the domestic economies of those states have rapidly declined. Globalization has imposed immense pressure in the transformation of local communities in the Third World, a situation resulting in the rapid commodification of production, urbanization, exploitation of wage labour, growth in poverty, environmental degradation, and class polarization in those communities.[152]

Many citizens feel that such programs are forced upon them from outside and have no sense of ownership of them, thereby dooming the programs from the start.

Second, such programs have caused the "delegitimization and undermining of the African state and the erosion of its capacity to provide basic and other forms of services."[153] Demands for reducing government services, while increasing external funds for the same services, appear to many as violations of sovereignty. Privatization of formerly public services may raise costs in the name of profit, placing necessities beyond the reach of the poor. Therefore, Zine Magubane argues that

> one point on which all theorists, without regard to ideological orientation, seem to agree is that states on the periphery of the global capitalist economy (and variously called *third world, underdeveloped,* or *developing states*) are going to be faced with newer and even more profound challenges to their economic sovereignty and efficacy.[154]

Government losses of revenue owing to privatization of enterprises reduce state capacity to meet the collective challenges of crime, environmental degradation, and national defense,[155] and a "weak state can neither protect the interests of the poor nor guarantee order and due process necessary for their empowerment."[156] In sum, Adejumobi, citing John Sleeman, lists three reasons for state involvement in providing social services: (1) preventing greater poverty, (2) reducing income inequalities, and (3) facilitating "a process of socioeconomic empowerment in society."[157]

Third, structural adjustment policies have exacerbated inequality within and between countries, between men and women, and between classes. International trade, critics contend, benefits rich countries. It favors African exports of commodities and agricultural products – the prices for which lag behind the cost of importing manufactured goods – and produces greater debt burdens. Trade also is said to foster intrastate inequality. In the case of South Africa, for instance, Magubane contends that emphasizing

> export orientation and competitiveness underscores the importance of the domestic market and domestic demand as an engine for economic growth. The lack of attention to the domestic market also tends to put policies of redistribution, which would enhance the purchasing power of the majority, on the back burner and therefore privileges a growth-first-redistribution-second approach over the growth-through-redistribution approach.[158]

Efforts to transform local enterprises into competitive exporters were based on a premise fostered by the World Bank that exports were limited owing to protection from imports. As a result, trade liberalization encouraged the importation of yet more manufactured goods.

> Virtually no attention was paid to the possibility that growth could be driven by an increase in domestic consumption demand, rather than by exports. No attention was given to the possibility that the redistribution of income and the promotion of higher wages (both components of an inward investment strategy) could provide the engine for economic growth, development, and redistribution.[159]

Structural adjustment, it is also claimed, exacerbates urban inequality. In the case of Nigeria, according to Mohammed Bello Yunusa: "The gap in access to urban infrastructures widened under the structural adjustment (SAP) regime."[160] Nor, according to critics, have structural adjustment policies reduced economic inequality between social classes or between men and women.[161] This argument, of course, fails to address the urban–rural gap noted earlier.

A fourth criticism is that structural adjustment policies such as currency devaluation, higher interest rates, higher debt loads, and higher agricultural prices[162] have actually reduced the standard of living of many Africans. Adejumobi concludes that "SAP has caused more harm and pain to the poor than any tangible benefits." "SAP," he insists, "has had severe negative effects on poverty in many African countries. It increased the rate of unemployment, deteriorated income levels, undermined the provision of social services, promoted inflation, and exacerbated income inequalities."[163] Logan and Mengisteab show that weak reform countries spent a higher percentage of government expenditure on health and education than strong reformers,[164] suggesting that "the theoretical basis of the [neoliberal] policy with respect to the provision of social welfare services is tenuous and rests basically on a foundation of sand."[165] However, it might be observed, the percentage is far less important than the total expenditure relative to the size and needs of the population, which might be very different in strong reform countries.

Many of these criticisms were based on Africa's experience in the 1980s, a period of global recession, widespread violence, and severe regional drought. Critics tend to ignore that intensive state intervention in African economies had previously failed, thereby undermining their arguments for returning to statist policies. An additional problem is the tendency of critics to conflate decreasing public spending to achieve greater efficiency with decreasing public services.[166] Household survey data are scarce and censuses are unreliable, limiting the validity of claims about poverty trends in Africa.[167] Ghai provides a balanced reading in declaring that peasants have done better than urban workers in most of Africa, that "owners of foreign assets" have benefited significantly, and that "losers include those producing for the shrinking domestic markets previously protected from foreign competition, pensioners, holders of fixed interest bonds and other assets which failed to keep up with accelerating inflation."[168] This is probably what the World Bank and IMF had expected.

Positive consequences of structural adjustment reforms include rising hard currency remittances made possible by decriminalizing the possession of foreign currency, capital accumulation based on trade liberalization, and greater revenue due to a reduction in corruption. There have also been improvements in urban transport systems owing to deregulation.[169] In sum, as Easterly observes: "There were some big successes, but also some big disasters."[170]

Be that as it may, neoliberal policies were frequently imposed prematurely in the development process, producing what Collier and Gunning term "poor sequencing of reforms." Premature "financial liberalization led to a fiscal crisis" that undermined political support for the program and deterred investment. "If financial liberalization had been postponed, fiscal adjustment would not have had to deal with the additional burden of a sharp increase in interest payments."[171]

Partly in response to criticism of the external imposition of conditions on loans, the World Bank and IMF in 1999 established the practice of Policy Reduction Strategy Papers (PRSPs) as part of their Enhanced Highly Indebted Poor Countries debt relief effort. Although still philosophically neoliberal and although the IMF and World Bank retain authority to make final decisions, the PRSPs "are prepared by the member countries through a participatory process involving domestic stakeholders as well as external development partners" and "describe the country's macroeconomic, structural and social policies and programs over a three year or longer horizon to promote broad-based growth and reduce poverty, as well as associated external financing needs and major sources of financing."[172] Countries are thus better able to avoid the "poor sequencing of reform."

For Africa to take greater advantage of globalization, it will need to devote substantial resources to developing infrastructure – roads, railways, ports – that will benefit trade. It also needs enhanced access to the markets of wealthy countries for agricultural products and greater regional cooperation and integration.[173] "For African countries, which are individually handicapped by small markets, weak basic infrastructure, and insufficient financial and human resources, regional integration can actually speed up globalization."[174]

Culturally, as well as economically, Africa is at globalization's margin. Notwithstanding the presence of Western films and music in major urban areas, Africa has a "negligible stake in the materialist culture of globalization."[175] Politically, Africa is more globalized than it is economically or culturally, although it is less so than any other region. Democracy has found greater support but is still rare, and poor governance, often tribal or clan in nature, remains a major problem. The Kikuyu–Kalenjin violence that swept Kenya after its 2008 elections[176] and the deadly clashes between Hausa-Fulani Muslims and Yoruba and Igbo Christians in the city of Jos in 2010[177] were vivid reminders of how widespread ethnic/religious tensions remain.

As noted above, Africa's condition may be changing. Ethan Kapstein's assessment is decidedly upbeat. "It is still a well-kept secret," he writes, "that the African continent has been in the midst of a profound economic transformation. Since 2004, economic growth has boomed at an average of six percent annually, on par with Latin America."[178] Between 2000 and 2008, Africa's annual output grew twice as fast as it had in the two previous decades and faster than the global average. Its 500 largest companies have grown at a rate of 8.3 percent a year since 1998.[179] Kapstein sees three factors as responsible for bringing about "the twilight of Afro-pessimism": urbanization, democratization, and the opening-up of African economies with the resulting growth of foreign investment.[180] But he cautions that continued improvement depends on the willingness of Europe and the United States to reduce protectionism and afford market access for African exports.[18]

Globalization has encountered severe criticism in recent years, leading some observers to see it as reversible, indeed as already being reversed. The terrorist attacks of 9/11 were viewed by some as a turning point, but the global economic crisis that began in late 2007 seemed far more threatening, a possible replay of the 1930s. The next chapter examines the ways in which recent events have affected globalization and weigh their overall impact on the direction of global political life.

NOTES

1. Roy Starrs, *Asian Nationalism in an Age of Globalization* (Richmond, UK: Curzon Press, 2001), 69.
2. David I. Sternberg, *Burma/Myanmar* (Oxford: Oxford University Press, 2010), 184.
3. Kirshner, "Globalization, Power, and Prospect," 322.
4. "Seeing the World Differently," *The Economist*, June 12, 2010, 65–7.
5. Alexander Cooley, "Globalization and National Security after Empire: The Former Soviet Space," in Kirshner, ed., *Globalization and National Security*, 201.
6. Leon Aron, "Everything You Think You Know about the Collapse of the Soviet Union Is Wrong," *Foreign Policy* 187 (July/August 2011), 68.
7. Eric Noreen, "Socializing Baltic Sea States into a Security Community: Aspects of Globalization," in Blum, ed., *Russia and Globalization*, 250.
8. See Alexey Fenenko, "Globalization, Identity, and Changing Understandings of Security in Russia," in Blum, ed., *Russia and Globalization*, 307–28.
9. "Russia Alarmed over New EU Pact," *BBC News*, May 22, 2009, http://news.bbc.co.uk/2/hi/europe/8061042.stm.
10. Edward Solovyev, "Russian Geopolitics in the Context of Globalization," in Blum, ed., *Russia and Globalization*, 301.
11. Douglas W. Blum, "Conclusion: Links between Globalization, Security, and Identity in Russia," in Blum, ed., *Russia and Globalization*, 346.
12. The group has become increasingly institutionalized and has added South Africa to its ranks. Owen Fletcher, "China Seeks Heft for 'BRICS'," *Wall Street Journal*, April 13, 2011, A12.
13. Konstantin Rozhnov, "Bric Tries to Shift Power Balance," *BBC News*, April 15, 2010, http://news.bbc.co.uk/2/hi/8620178.stm.
14. Blum, "Conclusion: Links between Globalization, Security, and Identity in Russia," 339, 340.

15 "2011 KOF Index of Globalization." Russia ranked 62nd of seventy-two states in the 2007 *Foreign Policy* Globalization Index.
16 World Economic Forum, "The Global Competitiveness Report 2010–2011," and Dutta and Mia, eds., *Global Information Technology Report 2008–2009*.
17 "Corruption Perception Index 2010 Results," *Transparency International*, http://www.transparency.org/policy_research/surveys_indices/cpi/2010/results.
18 Banyan, "More Black Tea than Jasmine," *The Economist*, March 5, 2011, 48.
19 Solovyev, "Russian Geopolitics in the Context of Globalization," 304.
20 "The 2008 Global Cities Index," 70.
21 Hedetoft and Blum, "Introduction: Russia and Globalization – A Historical and Conceptual Framework," 1.
22 Mikhail Troitsky, "Going 'Relativistic': The Changing Vision of 'Just International Order' in Russian Foreign Policy," in Blum, ed., *Russia and Globalization*, 207–31.
23 Gennady N. Konstantinov and Sergey R. Filonovich, "The Transformation of the Russian System of Higher Education," in Blum, ed., *Russia and Globalization*, 149.
24 Blum, "Conclusion: Links between Globalization, Security, and Identity in Russia," 335.
25 Hedetoft and Blum, "Introduction: Russia and Globalization – A Historical and Conceptual Framework," 17.
26 Blum, "Conclusion: Links between Globalization, Security, and Identity in Russia," 330, 329.
27 Ibid., 329.
28 Solovyev, "Russian Geopolitics in the Context of Globalization," 303.
29 Andrew E. Kramer, "Moscow's Ex-Mayor Faces Legal Scrutiny," *New York Times*, http://www.nytimes.com/2011/03/20/world/europe/20luzhkov.html.
30 See "The Putin v Medvedev Tandem," *The Economist*, April 9, 2011, 57–8.
31 Andrey Korotayev and Darya Khaltourina, "The Russian Demographic Crisis in Cross-National Perspective," in Blum, ed., *Russia and Globalization*, 70.
32 See Anatoly M. Khazanov, "A State Without a Nation? Russia after Empire," in Paul, Ikenberry, and Hall, eds., *The Nation-State in Question*, 79–105.
33 Blum, "Conclusion: Links between Globalization, Security, and Identity in Russia," 332.
34 Ibid., 332, 333. As this applies to Siberia, see Evgeny Vodichev and Vladimir Lamin, "Russian Identity and Siberia's Self-Identification: Historical Traditions in a Global World," in Blum, ed., *Russia and Globalization*, 111–38.
35 Ellen Barry, "Attacks Reawaken Fear of Caucasus Rebels," *New York Times*, March 29, 2010, http://www.nytimes.com/2010/03/30/world/europe/30mood.html.
36 Fenenko, "Globalization, Identity, and Changing Understandings of Security in Russia," 308.
37 James Richter, "Integration from Below? The Disappointing Effort to Promote Civil Society in Russia," in Blum, ed., *Russia and Globalization*, 182–8.
38 Ibid., 187–91.
39 Ibid., 194–5.
40 Ibid., 196.
41 Marc Morjé Howard, *The Weakness of Civil Society in Post-Communist Europe* (Cambridge: Cambridge University Press, 2003), 156.
42 Richter, "Integration from Below?" 199–200.
43 Vodichev and Lamin, "Russian Identity and Siberia's Self-Identification," 122.
44 "Russia Trade Exports and Imports," *EconomyWatch*, http://www.economywatch.com/world_economy/russia/export-import.html. See also US Department of State, "Background Note: Russia," March 16, 2011, http://www.state.gov/r/pa/ei/bgn/3183.htm.
45 Bradshaw, "Globalization, Change, and the Cohesion of the Russian Federation," 80.
46 Vladimir Putin, "Point of View," Government of the Russian Federation (April 2009), http://www.premier.gov.ru/eng/points/95/.
47 "Russian Exports," *Citi*, http://www.tradingeconomics.com/russia/exports. See also "Russia Trade Exports and Imports."
48 Bradshaw, "Globalization, Change, and the Cohesion of the Russian Federation," 87.

49 "Foreign Direct Investment in Russia: A Survey of CEOs 2008," Foreign Investment Advisory Council, http://www.fiac.ru/files/fiac_survey_2008_eng.pdf. See also *FDI.net*, Multilateral Investment Guarantee Agency, http://www.fdi.net/country/sub_index.cfm?countrynum=163. Most of the FDI in Russia comes from the Netherlands and Cyprus.
50 Michael Schwirtz, "New Trial for Tycoon Is a Test for Russia," *New York Times*, March 5, 2009, http://www.nytimes.com/2009/03/06/world/europe/06russia.html.
51 Michael Schwirtz, "Russia to Free Oil Magnate's Former Lawyer," *New York Times*, April 21, 2009, http://www.nytimes.com/2009/04/22/world/europe/22russia.html.
52 Bradshaw, "Globalization, Change, and the Cohesion of the Russian Federation," 106.
53 Blum, "Conclusion: Links between Globalization, Security, and Identity in Russia," 334.
54 Ramón Grosfoguel, "Developmentalism, Modernity, and Dependency Theory in Latin America," *Nepantia: Views from the South* 1:2 (2000), 356.
55 Ibid., 357.
56 Daniel Yergin and Joseph Stanislaw, *Commanding Heights*, rev. edn (New York: Free Press, 2002), 232–44.
57 José Bell Lara and Delia Luisa López, "The Harvest of Neoliberalism in Latin America," in Richard A. Dello Buono and Lara, eds., *Imperialism, Neoliberalism and Social Struggles in Latin America* (Boston, MA: Brill, 2007), 17.
58 William I. Robinson, *Latin America and Global Capitalism* (Baltimore, MD: Johns Hopkins University Press, 2008), 261.
59 Andy Klom, "Review: Latin America and International Trade: Regionalism and Beyond," *Latin American Research Review* 40:3 (2005), 354–6.
60 Robinson, *Latin America and Global Capitalism*, 55.
61 "So Near and Yet So Far: A Special Report on Latin America," *The Economist*, September 11, 2010, 3.
62 Ibid., 4.
63 Keeling, "Latin American Development and the Globalization Imperative," 2.
64 Carol Graham, "Globalization, Poverty, Inequality and Insecurity: Some Insights from the Economics of Happiness," in Machiko Nissanke and Erik Thorbecke, eds., *The Impact of Globalization on the World's Poor: Transmission Mechanisms* (New York: Palgrave Macmillan, 2007), 243.
65 Ibid., 252.
66 Keeling, "Latin American Development and the Globalization Imperative," 1.
67 "2011 KOF Globalization Index." The 2007 *Foreign Policy Index* ranked Chile 43rd, Mexico 49th, Argentina 54th, and Brazil 67th. Panama (30th) was the highest-ranking country in Latin America.
68 Blanke, Browne, Hanouz, Geiger, Mia, and Sala-i-Martin, *The Global Competitiveness Report 2009–2010*, and Dutta and Mia, eds., *Global Information Technology Report 2008–2009*.
69 Internet World Stats, http://www.internetworldstats.com/stats.htm.
70 Miguel Helft, "Where Google Is Really Big: India and Brazil," *New York Times*, September 14, 2009, http://bits.blogs.nytimes.com/2009/09/14/where-google-is-really-big-india-and-china/.
71 "Latin American Internet Usage Statistics," Internet World Stats, September 30, 2009, http://www.internetworldstats.com/stats10.htm.
72 Dani Rodrik, "Rethinking Growth Strategies," WIDER Annual Lecture 8 (Helsinki: United Nations World Institute for Development Economics Research, 2004), http://www.wider.unu.edu/publications/annual-lectures/en_GB/AL8/_files/78091862539831929/default/annual-lecture-2004.pdf, 3. Emphasis in original.
73 A. P. Thirlwall and Penélope Pacheco-Lopez, *Trade Liberalisation and the Poverty of Nations* (Northampton, MA: Edward Elgar Publishing, 2008), 21.
74 See James Petras and Henry Veltmeyer, "Imperial Globalization and Social Movements in Latin America," *Atlantic Free Press*, October 17, 2009, http://www.atlanticfreepress.com/news/1/11999-imperial-globalization-and-social-movements-in-latin-america.html.

75 Will Braun, "Campesinos vs Oil Industry," *Global Policy Forum*, December 5, 2004, http://www.globalpolicy.org/globalization/cases-of-globalization/28092.html. See also Raul Zibechi, "Privatizations," *Global Policy Forum*, November 1, 2004, http://www.globalpolicy.org/globalization/cases-of-globalization/28091.html, who describes the negative impact of privatization in Peru and Argentina.
76 Walden Bello, "Globalization in Retreat," *New Labor Forum* 16:3 (2007), 109–15.
77 Katie Baker, "Anti-US Trade Deal Grows during Recession," *Newsweek*, March 11, 2010, http://blog.newsweek.com/blogs/wealthofnations/archive/2010/03/11/anti-us-trade-deals-grow-during-recession.aspx, and "The Pacific Players Go to Market," *The Economist*, April 9, 2011, 41–2. Despite the proliferation of groupings including Mercosur, the Andean Community, and a nascent grouping of Pacific states (Chile, Peru, and Colombia), regional integration in Latin America is relatively shallow. Indeed, the regional groups are divided by ideology and history, as well as the lure of association with the United States.
78 "What Latin America Thinks about Globalization," *Global Envision*, January 16, 2007, http://www.globalenvision.org/library/8/1416.
79 Ibid.
80 John Ralston Saul, "The Collapse of Globalism and the Rebirth of Nationalism," *Harper's Magazine* (March 2004), http://www.johnralstonsaul.com/eng/articles_detail.php?id=6%E2%8C%A9=eng.
81 "The Globalization of Chilean Retailing," *Strategic Management*, December 12, 2007, http://www.wharton.universia.net/index.cfm?fa=viewArticle&id=1450&language=english.
82 Simon Schwartzman, "Globalization, Poverty, and Social Inequity in Brazil," Instituto de Estudos do Trabalho e Sociedade (IETS), Rio de Janeiro (February 2003), http://www.schwartzman.org.br/simon/pdf/globalization.pdf, 12–13.
83 Marcus Faro de Castro and Maria Izabel Valladao De Carvalho, "Globalization and Recent Political Transitions in Brazil," *International Political Science Review* 24:4 (2003), 467.
84 "Falling in Love Again with the State," *The Economist*, April 3, 2010, 37–8.
85 Mark London and Brian Kelly, *The Last Forest: The Amazon in the Age of Globalization* (New York: Random House, 2007), 27.
86 "So Near and Yet So Far," 6.
87 Ibid., 4. Also "Nobody's Backyard," *The Economist*, September 11, 2010, 13.
88 Paulo Prada, "For Brazil, It's Finally Tomorrow," *Wall Street Journal*, March 29, 2010, http://online.wsj.com/article/SB10001424052748704743404575127913634823670.html?mod=WSJ_hpp_MIDDLENexttoWhatsNewsTop. See also "Brazil Takes Off," *The Economist*, November 14, 2009, 15, and "Arrivals and Departures," *The Economist*, November 14, 2009, 9–10.
89 "Smile Turns to Frown," *The Economist*, January 16, 2010, 40.
90 "The Andean Laundry," *The Economist*, March 27, 2010, 42.
91 "The Tormented Isthmus," *The Economist*, April 16, 2011, 25–6, 28.
92 Cited in Juan Forero, "Across Latin America, Mandarin Is in the Air," *Washington Post*, September 22, 2006, http://www.washingtonpost.com/wp-dyn/content/article/2006/09/21/AR2006092101626.html. A similar phenomenon is visible in Indonesia where the study of Mandarin has increased as China's economic presence grows. Edward Wong, "Indonesians Seek Words to Attract China's Favor," *New York Times*, May 1, 2010, http://www.nytimes.com/2010/05/02/world/asia/02chinindo.html.
93 George Ritzer and Elizabeth L. Malone, "Globalization Theory: Lessons from the Exportation of McDonaldization and the New Means of Consumption," *American Studies* 41:2/3 (Summer/Fall 2000), 109.
94 Masoud Kavoossi, *The Globalization of Business and the Middle East* (Westport, CT: Quorum Books, 2000), 146.
95 Ibid.
96 See Valentine M. Moghadam, "Globalization and Women in the Middle East," *Middle East Women's Studies Review* 22 (September 2002), 2–5.
97 Marc Lynch, "Globalization and Arab Security," 171.

98 Ibid., 176.
99 "2011 KOF Globalization Index."
100 World Economic Forum, "The Global Competitiveness Report 2010–2011," and Dutta and Mia, eds., *Global Information Technology Report 2008–2009*.
101 Naomi Sakr, *Satellite Realms* (New York: I. B. Tauris, 2001), 16.
102 Anoushiravan Ehteshami, *Globalization and Geopolitics in the Middle East* (New York: Routledge, 2007), 6.
103 Kurt M. Campbell, "Globalization's First War?" *Washington Quarterly* 25:1 (Winter 2002), 7–14.
104 Lynch, "Globalization and Arab Security," 189.
105 Michael Howard, "What's in a Name?" *Foreign Affairs* 81:1 (January/February 2002), 12, 13.
106 Lieber and Weisberg, "Globalization, Culture, and Identities in Crisis," 294, 292–3. Emphasis in original.
107 "A Muslim Democracy in Action," *The Economist*, February 19, 2011, 59.
108 Aydinli, "Globalization of a Torn State," 160.
109 "A Commodity Still in Short Supply," *The Economist*, December 4, 2010, 58.
110 Clement M. Henry and Robert Springborg, *Globalization and the Politics of Development in the Middle East* (Cambridge: Cambridge University Press, 2001), 30.
111 Kavoosi, *Globalization of Business and the Middle East*, 3. See George T. Abed and Hamid R. Davoodi, *Challenges of Growth and Globalization in the Middle East and North Africa* (Washington, DC: International Monetary Fund, 2003).
112 Karen Aggestam, Laura Guazzone, Helena Lindholm Schulz, M. Cristina Paciello, and Daniela Pioppi, "The Arab State and Neo-Liberal Globalization," in Guazzone and Cristina Pioppi, eds., *The Arab State and Neo-Liberal Globalization* (Reading, UK: Ithaca Press, 2009), 326.
113 Anthony Shadid, "Exiles Shaping World's Image of Syria Revolt," *New York Times*, April 23, 2011, http://www.nytimes.com/2011/04/24/world/middleeast/24beirut.html.
114 "Libya – Protests and Revolt (2011)," *New York Times*, July 15, 2011, http://topics.nytimes.com/top/news/international/countriesandterritories/libya/index.html.
115 Bill Spindle, Nour Malas, and Farnaz Fassihi, "Protests Explode Across Syria," *Wall Street Journal*, April 23–4, 2011, A1, A11, and "The Squeeze on Assad," *The Economist*, July 2, 2011, 18–20.
116 "2011 KOF Globalization Index."
117 "2011 KOF Globalization Index," World Economic Forum, "The Global Competitiveness Report 2010–2011," and Dutta and Mia, eds., *Global Information Technology Report 2008–2009*. No data were available for Angola or the DRC for networked readiness or economic competitiveness.
118 Lockwood and Redoano (2005), The CSGR Globalisation Index.
119 Samuel M. Makinda and F. Wafula Okumu, *The African Union* (New York: Routledge, 2008), 35.
120 Said Adejumobi, "Governance and Poverty Reduction in Africa: A Critique of the Poverty Reduction Strategy," paper to the Inter-regional Conference on Social Policy and Welfare Regimes in Comparative Perspectives, University of Texas–Austin (April 2006), 7, 8, http://lanic.utexas.edu/project/etext/llilas/cpa/spring06/welfare/adejumobi.pdf.
121 "Internet Usage Statistics for Africa," *Internet World Stats* (2009), http://www.internetworldstats.com/stats1.htm. For the rest of the world the figure is almost 29 percent.
122 "The Lion Kings?" *The Economist*, January 8, 2011, 72.
123 Seyni N'Diaye, "The Role of Institutional Reforms," *Finance & Development* 38:4 (December 2001), http://imf.org/external/pubs/ft/fandd/2001/12/ndiaye.htm, and G. Dharam Ghai, *Structural Adjustment, Global Integration and Social Democracy*, UN Research Institute for Social Development (1992), 4, http://www.unrisd.org/unrisd/website/document.nsf/0/FA0468F70A7297D980256B64003E663C?OpenDocument, 19.
124 "The World Economy Calls," *The Economist*, March 27, 2010, 70.

125 N'Diaye, "The Role of Institutional Reforms." See also Paul Collier and Jan Willem Gunning, "Explaining African Economic Performance," *Journal of Economic Literature* 37 (March 1999), 64–111.
126 "Big Ambitions, Big Question-Marks," *The Economist*, September 5, 2009, 52.
127 For a critical analysis of state failure, see "Where Life is Cheap and Talk is Loose," *The Economist*, March 19, 2011, 67–8.
128 Avant, "The Marketization of Security," 130.
129 Tade Akin Aina, "Introduction: How Do We Understand Globalization and Social Policy in Africa," in Aina, C. S. L. Chachaga, and Elisabeth Annan-Yao, eds., *Globalization and Social Policy in Africa* (Dakar: Codesria, 2004), 5.
130 Ghai, *Structural Adjustment*, 4, http://www.unrisd.org/unrisd/website/document.nsf/0/FA0468F70A7297D980256B64003E663C?OpenDocument.
131 John Briggs and Ian E. A. Yeboah, "Structural Adjustment and the Contemporary Sub-Saharan African City," *Area* 33:1 (March 2001), 18.
132 N'Diaye, "The Role of Institutional Reforms."
133 Ibid.
134 Ibid. See also Saleh M. Nsouli and Françoise Le Gall, "Globalization and Africa: Overview of the Main Issues," *Finance & Development* 38:4 (December 2001), http://www.imf.org/external/pubs/ft/fandd/2001/12/nsouli.htm.
135 "Corruption Perception Index 2010 Results," *Transparency International*.
136 Mo Ibrahim Foundation, "Methodology," http://www.moibrahimfoundation.org/en/section/the-ibrahim-index/methodology.
137 "It's Better to Be Out to Sea," *The Economist*, September 29, 2007, 51.
138 Africa.com, "Ibrahim Index," http://www.africa.com/ibrahim_index. Former South African President Nelson Mandela was given an honorary award. See also "A Politician's Oscar," *The Economist*, October 27, 2007, 57.
139 Jeffrey D. Sachs and Andrew M. Warner, "Natural Resource Abundance and Economic Growth," Harvard University (November 1997), http://www.cid.harvard.edu/ciddata/warner_files/natresf5.pdf.
140 See Michael L. Ross, "The Political Economy of the Resource Curse," *World Politics* 51:2 (January 1999), 312–19.
141 See, for example, "Risky Toughness," *The Economist*, September 20, 2008, 65–6, and "Hints of a New Chapter," *The Economist*, November 14, 2009, 30–2.
142 Paul Collier, *The Plundered Planet* (Oxford: Oxford University Press, 2010), 6. Emphasis in original.
143 Craig Timberg, "Inside Mugabe's Violent Crackdown," *Washington Post National Weekly Review*, July 14–20, 2008, 6–7, and Karin Brulliard, "The Final Indignity," *Washington Post National Weekly Review*, January 19–25, 21.
144 "Get Still More Serious," *The Economist*, February 6, 2010, 14. For examples, see Sarah Childress, "In Africa Democracy Gains Amid Turmoil," *Wall Street Journal*, June 18, 2008, A1, A11, and "A Damned Close-Run Thing – And a Fine Example to the Rest Of Africa," *The Economist*, January 10, 2009, 41.
145 "The Democracy Bug Is Fitfully Catching On," *The Economist*, July 24, 2010, 47–8.
146 Ghai, *Structural Adjustment*, 6, and Briggs and Yeboah, "Structural Adjustment and the Contemporary Sub-Saharan African City," 21.
147 N'Diaye, "The Role of Institutional Reforms."
148 Said Adejumobi, "Economic Globalization, Market Reforms and Social Welfare Services in West Africa," in Aina, Chachaga, and Annan-Yao, eds., *Globalization and Social Policy in Africa*, 35.
149 Adejumobi, "Governance and Poverty Reduction in Africa," 11.
150 Ibid., 7.
151 Ikubolajeh Bernard Logan and Kidane Mengisteab, "IMF–World Bank Adjustment and Structural Transformation in Sub-Saharan Africa," *Economic Geography* 69:1 (January 1993), 5.
152 Adejumobi, "Economic Globalization, Market Reforms and Social Welfare Services in West Africa," 27.

153 Aina, "Introduction: How Do We Understand Globalization and Social Policy in Africa," 3. See also Mohammed Bello Yunusa, "Urban Development Policies and Infrastructures in Nigeria," in Aina, Chachaga, and Annan-Yao, eds., *Globalization and Social Policy in Africa*, 137.
154 Zine Magubane, "Globalization and the South African Transformation: The Impact on Social Policy," *Africa Today* 49:4 (2002), 93. Emphasis in original.
155 Ghai, *Structural Adjustment, Global Integration and Social Democracy*, 17.
156 Adejumobi, "Governance and Poverty Reduction in Africa," 12.
157 Said Adejumobi, "Privatisation Policy and the Delivery of Social Welfare Services in Africa: A Nigerian Example," *Journal of Social Development in Africa* 14:2 (1999), 92.
158 Magubane, "Globalization and the South African Transformation," 101.
159 Ibid., 102.
160 Yunusa, "Urban Development Policies," 135.
161 Adejumobi, "Governance and Poverty Reduction in Africa," 8, 9, and Adejumobi, "Privatisation Policy," 104.
162 Food became more expensive in urban areas. See Dejene Aredo, "Global and Local Factors and the Welfare of the Poor in Ethiopia: 1994–1997," in Aina, Chachaga, and Annan-Yao, eds., *Globalization and Social Policy in Africa*, 106.
163 Adejumobi, "Governance and Poverty Reduction in Africa," 12. Also Alfred Inis Ndiaye, "Economic Reforms and Social Policies in Senegal," in Aina, Chachaga, and Annan-Yao, eds., *Globalization and Social Policy in Africa*, 109–134.
164 Logan and Mengisteab, "IMF–World Bank Adjustment and Structural Transformation in Sub-Saharan Africa," figures 1 and 2, 6, 7.
165 Adejumobi, "Privatisation Policy and the Delivery of Social Welfare," 87.
166 Overstaffing of public services compared to "expenditures on non-staff inputs" is cited as a "dysfunctional" policy by Paul Collier and Jan Willem Gunning, "The IMF's Role in Structural Adjustment," *Economic Journal* 109 (November 1999), F635.
167 Ibid., F636, and Briggs and Yeboah, "Structural Adjustment and the Contemporary Sub-Saharan African City," 23–4.
168 Ghai, *Structural Adjustment, Global Integration and Social Democracy*, 17.
169 Briggs and Yeboah, "Structural Adjustment and the Contemporary Sub-Saharan African City," 22, 23.
170 Easterly, "What did Structural Adjustment Adjust?" 23.
171 Collier and Gunning, "The IMF's Role in Structural Adjustment," F634, F641.
172 International Monetary Fund, "Poverty Reduction Strategy Papers (PRSP)," updated January 7, 2010, http://www.imf.org/external/NP/prsp/prsp.asp.
173 Robert Sharer, "An Agenda for Trade, Investment, and Regional Integration," *Finance & Development* 38:4 (December 2001), http://www.imf.org/external/pubs/ft/fandd/2001/12/sharer.htm.
174 N'Diaye, "The Role of Institutional Reforms."
175 Briggs and Yeboah, "Structural Adjustment and the Contemporary Sub-Saharan African City," 19.
176 See Stephanie McCrummen, "Tribal Loyalties Persist," *Washington Post National Weekly Edition*, January 21–7, 2008, 20–1, Sarah Childress, "Violence in Kenya Exposes Tribes' Widening Wealth Gap," *Wall Street Journal*, January 30, 2008, A1, A18, and "The Politicians Just Don't Seem to Get It," *The Economist*, February 20, 2010, 45–6.
177 "Nigeria Ethnic Violence 'Leaves Hundreds Dead'," *BBC News*, March 8, 2010, http://news.bbc.co.uk/2/hi/8555018.stm.
178 Kapstein, "Africa's Capitalist Revolution," 119. See also "'Fast Economic Growth' in Africa," *BBC News*, November 14, 2007, http://news.bbc.co.uk/2/hi/africa/7093912.stm.
179 Schumpeter, "Uncaging the Lions," *The Economist*, June 12, 2010, 76.
180 Kapstein, "Africa's Capitalist Revolution," 121.
181 Ibid., 128.

CHAPTER 9

Two steps forward, one step back?

> One step forward, two steps back . . . It happens in the lives of individuals, and it happens in the history of nations and in the development of parties.[1]

> If one accepts the essential continuity of the forces that have created the increasingly integrated world, one cannot but see globalization as an unstoppable process.[2]

> The long movement toward market liberalization has stopped, and a new period of state intervention, regulation, and creeping protectionism has begun . . . Indeed, globalization itself is reversing.[3]

In recent years, numerous events and developments have challenged the globalization process, including the 9/11 terrorist attacks and America's subsequent "War on Terror," the collapse of the Doha trade negotiations,[4] a proliferation of interstate trade and monetary disputes, the rejection of the European Union[5] constitution by French and Dutch voters, Irish rejection of the Lisbon Treaty,[6] America's unilateralist foreign policies and the Iraq War, growing complaints about the outsourcing of jobs from the developed world,[7] increased resistance in the developed world to the flow of migrants and asylum seekers fleeing poverty and/or violence, and the failure of the Copenhagen environmental summit. Among the greatest threats to globalization have been growing protectionism and protectionist sentiments in reaction to the world financial crisis and its accompanying insecurity.[8] Another concern is increased US isolationism, revealed in a 2009 Pew poll in which a plurality (49 percent) of the American public for the first time in forty years said that the United States should "mind its own business internationally" and "let other countries get along the best they can on their own."[9] Among the most potent of symbols has been the tightening of controls at the US–Canadian border.[10] These developments might be read as suggesting that globalization is *not* overcoming national identities, that state frontiers are being strengthened, and that the world is again on a course of cultural fragmentation rather than uniting within a single, homogenized culture of modernity.

Predictably, the post-2007 financial crisis revived questions about the dark side of globalization and its future, and the need to reinvigorate state authority. It also renewed calls for managing globalization, greater transparency in international economic institutions, more regulation of financial transactions, and alternatives to neoliberal capitalism. Not surprisingly, as we saw earlier, the percentage of US citizens who view the free market system as the world's best dropped precipitously between 2002 and 2010, with the drop especially pronounced among those earning less than $20,000 per year.[11] Capitalism has lost favor in much of Europe as well. In retrospect, Strange was prescient when she concluded that "to let the financial markets run so far ahead, so far beyond the control of the state," is "mad."[12] Today, analysts recall how Strange, writing about the global financial system of the 1970s and 1980s, described that system as "casino capitalism,"[13] while in a similar vein Greider warned that "our wondrous machine, with all its great power and creativity, appears to be running out of control to some sort of abyss."[14]

Like Strange, John Plender wonders about the wisdom of neoliberal economics and the laissez-faire policies. "For the best part of three decades, policymakers in the developed world followed Ronald Reagan and Margaret Thatcher, in seeking to roll back the frontiers of the state. The triple mantra of privatisation, liberalisation and deregulation held sway." The crisis, Plender argues, began to raise thorny questions about the "triple mantra."

> [T]he problems that began in credit markets . . . now cast a cloud over the strong market orientation of western policy. Faith in the self-equilibrating power of the market is undoubtedly at . . . low ebb. So while New Deal- or Great Society-type policies may be out of the question, there remains the potential for the state to impose political accountability on technocratic policymakers, inflict more regulation on aberrant bankers and extend public ownership in response to the failure of politically sensitive corporations.

This leads Plender to ask whether "a more intrusive state is about to stage a comeback at the free market's expense, emulating the governmental response to the economic crisis of the 1930s." In fact, observes Plender, the "rise of emerging markets such as China, India, and Russia means that there is a growing proportion of the world economy in which governments play a central role in allocating resources, even if the trend in such countries is still broadly in a liberalising direction."[15] This may, of course, stifle bottom-up innovation and so actually to some extent slow the growth of these emerging economic giants.

Overall, the evidence is mixed about whether all these challenges have significantly curbed or slowed globalization, at least so far, but there has been little change in the rankings of countries in the globalization index. The most globalized are still small highly developed countries such as Singapore, Hong Kong, the Netherlands, Switzerland, Ireland, and Denmark. For the most part, they are also democracies. By contrast, the least globalized, including Iran, India, Algeria, Indonesia, Venezuela, Brazil, China, and Turkey – are large, for the most part relatively poor, and, in several cases, have unabashedly authoritarian governments.[16] Nevertheless, it should be emphasized that the globalization index is a state, not a system-level measure, and the factors it uses to measure globalization are controversial.

ANTI-GLOBALIZATION CURRENTS

The years following the global recession that began in late 2007 have seen accelerating currents of opposition to cultural, economic, and political globalization, as well as growing pessimism about globalization's future. These currents are not uniform, but the trends are related. Some involve fear of cultural homogenization and modernity as well as the undermining of local traditions and political elites, and others reflect a backlash against neoliberal economic policies, especially following the rapid deterioration of global economic conditions.

Roger Altman lists four anti-globalization consequences of the global economic crisis: (1) an end to "the era of laissez-faire economics," (2) a reversal in "the global spread of goods, capital, and jobs" and a decline in global trade[17] and migration, (3) a decline in global leadership, coordination, and coherence, and (4) an increase in "geopolitical instability."[18] He concludes that the "economic crisis" has been "a seismic global event." "Free-market capitalism, globalization, and deregulation have been rising across the globe for 30 years; that era has now ended, and a new one is at hand. Global economic and financial integration are reversing. The role of the state, together with financial and trade protectionism, is ascending."[19] Ó Tuathail, Herod, and Roberts similarly argue:

> With states increasingly impotent in the face of some global flows, the potential for backlash against many aspects of globalization – the downward leveling of wages, increased economic insecurity, overarching global "behemoths" (corporations, bureaucracies, and banks), "locked in" transnational liberalism, illegal immigration, cultural cosmopolitanism, and hybridity – is very high . . . [and that] has produced a retrenchant territorial parochialism often manifested in the form of strident nationalism.[20]

NATIONALISM AND ETHNICITY

Globalization might seem to imply that nationalism is waning, but, in fact, it remains a powerful ideology that appeals to innumerable people in both the developing and developed worlds. Its persistence reveals an intensification of identity politics in which individuals and groups assess goals and policies on the basis of "who they are." As Walker Connor argues, the essence of nationalism "is a psychological bond that joins a people and differentiates it, in the subconscious convictions of its members, from all nonmembers in a most vital way."²¹ Today, Rosenau observes, nationalism has become "a form of exclusionary localism" because "it emphasizes boundaries and the distinction between us and them."²² In Castells's words, "The age of globalization is also the age of nationalist resurgence, expressed both in the challenge to established nation-states and in the widespread (re)construction of identity on the basis of nationality, always affirmed against the alien."²³

Recent years have witnessed a revival of nationalism that involves, in Scholte's words, "defensive reactions against intrusions of the other who threatens to erase the self."²⁴ National myths, languages, and memorials have been dusted off, or reinforced, or (re)constructed in reaction to globalization. Nationalist sentiments have been encouraged and manipulated by political entrepreneurs such as Serbia's Slobodan Milošević, Georgia's Mikheil Saak'ashvili, Poland's Lech Kaczynski, and Russia's Vladimir Putin. Other former Soviet republics including Moldova, Estonia, Latvia, and Ukraine have also played the nationalist card and pointed to resurgent Russian power to mobilize nationalist sentiments and reinforce their political positions. Slovakia has rekindled old enmities with Hungary by trying to prevent the use of the Hungarian language by the country's Hungarian minority.²⁵ For their part, China's ruling elites are persistently asserting Han nationalism in relation to Tibetan and other minorities, and used the 2008 Beijing Olympics to showcase emerging China.

Nonetheless, "nation" – it cannot be emphasized too strongly – is not necessarily the same as "state." Few states are ethnically homogenous, and state boundaries are often not congruent with ethnic identities. States may be faced with demands for subgroup autonomy, communalism, and even secession.²⁶ In the words of one observer, on every continent "[n]ational movements are regaining popularity, and nations that had once assimilated and 'vanished' have now reappeared."²⁷ Today, as in past centuries, nationalism is a companion of rapid change. It was and remains "a subversive and revolutionary force."²⁸ Passionate separatist yearnings gripped Bosnian Muslims, Croatians, Albanians, Armenians, and Tibetans, reminding Patrick Daniel Moynihan of Milton's "Pandaemonium," that "was inhabited by creatures quite convinced that the great Satan had their best interests at heart."²⁹

Although carefully cultivated nationalism helped consolidate powerful European territorial states in the nineteenth century, the trend towards separation of the state and national identities accelerated after World War I. President Woodrow Wilson declared at the 1919 Versailles Peace Conference:

> There was not a man at the table who did not admit the sacredness of the right to self-determination, the sacredness of the right of any body of people to say that they would not continue to live under the Government that they were then living under.³⁰

With prescience, Wilson's Secretary of State Robert Lansing was aghast at the prospect. "Will it not breed discontent, disorder and rebellion?" he asked. "The phrase," he continued, "is simply loaded with dynamite. It will raise hopes which can never be realized. It will, I fear, cost thousands of lives."³¹ "If nations," writes Nigel Harris, "imply national States, there can be no State without a territory to administer, so a common territory is the precondition for asserting a claim to the right of national self-determination."³²

In the 1950s and 1960s, nationalism and national self-determination – enshrined in the UN Charter, Article 1(2) – were the ideological bases of decolonization and, therefore, seemed to target mainly the remains of European empires. In later years, however, both established and relatively new states have themselves become the target. There has been a veritable explosion in the number of groups seeking national homelands and the protection of national rights, including for indigenous and aboriginal peoples. Gurr identified over 200 politically active ethnic movements by the mid-1990s.[33] Strange argued that one reason why the "retreat of the state" is not fully recognized "is that while the governments of established states . . . are suffering this progressive loss of real authority, the queue of societies that want to have their own state is lengthening."[34] If Abkhazia and South Ossetia can be recognized as independent states, is there any limit to the number of potential "dwarf" polities? "If we don't find some way that the different ethnic groups can live together in a country," asked former US Secretary of State Warren Christopher, "how many countries will we have?" His answer: "We'll have 5,000 countries rather than the hundred plus we now have."[35]

Not only did the USSR split into quarreling nationalities, but also several of these remain at each other's throats – Armenians and Azeris, Georgians and Ossetians, Russians and Georgians, Russians and Ukrainians, and Russians and Moldovans. Moldovans are pulled towards Romania, and Russia remains separated from the breakaway Russian-supported Transdniestria. Ethnic conflict again threatens Bosnia,[36] and the Hungarian minority in Romania is inspired by Kosovo's independence to seek autonomy.[37] Even in the marchlands of Europe and Canada, there are "ethno-national" groups that claim that their culture is being swallowed up by national majorities – Spanish Basques, French Bretons and Corsicans, Northern Irish Catholics, Celtic Scots and Welsh, Canadian Québécois, Inuits and Native Americans. In Québec's case, efforts by the Francophone advocates of secession have had to confront the secessionist threats of non-Francophone English and other minorities (allophones), as well as the threat of the Cree and other indigenous Native American groups who claim large areas of Québec as theirs on the basis of the same right to national self-determination.

Not least in the developing world do ethnic and tribal loyalties threaten the integrity of many existing states. Bloody examples in Rwanda, Sri Lanka, Sudan, Somalia, and elsewhere illustrate how political entrepreneurs cynically use ethnic divisions. In India, the Bharatiya Janata Party has long enjoyed a popular base owing to Hindu nationalism. Hindu "fundamentalists"[38] resist globalized values even in Bangalore, the center of the country's high-tech industries.[39] Assam is the center of conflict between the country's largest tribal group, the Bodo, and local Muslims.[40] Neighboring Manipur is also wracked by violence,[41] and much of India's northeast is the scene of violent clashes with Maoist Naxalites.[42] Although Tamil separatism in Sri Lanka appears to have been crushed, Tamil aspirations for autonomy in that country remain strong. China continues to be bedeviled by tensions between Han settlers and Tibetans and Uighurs in Xinjiang who harbor separatist aspirations.[43] Myanmar's military leaders still contend with Karen insurgents.[44]

Meanwhile, belief in assimilation in the West is giving way to multiculturalism in which members of ethnic groups foster links with one another transnationally, while de-emphasizing the ties that bind them to fellow citizens in the countries in which they reside. As we have previously noted, owing to modern communications and transportation, these overseas communities can remain in touch with their homelands to an extent previously not possible, helping to explain why such communities assimilate more slowly than similar communities did in past centuries. Diasporas and migrant communities such as the overseas Chinese in Malaysia, Singapore, and Indonesia and the Vietnamese "ghost workers" in Russia[45] seek to keep alive national customs and traditions, which in some cases brings them into conflict with host countries. Thus, Islamic and African communities in Europe and North America find that traditional customs towards women are frowned upon and may be declared illegal.[46]

In sum, nationalism and ethnicity have been transformed from identities that fostered large territorial polities into identities that tend to foster parochialism, closure, and the thickening of vertical barriers. "Through glocalization," Urry observes,

> nation has become less a matter of the specific state uniquely determining that nation. And the notion of nation has . . . become more a matter of branding, as nation has become something of a free-floating signifier relatively detached from the 'state' within the swirling contours of the new global order.[47]

Nationalism and ethnicity need *not* imperil globalization. Ethnic networks enrich the exchange of information and ideas between host countries and homelands and facilitate transnational business arrangements.[48] People *do* have multiple identities that are drawn from many sources, and there is no inherent reason why one cannot identify oneself both as a Basque or a Scot, and a loyal citizen of Spain or the United Kingdom, respectively, *and* a European – or as a citizen of the world, for that matter.[49] Each identity provides particular benefits that the others do not. Benefits derived from broader linkages may, in fact, allow small states and local ethnic communities more real autonomy. Problems arise when nationalism and ethnicity are treated as Hobbesian categories, passion rather than reason rules,[50] and conflicts are regarded as zero-sum. This, in turn, often depends on the degree to which national, ethnic, or other identity cleavages crosscut or reinforce other social cleavages such as economic status.

The return of the state

Quite apart from the challenges of ethnic nationalism, there have been renewed efforts to firm up state borders and reassert state sovereignty and control of the economy. Altman argues that the "role of the state is expanding again" and Daniel Yergin concludes, as a result: "The era of easy globalization is certainly over."[51] The global economic crisis has tended to resuscitate the state and its presumed regulatory capacity, while raising fundamental questions about neoliberal capitalism.[52]

In truth, the state never "left" and so cannot be said to have "returned." For example, in thirteen developed states in North America and Europe, government spending as a percentage of gross domestic product (GDP) has consistently increased, from an average of 10.4 percent in 1870 to 44.1 percent in 2005 and 47.7 percent in 2009.[53] Nevertheless, state intervention throughout the developed world has to some extent increased in response to the threat of grave recession. French President Sarkozy, having run for office as a neoliberal, famously concluded that the central consequence of the financial crisis is "the return of the state, the end of the ideology of public powerlessness."[54] "Consolidated state" power, declared Vladislav Surkov, an adviser to Russia's Vladimir Putin, "is the only instrument of modernisation in Russia," and "it is the only one possible."[55]

Until the congressional election of 2010, growing state intervention was evident in the United States, where President Barack Obama moved towards a more activist and bigger government. The temporary nationalization of part of the banking and automotive industries, as well as proposed reforms of the financial system, were part of this picture. An ambitious national health program was narrowly adopted, albeit over fierce opposition that still threatens to dismantle key portions of the plan. However, swimming against the stream, Tea Party activists and resurgent right-wing Republicans, as well as the more moderate UK Conservative–Liberal government, insist that their central goal is to *shrink* government. But measured re-regulation of the financial sector is also a goal in the United Kingdom, Ireland, and elsewhere, where nationalization in some cases has gone even further than in the United States.

Where state intervention resumed, it indirectly involved what Bremmer called "a strategic rejection of free-market doctrine"[56] – or at least a strict interpretation thereof. In emerging economies, state capitalism is spreading, a system in which "governments do not so much reject the market as use it as an instrument of state power,"[57] a system similar to what Bobbitt calls the "mercantile market-state."[58] In this system, the state is both an economic player and an umpire of the rules, and values politics more than profit. Bremmer observes: "Governments, not private shareholders, already own the world's largest oil companies and control three-quarters of the world's energy reserves."[59] Such companies include Russia's Lukoil and Gazprom, and the China National Petroleum Corporation. Bremmer additionally stresses the growing impact of "sovereign wealth funds" (government investment portfolios) that already "account for one-eighth of global investment" and "are reshaping international politics and the global economy by transferring increasingly large levers of economic power and influence to the central authority of the state."[60] Some of the largest of the funds that are aggressively investing globally are held by the United Arab Republic, Norway, Kuwait, Singapore, and China.[61] Thus, in 2008 in the midst of the recession, the Abu Dhabi Investment Company, which had already invested $7.5 billion in Citigroup, bought a 90 percent share of New York City's Chrysler Building.[62]

Nowhere is state intervention in the economy more visible than in China. Recent years have seen a partial reversal of privatization, restrictions on direct foreign investment, an end to price liberalization, and a revival of state enterprises.[63] The Chinese state has taken charge of grain distribution and retains control of much of the country's economy through the financial system. "No matter their shareholding structure," writes Derek Scissors, "all national corporations in the sectors that make up the core of the Chinese economy are required by law to be owned or controlled by the state," including "power generation and distribution; oil, coal, petrochemicals, and natural gas; telecommunications; armaments; aviation and shipping; machinery and automobile production; information technologies; construction; and the production of iron, steel, and nonferrous metals."[64] In some cases, China is surpassing traditional leading manufacturers such as American and Japanese automakers in both production and sales,[65] as well as in exports of advanced technology products.[66]

China's model of state capitalism, as noted earlier, is attracting interest across the developing world. "China's market–authoritarian model," declares Stefan Halper, "provides rapid growth, stability, and the promise of a better life for its citizens," and, in doing so, *is shrinking the West.*"[67] China, he argues, "is the protagonist in a clash of values, governance, and two versions of modernity in the twenty-first century."

> On one side are the Western liberal founders of the global market-place. These actors take for granted their political and economic preeminence in the world they constructed after 1945. On the other side are the new non-Western market converts, from Asia to Latin America, which have learned how to extract the best from both market capitalism and one-party government, thus shattering the illusion that capitalism begets democracy.[68]

Governments, ranging from those of oil states like Russia and Venezuela to developing countries like Angola, Azerbaijan, Kazakhstan, and Morocco, are becoming deeply involved in state-managed investment decisions and are nationalizing and consolidating key industrial sectors. Hence "the champions of free trade and open markets have to prove these systems' value to an increasingly skeptical international audience."[69] In a variety of critical economic sectors, "a growing number of governments are no longer content with simply regulating the market" but "want to use the market to bolster their own domestic political positions."[70] This is evident in Russia where state–business links, as well as personal ties between politicians and business managers, have become ever denser. The result is a "client-patron dynamic" that "has brought politics, politicians, and bureaucrats into economic decision-making to an extent not seen since the Cold War"[71] and has made investment decisions subject to political motives.

To Halper, all this suggests that, with China's encouragement and example, "new centers of wealth in the developing world are diminishing the traditional leverage and centrality of Western economic power; meanwhile, today's emerging markets are increasingly drawn to a new and compelling doctrine of state-managed capitalism." In this model, "the government maintains central control over a partly liberalized economy, and the people accept a very non-Western kind of civic bargain: political repression in the public square in return for relative economic freedom and a rising quality of life."[72] Unlike Bremmer, who thinks free-market capitalism will eventually triumph, Halper suggests that state capitalism is more likely to do so.

State failure

Paradoxically, efforts in some regions to restore state capacity are paralleled by state failure elsewhere, especially in the developing world, where it isolates large numbers of people from the fruits of globalization. State failure is a relative concept, and should not be treated dichotomously.[73] It does, however, connote the absence of central authority and dysfunctional institutions in contexts that usually feature poverty and violence.[74] The absence of central authority in countries like Somalia, Afghanistan, and the western regions of Pakistan makes them attractive asylums for terrorists, narcotics traffickers, and even pirates, and threatens to spread violence and disorder into neighboring states or across entire regions.

On the US side of the Atlantic, Mexico is at war with the drug cartels and is thought by some to be in danger of becoming a failed state. Mexican cartels have extended their influence across the borders into Central America as well as the United States. When Secretary of State Hillary Clinton visited Mexico in March 2009, discussions suggested that the United States recognized that criminal violence in Mexico had become a US problem as well.[75] "Today, the United States–Mexico border has been pancaked between a collapsed economy to the north and brutal drug thugs to the south."[76] "Globalization," as Sven Bislev observes, "has meant an increasing flow across the border [Mexico–California], accelerating the problems of security that affect all sectors and groups in the region."[77] As a result, even US citizens feel it necessary to assure their personal security privately, a fact that, according to Bislev, is reflected in the proliferation of gated communities in southern California.

For the most part, failed states and their populations are almost beyond the reach of legitimate globalized networks. As in Mexico, Somalia, and Pakistan, "they provide a natural breeding ground for transsovereign problems such as international criminal activity, refugee flows, the spread of contagious disease, nuclear and drug trafficking, etc."[78] Failure to create national unity in the European sense and to build viable and stable states after the retreat of colonialism, followed by a post-Cold War upsurge in violence within and across states in much of Africa and parts of Asia – all are associated with national, tribal, and ethnic rivalries, revived by ambitious politicians seeking political power and loot. In Africa, Europe's colonizers imposed states and political borders that inhabitants never fully accepted but that reflected "commercial, religious, and military realities, the rivalries, power relationships, and alliances that prevailed among the various imperial powers and between them and Africans through the centuries preceding colonization proper."[79] The boundaries imposed divided ethnic groups or enclosed ethnic rivals within the same states, consequences of which are "the relative lack of congruence between the territory of a state and areas of exchange" and "markets that elude the states themselves."[80] Another is the "noncoincidence of the borders of states and natural borders."[81]

Governments of failed states are frequently in the hands of one of the ethnic or tribal contenders and are deemed illegitimate by members of other groups. Such states are unable to exercise authority over their territory or to provide security or essential services to citizens. States like these "can no longer reproduce the conditions for their own existence."[82] Not surprisingly, the "civil wars that characterize failed states usually stem from or have roots in ethnic, religious, linguistic, or other intercommunal enmity."[83]

Outside observers rightly regard most failed states as zones of war, instability, and chaos. As noted earlier, Somalia and Afghanistan harbor terrorists and jihadists, and Somalia is a haven for modern pirates. Virtually all failing states are multiethnic societies, and many are significant sources of valuable natural resources with a potential to attract foreign meddling or intervention. According to *Foreign Policy*'s 2011 Failed States Index, of the twenty "of the world's most vulnerable countries," fourteen are in Africa (Somalia, Chad, Sudan, Democratic Republic of Congo,

Zimbabwe, Central African Republic, Ivory Coast, Guinea, Nigeria, Niger, Kenya, Burundi, Guinea-Bissau, and Ethiopia), three are in Asia (Afghanistan, Pakistan, and Burma), two are in the Middle East (Iraq[84] and Yemen), and one (Haiti) is in the Caribbean.[85] The Brookings Institution has developed an Index of State Weakness in the Developing World based on twenty economic, political, security, and social welfare indicators.[86] According to this index, as of 2010 the ten weakest states are Somalia, Afghanistan, Democratic Republic of Congo, Iraq, Burundi, Sudan, Central African Republic, Zimbabwe, Liberia, and Côte d'Ivoire; fifteen of the twenty weakest states are in sub-Saharan Africa.[87]

Of course, such indexes do not tell us everything. In the case of Libya and Syria, none foresaw the collapse of the former into civil war or the violence that shook the latter in the wake of revolutions elsewhere in North Africa and the Middle East. Tunisia, Libya, and Bahrain ranked among the least likely failed states (ranked 108th, 111th, and 129th respectively), and Egypt and Syria ranked in the middle (45th and 48th respectively).[88]

"Neo-tribalism" lends credence to Robert Kaplan's apocalyptic vision of a world dominated by "poverty, the collapse of cities, porous borders, cultural and racial strife, growing economic disparities, weakening nation states," a world of "disease pandemics like AIDS, environmental catastrophes, organized crime."[89] "I believe," argues Kaplan, "that, for a number of reasons, we're going to see the weakening, dilution, and perhaps even crackup of larger, more complex, modern societies in the next 10 or 15 years in such places as Nigeria, Ivory Coast and Pakistan"[90] and that a combination of political upheavals, demographic factors, resource scarcity, and climate change will produce global chaos. The kind of chaos described by Kaplan is likely to afflict parts of the developing world like Somalia and Congo where a toxic combination of poverty, population growth, ecological disaster, and corruption foster state failure. "Caught in the maelstrom of the processes which are re-writing the rules of world order," argue Gearóid Ó Tuathail, Andrew Herod, and Susan Roberts, "are the old masters of global space, the state formations that have historically divided territories and organized economies, ruled sovereignly over populations and corporations, disciplined subjects, and consolidated identities."[91]

Opposition to immigration

Regarding immigration, writes Milena Novy-Marx, "the demographic disequilibria between the 'northern' and the 'southern' world regions may be forecast as a sure premise for future migratory pressure," and "between now and 2030, migratory flows, already described as unavoidable and inescapable, are expected to be the result of a decreasing working-age population (about 65 millions) in the 'northern' part of the world, and an enormous increase in the working-age population in the 'southern' part (about 1,037 million)."[92]

Although greater migration from poor to rich countries would profit the world, including wealthy countries dramatically in coming decades,[93] another manifestation of negative localism in reaction to globalization is opposition to immigration. It is symbolized in the United States by the law passed in Arizona that makes failure to carry immigration documents a crime and gives police authority to detain anyone suspected of entering the country illegally,[94] the high fence being built along much of the US border with Mexico, the US Senate's restriction on financial institutions that receive taxpayer bailout money from hiring high-skilled immigrants on temporary work permits,[95] and the more general failure at the national level to achieve any meaningful immigration reform.[96]

"Geographic proximity," writes Gordon Hanson,

> allows unauthorized migrants from Mexico to move to the United States relatively quickly. The existence of well-established migration networks enables US employers to communicate changes in their demand for labor to prospective migrants in Mexico. Migrants use these same networks to find jobs and housing in the United States.[97]

Such flows are, however, sensitive to global and national economic conditions.

What he termed a "challenge to America's national identity" was controversially articulated by Samuel Huntington.[98] In his view, Hispanics are establishing insulated cultural islands, and the sheer number of Hispanics in the United States threatens to undermine US culture. Huntington's provocative claim rested on his assertion that Hispanics do not assimilate into American society as did earlier waves of immigrants from Europe. The result would be "a culturally bifurcated Anglo-Hispanic society with two national languages."[99] The density of links across the US–Mexican border "could produce a consolidation of the Mexican-dominant areas into an autonomous, culturally and linguistically distinct, economically self-reliant bloc within the United States."[100] Huntington's analysis was an extension of his view that we are entering an era of clashing civilizations. To his critics, Huntington was a xenophobic nationalist, whose belief that American culture is rooted in Anglo-Protestant tradition is false and whose fears were overheated. To his supporters, he embodied the resentment towards a global tidal wave that threatens national identities, boundaries, and traditional values.

Negative localism is also evidenced in the widespread concern about "outsiders" that has spread across much of Europe since the years when Eric Haider's Freedom Party's sounding of this issue in Austria seemed like an isolated echo from the Nazi past. Rightist parties are springing up and enjoying considerable success at the polls in such previously unlikely places as Denmark, Sweden, and the Netherlands. As we have mentioned, the current debate over "multiculturalism" that has recently engaged the leading politicians of Britain, Germany, and France is but the latest reflection of deep-seated ethnic tensions.[101]

Ethnic xenophobia of resident national groups is one consequence of the large-scale movement of persons as refugees and illegal migrants across state frontiers, combined with fear of terrorism. Residents argue, like Huntington, that migrants do not or cannot assimilate into dominant cultures and create economic and social problems for their adopted societies, including lower wages, human smuggling, street crime, and spiraling welfare costs.

The economic downturn dramatically slowed migration to wealthy societies,[102] as unemployment grew and resentment against immigrants flared up – even in Singapore, one of the most globalized societies in the world. Indeed, by 2009 reverse migration had begun, much as had been the case during the Great Depression, a flow described by one observer as "deglobalization."[103] The governments of Spain and Japan even began to provide cash incentives for migrants to return home.[104] This reverse flow included Mexicans from the United States.[105] The number of illegal immigrants in the United States declined from 12 million in 2007 to about 11.1 million in 2009.[106] Although most Mexican-born residents in the United States remained, the flow from Mexico dropped from about 1 million to 636,000 between February 2006 and February 2009.[107]

Anti-migrant sentiment is partly a result of high unemployment. The United States has raised higher barriers for highly skilled and talented immigrants to remain in the country, at considerable cost to its business and technological sectors.[108] Washington has made it difficult for US companies to get H-1B visas for specialized foreign workers.[109] France dismantled a camp of undocumented migrants seeking entry to Great Britain near Calais[110] and systematically routed Roma from their enclaves in French territory. Italy has made it more difficult for outsiders to acquire residency permits, and riots erupted in Calabria and elsewhere against African migrants.[111] Foreign workers in Italy organized a strike to show how important their role is in the Italian economy.[112] For its part, Russia dramatically reduced work permits, and racist xenophobia is increasing in that country. In Asia, Malaysia also reduced work visas,[113] while Thailand witnessed deteriorating conditions for Burmese migrants.[114] Returnees have included "road builders from Bangladesh, domestic servants from the Philippines, factory workers from Indonesia and Vietnam, construction workers from Mexico, as well as bankers, lawyers and real-estate professionals from around the world who were working in Singapore and Dubai."[115] Such events reflect resistance to an important human dimension of globalization.

One consequence of reverse and reduced migration has been a significant reduction in the remittances sent home by migrants that constitute a major source of income for developing countries. The Philippines, for example, depends upon the roughly 8 million of its citizens living abroad to provide some 10 percent of total domestic output, rising from $7.6 billion to $17.3 billion between 2003 and 2009.[116] Remittances account for about 46 percent of Tajikistan's gross domestic product, 38 percent of Moldova's, and 24 percent of Lebanon's.[117] In the case of Mexico, remittances "generate more foreign exchange . . . than tourism or foreign direct investment."[118] As De Blij comments: "The remittances sent home by just one successful [migrant] can sustain an entire extended family in Mexico, India, China, the Philippines, or a host of other countries."[119] In the case of Haiti, where remittances accounted for more than a quarter of the country's national income in 2008, a decline of some 13 percent in the first few months of 2009 proved disastrous.[120] Overall, remittances from Latin American workers in the United States dropped an estimated 11 percent or about $7 billion in 2009.[121] The World Bank predicted a 5–8 percent decline in total remittances in 2009 from the estimated $305 billion in 2008. Its report concluded that "an outright fall in the level of remittance flows as projected now will cause hardships in many poor countries."[122] Only in 2011, as there was a measure of economic recovery, did remittances again rise.[123]

Whether a decline in remittances is entirely negative, especially in the long run, is unclear. Sarah Gammage's research on El Salvador, where remittances provide 16 percent of GDP, leads her to conclude that "remittances mitigate poverty and create opportunities for financial market expansion that have benefited the wealthy as well as some of the poor." Although remittances are praised by international institutions as "engendering novel mechanisms for leveraging development and affording new opportunities for dynamizing savings and investment in home economies, particularly in rural areas," Gammage's conclusion is darker: "Unfortunately, the analysis propagated by these institutions fails to explore factors that lead to mass out-migration and respond to the failure of neoliberal policies to promote lasting and sustainable growth." In her view, migration tends to be a "safety valve to create wealth for a few while ameliorating the costs of adjustment and liberalization."[124]

Migration is largely a product of demographic forces, economic distress, and violence. Currently, some 200 million people or 3 percent of the world's population reside outside their homelands.[125] Deteriorating environmental conditions have also created the phenomenon of "eco-migration."[126] Eco-migrants have fled their homes in such places as Bangladesh, the Philippines, and Africa's Sahel region. Meanwhile, the president of the Pacific island nation of Kiribati has called for the world to consider moving entire populations from island countries endangered by rising sea levels that are a perceived result of global warming.[127]

Populations are actually declining in some relatively wealthy countries like Italy, Russia, and Japan owing to factors such as urbanization, easy access to contraception, later marriage, and greater professional opportunities for women. Populations in such countries are seriously "graying." In the developed world, the consequences include spiraling costs for health care and social security and a declining tax base with fewer young people to fill jobs, especially lower-paying jobs. By contrast, burgeoning populations in Africa, the Middle East, and parts of Asia are producing a surplus of young workers in search of employment and higher wages. "These movements of people, often from former colonies," writes Tariq Modood, "whether welcome or not, have created a multiculturalism that is qualitatively different from the diversity of personal difference or lifestyles of historic, territorially based minorities that already characterize some Western European countries."[128] Owing to incompatible norms and practices, both in Europe and elsewhere, this threatens "returning to the impositions of the early modern and authoritarian state."[129]

Until recently, Europe was dominantly Christian and Caucasian, but large numbers of Muslims arrived after World War II as a result of guest-worker programs, filling poorly paid jobs that Europeans avoided. Although initially guest workers, notably Turks, were expected to be temporary residents, many remained and were joined by family members. During the economic stagnation of the 1970s, many former guest workers lost their jobs but decided to remain in Europe, where living standards were nonetheless higher than in their home countries. According to Robert Pauly, as a result of family reunification in the 1970s, "Muslims began to place greater emphasis on the role of Islam in their daily lives." This, in turn, "resulted in the cultivation of a more publicly visible version of Islam with greater potential for rejection by Western European societies dominated by white, Christian majorities." Moreover, "growth rates rose in Islamic communities, leading to pronounced increases in the proportions of Muslims in the populations of France, Germany and the United Kingdom over the last three decades of the twentieth century."[130] By 2005, Europe's

Muslim population had swelled to 15–20 million and is expected to grow from 6 to 8 percent of Europe's total population by 2030.[131] Muslims will account for more than 10 percent in several European countries. Some observers expect a doubling of Muslims in Europe between 2005 and 2025.[132] Excepting Germany, most Muslim immigrants in Europe originated in their host countries' former colonial territories – North Africans in France, Pakistanis in Great Britain, and Indonesians in the Netherlands.

The spread of jihadist sentiments in Europe's Muslim communities after 9/11 was part and parcel of the rapid and extensive movement of ideas in a globalized world. As Pauly suggests, it also reflected the difficulty younger generations had "in developing identities," since "they often feel caught between the culture of their ancestors and the contemporary Western European societies in which they were born and have since experienced during their formative years." Pauly adds: "Relegated to lives on the crime-ridden streets surrounding urban housing projects, young Muslims often have trouble identifying who they are," a fact that "undermines the potential for the creation of hybrid Euro-Islamic identities."[133]

Following terrorist incidents in Britain, Spain, and France, Europeans grew uneasy about the increasing numbers of Muslims in their midst, even as many of the children and grandchildren of the first generation of Muslim migrants were themselves becoming alienated from Western culture. Muslim communities in Europe became "the socially excluded areas of advanced capitalist societies."[134] "Jihadist networks," writes Robert Leiken, "span Europe from Poland to Portugal, thanks to the spread of radical Islam among the descendants of guest workers . . . In smoky coffeehouses in Rotterdam and Copenhagen, makeshift prayer halls in Hamburg and Brussels, Islamic bookstalls in Birmingham and 'Londonistan,' and the prisons of Madrid, Milan, and Marseilles, immigrants or their descendants are volunteering for jihad against the West."[135] "Impressions of Islam," Pauly observes, "as a foreign rather than indigenous faith pervade decision-making processes at all levels of government within EU borders."[136] One result has been a backlash among non-Muslims, and what we have observed to be the growing influence of right-wing and nationalist politics in much of Europe. Although Muslim communities in the United States do not appear as yet to have been penetrated by radical Islam ideas to the extent of Europe's Muslim communities, there have been incidents such as the recruitment of Somali-Americans by Somali jihadists and the murder of thirteen people at Fort Hood by an American Muslim military officer.[137]

Among Europeans and North Americans, fear of Muslim extremism is highest in Russia, Spain, and Germany, and is lowest in Canada, the United States, and Poland.[138] For their part, many Muslims in Europe – 51 percent in Germany, 42 percent in Britain, 39 percent in France, and 31 percent in Spain – believe that Europeans are hostile towards them. Only 7 percent of British Muslims believe they are "thriving,"[139] and links between conservative Pakistani Muslims living in northern England and their brethren in Pakistan are dense. In France, which has experienced repeated violence among young, often unemployed Muslims in the *banlieues* surrounding French cities, Muslim suspicions are intensified by bans on the wearing of head scarves in government facilities and on wearing full veils in public,[140] and President Sarkozy's description of the burqa, a garment that completely covers

Muslim women, as "a sign of subjugation" that is "not welcome on French territory."[141] Relations were exacerbated by the arrest for dangerous driving of a Muslim woman in Nantes who was wearing a niqab (full-face veil).[142] In Italy, a woman was fined for wearing a veil because it was not possible to identify her,[143] and an Egyptian woman was murdered in a German courtroom in July 2009 by an ethnic German man who was on trial for having verbally abused her a year earlier.[144]

Thus, large majorities of European Muslims – 81 percent in Britain, 69 percent in Spain, 61 percent in Germany, and 46 percent in France – identify themselves as Muslims first and only secondarily as citizens of their country.[145]

> For the second-generation Muslim migrants in Europe, a Muslim identity and a deliberate turn to Islam are perceived as a means to claim/maintain dignity in the face of exclusion. As an in-between group, neither accepted as French, Dutch, or German nor as Algerians, Moroccans, or Turks, many members of the second generation come to see themselves generally as Muslims and identify with 'things Muslim' and for a sense of belonging.[146]

NEOMERCANTILISM

Despite economic globalization, economic nationalism or neomercantilism has persisted. Evidence of economic nationalism includes the failure of the Doha Round of global trade talks that were begun in 2001, which "has already cost hundreds of billions of dollars in potentially increased global trade."[147] In Doha, it was originally decided that negotiations would focus on liberalizing trade in agriculture and services, both contentious issues, with an eye towards reaching agreement by 2005. However, none of the three impediments to an agreement that C. Fred Bergsten identified has been overcome:

> massive current account imbalances and currency misalignments pushing policy in dangerously protectionist directions in both the United States and Europe; the strong and growing anti-globalization sentiments that stalemate virtually every trade debate on both sides of the Atlantic and elsewhere; and the absence of a compelling reason for the political leaders of the chief holdout countries to make the necessary concessions to reach an agreement.[148]

The "most contentious issue" involved agricultural subsidies in the developed world that prevent developing countries from selling their products overseas and result in stagnation in their agricultural sector.[149] The causes of this stagnation, according to Goldin and Reinert, include "the bias against agriculture in most developing countries; and the extensive subsidization of agriculture in the developed countries." In their view, this "stagnation is an important explanation of the continued stubbornness of rural poverty and of the limitations to developing country participation in the world trading system."[150] Efforts to reach agreement collapsed in July 2006 when the United States and the EU failed to agree on agricultural subsidies and, in response, major developing countries like Brazil refused to open their markets further to developed countries' manufactured goods and services. Indeed, the EU and the United States added new farm subsidies. Moreover, bilateral trade agreements, especially in Asia, may further impede multilateral trade agreements.[151] One view is that the Doha failure threatens "long-term damage to the notion of multilateralism."[152] Others, however, decry "the 'bicycle theory' of trade negotiations – the view that the trade regime can remain upright only with continuous progress in liberalization."[153]

Since the onset of the global financial crisis, neomercantilism has experienced a revival, as countries sought ways around trade rules in order to advance their own economic interests. Overall, there was a rise in protectionism accompanying the deepening recession, although not as severe as some had expected.[154] According to the World Bank, seventeen members of the G-20 had adopted forty-seven protectionist measures between November 2008 and March 2009.[155] At the height of the crisis, economist Jeffrey Garten warned that, "if historians look back to today's severe downturn, with its crumbling markets, rising unemployment and massive government interventions, they could well be busy analyzing how globalization – the spread of trade, finance, technology and the movement of people around the world – went into reverse." He then suggested: "They would likely point to the growth of economic nationalism as the root cause," which in his view "is a frame of mind that casts doubt on the very assumption that we live in a single international market, and that relatively open borders are a virtue."[156]

Barry Buzan believes that contemporary neomercantilists "seek to make the international economy fit with the patterns of fragmentation in the political system by reducing the scope of the global market. They emphasize the integrity of the national economy and the primacy of state goals (military, welfare, societal). They advocate protection as a way of preserving integrity, but may be attracted to the construction of their own economy dominating at the centre."[157] In addition to state intervention, barriers to "the free flow of capital are rising fast," and "a retrenchment in cross-border credit is under way." "This," concluded *The Economist*, "is economic nationalism, but of insidious type . . . the purpose of which is to steer banks towards supporting businesses and jobs at home, not abroad."[158] Indeed, according to a World Trade Organization (WTO) report concerning the G-20, released in September 2009, "there has been policy slippage since the global crisis began. In some cases, G20 members have raised tariffs and introduced new non-tariff measures, and most of them have continued to use trade defense mechanisms. Two have re-introduced agricultural export subsidies."[159]

American public sentiment has grown increasingly negative towards free trade. In a 2010 poll, 53 percent of respondents said that free trade agreements harmed the United States (compared to 46 percent in 2007 and 32 percent in 1999), and over half of higher-income Americans (compared to 24 percent in 1999) – those usually most supportive of free trade – took this position.[160] Currently, all major trading states have developed new sophisticated non-tariff barriers to free trade, such as the US creative interpretation of "antidumping" rules. The United States also arguably violated North American Free Trade Agreement (NAFTA) rules by prohibiting Mexican trucks on American highways because of "safety" issues.[161] Mexico retaliated by placing tariffs on American industrial and agricultural exports. Such economic unilateralism led the WTO to warn that growing protectionism could "slowly strangle" international trade.[162]

China acceded to membership of the WTO in 2001 pledging to make its transition to a full market economy with all reasonable speed. A decade later, China still had a long way to go. Chinese currency was fixed to the dollar in 2008 at a rate that undervalued the renminbi/yuan somewhere between 25 and 50 percent (depending on the measure). This gave an "artificial" boost to Chinese exports. China's trade surplus soared, and the country's reserves of dollars and other foreign currencies accumulated to unprecedented levels. Meanwhile, China recovered remarkably well from a temporary decline in its export trade owing to the global recession. Only escalating pressures from the United States (which threatened countervailing duties), the G-20, and IMF finally persuaded the Chinese government in March 2011 to allow a gradual appreciation of the renminbi. This, in any event, seemed a prudent course to help stem what had come to be seen as an "overheated" Chinese economy accompanied by dangerous levels of inflation. Meanwhile, China has used the controversy over exchange rates to suggest that leading economic states and the IMF begin to think about a new global monetary system that would include a wider basket of currencies including the renminbi.[163] In many respects, China remains a tightly controlled economy. The government manages capital flows and dictates to foreign firms which economic sectors and geographic areas of the country are open for their investment.[164] Prices of water, electricity, and fuel – as well as a host of consumer items – are controlled, and well over 100,000 enterprises remain state-owned.

For its part, the United States has been vigorously criticized, especially at the G-20 meeting in Seoul in November 2010 – by major exporters like China and Germany and by emerging economies like Russia and South Korea – for efforts by the US Federal Reserve to stimulate domestic economic activity through the QE2 (Large Scale Asset Purchase, also known as "quantitative easing") purchase of large amounts of US Treasury bonds. Critics alleged that this was a disguised attempt to devalue the US dollar.[165] Pledging "to pursue the full range of policies conducive to reducing excessive imbalances," the G-20 has sought to give additional responsibility to the IMF to monitor countries' exchange rate policies and to give emerging economies a greater decision-making role in that institution.[166] The intent – however elusive its implementation – is to head off "currency wars" and, more specifically in the meantime, to help push the renminbi higher and keep the dollar stable.

The EU and the United States filed a complaint with the WTO about Chinese limitations on exports of nine raw materials for the steel industry.[167] The US, the EU, and Japan were also disturbed when China announced that those who sell high tech equipment to the Chinese government must prove that their products contained "indigenous innovation," a rule that would curb China's imports of high-tech products.[168] China has intermittently limited the export of rare earths needed in high-technology industries.[169] More recently, China has been accused of providing illegal subsidies to its clean energy industries.[170]

The WTO did decide in favor of an American complaint regarding China's limitations on imports of books and movies ("pirated" copies of which are commonly available); this is part of a much larger trade dispute concerning China's alleged failure to protect intellectual property.[171] China has lost two recent WTO cases involving taxes on imported automobile parts and enforcement of counterfeiting laws, and, as of 2010, had agreed to alter these policies. Finally, China's efforts to increase its global market share during the economic crisis by reducing prices exacerbated trade frictions with the United States and Europe.[172] With its trade deficit rising by a third in 2010 and imports from China reaching $364.9 billion that year,[173] the American commitment to free trade has been sorely tested.

Overall, China has been more protectionist during the recession than the United States.[174] Nevertheless, China also has reasons for complaint about the policies of its trading partners. Beijing has imposed anti-dumping duties on US poultry[175] and has filed complaints against the United States and the EU about import tariffs[176] and anti-dumping tariffs on selected Chinese exports, including EU tariffs on Chinese shoe exports.[177]

In Britain, there have been protests against foreign workers,[178] and a British minister suggested that his government would review whether foreign ownership of British companies might be disadvantageous for the country, reflecting "growing scrutiny in the U.K. of a decades-long mantra that foreign ownership is neutral for domestic companies."[179] In Russia, the government triggered protests in Vladivostok by placing high tariffs on the import of popular used Japanese autos,[180] and, according to an EU trade official, "Putin visits a combine harvester factory and decides on the spot he'll raise tariffs."[181] Tensions have also grown in US–EU[182] and US–Indian trade relations.[183] Bremmer summarizes the protectionist wave as follows:

> China has reinstated tax relief for certain exporters. Russia has limited foreign investment in 42 "strategic sectors" and imposed new duties on imported cars, pork, and poultry. Indonesia has imposed import tariffs and licensing restrictions on over 500 types of foreign products. India has added a 20 percent levy on soybean oil imports. Argentina and Brazil are publicly considering new tariffs on imported textiles and wine. South Korea refuses to drop trade barriers against U.S. auto imports. France has announced the creation of a state fund to protect domestic companies from foreign takeover.[184]

Striking evidence of economic nationalism in the key agricultural sector emerged with dramatic increases in grain and commodity prices in 2008. Confronted with domestic unrest, countries as varied as Ukraine, Argentina, Pakistan, India, and China[185] reacted by imposing export taxes and export bans on grains and fertilizers, thereby worsening food shortages elsewhere, especially in East Africa. Russia imposed a similar export ban two years later.[186] Even the member states of the EU "have broken ranks, opting in ugly disarray for self-interested policies to protect their own citizens and banks first."[187]

Of greatest concern, perhaps, has been the apparent American retreat from free trade. Washington, for example, decided to place tariffs on Chinese-made tires in response to lobbying by the United Steelworkers who claim Chinese tire imports had cost 5,000 jobs since 2004. In taking action, Washington for the first time invoked a safeguard provision that was part of its agreement supporting China's 2001 entry into the WTO by which US companies or workers harmed by Chinese imports can ask for protection by showing that they had suffered a "market disruption." The action, described by *The Economist* as "playing with fire,"[188] "economic vandalism," and "a wrongheaded decision"[189] by the Obama administration, triggered a nationalist outburst of anti-American sentiment in China, including demands that China sell its vast holdings of US securities. The WTO, however, ruled that the American tariff was legal.[190] Beijing, in tit-for-tat retaliation, threatened to impose tariffs on American exports of chicken and car parts[191] and to investigate US and EU dumping of chemical products and optical fiber, following the beginning of a US investigation of Chinese subsidies of aluminum exports.[192]

Matters were further exacerbated by a US decision to redefine solar panels in a manner that would increase the tariff on their importation from China[193] and by imposition of antidumping duties on Chinese steel that China described as "abusive protectionism."[194] Antidumping duties were imposed first on Chinese exports of tubular steel and later on exports of drill pipe.[195] China responded by taxing selected steel imports from the US and Russia.[196] American policy was described as "the tip of a coming protectionist iceberg" in a report by Global Trade Alert, a team of trade analysts associated with the World Bank and the British government.[197] The trade conflict could infect Sino-American political relations, although both sides seem aware of this ominous possibility.

At best, cooperation in the face of global recession was spotty, and economic nationalism reared its head as global financial and economic conditions worsened.[198] Germany, for instance, refused to adopt fiscal-stimulus programs as vigorous as those of other European governments, and, for a time, its export-driven economy seemed especially susceptible to recession.[199] Germany also resisted aiding Hungary or other recent EU members,[200] and Greece's 2010 financial crisis opened political fissures within Europe.[201] The European Union did, however, finally cooperate in the face of the prospect of Greek sovereign default by creating a fund managed to rescue member states beset by similar financial woes.[202] Whether that plan can weather additional market stresses affecting government borrowing in Portugal and Spain – and even Italy and France – remains to be seen. Many observers argue that only a full-fledged European financial union has any real chance of coping with the challenges that lie ahead.

In Asia, at least a vague form of cooperation appeared more quickly as Japan, South Korea, and China agreed to work together in responding to recessionary strains.[203]

As the economic conditions deteriorated in 2009, there appeared "a wave of barriers to world commerce" by countries "scrambling to safeguard their key industries – often by damaging those of their neighbors."[204] The initial US economic stimulus plan, for example, included a "Buy American" requirement that probably violated WTO rules,[205] angering even close American allies like Canada.[206] The original House version of an energy bill contained a provision that would impose tariffs on the imports of countries that do not accept limits on global warming pollution.[207] "Buy American" was echoed in Asia by "Buy local" campaigns, especially in Vietnam and Malaysia.[208] It is hardly surprising that economic unilateralism was reciprocated.[209]

Finally, opposition in the US Congress to concluding bilateral trade agreements with countries such as Colombia and South Korea (both ratified in late 2011),[210] along with unwillingness to make hard decisions to rescue the Doha Round suggest that Washington may no longer be willing to exercise hegemonic leadership in maintaining a liberal economic system. Without a hegemon to lead, economic liberalism may slow or even erode. That said, the Obama administration has to date avoided any major changes in the US commitments to existing trade agreements, including NAFTA, and has in general reconfirmed its commitment to the free trade ideal.

A key question is whether the economic nationalism that accompanied the global financial and economic crisis is part of a long-term trend or is merely a temporary retreat in the face of economic hard times. Although economic nationalism was widespread even before the crisis, as shown by the stalemate over Doha, elements of it are likely to remain after a recovery. However, there are reasons to believe that economic nationalism will moderate as the crisis ebbs. Indeed, the extent of the decline in trade was, ironically, partly due to globalization of the supply chain, diminished demand leading to reduced inventories, and a significant decline in imports.[211] Despite the precipitous decline in overall trade in 2008 and much of 2009 that elicited comparisons with the Great Depression, by the third quarter of 2009, global trade appeared to have ceased declining and had again begun to grow,[212] and global demand also seemed to be recovering. Still, protectionist barriers, once in place, are difficult to remove, and the disagreements they spawn inevitably leave political scars.

ENVIRONMENTAL NATIONALISM

Economic pressures and the emergence of China and India[213] as economic powers and as leading producers of carbon gases have complicated the already difficult and complex task of achieving cooperation in dealing with regional[214] and global environmental challenges. Developing countries, many of which resist limits on carbon emissions owing to the impact on economic development, are also the greatest victims of the problem.[215] Even Europe, a center of environmental concern and activism, has found cooperation difficult. Economic costs are perhaps the greatest obstacle to environmental progress. Indeed, there is an inverse relationship between the level and direction of economic activity and environmental cooperation. This relationship can be loosened if environmental investment can be "sold" to publics as contributing to prosperity, an effort undertaken by the Obama administration. However, in the midst of financial hard times, it is difficult to find the private investment for new environmentally friendly technologies.

In 2007, China passed the United States as the world's leading emitter of carbon gases. The two countries engaged in negotiations about limiting such gases in preparation for achieving new global standards at a meeting in Copenhagen in December 2009 to replace the Kyoto Protocol which expires in 2012, but agreement proved elusive. China and India pointed out that Americans are far higher per capita sources of carbon gases, while Americans stressed that China's and India's rates of increase are higher.[216] The core problem in negotiations between the developed and developing worlds is that the former want the latter to reduce emissions of greenhouse gases, while the latter contend that limits would preclude their economic growth and opportunity to catch up with wealthy states. This remains a major obstacle, for instance, in efforts to limit deforestation of Brazil's Amazon region. Farming and logging interests, as well as inadequate resources for environmental protection, undermine the government's policies and laws.[217]

Although the Obama administration is more favorable to limiting greenhouse emissions than its predecessor, it faces significant congressional and public opposition to taking the lead in coping with global warming. And American subsidies for biofuels like ethanol, though intended to increase the country's energy independence, also raise grain prices and produce hunger in poor countries where individual incomes are already depressed by the global recession.[218] By one estimate there was an increase of 100 million who suffered from hunger during the global recession.[219] China is prepared to initiate "green" policies at home (and is under domestic pressure to do so) and to work bilaterally with the United States towards reaching an arrangement, but remains unwilling to accept quantitative limits on emissions. Unilateral policies announced by Mexico, Brazil, and Peru are promising. And the EU, in a meeting in December 2008, remained committed to cutting greenhouse gases by 20 percent over 1990 levels, obtaining 20 percent of energy from renewable sources, and making efficiency savings of 20 percent over forecast consumption by the year 2020.[220]

Thus with environment, as other fields, the picture is decidedly mixed. In recent years, globalization has advanced in some areas and stalled or even retreated in others. Our final chapter will attempt to bring all the evidence together and make some predictions about the future.

NOTES

1 Vladimir Ilyich Lenin, "A Few Words on Dialectics. Two Revolutions," *One Step Forward, Two Steps Back*, http://www.marxists.org/archive/lenin/works/1904/onestep/r.htm.
2 Chanda, *Bound Together*, xiii–xiv.
3 Altman, "Globalization in Retreat," 2.
4 "WTO Abandons Plan for Trade Talks," *BBC News*, December 12, 2008, http://news.bbc.co.uk/2/hi/bUSiness/7779748.stm.
5 The EU is already something of an anomaly of a globalizing era. The European Union, writes Stephen Krasner, "has territory, recognition, control, national authority, extranational authority, and supranational authority . . . Is it a state, a commonwealth, a dominion, a confederation of states, a federation of states?" See Krasner, *Sovereignty: Organized Hypocrisy*, 235. Held et al., *Global Transformations*, 74, conclude that "it is best described neither as an international regime nor as a federal state, but as a network of states involving the pooling of sovereignty." See also Nederveen Pieterse, *Globalization and Culture*, 12.
6 The initial Irish rejection in 2008 was reversed a year later. The Lisbon Treaty was finally adopted in November 2009.
7 Paul Krugman argues that unemployment in Europe and wage inequality in the United States are less the result of cheap exports from low-wage exporters than of technological change and "slicing up the value added chain." See P. Krugman, "Growing World Trade: Causes and Consequences," in William C. Brainard and George L. Perry, eds., *Brookings Papers on Economic Activity 1995* (Washington, DC: Brookings Institution Press, 1995), 327–62. See also Rodrik, *Has Globalization Gone Too Far?*, 16 ff.

8 Thus, *The Economist* of February 7, 2009 was ominously headlined "The Return of Economic Nationalism." See also "The Return of Economic Nationalism" (9–10) and "Homeward Bound" (69–70), *The Economist*, February 7, 2009. See also Irwin, "Goodbye, Free Trade?" C1–C2.

9 Pew Research Center, "America's Place in the World 2009" (December 2009), 1, http://people-press.org/reports/pdf/569.pdf. See also "Pay Any Price? Pull the Other One," *The Economist*, December 12, 2009, 33–4.

10 "Stop, Border Ahead," *The Economist*, May 30, 2009, 37.

11 "Market of Ideas," 70. Among capitalism's strongest supporters are China, Germany, and Brazil.

12 Susan Strange, *Mad Money: When Markets Outgrow Governments* (Ann Arbor, MI: University of Michigan Press, 1998), 1.

13 Susan Strange, *Casino Capitalism* (Manchester, UK: Manchester University Press, 1997).

14 Greider, *One World Ready or Not*, 12.

15 John Plender, "The Return of the State: How Government Is Back at the Heart of Economic Life," *Financial Times*, August 21, 2008, http://www.ft.com/cms/s/0/73dfc892-6fb2-11dd-986f-0000779fd18c,dwp. Philip Cerny takes issue with Plender, arguing: "Today, the underlying aim of state intervention is not to replace the market, but to make it work more efficiently . . . Relationships between the state, international institutions and the economy are . . . fundamentally different from earlier forms of state intervention. In this context, paradoxically, moral hazard is unavoidable – in the name of ever-increasing marketisation." See P. Cerny, "Nature of State Intervention Has Changed Since the Pre-1980s," *Financial Times*, August 26, 2008, http://www.ft.com/cms/s/0/586987e6-7305-11dd-983b-0000779fd18c.html.

16 "The Globalization Index," 70–1. Several of these countries are growing rapidly. See, for example, "Brazil Takes Off," *The Economist*, November 14, 2009, 15.

17 The expansion of global trade resumed in 2010, led by China and India. See Sewell Chan, "Rebound in World Trade Is Seen," *New York Times*, March 26, 2010, http://www.nytimes.com/2010/03/27/business/global/27wto.html.

18 Altman, "Globalization in Retreat," 5, 6. In addition, global flows of direct foreign investment (FDI) declined 39 percent in 2009, from $1.7 trillion in 2008 to just over $1 trillion. See Paul Hannon, "Foreign Investing Falls 39%," *Wall Street Journal*, January 20, 2010, A13.

19 Altman, "Globalization in Retreat," 7.

20 Ó Tuathail, Herod, and Roberts, "Negotiating Unruly Problematics," 20.

21 Walker Connor, "Beyond Reason: The Nature of the Ethnonational Bond," in John Hutchinson and Anthony D. Smith, eds., *Ethnicity* (Oxford: Oxford University Press, 1996), 70.

22 Rosenau, *Distant Proximities*, 107.

23 Castells, *The Power of Identity*, 30.

24 Scholte, "The Geography of Collective Identities in a Globalizing World," 580.

25 "Hovorte po slovensky!" *The Economist*, August 1, 2009, 47.

26 Ironically, the smaller polities resulting from secession may thrive in the context of regional or global economic systems that provide economies of scale previously afforded only by larger states.

27 Yael Tamir, *Liberal Nationalism* (Princeton, NJ: Princeton University Press, 1993), 3.

28 Roman Szporluk, "Thoughts about Change: Ernest Gellner and the History of Nationalism" in John A. Hall, ed., *The State of the Nation: Ernest Gellner and the Theory of Nationalism* (Cambridge: Cambridge University Press, 1998), 27.

29 Moynihan, *Pandaemonium: Ethnicity in International Politics* (New York: Oxford University Press, 1993), 174.

30 Woodrow Wilson, "Appeal for Support of the League of Nations at Pueblo, Colorado," in Mario DiNunzio, ed., *Woodrow Wilson: Essential Writings and Speeches of the Scholar-President* (New York: NYU Press, 2006), 415.

31 Cited in David D. Binder, with Barbara Crossette, "As Ethnic Wars Multiply, US Strives

for a Policy," *New York Times*, February 7, 1993, http://query.nytimes.com/gst/fullpage.html?res=9F0CEFD9113AF934A35751C0A965958260&sec=&spon=&pagewanted=all.

32 Nigel Harris, *National Liberation* (London: I. B. Tauris, 1990), 9.
33 Ted Robert Gurr, *Minorities at Risk* (Washington, DC: United States Institute of Peace Press, 1996).
34 Strange, *Retreat of the State*, 5.
35 Cited in Binder, "As Ethnic Wars Multiply." Nairn and James, *Global Matrix*, 12, write of "minnows inherently incapable of 'classical' nationalism and its accompanying prescriptions."
36 Craig Whitlock, "We Must Not Let Things Fall Apart," *Washington Post National Weekly Edition*, August 31–September 6, 2009, 20.
37 Nicholas Kulish, "Kosovo's Actions Hearten a Hungarian Enclave," *New York Times*, April 7, 2008, http://www.nytimes.com/2008/04/07/world/europe/07iht-07hungarians.11716058.html.
38 Castells, *The Power of Identity*, 13, defines "fundamentalism" *as the constructions of collective identity of individual behavior and society's institutions to the norms derived from God's law, interpreted by a definite authority that intermediates between God and humanity*." Emphasis in original.
39 Emily Wax, "A Conservative Uprising in Bangalore," *Washington Post National Weekly Edition*, May 11–17, 2009, 18.
40 See Geeta Anand, "India's Tribal People Caught in War's Crossfire," *Wall Street Journal*, June 23, 2010, A13.
41 "Not Free to Starve," *The Economist*, November 7, 2009, 43.
42 "A Ragtag Rebellion," *The Economist*, June 27, 2009, 47–8.
43 Gordon Fairclough, "China's Ethnic Tension Isn't Limited to Tibet," *Wall Street Journal*, April 5–6, 2008, A5.
44 "On the Run," *The Economist*, June 27, 2009, 50.
45 "Secret World of Vietnamese Workers in Russia," *BBC News*, April 4, 2010, http://news.bbc.co.uk/2/hi/8482466.stm.
46 For a comparison of the challenges of assimilating immigrants in Europe and the United States, see Nancy Foner, "Challenges of Integration: The Second Generation in the United States and Europe," in Joseph Chamie and Mary G. Powers, eds., *International Migration and Development: Continuing the Dialogue: Legal and Policy Perspectives* (New York: Center for Migration Studies, 2008), 159–68.
47 Urry, *Global Complexity*, 87.
48 Lexington, "The Hub Nation," *The Economist*, April 24, 2010, 32.
49 John W. Books, "Globalization and Alternative Approaches to the Transformation of Nation-States," in Kennedy and Danks, eds., *Globalization and National Identities*, 216.
50 Donald L. Horowitz, *Ethnic Groups in Conflict*, 2nd edn (Berkeley, CA: University of California Press, 2000), 186, 17.
51 Cited in Bob Davis, "Global Ties under Stress as Nations Grab Power," *Wall Street Journal*, April 28, 2008, A1.
52 Steven Erlanger and Nicholas Kulish, "Sarkozy and Merkel Try to Shape European Unity," *New York Times*, March 30, 2009, http://www.nytimes.com/2009/03/31/world/europe/31europe.html.
53 "Taming Leviathan: A Special Report on the Future of the State," *The Economist*, March 19, 2011, 4.
54 Cited in "Leviathan Stirs Again," *The Economist*, January 23, 2010, 23.
55 Cited in "Another Great Leap Forward?" *The Economist*, March 13, 2010, 27.
56 Ian Bremmer, "State Capitalism Comes of Age: The End of the Free Market?" *Foreign Affairs* 88:3 (May/June 2009), 40. See also Bremmer, *The End of the Free Market: Who Wins the War Between States and Corporations?* (New York: Portfolio, 2010).
57 "Leviathan Stirs Again," 24.
58 Bobbitt, *The Shield of Achilles*, 283. Bobbitt contrasts this to the neoliberal "entrepreneurial state."

59 Bremmer, "State Capitalism Comes of Age," 40.
60 Ibid.
61 David Cho and Thomas Heath, "Cash Hoarders," *Washington Post National Weekly Edition*, November 5–11, 2007, 23–4.
62 "A Bigger World," 22.
63 "Nationalisation Rides Again," *The Economist*, November 14, 2009, 52–3.
64 Derek Scissors, "Deng Undone: The Costs of Halting Market Reform in China," *Foreign Affairs* 88:3 (May/June 2009), 28.
65 See Kendra Marr, "The Auto Empire," *Washington Post National Weekly Edition*, May 25–31, 2009, 25.
66 "U.S. Trade Deficit Narrowed in September," *New York Times*, November 10, 2010, http://www.nytimes.com/2010/11/11/business/economy/11econ.html?ref=business.
67 Stefan Halper, *The Beijing Consensus: How China's Authoritarian Model Will Dominate the Twenty-First Century* (New York: Basic Books, 2010), x, xi. Emphasis in original.
68 Ibid., 2. For an analysis that sees China's repressive policies as a reflection of fear, see "What Are They Afraid of?" *The Economist*, February 20, 2010, 37–8. See also Walker, "Globalization 3.0."
69 Bremmer, "State Capitalism Comes of Age," 41.
70 Ibid., 42.
71 Ibid., 44.
72 Halper, *The Beijing Consensus*, 2–3.
73 "Where Life Is Cheap and Talk Is Loose."
74 See "The Economics of Violence," *The Economist*, April 16, 2011.
75 "Taking on the Narcos, and Their American Guns," *The Economist*, April 4, 2009, 43–4.
76 Tom Miller, "Twilight Zone," *Washington Post National Weekly Review*, February 16–22, 2009, 27.
77 Sven Bislev, "Globalization, State Transformation, and Public Security," *International Political Science Review*, 25:3 (2004), 288.
78 Maryann K. Cusimano, "Beyond Sovereignty: The Rise of Transsovereign Problems," in Cusimano, ed., *Beyond Sovereignty*, 4.
79 Achille Mbembe, "At the Edge of the World: Boundaries, Territoriality, and Sovereignty in Africa," trans. Steven Rendall, in Appadurai, ed., *Globalization*, 29.
80 Ibid., 25, 26.
81 Ibid., 38.
82 Jonathan Di John, "Conceptualising the Causes and Consequences of Failed States: A Critical Review of the Literature," *Development as State-Making* 25 (January 2008), Crisis States Research Centre, http://www.crisisstates.com/download/wp/wpSeries2/wp25.2.pdf, 10.
83 Robert I. Rotberg, "The Failure and Collapse of Nation-States: Breakdown, Prevention, and Repair," in Rotberg, ed., *When States Fail* (Princeton, NJ: Princeton University Press, 2003), 5. Not all failed states are characterized by violence and insecurity.
84 Regional and ethnic loyalties continue to afflict Iraq. See, for example, Amit R. Paley, "'On the Verge of Exploding' in Iraq," *Washington Post Weekly Edition*, September 22–8, 2008, 21–2.
85 "Failed States: The 2011 Index," *Foreign Policy* 187 (July/August 2011), 48.
86 Brookings Institution, "Index of State Weakness in the Developing World (20 Indicators)," http://www.brookings.edu/~/media/Files/rc/reports/2008/02_weak_states_index/02_weak_states_index_indicator_scores_pullout.pdf.
87 Brookings Institution, "Index of State Weakness in the Developing World," August 24, 2010, http://www.brookings.edu/reports/2008/02_weak_states_index.aspx.
88 Blake Hounshell, "Dark Crystal," *Foreign Policy* 187 (July/August 2011), 50.
89 Robert D. Kaplan, *The Ends of the Earth* (New York: Vintage Books, 1996), 436.
90 "Mr. Order Meets Mr. Chaos," *Foreign Policy* 124 (May/June 2001), 54.
91 Ó Tuathail, Herod, and Roberts, "Negotiating Unruly Problematics," 1.

92 Milena Novy-Marx, "MacArthur Initiative on Global Migration and Human Mobility," in Chamie and Powers, eds., *International Migration and Development*, 56.
93 Ian Goldin, Geoffrey Cameron, and Meera Balarajan, *Exceptional People: How Migration Shaped Our World and Will Define Our Future* (Princeton, NJ: Princeton University Press, 2011), 162–3.
94 Randal C. Archibold, "Arizona Enacts Stringent Law on Immigration," *New York Times*, April 23, 2010, http://www.nytimes.com/2010/04/24/us/politics/24immig.html.
95 As a result of the economic recession, anti-immigrant sentiment, the cost of employing skilled foreign workers, the US quota for visas for skilled foreigners was not reached in 2009 for the first time since 2003. See Miriam Jordan, "Slump Sinks Visa Program," *Wall Street Journal*, October 29, 2009, A1, A4.
96 For a comparison of the challenges of assimilating immigrants in Europe and the United States, see Nancy Foner, "Challenges of Integration: The Second Generation in the United States and Europe," in Chamie and Powers, eds., *International Migration and Development*, 159–68.
97 Gordon H. Hanson, "Illegal Migration from Mexico to the United States," *Journal of Economic Literature* 44:4 (December 2006), 872.
98 Samuel P. Huntington, *Who Are We? The Challenges to America's National Identity* (New York: Simon & Schuster, 2005), 221.
99 Ibid.
100 Ibid., 247. For a spirited defense of the virtues of immigration into the US, see "A Ponzi Scheme that Works," *The Economist*, December 19, 2009, 41–4.
101 "Multikulturell? Wir?" *The Economist*, November 13, 2010, 59–60.
102 Sebastian Moffett, "Crisis Slowed Migration to Industrialized Nations," *Wall Street Journal*, July 13, 2011, A10.
103 Anthony Faiola, "A Global Economy in Retreat," *Washington Post National Weekly Review*, March 9–15, 2009, 6.
104 Patrick Barta and Joel Millman, "The Great U-Turn," *Wall Street Journal*, June 6–7, 2009, A1, A10. In 2009, illegal immigration from Mexico was at the lowest level in a decade. Miriam Jordan, "Illegal Immigration from Mexico Hits Lowest Level in Decade," *Wall Street Journal*, July 23, 2009, A2. According to one study, Mexican emigration dropped 42 percent between 2007 and 2009. See "The People Crunch," *The Economist*, January 17, 2009, 58. Reverse migration could cease if the emerging economies from which migrants originated experience a dramatic economic decline.
105 Miriam Jordan, "As U.S. Job Opportunities Fade, More Mexicans Look Homeward," *Wall Street Journal*, February 13, 2009, A14, and Julia Preston, "Mexican Data Say Migration to U.S. Has Plummeted," *New York Times*, May 14, 2009, http://www.nytimes.com/2009/05/15/us/15immig.html.
106 Julia Preston, "Number of Illegal Immigrants in U.S. Fell, Study Says," *New York Times*, September 1, 2010, http://www.nytimes.com/2010/09/02/us/02immig.html?hp.
107 Tara Bahrampour, "Staying Put," *Washington Post National Weekly Edition*, July 27–August 2, 2009, 25.
108 Vivek Wadhwa, "Brain Drain," *Washington Post National Weekly Edition*, March 16–22, 2009, 27.
109 Carl Bialik, "Work-Visa Numbers Get Squishy – and Get Played," *Wall Street Journal*, April 1, 2009, A19.
110 Nadim Audi and Caroline Brothers, "French Police Dismantle Migrant Camp," *New York Times*, September 22, 2009, http://www.nytimes.com/2009/09/23/world/europe/23france.html.
111 "Southern Misery," *The Economist*, January 16, 2010, 50. See also "Fear of Foreigners," *The Economist*, March 5, 2011, 60.
112 Elisabetta Povoledo, "Immigrants Rally for a Nationwide Strike in Italy," *New York Times*, March 1, 2010, http://www.nytimes.com/2010/03/02/world/europe/02iht-italy.html.
113 Liz Gooch, "Malaysia's Labor Restrictions Hurt Business," *New York Times*, August 31, 2009, http://www.nytimes.com/2009/09/01/business/global/01iht-labor.html.

114 "Inhospitality," *The Economist*, February 27, 2010, 50.
115 Barta and Millman, "The Great U-Turn," A10.
116 Norimitsu Onishi, "Toiling Far from Home for Philippine Dreams," *New York Times*, September 18, 2010, http://www.nytimes.com/2010/09/19/world/asia/19phils.html.
117 "The People Crunch," 59.
118 Hanson, "Illegal Migration from Mexico to the United States," 872.
119 De Blij, "The Power of Place," 13.
120 Mary Beth Sheridan, "A Dire Situation," *Washington Post National Weekly Edition*, April 27–May 3, 2009, 19. See also Sabrina Tavernise, "Cash Flow from Tajik Migrants Stalls," *New York Times*, December 25, 2008, http://www.nytimes.com/2008/12/25/world/asia/25tajikistan.html.
121 Miriam Jordan, "Latin American Workers Send Home Less Money from U.S.," *Wall Street Journal*, August 12, 2009, A10.
122 Dilip Ratha and Sanket Mohapatra, "Revised Outlook for Remittance Flows 2009–2011: Remittances Expected to Fall by 5 to 8 percent in 2009," *Migration and Development Brief 9*, World Bank, March 23, 2009, http://siteresources.worldbank.org/INTPROSPECTS/Resources/MD_Brief9_Mar2009.pdf.
123 Miriam Jordan and Paulo Trevisani, "Buoyed by Recovery, Migrants Send Home More Money," *Wall Street Journal*, May 14, 2011, A2.
124 Sarah Gammage, "Exporting People and Recruiting Remittances: A Development Strategy for El Salvador?" *Latin American Perspectives* 33:6 (November 2006), 96.
125 "The People Crunch," 58.
126 "A New (Under) Class of Travelers," *The Economist*, June 27, 2009, 67–8.
127 Shankar Vedantam, "In Search of a Better Place to Live," *Washington Post National Weekly Edition*, March 2–8, 2009, 21.
128 Tariq Modood, "Introduction: The Politics of Multiculturalism in the New Europe," in Tariq Modood and Prina J. Werbner, eds., *The Politics of Multiculturalism in the New Europe* (London: Zed Books, 1997), 1.
129 Peter Baldwin, "The Return of the Coercive State: Behavioral Control in Multicultural Society," in Paul, Ikenberry, and Hall, eds., *The Nation-State in Question*, 110.
130 Robert J. Pauly, Jr., *Islam in Europe: Integration of Marginalization?* (Aldershot, UK: Ashgate Publishing, 2004), 161–2. The highest Muslim population in Europe is in Russia, accounting for almost 12 percent of the country's population. See "A Shifting Locus," *The Economist*, October 10, 2009, 62–3.
131 "A Waxing Crescent," *The Economist*, January 29, 2011, 59.
132 Robert S. Leiken, "Europe's Angry Muslims," *Foreign Affairs* 84:4 (July/August 2005), 122.
133 Pauly, *Islam in Europe*, 164, 165.
134 Castells, *The Power of Identity*, 21.
135 Leiken, "Europe's Angry Muslims," 120. French officials fear that Islamic radicalism is being fueled in overcrowded prisons. See "Jailhouse Jihad," *The Economist*, September 20, 2008, 69.
136 Pauly, *Islam in Europe*, 170.
137 Thomas L. Friedman, "America vs. the Narrative," *New York Times*, November 28, 2009, http://www.nytimes.com/2009/11/29/opinion/29friedman.html. For a comparison of Muslim assimilation in Europe and the United States, see Rey Koslowski, "Global Mobility and the Quest for an International Migration Regime," in Chamie and Powers, eds., *International Migration and Development*, 132–3.
138 Pew Global Attitudes Project, 2005, "Islamic Extremism: Common Concern for Muslim and Western Publics" (July 14), http://pewglobal.org/reports/display.php?ReportID=248.
139 "Pious, Loyal and Unhappy," *The Economist*, May 9, 2009, 59.
140 "Running for Cover," *The Economist*, May 15, 2010, and Edward Cody, "French Lawmakers Advance Public Ban on Full-Face Islamic Veils," *Washington Post*, July 14,

2010, http://www.washingtonpost.com/wp-dyn/content/article/2010/07/13/AR2010071301103.html.

141 Cited in "No Cover Up," *The Economist*, June 27, 2009, 58. A similar argument was made by France's Urban Regeneration Minister Fadela Amara, herself a Muslim. See "French Minister Urges Burka Ban," *BBC News*, August 17, 2009, http://news.bbc.co.uk/2/hi/europe/8203290.stm.Gender rights in France have also triggered a quarrel over the issue of providing hymenoplasty for non-virgin Muslim women seeking to get married. See Stacy Meichtry and Max Colchester, "Secular, Muslim Culture Clash Ensnares French Doctors," *Wall Street Journal*, June 10, 2008, A11.

142 "French Police Fine Muslim Driver for Wearing Veil," *BBC News*, April 23, 2010, http://news.bbc.co.uk/2/hi/8641070.stm.

143 "Police Stop Veiled Woman in Italy," *BBC News*, May 3, 2010, http://news.bbc.co.uk/2/hi/europe/8658017.stm.

144 "'Hijab Martyr' Rally due in Cairo," *BBC News*, July 9, 2009, http://www.webcitation.org/query?url=http%3A%2F%2Fnews.bbc.co.uk%2F2%2Fhi%2Fmiddle_east%2F8141900.stm&date=2009-12-31.

145 Pew Global Attitudes Project, 2006, "Muslims in Europe: Economic Worries Top Concerns about Religious and Cultural Identity" (June 6), http://pewglobal.org/reports/display.php?ReportID=254.

146 Koslowski, "Global Mobility and the Quest for an International Migration Regime," 133.

147 Bremmer, "State Capitalism Comes of Age," 52.

148 C. Fred Bergsten, "Rescuing the Doha Round," *Foreign Affairs* 84:7 (December 2005), http://www.foreignaffairs.org/20051201faessay84702/c-fred-bergsten/r, 1. See also Alan Tonelson, "The Real Lessons in the Doha Round's Failure," *AmericanEconomicAlert* (August 15, 2006), http://www.americaneconomicalert.org/view_art.asp?Prod_ID=2537.

149 Arvind Panagariya, "Liberalizing Agriculture," *Foreign Affairs* 84:7 (December 2005), http://www.foreignaffairs.org/20051201faessay84706/arvind-panagariya/liberalizing-agriculture.html, 4.

150 Ian Goldin and Kenneth A. Reinert, *Globalization for Development: Trade, Finance, Aid, Migration, and Policy*, rev. edn (New York: Palgrave Macmillan, 2006), 36.

151 "The Noodle Bowl," *The Economist*, September 5, 2009, 48.

152 Peter D. Sutherland, "Correcting Misperceptions," *Foreign Affairs* 84:7 (December 2005), http://www.foreignaffairs.org/20051201faessay84705/peter-d-sutherland/correcting-misperceptions.html, 1.

153 Dani Rodrik, "Don't Cry for Doha," *Policy Innovations*, August 19, 2008, http://www.policyinnovations.org/ideas/commentary/data/000077. See also Philip G. Cerny, "Thinking Outside the Bicycle: Shifting Gears on Global Trade Talks," *Policy Innovations*, December 10, 2008, http://www.policyinnovations.org/ideas/commentary/data/000097.

154 See, for example, Bob Davis and Carrick Mollenkamp, "Financial Protectionism Is Latest Threat to Global Recovery," *Wall Street Journal*, February 2, 2009, A2. Global trade declined roughly one-third between May 2008 and May 2009. See "Unpredictable Tides," *The Economist*, July 23, 2009, 67.

155 Mark Landler, "Trade Barriers Rise as Slump Tightens Grip," *New York Times*, March 22, 2009, http://www.nytimes.com/2009/03/23/world/23trade.html.

156 Jeffrey E. Garten, "The Dangers of Turning Inward," *Wall Street Journal*, February 28–March 1, 2009, W1.

157 Barry Buzan, *People, States and Fear* (New York: Columbia University Press, 2008), 252.

158 "Homeward Bound," *The Economist*, February 7, 2009, 69, 70.

159 World Trade Organization, "G20 Governments Refrain from Extensive Use of Restrictive Measures, But Some Slippage Evident," September 14, 2009, http://www.wto.org/english/news_e/news09_e/trdev_14sep09_e.htm.

160 Sara Murray and Douglas Belkin, "Americans Sour on Trade," *Wall Street Journal*, October 4, 2010, A1–A2.

161 Elizabeth Williamson, "Truck Dispute Previews Trade Battle," *Wall Street Journal*, July 9, 2010, A5.
162 Cited in John W. Miller, "WTO Details Rising Protectionism, Pushes Countries to Reverse Course," *Wall Street Journal*, March 26, 2009, A8.
163 Lingling Wei, "New Move to Make the Yuan a Global Currency," *Wall Street Journal*, January 12, 2011, A1, A11.
164 "Hard to Swallow," *The Economist*, March 21, 2009, 68–9. Coca-Cola had sought to acquire China's largest juice company.
165 Jonathan Weisman, "Fed Global Backlash Grows," *Wall Street Journal*, November 9, 2010, A1, A15.
166 Sewell Chan, "G-20 Vows to Avoid a Currency War," *New York Times*, October 23, 2010, http://www.nytimes.com/2010/10/24/business/global/24g20.html.
167 John W. Miller, "U.S., EU Complain to WTO about China," *Wall Street Journal*, November 5, 2009, A14.
168 Loretta Chao, "China's Curbs on Tech Purchases Draw Ire," *Wall Street Journal*, December 11, 2009, A11.
169 Keith Bradsher, "China to Put New Limits, but Not Export Ban, on Rare Minerals," *New York Times*, September 4, 2009, http://www.nytimes.com/pages/business/index.html?excamp=GGBUbusinessnews&WT.srch=1&WT.mc_ev=click&WT.mc_id=BI-S-E-GG-NA-S-business_news.
170 Michael Wines and Xiyun Yang, "China Escalates Fight with U.S. on Energy Aid," *New York Times*, October 17, 2010, http://www.nytimes.com/2010/10/18/business/global/18trade.html.
171 See, for example, John W. Miller, Peter Fritsch, and Lauren A. E. Schuker, "Hollywood Upstages Beijing," *Wall Street Journal*, August 13, 2009, A1, A6, and "Let Me Entertain You," *The Economist*, August 15, 2009, 36, and Michael Wines, "Suit Says Two Chinese Firms Stole Web-Blocking Code," *New York Times*, January 6, 2010, http://www.nytimes.com/2010/01/07/technology/companies/07censor.html.
172 See John W. Miller, "Protectionism Hurts Efforts to Pressure China," *Wall Street Journal*, November 9, 2010, A15.
173 "US Trade Deficit Widened by 33% in 2010," *BBC News*, February 11, 2011, http://www.bbc.co.uk/news/business-12431066.
174 "Repelling Borders," *The Economist*, April 10, 2010, 75–6.
175 Geoff Dyer, "China to Impose Duties on US Chicken," *FT.com*, February 5, 2010, http://www.ft.com/cms/s/0/105a0522-1208-11df-b6e3-00144feab49a.html. See also "Major Trade Disputes Between China and the US," *FT.com*, February 8, 2010, http://www.ft.com/cms/s/0/b585524e-b3ea-11de-98ec-00144feab49a.html?catid=14&SID=google.
176 John W. Miller, "China Takes Aim at Trade Barriers to Keep U.S., EU Markets Open," *Wall Street Journal*, August 1–2, 2009, A6.
177 John W. Miller, "China Complains to WTO about EU Tariffs," *Wall Street Journal*, February 5, 2010, A12.
178 "Discontents, Wintry and Otherwise," *The Economist*, February 7, 2009, 48–9.
179 Alistair MacDonald, "U.K. Reviews Foreign Ownership of Firm," *Wall Street Journal*, September 25, 2009, A9.
180 Philip P. Pan, "Blaming the Kremlin," *Washington Post National Weekly Review*, June 29–July 12, 2009, 20–1.
181 Cited in John W. Miller, "Nations Rush to Establish New Barriers to Trade," *Wall Street Journal*, February 6, 2009, A1.
182 In August 2010, the WTO ruled in favor of the US, Japan, and Taiwan in their complaint against EU tariffs on electronic imports. See "W.T.O. Rules Against European Union on Tariffs for Electronics," *New York Times*, August 16, 2010, http://www.nytimes.com/2010/08/17/business/global/17wto.html?emc=eta1.
183 See Rama Lakshmi, "In Reprisal, India Probes U.S. Trade Barriers," *Washington Post*,

May 8, 2009, http://www.washingtonpost.com/wp-dyn/content/article/2009/05/07/AR2009050704035.html.

184 Bremmer, "State Capitalism Comes of Age," 52. Bremmer (54) predicts, however, that China and Russia are likely to return to the free-market path unless state capitalism affords sustained growth.

185 China imposed controls on food prices in January 2007 but lifted them in December 2008.

186 Liam Pleven, Ira Iosebashvili, and Tom Polansek, "Putin Extends Wheat-Export Ban," *Wall Street Journal*, September 3, 2010, C1, C6.

187 Nicholas Kulish and Graham Bowley, "Facing a Financial Crisis, European Nations Put Self-Interest First," *New York Times*, October 8, 2008, http://www.nytimes.com/2008/10/08/world/europe/08unity.html. See also Steven Erlanger, "Economy Shows Cracks in European Union," *New York Times*, June 9, 2009, http://www.nytimes.com/2009/06/09/world/europe/09union.html.

188 "Playing with Fire," *The Economist*, September 19, 2009, 37.

189 "Economic Vandalism," *The Economist*, September 19, 2009, 13.

190 Sewell Chan, "W.T.O. Rules on Chinese Tire Imports Legal, U.S. Says," *New York Times*, December 13, 2010, http://www.nytimes.com/2010/12/14/business/global/14trade.html?ref=business.

191 Ian Johnson "China Strikes Back on Trade," *Wall Street Journal*, September 14, 2009, A1, A4. For the union's position see *Underdog*, August 2009, http://wwwsecondchance.blogspot.com/. There is concern that additional American industries will seek similar protection. See Terence Poon, Ian Johnson, and Peter Fritsch, "China Seeks Talks with the U.S. at W.T.O. over Tire Tariff," *Wall Street Journal*, September 15, 2009. A5.

192 J. R. Wu, "China Sets Antidumping Probe," *Wall Street Journal*, April 23, 2010, A12.

193 Keith Bradsher, "Solar Panel Tariff May Further Strain U.S.–China Trade," *New York Times*, October 1, 2009, http://www.nytimes.com/2009/10/01/business/global/01tariff.html.

194 Tom Barkley, "U.S. Weighs Trade Fight Over Steel," *Wall Street Journal*, October 8, 2009, A6, and Aaron Back and Patricia Jiayi Ho, "Beijing Slams U.S. Tariffs in Growing Clash," *Wall Street Journal*, November 7–8, 2009, A6.

195 Robert Guy Matthews, "U.S. Hits China with Steel Penalty," *Wall Street Journal*, June 9, 2010, A4, and "U.S. Sets Hefty Duties on Chinese Steel Pipe," *Financial Times*, June 18, 2010, http://www.ft.com/cms/s/0/1640c36a-4433-11df-b327-00144feab49a.html. The WTO upheld the legality of these tariffs. See Sewell Chan, "U.S. Prevails in Trade Dispute with China," *New York Times*, October 22, 2010, http://www.nytimes.com/2010/10/23/business/global/23pipe.html.

196 Bloomberg News, "China to Tax Some Imports from U.S. and Russia," *New York Times*, December 10, 2009, http://www.nytimes.com/2009/12/11/business/global/11steel.html.

197 John W. Miller, "Protectionist Measures Expected to Rise, Report Warns," *Wall Street Journal*, September 15, 2009, A5.

198 See, for example, Bob Davis and Carrick Mollenkamp, "Financial Protectionism Is Latest Threat to Global Recovery," *Wall Street Journal*, February 2, 2009, A2.

199 Marcus Walker, "As Exports Decline, Germany Slips into Recession," *Wall Street Journal*, November 14, 2008, A6.

200 Charles Forelle, "EU Rejects a Rescue of Faltering East Europe," *Wall Street Journal*, March 2, 2009, A1.

201 Brian Blackstone, "Greek Woes Deter New Euro Members," *Wall Street Journal*, March 20–1, 2010, A10, and Nicholas Kulish and Steven Erlanger, "In Greek Pact, Compromises and Intrigues," *New York Times*, July 22, 2011, http://www.nytimes.com/2011/07/23/business/global/european-leaders-achieve-greek-deal-through-compromise.html.

202 Charlemagne, "Financial Fortress Europe," *The Economist*, May 15, 2010, 61.

203 "Asian Giants Agree Economic Plan," *BBC News*, December 13, 2008, http://news.bbc.co.uk/2/hi/asia-pacific/7781027.stm.

204 John W. Miller, "Nations Rush to Establish New Barriers to Trade," *Wall Street Journal*, February 6, 2009, A1. In only a few months Russia introduced 28 tariff increases and US–EU trade disputes multiplied.
205 "Buying American," *The Economist*, January 31, 2009, 40. The final legislation modified this with language stating that the rule be applied in a manner consistent with US international trade agreements.
206 Anthony Faiola and Lori Montgomery, "A North American Trade War," *Washington Post National Weekly Edition*, May 25–31, 2009, 23–4.
207 John M. Broder, "Obama Opposes Trade Sanctions in Climate Bill," *New York Times*, June 28, 2009, http://www.nytimes.com/2009/06/29/US/politics/29climate.html?hp.
208 By contrast, China resisted calls for protectionism. See "The Next Great Wall," *The Economist*, March 14, 2009, 67–8.
209 See, for example, Peter Fritsch and Corey Boles, "How 'Buy American' Can Hurt U.S. Firms," *Wall Street Journal*, September 16, 2009, A5.
210 South Korea and the Obama administration reached an agreement on forming a free trade zone in late 2010.
211 "Unpredictable Tides," 67–8.
212 Paul Hannon and John W. Miller, "World Trade Volume Climbs 2.5%," *Wall Street Journal*, August 27, 2009, A7.
213 See, for example, Matthew Rosenberg, "India Rejects U.S. Proposal of Carbon Limits," *Wall Street Journal*, July 20, 2009, A7.
214 Asia, for example, suffers from a vast blanket of haze caused by a "noxious cocktail of soot, smog and toxic chemicals." See Andrew Jacobs, "Report Sees New Pollution Threat," *New York Times*, November 14, 2008, http://www.nytimes.com/2008/11/14/world/14cloud.html.
215 "A Bad Climate for Development," *The Economist*, September 19, 2009, 69–70.
216 "Heating Up or Cooling Down?" *The Economist*, June 13, 2009, 45, and "Wanted: Fresh Air," *The Economist*, July 11, 2009, 60, 62. Both India and China oppose strict quantitative limits to greenhouse gas emissions. See, for example, Michael Wines, "China Sees Progress on Climate Accord, but Resists an Emissions Ceiling," *New York Times*, August 5, 2009, http://www.nytimes.com/2009/08/06/world/asia/06china.html.
217 Joshua Partlow, "Protected, Yet Destroyed," *Washington Post National Weekly Edition*, February 23–March 1, 2009, 9–10.
218 Elisabeth Rosenthal, "U.N. Says Biofuel Subsidies Raise Food Bill and Hunger," *New York Times*, October 7, 2008, http://www.nytimes.com/2008/10/08/world/europe/08italy.html.
219 "World Hunger 'Hits One Billion'," *BBC News*, June 19, 2009, http://news.bbc.co.uk/2/hi/europe/8109698.stm. Of the roughly 1 billion people who suffer from hunger, some 642 million live in the Asia–Pacific region and 265 million live in sub-Saharan Africa.
220 "Fiddling with Words as the World Melts," *The Economist*, December 20, 2008, 108–9. However, the EU made a variety of concessions to some of its members, especially in Eastern Europe, that fear loss of jobs and industry and higher energy costs.

CHAPTER 10

The balance sheet

Taking globalization theory seriously by (re-)positioning it in traditional and recent themes of social theory and seeing a global social whole as its point of reference means that globalization theory is far from being an intellectual fad. Quite to the contrary, it is still far from having reached its apex and continues to provide the main ground of engagement with social and political change understood in a "global" sense.[1]

And what was unimaginable just a few years ago is now becoming a real possibility, i.e. the iron law of the globalization of the free market is in danger of collapsing and with it the associated ideology . . . Protectionism is experiencing a revival; some call for new transnational institutions to control global financial flows, whereas others plead for transnational insurance systems or a renewal of international institutions and regimes. The result is that the era of free-market ideology is becoming a distant memory and is being overshadowed by its opposite, namely, the *politicization* of the global market economy.[2]

Historian Niall Ferguson in 2005 asserted: "The possibility is as real today as it was in 1915 that globalization, like the Lusitania, could be sunk."[3] Given the recent crisis in the world of global finance and its role in engendering what some are now terming the Great Recession, there is irony in Ferguson's observations about the onset of the Great War: "[M]ost investors were completely caught off guard when the crisis came. Not until the last week of July 1914 was there a desperate dash for liquidity; it happened so suddenly and on such a large scale that the world's major stock markets, New York's included, closed down for the rest of the year." Ferguson presciently warned that "today's international fiat-money system is significantly, and dangerously, crisis-prone" and subject to "contagion."[4] Among the similarities that Ferguson detected between the contemporary era and the one that gave major pause to the earlier epoch of globalization are: (1) continued protectionism, (2) monetary instability, (3) rapidly advancing military technology, and (4) US dependence on foreign investment. He noted one difference that casts a greater shadow on the present, the enormous current account deficit of the world's leading economic power and the prospect of a dramatic weakening of the world's leading reserve currency and the emergence of rival currencies.

The global economic and financial crisis provides a strong test of Ferguson's prediction. Global trade, migration, tourism, direct investment, and other indicators of globalization declined precipitously, at least initially. Paul Krugman writes about the 2008 global spike in food prices:

> Consider how things have played out . . . For years we were told that self-sufficiency was an outmoded concept, and that it was safe to rely on world markets for food supplies. But when the prices of wheat, rice and corn soared, Keynes's "projects and politics" of "restrictions and exclusion" made a comeback: many governments rushed to protect domestic consumers by banning or limiting exports, leaving food-importing countries in dire straits . . . Most of us have proceeded on the belief that, at least as far as economics goes, this doesn't matter – that we can count on world trade continuing to flow freely simply because it's so profitable. But that's not a safe assumption.[5]

If Ferguson's fears are correct, that crisis will leave scars that will slow, if not in some ways reverse globalization for a significant period of time. This does not, of course, mean that globalization in all of its dimensions would necessarily decline or reverse, nor does it rule out globalization resuming broad acceleration when general conditions are seen to improve.

Additional assessments about the lasting effects of the financial crisis and the possible shape of the future are already emerging. G. John Ikenberry, for example, asks whether the "liberal world order" is likely to outlast American hegemony or, perhaps more accurately, the current US role as *primus inter pares*. He takes it for granted, as do we, that "wealth and power are moving from the North and the West to the East and the South and that the old order dominated by the United States and Europe is giving way to one increasingly shared with non-Western states." Some have suggested that Brazil, China, India, and others will "push world politics in an illiberal direction." Ikenberry labels this is as "panicked narrative" that "misses a deeper reality." "The struggle over international order today is not about fundamental principles. China and the emerging great powers do not want to contest the basic rules and principles of the liberal international order; they wish to gain more authority and leadership within it." Ikenberry believes that the emerging economies "have all become more prosperous and capable of operating inside the existing international order – benefiting from its rules, practices, and institutions."[6]

Nancy Birdsall and Francis Fukuyama generally share Ikenberry's assessment, although with significant variations. They begin by making the important observation that "[n]o leader of a major developing country has backed away from his or her commitment to free trade or the global capitalist system." In fact, "the established Western democracies are the ones that have highlighted the risks of relying too much on market-led globalization and called for greater regulation of international finance." Nevertheless, they recognize that the US model of capitalism has competitors and that emerging markets "will become less focused on the free flow of capital, more concerned with minimizing social disruption through social safety net programs, and more active in supporting domestic institutions."[7]

Let us now summarize several key issues about globalization that we have emphasized throughout this book. Globalization is a multidimensional phenomenon and is *not* a unilinear process, much less one that will take us to Nirvana.[8] Instead, as Philip Cerny argues, "it is a multilayered, asymmetric admixture of international, transnational, domestic and local processes."[9]

In some respects, globalization has been with us since the earliest days of humankind. Typically, some dimensions of globalization move forward, while others slow or stop for at least a while, and a few retreat. The major currents shaping globalization have in fact not been antithetical but are instead dialectically related. As Benjamin Barber famously expressed it, "the planet is falling precipitously apart and coming reluctantly together at the very same moment"[10] – and the two tendencies, captured in James Rosenau's fragmegration concept, are intimately related.

Contemporary global processes, today as in the past, consist of apparent contradictions. Fission produces fusion and vice versa; centralization of authority makes for diffusion of authority and vice versa; fragmentation creates pressures for integration; and so forth. "In the nineteenth century," writes Paul James,

> there had been a rapid process of globalization, which met almost immediate resistance. The interventionist state derived a great deal of legitimation from the process of globalization, and became increasingly an impediment to integration. It was in the Great Depression that those who opposed the freedom of migration, and of goods and capital transactions, saw the opportunity to move the pendulum back.[11]

Stanley Hoffmann, in an insightful essay written shortly after 9/11, captures these contradictions and the "pendulum" effect, especially in relation to global terrorism. "If globalization often facilitates terrorist violence," Hoffmann declares,

> the fight against this war without borders is potentially disastrous for both economic development and globalization. Antiterrorist measures restrict mobility and financial flows, while new terrorist attacks could lead the way for an antiglobalist reaction comparable to the chauvinistic paroxysms of the 1930s.[12]

Jihadists who avowedly seek to restore the medieval caliphate actually reinforce the interstate system they oppose. Thus, "the beneficiaries of the antiterrorist 'war' have been the illiberal, poorer states that have lost so much of their sovereignty of late. Now the crackdown on terror allows them to tighten their controls on their own people, products, and money."[13] States, like the Kyrgyz Republic that aided the United States as a base to support the war in Afghanistan, "can give themselves new reasons to violate individual rights in the name of common defense against insecurity,"[14] thereby reversing the globalization of human rights and the global governance for enforcing them. "Thus," concludes Hoffmann, "terrorism is a global phenomenon that ultimately reinforces the enemy – the state – at the same time as it tries to destroy it."[15]

When all is said and done, it is difficult to generalize about the impact of globalization on states. Globalization has been facilitated by state behavior even as it constrains state autonomy and reduces state capacity.[16] For national leaders, the claim that globalization limits autonomy provides justification for policies they wish to undertake while denying responsibility for them. In time, leaders may come to believe those claims, thereby privileging structure over agency. This leads to the odd paradox that states constrain themselves or, at a minimum, have voluntarily followed policies that limit their autonomy. John Campbell is thus moved to argue that "one very important reason that the forces of globalization ebb and flow is that states actually have some control over them."[17]

Maria Gritsch offers a stronger variant of this argument from a realist perspective. In her view, globalization, far from reducing state autonomy, reflects "politically connected aspects of advanced capitalist states' project to acquire greater intra-national power and autonomy."[18] Institutions like the WTO and IMF, she suggests, are not independent sources of governance but coercive instruments of major states seeking competitive advantages over weaker states. Gritsch defines globalization "as a soft geo-politics, or states' zero-sum pursuit of geo-political power on non-militaristic terrain,"[19] and she interprets states' provision of social services during earlier centuries, not as growing state capacity, but as an unwilling concession to domestic actors such as labor unions that limited state autonomy. Hence: "Even as states and capitalists reluctantly share power with citizens, and grant entitlements, they continuously attempt to rescind these concessions through a wide range of political and legislative tactics designed to increase their own political and economic power."[20] Globalization, Gritsch concludes, actually increases the autonomy of major states by allying them with the interests of their capitalists, thereby reducing the limits imposed by domestic actors. Moreover, "states' and capitalists' greater control over economic decision-making, and increased autonomy from intra-national constraints, may enable them to voluntarily undo domestic relationships of dependency, reciprocity, contestation and power-sharing with territorially based nations."

> By implementing globalization, states, themselves, establish conditions allowing them to call into question traditional state functions. Thus, states' ostensibly diminished capacity may reflect states' diminished propensity, combined with greater, not lesser, power over society and increased ability to withdraw from intra-national relationships of obligation and contestation.[21]

As Colin Hay contends, "there is no agreed or emerging consensus on globalization's impact on the state," and, in addition to the role of normative judgments, our view of this issue "is likely to relate, among other things, to our evaluation of the extent and significance of genuinely global institutions of governance, the relative significance of regional institutions, and the degree to which the emergence of global institutions might be seen to give rise to a politics independent of, and irreducible to, that between discrete nation states, or regions."[22] Michael Mann's caution regarding the need to be historically sensitive and to recognize differences among states and regions is worth recalling, as is his claim that many of those who most strongly believe that globalization is eroding the state are European and that the European experience is idiosyncratic.[23] Nevertheless, overall, as Maryann Cusimano concludes: "Sovereignty is changing in real and fundamental ways." Contemporary states are not Westphalian polities, "but the sovereign state will not become obsolete, and no single replacement organizational unit will arise, anytime soon." Sovereignty remains important, "but there will be a 'return to history' in the sense of a return to crosscutting, non-hierarchical, ad hoc, and relative forms of order and organization."

> The state is alive, but is increasingly contracting out; and a decentralized state less connected to territory and to traditional state functions is something different than the sovereign state we have known in the twentieth century, although it is something less than the wholesale eviction of the idea of sovereignty.[24]

States remain but have been thoroughly penetrated by global forces. They may evolve as in the past by adapting to changed conditions, *but they are not disappearing, nor do they need to do so for globalization to persist.*

Neither realists for whom history is largely an unchanging set of structural "truths," nor liberals who see the world as going "somewhere" capture the complex mix of change and continuity that characterizes the temporal dimension of global politics. Understanding globalization requires making sense of its historical evolution.

There is no teleology to globalization, only contingencies, possibilities, and trends. Thus, the fall of the Berlin Wall in 1989 suddenly ended what seemed an endless bipolar hostility, just as 9/11 suddenly brought an end to the optimism and enthusiasm that had accompanied the Cold War's end. "There is simply," as Ronaldo Munck puts it, "no unified coherent and unilinear globalization strategy waiting to be applied as 'made in USA' modernization theory was in the 1950s."[25] In different eras and under different conditions, authority may expand or contract, polities may expand or shrink, and structures may grow more integrated or may fragment.

THE POLITICAL DIALECTIC

Political globalization, as we have seen, has taken a variety of forms, including the central role of international and regional institutions such as the IMF and the WTO in fostering a neoliberal world, as well as in institutions like the UN, the EU, the African Union, and NATO in imposing order by undertaking humanitarian intervention, aiding reconstruction of failed states, and combating "rogue" regimes. It has also taken the form of an incipient global civil society built on networks of nongovernmental organizations.

However, efforts by international institutions, NGOs, or states to foster global governance can produce a backlash. For example, the effort of the International Criminal Court to prosecute Sudan's president for human-rights abuses in Darfur inadvertently increased his popularity at home and produced anger in the Arab world.

Similarly, the claims of Spanish magistrates to have authority to prosecute foreign citizens for alleged abuses have enraged "officials in the countries they target" and triggered "a political backlash in a nation uncomfortable acting as the world's conscience."[26] Thus, John Ruggie is pessimistic about the future, concluding: "Global governance failures, geopolitical changes, and identity politics are pulling global governance back toward more of a statist model" even as "human needs as well as the scope of economic activity and the interests of economic actors strive for a more effective organization of transnational spaces."[27]

Although individual countries like North Korea, Burma, and Zimbabwe may close themselves off from globalization, the costs of doing so are high. As Jonathan Kirshner explains: "Resistance to globalization – efforts by states to keep borders (more or less) closed to flows of data, money, and people is certainly possible; the 'level' of globalization does not operate by fiat imposing openness upon all so much as it raises in general the opportunity costs of such closure."[28]

Another example of the dialectical nature of political change is revealed in the shifting balance between multilateralism and unilateralism. The period between the end of the Cold War and 9/11 might be described as a multilateral era, the highlight of which was multilateral cooperation in forcing Iraq out of Kuwait and bringing an end to the Bosnian and Kosovo conflicts. By contrast, after 9/11, unilateralism became dominant, ranging from US unwillingness to ratify the ban on testing of nuclear weapons or join the International Criminal Court, to its invasion of Iraq. More recently, the election of Barack Obama and NATO's intervention in Libya looked to have initiated a new era of multilateralism. Or will increased US right-wing isolationism and the embarrassingly messy Libyan operation put paid to any such outcome?

In a more traditional "realist" sense, there appears to be an historical cycle in which the concentration of power ("unipolarity" and "bipolarity") is gradually diffused ("multipolarity") and then again concentrated. Concentration of power may produce "imperial overstretch"[29] and greater diffusion of global power. Although Kennedy's well-known analysis remains controversial, historical epochs ranging from postwar concentration of power by two superpowers and the rise and decline of Rome to the erosion of Soviet–American bipolarity and subsequent American hegemony loosely support his thesis. From a dialectical perspective, it appears that power concentration produces fear and resentment that mobilizes opposition to hegemonic control, while power diffusion produces disorder that enhances the prospect of hegemonic leadership.

THE CULTURAL DIALECTIC

Cultural globalization rests on the spread of neoliberal capitalism based on values such as political democracy, individualism, secularism, and consumerism. Such values are, at once, seen to be necessary for economic development but are contentious because they may undermine traditional cultures and mores that anchor communities psychologically and reinforce the authority of traditional elites.[30] Nationalism is a dangerous luxury in a globalizing world, yet at least some "nations" are in danger of losing what makes them distinctive in terms of religion, history, and language.

Migration from poor to rich regions obliges young workers and taxpayers to support growing welfare costs in aging societies but simultaneously dilutes traditional cultures and poses problems of assimilation. The influx of Latinos into the United States and of Africans and Muslims into Europe involve cultural contradictions that produce social tensions. The Swiss voted to ban minarets[31] and the French banned headscarves in schools,[32] but both states still need Muslim migrants to fill jobs that locals refuse and to cope with the demographic dilemma in which they find themselves. Even the Japanese, traditionally among the most reluctant to admit foreign workers, are beginning to rethink the issue, recognizing that there are few other alternatives given their aging workforce.[33] Migrants keep labor costs low while providing remittances to communities in their homelands. The alternative may be less palatable, the outsourcing of jobs from developed to developing countries with surplus labor.

THE MILITARY DIALECTIC

Military globalization rests on "global infrastructures of command, control, communication, logistics, and military organization."[34] It is also reflected in the outsourcing of defense production, the sharing of military innovations, and collaboration in developing new military technologies. Globalization in this sphere takes the form of transnational violence that is becoming more frequent even as the frequency of interstate warfare declines. States are losing their capacity to manage and limit violence, even as private security organizations, terrorists, criminal gangs, and ethnic secessionists become sources of "private violence"; and government agencies, including America's CIA, have outsourced tasks, including (reportedly) the assassination of Al Qaeda leaders.[35]

But there is a contradiction here, too, for as Robert Keohane suggests, "as the state loses it monopoly on means of mass destruction, the response to terrorism is strengthening the powers of states, and the reliance of people on government."[36] Thus, states battling terrorism have sought to regulate transnational financial networks that are believed to assist terrorists and have erected a variety of barriers to international travel including new rules for documentation and inspection. State surveillance of citizens, as well as domestic and foreign intelligence activities, has intensified. "Since the same global infrastructures which enable the outsourcing of production also make possible the transnational organization of violence, it is hardly surprising that states will seek to limit their citizens' vulnerability by making borders, physical or virtual, more impermeable."[37]

THE ECONOMIC DIALECTIC

Even in the absence of the global economic crisis, it is likely that resistance would have grown to any world dominated by neoliberal capitalism in its most extreme form. Environmentalists who believe the outsourcing of industry to developing countries facilitates evasion of environmental regulations; union members in developed countries who see their jobs disappear[38] and are convinced that lower labor costs elsewhere derive from exploitation of local workers, including children, and from an absence of welfare and safety rules; and local businesses that cannot compete with global goliaths – these will oppose economic globalization. Yet even as jobs leave the developed world, wages rise in the countries to which they flow until at some point at least some of the jobs come home; meanwhile, new types of job opportunities tend to arise. Thus, Hal Sirkin, a business consultant, predicts that "around 2015, manufacturers will be indifferent between locating in America and China for production for consumption in America."[39]

Global trade also appears to run in cycles. The late nineteenth and early twentieth centuries witnessed a dramatic growth in global trade. The period from the onset of World War I until World War II saw an equally dramatic decline in trade, followed by its great postwar increase that lasted until the global economic crisis began in late 2007. Again there was a dramatic downturn. Between February 2008 and February 2009, exports of the world's fifteen leading export countries declined by a third.[40] However, as the global economy slowly recovers, the volume of trade once more is rising, even though trade patterns are shifting (for example, Asians increasingly trade with one another rather than with Europe). The future of economic globalization seems to be improving as the global recession eases, a trend evident by 2010. Gregg Easterbrook takes an optimistic view of this, convinced that the global economic crisis is only a blip on the radar screen and that globalization will again accelerate. It is, he thinks, like a "Sonic Boom – noisy, superfast, covering huge amounts of territory."[41]

Changing trade patterns over the past century have been accompanied by shifts between bilateral and regional arrangements to multilateral governance. The period from World War I to the end of World War II featured the former, while the era following the Bretton Woods agreement featured the latter. Nevertheless, after a long string of successful multilateral trade rounds, the Doha Round begun in 2001 lurched to a halt after years of negotiations. A dialectical process was unintentionally described by *The Economist*:

> The failure of this round was rooted in the success of the last. The 1994 Uruguay round . . . required countries to convert their farm quotas and other barriers into straightforward tariffs. Nervous about unanticipated floods of imports, countries were allowed to impose "special safeguard" duties to protect themselves in the event of a surge. Intended as a temporary fix, these duties soon became a long-term crutch for politically touchy commodities, such as sugar . . . The shadow of the Uruguay round arguably extended beyond this nettlesome detail. Many developing countries believe that the earlier round was lopsided, doing little to constrain the farm policies of the rich world even as it placed heavy obligations on the poor in areas such as intellectual property (IP).[42]

Perhaps Susan Schwab, former US Trade Representative, is right in insisting that "it is time to give up trying to 'save' Doha." "Negotiators obsess over how to keep the dead cat from landing on their doorstep. But the pretense that the deal will somehow come together is now a greater threat to the multilateral trading system than acknowledging the truth." The strategy henceforth, she argues, should be to "launch new multilateral initiatives to restore trust in the WTO and preserve it as a dynamic venue for both improving and enforcing the rules governing international trade."[43] Indeed, everything suggests that the WTO for the foreseeable future will be less about reducing general barriers to trade and more about adjudicating disputes regarding specific commodities, products, and services within the existing rules. Nevertheless, it remains as necessary today as it has been in recent decades to accommodate "the coexistence of a territorially based political system with an economic system that is increasingly global in scope."[44]

THE ENVIRONMENTAL DIALECTIC

Economic growth and development exacerbate environmental problems, but also help provide countries with resources to cope with those problems. Optimists (some might say dreamers) see globalization as "promoting integration and co-operation as well as common environmental norms and standards, which are enhancing the capacity of a system of sovereign states to manage problems such as ozone depletion and climate change."[45] New technologies and information to manage environmental stress are available to developing societies. At a minimum, the formation of environmental epistemic communities has fostered greater understanding of and concern for ecological issues on a global scale.

The rich use more resources and produce more waste per capita than the poor. However, initial stages of economic growth tend to produce more pollution "because governments focus on increasing industrial growth and national income rather than on pollution controls." As wealth increases, "pollution begins to fall" because population growth rates decline, more citizens grow concerned, and governments acquire the technologies and wealth to address environmental problems.[46] Currently, emerging economies like India and China are major polluters, while mature economies like those of the European Union are reducing their impact on the environment. Economic crises may reduce pollution as economic activity slows, but at the same time may accelerate resource depletion. This happened in Indonesia during the 1997–8 Asian economic crisis when environmental regulations were ignored and people sought to use less expensive ways to produce and harvest what they needed.[47]

Overall, not all poor countries will necessarily grow sufficiently wealthy to bring about a reduction in pollution, and, in any event, the process may be so slow that ecological stress such as increased global warming, the loss of biodiversity, and resource exhaustion will outstrip any capacity to manage it. Another apparent contradiction lies in the fact that free trade, in theory, should accurately reflect resource scarcities and pollution costs, while also producing corporate outsourcing to poor countries with lower environmental standards.[48]

ENFIN

Martin Coward is almost certainly correct in rejecting the dichotomy "between state-centric and supra-territorial accounts of global politics," which he sees as based on a "mythical-fictional understanding on the nature of the global order."

On the one hand, state-centric accounts are predicated upon a notion of the judicial authority of the sovereign nation state shown to be problematic by extant economic and cultural interconnections. On the other hand, the globalist account rests on the refutation of a mythical-fictional notion of sovereignty – the Westphalian system – without which its claims to novelty or explanatory adequacy look distinctly frail. Indeed, the novelty of notions of globalisation as a supra-territorial regime look problematic as soon as one recognises that the purported territoriality of pre-globalisation global politics was itself already permeated with transnational interconnections.[49]

The longstanding debate over whether we live in a globalized or state-centric world has always involved something of a false choice. If it had not been such an earnest debate, we would be inclined to call it silly. Like most dichotomies, it offers scholars a sterile option of "either/or" instead of a dynamic continuum that varies towards or away from one extreme to the other over time. Statism and globalization, Coward argues, "represent inverse models of understanding of global order, one predicated on the refutation of the other."[50] As "models," they are strategic simplifications of reality that provide clues of theoretical connections, but neither model has any dynamic or feedback element. Each model, then, although a caricature of global order, requires the other if it is to have meaning.[51] For Coward, the answer lies in recognizing that states are complex networks with porous boundaries whose institutions and agencies are indeed linked to one another in complex ways.[52]

Well, yes, but it is rather more complicated than that. States and their institutions and agencies are by no means the only actors. We do not have just an interstate and intergovernmental world, and there are profound systemic trends and forces at work shaping the present and the future. Much better to recognize that political space (interacting with economic space, cultural space, and so on) has been in constant flux and has needed frequent remapping since the dawn of time,[53] down to our contemporary era when we are even having to incorporate cyberspace.[54]

Globalization has already revolutionized global politics. Interconnectedness, a key component of globalization, continues to intensify despite its detractors. The spread of modern technologies does help to make national frontiers more porous and produces a "compression of the world and the intensification of the consciousness of the world."[55] Barring some "unthinkable" catastrophe – like global nuclear war, the worst projections of climate change, asteroid collision, or alien invasion from outer space – those technologies will surely continue to develop.

According to Switzerland's KOF Index, globalization continues to thicken.[56] Problems associated with globalization – like the rapid spread of disease and economic crises, transnational crime, migration from poor to wealthy societies, environmental stress – are almost certain to become more pressing. All are inherently global problems that beg for global solutions, even as global governance institutions remain relatively weak. As for states, they have trouble enough dealing with the relatively few issues that might be considered genuinely domestic; and most of their governments are suffering a major crisis of legitimacy. At the end of the day, state capacity may be far more limited than almost anyone expects. Publics are restive the world over, even in the developed world – e.g. the US Tea Party movement – and perhaps currently more inclined to destroy institutions at any and all levels rather than to construct and empower them.

As the revolutions that began in North Africa and spread to the Arabic Middle East in 2011 remind us, democratic aspirations continue to spread and animate political life. Yet, of course there are other models out there. China's rise seems to offer an exchange of political freedom for economic prosperity and social stability. Disorder, religious fanaticism, ethno-nationalism, and/or another economic collapse could lead to even uglier authoritarian "solutions." This was the path that the public in Germany chose to follow after the Great Depression in what Eric Fromm described as an "escape from freedom."[57] It was the path taken by Chile, Uruguay, and Argentina in the 1970s. Contemporary Russia also illustrates how creeping authoritarianism can occur in the name of restoring "order."

Democratic norms are also sorely tested by ethnic and religious "neo-tribalism" in regions such as Darfur, Bosnia, Congo, and Tibet. "We live in unruly times and, increasingly, in unruly places and space."[58] At present, it is not clear whether major states have the political will or vision to oppose oppressive regimes like that in Zimbabwe or provide the wherewithal for international institutions to manage the use of force during subnational strife. Humanitarian intervention has been haphazard, depending on the attitude of major powers like the United States (which opposed declaring Rwanda the victim of genocide against Tutsis yet supported intervention in Libya) and China (which opposed intervention in Darfur). The record as revealed by analysis of cases, as Wayne Sandholtz points out, is hardly encouraging:

> The impassioned controversies surrounding humanitarian intervention are evidence that human rights norms have not yet displaced other principles of legitimate sovereignty, in particular the territorial norm . . . [and that although] the society of states has on several occasions been willing to suspend the territorial sovereignty of governments involved in massive human rights abuses, it has done so while making clear that each such intervention must be justified as an exception to the norm of nonintervention.[59]

Global transformation and changing patterns of authority, identities, and resource distribution in *any* era, of course, provoke anxiety and turmoil. *Complexity produces misunderstanding; misunderstanding creates unpredictability; unpredictability breeds instability; and instability threatens conflict.*

Kirshner is correct in concluding that globalization "is neither inevitable nor irreversible."[60] Globalization, like domestic politics, defies simple predictions. We have argued elsewhere that there can be no final answer to the "agent–structure question," because each influences the other in complex ways. "Structure conditions behavior but does not determine it," and "people – in the streets, in voting booths, in stores, and elsewhere – are the wellsprings."[61] "Only if the future is open," as Doreen Massey observes, "is there any ground for a politics which can make a difference."[62]

For this reason, we accept Cerny's view that the "evolution of globalisation, unlike Darwinist evolution, is not a random process of natural selection."

In terms of the philosophy of science, it is more Lamarckian. It involves conscious actors, whether individuals or groups, who can interpret structural changes, multiple equilibria and opportunities creatively; change and refine their strategies; negotiate, bargain, build coalitions, and mobilise their power resources in ongoing interactions with other actors; and – both in winning and losing – affect and shape medium-term and long-term outcomes . . . The globalisation process will continue to develop and grow, but it will be shaped more and more by the interaction of an expanding, pluralistic constellation of actors operating across increasingly diverse, "multinucleated" transnational spaces, opening up a range of alternative outcomes and multiple equilibria.[63]

The world, while not fully "flat" as Friedman believes it to be, is not becoming round again or spiky or square – or whatever. It is *none of these* and in a sense *all of these and more* (all right, perhaps not square), because globalization – this cannot be repeated often enough – *is a multidimensional phenomenon that develops along various continua in a dialectical fashion*. It slows, it speeds up, it halts, and it may even be reversed along some continua and not along others. As for its normative impact, globalization is neither good nor bad, a boon nor a curse to humanity, but in itself is morally neutral – because there is no "itself" to consider. Various *aspects* of globalization are good, bad, and indifferent, depending in no small part upon which values we hold dear. Whatever else might be said, globalization expands the range of possibilities. Kessler suggests that "globalization processes are arguably now creating, for the first time in human history, the detailed social infrastructure of a single unified humanity: a network of mutual human interdependence and of worldwide involvement in one another's fate."[64] We are entranced by the vision of the world as "an immense global intercultural festival,"[65] but others will worry about the fate of the olive tree they value most.

NOTES

1. Matthias Albert, "'Globalization Theory': Yesterday's Fad or More Likely than Ever?" *International Political Sociology* 1:2 (2007), 180.
2. Beck, *World at Risk*, 200. Emphasis in original.
3. Niall Ferguson, "Sinking Globalization," 66. See also Justin Rosenberg, "Globalization Theory: A Post Mortem," *International Politics* 42:1 (March 2005), 2–74.
4. Ferguson, "Sinking Globalization," 72.
5. Krugman, "The Great Illusion."
6. G. John Ikenberry, "The Future of the Liberal World Order," *Foreign Affairs* 90:3 (May/June 2011), 56–8.
7. Nancy Birdsall and Francis Fukuyama, "The Post-Washington Consensus: Development after the Crisis," *Foreign Affairs* 90:2 (March/April 2011), 45–6.
8. Charles F. Doran identifies two historical paths – cyclical and evolutionary. See C. F. Doran, *The Politics of Assimilation: Hegemony and Its Aftermath* (Baltimore, ND: Johns Hopkins University Press, 1971), 11, and Doran, "Economics, Philosophy of History, and the 'Single Dynamic' of Power Cycle Theory: Expectations, Competition, and Statecraft," *International Political Science Review* 24:1 (2003), 19–20.
9. Philip G. Cerny, "Political Agency in a Globalizing World: Toward a Structurational Approach," *European Journal of International Relations* 6:4 (December 2000), 439. See

also Cerny, "Structuring the Political Arena: Public Goods, States and Governance in a Globalizing World," in Ronen Palan, ed., *Global Political Economy: Contemporary Theories* (London: Routledge, 2000), 21–35.
10 Barber, *Jihad vs. McWorld*, 4.
11 James, *The End of Globalization*, 198–9.
12 Hoffmann, "Clash of Globalizations," 112.
13 Ibid., 112–13.
14 Ibid., 113.
15 Ibid.
16 T. V. Paul argues that advanced capitalist states have wittingly abetted globalization. See T. V. Paul, "States, Security Function, and the New Global Forces," in Paul, Ikenberry, and Hall, eds., *The Nation-State in Question*, 139–65.
17 John L. Campbell, "States, Politics, and Globalization: Why Institutions Still Matter," in Paul, Ikenberry, and Hall, eds., *The Nation-State in Question*, 247.
18 Maria Gritsch, "The Nation-State and Economic Globalization: Soft Geo-Politics and Increased State Autonomy?" *Review of International Political Economy* 12:1 (February 2005), 3.
19 Ibid., 9.
20 Ibid., 6.
21 Ibid., 17.
22 Colin Hay, "Globalization's Impact on States," in Ravenhill, *Global Political Economy*, 316.
23 Mann, "Has Globalization Ended the Rise and Rise of the Nation-State?" 473, 477, 486–7.
24 Maryann K. Cusimano, "Sovereignty's Future: The Ship of Theseus and Other Conclusions," in Cusimano, ed., *Beyond Sovereignty*, 328.
25 Munck, *Globalization and Contestation*, 4.
26 Whitlock, "To the Ends of the Earth," 20.
27 John Gerard Ruggie, "Foreword," in Weiss and Thakur, *Global Governance and the UN*, xix.
28 Kirshner, "Globalization and National Security," 5.
29 Paul Kennedy, *The Rise and Fall of the Great Powers: Economic Change and Military Conflict from 1500 to 2000* (New York: Random House, 1987).
30 Some observers argue that globalization has penetrated most deeply into everyday lives in terms of culture. See G. Honor Fagan, "Globalization, Identity and 'Ireland'," in Kennedy and Danks, eds., *Globalization and National Identities*, 113–23.
31 "The Return of the Nativists," *The Economist*, December 5, 2009, 70–1.
32 "French Scarf Ban Comes into Force," *BBC News*, September 2, 2004, http://news.bbc.co.uk/2/hi/3619988.stm.
33 "Don't Bring Me Your Huddled Masses," *The Economist*, January 3, 2009, 31.
34 Held and McGrew, *Globalization/Anti-Globalization*, 52.
35 Joby Warrick and R. Jeffrey Smith, "Outsourcing Assassinations," *Washington Post National Weekly Review*, August 24–30, 2009, 33.
36 Robert O. Keohane, "The Globalization of Informal Violence, Theories of World Politics, and the 'Liberalism of Fear'," in Robert O. Keohane, ed., *Power and Governance in a Partially Globalized World* (New York: Routledge, 2002), 284.
37 McGrew, "Organized Violence in the Making (and Remaking) of Globalization," 24. McGrew (25) notes that "the assertion of U.S. unilateral power" helped to restore an "awareness of the geopolitical unity of the world."
38 See, for example, Louis Uchitelle, "Pipe Made in India Incenses an Illinois Steel Town," *New York Times*, April 16, 2009, http://www.nytimes.com/2009/04/16/business/economy/16pipe.html.
39 Cited in "Moving Back to America," *The Economist*, May 14, 2011, 79.
40 Floyd Norris, "Off the Charts: Trade Is Falling Fast across the Globe," *New York Times*, April 11, 2009, http://www.nytimes.com/2009/04/11/business/economy/11charts.html.

41 Gregg Easterbrook, *Sonic Boom: Globalization at Mach Speed* (New York: Random House, 2010), 4.
42 "The Doha Round... and Round... and Round," *The Economist*, August 2, 2008, 71.
43 Susan C. Schwab, "After Doha: Why the Negotiations Are Doomed and What We Should Do about It," *Foreign Affairs* 90:3 (May/June 2011), 105.
44 Robin Brown, "Globalization and the End of the National Project," in John MacMillan and Andrew Linklater, eds., *Boundaries in Question: New Directions in International Relations* (London: Pinter Publishers, 1995), 58.
45 Peter Dauvergne, "Globalization and the Environment," in Ravenhill, ed., *Global Political Economy*, 449.
46 Ibid., 461. This is known as the Environmental Kuznets Curve. For its application to economic inequality, see Galbraith, "Global Inequality and Global Macro Economics," 150–1, and Thompson, "Global Inequality, the 'Great Divergence' and Supranational Regionalization," 178–80.
47 John Ravenhill, "The Study of Global Political Economy," in Ravenhill, ed., *Global Political Economy*, 7.
48 TNCs, however, usually follow higher environmental standards than poor countries require.
49 Martin Coward, "International Relations in the Post-Globalisation Era," *Politics* 26:1 (2006), 55.
50 Ibid., 57.
51 Justin Rosenberg, *The Follies of Globalisation Theories: Polemical Essays* (London: Verso, 2000), 27–44. See also Rosenberg, "Globalisation Theory: A Post-Mortem."
52 Coward, "International Relations in the Post-Globalisation Era," 59.
53 Anthony Giddens captures this essential fact: "In pre-modern societies, space and place largely coincide, since the spatial dimensions of social life are, for most of the population, and in most respects, dominated by 'presence' – by localized activities. The advent of modernity increasingly tears space away from place by fostering relations between 'absent' others, locationally distant from any given situation of face-to-face interaction." See Giddens, *The Consequences of Modernity*, 18.
54 Nicholas P. Negroponte, *Being Digital* (New York: Knopf, 1995), 4. See Ferguson and Mansbach, *Remapping Global Politics*, 66–106, and Doreen Massey, *For Space* (London: Sage Publications, 2005), 47–8.
55 Roland Robertson, *Globalization: Social Theory and Global Culture* (London: Sage Publications 1992), 8.
56 KOF Swiss Economic Institute, "KOF Index of Globalisation 2009," (January 27, 2009), http://www.kof.ethz.ch/news/.
57 Erich Fromm, *Escape from Freedom* (New York: Farrar & Rinehart, 1941).
58 Ó Tuathail, Herod, and Roberts, "Negotiating Unruly Problematics," 1.
59 Wayne Sandholtz, "Humanitarian Intervention: Global Enforcement of Human Rights," in Brysk, ed., *Globalization and Human Rights*, 222.
60 Kirshner, "Globalization and National Security," 5.
61 Ferguson and Mansbach, *Remapping Global Politics*, 72.
62 Massey, *For Space*, 11.
63 Cerny, "Multi-Nodal Politics," 449.
64 Clive V. Kessler, "Globalization: Another False Universalism?" *Third World Quarterly* 21:6 (December 2000), 939.
65 Fredric Jameson, "Globalization as a Philosophical Issue," in Fredric Jameson and Masao Miyoshi, eds., *The Cultures of Globalization* (Durham, NC: Duke University Press), 66.

INDEX

Abbate, Janet, 124n
Abed, George T., 244n
Abkhazia, 251
Abouharb, M. Rodwan, 181n
   on international economic institutions and human rights, 164
Abu Dhabi Investment Company, 253
Acharya, Amitav, 217n
   on local actors in Central Asia, 205
Adams, Laura, 216n
Adamson, Fiona, 182n
   on migration rates, 168
Addison, Tony
   on economic inequality, 160
Adejumobi, Said, 244n, 245n, 246n
   on structural adjustment in Africa, 236, 237, 238
Afghanistan, 114, 254
African Union, 234, 281
Africa, sub-Saharan,
   early migrations from, 42
   level and impact of globalization, 234–39
   civil society, 234
   regionalization, 234
   failing states, ethnic conflict, and civil wars, 234–35
   "resource curse," 235
   and structural adjustment, 235, 237, 238
   needed reforms, 235, 239
   on the cultural periphery, 239
   economic improvement, 234, 239
   "failed states" in, 255–56
AFL-CIO, 174
Aggestam, Karen, 244n
   on governance in Arab states., 233
Agriculture,
   globalization of, 171–72
   barriers to and Doha Round, 261
AIDs, 66, 153, 167

Aina, Tade Akin, 244n, 245n
   on globalization in Africa as neo-imperialism, 235
   structural reform in Africa, 235
Akcali, Pinar, 216n
ALBA, 229
Albania, 250
Albert, Matthias, 288n
   on globalization theory, 277
Alexander, Marcus, 126n
   on Russia and ICT, 117
Alexander the Great,
   campaigns of conquest and empire, 48
   successor regimes, 48
Alexandria, ancient commercial center, 48
Algeria, 53, 204, 244, 261
Al-Jazeera, 115, 232
Allworth, Edward, 216n
Al Qaeda, 31, 135, 181, 187, 283
Alter-globalization, 153, 172–76, 229, 249
Altman, Roger C., 107n, 268n
   on erosion of US economic power, 95–96
   future of globalization, 247
   consequences of global economic crisis, 249
   state revival, 252
Al-Zawahiri. Ayman
Amazon, firm, 123
Amin, Samir, 37n, 149n
Amnesty International, 81
Amsterdam Exchange Bank, 56
Anand, Geeta, 269n
Anand, Sudkir, 179n
Anderson, James, 38n, 101n
Anderson, Kenneth, 105n, 178n
   on NGOs and global civil society, 88
Anderson, Perry, 14n
Andersson, Martin, 213n
Andretta, Massimiliano, 184n

INDEX

Andrews, David M., 178n
  on the "democratic deficit," 156
Andrews, Edmund L., 102n
Angell, Norman
  on global economy and war, 61
Angola, 78, 202, 234, 244n, 254
Annan-Yao, Elisabeth, 245n
Ansfield, Jonathan, 126n, 214n
Antigua, 33
Anheier, Helmut K., 104n
Annan-Yao, Elisabeth, 244n
Appadurai, Arjun, 12n, 14n, 15n, 33n, 148n
  demise of the nation-state, 8
  "objects in motion," 10
  the global and the local, 133
Arabs, early warriors/traders, 52, 53
"Arab Spring," 84–85, 115, 233–34, 287
Archibold, Randal C., 270n
Archibugi, Daniele, 127n, 178n, 211n
  on global innovation scores, 119
Areddy, James T., 129n
Aredo, Dejene, 246n
Argentina, 287
Armenia, 250, 251
Arms trade, transnational, 99, 169
Armstrong, John A., 69n
Armstrong, Sarah, 105n, 151n
  on cultural homogenization, 89
  cultural protectionism, 144
Aron, Leon, 240n
Arrighi, Giovanni, 100n
ASEAN, 11, see especially 194–204
Asia,
  1997–98 economic crisis, 66, 118, 154, 161, 195, 200, 282
  level and impact of globalization, 194–204
"Asian Tigers," 236
"Asian values," 76, 195–96, 199
Askew, Kelly Michelle, 147n
Assange, Julian, 116
Assyrians, 45
Atkinson, A.B., 179n
Audi, Nadim, 271n
Australia, 55, 91, 111, 116, 201
  education hub, 33
  early migrations to, 42–43
Austria, 257
Authority patterns
  concept of, 3
  shifting patterns, 4
Avant, Deborah, 37n, 178n, 244n
  on globalization and the military, 27
  civil wars in Africa, 235
Avian flu, 66
Axford, Barry, 150n
Axtmann, Roland, 14n, 103n, 184n
  on state survival, 9
Aydinli, Ersel, 148n, 244n
  Turkey as East–West bridge, 233
Ayres, Jeffrey, 179n
  on criticism of globalization, 157
Azerbaijan, 92, 205–06, 207, 216n, 217n, 221, 254
Azeris, 251
Aztecs, 54, 55

Babylon, 44–46
Back, Aaron, 275n
Badie, Bertrand, 14n
Bahrain, 44, 85, 233, 256
Bahrampour, Tara, 271n
Baildon, Mark, 100n, 213n
Baker, Gideon, 102n, 104n, 106n, 242n
  on "globalization from below," 86
  global civil society, 86
Balarajan, Meera, 270n
Balbones, Salvatore J., 179n
Baldwin, Peter, 272n
Bales, Kevin, 181n
Bangalore, 219n, 251, 269n
Bangladesh, 165, 207, 258, 259
Banking, early history of, 53, 56
Bank of England, 19
Barber, Benjamin, 105n, 150n, 289n
  on cultural homogenization, 89
  the global and the local, 142, 279
Barbieri, Katherine, 183n
  on trade and peace, 170
Barboza, David, 126n, 127n, 212n
Baring Brothers, 1893 collapse of, 61
Barkley, Tom, 275n
Barnes, Brooks, 38n
Barnes, Julian E., 107n
Barry, Ellen, 126n, 241n
Barta, Patrick, 271n
Bartlett, Christopher A., 103n, 149n
  on "global chess," 83
  on local and global in TNCs, 139
Basques, 251
Basu, Kaushik, 218n
Batson, Andrew, 215n
Bauman, Zygmunt, 33n
  on globalization's reach, 16

INDEX

Baylis, John, 35n
Beck, Ulrich, 108n, 183n, 210n, 288n
   on risk society, 97–98
   human rights, 98
   globalization in Europe, 188
   globalization's future, 277
Beeley, Brian, 38n
Belarus, 98, 221, 226
Belgium, 189
Belkin, Douglas, 273n
Bell, Alexander Graham, 112
Bell, Duncan S. A., 34n
Bello, Walden, 102n, 242n
   neoliberalism in Latin America, 229
Berezhovsky, Boris, 223
Bergsten, C. Fred, 15n, 216n, 273n
   on globalization and trade, 11
   China as obstacle to globalization, 203
   the Doha Round, 203, 261
Bhalla, Surjit S, 180n
Bhagwati, Jagdish, 105n, 177n, 184n
   on globalization's critics, 88, 152–53, 173
Bhattacharyya, Gargi, 183n
   on human trafficking
Bialik, Carl, 271n
"Bicycle theory" of trade negotiations, 261
Bilderberg group, 80
Bill & Melinda Gates Foundation, 86, 104n
Bilton, Nick, 125n
Binder, David D., 268n
Bin Laden, Osama, 153
Birdsall, Nancy, 288n
Birkinshaw, Julian, 83, 103n, 149n
Birnbaum, Pierre, 14n
Bislev, Sven, 270n
   on security at US-Mexican border, 255
Blackstone, Brian, 275n
Blaney, David, 125n
Blanke, Jennifer, 101n, 212n, 215n, 242n
Blattner, Joachim, 38n
   on globalization, identities, and
     institutionalization, 31–32
Blum, Douglas W., 37n, 105n, 106n, 150n,
   177n, 212n, 215n, 217n, 240n, 241n
   cultural homogenization, 89, 143, 194
   cultural protectionism, 143
   cultural hybridization in Central Asia, 204–05
   Russia's hybridized identity, 222
   Russia's view of globalization, 226
   Russia's "managed democracy," 223
   Russia's "war on terrorism," 223
   on Chechnya, 223, 224

Blumenstein, Rebecca, 107n
Bobbitt, Philip, 13n, 14n, 269n
   on state evolution, 5–6
   princely state, 5
   territorial state, 6, 8
   kingly state, 6, 8
   state-nation, 7, 8
   nation-state, 8
   mercantile-market state, 253
Bob, Clifford, 181n, 182n
   on globalization and human rights, 162, 164
Boles, Corey, 276n
Bolivia, 228–29, 230
Books, John W., 269n
Booth, William, 37n
Bordo, Michael D., 35n
Bornschier, Simon, 211n
Bosnia, 250, 282 and Herzegovina
Botswana, 235
Bourse, first stock market, 56
Bowley, Graham, 13n, 275n
Bradford, Scott, 36n
   on globalization and trade, 25
Bradshaw, Michael, 37n, 241n
   Russia's complex view of economic
     liberalization, 226
Bradsher, Keith, 13n, 107n, 108n, 214n, 274n,
   275n
Brainard, William C., 267n
Brandolini, A., 179n
Brauman, Leigh, 148n
Braun, Will, 242n
   on Bolivian oil sales, 228–29
Braund, David C., 71n
Brazil, 24
   political and economic reform, 230
   growing political and economic status, 230
   Amazon deforestation, 266
Bremmer, Ian, 269n, 270n, 273n, 274n
   on state capitalism, 253
   Neomercantilism, 264
Brennan, Denise, 181n
Bretton Woods Conference (1944), 63
BRICs, 64, 80, 83, 119, 222, 230
Briggs, John, 235, 245n, 246n
British East India Company, 58
British Empire, 58–59
Broad, Robin, 105n
Broad, William J., 128n
Broader, John M., 108n, 275n
Brook, Chris, 38n
Brookings Institution, 80, 256

Brooks, Stephen, 100n, 101n
  on international institutions, 79
Brothers, Caroline, 271n
Brown, Chris, 151n
  globalization skeptic, 145
Brown, Lester R., 182n
Brown, Robin, 290n
Browne, Andrew, 107n
Browne, Clara, 101n, 212n, 215n, 242n
Bruges, "second venice," 56
Brulliard, Karen, 245n
Brunei, 197
Bruner, Henry, 103n
Brunn, Stanley D., 148n
  on the global and local as a continuum, 134
Brysk, Alison, 100n, 103n, 150n, 181n, 182n, 290n
  globalization and localization, 143
Buckman, Greg, 184n
  on the counter-globalization movement, 173
Bull, Hedley, 148n
  on international society, 2
  "new medievalism," 133
Buddhism, early, 52
Bumiller, Elisabeth, 128n
Burbach, Roger, 37n, 181n
Burling, Tom
  on US vulnerability to cyberattack, 121
Burma, 282
Burns, John F., 128n, 129n
Burundi, 256
Bussey, Jane, 149n
Bustillo, Miguel, 149n
Buzan, Barry, 273n
  on neomercantilists, 262
Byzantine Empire, 52, 53, 68

Cabezas, Amalia Lucia, 181n
Caldor, Mary, 85
Callinicos, Alex, 100n, 105n
  on neoliberalism, 76
  cultural homogenization, 89–90
Cambodia, 171, 213n
Camels, as boon to ancient trade, 48
Cameron, David, 192
Cameron, Geoffrey, 270n
Campbell, John L., 289n
  on state control of globalization, 280
Campbell, Kurt M., 43n
  globalization, Islamic culture and militant Islam. 232
Canada
  Québécois, 251
  border with US, 142, 247
Canon, 83
Cape Verde, 235
Capital, mobility of, 66
Capitalism,
  forms of, 69, 76
  disillusionment with neoliberal form, 248
Cardoso, Fernando Henrique, 230
Carlisle, Kate, 106n
Carnegie Foundation, 80–81
Carthage, 46, 71n
Carvajal, Doreen, 102n, 216n
Castells, Manuel, 33n, 38n, 100n, 105n, 127n, 148n, 184n, 268n, 269n, 272n
  on identity and identities, 30
  identity and Islam, 31
  "end of patriarchalism," 87
  network society, 100n
  technological revolution, 117
  ICT and global finance, 117–18
  globalization and localization, 132
  the *Zapatistas*, 174
  globalization and nationalism, 250
Castle, Stephen, 216n
Castro, Marcus Faro de, 243n
Cayman islands, 33
Cell phones, 111
Center for International Dialogue, 79
Centers for Disease Control and Prevention, 81
Central African Republic, 255, 256
Central America
  conditions in, 230, 255
Central Asia
  level and impact of globalization, 204–07
  globalization challenges, 204
  identities, 204–05
  nationalism, 204, 206–07
  democratization levels, 205
Central Europe
  level and impact of globalization, 192–94
Cerny, Philip, 13n, 36n, 106n, 150n, 151n, 178n, 179n, 273n, 288n, 290n
  on levels of analysis, 3–4
  state capacity and globalization, 268
  transgovernmental linkages, 93
  the global and local, 144
  reforming globalization, 155
  the "competition state," 157
  evolution of globalization, 279, 287–88
Chachaga, C. S. L., 244n, 245n

Chad, 234, 235, 255
Chambers, Simon, 104n
Chamie, Joseph, 270n, 272n
Chan, Sewell, 107n, 268n, 274n, 275n
Chanda, Nayan, 69n, 70n, 71n, 72n, 74n, 124n, 184n
  on origins of globalization, 40
  early trade, 42
  ancient Athenian currency, 47
  globalization and religion, 42, 51
  Ottoman Empire, 54
  motives for globalization, 40, 42, 58, 110
  future of globalization, 247
Chandler, David, 102n, 104n
  on global civil society, 86
Changchun, Li, 120
Chao, Loretta, 274n
Cha, Victor, 108n
  on human mobility and interaction, 97
  globalization and interstate war, 99
Chávez, Hugo, 229
Chazen, Guy, 178n
Checchi, Daniele, 180n
Checkel, Jeffrey T., 217n
Chen, Shaohua, 180n
Cheng, Jonathan, 13n
Childress, Sarah, 101n, 246n
Chile, 229–30, 287
China, 24
  education hub, 33
  ancient empires, 50–51, 87
  early trading voyages, 54
  retreat from outside contact, 54, 68
  re-engagement with the West, 65
  crackdown on ICT, 8, 115, 117, 120, 199
  income inequality, 66–67, 158, 159, 160, 161, 200, 203
  joining WTO and trade disputes, 79, 200, 263–65
  ICT and R&D, 202
  intelligence hacking, 119
  NGOs, 87
  U.S. debt, 94, 253
  expanding global interests of, 93–94
  economic growth in, 165, 194
  labor shortage, 165
  effect of 2007 economic crisis, 198, 203
  pro-democracy tensions, 200
  and globalization, 194–96, 198, 200–01, 203
  globalization and localization in China, 198
  state capitalism, 200–01, 253–54
  economic reform, 200–01
  carbon emission and energy use, 266–67, 285
  call for a new global currency, 201, 262
  currency disputes with US, 93, 201, 262
  and Africa, 202–03
  territorial disputes, 95
  Beijing Olympics, 250
  and Latin America, 230–31
  nationalism, 250
  national minorities, 31, 251
China National Petroleum Corporation, 253
Chissano, Joaquim, 235
Cho, David, 269n
Christianity, early, 51, 141
Christopher, Warren
  on ethnic separatism, 251
Chrysler Building, 253
Chua, Amy
Cingranelli, David, 181n
  on international economic institutions and human rights, 164
Ciochetto, Lynne, 219n
Cities, global, 25, 100n, 140, 143, 163, 190, 211n, 215n, 222
Civil society, global, 3, 81, 85–89
  definitions of, 85–86
Clark, David, 15n
Clark, Ian, 33n, 150n
  on globalization and fragmentation, 142–43
Clarke, Richard A., 128n, 129n
  on cyberwar and security, 120, 122
Clinton Foundation, 87, 104n
Clinton, Hillary, 87
  on women and human rights, 87
Coca-Cola, 78, 83, 166, 273n
Cochrane, Allan, 38n, 101n
Coclanis, Peter, 197, 213n
  on Southeast Asia's export strategy
Cody, Edward, 272n
Cohen, Noam, 126n, 129n
Cohen, Stephen, 182n
Colás, Alejandro, 104n, 105n
  on global civil society, 85
  NGOs, 88
Colchester, Max, 272n
Cold War, 62, 90, 281, 282
Cole, August, 128n, 129n
Collier, Paul, 103n, 245n, 246n
  on elections and political violence, 84
  "resource curse," 236
  sequencing of reforms in Africa, 238–39
Collins, Kathleen, 217n
Colombia, 183n, 208, 229, 242n, 265

295

Columbus, Christopher, 54
Comor, Edward, 36n
   on information, 23
Communications revolution, 65
Concert of Europe, 61
Confucius and Confucianism, 195
Congo, Democratic Republic of, 78, 84, 234, 235, 255, 254,287
Connors, Michael, 124n, 215n
   on technology and globalization, 110
Connor, Walker, 268n
   on defining nationalism, 249–50
Cook, Robin, 168
Cooley, Alexander, 35n, 240n
   on the state, 21
   globalization and the Soviet Union, 221
Copenhagen Climate Conference (2009), 97, 266
Cornia, Giovanni Andrea, 180n
   trade liberalization and inequality, 160
   economic inequality, 160
Costa Rica, 208, 230
Coulby, David, 147n
Council of Europe,
   on multiculturalism, 192
Coward, Martin, 290n
   on dichotomizing "state-centric" and "supra-territorial," 285–86
Cowen, Tyler, 37n, 105n, 182n
   on trade and culture, 90
   cultural homogenization, 90, 167
Cox, Kevin R., 149n
Cox, Robert, 100n
   on neoliberalism, 76–77
Crawford, David, 39n
Crete, Minoan, 46
Crime, transnational, 97, 99, 118
Croatia, 250
Cronin, Audrey Kurth, 108n
Crosby, Alfred, 72n-73n
   on "Columbian exchange,' 55–
Crossette, Barbara, 268n
CSGR Globalisation Index, 34n, 193, 212n, 234, 244n
Cuba, 116, 227, 230
Culture and cultural globalization
   homogenization of, 27, 89–92, 282–83
   globalization and localization, 143–45
Curtin, Philip D., 70n
Cusimano, Maryann K., 183n, 270n, 289n
   on changes in sovereignty, 281
Cutler, Claire, 101n
Cybercrime, 118

Cyber-espionage, 122
   Ghost-Net, 120
Cyberwar
   Stuxnet, 121
   and Estonia, 121
   and Georgia, 121
Cyprus, 46
Czech Republic, 189, 192, 221

Danks, Catherine J., 150n, 268n
Darfur, 281, 287
Dauvergne, Peter, 290n
Davis, Bob, 102n, 268n, 273n, 275n
Davoodi, Hamid R., 244n
De Blij, Harm, 106n, 182n, 211n, 218n, 271n
   on globalization and English, 92, 166
   migrant remittances, 258
De Carvalho, Maria Izabel Valladao, 243n
De la Mothe, John, 211n
Dello Buono, Delia, 241n
Dello Buono, Richard A., 241n
Democracy
   "democratic deficit," 81, 113, 155–56
   spread of, 84–85
   and neoliberal economics, 84
   "democratic peace," 84, 171
   e-democracy, 156
   prospects in hard times, 287
Denemark, Robert, 210n
Deng Xiaoping, 107n
Denmark, 78, 257
Denni, Mario, 127n, 211n
   on global innovation scores, 119
Dependency theory, 226, 228
Derné, Steve D., 219n
   on English in India, 209
Deutsch, Karl W., 34n
   on integration theory, 1–2
Devetak, Richard, 148n
Dhumale, Rahul, 180n
Diamond, Jared, 70n, 72n
   on origins of globalization, 43
   early agriculture, 43
   bridging the Atlantic, 55
Diasporas, financial flows via, 26
Dicken, Peter, 15n, 35n, 36n
   on views of globalization, 21–22
   on transnational corporations, 24
Dickerman, C. Robert, 106n
Dilmun, early trade hub, 44
Di John, Jonathan, 270n

Dikhanov, Yuri, 180n
DiNunzio, Mario, 268n
Disease, transnational
    H1N1 influenza, 169, 170
    HIV/AIDS, 68, 153,169, 181n, 256
    SARS, 66, 170
Dissanayake, Wimal, 219n
Distance, relative decline of, 112
Dittmer, Lowell, 213n, 214n
    on globalization in East Asia, 198
    Asian values, 199
Djibouti, 233
Dobson, Hugo, 87, 104n, 214n
    on NGOs and civil society, 87
Doezema, Jo, 183n
Doha Round trade negotiations, 15n, 203, 247, 261–65, 273n, 284, 290n
Dolezal, Martin, 211n
Dollar, David, 180n
    on economic inequality, 160
Donnelly, Jack, 69n, 163, 181n
    on globalization, 40
Doran, Charles F., 288n
Dordoy, Alan, 149n
Doshi, Tilak, 197, 213n
Douglas, Ian, 101n
    on global governance, 78
Douglass, Mike, 213n
    on state, civil society, and capital in Southeast Asia, 198
Dowling, J. Malcolm, 218n
Doyle, Michael W., 178n
Drainville, André, 184n
Dreazen, Yochi, 128n, 129n
Drew, Kevin, 127n
Dubai, 258
Dutch East and West India Companies, 58
Dutta, Soumitra, 127n, 213n, 216n, 217n
    on ICT
Dyer, Geoff, 274n

Eades, Jeremy Seymour, 15n, 213n
East Asia
    level and impact of globalization, 198–204
    and Asian values, 195–96, 199
    Easterbrook, Gregg, 290n
    on global economic crisis, 284
Easterly, William, 102n, 246n
    structural adjustment in Africa, 238
Eastern Europe, *See* Central Europe
East-West Institute, 123
Eastwood, Robert, 180n

Eatwell, John, 36n
Ecuador, 230
Education, impact of, 132
Edwards, Chris, 213n
Efrati, Amir, 182n
Egypt
    ancient, 44–46, 48, 52
    globalization status, 232
    revolution in, 115, 256
Ehrenreich, Barbara, 148n, 151n
    on female migrants, 163
Ehteshami. Anoushiravan, 243n
    globalization challenge to Middle East, 232
Eichengreen, Barry, 35n
Eileprin, Juliet, 182n
Elden, Stuart, 149n
    on deterritorialization, 137–38
Ellick, Adam B., 126n
El Salvador, 230, 254, 258, 272n
Empires, Age of, 57–60
Empiricism, 4
England
    Glorious Revolution of 1688, 7, 58
    Corn Laws, 40, 60
    Seven Years War, 58
English and globalization, 91–93, 190
    and "globish," 91
    in India, 92, 197, 209
Environment and globalization, 67, 96, 139, 167, 247, 283, 285
    environmental nationalism, 266–67
Epstein, Barbara, 184n
    on anarchists, 173
Epstein, Juliet, 108n
Epstein, Rachel, 37n
    on global business, 27
Equatorial Guinea, 234
Erikkson, John, 127n
Erlanger, Steven, 211n, 268n, 275n
Erman, Eva, 73n
Esping-Andersen, Gøsta, 180n
    on economic inequality, 159
Estonia, 128n, 132, 148n, 192, 193, 212n
    and Russian cyberattack, 121
    and globalization, 193, 250
Ethiopia, 84, 171, 172, 202, 234, 246n, 256
Etling, Bruce, 126n
European Central Bank (ECB), 18, 19, 191
European Union (EU), 11, 18, 19, 24, 64, 65, 66, 138, 156, 186–94, 221, 225, 247, 263, 267, 267n, 281, 285

Eurozone
   growth rate, 186–94
   and sovereign debt crisis, 66, 68, 80, 118, 265
Evans, Kelly, 33n
Evron, Gadi, 128n

Facebook, 110, 111, 115, 116, 123, 124, 125n, 126n, 128n, 209
Fagan, G. Honor, 289n
"Failed states," 8, 254–56
Faiola, Anthony, 102n, 271n, 275n
Fairbrother, Richard, 181n
Fairclough, Gordon, 268n
Fairs, medieval, 56
Falk, Richard, 181n
   on human rights, 163
Falun Gong, 115
Faris, Robert, 126n
Fassihi, Farnaz, 244n
Fathi, Nazila, 126n
Featherstone, Mike, 105n, 106n, 125n, 149n, 150n
   on globalization flows to and from core and periphery, 92, 113
   polyculturalism, 91
Feder, Barnaby J., 12n
Federal Reserve Bank (US), 19, 263
Fee, Lian Kwen, 15n
Fenenko, Alexey, 240n, 241n
   on threats to Russian security, 224
Ferguson, Niall, 35n, 70n, 71n, 72n, 73n, 105n, 288n, 290n
   on globalization perspectives, 20
   origins of globalization, 20
   Babylon, early finance, 44
   Crusades, 52
   war and finance, 57
   British Empire, 58
   on global war, 58
   globalization's future, 277–78
Ferguson, Yale, 12n, 13n, 70n, 71n, 72n, 74n, 105n, 124n
   intellectual history of, 2–5
Fernandez, Luis Alberto, 184n
   on the counter-globalization movement, 173–74
Fidler, Stephen, 39n, 102n
Filippetti, Andrea, 127n, 211n
   on global innovation scores, 119
Filonovich, Sergey R., 240n
Finland, 78, 119, 190

Finley, M. I. 74n
   on ancient economies vs. modern economies, 68
Fishman, Joshua A., 106n
Fletcher, Owen, 240n
Flextronics International, 83
Florence, banking pioneer, 53
Florida, Richard, 34n
Flynn, Stephen, 183n
   on the drug trade, 169
Foner, Nancy, 269n, 271n
Fong, Mei, 34n
Fordist/post-Fordist production, 65
Foreign Policy Global Cities Index, 190, 222
Foreign Policy 2007 Globalization Index, 189–90, 201–02
Foreign Policy 2011 Failed States Index, 255–56
Forelle, Charles, 211n, 275n
Forero, Juan, 37n, 183n, 243n
Forrester, Viviane, 177n
Foucault, Michel
   on characteristics of modernity, 78
Fourth World Conference on Women, 87
Fox, Jonathan, 102n
   on global civil society, 81
"Fragmegration," concept of, 8–9, 30, 57
Fragmentation, 3, 17
France, 14, 61, 126, 188, 189, 190, 196, 201, 202, 203, 264, 272n
   "Capetian project," 6
   Thirty Years' War, 6
   Seven Years' War, 58
   "muliculturalism," 192, 257–61
   Eurozone crisis, 76, 265
Frank, Andre Gundar, 210n
Frankel, Jeffrey, 35n
Fraser, Nancy, 177n
   on globalization and justice, 153
Freedom House, 84
Free Trade Area of the Americas (FTAA), 174, 227
French Revolution, 57
Frey, Timotheos, 211n
Frieden, Jeffrey, 73n
   on nineteenth-century global trade, 60, 61
   liberalization of financial markets, 65–66
Friedman, Benjamin M., 127n
Friedman, Edward, 214n, 214n
   on democracy in East Asia and China, 199
Friedman, Milton, 193
Friedman, Thomas L., 15n, 33n, 130n, 150n, 218n, 272n

on meaning of globalization, 12
"flat world," 75 118–19, 230, 288
"olive tree" vs. Lexus, 123, 142, 288
technology and globalization, 109
the global and local, 123–24
on India, 208
Fritsch, Peter, 274n, 275n, 276n
Fromm, Erich, 287, 290n
Fu, Wayne, 106n, 210n
  Measuring cultural globalization, 91–92, 188
Fukuyama, Francis, 34n, 288n

G-7 (8), 80
G-20, 173, 174, 230, 262, 263, 273n
Gabel, Medard, 103n
Gaines, Steven D., 108n
Galbraith, James, 179n, 290n
  On economic inequality, 158
Galeotti, Mark, 183n
Gammage, Sarah, 272n
  on migrants from El Salvador, 258–59
Ganguly-Scrase, Ruchira, 219n
Garnsey, Peter, 71n
Garten, Jeffrey, 273n
Gazprom, 225, 253
Geiger, Thierry, 101n, 212n, 215n, 242n
Gelleny, Ronald, 181n
Gellner, Ernest, 125n
General Agreement on Tariffs and Trade (GATT), 63, 77
Georgia, 128n, 206, 221, 224
  and Russian cyberattack, 121
  war with Russia, 96, 98
  and localization, 146, 250, 251
Germain, Randall D., 104n, 130n, 149n
  on global civil society, 85
Germany, 8, 57, 59, 60, 61, 76, 78, 83, 257
  and Eurozone financial crisis, 265
Geyer, Michael, 14n
  on war and technology
Ghai, G. Dharam, 244n, 245n, 246n
  structural adjustment in Africa, 235
  "winners" and "losers" in Africa, 238
Ghana, 92, 202, 208, 215n
Ghemawat, Pankaj, 180n
  on market concentration, 161
Ghoshal, Sumantra, 103n, 149n
  on "global chess," 83
  local and global in TNCs, 139
Ghosh, Jayati, 218n
Giacomello, Giampiero, 127n

Giddens, Anthony, 36n-37n, 38n, 178n, 290n
  globalization, time ,and space28
Gillani, Waqar, 126n
Gills, Barry, 34n, 38n, 103n, 148n, 184n
  on roots of globalization, 18
  globalization and democracy, 84
  globalization and localization, 132
Giridharades, Anand, 107n
Glanz, James, 128n
Glasius, Maries, 104n
Global Competitiveness Report, 78, 101n, 211n, 21n, 213n, 215n, 216n, 217n, 240n, 242n, 243n, 244n
Global economic and financial crisis, 10, 19, 20, 66, 76, 77, 80, 95, 96, 118, 154, 179, 186, 191, 194, 198, 200, 202, 203, 207, 227, 239, 240, 248, 249, 252, 262, 263, 265–66, 278, 283–86
Global economy, reasons for expansion, 64–65
Global Information Technology Report, 119, 127n, 212n, 213n, 215n, 216n, 217n, 240n, 242n, 243n, 244n
Globalization
  origin of term, 1, 4
  definitions of, 16–17–26, 40–42
  dimensions of, 16–17, 26–28, 41, 68
  evolutionary, non-unilinear process, 41, 68, 279
  different from internationalization, 5
  ebbs and flows, 41, 140–41, 280
  distinct from "globality," 41–42, 75
  reversibility, 41, 140–41, see especially Chapters 9 and 10
  see also "Global economic and financial crisis"
  geographical scope, 42
  transactions, volume and density of, 42
  pace and direction of change, 41, 42
  identities and institutionalization, 32
  cosmopolitanism and citizenship, 33
  as Westernization or Americanization, 18, 28, 41
  relation to hegemony, 147
  controversy about, 1, 4, 5, 18–21, 153, 171
  dialectical relationship with localization, 69, 124, see especially Chapter 5, 168–69
  effect on autonomy of states, 280
  threat of cultural homogenization, 89–92, 153, 166–67, 282–83
  "winners" and "losers," 147, 191
  and the military, 283
  and territory, 112
  trade, production, and economic efficiency, 171–2

299

respatialization, 18, 29, 41–43, 171–72
and religion, 153
and technology, see especially Chapter 4, 167
and health, 169–70
and the environment, 153
and "race to the bottom," 164–66
and language, 166
and crime, 167–69
and terrorism, 169
diffusion of global power, 95–96
and human rights, 162
and migration, 162–63, 191–92
and borders, 145–47
normative issues of, 5, see especially Chapter 6
and war, 171
as structural violence, 161–62
and nationalism, 171
regional differences, 42, 177, see especially Chapters 7–8
and terrorism, 279
dialectical aspects of, see especially Chapter 9
future of, see especially Chapter 10
Globalization Innovation Scoreboard, 127n, 211n
"Global justice movement" See alter-globalization.
Glocalization, 138–40
Godemont, François, 213n, 214n
on Asian values, 195–96
Goetz, Anne Marie, 102n
on "complex multilateralism, 79
Gokulsing, K. Moti, 219n
Gold monetary standard (1875–1914), 60
Goldberg, Pinelopi Koujianou, 182n
Goldblatt, David, 34n, 36n, 37n, 38n, 103n
on dimensions of globalization, 26
Goldin, Ian, 270n, 273n
on agricultural stagnation, 261
Golding, Peter, 182n
Goldmann, Kjell, 14n, 106n, 178n
on sovereignty and autonomy, 8
Goldstein, Judith, 14n
Gooch, Liz, 271n
Google, 110, 115, 116, 117, 120, 123, 124, 128n, 199, 228
Gorman, Siobahn, 128n, 129n
Governance, global, 3, 11, 25–26, 29–30, 32, 39n, 69–70, 76, 78–85, 88, 93–94, 96, 102n, 103n 133–34, 140, 143–45, 152, 156, 159, 167, 170, 173, 177, 204, 235, 279–81, 284, 286
Graham, Carol, 242n
on educational differences in Latin America, 227–28

Grammaticas, Damien, 218n
Grande, Edgar, 210n, 211n, 212n
globalization in Europe, 188
Gray, John, 179n
Great Depression (1930s), 68, 77, 118, 279, 287
Great Recession, see Global economic and financial crisis
Greece
ancient, 41, 46, 47
financial crisis in, 76, 80, 118, 156, 189, 190, 265
Greider, William, 36n, 178n, 179n, 268n
on global finance, 157
Grier, Peter, 126n
Griswold, Daniel T., 210n
US globalization trends. 186
Gritsch, Maria, 289n
on state manipulation of globalization, 280
Grosfoguel, Ramón, 241n
on the rise of dependency theory, 226–27
Group of 20, 80
Grueber, Martin, 210n, 212n
Guatemala, 54, 81, 229, 230
Guazzone, Laura, 244n
Guégan, Jean-François, 108n
Guéhenno, Jean-Marie, 210n
Guernier, Vanina, 108n
Guillén, Mauro F., 101n
Guinea-Bissau, 59, 84, 222, 234, 255, 256
Gunnarsson, Christer, 213n
Gunning, Jan Willem, 246n
Gupta, Dipankar, 219n
Gurr, Ted Robert, 268n
on number of ethnic movements, 251
Gusinsky, Vladimir, 223
Guth, Robert A., 104n
Guthrie, Doug, 105n, 125n, 212n, 214n, 215n
economic systems as cultural systems, 194
democracy in China, 199

Haederle, Michael, 70n
Hague Conferences (1899, 1907), 61
Haider, Eric, 257
Haiti, 59, 254, 258
Hall, John A., 105n, 268n, 272n, 289n
Hall, Rodney Bruce, 14n
on territorial-sovereign states, 8
Hall, Stuart, 34n
Halper, Stefan, 270n
on China's state capitalism, 254

INDEX

Hamilton, David S., 33n, 35n, 36n, 182n, 183n, 210n, 211n, 215n
  on global business, 22
  impact of globalization, 165
  globalization in Western Europe, 189
  difference among European states
Hannah, Matthew, 13n
  on globalization and organizations, 4
Hannerz, Ulf, 217n
Hannon, Paul, 268, 275n
Hanouz, Drzeniek, 101n, 212n, 215n, 242n
Hansa, medieval trading group, 56
Hanson, Gordon, 271n
  on Mexican migration, 257
Hardt, Michael, 101n, 148n
  on neoliberalism, 77
  globalization and localization, 132
Harrapan civilization, 44
Harris, Nigel, 268n
  on national self-determination, 250
Harris, Phil, 182n
Hart, Jeffrey A., 101n
Harvey, David, 100n, 149n, 184n
  on neoliberalism, 76
  "time-space compression," 136
Hasenclever, Andreas, 103n
Haufler, Virginia, 103n
Hauser, Christine, 103n
Hay, Colin, 289n
  on globalization's impact on the state, 280
Heath, Thomas, 269n
Hedetoft, Ulf, 177n, 240n
  on globalization threat scenarios
  Russia's "war on terrorism," 223
Hegel, G. W. F.
  on civil society, 85
Held, David, 12n, 15n, 34n, 35n, 36n, 37n, 38n, 39n, 100n, 101n, 103n, 105n, 125n, 149n, 151n, 177n, 178n, 179n, 180n, 181n, 185n, 289n
  on globalization after 9/11, 10
  role of territory, 113
  definitions of globalization, 17
  dimensions of globalization, 25, 26
  hyperglobalism, 18
  globalization skeptics, 18
  transformationalists, 18, 40
  technology and globalization, 113
  economic deterritorialization, 137
  "spatio-temporal" dimensions of globalization, 146–47
  normative views of globalization, 176
  the European Union, 267
Helft, Miguel, 242n
Helgesen, Geir, 214n
Helleiner, Charles, 127n
Henning, C. Randall, 178n
  on the "democratic deficit," 156
Henry, Clement M., 244n
Henry VIII, and the English Church, 57
Heritage Foundation, 81
Herod, Andrew, 14n, 124n, 268n, 270n, 290n
  on revival of nationalism, 247
  state failure, 256
Hertz, Noreena, 178n
  on corporations and globalization, 154
Hewson, Martin, 102n
Hiroshima, 62
Hirst, Paul, 15n, 35n, 36n
  on history of globalization, 10–11
  globalization skeptic, 19–20
  multinational corporations, 36n
History,
  role of
  overcoming selectivity, 4
  necessity of historical analysis, 4–5
  problems involved in using history, 67–68
  and globalization, 5, 67–69
Hitler, Adolf, 250
Hizbullah, 169
Hobson, John, 101n
  on state capacity and globalization, 77
Hochschild, Arlie Russell, 148n, 151n
  on migration, 135
  female migrants, 163
Hoffmann, Stanley, 150n, 184n, 289n
  on contradictions in globalization, 143, 176
  terrorism and globalization, 279
Ho, K.C., 213n
  on state, civil society, and capital in Southeast Asia, 198
Ho, Patricia Jiayi, 275n
Hollinger, Peggy, 212n
Holm, Hans-Henrik, 178n
Holton, Robert J., 34n
Holy Roman Empire, 52, 56
Honduras, 230
Hong Kong, 28, 120, 190, 195, 204, 202, 249
Hoogvelt, Ankie, 181n
Hoover Institution, 80
Hopkins, Raymond F., 106n
Horowitz, Donald L., 268n
Hounshell, Blake, 270n

INDEX

Howard, Marc Morjé, 241n
  on Russian civil society, 225
Howard, Michael, 243n
  roots of militant Islam, 232
Hudson, Alan, 148n
Hughes, Christopher W., 148n
Hu Jintao, 202
Human rights,
  Role in legitimizing military invasions, 98
  erosion of, 162–63, 287
human trafficking, 168
  child labor, 164
  sweatshops, 164
  "sex tourism," 163–64
Humphrey, Caroline, 148n
  on the global and the local, 135
Hungary, 53, 61, 189, 190, 192250, 251
Huntington, Samuel, 150n, 151n, 171n
  on cultural homogenization and localization, 143
  clash of civilizations, 143–44, 231
  Hispanic challenge, 257
Hutchinson, John, 125n, 268n
Hyperglobalism, 17, 21–25, 26

IBM, 82
ICann, 130n
Iceland, 55
  financial crisis in, 76, 118, 119
ICT
  impact of, see especially Chapter 4
  "digital divide," 11, 199, 167
  and geography, 112–13
  and political participation, 114–17
  economic implications, 117–19
  and the global financial crisis, 118
  and criminal activity, 118
  security implications, 120–23
  "video terrorism, 127"
Identity
  changing, 4
  multiple identities, 252
Ikenberry, G. John, 105n, 272n, 288n, 289n
  on globalization and cultural homogenization, 89–90
  liberal world order and US hegemony, 278
Ilkhamov, Alisher, 217n
Import-substitution industrialization (ISI), 226–27
Inayatullah, Naeem, 125n
  on the Internet and authority, 112
  constructions of space, 112

Inca Empire, 54, 55
Income inequality
  US, China, poorest countries, 66–67, 157–61
  Relation to trade liberalization, 67
Industrial Revolution, 59
Inequality, economic, 67
India, 24
  and ICT and R&D, 207
  economic growth in, 207–09
  relations with China, 208
  "License Raj," 207
  economic liberalization, 207
  inequality and poverty in, 161, 208
  Dalits, caste system, 208, 217n-18n
  role of English, 209
  Bollywood, 209
  Bharatiya Janata Party, 251
  secessionist movements, 251
  carbon emissions, 266, 285
Indian Oil, 83
Indonesia, 31, 252, 285
Indus Enterprise, 80
Information and Technology Agreement, 110
Information revolution, 65
Infosat MSAT Mobile System, 112
Inglehardt, Ronald, 216n
Inman, Philip, Phillip, 212n
Inmarsat, 112, 125n
Inoguchi, Takashi, 212n
International Accounting Standards Committee, 82
International Chamber of Commerce, 82
International Criminal Court (ICC), 81, 281, 282
International Governmental Organizations
  rise of, 61
  proliferation of, 63
Internationalization, as distinct from globalization, 5
International Monetary Fund, 19, 281
  creation of, 63, 78
  as neoliberal advocate, 165, 174, 239
  as instrument of major states, 280
  conditionality and structural adjustment programs, 80, 87–88, 156, 161, 164, 229
  on Africa, 236, 239
  and 1997 Asian financial crisis, 154
  role in Eurozone financial crisis, 189
International Trade Organization (ITO-proposed), 62
International regimes, 29, 81, 165
Internet
  origins of, 110
  impact on globalization, 22

302

growth of, 110–111
effects of globalization on
and geography, 112–13
and political participation, 113–14
impact on the economy, 117–19
and espionage, 120–24
and crime, 118
security implications of, 120–23
regulation, 124
Iran, 43, 46, 52, 59, 84, 87, 95, 100, 121, 123, 232
crackdown on ICT, 115–16
Iraq, Anglo-American intervention in (2003–2010), 27, 98, 114, 247
Ireland, 91, 132, 249
financial crisis in, 76, 80, 89, 118, 156, 189, 253
Iriye, Akira, 217n
Irwin, Douglas A., 35n, 215n
Isemeyer, Axel H., 36n
Islam
early, 51– 53, 68, 197
globalized vision of, 31, 153, 173, 232
extremists, 123, 143, 152, 154, 169, 223
moderates, 134, 233
uneasiness about, 192, 204–05, 224, 234, 252, 259, 260–61
Ismail, Rahil, 100n, 213n
Israel, 51, 231, 232, 233
Italy
history, 6, 8, 46–47, 49, 52–54, 57, 59, 61
financial crisis in, 26, 118, 189–90, 265
immigration, 258–60
Ivory Coast, 78, 236, 255, 256

Jackson, Patrick, 129n
Jackson, Robert, 14n
"quasi-states," 8
Jacobs, Andrew, 104n, 128n, 184n, 276n
Jade Road, 51
Jaggar, Alison M., 180n
James, Harold, 289n
Jameson, Fredric
James, Paul, 35n, 103n, 150n, 268n
on dimensions of globalization, 18–19
reversibility of globalization, 140–41, 279
nationalist revivals, 268n
Japan
education hub, 33
globalization in, 19, 195
trade growth rate, 64
immigration, 257

Jensen, Nathan M., 101n
Jessop, Bob, 137, 149n
Johnson, Ian, 210n, 275n
Johnston, Hank, 184n
Jones, R. J. Barry, 70n
Jonson, Lena, 216n
Jönsson. Kristina, 178n, 213n, 214n
Jordan, 231–32, 233
Jordan, Bill, 14n
Jordan, Mary 102n
Jordan, Miriam, 270n, 271n, 272n
Judaism, early, 51
Juris, Jeffrey, 125n
Jun, Li, 122

Kaczynski, Lech, 250
Kagarlitsky, Boris, 37n, 181n
Kahler, Miles, 103n, 178n
Kaldor, Mary, 104n
Kamp, Marianne, 216n
Kanbur, Ravi, 179n, 180n
on "spatial inequality," 159
Kansas, Dave, 15n
Kant, Immanuel, 85
Kaplan, Robert D., 270n
apocalyptic future, 256
Kapstein, Ethan, 125, 179n, 246n
on ICT technology in Africa, 111
Africa's economic transformation, 239
Kapur, S. L., 218n
on Indian economic growth, 207
Karides. Marina, 184n
Kassianova, Alla, 37n
Kavoosi, Masoud, 243n
on globalization in the Middle East, 231, 233
Kaya, Ayse, 177n, 179n, 180n
Kazakhstan, 206–07, 254
Keane, John, 102n, 104n
Kearney, M., 149n
Keck, Margaret E., 104n
Keeling, David J., 147n, 242n
on globalization and localization, 132, 227
Latin America's economic shift, 228
Keil, Roger, 151n
Kellner, Douglas, 184n
on globalization from below, 175–76
Kelly, Brian, 243n
on Brazil and the Internet, 230
Kempadoo, Kamala, 183n
Kennedy, Paul, 150n, 268n, 289n
on imperial overstretch, 282

Kennedy-Pipe, Caroline, 15n
  on globalization and war, 10
Kenny, Michael, 104n, 149n
  on global civil society, 85
Kenya, 79, 81, 84, 111, 172, 222, 234, 239, 255
Keohane, Robert O., 35n, 106n, 289n
  on complex interdependence and transnationalism, 2, 21
  defining globalization, 21
  globalism, 21
  terrorism and state authority, 283
Kessler, Clive V., 290n
  on globalization and humanity's unity, 288
Keynes, John Maynard, 141
Khaltourina, Darya, 241n
  on Russia's mortality rate, 223–24
Khazanov, Anatoly M., 241n
Khodorkovsky, Mikhail, 226
Khong, C.O., 213n
Kiel, Roger, 145
Kiiski, Sampsa, 160
Kilgannon, Corey, 129n
Kimberly Process, 78, 101n
Kinvall, Catarina, 166, 178n, 182n, 183n, 214n
Kinzie, Susan, 39n
Kiong, Tong Chee, 15n
Kiribati, 259
Kirkbride, Paul, 147n
Kirkegaard, Jacob Funk, 124n
Kirkpatrick, David D., 125n
Kirshner, Jonathan, 37n, 108n, 126n, 127n, 182n, 213n, 214n, 240n, 289n, 290n
  on economics and politics, 27
  Internet strategies, 117
  cyberspace and security, 120
  globalization and interstate war, 99
  impact of globalization on costs and benefits, 220, 282
  reversibility of globalization, 287
Kishwar, Madhu Purnima, 218n
Kitson, Michael, 178n
Klein, Naomi, 177n
  on globalization's "virtual fences," 152
Klom, Andy, 242n
Kluver, Randolph, 106n, 210n
  measuring cultural globalization, 91–92, 188
Knake, Robert K., 128n, 129n
  on cyberwar and security, 120, 122
Knox, Paul L., 15n
Kobrin, Stephen, 127n, 130n, 148n
  on ICT and economics, 117
  electronic money, 117
  regulation of the Internet, 124
  "medieval" global political economy, 133
KOF Globalization Index, 189, 192, 196, 201, 204, 207, 222, 228, 232, 234, 286
Kofman, Eleonore, 36n
Konstantinov, Gennady N., 240n
Korotayev, Andrey, 241n
  on Russian mortality rate, 223–24
Koslowski, Rey, 272n, 273n
Kosovo, 251, 282
Kraay, Aart, 180n
  on economic inequality, 160
Kramer, Andrew E., 129n, 241n
Krasner, Stephen, 15n, 103n
  on state continuity, 9–10
  sovereignty, 10
  international regimes, 81, 267
Krauthammer, Charles, 107n
Krebs, Brian, 129n
Krepinevich, Andrew, 107n, 129n
  on cyberwar and the U.S., 122
  the diffusion of global power, 95
Kriesi, Hanspeter, 211n
Krishnan, Unni, 218n
Krongkeaw, Medhi
Krugman, Paul, 107n, 150n, 288n
  on globalization and erosion of US power, 96
  the reversibility of globalization, 96, 141
  European unemployment and US inequality, 267
  food prices, 278
Kulish, Nicholas, 269n, 275n
Kumar, Ashwani, 104n
Kunanbaev, Abai, 206
Kuper, Andrew, 178n
Kuwait, 253, 282
Kuznets Curve, 290n
Kymlicka, Will, 104n
Kyoto Protocol (1992), 97, 266
Kyrgyz Republic, 54, 204–06, 221–22, 279

Lachat, Romain, 21n
LaFraniere, Sharon, 126n, 214n
Lake, David A., 103n, 178n
Lakshmi, Rama, 218n, 274n
Lamin, Vladimir, 241n
  on EU–Russian relations, 225
Lamont, James, 217n
Lampert, Donald E., 12n
Languages
  English dominant, 91–93, 166
Local revivals, 92–93

Landler, Mark, 107n, 126n, 215n, 273n
Lan, Pei-Chia, 148n
Lansing, Robert
    on national self-determination, 250
Laos, 196, 222
Laqueur, Walter, 212n
    on migrants to Europe, 192
Lara, José Bell, 241n
    on neoliberalism in Latin America, 227
Lash, Scott M., 149n
Latin America,
    and dependency theory, 226–27
    evolving economic policies, 226–27
    education disparities, 227–28
    level and impact of globalization, 226–31
    debt crisis, 227
    politico-economic trends, 229–30
    attitudes towards globalization, 229
    differing economic policies, 227
    and China, 230–31
    culture, 231
Latvia, 250
Lauricella, Tom, 15n
Lawrence, Robert, 36n
    on the global economy, 25
Law, Vivien, 216n
League of Nations, 61–62
Lebanon, 45, 169, 232, 258
Lechner, Frank, 147n, 149n
    on coexistence of global and local in Japan, 131
Le Gall, Françoise, 245n
Legitimacy, concept of, 3
Lieber, Robert J. 91, 151n, 232–33, 243n
Leiken, Robert S., 272n
    on militant Islam in Europe, 260
Lenin, Vladimir Ilyich, 247
Levels of analysis, 3–4
Levi, Margaret, 184n
Levitt, Theodore, 1, 12n
Levy, Clifford J., 148n
Lewis, David, , 70n, 71n, 72n, 74n
    on the origins of globalization, 43ff
    Mesopotamia, 43–44
    early trade, 43ff
    the Iron Age, 47
    ancient Greek "market revolution," 47
    different varieties of capitalism, 69
    Roman Empire, 49
Libya
    civil war in, 234, 256, 282
Li Changchun, 120

Lieber, Robert J., 105n, 106n
    globalization and localization, 144
Liebfried, Stephan, 101n
Liechtenstein, 33
Lindholm, Charles, 177n
    on the "global justice movement," 153
Linklater, Andrew, 290n
Lipton, Michael, 180n
Lisbon Treaty, 247
List, Regina, 102n
    on "associational revolution," 81
Lithuania, 193
Lobjakas, Ahto, 128n
Lockwood, Ben, 211n, 212n, 244n
Logan, Ikubolajeh Bernard, 245n, 246
    on structural adjustment in Africa, 236–37, 238
London, Mark, 243n
    on Brazil and the Internet, 220
López, Delia Luisa, 241n
    on neoliberalism in Latin America, 227
Lukoil, 253
Lula da Silva, Luiz Inácio, 230
Luong, Pauline Jones, 216n
Luttwak, Edward, 178n
    on "turbo-capitalism," 154
Lutz, Helma, 181n
    on female migrants, 163
Luxembourg, 189
Luzhkov, Yuri, 223
LVMH, 83
Lynch, Marc, 38n, 243n
    on Islam and globalization, 232
    the Arab Middle East, 231

MacDonald, Alistair, 274n
Macedonia, 193
MacFarquhar, Neil, 183n
Machiavelli, Niccolò
    ragione di stato, 6
MacKay, Christopher, 72n
MacMillan, John, 290n
MAD, strategic doctrine, 62
Madagascar, 84
Madsen, Frank, 183n
    on transnational crime, 168–69
Maffesoli, Michel, 150n
Magubane, Zine, 245n, 246n
    on structural reform in Africa, 237–38
Maher, Kristen Hill, 181n
Mahler, Vincent A., 179n
Makarenko, Tamara, 183n

305

Makinda, Samuel, 244n
Malas, Nour, 244n
Malaysia, 197, 252, 258
Mali, 5, 171
Malone, Elizabeth L., 243n
  on Latin American cultural hybridization, 231
Mandela, Nelson, 245n
Mann, Catherine L., 124n
  on ICT and globalized economy
Manning, J. G., 74n
Mann, Michael, 57n, 73n, 124n, 289n
  on state erosion, 9, 280–81
  war and the state, 56
  historical sensitivity
Mansbach, Richard W., 12n, 13n, 70n, 71n, 72n, 74n, 105n, 124n, 290n
  intellectual history of, 2–5
Mao Zedong, 200
Markoff, John, 126n, 127n, 128n, 129n
Marr, Kendra, 269n
Martell, Luke, 37n
  on "third wave" of globalization theory, 26
Martin, Andrew, 108n
Marxism, Marxists, 21, 23, 36n, 76, 77, 153, 175, 226
Massey, Doreen, 38n, 290n
  on the "global sense of place," 31
  on an "open" future, 287
Matthews, Robert Guy, 275n
Maurais, Jacques, 106n
  on English, 92
Mauritius, 234, 235
Mayer, Peter, 103n
Mazlish, Bruce, 217n
Mbembe, Achille, 270n
McChrystal, Stanley A., 129n
  on technology and the military, 123
McCorquodale, Robert, 181n
McCrum, Robert, 106n
  on globalization and English, 91
McCrummen, Stephanie, 246n
McGivering, Jill, 215n
McGrew, Anthony, 12n, 15n, 34n, 35n, 36n, 37n, 38n, 100n, 101n, 103n, 105n, 181n, 183n, 184n, 213n, 289n
  on globalization after 9/11, 10
  polycentric globalization, 194–95
  dimensions of globalization, 26
  war and globalization, 27, 170
  economic deterritorialization, 137
  normative views of globalization, 176

McKay, Betsy, 13n, 183n
McKay, Christopher, 72n
McKinley, James C., Jr., 13n, 183n
McMahon, Dinny, 107n
McNeill, J. R., 33n, 73n
  on "human web," 62
McNeill, William H., 33n, 72n, 73n
  medieval Venice, 52
  "human web," 62
Medical tourism, 33
Medvedev, Dmitry
  on Russian competitiveness, 222
Mehta, Nalin, 209
Meichtry, Stacy, 272n
Mellor, Mary, 149n
  on the local and global in environmental groups
Mengisteab, Kidane, 245n, 246
  on structural adjustment in Africa, 236–37, 238
Menz, Georg, 151n
  on global and local, 144
Menzies, Gavin, 72n
Mercantilism, 60
Mercosur, 11
Merkel, Angela, 192
Mesomaerica, early regional system, 54
Metha, Nalin, 219n
Mexico,
  financial crisis (1995), 66, 118
  and drug cartels, 168, 255
  see Zapatistas
  migration from, 258
Meyer, Klaus, 182n
  On TNCs, 165
Mesopotamia, ancient, 41, 43–44, 51
Mia, Irene, 101n, 127n, 212n, 213n, 216n, 217n, 242n
Microstates, 11
Middle East
  early civilizations and empires, 43–47
  level and impact of globalization, 31, 231–34
  democratic "contagion,"233–34
Midford, Paul, 213n
  on Japanese goals, 195
Migration
  early, 42–43
  dangers of, 27, 167–68
  post-WWI expansion, 65
  reasons for, 135
  remittances, 26, 136, 168, , 238, 258–59, 283
  opposition to, 247, 256–61, 282

eco-migration, 258
  and aging populations, 168
  Muslim to Europe, 258
Milanovic, Branko, 179n, 180n
  measurements of inequality, 158–59, 160
Miller, Claire Cain, 125n
Miller, John W., 34n, 273n, 274n, 275n, 276n
Miller, Tom, 270n
Millman, Joel, 271n
Milner, Wesley, 181n
  on trade and human rights, 163
Milošević, Slobodan, 250
Mitchell, Stephen, 71n, 72n
  on the rise of the medieval Islamic state 52
Mitchie, Jonathan, 178n
Mittelman, James H., 38n
Miyoshi, Masao, 290n
Modood, Tariq, 272n
  on migration and multiculturalism, 258
Moffett, Sebastian, 124n, 271n
Mogae, Festus, 235
Moghadam, Valentine M., 243
Mohapatra, Sanket, 272n
Mo Ibrahim Foundation, 235, 245n
Moldova, 250, 251
  Transdniestria, 251
Mollenkamp, Carrick, 273n, 275n
Montenegro, 193
Montgomery, Lori, 275n
Moore, Karl, 70n, 71n, 72n, 74n
  on the origins of globalization, 43ff
  Mesopotamia, 43–44
  early trade, 43ff
  Iron Age, 47
  ancient Greek "market revolution," 47
  different varieties of capitalism, 69
  Roman Empire, 49
Morcom, Anna, 219n
Morocco, 232, 254
Morozov, Evgeny, 126n
  on "the Google doctrine," 116–17
  ICT and authoritrianism, 117
Morris, Ian, 74n
Morris, Michael A., 106n
  on globalization and English, 92
Morrison, Allen J., 148n
  on globalization and international corporations, 133
Morton, Adam David, 184n
Mosca, Lorenzo, 184n
Moscow, 222
Moses, Jonathan W., 148n

Mosley, Layna, 101n
  on neoliberalism, 77
  state capacity and globalization, 77
Movement for the Survival of the Ogoni People, 164
Moynihan, Daniel P.
  on ethnic separatism, 250
Mozambique, 234, 235
MSAT Mobile System, 112, 125n
Mubarak, Hosni, 115
Muhammad, Prophet, 52, 115
Munck, Ronaldo, 15n, 100n, 105n, 149n, 178n, 184n, 289n
  on "social facts" of globalization, 10
  criticism of market capitalism, 76
  human rights and NGOs, 87
  "local transnationalism," 138–39
  democracy and development
  globalization strategy, lack of, 281
Murphy, Craig N., 102n
Murphy, Gillian Hughes, 184n
Murray, Sara, 273n
Musa, Mohammed, 182n
Muslims, in Europe, 258–61
Myanmar
  Karen insurgents, 251
Mycenaeans, 46
Mydans, Seth, 125
MySpace, 209

Nacos, Brigitte L., 104n
North American Free Trade Area (NAFTA), 11, 18, 138, 262, 265, 281
Nagasaki, 62
Naím, Moisés, 13n, 35n, 108n, 127n, 183n
  "neighborhood effect," 118
  globalization and crime, 118
  human trafficking, 168, 169
Nairn, Tom, 35n, 268n
  dimensions of globalization, 18–19
Naisbitt, John, 104n, 147n, 214n
  on "globalization from below," 86
  globalization and localization in China, 198
Nakashima, Ellen, 129n
Nationalism and ethnic identity
  contemporary revival of, 170–71, 249–52
National self-determination, 250–51
North Atlantic Treaty Organization (NATO), 62, 221, 229, 282
Naughton, John, 124n
Nayar, Pramad K., 219n
Ndiaye, Alfred Inis, 246n

N'Diaye, Seyni, 244n, 245n, 246n
  globalization challenges in Africa, 234, 235
  need for reform in Africa, 235
Nederveen Pieterse, Jan, 12n, 33n, 37n, 108n, 148n, 149n, 151n, 179n, 210n, 267n
  definitions of globalization, 16
  dimensions of globalization, 16–17
  "essential problem" of globalization, 27
  globalization and violence, 99
  globalization and localization, 132, 138
  cultural interaction, 136, 142
  cultural paradigms, 144, 231
  global inequality, 158
  regional differences, 186
Negri, Antonio, 101n, 148n
  on neoliberalism, 77
  globalization and localization, 132
Negroponte, Nicholas P., 290n
Neomercantilism
  revival of, 261
Neorealism, 2
Nesadurai, Helen, E. S., 213n
Netflix, 123
Netherlands, the, 257
Newman, Abraham L., 106n
Newman, David, 148n
Newman, Edward, 212n
Nickel, James, 13n
  on global governance, 16n
Nigeria, 192, 202–03, 234, 236, 238, 255, 256
  and human rights, 31, 84, 164
  "resource curse," 235
  unrest, 256
Nike Inc., 171, 181n
Nissanke, Machiko, 216n, 242n
Noah, Timothy, 73n
Nokia
Nongovernmental organizations, 79, 156, 281
  proliferation of, 63–64
  relationships with IGOs, 79, 81
  role in globalization
  and global civil society, 86–87
  and human rights, 87
  "local transnationalism," 138–39
Noreen, Erik, 240n
Norris, Floyd, 215n, 216n
Norse, early contacts with North America, 54–55
Normative and empirical theory, 4
Norris, Floyd, 289n
North America
  globalization in, 19, 23
North Korea, 100, 121, 150n, 200, 201, 220, 282

Norway, 119, 190, 211n, 253
Novy-Marx, Milena, 270n
  on migration, 254
Nsouli, Saleh M., 245n
Núñez, Orlando, 37n, 181n
Nye, Joseph S., 35n, 105n

Obama, Barack
  on cybersecurity, 122–23
  and activist state, 253
  and multilateralism, 282
O'Brien, Robert, 72n, 73n, 101n
  on Abu-Lughod's map, 54
  "complex multilateralism," 79
  economic growth after 1945, 64
  TNCs, 65
Ohmae, Kenichi, 14n
  on the demise of the state, 8
Okumu, F. Wafula, 244n
Oliker, Olga, 216n
Olivera, Oscar, 229
O'Neill, Jim, 102n
Onishi, Norimitsu, 126n, 271n
Ooi, Giok Ling, 100n, 213n
on state, civil society, and capital in Southeast Asia, 198
Organization of African States, 234
Organization of American States (OAS), 62
Organization for Economic Cooperation and Development (OECD), 26, 110, 229
Organization of Petroleum Exporting Countries (OPEC), 20
Ó Riain, Sean, 106n
  on "embedded liberalism," 93
Oshi, Nana, 182nOsiander, Andrea, 179n
Ossetians, 251
Oster, Shair, 212n
Ottoman Empire, 53
ÖTuathaul, Gearóid,, 14n, 102n, 125n, 268n, 270n, 290n
  technology and crime
  revival of nationalism, 249
  state failure, 256
Owens, Patricia, 35n
Özdemir, Cem, 192

Paasi, Anssi, 38n
  on identities, 31
Pacheco-Lopez, Penélope, 242n
Paciello, M. Cristina, 244n
Page, Jeremy, 107n
Pakistan, 31, 254, 255, 256

Pal, Parthapratim, 218n
Palan, Ronen, 289n
Palfrey, John, 126n
Pal, Parthapratim
Panagariya, Arvind, 273n
Panama Canal, 60
Panama Congress (1826), 60
Pan American Union, 61
Panda Burns Incense, computer worm, 122
Pandemics, threat and response, 66
Pangalangan, Raul C., 182n
　on enforceable global standards, 165
Pan, Philip P., 274n
Papastergiadis, Nikos, 148n, 149n
　on migration, 135
　"dematerialization" and "deterritorialization," 137
Papua New Guinea, 222
Paret, Peter, 14n
Pariser, Eli, 130n
Parker, John, 37n
Parry, J. H., 73n
Partlow, Joshua, 276n
Pasha, Mustapha Kamal, 38n, 178n
　on identities and Islam, 31, 177n
Patriarch, Greek Orthodox, 52
Paul, T. V., 105n, 289n
Pauly, Louis W., 178n
　on the "democratic deficit," 156
Pauly, Robert J., Jr, 272n
　on Muslims in Europe, 259
Pavcnik, Nina, 182n
　on "race to the bottom"
Pei-Chia Lan, 148n
Pempel, T. J., 180n
"Perfect Citizen," 121
Perraton, Jonathan, 34n, 35n, 37n, 38n, 103n
Perry, George L., 267n
Persian Empire, 47, 48, 51, 52
Petra, caravan trade hub, 48
Petras, James, 242n
Peru, 54, 58, 173, 229, 242n, 267
Peyrouse, Sébastien, 216n
Pfanner, Eric, 130n
Phoenicians, 46–47, 71n
Philippines, 258
Pianta, Mario, 178n
Pinnington, Paul, 147n
Pioppi, Daniella, 244n
Pirages, Dennis, 183n
Plender, John,
　on neoliberal economics, 248, 268

Pleven, Liam, 274n
Pleyers, Geoffrey, 177n
　on alter-globalization, 154
Pogge, Thomas W., 179n, 181n
Pogue, David, 124n
Poland, 193, 250
Polansek, Tom, 274n
Polanyi, Karl, 178n
　on the dialectic between global and local, 140
　"double movement," 140
　self-adjusting market, 140, 154
Policy Reduction Strategy Papers, 239, 246n
Polities and polity types, 3, 4, 5, 42, 69
Political space, 3, 94, 112–13, 286
Polo, Marco, 53
Pomfret, John, 107n
Poon, Terence, 275n
Pope, Catholic, 52, 53
Population decline, 258
Portugal, 260
　Empire, 55, 57–59
　financial crisis in, 61, 76, 80, 118, 156, 189, 190, 231, 265
Positivism, 4
Postinternational politics, 2, 32, 109
Poveda, Miguel Angela, 231
Povoledo, Elisabetta, 271n
Power, diffusion of, 94–96
Powers, Mary G., 270n, 272n
Prada, Paulo, 243n
Prakash, Aseem, 101n
Preston, Julia, 271n
Princeton/Washington Mapping Globalization project, 41, 70n
Printing press, 110
Puchala, Donald J., 34n
Puniyani, Ram, 219n
Putin, Vladimir, 241n
　manipulation of Russian nationalism, 117, 223, 224, 250
Putzel, James, 183n, 184n
　on neoliberalismn and the state, 170, 172

Qatar, 33, 115
Quinlan, Joseph P., 33n, 35n, 36n, 182n, 183n, 210n, 211n, 215n
　on global economy, 22
　impact of globalization, 22, 165
　globalization in Western Europe, 189

Rachman, Gideon, 106n
　on the Chinese economy, 94–95

Rae, David, 211n
  on regional variations in coping with globalization, 190
Raghavendra, M. K., 219n
Ramstad, Evan, 128n
Rana, Pradumma B.
Ratha. Dilip, 272n
Ravallion, Martin, 180n
Ravenhill, John, 290n
Realism, 2, 4, 36n, 282
Redoano, Michela, 212n, 244n
Reich, Robert,, 60n
Renaissance, 41, 57, 141
Reinert, Kenneth A., 273n
  on agricultural stagnation, 261
Reis, Elia P., 150n
  on the dialectic between global and local, 141–42
Rendall, Steven, 270n
Rengger, Nicholas, 15n
  on globalization and war, 10
Resch, Inka, 106n
Reuveny, Rafael, 127n
  on technology and globalization, 119
  an "unflat" world, 119
Rhodes, 48, 49
Ricardo, David,
  theory of comparative advantage, 60
Richard, David L., 181n
  on trade, investment, and improved women's status
Richburg, Keith B., 127n
Richter, James, 241n
  on civil society in Russia, 225
  globalization tensions in Russia, 225
Ricks, David A., 148n
  on globalization and international corporations, 133
Rieger, Elmar, 101n
Rieff, David, 105n, 178n
  on NGOs and global civil society, 88
Risse, Thomas, 34n, 36n, 101n, 104n, 105n
  on the origins of globalization, 17
  structuralists and agency in globalization, 77–78
  cultural homogenization, 71
Rittberger, Volker, 103n
Ritzer, George, 243n
  on Latin American cultural hybridization, 231
Robertson, Roland, 149n, 290n
  technologies and frontiers

Roberts, Susan M., 14n, 102n, 124n, 268n, 270n, 290n
  on governance of world trade, 77–78
  revival of nationalism, 249
  state failure, 256
Robinson, William L., 241n, 242n
  on neoliberalism in Latin America, 227
Rodrik, Dani, 35n, 178n, 242n, 273n
  on winners and loser in globalization, 154
  Latin American economic growth, 228
  "bicycle theory" of trade, 261
Roman Empire, 48–50, 51, 52, 68, 87, 141
Romania, 191, 193, 251
Root, Franklin R., 148n
Ropp, Stephen C., 104n
Rosenau, James N., 12n, 14n, 34n, 37n, 38n, 70n, 74n, 101n, 105n, 124n, 125n, 150n, 151n, 181n, 268n
  dedication to, v, 2
  on postinternational politics, 2, 32
  states and fragmegration, 8–9, 30, 142
  postinternational politics
  authority structures, 145
  definition of globalization, 17
  "distant proximities," 42
  "domestic–foreign frontier," 32, 146
  global economy, 25–26, 32–33
  sovereignty, 29–30, 32
  dimensions of globalization, 32
  present vs past as "difference in kind," 68
  governance, 78–79
  cultural homogenization, 90
  "fragmegration," concept of, 8–9, 30, 57
  the age of fragmentation, 141, 279
  boundaries, 32, 145
  globalization and localization, 32, 42, 146
  normative issues, 146
  globalization and human rights
  "skill revolution," 113–14, 162
  nationalism as exclusionary localism, 250
Rosenberg, Matthew, 276n
Rosenberg, Justin, 290n
Rosenthal, Elisabeth, 276n
Ross, George, 210n
Ross, Michael L., 245n
Rotberg, Robert I., 270n
Roth, Kendall, 148n
  on globalization and international corporations, 133
Royal Philips Electronics, 83
Roy, Oliver, 38n, 217n

INDEX

on Islamic neofundamentalism, 31
Central Asia in Soviet period, 206
Rozhnov, Konstantin, 240n
Rozman, Gilbert, 212n
Rudra, Nita, 182n
  on reduced welfare assistance, 165
Ruggie, John, 106n, 289n
  on "embedded liberalism," 93
  global governance, 281–82
Rugman, Alan M., 35n, 83, 103n, 183n
Ruigrok, Winfried,
Runci, Paul, 183n
Rupert, James, 217n
  on origins of Central Asian republics, 206
Rupert, Mark, 184n, 217n
Russell, Robert W., 106n
Russia
  and cyberwar, 121
  cyberwar negotiations with U.S., 122–23, 124
  Chechnya, 223–24
  level and impact of globalization, 221–26
  post-Soviet identity, 221
  relations with "near abroad" and former bloc members, 221
  Commonwealth of Independent States, 221–22
  Shanghai Cooperation Organization, 222
  "managed democracy," 223, 287
  as a multinational state, 31, 223, 224
  civil society, 224–25
  view of NGOs, 224
  "war on terrorism," 223
  state capitalism, 253, 254
  bid for WTO membership, 226
  natural resource supplier, 225–26
  immigration concerns, 258
  protectionism, 264
Rwanda, 202, 234, 251, 287
Ryan, Yasmine, 181n

Saak'ashvili, Mikheil, 250
Sachs, Jeffrey D., 245n
Sakr, Naomi, 243n
Sala-i-Martin, Xavier, 101n, 212n, 242n
Saller, Richard, 71n
Salamon, Lester, 101n, 104n
  "associational revolution," 81
Sánchez de Lozada, Gonzalo, 228
Sandholtz, Wayne, 282, 290n
Sanger, David E., 107n, 128n, 129n
Sang-Hun, Choe, 39n

Sarkozy, Nicolas, 192, 252–53, 260
SARS, 66, 170
Sassen, Saskia, 13n, 15n, 34n, 35n, 36n, 73n, 104n, 106n, 147n, 148n, 149n, 150n, 151n, 179n, 181n
  on kingly states, 6
  world cities, 11, 25, 140
  global integration, 25
  transgovernmental linkages, 93–94
  the global and the local, 133, 137, 145
  denationalization, 34n, 137
  on women and migrants, 163
Saudi Arabia, 232, 233
Saul, John Ralston, 243n
  on Latin American debt crises, 229
Sax, Dov F., 108n
Schatz, Edward, 217n
Scheidel, Walter, 74n
Schlapak, David A., 216n
Schmidt, Howard, 122
Schmidt, Katherine A., 106n
Schmuckler, Sergio L., 180n
  on market imperfections, 162
Scholte, Jan Aart, 12n, 34n, 35n, 36n, 38n, 69n, 70n, 73n, 101n, 102n, 105n, 150n, 151n, 268n
  on identity, 3
  "complex multilateralism," 79
  definitions of globalization, 18, 40–41
  internationalization, 18
  liberalization, 18, 20, 24
  universalization, 18, 29
  westernization (or modernization), 18, 89
  respacialization, 18, 29, 78, 146
  globality, 30
  governance, 78
  transnational corporations, 139
  globalization and localization, 139, 146
Schuker, Lauren A. E., 274n
Schulz, Helena Lindholm, 244n
Schwab, Susan C., 290n
  on the Doha Round, 284–85
Schwartzman, Simon, 243n
Schwartz, Nelson D. 214n
Schwirtz, Michael, 241n
Scissors, Derek, 269n
  on China's state capitalism, 253
Scots, 251
Scrase, Timothy J., 219n
  on Indian middle class
Seckinelgin, Hakan, 104n
Security, changing nature of, 97–100

311

INDEX

Segal, Adam, 214n
    on impact of globalization on China, 198–99
Segal, Paul, 179n
Seligman, Adam A., 104n
Senegal, 171
Sengupta, Somini, 15n
Sen, Jai, 184n
Seychelles, 235
Shadid, Anthony, 244n
Shane, Scott, 125n, 183n
Shanker, Thom, 108n, 128n, 129n
Shapiro, Carl, 127n
Shapiro, Robert Y., 104n
Sharer, Robert, 246n
Shari, Ishak, 213n
    on economic development and crisis in Southeast Asia, 197
Shaw, Brian, 100n
Shaw, Ian, 70n
    on ancient Egypt, 31
Shaw, Martin, 104n, 105n, 148n, 183n, 213n
    on globalization and liberalization, 86
    global civil society, 88
    globalization of authority, 134, 170, 171
    globalization and extraterritorial action, 134
    limiting violence, 170
Sheehan, James, 14n
    on kingly states, 6
    state-nations, 7
Sheridan, Mary Beth, 105n, 271n
Shiels, Maggie, 127n, 128n
Shue, Vivienne, 203, 216n
Sikkink, Kathryn, 104n
Sil, Rudra, 105n
    on globalization and NGOs, 88
Silk Road, 51
Silver, Beverly, 154, 164, 178n, 182n
Siméant, Johanna, 103n
Simon, Stephanie, 183n
Sinclair, Timothy J., 101n, 102n
Singapore, 172, 195, 196, 197, 252, 253, 257, 258
Singer, J. David, 12n
Singh, Ajit, 180n
Sinopec, 83
Sirkin, Hal, 284
Skeptics, globalization, 17–21, 26
Slave trade ("triangular trade"), 59–60
Sleeman, John, 237
Slovak Republic, 250
Slovenia, 193

Smadja, Claude, 178n
Smil, Vaclav, 124n
    on technology and globalization, 110
Smith, Adam, 60
Smith, Anthony D., 125n, 268n
Smith, Graham, 216n
Smith, Jackie, 177n, 178n, 184n
    on transnational activism and democratic participation, 153
Smith, Katherine F., 108n
Smith, R. Jeffrey, 289n
Smith, Richard L., 70n, 71n, 72n
    on world systems, 42
    on the origins of globalization, 42
    on the ancient Mediterranean, 43
    on globalization and war, 45
    on ancient Egypt, 44
    on the late Bronze Age, 46
    on ancient trade routes, 50
Smith, Steve, 35n
Smoot-Hawley tariff, 21, 62
Soederberg, Susanne, 151n
    on global and local, 144
Sollie, Martie, 211n
    on regional variations in coping with globalization, 190
Solovyev, Edward, 240n, 241n
    on Russia's identity, 223
    impact of globalization on Russia, 222
Somalia
    as a failed state, 172, 251, 254, 255
Sommerville, Quentin, 126n
Sony, 82
Sorensen, Georg, 178n
South Africa, 234, 237
South American Union, 229
South Asia
    globalization in, 207–09
Southeast Asia
    globalization in, 196–98
South Korea,
    and Asian financial crisis, 195, 200
    per capita income growth, 207
South Ossetia, 250
Sovereign debt crisis, 66
Spain, 61, 211, 252, 257, 260, 261
    History, 6, 46, 53–56, 58–59, 231
    financial crisis in, 189, 265
Spar, Debora, 181n
    on the "spotlight phenomenon," 164
Spindle, Bill, 244n
Springborg, Robert, 244n

Spruyt, Hendrik, 35n, 73n
  on globalization and the state, 21
Sreberny-Mohammadi, Annabelle, 147n, 182n
Sri Lanka, 207
  Tamil separatism, 251
Standard & Poors, 156
Stanislaw, Joseph, 241n
Starr, Amory, 184n
Starr, Chester, 71n
  on the Roman empire, 48–49
Starrs, Roy, 240n
  on American and Asian globalization, 220
State,
  origins, 5–8, 56–57
  link to empires, 57
  role and nature of, 2
  sovereignty, 2, 19, 21, 82, 171–72
  state-centric realism, 2, 4
  autonomy and capacity, 2, 5, 15, 19, 21
  interactions with globalization, 280–81, 286
  transgovernmental linkages
  fragmentation of, 249–52
  separation from nation, 255
  revival of, 247–54
  "failed states,", 254–56
Steger, Manfred, 35n, 101n, 149n, 177n
  on views of globalization, 34n, 78, 136
  distinction between "globalization" and "globalisms," 153–54
Sternberg, David I., 240n
  on globalization and Myanmar, 220
Stevenson, Nick, 149n
  on technology and culture, 136
Stiglitz, Joseph, 177n
  criticism of globalization, 152
Stone, Brad, 36n
Strange, Susan, 33n, 38n, 101n, 178n, 268n
  on international political economy, 2
  definitions of globalization, 16
  identity loyalty, 31
  neoliberalism, 77
  retreat of the state, 77, 154, 177
  "casino capitalism," 247
  "mad money," 268
  national self-determination, 251
Stub, Sara Toth, 101n
Studt, Tim, 212n
Sudan, 251, 281
Suez Canal, 60
Sullivan, Kevin, 102n
Sumer, ancient, 41–42

Summers, Lawrence
  on diffusion of global power, 94
Suny, Ronald G., 105n, 216n, 217n
  on cultural homogenization and identity, 90
Surkov, Vladislav
  on state power and Russian modernization, 253
Sutcliffe, Bob, 179n, 180n
  on economic inequality, 158
Sutherland, Peter D., 273n
Sutton, Philip, 38n
  on globalization and Islam, 31
Suzlon, 83
Swank, Duane, 101n
  on globalization and welfare, 77
Swartz, Spencer, 212n
Sweden, 56, 257
Swedish Risbank, 56
Switzerland, 23
Swyngedouw, Erik, 149n
  on glocalization, 138
Syria, 232
  history, 44, 45, 48, 50, 52, 71
  violence in, 233–34, 256
Szporluk, Roman, 268n

Tabb, William, 103n, 184n
  on sovereignty and globalization, 82
  merchant law, 82
Taiwan, 66, 96, 195, 199, 201, 202, 207, 213n, 215n, 274n
Tajikistan, 204, 206, 222, 258
Talalay, Michael, 106n, 130n
  on cultural integration, 123
  globalization and English, 92
Taliban, 123, 169
Tamir, Yael, 268n
Tang, Rong, 184
Tata group, 83, 194
Tavernise, Sabrina, 126n, 271n
Taylor, Alan M., 35n
Taylor, Lance, 36n
Taylor, Peter, 15n, 38n
  dimensions of globalization, 30
Taylor, Rupert, 104n, 184n
Territory
  significance of, 3, 21
  and the Internet, 112–13
Terrorism, 2, 94, 97–99, 112, 114, 123, 151n, 153, 167–69, 192, 223–24, 240, 257, 279, 283

Teshke, Benno, 14n
  origin of modern states, 7
Thai, Hung Cam, 181n
Thailand, 66, 67, 81, 168, 169, 195, 196, 207, 258
Thakur, Ramesh, 103n
  on global governance, 81–82
Thatcher, Margaret, 248
Thirlwall, A. P., 242n
Thirty Years' War, 6
Thompson, Grahame, 35n, 179n
Thompson, John R., 216n
Thompson, William, 34n, 127n, 290n
  on the roots of globalization, 18
  technology and globalization, 119
  an "unflat" world, 119
Thorbecke, Erik, 216n, 242n
Thurow, Roger, 104n
Tibet, 115, 250, 251, 287
Tilly, Charles, 73n, 183n
  on the emergence of the state, 57
  the state and war, 57, 170
Timberg, Craig, 215n, 245n
Toepler, Stefan, 104n
Tokyo fish market (Tsukiji), 131
Tomlinson, John, 37n, 38n, 105n, 149n, 151n
  cultural homogenization, 90–91
  globalized culture and "telemediazation," 136
Tourraine, Alain, 177n
  on alter-globalization, 153
Trade, 24, 43–44, 50, 60, 247, 261–66, 284
Transformational theory, 18, 25–26, 28–33
Transgovernmental linkages, 93–94
Transnational corporations (TNCs)
  in Latin America, 2
  in Middle East, 231
  strategies, 24, 132
  late nineteenth/early twentieth centuries, 60
  post-WWII expansion, 65, 82–83
  and global governance, 82
  global or regional, 82–83, 139
  and "race to the bottom," 165
Transparency International, 235
Transportation revolution, late 19th/early 20th centuries, 61
Treaty of Utrecht and balance of power, 7
Treaty of Westphalia, 7
Trevisani, Paulo, 272n
Trilateral Commission, 80
Troitsky, Mikhail, 240n
Tunisia, 256
  democratic reform in, 115, 233

Turkey, 71n, 126n, 217, 221, 249
  unique role in the Middle East, 134, 233
  Ottoman Turkey, 53
  globalization status, 134, 232, 233
Turkmenistan, 204, 206, 216n
Twiss, Sumner B., 148n
Twitter, 110, 115, 116, 117, 126n
Tyler, Patrick E., 105n

Uchitelle, Louis, 289n
Uhlin, Anders, 73n
Uighurs, 115, 251
Ukraine, 193, 225, 250, 251
United Arab Republic, 253
United Kingdom, 33, 91, 252, 259
  education hub, 33
  Conservative-Liberal Coalition, 253
  "multiculturalism," 257
United Nations, 88
  establishment of, 62–63
  global policing, 81
  influence of, 281
  Charter Art. 1(2) on national self-determination, 250
United Nations Economic Commission for Africa, 236
United States, 10, 19, 27, 33, 41, 64, 66, 78, 79, 81, 83, 89– 92, 94–97, 100, 119, 132, 134, 156, 160, 167, 169, 176, 186–87, 190–92, 194, 195, 197, 201, 203, 204, 211n, 222, 227, 229, 230, 232, 239, 247, 253, 255–58, 260–64, 266, 267n, 272n, 278, 279, 282, 287
  rise of, 59
  role in early 20th century, 59–62
  as a hegemon, 59, 89, 96, 147, 278
  independence, expansion, "empire," 59
  sub-prime mortgage crisis, 10, 65, 118, 162
  Federal Reserve "quantitative easing" (QE2), 263
  9/11 attacks, 10, 239, 247, 279, 282
  income inequality, 66
  and international students, 33
  and WikiLeaks, 116
  and cyber-security, 121–24
  cyberwar negotiations with Russia, 122–23, 124
  and diffusion of global power 94–96
  and China, 94–96, 159, 202, 225, 262–65
  anti-proliferation policy, 100
  borders with Canada and Mexico, 142, 247, 257

and migrant rights, 163, 258
Tea Party Movement, 177, 253, 286
trade agreements with Peru and Colombia, 229, 265
trade agreement with South Korea, 265
"War on Terror," 247
growing isolationism, 282
unilateralism, 247
protectionism and protectionist sentiment, 262, 263
Urry, John, 38n, 149n, 150n, 176, 184n, 269n
  on governance, 30
  glocalization, 139–40
  information technologies, 139–40
  glocalization and nations, 251
Uruguay, 284, 287
Uzbekistan, 98, 204–06, 222

Van Agtmael, Antoine W., 101n
Van Creveld, Martin, 106n
  on transgovernmental linkages, 93
Van de Mieroop, Marc, 71n
  on ancient global politics, 45
Van der Zwart, Alex, 36n
Van Tulder, Rob 35n, 36n
Vargas Llosa, Mario, 166–67, 182n
Varian, Hal K., 127n
Veltmeyer, Henry, 242n
Venables, Anthony J., 179n, 180n
  on "spatial inequality," 159
Vendatam, Shankar, 72n
Venezuela, 229, 230, 254
Venice, "hinge of Europe," 52, 53
Verbeke, Alain, 103n, 183n
  on TNCs, 83
Versailles Peace Conference (1919), 250
Vertigans, Stephen, 38n
  on globalization and Islam, 31
Vietnam, 52, 90, 95, 165, 167, 196, 202, 252, 258, 265
Viles, Heather, 37n
  on definitions of globalization, 28
"Virtual" vs "real" global economy, 66
Visudtibhan, Kanoknart, 148n
Vodichev, Evgeny, 241n
  on EU–Russian relations, 225
Vonada, Dorian C., 179n
Von Reden, Sitta, 74n

Wade, Robert H., 179n, 180n, 210n
  on neoliberalism, 158
Wadhwa, Vivek, 271n

Walker, Marcus, 275n
Walker, Martin, 213n
  on state capitalism, 195
Wallerstein, Immanuel, 210n
Walzer, Michael, 151n
Ward, Karen, 147n
Warfare, growth of "irregular" forms, 98, 99
Warner, Andrew M., 245n
Warrick, Joby, 289n
Warwick CSGR Globalisation Index, 193, 234
Washbourne, Neil,, 149n
  on "translocal" groups, 139
Wassener, Bettina, 210n, 212n
Waterman, Peter, 184n
Watts, Jonathan, 127n
Watts, Susan, 129n
Wax, Emily, 218n, 269n
"Weapons of mass destruction" (WMD), diffusion of, 98, 100
Webster, Frank, 149n, 179n
Wei, Lingling, 273n
Weinstein, Michael M., 177n
Weisberg, Ruth, 105n, 106n, 151n, 243n
  on globalization and English, 91
  roots of militant Islam, 232–33
Weisman, Jonathan, 39n, 273n
Weiss, Linda, 12n, 101n, 213n, 214n
  on territory, 3
  state capacity and globalization, 77
  globalization and the state, 77
Weiss, Thomas, 103n
  on global governance, 81–82
  international public policy, 83–84
Welsh, 251
Wendt, Alexander, 88
Werbner, Prina J., 272n
Westphalian polity *See* state
Weyker, Shayne, 182n
Whatmore, Sarah, 38n
Whitlock, Craig, 151n, 268n, 289n
Widodo, Johannes, 213n
  culture in Southeast Asia, 197
Wilk, Richard R., 147n
Wilson, Woodrow 250, 268n
WikiLeaks, 116
Wildavsky, Ben, 39n
  on globalization and education, 33
Willetts, Peter, 104n
  on NGOs, 85
Williams, Jeffrey, 158
Williams, Marc, 72n, 73n, 102n, 150n
  on Abu-Lughod's map, 54

economic growth after 1945, 64
"complex multilateralism," 79
TNCs, 65
territoriality and globalization, 140
Williamson, Elizabeth, 273n
Williamson, Jeffrey G., 179n
on globalization and convergence, 158
Wilson, Woodrow, 250, 268n
Wines, Michael, 107n, 126n, 214n, 274n, 276n
Wirth, David A.,, 182n
on globalization and environment, 165–66
Wohlforth, William, 102n
on international institutions, 79
Wojciech, S., 102n
on "associational revolution," 81
Wold, Charles, Jr., 213n
Wolf, Martin, 13n, 15n, 35n, 73n, 105n, 124n, 182n, 183n, 184n, 213n
assaults on globalization, 173
recent economic growth (Prometian"), 64
technology and globalization, 109
child labor, 182n
Women's rights, 87–88, 163
Wong, Edward, 107n, 126n, 243n
World Bank (IBRD), 138, 281
establishment of, 63, 79
influence and structural adjustment policies, 80, 87, 165, 17, 239
accountability, 81
as instrument of major states, 280
and global spread of values, 87
economic inequality, 161
on Africa, 236, 237, 238, 239
on remittances, 258
on protectionism, 262
World cities, 25, 140, 145, 190, 201, 211n, 222, 240n
as global–local sites, 11
World Economic Forum, 23, 119, 174, 211n, 240n
World Social Forum
Charter of Principles, 174–75

World Trade Organization, 19, 138, 146–47, 156, 173, 203, 226
influence of, 77, 164
consultation with NGOs, 88
as neoliberal advocate, 161
on protectionist measures, 282
WTO complaint process, 262, 263, 284
Worth, Robert F., 125n
Wright, Robert, 12n, 70n
on the origins of globalization, 12n, 43
hunter-gatherers, 43
Wu, J. R., 275n

Yamashita, Shinji, 213n
glocalization in Southeast Asia, 197
Yang, Xiyun, 274n
Yardley, Jim, 107n
Yearly, Steven, 108n
Yeboah, Ian E. A., 245n, 246n
on Africa and global culture
Yeltsin, Boris, 224
Yemen, 85, 99, 233, 256
Yergin, Daniel, 241n
on state revival, 251
Yew, Lee Kwan,
on Asian values, 195
Youngs, Gillian, 36n
YouTube, 115, 209
Yugoslavia, 11, 15n
Yunusa, Mohammed Bello, 245n, 246n
on structural reform and Nigeria, 238
Yu, Peter Kien-hong, 33n, 106n

Zambeta, Evie, 147n-147n
Zapatistas, 173, 174
Zarembka, Joy, M., 181n
Zhou Xiao-chuan
Zibechi, Raul, 242n
Zimbabwe, 236, 282, 287
Zúquette, José, 177n
on the "global justice movement," 153
Zürn, Michael, 178n